D0463158

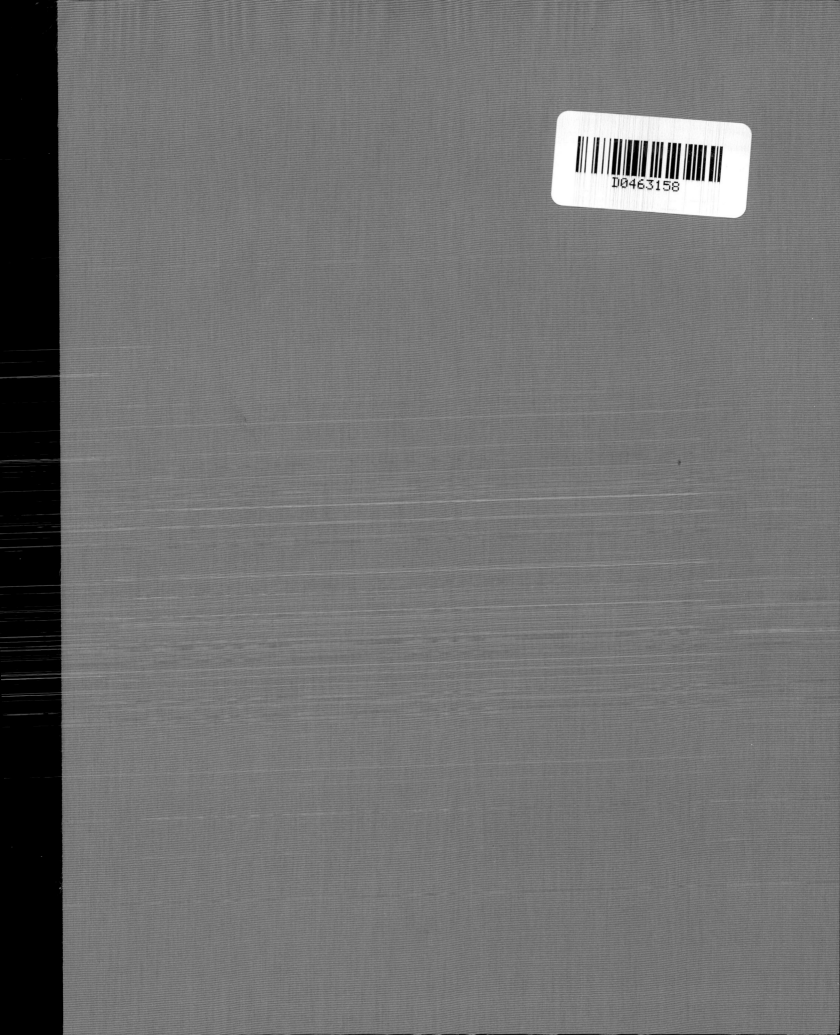

Holman Bible Atlas
Broadman & Holman Publishers
Nashville, Tennessee 37234

Graphic on page 28 adapted from David C. Hopkins, "Life on the Land: The Subsistent Struggles of Early Israel," *Biblical Archaeologist,* vol. 150 #3 (September 1987): 186.

Photo and art credits (All Rights Reserved):

Biblical Illustrator:

27, bottom left; 29 top; 49; 74, bottom; 85; 161, bottom left; 178, top left; 192; 195; 203, bottom left; 209; 260; 266, top right.

British Museum:

57, bottom right; 149

Brisco, Thomas V., Professor of Biblical Backgrounds and Archaeology, Southwestern Baptist Theological Seminary, Fort Worth, Texas 76122:

7, top, bottom; 8; 10; 12; 16; 17, bottom right; 18 , top, bottom; 19, bottom right; 21, top, bottom; 22, top left; 23, top right; 25; 27; 29, bottom left; 30, top, bottom; 31; 32; 33 bottom left; 39; 40; 45 top left, bottom right; 47, bottom right; 54, top right, bottom right; 57, bottom right; 60; 63; 65; top left, bottom right; 67; 68, top, bottom; 69; 77; 78; 80; 88; 101; 102; 109, top, bottom; 110; 112, top, bottom; 114, top left, bottom right; 120; 128; 134, top left; 146, top right; 148, bottom left; 149; 190; 201; 202, top, bottom; 203, top right; 204, top, bottom; 205; 210; 213; 215, top left; 217, top, bottom; 219; 221, bottom left; 222, top, bottom; 223; 227, top left; 228; 230, top, bottom; 231; 232, top, bottom; 233; 235, top, bottom; 247; 248, top, bottom; 251; 252, top, bottom; 253, top, bottom; 254, top, bottom; 255, top, bottom; 257; 262, top, bottom; 263; 266, bottom left; 267; 270.

Illustrated World of the Bible Library:

22, bottom; 23 bottom left; 37; 43, top, bottom; 51, top, bottom; 57, top left; 58, top left; 61, top, bottom; 71, bottom left; 74 top; 81; 91; 95; 123; 127; 129; 134, lower right; 142; 146, bottom left; 148, top right; 156; 167, top, middle; 173; 178, bottom right; 181; 215, bottom right; 237.

Latta, Bill:

113; 206; 227, bottom.

Severance, Murray:

167, bottom left.

Tolar, William B.:

5; 265.

University of Chicago:

161, upper right.
All rights reserved.

ISBN # 1–55819–709–5

Dewey Classification: BIBLE—ATLASES
Dewey Number: 220.91

Library of Congress Cataloging-in Publication Data
Brisco, Thomas C.
Holman Bible atlas / Thomas C. Brisco.
p. cm.
Includes index.
ISBN 1–55819–709–5 (hardcover)
1. Bible—Geography—Maps. I. Title. II. Title: Bible atlas.
G2230.B63 1997 <G&M>
220.9'1'0223—dc21 97–25035
CIP
Maps

9 10 11 12 09 08 07 06 05

To Judy, my wife and dearest friend,
and our two children, Carole and Brian,
constant sources of joy

TABLE OF CONTENTS

PART ONE: The Biblical Setting

PART TWO: The Old Testament Period

PART THREE: The New Testament Era: The World of Jesus and the Early Church

LIST OF SIDEBARS

LIST OF CHARTS

LIST OF MAPS

LIST OF ABBREVIATIONS

ANET .... *Ancient Near Eastern Texts Relating to the Old Testament,* ed. James B. Pritchard. 3rd ed. Princeton: Princeton University Press, 1969.

ANT. ...... *Jewish Antiquities,* by Josephus. Loeb Classical Library: Harvard University Press.

JW .... *Jewish Wars,* by Josephus. Loeb Classical Library: Harvard University Press.

Strabo .... *Geography,* by Strabo. Loeb Classical Library: Harvard University Press.

CAH ...... *The Cambridge Ancient History,* eds. I. E. S. Edwards, C. J. Gadd, N. G. L. Hammond, and E. Sollberger. 3rd ed. Cambridge: Cambridge University Press, 1971.

PREFACE

This *Atlas* is offered out of the deep conviction that the Bible's message is timeless and eternally relevant. Yet God conveyed that timeless message in very specific geographical and historical settings. To understand the Bible today we must hear its words in light of the ancient setting. Over twenty years of teaching biblical studies in college, seminary, and churches has convinced me that an atlas can be a powerful lens through which to view the Bible in its original environment. In what follows the reader will find over 130 maps, almost as many photographs, and numerous charts and illustrations all designed to make the biblical world accessible to students of the Bible.

I have written this *Atlas* for the interested lay person and beginning level student of the Bible in colleges and seminaries. Accordingly, I have avoided technical jargon and overly complex discussion of issues that have a legitimate place among scholars, but which can be distracting to students with little or no background. The goal has been to provide the geographical and historical data necessary to comprehend the Bible's unfolding story.

Part I describes the physical realities of the biblical world—geography, climate, economics, and routes. Against this foundation, Part II traces the biblical story from the pages of Genesis through the triumph of Christianity in the fourth century A.D. The text narrates the historical events of the Bible. The interaction of ancient Israel with the dominant powers of the day—Egypt, Assyria, Babylon, Persia, Greece, and Rome—receives special emphasis, but attention is given also to Israel's lesser neighbors including the Phoenicians, Arameans, and the Transjordan Kingdoms. Maps based on the text are provided for each section. Many maps provide more information than can be found in the accompanying narrative. Most maps are coordinated with relevant biblical texts in the map legend. I greatly encourage students to read the biblical texts as they use the *Atlas*. There is no substitute for studying the Bible itself.

Other features of the *Atlas* include side-bars—short articles giving more information on something mentioned in the text. A glossary and bibliography arranged by topics for students and teachers who desire greater knowledge about a particular subject are provided at the back. Numerous charts provide overviews of periods or additional information relevant to the text. Chronology (dating events) is always a problem for historians. The dates utilized in this *Atlas* conform primarily to those found in the *Cambridge Ancient History*, 3rd edition. I have followed John Bright's *History of Israel*, 3rd edition for the kings of Israel and Judah. We made an editorial decision to use approximate dates e.g., 1850 B.C. rather than "mid-eighteenth century," believing the former is less confusing to new students.

All scriptural quotations are taken from the Revised Standard Version; spellings of biblical place names conform to those found in the R.S.V. I have chosen to use static terms for certain well-known physical features, thus "Mediterranean Sea" not "Upper Sea" or "Great Sea." The term "Palestine" as used in the *Atlas* has no modern political associations, but was chosen as the best term to describe the southern Levant.

Finally, I have the joyful task of extending my deepest gratitude to many people whose expertise and effort made the *Atlas* possible. I am indebted to Holman Publishers for affording me the opportunity to produce the *Atlas* and especially to two fine editors, Trent Butler (Managing Editor of the Bible Division), and Steve Bond (Managing Editor of the Reference Division). Trent guided the project for nearly eight years; Steve oversaw the final two years of the project, coordinating the innumerable details in a project this size and functioning as liaison to the cartographers and graphic artists. I am deeply grateful for their wise counsel and constant encouragement. Many thanks also to the talented people at GeoSystems, Keith Winters (Senior Project Manager), Kevin Lear (Project Manager), and special map consultant Barry Beitzel. Kevin and his gifted cartographers worked diligently to create maps conveying the ideas explained in the text. Professor Beitzel's expertise in the area is well established; I am grateful for the benefit of his insight and experience. Likewise the people at Multnomah Graphics led by Mike Petersen and John R. Kohlenberger III are to be commended for their fine work designing the layout of the *Atlas*. Thanks also go to James McClemore and Brent Bruce of the *Biblical Illustrator* as well as Marsha Ellis-Smith who helped secure several illustrations. My colleague Bruce Corley read and provided comments on the New Testament section for which I am grateful. Three capable secretaries—Stephanie Faulls, Beverly Gill, and Sherri Hall—typed the manuscript; Sherri also cheerfully assisted in innumerable details that accompanied the final stages of the work. Any deficiencies of the *Atlas* are surely my own and not the result of the fine assistance I have received from all of the above.

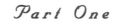

Part One

THE BIBLICAL SETTING

INTRODUCTION

The Bible is an intensely geographical book as even a casual glance makes clear. It tells the story of God's redemptive work in human history. This story is revealed through the nation of Israel, the early church, and supremely in Jesus Christ. Specific geographical and cultural settings form the backdrop of this divine drama. Geographic position often plays a crucial part in the history of any people. Cultural influences, military and economic alliances, and the political importance of a given people all are determined to some degree by geographical location. Moreover, physical environment left a deep imprint on ancient societies since they were linked much more closely to the land than we are today. Terrain determined the location of villages and cities as well as the roads that linked them. Climate, soil conditions, and availability of water affected agriculture, location of settlements, everyday diet, even religious beliefs. The land provided the raw materials for household utensils, tools, weapons, houses, and other necessities of daily living. Not surprisingly then, students of the Bible must learn something of the physical setting of the biblical world to understand the story it narrates.

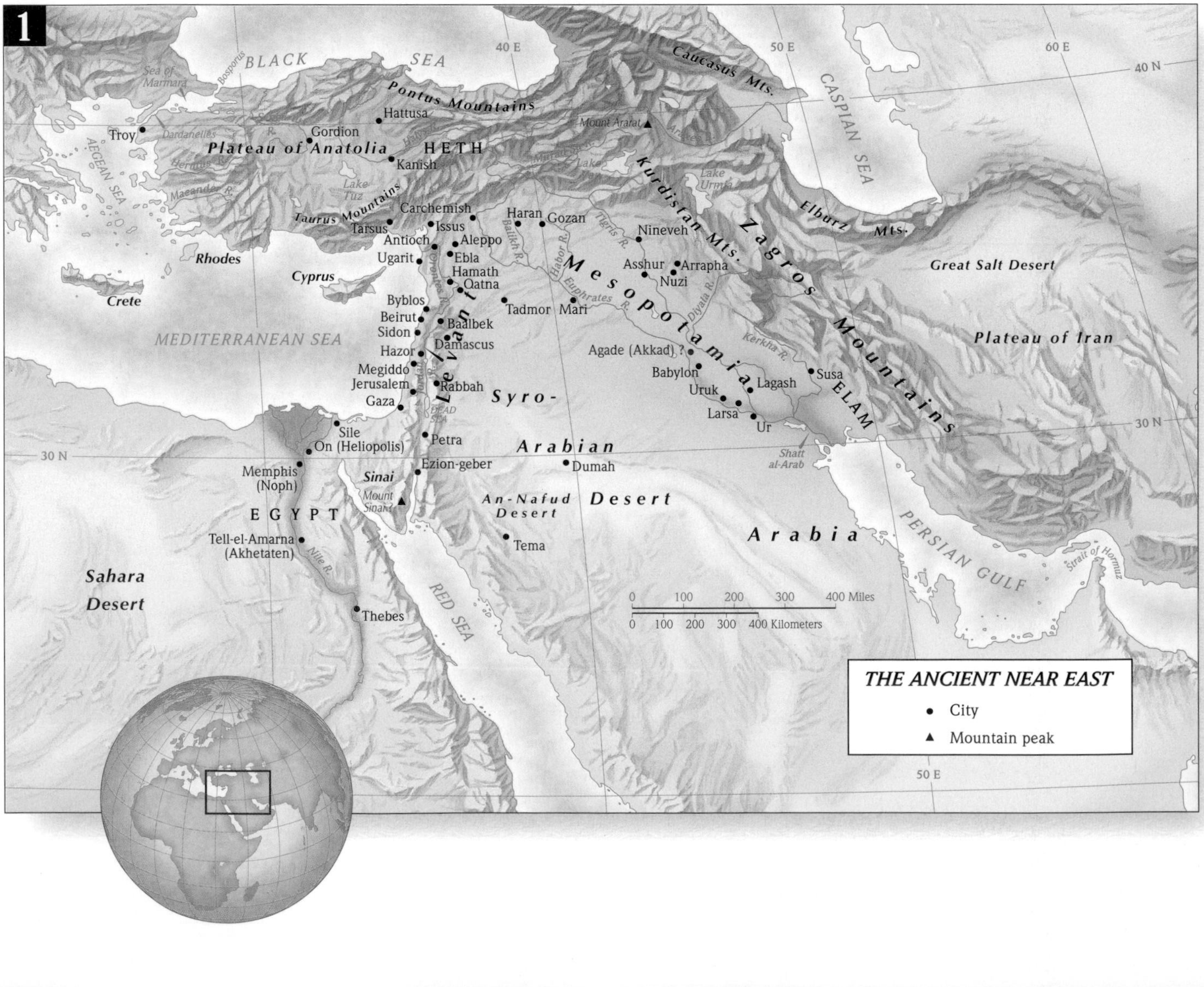

Chapter One

THE FACE OF THE ANCIENT NEAR EAST

Most of the biblical drama unfolded in the Ancient Near East. Today the modern states of Egypt, Israel, Jordan, Saudi Arabia, Lebanon, Syria, Iraq, Iran, and Turkey occupy that area. The Ancient Near East has been called the "Cradle of Civilization" because many important cultural and technological advances took place there. We now know that comparable innovations occurred in other parts of the world, yet the Near East retains a central place in human history. There the influence of three continents—Africa, Asia, and Europe—converge.

The Fertile Crescent

James Breasted coined the phrase "Fertile Crescent" to describe a band of land where conditions favored the establishment of early agricultural settlements. Water, either from rainfall or irrigation, and a favorable climate encouraged the development of village life. Stretching northwest from the Persian Gulf (the "Lower Sea"), the crescent includes the lands bordering the Tigris and Euphrates Rivers known as Mesopotamia. In southern Turkey the crescent bends south along the eastern Mediterranean coast. Here lies a narrow strip of land caught between the sea and desert called the Levant. Ancient Syria formed the northern half of the Levant, while Palestine occupied the southern portion. The intrusion of the Syro-Arabian Desert from the south gives the crescent its characteristic shape, while mountain ranges

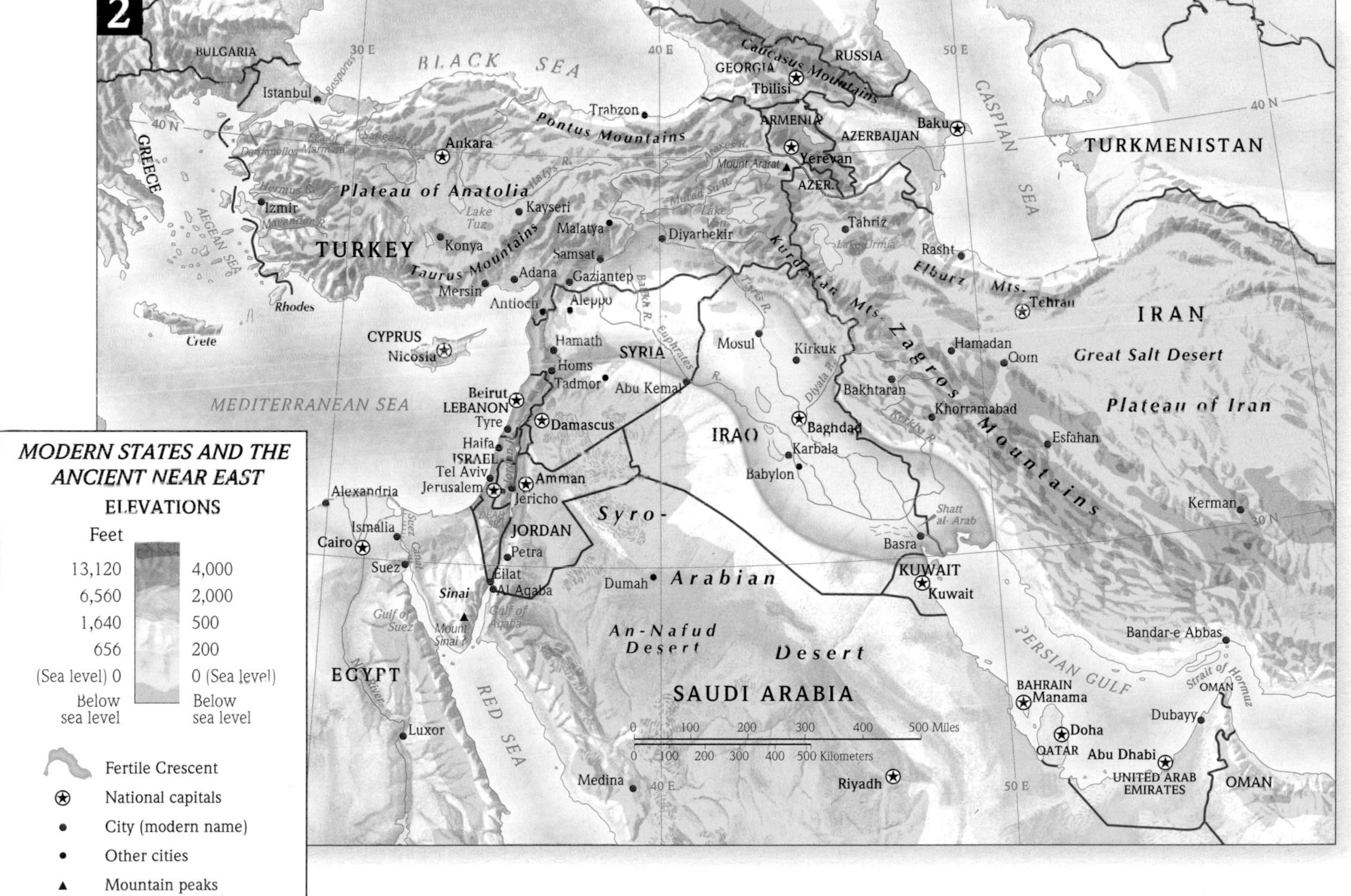

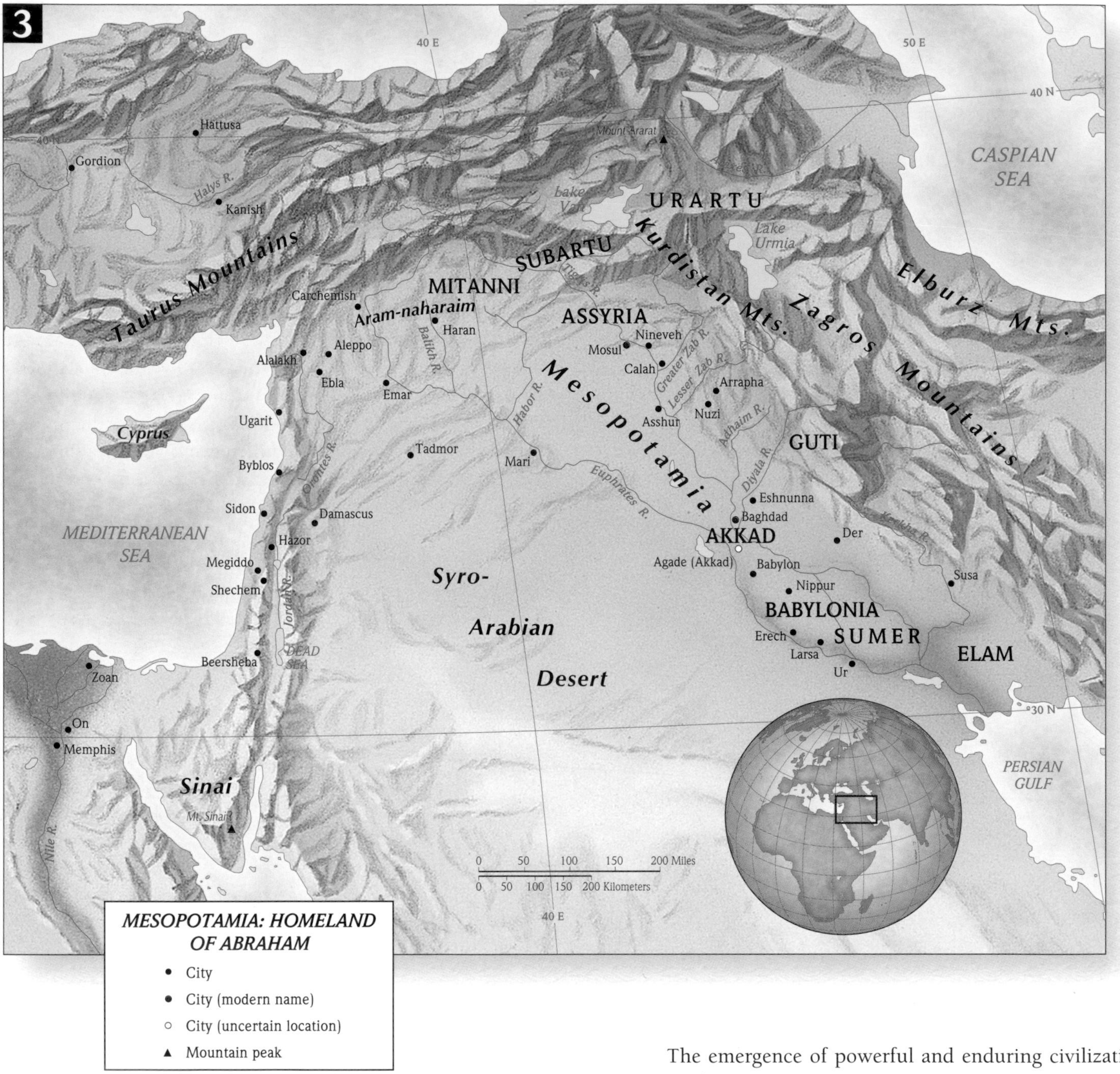

3

MESOPOTAMIA: HOMELAND OF ABRAHAM

- • City
- • City (modern name)
- ○ City (uncertain location)
- ▲ Mountain peak

(Taurus, Kurdistan, and Zagros Mountains) mark the limits to the north and east.

Beyond the Sinai, south of the Fertile Crescent, lay Egypt. Favored by nature with the Nile River and its abundant water, Egypt played a vital part in the Ancient Near East. From about 3200 B.C., Egypt, like Mesopotamia, became a powerful center of civilization. Historically, the cultures of Egypt and Mesopotamia dominated the history of the Ancient Near East, at least until the campaigns of Alexander the Great (334–323 B.C.).

The emergence of powerful and enduring civilizations in Egypt and Mesopotamia gave strategic importance to Palestine. Palestine was a "land bridge" linking the two great cultural centers. The major international route, the International Coastal Highway, crossed portions of Palestine. This geographical fact is crucial to the history of Palestine. As part of the corridor connecting Egypt and Mesopotamia, Palestine possessed a strategic importance far greater than its size or relatively few resources might suggest. Palestine sat astride the vital economic and military arteries of the Near East. Historically, this meant two things: (1) the people living in Palestine felt the imprint of many cultures, and (2) the major powers sought control of this small land.

Mesopotamia: Home of Abraham

Mesopotamia was an integral part of the biblical landscape in many periods. Genesis locates Abraham's homeland in Mesopotamia (Gen. 11–12). Mesopotamian kings from Assyria and Babylon appear frequently in the historical and prophetic books of the Old Testament. Jewish captives from Jerusalem spent many years in exile near Babylon. Descendants of those exiles were present at Pentecost.

Mesopotamia, literally the land "between the rivers," describes those lands bordering the Tigris and Euphrates Rivers. Today Iraq, northern Syria, and extreme southeastern Turkey occupy the area of ancient Mesopotamia. To the south and west the great expanse of the Syro-Arabian desert forms the border beyond which settled life based on agriculture is not possible. To the north and east, mountains ring Mesopotamia. In Bible times these mountains harbored less-advanced peoples who often threatened Mesopotamian kingdoms. Mesopotamia gave birth to many great civilizations, including the Sumerian, Akkadian, Babylonian, and Assyrian.

TIGRIS AND EUPHRATES

The Tigris and Euphrates Rivers dominate Mesopotamia. Both rivers originate in the high mountains of eastern Turkey and flow south-southeastward to the Persian Gulf. Large distances separate the rivers for most of their journey, but near Baghdad they converge to within twenty miles of each other before diverging again. Near the head of the Persian Gulf, the rivers merge into a marshland, a feature characteristic of both ancient and modern times. The Euphrates (1,780 miles long) is longer and slower than the Tigris, but more suited for transportation. Two major tributaries, the Balikh and Habor, join the Euphrates in northwest Mesopotamia. The Tigris (1,150 miles long) is much swifter, descending through the steppes running parallel to the Zagros Mountains. Four tributaries—the Greater and Lesser Zab, the Adhem, and the Diyala—enter the Tigris from these mountains. The influence of the Tigris and Euphrates, with their tributaries, is such that virtually all important cities of Mesopotamia can be found along their courses. Indeed, whenever a river changed its course, as the Euphrates on occasion did, it isolated the cities, which then declined or were abandoned for economic reasons.

Both the Tigris and Euphrates flooded annually. Autumn and winter rains in combination with melting snows of the high northern mountains produced a large volume of water that had to be harnessed. This inundation was unpredictable, at times being inadequate and at other times, violent. The timing of the flood in Mesopotamia was not as helpful for agriculture as in Egypt. Consequently, the inhabitants of central and southern Mesopotamia maintained a sophisticated system of canals, dikes, and dams from earliest times to protect their cities and to distribute water to thirsty fields. Ancient flood stories like the Gilgamesh Epic abounded in Mesopotamia. They expressed the ancients' fascination with and fear of these floods.

NORTH AND SOUTH MESOPOTAMIA

Southern and northern Mesopotamia differ in terms of geography, climate, and natural resources. The dividing line between the two sections is roughly near modern Baghdad. The southern portion from Baghdad to the Persian Gulf (approximately 350 miles by scale) is a flat plain formed by sediments deposited by the rivers and soil blown from the desert. Summers here are very hot (95°F average in July), but winters are mild. Rainfall is scarce, decreasing the farther south one goes; thus crops have depended entirely on irrigation. Still visible from the air are the numerous irrigation canals, long since silted up, required for agriculture. This intense irrigation and flooding resulted in an increase in the salt content of the land (salinization), which eventually hindered crop production.

Southern Mesopotamia lacks many resources. Few building materials were available; houses, temples, and palaces were all built of mud brick. Metals and timber had to be imported. However, the irrigated fields produced excellent crops of barley, the basic staple used for cakes and beer, and some wheat. Dates, which grew in abundance, and sesame oil supplied essential carbohydrates for the diet. Fish from the marshlands and rivers provided much of the meat. Properly

Euphrates River.

utilized, this land supported a significant population, with surpluses for export. Successively, the Sumerian, Akkadian, and Babylonian civilizations arose in southern Mesopotamia, bequeathing a great cultural heritage to the Near East. Cities like Babylon and Ur testify to the land's vitality.

North of Baghdad, uplands and steppes contrast with the flat plain of the south. Rolling hills emerge from the high mountains that border Mesopotamia to the north. Rainfall amounts are higher here, with some sections receiving up to twenty inches annually, although many areas receive much less. The summers are somewhat milder than in the south, but winters are harsher due to higher elevations.

Near Mosul in the Middle Tigris Valley, Asshur, Nineveh, and Calah (Nimrud) mark the heartland of ancient Assyria. Timber and building stones offered royal architects materials for the impressive palaces, temples, and administrative centers of the Assyrian kings; however, common people used mud brick for their houses.

Portions of Assyria produced crops of barley and wheat, but seldom in quantities to be totally self-sufficient. Also, the metals necessary for weapons and implements—copper, iron, tin, zinc, and lead—had to be imported along with cedar and supplemental food supplies. This meant that the Assyrians often sought to expand their control southward to Babylonia or westward to the Mediterranean Sea to obtain vital commodities through major trade routes.

Due west of Assyria lay northwest Mesopotamia with its grassy steppes and fertile lands associated with the Balikh and Habor Rivers. Abundant winter rains, a high water table, and numerous small streams make this region especially attractive for raising cattle and sheep. The Bible associates Abraham closely with this region. The biblical term *Aram-naharaim* (Gen. 24:10; Deut. 23:4), often translated "Mesopotamia," refers to the land of the Balikh and Habor Rivers.

Egypt: Land of Bondage

As the home of one of the world's enduring civilizations, Egypt looms large on the biblical landscape. For over three thousand years Egyptian history unfolded, casting its spell over the

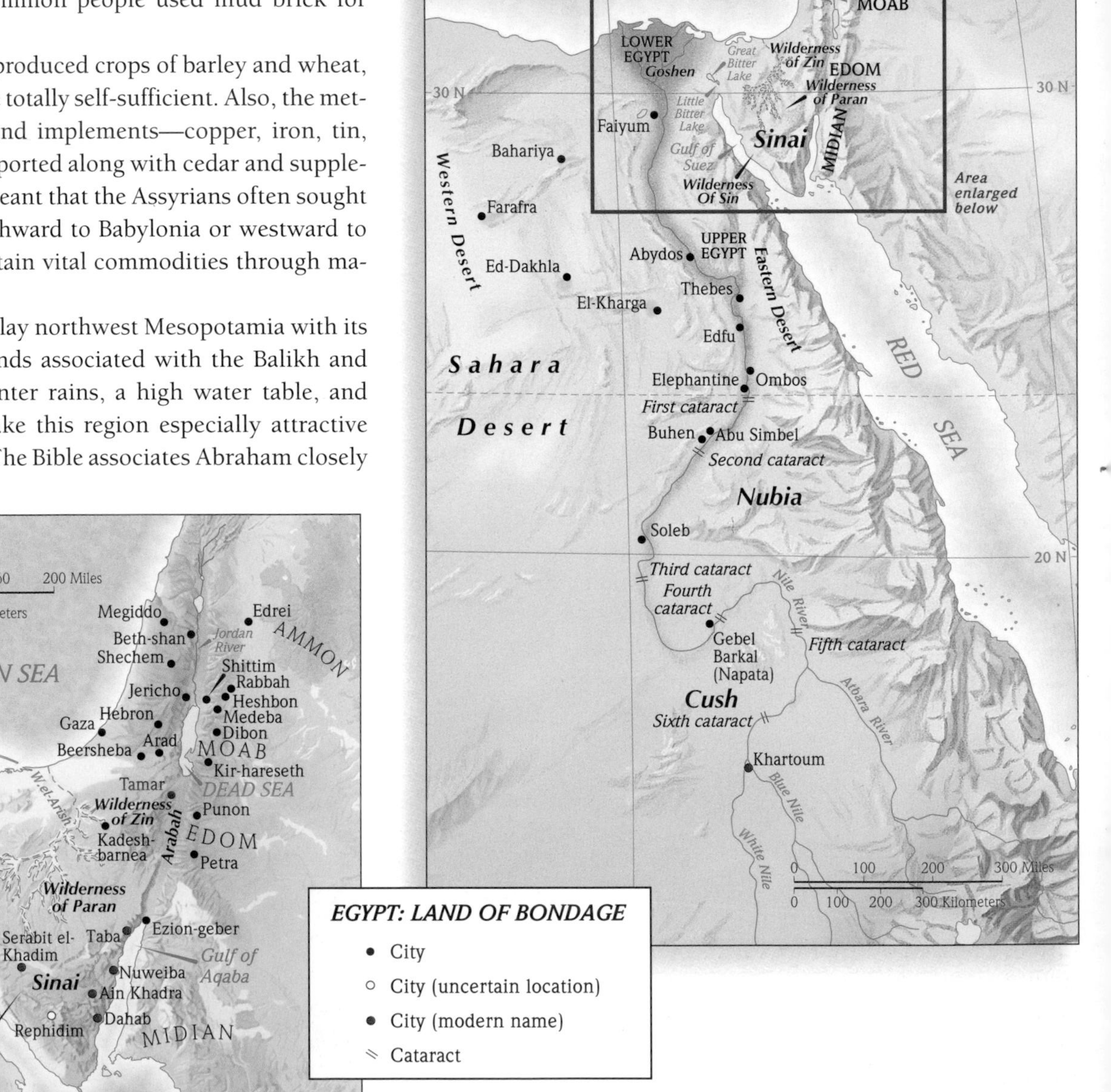

EGYPT: LAND OF BONDAGE

- City
- City (uncertain location)
- City (modern name)
- Cataract

An air view of the Nile Valley taken near Thebes. Notice the sharp differentiation between the lands nourished by the Nile River and the deserts that surround the valley.

ancient world. By the time Abraham journeyed to Egypt, the pharaohs had ruled for over a thousand years. With its close geographical proximity, this ancient culture left a deep impression on the people of Palestine. The biblical references concerning Joseph and Moses illustrate the interconnections between the lands. Egyptian kings repeatedly meddled in the affairs of Palestine, attempting to exploit key trade routes and maintain a buffer zone of security.

THE TWO LANDS

The land that spawned such a vital civilization is geographically unique. Egypt is "the gift of the Nile," observed the Greek historian Herodotus in the fifth century B.C. The waters of the Nile extend like a finger of life through the stone and sand of North Africa's deserts. From the first cataract near Aswan northward 750 miles to the Mediterranean Sea, ancient Egypt comprised the arable land touched by the Nile.

Geographically, Egypt consisted of two distinct parts, with the dividing line near modern Cairo. North of Cairo, the Nile formed a great Delta composed of deep alluvial sediments deposited through the millennia. Several branches of the Nile flowed through the Delta, or "Lower Egypt," in antiquity, although only two remain today. Dense undergrowth prevented development in earlier times, but eventually several key cities emerged, such as Sais, Bubastis, and the biblical store cities of Pithom and Raamses (Exod. 1:11). The northeastern Delta, the part of Egypt most readily accessible to Palestine, is the land of Goshen to which the patriarchs frequently traveled (Gen. 45:9–11; 46:31ff).

South of Cairo, the encroaching deserts restrict settlement to the Nile Valley, a narrow ribbon of land affected by the annual flood on either side of the river. The Nile Valley, or "Upper Egypt," never is more than a few miles wide. Scattered along the banks of the Nile, the great Egyptian cities with their monumental temples still inspire awe. Abydos, Edfu, and especially Thebes (biblical No-amon), with its temple of Amon-Re, embodied the power of Egypt in her era of greatest strength. Opposite Thebes in the cliffs of the western desert, the pharaohs of the New Kingdom carved their tombs in the Valley of the Kings. These Egyptian cities tended to be smaller than their Mesopotamian counterparts; in fact, most Egyptians lived in small villages. Still, through the centuries Egypt's monumental architecture, not normal village life, has gripped the imaginations of historian and poet alike.

THE GIFT OF THE NILE

Egypt's greatest resource was the Nile, which linked the cities and villages along its length. The Nile provided transportation and communication as the principal highway of the land. Natural currents carried traffic northward, while prevailing north winds permitted travel upriver (southward). The annual inundation of the Nile provided the river's chief benefit to the land. Each year, with uncanny regularity, the Nile flooded, replenishing the land with water and a thin layer of new soil. The causes of this unique phenomenon are found far to the south of Egypt.

The Nile is a composite river that draws water from

The Nile River at Thebes with the temple of Luxor in the background.

several different streams. The White Nile provides a steady source of water from the lakes of equatorial Africa that are fed by constant rains. Near Khartoum in the Sudan, two other rivers—the Blue Nile and the Atbara—join the White Nile. During the spring, melting snows and rains in the Ethiopian highlands swell the Blue Nile and the Atbara with water, their swift currents carrying soil and organic materials. The Nile rises as their waters rush northward toward the Mediterranean.

From July to September the waters covered the land along the river's banks, soaking the fields and depositing a layer of rich silt. When the waters retreated, the Egyptian farmers reestablished the boundaries of their fields and prepared the land for planting. Since all agriculture depended on the annual flood, the Egyptians developed devices (Nilometers) to predict its height. A rise of seven to eight meters was ideal. A higher flood could be destructive, while a rise of less than six meters could provoke a famine like that mentioned in Genesis 41:53.

The annual inundation of the Nile was one of several factors that gave stability to Egyptian civilization. A favorable climate was another. Although rainfall is sparse throughout the land and summer temperatures can be very hot, the long sunny days and mild winters were ideal for growing crops. Egypt was immune from the storms and extreme variations of climate found in other parts of the Near East. Moreover, deserts bordered the land of Egypt on the east and west, while the Mediterranean Sea was an effective barrier to the north.

Six cataracts in the Nile River to the south, protected by strategically fortified garrisons, controlled any approach to Egypt from that direction. Access to Egypt came primarily through the northeast Delta. Here the great trade routes crossing the Sinai from Palestine entered Egypt, linking the land with the other cultures of the Near East. Those same trade routes could be used to attack Egypt as well. Consequently, the Egyptians repeatedly sought to extend their control beyond Sinai into Palestine and Syria, thereby ensuring security and an enduring connection to vital goods.

The Levant

The term "Levant" describes the habitable land along the eastern Mediterranean coast sandwiched between the Mediterranean Sea on the west and the Syro-Arabian Desert to the east. Syria and Lebanon comprised the northern sections of the Levant while Palestine (see chap. 2) anchored the southern end. The Levant served as a land bridge, connecting the great cultural centers located in Mesopotamia and Egypt. The great trunk route—the International Coastal Highway—followed the natural passageway through the region. Although not blessed with large rivers, most sections of the Levant normally received adequate rainfall for crop production, while several smaller rivers interspersed between higher mountains provided additional water.

SYRIA AND LEBANON

The modern states of Syria and Lebanon occupy most of the northern Levant today, although portions lay in southern Turkey. The Amanus Mountains (up to 7,000 feet) marked the northern limits of ancient Syria. A pass through these mountains led to the Cilician Plain which in turn gave access up to the Anatolian Plateau through the Taurus Mountains via the vital Cilician Gates. Syria proper lay south and west of the Euphrates River. The great city of Carchemish, on the Euphrates, connected Syria with Assyria by way of Haran across the steppe land known as Al-Jazirah. A series of mountains dominates Syria's western sector along the coast including the Amanus Mountains, the Nuseiriyeh Mountains (up to 5,300 feet), and Mons Cassius (5,771 feet). The Orontes River descends from the Beqa Valley, emptying into the Plain of Antioch. Ancient Ugarit, where excavations yielded important religious texts detailing the myths of Baal, was a key Syrian port. Inland, the International Coastal Highway passed through Hamath, Ebla, and Aleppo, all lying in valleys and plains east of the mountains. Caravans traversed the Syrian desert along an important route that connected Mari with Damascus by way of Tadmor/Palmyra, one of the great cara-

Snow capped Mt. Hermon from a distance.

van cities of the ancient world. The great Syrian Desert tableland south and east of this caravan route made travel virtually impossible.

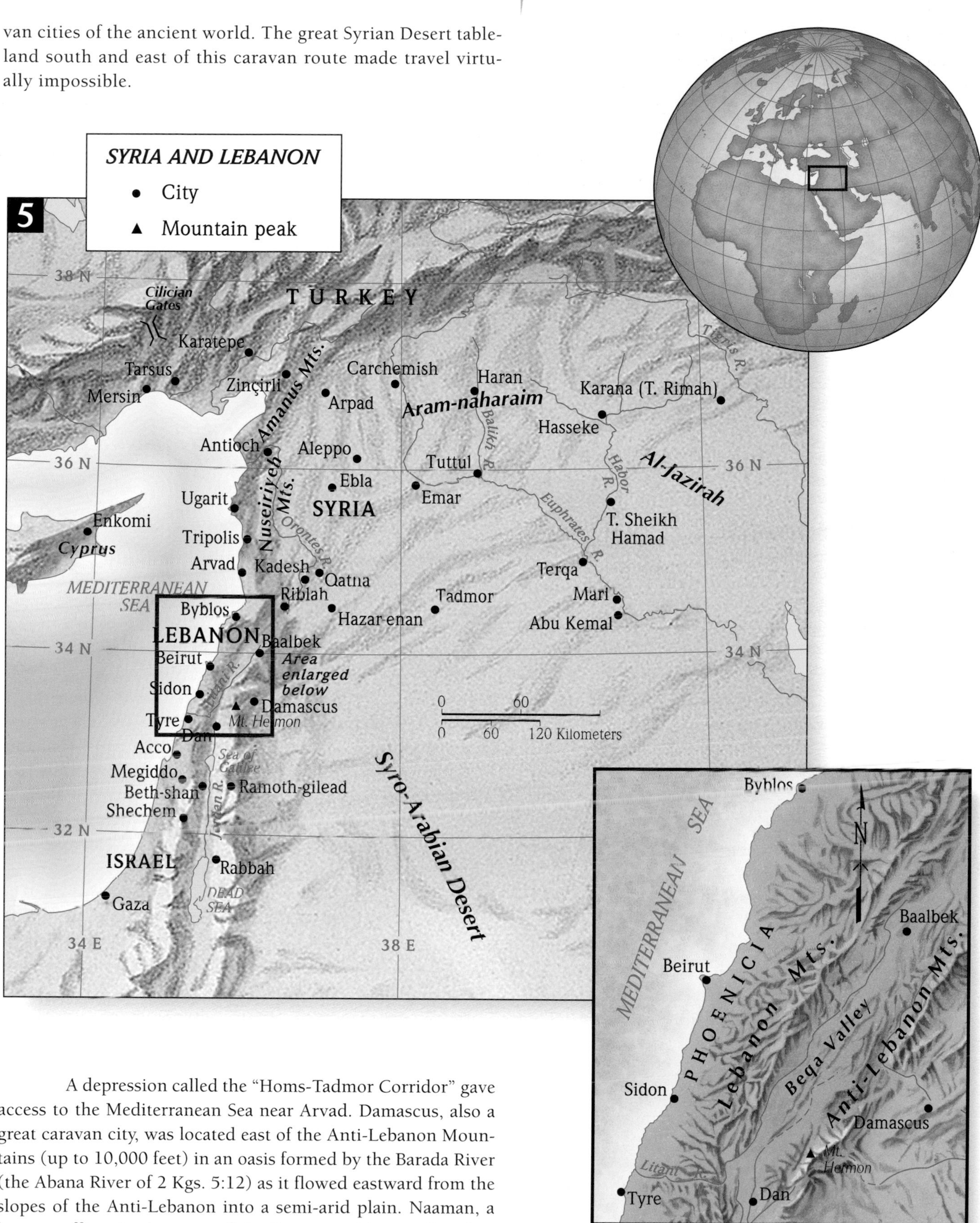

A depression called the "Homs-Tadmor Corridor" gave access to the Mediterranean Sea near Arvad. Damascus, also a great caravan city, was located east of the Anti-Lebanon Mountains (up to 10,000 feet) in an oasis formed by the Barada River (the Abana River of 2 Kgs. 5:12) as it flowed eastward from the slopes of the Anti-Lebanon into a semi-arid plain. Naaman, a leprous officer in the army of the Damascus kings, referred to the fresh water of the Abana and Pharpar Rivers that sustained

Byblos, a Phoenician port city just north of Beirut. Beyond the Bronze Age temples in the foreground, notice the sloping Lebanon Mountains that descend to the seacoast.

Damascus (2 Kgs. 5:1–14). The identity of the latter river is uncertain, but may refer to the el-Awaj south of Damascus.

Lebanon was a mountainous enclave tucked between the sea and the desert. Two high chains of mountains—the Lebanon Mountains (highest peak 10,115 feet) and the Anti-Lebanon Mountains (up to 10,000 feet) bisect the region north to south. Mt Hermon (9,263 feet) lies at the southern end of the Anti-Lebanon chain. The name "Lebanon" comes from a Hebrew root meaning "white," likely a reference to the snow-capped peaks of the region. The mountains were the source of the famous "cedars of Lebanon," prized throughout the Ancient Near East. Their great size made the cedars desirable for construction of ships and large public buildings such as temples and palaces. Solomon used cedars from Lebanon in his temple and palace (1 Kgs. 5:6; 7:11). The Egyptians coveted the cedars, using them for sacred barques (sacred boats used in transporting the image of a god) among other things. Byblos, port of access for the cedars, shows much Egyptian influence in the second millennium B.C.

The fertile Beqa Valley lies between the Lebanon and Anti-Lebanon Mountains. Well-watered at an elevation of 3,000 feet, the Beqa serves as a watershed for the region. The Orontes River flows northward from the Beqa while the Litani River drains the valley southward, curving west to join the sea just north of Tyre. Baal-bek, with its magnificent Roman temples, sits near the middle of the Beqa.

The cultural identity of Syria varied historically; but from at least the beginning of the Iron Age (ca. 1200 B.C.), the Arameans increasingly dominated the region. Aramean kingdoms like Aram-Damascus, Aram-zobah, and Hamath appear repeatedly in the biblical record.

The Phoenicians inhabited the narrow coast of Lebanon. The Lebanon Mountains restricted the available agricultural land. Phoenicia faced the sea; numerous natural harbors—Tyre, Byblos (Gebal), Sidon, Beyrutus, and Arvad—induced the Phoenicians to take to the sea. Ultimately, the Phoenicians became perhaps the greatest merchant seafarers of the ancient world. Phoenician merchants plied the Mediterranean basin planting colonies (Carthage, Cadiz, Marseilles) as they went (see "The Phoenician Culture," p. 127). Israel developed a close commercial relationship with Phoenicia as early as the time of Solomon. The Phoenicians needed Israel's agricultural surplus while Israel profited from a link with Phoenicia's trading ventures.

International Highways

THE INTERNATIONAL COASTAL HIGHWAY (*VIA MARIS*)

Two major international highways connecting Egypt and Mesopotamia traversed Palestine. Until recently the most important international highway system was called the *Via Maris*, or "way of the sea" (Isa. 9:1), which extended from the northeastern Delta of Egypt into Mesopotamia. This name is still used in many books and articles, but recent work has demonstrated that the term *Via Maris* is a misnomer originating in the Middle Ages. A better name for this great trunk route is the "International Coastal Highway." This artery carried trade goods vital to the economy of the Near East, while the armies of powerful kingdoms marched along its length. The initial portions of the route hugged the coast of Sinai, passing through Gaza and the southern coast of Palestine. Near Aphek, conditions forced the route further inland, skirting the Sharon Plain, to enter the Jezreel Valley through a vital pass (the Aruna Pass) controlled by Megiddo.

Branches of the International Coastal Highway radiated out of the Jezreel Valley northwestward toward the Phoenician cities (Tyre, Sidon) and southeastward into the Jordan Valley near Beth-shan. Another branch extended past the northwest shore of the Sea of Galilee to Hazor and Dan before crossing over to Damascus. From Damascus, two main branches of the International Coastal Highway continued into Mesopotamia. The more difficult but shorter route crossed the desert by Tadmor (Palmyra) to Mari. The longer, more secure branch headed north through Syria by way of Qatna, Hamath, and Aleppo, from whence the route turned southeast to the great cities—Mari, Babylon, Ur—along the Euphrates. The importance of the International Coastal Highway can be gauged by the influence of the great cities located along its path.

6

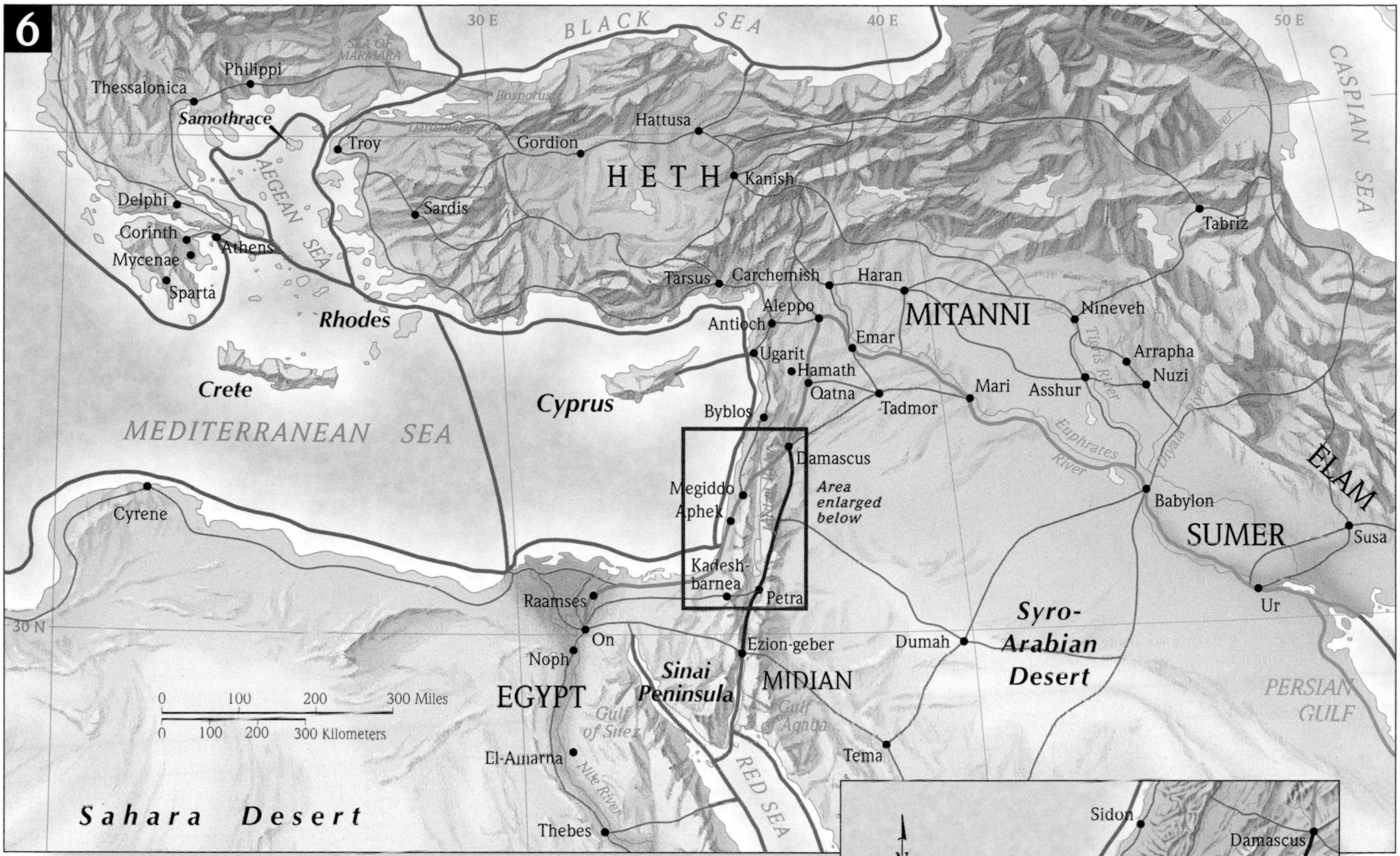

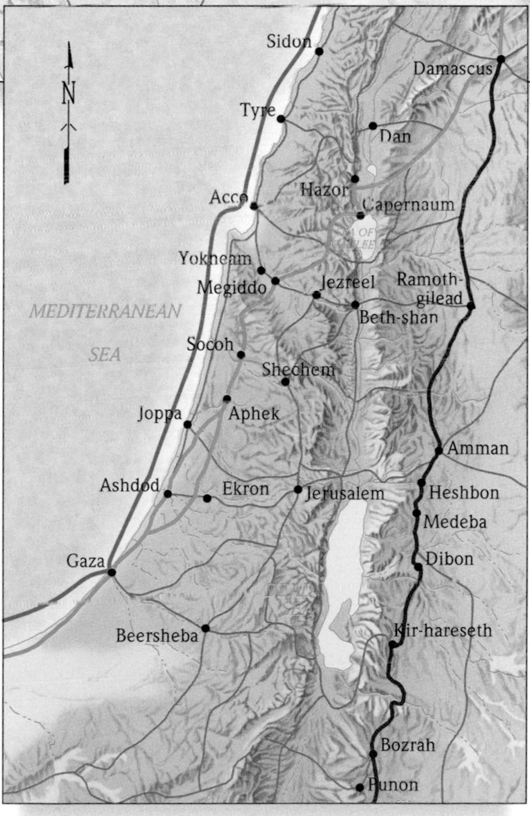

"INTERNATIONAL ROUTES"

- City
- International Coastal Highway
- King's Highway
- Sea routes
- Other routes

THE KING'S HIGHWAY

A second, less important interregional highway linked Arabia with Damascus. This "King's Highway" (Num. 21:22) extended from Ezion-geber at the top of the Gulf of Aqabah through the Transjordan to Damascus. Important cities along this route included Kir-hareseth, Dibon, Heshbon, Ramoth-gilead, Ashtaroth, and Karnaim. Caravans conveyed spices and perfumes as well as other goods from the Arabian Peninsula along this route. Though of less importance militarily than the International Coastal Highway, the economic potential of the King's Highway occasioned many conflicts between Israel, Damascus, and other minor kingdoms of the Transjordan region.

Chapter Two

NATURAL REGIONS OF PALESTINE

Introduction

Having gained an overview of the geography of the Ancient Near East, we now focus on Palestine—the geographical epicenter of our faith. "Judea," "Galilee," and "Samaria" evoke vivid images of biblical events. The hills and valleys of this land heard the thunder of Amos' prophetic voice. The deserts witnessed the courageous preaching of John the Baptist as he prepared the way for the Lamb of God. The cities echo with the memories of David, Solomon, and Herod the Great, from whose imagination great buildings sprang. Along the dusty roads of this land the disciples followed Jesus of Nazareth, whose words and deeds mark the decisive intervention of God in human affairs.

According to the biblical description, Palestine is "a land of brooks of water, of fountains and springs, flowing forth in valleys and hills" (Deut. 8:7; cf. Deut. 11:10–17) and much more. Few areas on earth of comparable size contain more geographic diversity than Palestine. The small dimensions of the area makes the variety of landforms all the more striking. Ranging in width from 80 to 100 miles with a maximum length of 250 miles, Palestine is about the size of New Jersey. Yet within its borders, desert areas contrast with broad, fertile plains; mountain ranges and high plateaus tower above the lowest place on the earth's surface—the Dead Sea. (See also "The Tribal Allotments of Israel," p. 85)

The Plain of Sharon viewed from Aphek. The headwaters of the Yarkon River emerge from springs beside Tel Aphek.

Major Geographical Regions and Subdivisions

A study of Palestine's geology shows that the main physical features of the land run north to south. A cross sectional view (see map 8) reveals four major longitudinal zones: (1) the Coastal Plain, (2) the Western Mountains, (3) the Jordan Rift, and (4) the Eastern Plateau. The Jordan Rift is the most pronounced feature of the landscape and divides the land into two parts: Cisjordan, the area west of the Jordan Rift, and Transjordan, the inhabitable land between the rift and the deserts to the east. Most of the geographic features in Palestine represent a subdivision of the four major zones; however, four features—the Jezreel Valley, the Shephelah, the Negeb, and the Southern Wilderness—cannot be fitted easily in these zones and are listed separately below.

THE COASTAL PLAIN

The Coastal Plain of Palestine extends from the Ladder of Tyre in the north, southward to the Sinai, interrupted only by Mount Carmel as it juts out into the Mediterranean Sea. Few natural harbors can be found along the coast, however, and the presence of sand dunes and hard limestone ridges (*kurkar*) prohibited most settlement directly on the coast. These conditions meant that the people living in Palestine were seldom great seafarers. The fertile soil and abundant water, characteristic of the Coastal Plain, did ensure dense settlement in most periods.

Israel controlled portions of the plain only in times of political and military strength. More frequently, powerful

7

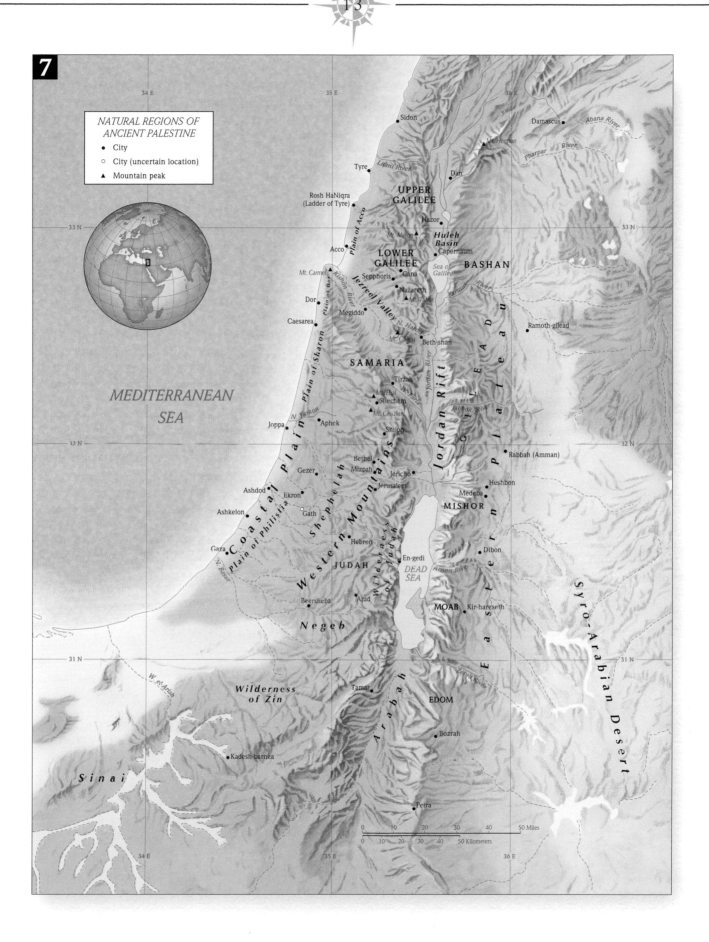

NATURAL REGIONS OF ANCIENT PALESTINE

- ● City
- ○ City (uncertain location)
- ▲ Mountain peak

34 E
35 E
36 E
33 N
32 N
31 N

Sidon
Damascus
Abana River
Mt. Hermon
Pharpar River
Tyre
Litani River
Dan
UPPER GALILEE
Rosh HaNiqra (Ladder of Tyre)
Plain of Acco
Hazor
Mt. Meron
Huleh Basin
Acco
LOWER GALILEE
Capernaum
BASHAN
Sea of Galilee
Cana
Sepphoris
Mt. Carmel
Kishon River
Jezreel Valley
Nazareth
Mt. Tabor
Yarmuk River
Dor
Plain of Dor
Megiddo
Caesarea
N. Harod
Mt. Gilboa
Beth-shan
Ramoth-gilead
SAMARIA
Plain of Sharon
Jordan River
Tirzah
Mt. Ebal
Shechem
Mt. Gerizim
W. Faria
Jordan Rift
Jabbok River
GILEAD
MEDITERRANEAN SEA
N. Yarkon
Joppa
Aphek
Shiloh
Rabbah (Amman)
Bethel
Mizpah
Gezer
Jericho
Jerusalem
Heshbon
Ashdod
Ekron
Medeba
MISHOR
Ashkelon
Gath
Coastal Plain
Shephelah
Western Mountains
Hebron
Wilderness of Judah
Gaza
Plain of Philistia
En-gedi
Dibon
N. Besor
JUDAH
DEAD SEA
Arnon River
Eastern Plateau
Arad
Beersheba
MOAB
Kir-hareseth
Negeb
Syro-Arabian Desert
W. el-Arish
Wilderness of Zin
Tamar
Zered River
Arabah
EDOM
Bozrah
Kadesh-barnea
Sinai
Petra

0 10 20 30 40 50 Miles
0 10 20 30 40 50 Kilometers

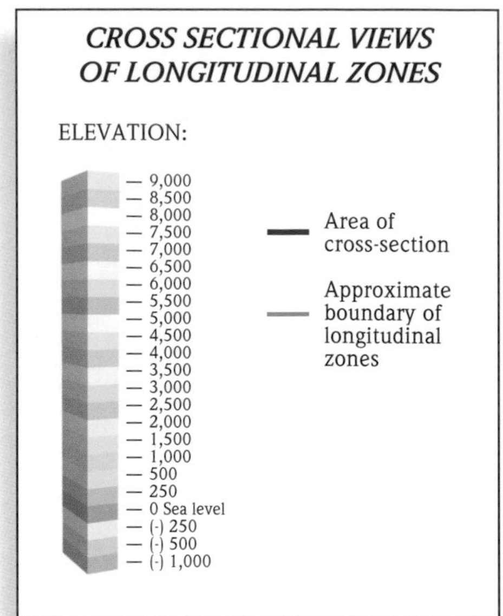
CROSS SECTIONAL VIEWS OF LONGITUDINAL ZONES
ELEVATION:
— 9,000
— 8,500
— 8,000
— 7,500
— 7,000
— 6,500
— 6,000
— 5,500
— 5,000
— 4,500
— 4,000
— 3,500
— 3,000
— 2,500
— 2,000
— 1,500
— 1,000
— 500
— 250
— 0 Sea level
— (-) 250
— (-) 500
— (-) 1,000
Area of cross-section
Approximate boundary of longitudinal zones

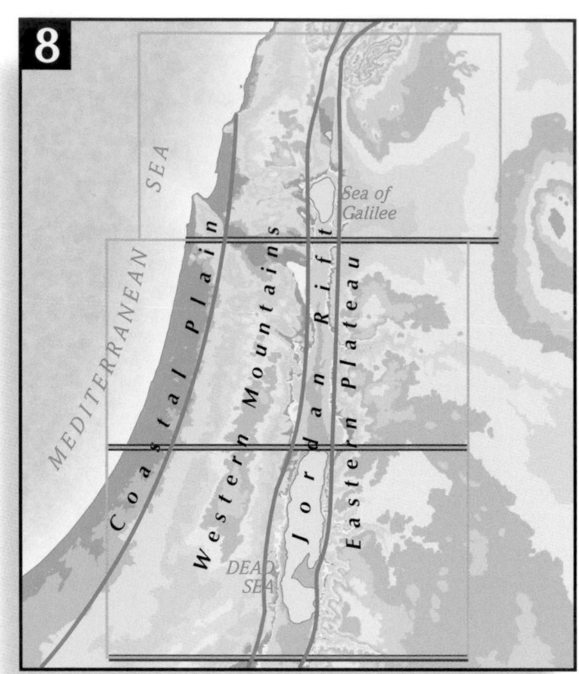
8
MEDITERRANEAN SEA
Sea of Galilee
DEAD SEA
Coastal Plain
Western Mountains
Jordan Rift
Eastern Plateau

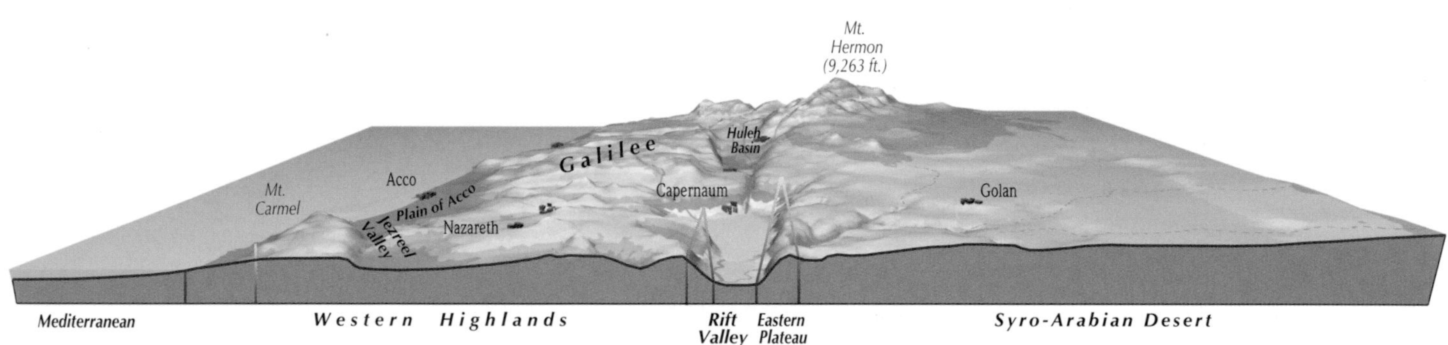
Mt. Hermon (9,263 ft.)
Huleh Basin
Galilee
Acco
Plain of Acco
Mt. Carmel
Jezreel Valley
Nazareth
Capernaum
Golan
Mediterranean
Western Highlands
Rift Valley
Eastern Plateau
Syro-Arabian Desert

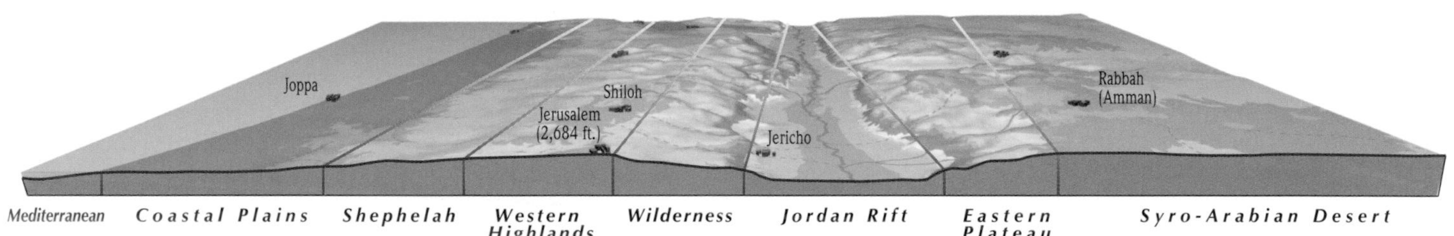
Joppa
Shiloh
Jerusalem (2,684 ft.)
Jericho
Rabbah (Amman)
Mediterranean
Coastal Plains
Shephelah
Western Highlands
Wilderness
Jordan Rift
Eastern Plateau
Syro-Arabian Desert

Shephelah
Western Mountains
Beersheba
Negeb
Zoar
Western Highlands
Wilderness
Jordan Rift (Arabah)
Eastern Plateau
Syro-Arabian Desert

foes like Egypt or Assyria dominated this region. The Philistines and Phoenicians encroached upon the plain throughout much of the first millennium B.C. The Coastal Plain consists of three sections: the Plain of Acco, the Plain of Sharon, and the Philistine Plain.

Plain of Acco (see map 9). The Plain of Acco occupies a narrow strip between the Ladder of Tyre in the north and Mount Carmel to the south. In Joshua's division of the land, the tribe of Asher received the Plain of Acco, but historically and culturally, the small cities of the region were closely related to their Phoenician neighbors to the north. Most of these cities clustered along the eastern portion of the Acco Plain, but the city of Acco (later, Ptolemais) and Achzib were along the coast.

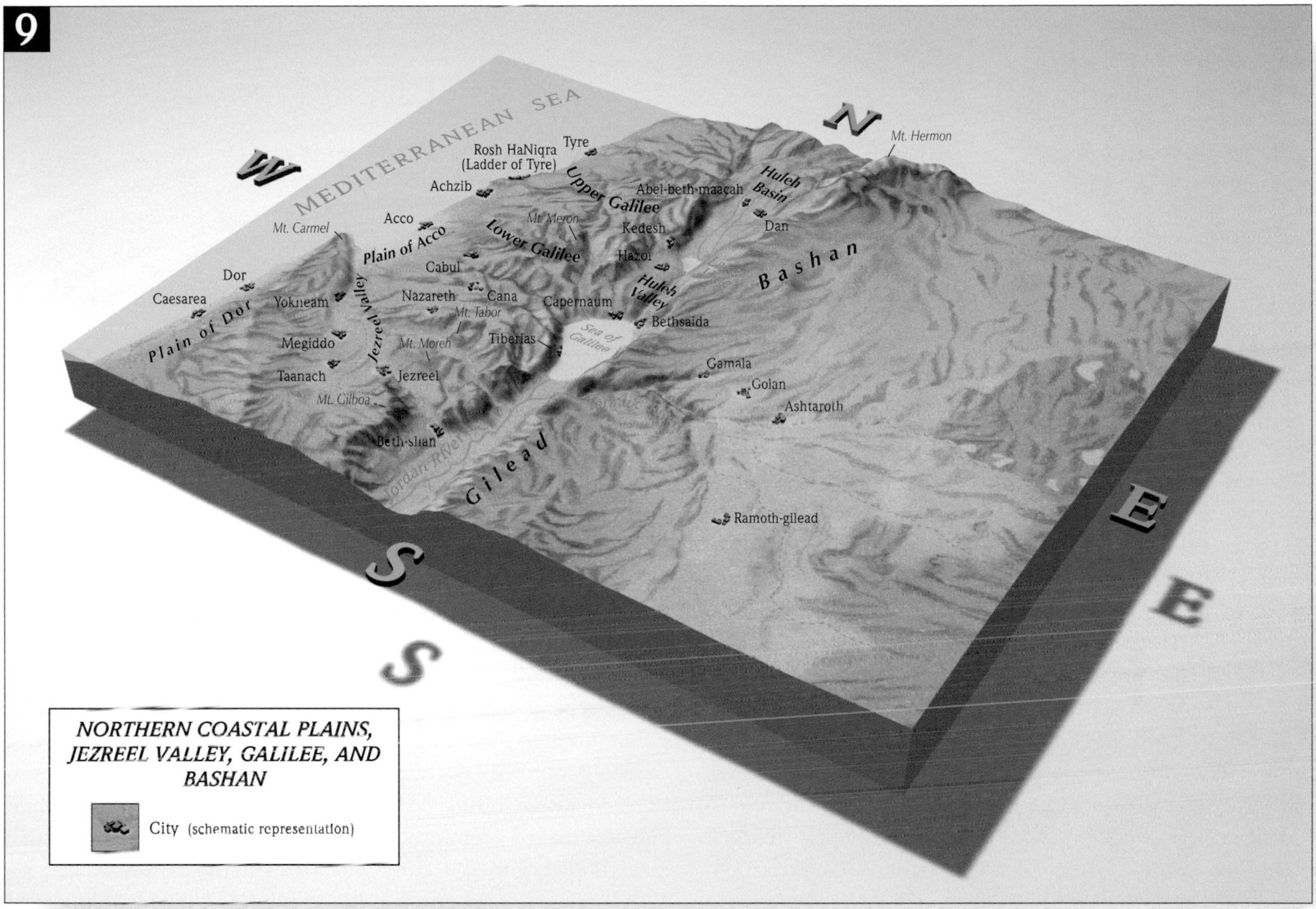

The Sharon Plain (see map 10). The Sharon Plain extends south of Mount Carmel to the Yarkon River. Until New Testament times the Sharon Plain was sparsely inhabited. Because of the deposition of sand along the coast, numerous streams of the region had a tendency to dam at their mouths. As a result, marshes and swamps formed in the western sector where dense undergrowth and oak thickets flourished. The lush vegetation of the Sharon inspired biblical poets (Song of Sol. 2:1) but discouraged settlement. The International Coastal Highway skirted the Sharon eastward where the few cities of the plain were located. Aphek, at the head of the Yarkon River, was the region's most important city in the Old Testament period. By New Testament times the marshes had been drained. Herod built the impressive port of Caesarea on the coast, giving to Palestine a much needed major harbor.

9

NORTHERN COASTAL PLAINS, JEZREEL VALLEY, GALILEE, AND BASHAN

City (schematic representation)

The Plain of Dor (see map 10), tucked beneath the western slopes of Mount Carmel, is sometimes considered a part of the Sharon Plain. Other geographers consider the plain a separate geographical entity. One of the most important harbors of Palestine, Dor gave the plain a strategic importance.

The Plain of Philistia (see map 11). By 1150 B.C. the Philistines settled the southern coastal region of Palestine, and, eventually the broad plain stretching south to the Sinai bore their name. The major international trade route, the International Coastal Highway, split into two branches as it crossed the Philistine Plain. The key cities of this region—Gaza, Ashkelon, Ashdod, Gath, and Ekron—play important roles in biblical history and are located along the International Coastal Highway. Unlike the Sharon Plain, drainage was not a problem, and the rich alluvial soil provided abundant grain crops for the large population inhabiting the region.

A general view of the Jezreel Valley viewed from near Megiddo.

JEZREEL VALLEY (VALLEY OF ESDRAELON)

(SEE MAP 9)

Considered by some an extension of the Coastal Plain, the beautiful Jezreel Valley is a major feature of Palestine's geography, possessing historical and economic importance. The valley runs from the northwest to the southeast, connecting the Plain of Acco to the Jordan Rift near Beth-shan. The valley consists of two distinct parts: western Jezreel and eastern Jezreel. The city of Jezreel ("God sows") was located in the valley where the two parts meet. The western Jezreel is a broad triangle of land tucked between Mount Carmel on the south and lower Galilee to the north. The eastern Jezreel is much narrower. Mount Tabor, the Hill of Moreh, and Mount Gilboa intrude on the Jezreel Valley in the east as it descends to the Jordan Rift. Routes radiated through the Jezreel in all directions, giving the valley a strategic importance. Key cities—Megiddo, Yokneam, and Ibleam—guarded passes through Mount Carmel. The International Coastal Highway entered the Jezreel at Megiddo. This important city guarded the main pass leading to the valley and was the scene of many battles. The name Armageddon ("Mountain of Megiddo") used in Revelation 16:16 recalls the numerous conflicts fought over control of this strategic valley.

Fertile soil and abundant water supplies made the valley agriculturally productive, especially for barley and wheat crops. Numerous springs in the valley fed two small streams flowing to the east and west. The Kishon drained the western Jezreel, while the Harod (Jalud) emptied to the east. This abundance of water created marshes at times. Heavy rains occasionally caused these streams to flood, as described in Deborah's victory over the Canaanites recorded in Judges 4 and 5.

THE WESTERN MOUNTAINS

This central spine of mountains ranging from 1,500 to 4,000 feet in altitude runs the length of western Palestine, broken only by the Jezreel Valley. The Israelite tribes originally settled here and began clearing the forests natural to the region (Josh. 17:14–15). The Western Mountains with their three major divisions—Galilee, Samaria, and Judah—played the major role in biblical history.

Galilee (see map 9). North of the Jezreel Valley lies Galilee, a region with two distinct characteristics. Upper Galilee is a high, uplifted plateau isolated by its height from surrounding regions. Mount Meron, the highest point, rises to an elevation of 3,963 feet. Well watered and heavily forested in antiquity, Upper Galilee played a less prominent historical role due to its relative isolation. By contrast, the gentle hills and broad, fertile valleys of Lower Galilee are more familiar to biblical students. The rolling hills, oriented east and west, do not exceed 2,000 feet and often are much lower. Bisecting valleys (Beth Kerem Valley, Beth Netofa Valley) made travel easy. Vineyards, olive trees, and wheat flourished in the favorable climate and soil. Villages and towns like Nazareth, Cana, and the provincial capital, Sepphoris, dotted the landscape.

Samaria (Hill Country of Ephraim) (see map 10). The regions of Samaria and Judah constitute the Western Mountains south of the Jezreel. These mountains, composed of soft sedimentary rock, have been scoured by rainfall forming *wadis* that penetrate the mountains from east and west. The term *wadi* refers to gullies formed by runoff erosion. Normally dry, wadis can

10

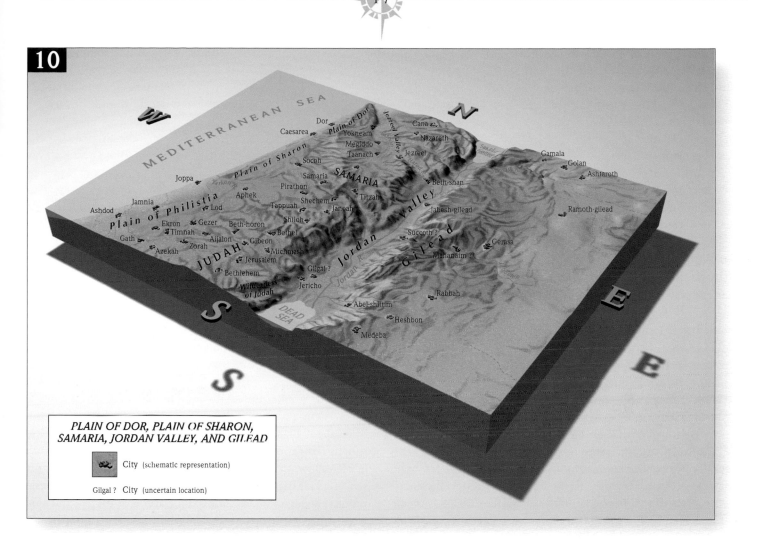

PLAIN OF DOR, PLAIN OF SHARON, SAMARIA, JORDAN VALLEY, AND GILEAD

City (schematic representation)

Gilgal ? City (uncertain location)

become raging torrents, especially in semidry regions. Some of these wadis are wide, allowing easy travel; others are narrow, steep, and easily defended. An important road—the Ridge Road—following the crest or watershed, links Samaria and Judah. Many biblical cities lie along or near this route: Hebron, Bethlehem, Jerusalem, Bethel, Mizpah, Shiloh, and Shechem.

The two sides of the Western Mountains are noticeably different. The western side of the mountains catches the rain from the Mediterranean Sea, but the area east of the crest receives little rain as it plummets down into the Rift. As a result, the lands east of the crest are increasingly desertlike, especially as one moves south.

Samaria, or the Hill Country of Ephraim, begins with the Gilboan Mountains (about 1,600 feet) and rises in altitude to more than 3,300 feet near Bethel. The northern part

The Valley of Shiloh in the hill country of Ephraim.

of Samaria, the tribal area of Manasseh, is lower and more accessible than the southern sector. Here a softer limestone eroded more easily, creating extensive valleys; convenient roads followed these valleys. The Wadi Farah, an especially important conduit, links Samaria with the Transjordan (Gilead) by way of the Wadi Jabbok across the fords near Adam. All the capitals of the Northern Kingdom, Israel (Shechem, Tirzah, and Samaria), were located in north Samaria. Shechem lies between Mount Ebal (3,083 feet) and Mount Gerizim (2,890 feet), scene of the blessings and curses of Deuteronomy 27–28. The Samaritans built a temple on Mount Gerizim, later destroyed by John Hyrcanus in 128 B.C.

The Judean Mountains northwest of Jerusalem.

South of Manasseh a harder limestone withstood erosion, producing a high, more isolated plateau (3,000 feet) with steep slopes on both sides. The tribe of Ephraim settled here. Shiloh, Bethel, and Mizpah, located along the Ridge Road, appear frequently in Old Testament history. Settlers took advantage of the exceptionally rich soil to produce abundant crops. They farmed the valleys and built terraces on the hillsides, reaping a bounty of wheat, barley, and olives.

Judah (see map 11). The gentle depression called the "Saddle of Benjamin" separates Samaria from Judah. Judah, or Mount Judah, is a mountainous highland; altitudes range from 2,000 to 3,400 feet with the higher elevations found near Hebron in the south. The major cities—Jerusalem, Beth-zur, and Hebron—are located along or just off the Ridge Road that follows the crest of the mountains.

Judah is one of the most protected regions in Palestine. The Wilderness of Judah, a dry, desolate area stretching down to the Dead Sea, functions as a formidable barrier to the east. The mountains plunge precipitously more than 3,500 feet from Jerusalem down to Jericho in the Rift below. The few settlements of this desert region clustered just east of the watershed. Brigands, outcasts, and Jewish freedom fighters sought refuge in this barren region, known as Jeshimon in the Old Testament (1 Sam. 23:19). The Shephelah (see below) restricts access to Judah from the west, while the Negeb and deserts protect the region to the south. Judah is more rugged and somewhat drier, with less available agricultural land than Samaria. However, the soil is fertile, and terrace farming provides ample space for the cultivation of vines, fruit trees, and grain crops.

The rugged terrain characteristic of the Wilderness of Judah.

SHEPHELAH (SEE MAP 11)

The Shephelah is a strip of foothills along the western flank of Judah. The term means "Lowlands" and must have been given by inhabitants living in the higher elevations of Judah. These rolling hills form an effective barrier separating Judah from the Philistine Plain. Four valleys (wadis) cut through the Shephelah giving access to the cities of Judah: the Aijalon, the Sorek, the Elah, and the "Way to Hebron."

Control of the Shephelah was vital to the security of Judah. Heavily fortified towns such as Lachish, Azekah, Socoh, and Timnah protected each valley. Frequently these cities bore the brunt of armies attacking Judah; the spade of the archaeologist has revealed evidence of their frequent destruction. Early on, the Philistines fought with the tribes of Israel for control of this

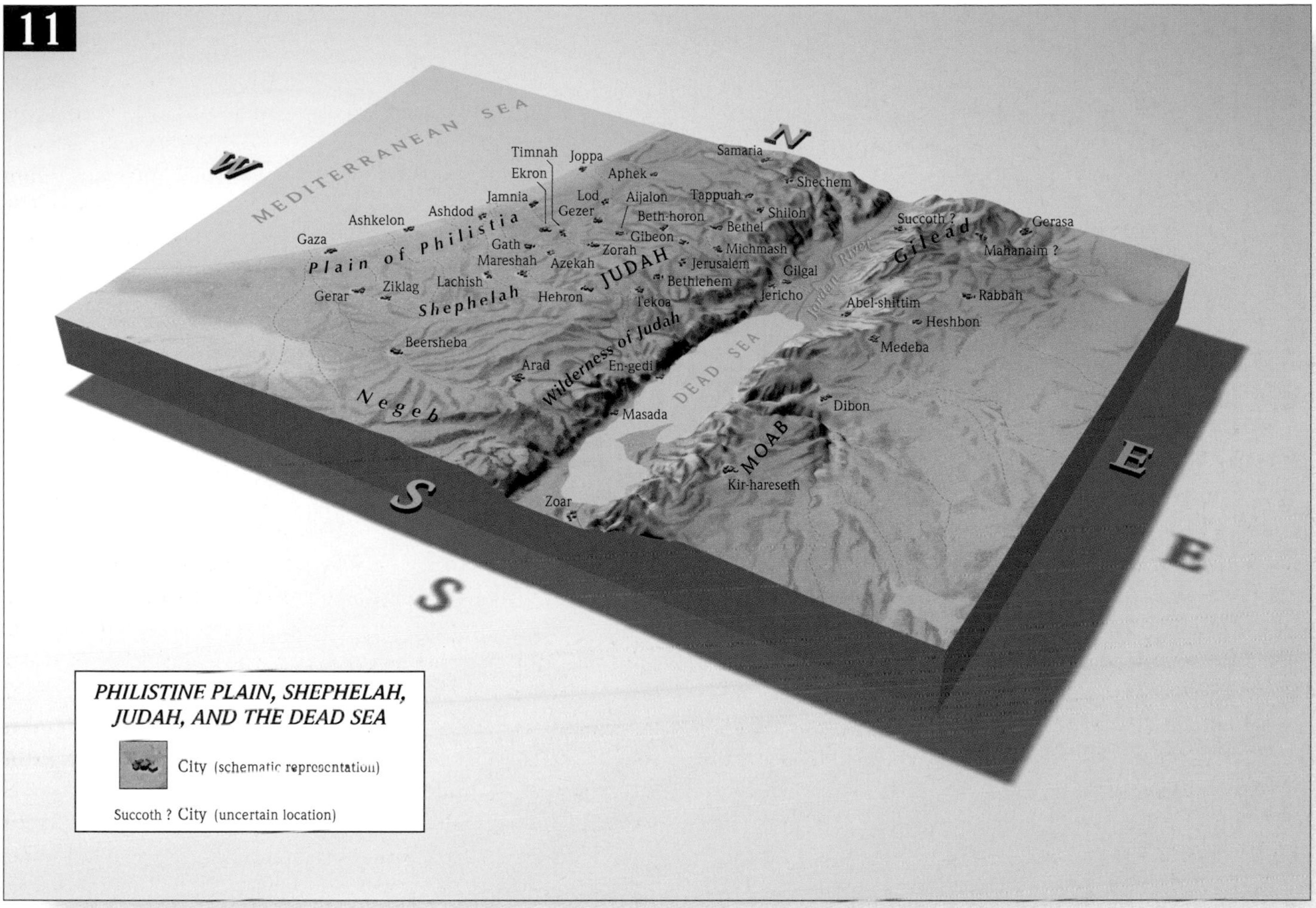

11

PHILISTINE PLAIN, SHEPHELAH, JUDAH, AND THE DEAD SEA

City (schematic representation)

Succoth ? City (uncertain location)

vital region. Several of the battles fought between the Philistines and the Israelite tribes that are recorded in Judges and Samuel took place in the Shephelah. David fought Goliath in the Valley of Elah (1 Sam. 17). Earlier many of Samson's exploits took place in the vicinity of Timnah along the Sorek Valley (Judg. 14–15).

NEGEB (SEE MAPS 11 AND 12)

Modern geographies apply the term *Negeb* to a triangle of land extending south from Judah to the Gulf of Aqabah. The biblical use of the term, however, is more restricted. Negeb refers to the region around Beer-sheba and Arad. Beer-sheba receives about ten to twelve inches of rain annually, an amount considered marginal for agriculture but adequate for grazing flocks. Abraham and Isaac sojourned in the Negeb with their clans and livestock. Water was a perennial problem for inhabitants of the Negeb, but scattered wells along the major wadis and, later, the use of cisterns permitted settlements. Nomadic tribes inhabiting the desert fringe, like the Amalekites, often raided settlements in the Negeb. David repulsed the Amalekites after an attack on Ziklag, a city of the Negeb (1 Sam. 30).

View of the Negeb from Beer-sheba, the most important city of the Negeb. Remains of the store facilities and gate complex dating from the Iron II Period (approximately 900–600 B.C.) are in view.

12

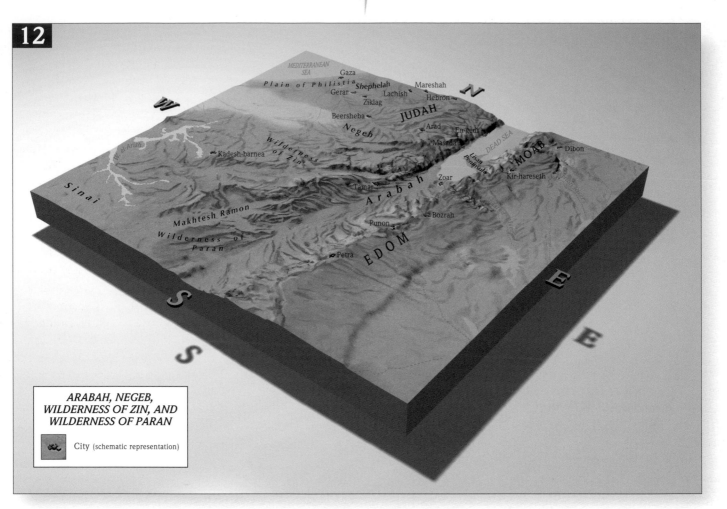

ARABAH, NEGEB, WILDERNESS OF ZIN, AND WILDERNESS OF PARAN

City (schematic representation)

By New Testament times, the region of the Negeb was known as Idumea. Herod the Great was an Idumean, a people despised by the Jews for their Edomite heritage.

THE SOUTHERN WILDERNESS (SEE MAP 12)

South of Beer-sheba, rainfall amounts drop sharply, and the landscape becomes increasingly rugged. The Bible refers to this area as "wilderness." The Wilderness of Zin stretches southeast of Beer-sheba, while portions of the Wilderness of Paran intrude from the Sinai near Kadesh-barnea. Jagged peaks, desolate plateaus, and craterlike depressions punctuate this foreboding land. During New Testament times the Nabateans, an Arab people, inhabited portions of the Negeb, the southern wildernesses, and the Transjordan. They controlled the Arabian trade routes from Petra to Gaza. The Nabateans were also adept agriculturalists in marginal desert regions. Their innovative irrigation techniques (e.g., dams, catch basins, etc.) made the southern deserts bloom.

THE JORDAN RIFT

Nature has divided Palestine into two segments by a deep cleft, the Jordan Rift. This cleft in the earth's surface is part of a great fissure extending from eastern Turkey into Africa. In Palestine most of the Rift lies below sea level, reaching a maximum depth of 1,300 feet at the Dead Sea. The higher mountains and plateaus to the east and west of the Rift make the effect more dramatic. Most of the perennial rivers and bodies of water of Palestine are found in the Jordan Rift, which drains 70 percent of the land. Five divisions of the Rift should be noted: the Huleh Basin, the Sea of Galilee, the Jordan Valley, the Dead Sea, and the Arabah.

The Huleh Basin (see map 9). The Huleh Basin is a depression caught between Upper Galilee and the Eastern Plateau. Mount Hermon (9,232 feet) flanks the basin on the northeast. Numerous springs dot the area, fed by the melting snows of Mount Hermon. Principal springs emerge in southern Lebanon (Nahr al-Hasbani), Dan (Nahr al-Qadi), and near Caesarea Philippi (Nahr al-Baniyas) and are the source of the Jordan River. In antiquity, the waters collected in the southern end of the basin forming a marshy lake, Lake Huleh. Today the marshes have

A view of the northwest portion of the Sea of Galilee at sunset.
The Plain of Genneseret and the Horns of Hattin are visible in the distance.

been drained, but in ancient times they hindered travel, promoted disease, and foiled settlement in the center of the basin. Yet the climate, refreshing springs, and fertile soil invited the establishment of cities, especially away from the marshes. Hazor, Dan, Abel-beth-maacah, and Ijon all were located along the perimeter of the basin. At the southern end of the basin the Jordan River begins a rapid descent southward. The name *Jordan* probably comes from a Hebrew verb meaning "to descend," appropriate for a river that drops forty feet per mile in some places.

The Sea of Galilee (see map 9). This famous body of water is a freshwater lake thirteen miles long and seven miles wide. The surface of the lake is 690 feet below sea level, surrounded on all sides by higher land. In the Bible, the lake bears several names: Sea of Galilee (Mark 1:16), Sea of Tiberias (John 6:1), Sea of Chinnereth (Deut. 3:17), Lake Gennesaret (Luke 5:1), or simply "the lake" (Luke 5:2). A branch of the International Coastal Highway skirted the northwest shore of the lake by the Plain of Gennesaret. Capernaum, Magdala, and Bethsaida were located along the north/northwest shore. Local towns and villages depended on the fishing industries and agriculture products provided by the lake. Even today the lake's classic beauty calls to mind the miracles and teachings Jesus performed along its shores.

The Jordan Valley (see maps 9–10). For approximately seventy miles the Jordan River winds its way south from the Sea of Galilee to the Dead Sea through the Jordan Valley. The volume of the Jordan doubled with the influx from the Yarmuk River in antiquity, but modern water conservation techniques greatly restrict the present water volume. The northern half of the Jordan Valley is well watered and fertile, with numerous traces of ancient settlements. Key cities (Adam, Succoth, Zarethan, Beth-shan) developed at points where natural routes connected the highlands to the east and west. The Jordan cut a deep gorge (in Arabic, *Zor*) that contained dense thickets of trees and shrubs, the "pride of the Jordan" (Jer. 49:19). In biblical times this dense vegetation harbored wild animals, including lions (Jer. 50:44). The southern Jordan Valley is drier, almost desertlike. Jericho flourishes in an oasis nourished by several springs in the midst of this arid landscape.

The Dead Sea (see maps 11–12). The Dead Sea is unique among the bodies of water on earth. About 50 miles long and 10 miles wide, the surface of the sea lies 1,300 feet below sea level—the lowest place on the earth's surface. The Lisan Peninsula protrudes into the sea from the east, dividing the Dead Sea into two unequal parts. The larger northern portion of the sea reaches depths of 1,300 feet, but the smaller southern sector averages less than thirty feet. Oppressively hot temperatures and dry climate grip the entire region. The barren, ragged landscape possesses an eerie beauty all its own.

Known in the Bible as the "Salt Sea" or "Sea of the Arabah" (Deut. 3:17), the Dead Sea receives water from several freshwater tributaries and springs. Among the larger streams, the Jordan flows in from the north, while the Arnon and Zered enter the sea from the east. However, the rivers have no exit. The waters absorb salts and other

The Jordan River just north of the Sea of Galilee.

View of the southern end of the Dead Sea from Masada.
The Lisan Peninsula that divides the Dead Sea into two parts—a deeper northern section and a much shallower southern section—can be seen in the photograph.

ratio several times saltier than normal sea water and almost twice as salty as the Great Salt Lake.

These conditions discouraged habitation except where freshwater springs (En-gedi, Ain Feshkha) made settlement possible. Refugees, like David as he fled Saul (1 Sam. 26), found safety in the numerous caves of the region. Later, the Qumran sectarians hid their library in caves along the northwest shore. Beginning in 1947, shepherd boys discovered scrolls today known as the "Dead Sea Scrolls." Herod the Great built two fortresses, Masada and Macherus, along the shores of the Dead Sea.

Arabah (see map 12). The Jordan Rift continues south of the Dead Sea 110 miles to the Gulf of Aqabah. The Bible calls this region the Arabah, a dry and desolate region. Occasionally the Bible uses the term *Arabah* in a broader sense, including parts of the Jordan Valley north of the Dead Sea (Josh. 18:18), but here the more restricted sense is used.

chemicals from numerous deposits in the region. The extreme heat of the region concentrates the chemicals by evaporation with the result that the Dead Sea consists of 26 to 33 percent salts—a

Immediately south of the Dead Sea, the Arabah is below

The Arabah.

sea level, but a gradual elevation rises above sea level midway to the gulf. The red Nubian sandstone of Edom on the east and the highlands of the Negeb to the west contrast with the monotonous landscape of the Arabah.

Extremely dry and isolated, the Arabah, nonetheless, possessed strategic importance for several reasons. In biblical times the Arabah held important copper deposits located near Punon and Timna. Ezion-geber, a seaport built by Solomon on the Gulf of Aqabah, received the wealth of Arabia and Africa through the fleet stationed there. Highways linking Ezion-geber with Judah ran the length of the Arabah. Control of the Arabah was, therefore, economically important to the court of Jerusalem.

A Nabatean temple—"the Khasneh"—carved out of the sandstone cliffs at Petra.

EASTERN PLATEAU (TRANSJORDAN)

The lands rising sharply to the east of the Jordan Rift form a high plateau or tableland often called Transjordan. This plateau, ranging in height from two thousand to more than five thousand feet, towers above the Jordan Rift, then slopes gradually eastward to the Syro-Arabian desert. Four large wadis—Yarmuk, Jabbok, Arnon, and Zered—bisect the plateau, carrying the runoff into the rift. Considerable amounts of rain fall on the plateau as clouds reform in the higher altitudes beyond the rift. The northern and central sections are well watered (twenty to forty inches in Bashan, twelve to twenty inches in parts of Gilead). Further south, the encroaching desert restricts rainfall amounts. The larger cities developed along the important commercial route known as the King's Highway, which traversed the top of the plateau from the Gulf of Aqabah to Damascus. The wadis helped divide the region into four major sections: Bashan, Gilead, Moab, and Edom.

Bashan (see map 9). Bashan is the northernmost region of the Eastern Plateau. Lying between the towering slopes of Mount Hermon (9,263 feet; also known as Sirion and Senir [Deut. 3:9]) and the Yarmuk River, Bashan is a fertile land blessed with abundant water and rich volcanic soil. Extinct volcanic cones protrude from the landscape, while oak trees graced portions of the Bashan in biblical times (Isa. 2:13). Often, biblical writers referred to the well-fed cattle that grazed in the Bashan (Amos 4:1; Ezek. 39:18). During the Old Testament period, Israel seldom controlled this region, although portions of Bashan originally were allotted to the half-tribe of Manasseh. The Arameans, especially the kings of Damascus, controlled the Bashan from about 900 to 732 B.C. Herod's son Philip governed this land during the New Testament era when various parts

The Arnon Gorge. The deep chasm created by the Arnon River was the boundary between the Moabites to the south and the Israelite territory of Reuben to the north.

of the region bore the names Gaulanitis, Trachonitis, Auranitis, and Batanea.

Gilead (see map 9–10). Gilead, a mountainous region noted for its heavy forests in ancient times, stretches south of the Yarmuk to the top of the Dead Sea. A natural passage links Gilead with the lands west of the Jordan. The Jabbok River (Nahr ez-Zerka), dividing Gilead into two parts, lies opposite the Wadi Farah, which affords easy access to Samaria. The Israelite tribes of East Manasseh and Gad, who settled Gilead, thus maintained contact with their kinsmen beyond the Rift. The Kingdom of Ammon, centered on Rabbah, occupied the lands bordering the desert southeast of Gilead. By New Testament times, portions of Perea and the Decapolis fell within Gilead.

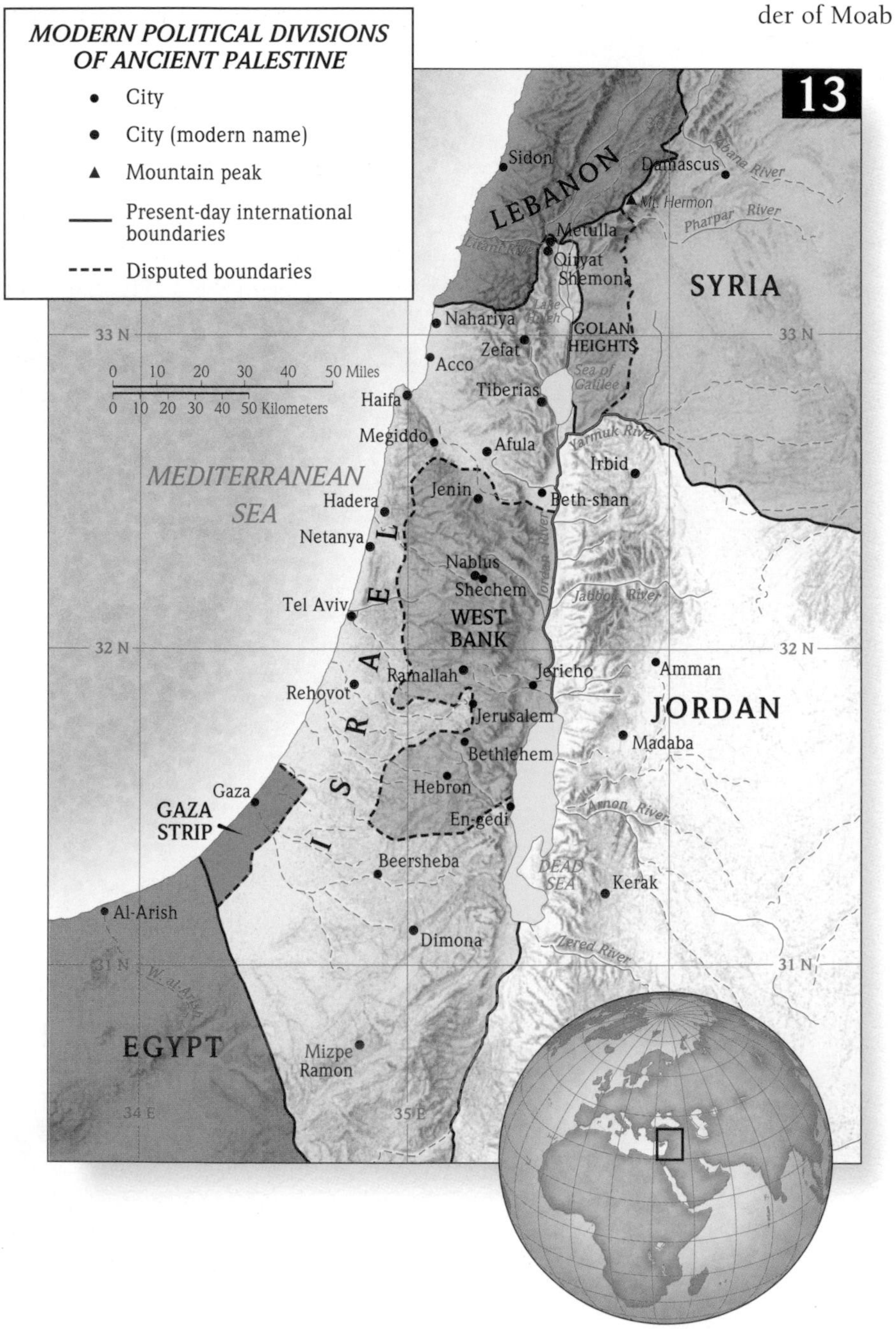

Moab (see map 11). The region due east of the Dead Sea is Moab, a land divided by the deep gorge of the Arnon River (Wadi Mujib). The southern boundary of Moab is the Zered (Wadi al-Hesa), which separates Moab from Edom. Precipitous wadis leading to the Dead Sea scour the land, making both travel and settlement difficult along the western edge. The eastern border of Moab is ill defined as the habitable land blends gradually to desert.

MODERN POLITICAL DIVISIONS OF ANCIENT PALESTINE

- City
- City (modern name)
- ▲ Mountain peak
- Present-day international boundaries
- Disputed boundaries

13

Between the western scarp and desert lies a plateau where conditions favored sheepherding and cereal crops. The story of Ruth the Moabitess illustrates the agricultural potential of Moab. North of the Arnon, a high flat tableland, in Hebrew *Mishor* (Josh. 13:21), provided the best agricultural lands of Moab. Important cities of the Mishor include Heshbon and Dibon. Although the Moabites claimed this region, the Israelite tribe of Reuben settled north of the Arnon, leading to frequent hostilities between Israel and Moab over control of this territory (2 Kgs. 3:4–27).

Edom (see map 12). South of the Zered, striking red Nubian sandstone mountains decorate the land of Edom. The name *Edom* comes from the Hebrew word meaning "red." Occasionally, underlying granite rocks protrude through the earth's crust giving the region a more dramatic visual impact. Some mountains reach heights in excess of five thousand feet. Tucked between the desert and the Arabah, Edom is something of a fortress consisting of a narrow band of mountains affording protection to its inhabitants. Sufficient rainfall occurs in the western area to produce small clumps of juniper, oak, and hawthorn forests. Seir is another name for Edom (Gen. 32:3), although sometimes the name refers to land south of Judah (Deut. 1:2, 44; Josh. 11:17). The Edomites, descendants of Esau and ancestral enemies of Israel and Judah, built their cities in the rugged mountains of this region. Later, the Nabateans carved out of the living rock the city of Petra—a feast of beauty with its multicolored sandstone monuments.

Chapter Three

LIFE IN ANCIENT PALESTINE

People today have great difficulty understanding life in ancient societies. Our urban world of computers, advanced technology, and heavy industry separates us decisively from that of ancient people. Their world centered on the village, and their livelihood came primarily from agriculture and herding of animals (pastoralism). The seasons of the year determined the pace of life; changes occurred slowly. Although the coming of Greece and Rome altered society in some ways, life in Palestine tended to be tied closely to the land—essentially rural and agrarian.

Location of Settlements

Palestine was not a land of large cities, like Babylon or Ur. Most settlements were small villages or towns that sprang up where four factors essential to habitation—water, food, defense, and transportation—converged. An adequate water supply was a primary concern in a land not blessed with an abundance of water. Springs, small rivers, and wells usually met this need, although the development of cisterns to catch and store rainwater permitted towns to be established apart from normal sources of water. Security, likewise, was a basic necessity. A preference for a place easily fortified was a marked feature of site selection, at least until the Graeco-Roman period. Since villages and towns depended on a ready food supply, people settled near good farming land. Finally, a location on or near trade routes gave an outlet for surpluses and access to goods not available locally.

Sites especially favored by these four elements were occupied for centuries, even millennia. When a city was abandoned or destroyed, people returned to build again. Over the years the debris, held in place by fortification walls, arose in the form of flat-topped mounds that archaeologists term "tells" (or "tels"). Most tells were quite small, less than ten acres. The Philistine city Ekron, covering fifty acres, was among the largest tells in Palestine. Hazor covered thirty acres, although its "Lower City" increased the Canaanite city to two hundred acres in size, the largest site in Palestine prior to Graeco-Roman times. Some cities, such as Hazor, Megiddo, Samaria, and Jerusalem, possessed such strategic, political, or economic importance that they grew larger. Smaller villages and towns depended on their larger neighbors for protection in times of distress and as markets for goods.

Tell Batash—biblical Timnah—beside the Sorek River that runs westward through the Sorek Valley of the Shepheleh.

Climate

Climate played a dominant role in Palestine. Unlike Egypt and Mesopotamia, where larger rivers provided a constant source of water, life in Palestine depended on seasonal rains (Deut. 11:11, 14; Jer. 5:24). The subtropical climate of Palestine has two principal seasons: a hot, dry summer and a winter punctuated by periodic rain. Normally no rainfall occurs between mid-May and mid-October.

The summer drought is broken by what the Bible calls the "early rains." The "early rains" (Heb. *yoreh)* come usually in October, relieving the parched soil and allowing farmers to prepare the soil for planting. The bulk of the annual rain, over 70 percent, falls from December to February. The "later rains" appear in March to mid-April, ending rainfall in Palestine for the year (Hos. 6:3).

All parts of Palestine do not receive equal amounts of rain. Rainfall amounts are influenced by elevation and location. As a general rule, those regions nearer the coast, higher in elevation, and further north receive the most rainfall. Upper Galilee, with an annual rainfall of more than forty inches, illustrates this rule well. Conversely, areas nearest the desert on the east, lower in elevation, and farther south receive the least rain; for example, the Dead Sea region receives less than four inches annually. In general, a minimum of twelve inches of annual rainfall is required for agricultural purposes—particularly for the important grain crops, wheat and barley. Dew provides moisture in some areas, nourishing plants, especially in the hot summer months. Hosea compares God to the dew as a symbol of His renewing powers (Hos. 14:5). Some parts of Palestine are desert or semiarid. Lands south of Beer-sheba, the Arabah, portions of the Jordan Valley, southern Transjordan, and even sections of the eastern side of the Western Mountains receive insufficient amounts of rain to sustain agriculture apart from some type of irrigation.

Temperatures fluctuate greatly in Palestine due to the varied elevation and relative proximity of either the desert or the sea. Winters are mild along the coast and in the Jordan Rift, but the higher elevations have harsher conditions, including an occasional snow. Summer temperatures are pleasant along the coast and in the higher regions, but become oppressive in the Jordan Valley, the Dead Sea, and the Arabah.

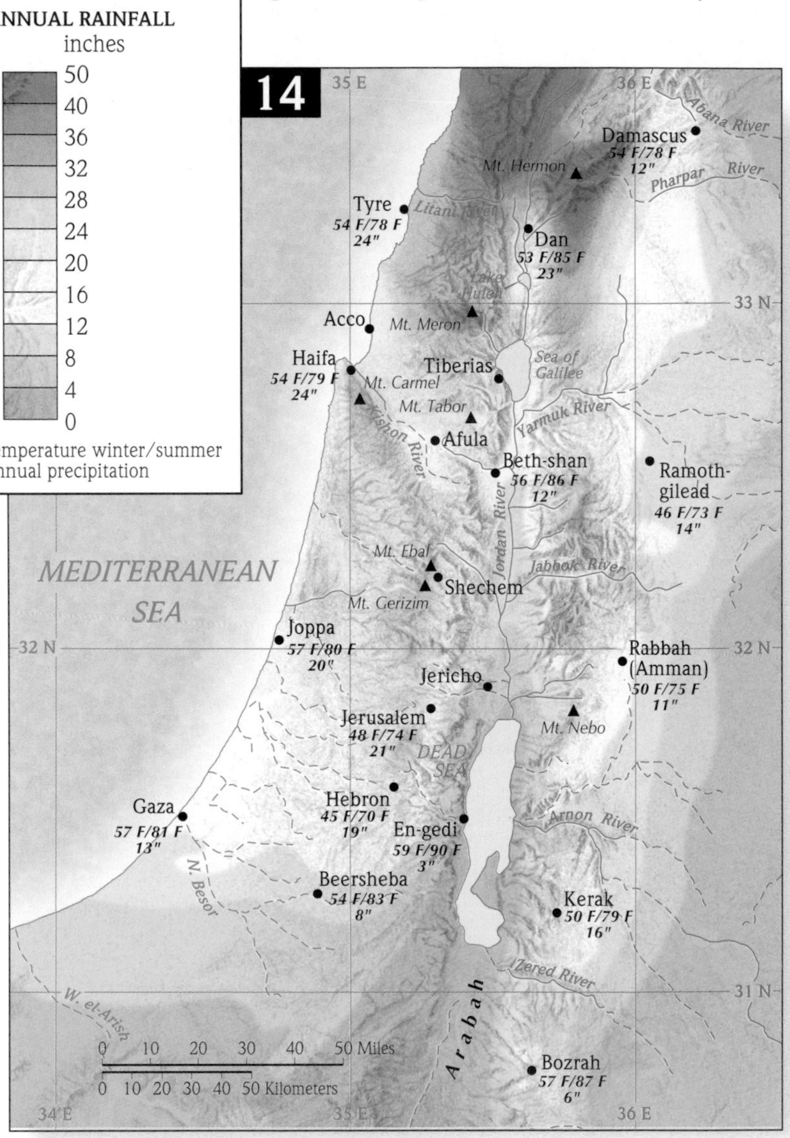

Basic Economy and Food Supplies

Biblical descriptions emphasize the agricultural potential of the promised land. Palestine is "a land of wheat and barley, of vines and fig trees and pomegranates, a land of olive trees and honey" (Deut. 8:8). These seven products of the land emphasize the importance of field crops, vineyards, and orchards to the economy. Grain, wine, and olive oil provided the staples of a daily diet.

Palestine's broad valleys and plains provided large fields for agriculture, but in the more mountainous regions small terraced fields retained by rock walls were most common. The terrace not only gave space but also retained precious water and prevented soil erosion as long as the walls were maintained. As a rule, crops depended on rainfall (dry farming), but some irrigation techniques were used occasionally.

FIELD CROPS

Cereal crops like barley and wheat were the basis of most ancient diets. Barley matures more quickly than wheat and can thrive in soil and rain conditions not tolerated by wheat. Both were used to make bread and porridge, or the grains could be eaten parched. Fermented barley produced a beer. Various legumes such as beans, lentils, peas, and bitter vetch were grown, along with other vegetables like leeks, melons, and cucumbers. Other crops included spices (coriander and cummin) and flax for clothing.

A Bedouin encampment in the Judean wilderness.

TREES AND VINES

The Israelites cultivated various trees and vines whose produce added to the food supply. The olive tree, grape vine, and date palm were especially important. The olive tree was a symbol of beauty and abundance in the Bible (Hos. 14:6; Ps. 52:8) and was the first tree to be asked to rule over others in Jotham's famous fable (Judg. 9:8–9). Although olives were eaten, more prized was the oil, produced by crushing the olive. Olive oil was used as a fuel in lamps, for cooking, and medicinally. The importance of the olive is revealed by the numerous olive presses discovered at many sites in Israel.

Grapes were occasionally used as a fruit, but their juice was used primarily to make wine. The vine and its fruit appear throughout the Bible as a symbol of abundance, peace, prosperity, and stability. Jesus used the grapevine to express the beautiful relationship between Himself and His followers (John 15). Dates were a major source of carbohydrates. The "honey" mentioned in descriptions of the promised land (Exod. 3:8; Num. 13:27) possibly was honey made from dates. Other native trees bore figs, pomegranates, carob, and various nuts such as almonds, pistachios, and walnuts.

The Gezer calendar.

PASTORALISM

Tending sheep, goats, and cattle (pastoralism) was another important basis of life in Palestine. Especially in the southern marginal land and in Transjordan, Israelite flocks and herds dotted the landscape. Seldom eaten except on rare festive occasions, these animals were prized for their secondary products: milk, cheese, wool, and hair.

COTTAGE INDUSTRIES

Though agriculture and pastoralism constituted the major basis of ancient Palestine's economy, all towns required other skilled occupations. Craftsmen, such as metal workers, potters, woodcraftsmen, and stonemasons, could be found in each village or town. The textile industry seems to have been especially well developed. Cloth and garments from Palestine appear frequently in Assyrian tribute lists.

Undoubtedly, the people of Palestine exported pottery and textiles along with crop surpluses of wheat, wine, olive oil, balm, and perhaps date honey in exchange for goods not readily available, such as timber, luxury items, spices, metals, and perfumes (Ezek. 27:17).

The Agricultural Year

"For everything there is a season" wrote the author of Ecclesiastes (3:1). Indeed, daily life in the villages and towns of Palestine revolved around the particular agricultural tasks thrust upon the people in unending cycle. The Gezer Calendar, dated by archaeologists to 925 B.C., contains a list of the chores required throughout the agricultural year. Although the seven lines of old Hebrew script are difficult to read precisely, a recent writer suggests the following translation:

"two months of ingathering (olives)"
"two months of sowing cereals"
"two months of late sowing"
"a month of hoeing weeds"
"a month of harvesting barley"
"a month of harvesting (wheat) and measuring (grain)"
"two months of grape harvesting"
"a month of gathering summer fruit."[1]

[1]Borowski, *Agriculture in Iron Age Israel,* p. 38.

This cycle of plowing, sowing, and harvesting involved the entire population in ancient times. The graphic below correlates various aspects of the agricultural year, giving an impression of seasonal demands. Pastoral activities and tasks associated with the cultivation of vineyards and orchards also are included. The ancient Israelite calendar was based on the phases of the moon (a lunar calendar), but the solar year determined the agricultural cycle. This required adding an additional short month periodically to the lunar calendar and explains why Hebrew months do not correlate exactly with our modern calendars based on the solar year.

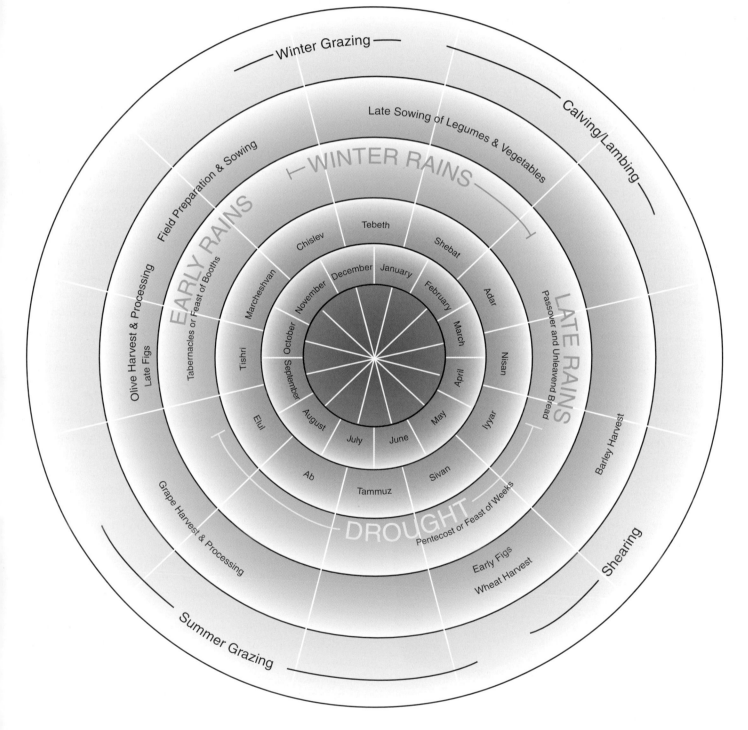

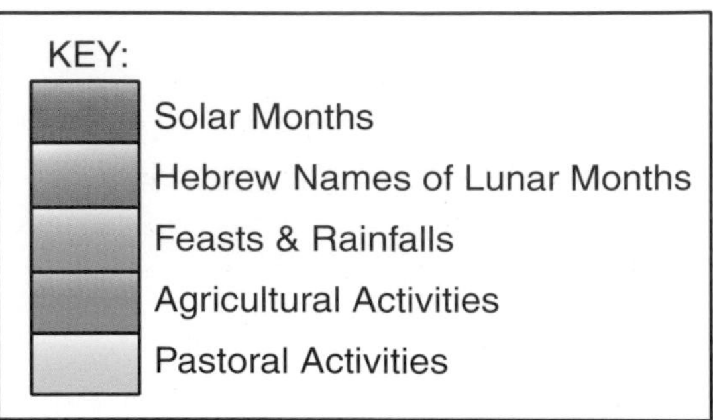

FALL AND WINTER ACTIVITIES

Note the heavy demands on Israel's farmers beginning in September-October with the olive harvest and increasing with field preparation in October-November. Families gathered olives by beating the tree limbs with sticks to shake the fruit loose. Olive presses, located in every village, were used to convert the olives to precious oil, which was stored in large jars. With the early rains, farmers used wooden plows with metal points, usually drawn by oxen, to till the soil in preparation for sowing. Wheat and barley seed was broadcast and then covered with earth, either by means of a second plowing or by using animals to trample on it. Garden crops requiring less time for maturation, such as lentils, peas, and flax, were planted in the winter months.

An olive press.

SUMMER ACTIVITIES

During the summer months grapes were harvested and pressed to yield their juice. Large storage jars placed in rock-cut cellars held the juice for fermentation. Pomegranates, figs, and dates were collected as late summer turned to fall, thus completing the agricultural cycle.

SPRING ACTIVITIES

Harvesttime again required the efforts of all the villagers. Harvesting barley and wheat commenced in late March or April and continued through May. After reaping, the grain was taken to threshing floors where the grain was removed from the stalk, either by means of animals treading on the stalks (Hos. 10:11), by threshing sleds drawn over the crop (Isa. 28:27), or by sticks used to beat the stalks (Ruth 2:17). The remaining chaff was separated from the grain by winnowing, using large wooden forks. Grain was stored in jars, cellars, small grain pits, larger silos, or stone houses until needed.

Agriculture and Israel's Pilgrim Feasts

Major religious festivals marked key events in the agricultural year. The Old Testament commanded attendance at three great pilgrim festivals, all of which originally possessed agricultural or pastoral significance (Exod. 23:14–17; Deut. 16:13–17). Passover with its companion Feast of Unleavened Bread not only commemorated the Exodus from Egypt but also marked the beginning of the barley and wheat harvest. The Feast of Weeks, or Firstfruits (Pentecost), celebrated seven weeks after Passover, culminated the cereal harvesttime. Later, in the fall, the Feast of Ingathering, or Booths (Tabernacles), perhaps the most joyous of all festivals, recalled with thanksgiving the experience of God's care in the wilderness. Celebrated at the end of the year, Ingathering signaled the conclusion of harvesttime and anticipated the beginning of a new agricultural cycle.

Concern for crops, fields, vineyards, orchards, and flocks dominated Israelite society from earliest times throughout the Old Testament period. The new opportunities presented by the coming of Greece and Rome greatly diversified Jewish life. The Jews engaged more and more in commerce and banking, among other specialized occupations. Still, agriculture, especially in Palestine, retained a prominent place, as numerous New Testament allusions to agricultural practices attest.

A threshing floor in use near Gibeon.

Archaeology: Recovering Ancient Societies

Since about 1860, the spade of the archaeologist has provided a wealth of material enriching biblical studies. The remains of long-dead civilizations and forgotten cities have given life to the biblical text. Thanks primarily to archaeology, we are in a much better position than ever before to understand the Bible and its world.

THE TELL

Today most ancient sites in the Near East are represented by mounds called tells. Tells are composed of several superimposed layers containing the material remains of those who lived at the site. Tells come in different sizes and contain varying depths of ancient remains. Some tells were inhabited only briefly, while others hold debris deposited over thousands of years. The task of archaeologists is twofold: (1) to dissect a portion of the tell, scientifically recovering all the ancient remains and carefully recording the findings, and (2) to give a coherent interpretation to the data. The ultimate goal of archaeology is to reconstruct and understand ancient societies in as much detail as possible.

The ancient tell of Beth-shan.
The Old Testament tell towers above the Decapolis city of Scythopolis whose ruins are visible in the foreground.

IDENTIFYING PLACE NAMES

Archaeologists cannot determine the ancient names of many tells they excavate. Unless the excavation yields written evidence providing the ancient name of a tell—a rare event—the archaeologist must rely on several lines of evidence to identify the site. Foremost are ancient sources, including the Bible, which mention towns and cities. These sources provide information about the geographical location of the city, often in considerable detail, and suggest the specific historical periods when the site was inhabited.

Occasionally, an archaeologist receives help when the ancient name is preserved in a modern Arabic equivalent attached either to the tell or perhaps given to a nearby village. Still another source of information comes from later written sources that identify biblical sites. Early Christian writers, like Eusebius, and pilgrims to the Holy Land naturally sought out the locations of biblical cities and events. Unfortunately, their knowledge often depended on faulty traditions, but their records can furnish vital clues if carefully evaluated. With the information gained from the above sources, the archaeologists can correlate the data gained from excavation and make a reasonable guess of the ancient name of the tell.

STRATIGRAPHY AND TYPOLOGY

Excavation proceeds on a scientific basis by employing the twin principles of stratigraphy and typology. Stratigraphy refers to the different layers or strata that make up the tell. The first task of field work is to untangle the different layers found in the tell and establish a stratigraphic sequence. Each layer represents a separate part of the site's overall history and must be distinguished from other layers to avoid confusion.

A baulk illustrating stratigraphy. The tags indicate floors and floor makeup of a building in use over a period of time.

Archaeologists normally excavate in 5 x 5 meter squares and leave a catwalk or balk either of 1/2 or 1 meter unexcavated along the perimeter. The balk reveals the different layers to the trained eye. All objects and remains recovered from each layer are kept separate, their exact locations carefully noted. During the last forty years, greater emphasis has been given to the principle of stratigraphy, thanks to the pioneering efforts of Kathleen Kenyon, resulting in greater precision and more accurate results.

DATING THE STRATA

Next, the archaeologists must date their material before it can be useful. In 1890, Flinders Petrie recognized that the key to dating each layer resided in the most common artifact found in an excavation: pottery. He noticed that each layer in a tell tended to have distinct

Two chalices *in situ* on a plaster surface at Tell Batash. The chalices are typical of the forms for this vessel in the Iron II Period (approximately 900–600 B.C.).

pottery forms in it. These allowed comparison with pottery found in other sites. This comparison of objects—known as typology—has been successfully applied to thousands of sites.

W. F. Albright and G. Ernest Wright classified the basic types of pottery and developed a relative chronology for the Near East, and for Palestine in particular. Further refinements now permit the archaeologists to date material rather accurately back to about 2000 B.C. primarily on the basis of pottery. For the earlier periods certain physical or chemical processes such as carbon 14 and thermoluminescence become important, although the results are more general. Today, the basic chronological sequence for the Near East has been worked out in considerable detail.

ARCHAEOLOGY AND THE BIBLE

The data recovered from archaeological excavations can be used by the biblical scholar in many ways. Archaeology has provided the basic chronology for both the Old and New Testaments. Our knowledge of the biblical languages—Hebrew, Aramaic, and Greek—has greatly increased through ancient texts discovered in excavations. Entire civilizations mentioned in the Bible have been resurrected by the work of the archaeologist. Occasionally archaeology has provided data that has clarified the meaning of a biblical text. The meaning of the term *Millo* in 2 Samuel 5:9 formerly puzzled scholars. Discovery of a vast stone terrace that supported structures in David's Jerusalem—the "millo"—makes clear what the ancient term meant.

Perhaps most importantly, archaeology has brought the biblical world to life and allowed us to understand it on its own terms. The illustrative value offered by archaeology cannot be overemphasized. Through archaeology the biblical text and the world in which it was written have been given flesh by the dedication of countless excavators working on thousands of ancient sites.

CHART 1: THE ARCHAEOLOGICAL PERIODS OF THE NEAR EAST WITH SPECIAL REFERENCE TO PALESTINE*

Term	Approximate Dates
Paleolithic (Old Stone Age)	?–18,000 B.C.
Epipaleolithic (formerly Mesolithic—Middle Stone Age)	18,000–8300 B.C.
Neolithic (New Stone Age)	8300–4500 B.C.
Chalcolithic (Copper Stone Age)	4500–3300 B.C.
Early Bronze Age	3300–2000 B.C.
Middle Bronze Age	2000–1550 B.C.
Late Bronze Age	1550–1200 B.C.
Iron Age	1200–586 B.C.
Babylonian and Persian Periods	586–332 B.C.
Hellenistic Period	332–63 B.C.
Roman Period	63 B.C.–A.D. 324
Byzantine Period	A.D. 324–638

*The dates in the chart are those found in *The New Encyclopedia of Archaeological Excavations in the Holy Land,* with the exception that the Early Bronze Age is extended to 2000 B.C., covering the Early Bronze IV-Intermediate Bronze period. Dates for the periods prior to the Neolithic vary, often widely, depending upon one's view of human origins. (Stern, *The New Encyclopedia of Archaeological Excavations in the Holy Land,* Vol. 2.)

Part Two

THE OLD TESTAMENT PERIOD

The Fourth Dynasty pyramids at Giza (ca. 2600 B.C.). The pyramid of Menkaure with three subsidiary pyramids occupies the foreground, while the pyramids of Khephren and Kufu (Cheops) rise in the distance.

Chapter Four

BEFORE ABRAHAM

Beginnings

"In the beginning God created," the opening words of Genesis (1:1), move us at once to the question of origins. In an unparalleled panorama, Genesis 1–11 sets the stage for understanding the drama of God's plan of redemption begun in Abraham. Yet long before Abraham journeyed to Canaan, a whole series of cultures and civilizations developed in the Near East. Because much of this time preceded the development of writing, scholars use the term *prehistory* to describe this period. Our knowledge of these developments comes solely through archaeology.

Archaeologists subdivide prehistory into several periods based on developments that distinguish one period from another. The names of these periods end in the Greek word *lithic*, meaning "stone," because many basic utensils and weapons during this time were made of stone. However, the key elements distinguishing one period from another most often relate to other matters.

The Neolithic tower at Jericho, uncovered in the excavations by Kathleen Kenyon.

THE GARDEN OF EDEN

Genesis describes a garden God provided for the first human couple. From the writers, perspective in Canaan, the garden lay to the east in a place called Eden (Gen. 2:8). The term *Eden* may come from the Hebrew word for "delight"; alternatively, the word may have derived from a Babylonian word *edine* meaning "plain," or perhaps "Eden" is related to a West Semitic word suggesting a well-watered place. The Garden of Eden (Gen. 2:15), therefore, was a place of life-giving water and fertile land where God abundantly provided for Adam and Eve.

The writer describes a river that flowed forth from the Garden that separated into four rivers: the Pishon, the Gihon, the Tigris, and the Euphrates. The last two rivers are well known; they originate in the Armenian mountains of eastern Turkey and flow through Mesopotamia to the Persian Gulf (see map 1). The other two rivers are unknown. The Pishon traveled through Havilah, a name that occurs twice in the Table of Nations (Gen. 10:6, 29). Proposals for the two Havilahs include the area of northern Arabia and the African coast. The Gihon traversed the land of Cush, most often associated with Nubia, south of Egypt (Gen. 10:6). An alternate suggestion based on Genesis 10:8 identifies another Cush with the Kassites of central and southern Mesopotamia.

The geographical details—a river that separates into four headwaters—cannot be easily matched with the present geography of the Middle East. Several proposed locations for the Garden of Eden have been offered. One idea locates the Garden in the Armenian Mountains near the headwater of the Euphrates and Tigris Rivers. In this scenario Pishon and Gihon might be identified with other rivers arising in this mountainous region.

A second proposal places the Garden of Eden in southern Mesopotamia. If the name *Eden* comes from the Babylonian word for "plain," this idea gains strength. Furthermore, from the vantage point of Canaan, southern Mesopotamia lies east. The Tigris and Euphrates flow through Mesopotamia. Perhaps the Gihon and Pishon refer to rivers flowing out of the southern Zagros Mountains into the plain. An alternate suggestion is that two of the numerous irrigation canals are the Pishon and Gihon.

A third view takes a broader approach, suggesting that the description locates the Garden of Eden only generally in the Ancient Near East. The name *Cush* suggests to some scholars that the two unidentified rivers are the White and Blue Niles of Africa. Since the location of the Tigris and Euphrates are known, this view locates the Garden of Eden generally in the Near East, the cradle of ancient civilizations.

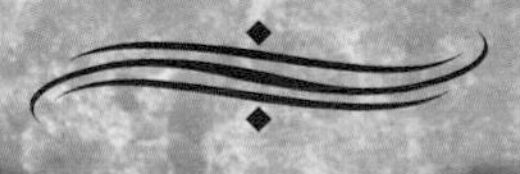

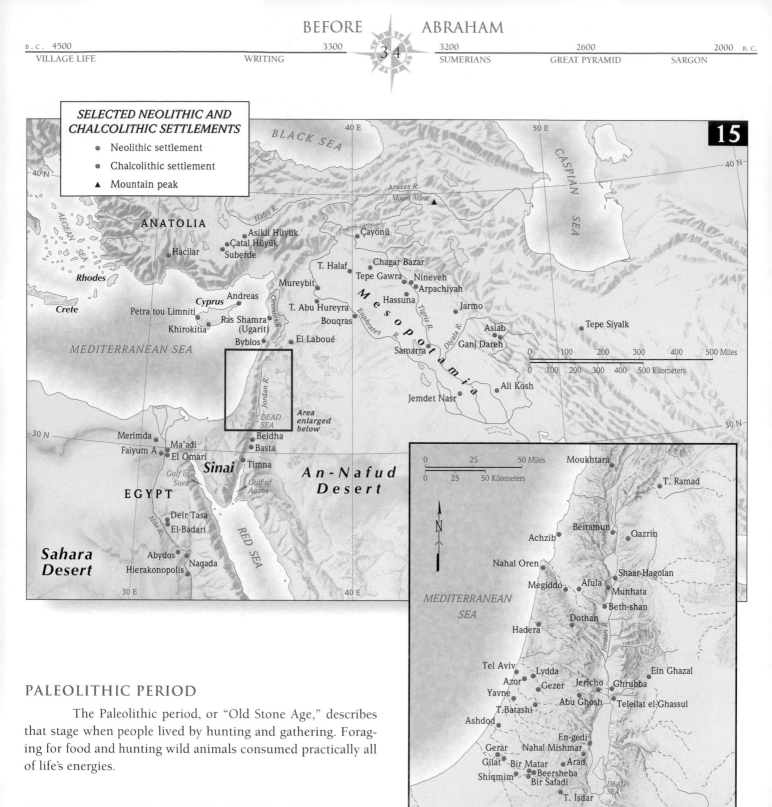

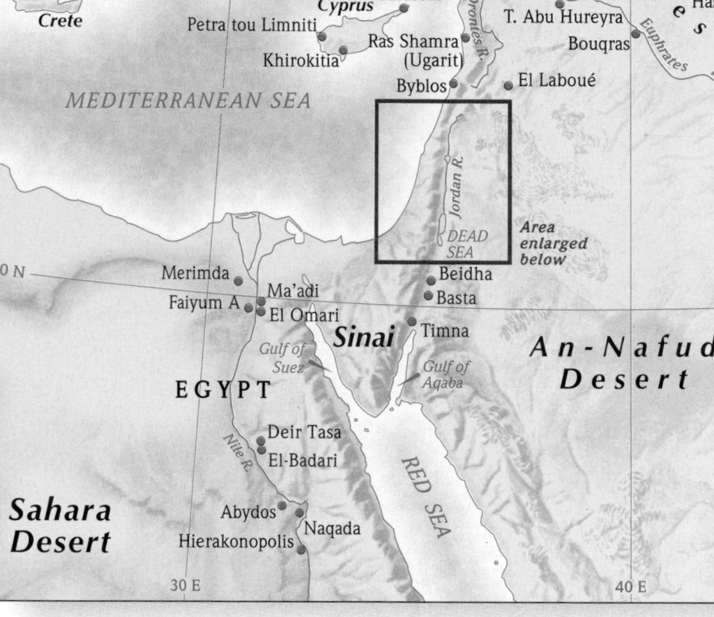

PALEOLITHIC PERIOD

The Paleolithic period, or "Old Stone Age," describes that stage when people lived by hunting and gathering. Foraging for food and hunting wild animals consumed practically all of life's energies.

EPIPALEOLITHIC PERIOD (FORMALLY "MIDDLE STONE AGE")

By the Epipaleolithic period (ca. 15,000–8300 B.C.) people learned to make better use of the resources that surrounded them. Fishing and collecting wild wheat and barley allowed more stable communities. Evidence of a few round houses appears for the first time. The Natufian culture of Palestine represents a transitional phase between a society based strictly on hunting and gathering and one based on agriculture and animal husbandry.

NEOLITHIC PERIOD

Gradually, as populations increased and new ideas emerged, permanent villages appeared whose people lived by farming. The Neolithic period, or "New Stone Age," (ca. 9000–4500 B.C.) arrived in the Near East. During this period the domestication of both plants and animals provided a stable food supply and permitted long-term settlements. Villages supported by agriculture dotted the Near East, principally in zones favored by adequate rainfall. Pottery also came into use during the Neolithic period. A few Neolithic settlements were surprisingly large. By 7500 B.C. Jericho covered six acres and was heavily fortified by a wall with massive round towers made of stone. In the Transjordan the thirty-acre site of Ain Ghazal yielded a major collection of plaster human statues, several nearly a meter in height, perhaps associated with ancestor worship. Catal Huyuk in central Turkey extended over thirty-two acres. Most Neolithic villages, however, were much smaller. Important Neolithic sites include Jarmo, Hassuna, Samarra, Nineveh, Ugarit, and Byblos.

Not all people settled into village life; some became herders of sheep and goats, moving from time to time in search of grazing land. This contrast between settled farmers and seminomadic herders was embedded deeply in both the societies of the Near East and the Bible.

CHALCOLITHIC PERIOD

The Chalcolithic period, or "Copper Stone Age," (ca. 4500–3300 B.C.) brought several important changes. The first known use of metal (copper) for utensils and weapons occurred in this period. Settlements in the Near East became more numerous and somewhat larger, although, curiously, they were seldom well fortified. Although Chalcolithic sites both large and small were found throughout the Near East, in Mesopotamia a remarkable series of cultures emerged identifiable by their beautiful multicolored pottery. Northern Mesopotamia was the home of cultures known by the names Hassuna, Samarra, and Halafian. From about 4200 B.C. to 3000 B.C. the most important cultural advancements occurred in southern Mesopotamia. Sites like Al'Ubaid and Uruk, the biblical Erech (Gen. 10:10), provide examples of mud-brick temples beautifully decorated by colored cones arranged in geometric designs.

By 3500 B.C. the Sumerians settled in southern Mesopotamia, where they developed an elementary writing system and erected larger temples. Biblical Shinar (Gen. 10:10; 11:2; 14:2) evidently refers to southern Mesopotamia, reflecting knowledge that many important cultural advances came from this region. The stage for the development of more sophisticated societies had been set.

In Palestine, metalsmiths produced a remarkable number of copper objects in the Chalcolithic period, some of which were found in a cave near En-gedi on the Dead Sea. The objects apparently were used in a nearby Chalcolithic temple. Several sites in the vicinity of Beer-sheba show high craftsmanship-especially in ivory work from this era. The large Chalcolithic settlement at Teleilat Ghassul (fifty acres) northeast of the Dead Sea had temples with wall paintings richly decorated with fantastic creatures, eight-pointed stars, and ritual masks. However, the cultural achievements in Mesopotamia during the Chalcolithic far outstrip any other region of the Near East.

The Rise and Decline of Early Civilizations: The Early Bronze Age (3300–2000 B.C.)

THE URBAN REVOLUTION

From about 3300 to 2200 B.C. an "Urban Revolution" produced the first true civilizations in the Near East. Towns and a few larger cities developed alongside the smaller villages of earlier periods. Improved agricultural practices generated food surpluses that could support a larger population or be traded for goods not locally available. The food surplus and increased societal needs provided a demand for occupations other than agriculture. Craftsmen, administrators, architects, and scribes served the needs of increasingly complex societies. Although these changes took place gradually over several hundreds of years and did not affect every part of the Near East equally, they signal the first truly urban period.

Not surprisingly, our first evidence of these developments comes from regions dominated by great river systems: southern Mesopotamia and Egypt. These rivers stimulated the development of civilizations in many ways. Communication and transportation were relatively easy along the course of the rivers; trade flowed smoothly from village to village. Moreover, the rivers provided an abundance of water for irrigation in these naturally dry lands. Irrigation produced greater crop yields than natural rainfall, resulting in agricultural surpluses to be used for export or to support other sectors of society. To build and maintain a sophisticated agricultural system requires large-scale cooperation and a strong, centralized authority. These factors, and others, facilitated the emergence of cities as centers of political power and expanding trade. During what archaeologists call the Early Bronze Age (ca. 3300–2000 B.C.), remarkable civilizations flowered in Mesopotamia and Egypt.

MESOPOTAMIA

The Sumerians. The Sumerian civilization dominated southern Mesopotamia from about 3500 to 2371 B.C. The Sumerians laid the foundations of their culture just prior to 3000 B.C. with the invention of writing, monumental buildings, and the development of a complex social structure headed by a king. Important cities such as Kish, Uruk (biblical Erech), Nippur, Lagash, and Ur formed the basis of Sumerian civilization. Canals connected the cities located in the plain away from the rivers.

THE TABLE OF NATIONS

Genesis 10 presents a list of nations descended from the three sons of Noah: Japheth, Ham, and Shem. This "Table of Nations" is unique in the ancient world and contains seventy names of ancestral heads of nations and peoples known to Israel. The list proceeds from the less important, for the purposes of the writer, to the most important. The fourteen descendants of Japheth are named first. Japheth's descendants generally are associated with areas north and northwest of Canaan, including mainland Greece, Asia Minor (modern Turkey), certain Mediterranean islands (Crete, Cyprus, and Rhodes), and the mountainous areas from Armenia to the Caspian Sea.

The list next names thirty descendants of Ham. The Hamites generally are located in North Africa (Egypt and the Sudan), along the coast of Somaliland and the west Arabian coasts, and in certain sections of Mesopotamia. Canaan along with many of the people-groups Israel encountered as she entered the promised land (Amorites, Jebusites, Perizzites, Hivites, Girgashites, and others) are listed as Hamites.

The last and most extensive part of the list contains twenty-six descendants of Shem, the ancestor of Israel. Genesis 11:10–26 connects Shem with Abram (Abraham), who received God's gracious covenant of blessing and hope for the human race (Gen. 12:1–3).

Identification of many of Shem's descendants remains uncertain. Some of the names seem to refer to areas of northwest Mesopotamia (Eber, Peleg, Aram). Elam was at the bend of the Persian Gulf, while Asshur and Arpachshad are in the upper Tigris region. Several names can be located plausibly in Somaliland (Havilah, Ophir). The thirteen sons of Joktan are related to the tribes of the Arabian Peninsula.

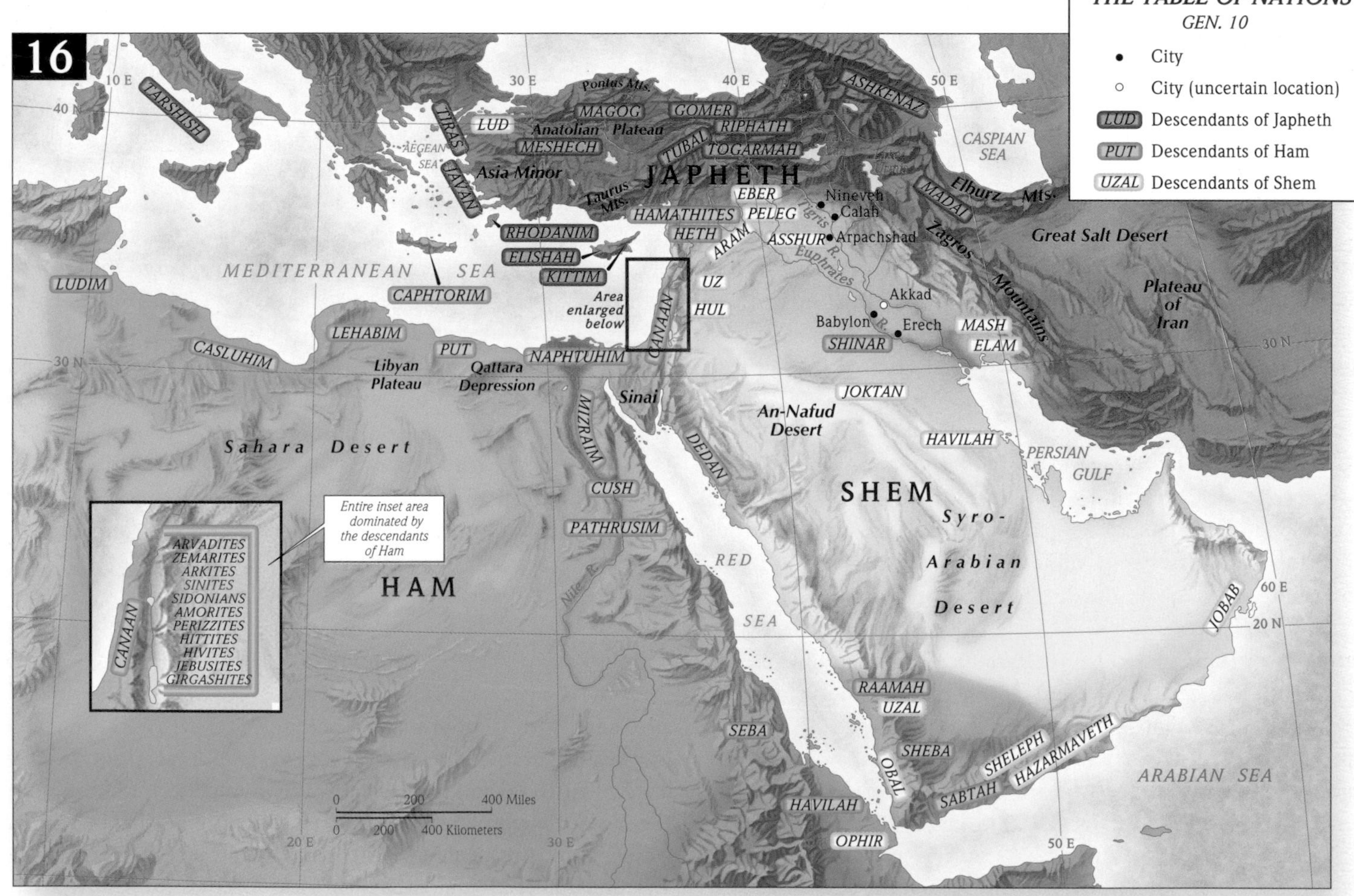

The Sumerian civilization actually was a confederation of independent city-states; each city had its own king who ruled the surrounding land and villages. At the center of each city-state stood the temple dedicated to the chief god or goddess of the city. Both political and economic power centered in the temples, and the king personally performed many priestly functions. Nippur, the center of worship for the greatest of the Sumerian gods, Enlil, possessed a favored status; kings of other city-states sought recognition at Nippur. Although the city-states theoretically were independent, kings frequently warred against one another in territorial feuds, often seeking to extend their influence.

The Classical Sumerian Age extended approximately from 2900 to 2350 B.C. during which time Sumerian culture reached a high point. Most Sumerian cities had a high stepped tower, or ziggurat, near the city center. Atop the ziggurat was a shrine often dedicated to the worship of the city's patron deity. Some scholars suggest that the Tower of Babel in Genesis 10 was a ziggurat.

The most impressive evidence of Sumerian culture comes from the Royal Tombs of Ur, excavated by Leonard Woolley in 1928. These tombs contained beautiful objects of art and equipment buried with members of royalty at Ur. Gold jewelry and daggers, helmets made of electrum, and lyres decorated with bull heads illustrate the artistic skills of Sumerian craftsmen.

The Sumerians produced a wide variety of literature ranging from ordinary economic documents to great epics. Our earliest examples of law codes, medical treatises, and agricultural manuals come from Sumerian writers. Sumerian theologians wrestled with some of life's basic questions and developed a body of literature that expressed Sumerian concepts about people and their world. Our earliest version of the story of a great flood comes from Sumer. The Sumerians left a lasting imprint on many other cultures through their literary heritage.

The Akkadians. The Akkadian period, about 2371 to 2230 B.C., followed the Classical Sumerian Age in Mesopotamia. The Akkadians (cf. Gen. 10:10), a people of Semitic stock, coexisted peacefully with the Sumerians for centuries. Larger populations of Akkadians inhabited central and northern Mesopotamia. About 2371, a local Akkadian governor named Sargon gained control of Kish and defeated the most important Sumerian ruler, Lugalzagessi of Uruk. Eventually, Sargon subdued all the Sumerian cities and united most of Mesopotamia under his power.

A beautiful example of Sumerian craftsmanship recovered from the royal burials at Ur. The ram is made from wood, gold, silver, lapis lazuli, and sea shells.

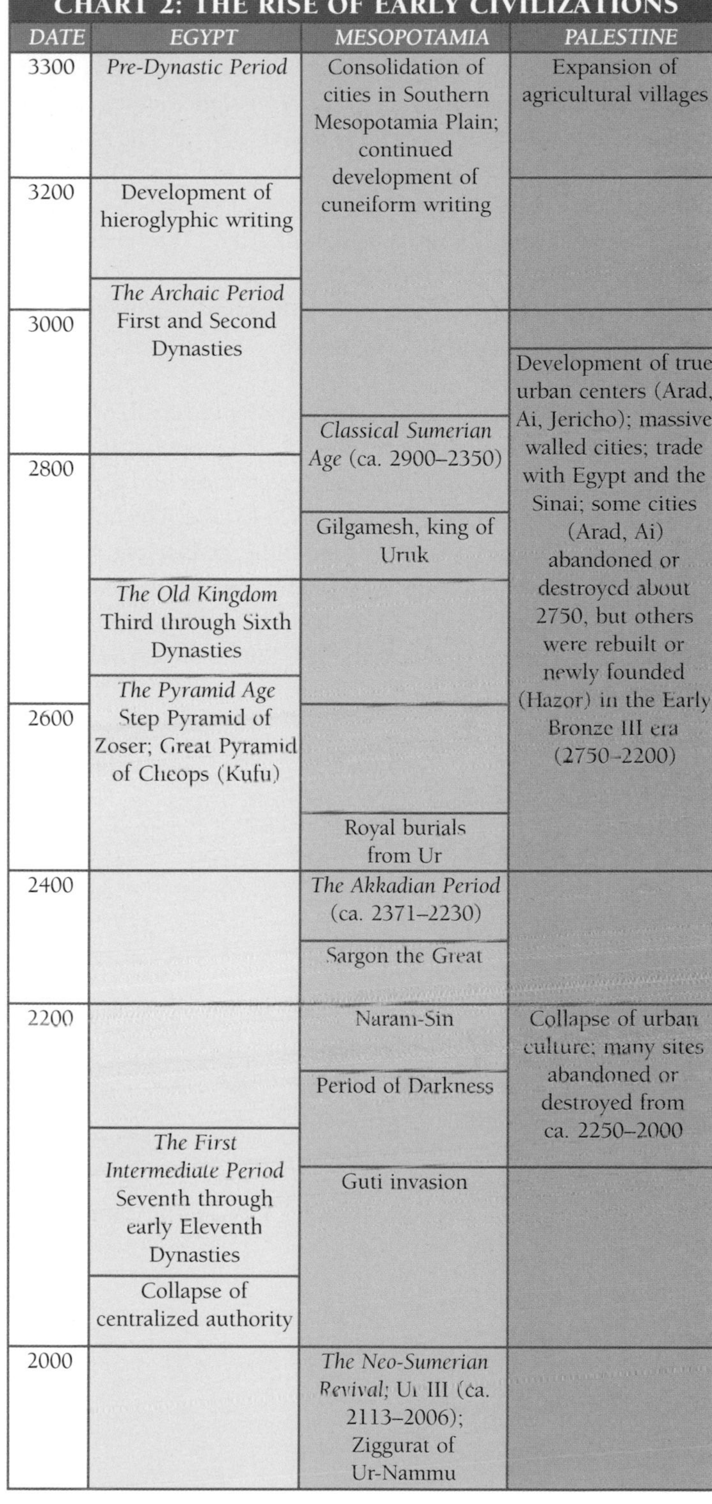

CHART 2: THE RISE OF EARLY CIVILIZATIONS

DATE	EGYPT	MESOPOTAMIA	PALESTINE
3300	*Pre-Dynastic Period*	Consolidation of cities in Southern Mesopotamia Plain; continued development of cuneiform writing	Expansion of agricultural villages
3200	Development of hieroglyphic writing		
	The Archaic Period First and Second Dynasties		
3000			Development of true urban centers (Arad, Ai, Jericho); massive walled cities; trade with Egypt and the Sinai; some cities (Arad, Ai) abandoned or destroyed about 2750, but others were rebuilt or newly founded (Hazor) in the Early Bronze III era (2750–2200)
		Classical Sumerian Age (ca. 2900–2350)	
2800			
		Gilgamesh, king of Uruk	
	The Old Kingdom Third through Sixth Dynasties		
	The Pyramid Age Step Pyramid of Zoser; Great Pyramid of Cheops (Kufu)		
2600			
		Royal burials from Ur	
2400		*The Akkadian Period* (ca. 2371–2230)	
		Sargon the Great	
2200		Naram-Sin	Collapse of urban culture; many sites abandoned or destroyed from ca. 2250–2000
		Period of Darkness	
	The First Intermediate Period Seventh through early Eleventh Dynasties		
		Guti invasion	
	Collapse of centralized authority		
2000		*The Neo-Sumerian Revival;* Ur III (ca. 2113–2006); Ziggurat of Ur-Nammu	

Known to historians as Sargon the Great, he and his descendants ruled the Akkadian Empire for approximately 160 years. Sargon established a new capital at Agade, whose precise location is unknown, although it must be in central Mesopotamia. Sargon and his grandson Naram-Sin campaigned eastward into ancient Elam and westward as far as northern Syria. The Akkadian Empire bequeathed to later Mesopotamian cultures two important legacies: (1) the concept of one strong ruler who controlled a large territory, and (2) the Akkadian language. Later Babylonian and Assyrian kings styled themselves "king of Sumer and Akkad, king of the four corners of the earth." Akkadian became the common language of diplomacy, economics, and literature until the first millennium B.C.

The Akkadian Empire collapsed after the death of Naram-Sin. The causes of the collapse are obscure, but mountainous tribesmen called Gutians overran most of Mesopotamia and a period of decline in civilization ensued (ca. 2230–2113 B.C.). The hold of the Guti over Mesopotamia was broken by Utuhegal, king of Uruk, who appointed Ur-Nammu as military governor over Ur. Ur-Nammu established the Third Dynasty of Ur (Ur III) inaugurating a period of cultural achievements known as the Neo-Sumerian Revival (2113–2006 B.C.). The earliest certain examples of ziggurats (towers consisting of a series of superimposed platforms made of mud brick with a temple on top) come from this era, including the famous ziggurat at Ur. One of the earliest known codes of law, the fragmentary "Law Code of Ur-Nammu," dates from this era along with beautiful examples of the sculptor's art.

EGYPT

Prior to 3100 B.C. Egypt consisted of local districts or nomes controlled by local chieftains in the largest town of the area. A few of these chieftains became powerful enough to dominate the districts in an entire region. Gradually, separate kingdoms ruled by warriors appeared in the Delta of the north and others in the Nile Valley of the south. These warriors/chieftains struggled intermittently until an ambitious king of the south—by tradition named Narmer—conquered the north, resulting in the unification of the "Two Lands." Narmer is often identified, perhaps erroneously, with Menes of Greek tradition

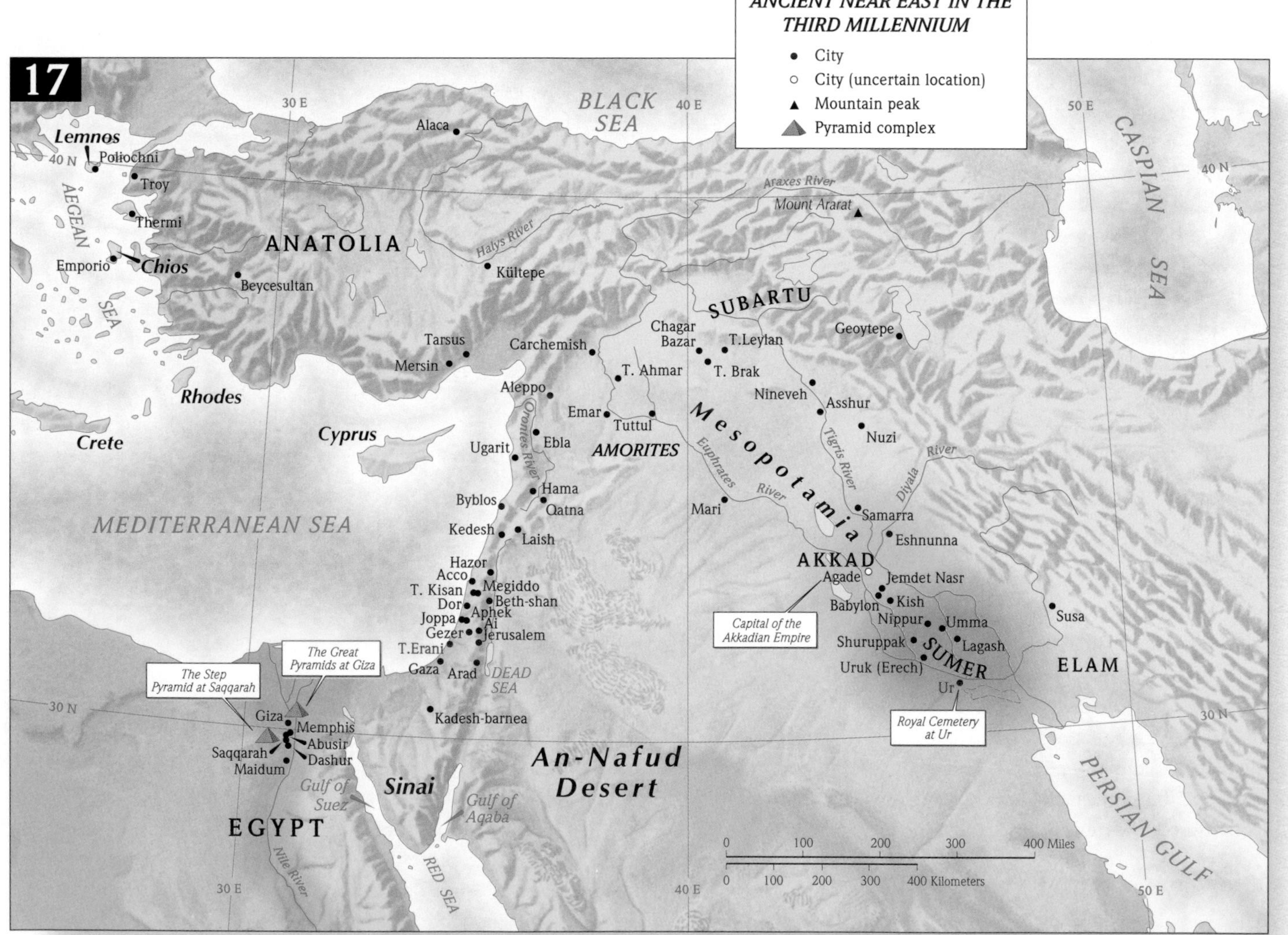

(the Greeks considered Menes to be the first king of Egypt). Narmer founded the First Dynasty of Egypt and built a new capital at Memphis just south of modern Cairo. These actions inaugurated an Egyptian civilization that would remain more or less intact for three thousand years.

We know little about the first two dynasties of Egypt, an era covering perhaps four hundred years known as the Archaic Period. By this time the Egyptians had devised a writing system today called hieroglyphics. The tombs of the kings and officials of the First and Second Dynasties found at Saqqarah and Abydos provide most of our information. Although the evidence suggests some internal power struggles, Egypt remained united.

The essential foundation of unification was the Egyptian concept of kingship. The Egyptians viewed each king, or pharaoh, as a god who ruled the land according to the divine principles of justice, truth, and the natural order. The land's fertility and prosperity, as well as national security, depended on the king. The Egyptians developed an elaborate mythology to express their ideas about kingship. The king was regarded as a god, the incarnation of the falcon god Horus and the son of Re, a sun god. This concept of divine kingship was a central feature of Egyptian civilization. Ruling as absolute monarch, the king mediated the benefits of the gods to the people, ensuring peace and prosperity.

The Old Kingdom. The pyramids of Egypt embody the social structure of Egypt headed by a divine ruler. During the Third through the Sixth Dynasties, or the Old Kingdom (ca. 2686–2181 B.C.), the Egyptians built most of the massive pyramids—tombs for their departed kings. The Step Pyramid at Saqqarah, built by Imhotep (ca. 2660 B.C.) for his master Zoser of the Third Dynasty, was one of the earliest monumental stone buildings. The first true pyramids were erected in the Fourth Dynasty on the edge of the Western desert. The most famous of these structures is the Great Pyramid of Giza near Cairo, erected about 2600 B.C. as a tomb and monument for Cheops (Kufu). Originally 485 feet tall, the Great Pyramid measures 755 feet on each side and covers over thirteen acres of land (see photograph on p. 32).

Each pyramid was the central feature of a large complex of structures associated with the king. Worship of the dead king continued in temples located at the foot of the pyramid. The tombs of high officials and royal family members who hoped to follow the king into the life beyond surround the pyramids. These pyramid complexes of the Old Kingdom reflect the supreme importance of the pharaoh as the divine king through whom the gods ruled Egypt.

The Step Pyramid of Zoser at Saqqarah.

The Pyramid Age established many norms for Egyptian civilization throughout its history. The Egyptians were essentially a conservative people. Styles and customs of art, architecture, religion, and society that were developed in the Old Kingdom continued in later periods. True, new ideas emerged later, and certain modifications of styles did occur, but a sameness marks Egyptian culture that is not found elsewhere in the Near East. The land of Egypt with its favorable climate and unfailing river encouraged a static view of life. The divine order manifested in the Egyptian concept of kingship reinforced the timeless reality of Egyptian culture. Moreover, the relative isolation of Egypt due to effective barriers protecting against intrusion from all directions, except the northeast, helped ensure that change came slowly. When Moses led the Hebrew people out of Egypt over one thousand years after the Great Pyramid had been built, he contended with a civilization whose essential features were established in the Old Kingdom.

Egypt's First Intermediate Period. Toward the end of the Sixth Dynasty the power of the pharaoh declined rapidly. Powerful nobles set themselves up as rulers over large areas. This decline in centralized authority resulted in a political fragmentation of Egypt; numerous petty rulers claimed the title of king. At

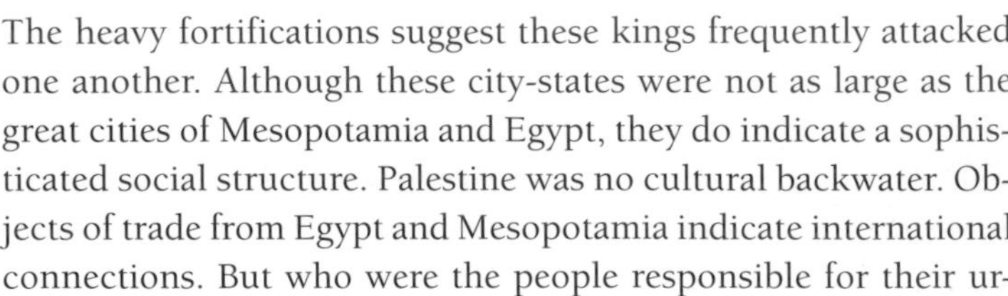

the same time, peoples from the Sinai and southern Palestine migrated into Egypt and settled down. The Egyptians referred to these peoples contemptuously as "sand crossers" or "Asiatics" and later blamed them for the decline of Egyptian civilization. Known as the First Intermediate Period, this era included the Seventh through the early Eleventh Dynasties (ca. 2200–2040 B.C.). The First Intermediate Period was the first of several breakdowns of central authority in the course of Egyptian history and coincided generally with a decline in urban society throughout the Near East just before 2000 B.C.

PALESTINE AND SYRIA

Shortly after 3000 B.C., Palestine underwent its own urban revolution. Unfortunately, unlike Egypt and Mesopotamia, Palestine so far has produced no written documents to aid us in interpreting the archaeological evidence from this period. However, the archaeological data is clear. Beginning about 3000 B.C., several large, heavily fortified towns appeared alongside the numerous villages. Most of these towns were along the coastal plains or in the great valleys where the presence of good water supplies and fertile land invited settlement (Megiddo, Beth-yerah, Yarmuth, Jericho, Gezer, and Hazor, among others). A few sites such as Arad and Ai were located in more arid or mountainous sectors. Almost all these sites had heavy fortifications, with walls up to thirty feet thick. Inside the fortifications, archaeologists have discovered temples and larger buildings, usually interpreted as palaces of the local king.

Politically, Palestine in the Early Bronze Age was a collection of city-states with its own king. Each king controlled the smaller agricultural settlements of the surrounding countryside. The heavy fortifications suggest these kings frequently attacked one another. Although these city-states were not as large as the great cities of Mesopotamia and Egypt, they do indicate a sophisticated social structure. Palestine was no cultural backwater. Objects of trade from Egypt and Mesopotamia indicate international connections. But who were the people responsible for their urban development? Many scholars regard them as the ancestors of the Canaanites and call them "Proto-Canaanites."

The "sacred area" at Megiddo. Two of three Early Bronze Age temples and a raised platform, probably a sacrificial altar, are in view.

Palestine also experienced a serious erosion of urban life in this period. From 2250 to shortly after 2000 B.C. virtually every town in Palestine suffered a violent destruction or sharp decline. Why? We are not sure, but this period coincides with the general decline of civilization elsewhere at this time. Undoubtedly a number of factors contributed to this decline. Short-term climate changes (drought), the ebbing power of aging civilizations, or disruption of economic and social relationships may have played roles.

One site in Syria, Tell Mardikh, has yielded evidence of a city-state that controlled much of northern Syria in this period. Tell Mardikh represents the ruins of ancient Ebla, a city formerly known only from Mesopotamian documents. A cache of several thousand clay tablets found at the site, written in Sumerian and Eblaite, sheds much needed light on Syria during this era. From about 2500 to 2200 B.C. Ebla was the center of a powerful economic empire that rivaled the Akkadian Empire. Biblical scholars have been interested in the numerous geographical references in the Ebla texts, including early references to sites in Palestine. They also have strong interest in the Eblaite language itself.

Chapter Five

THE WORLD OF THE PATRIARCHS

The familiar figures of the patriarchs Abraham, Isaac, Jacob, and Joseph emerge out of the mists of Israel's earliest memories. Genesis 12–50 traces the journeys of these ancestral forefathers as they sought a land promised by God (Gen. 12:1; 15:7). Their migrations carried them from Mesopotamia to Egypt on several occasions, although the focus remained on Canaan, the land that their descendants would eventually possess. We are completely dependent upon Genesis for our knowledge of these great biblical figures since not a single reference to the patriarchs has been discovered outside the Bible. This is not surprising, given the emphatic biblical affirmation that God chose His people from the least of all the peoples of the earth (Deut. 7:7).

Israel's ancestors came from the peripheral edges of history even though they were at the theological center of God's redemptive plan. Yet this historical anonymity makes it difficult to place the patriarchs within their proper milieu. Several scholars believe Genesis 12–50 reflects the Middle Bronze Age (2000–1550 B.C.) and place the migrations of the patriarchs within this period.

CHART 3: PERIOD AT A GLANCE
THE MIDDLE BRONZE AGE 2000 TO 1550 B.C.

DATES	MESOPOTAMIA	EGYPT	PALESTINE
2100	*Third Dynasty of Ur* (2113–2006) Ur-Nammu		Emergence of urban centers after two centuries of decline; Abraham, Isaac, and Jacob's migrations (?)
2000		*Middle Kingdom:* Late Eleventh and Twelfth Dynasties (ca. 2000–1786)	
	Increasing domination over Mesopotamia by Amorites		
		Tale of Sinuhe	
1900		Execration Texts	
1800	*Old Babylonian Kingdom* Hammurabi (1792–1750)	*Second Intermediate Period;* Thirteenth through Seventeenth Dynasties	*Classical Canaanite Era;* many heavily fortified cities; introduction of Bronze technology
	(Zimri-lim, king of Mari)		
		infiltration of Asiatics (Hyksos)	
	Law code of Hammurabi		
	Babylonian Literary Epics: Gilgamesh Epic; Enuma Elish		
1700		Egyptian unity collapses; Hyksos kings rule the Delta and central Egypt from Avaris; native Egyptian kings maintain some control on southern Egypt	
1600		(Descent of Joseph and his brothers into the Delta of Egypt?)	Indication of earliest writing in Palestine
1550	Sack of Babylon by the Hittite king Mursilis I	Kings of the Seventeenth Dynasty (Kamose, Seqenenre, and Ahmose) drive Hyksos from the Delta, attacking Hyksos strongholds in southern Palestine	

The Middle Bronze Age in Mesopotamia and Egypt

MESOPOTAMIA

After the collapse of urban civilization, powerful states reappeared beginning about 2000 B.C. In southern Mesopotamia the city-state of Ur had already gained control of the surrounding territory. Ur Nammu, greatest king of the Third Dynasty of Ur (ca. 2113–2006 B.C.), erected a great ziggurat (temple tower) and encouraged art and literature. (See chap. 4, p. 38)

The Amorites. The power of Ur ebbed under increasing pressure from new groups of people who came into Mesopotamia and changed the political landscape. Particularly important were the Amorites, a Semitic people perhaps originally from the fringes of the Syro-Arabian Desert west of Mesopotamia. Tribally oriented and seminomadic, moving with small herds of sheep and goats, these Amorites gradually penetrated Mesopotamia, overthrowing the rulers of city-states and establishing Amorite dynasties at Isin and Larsa. During a span of two hundred years (2000–1800 B.C.) Amorites dominated most cities in Mesopotamia.

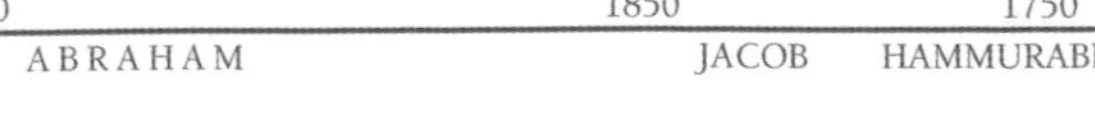

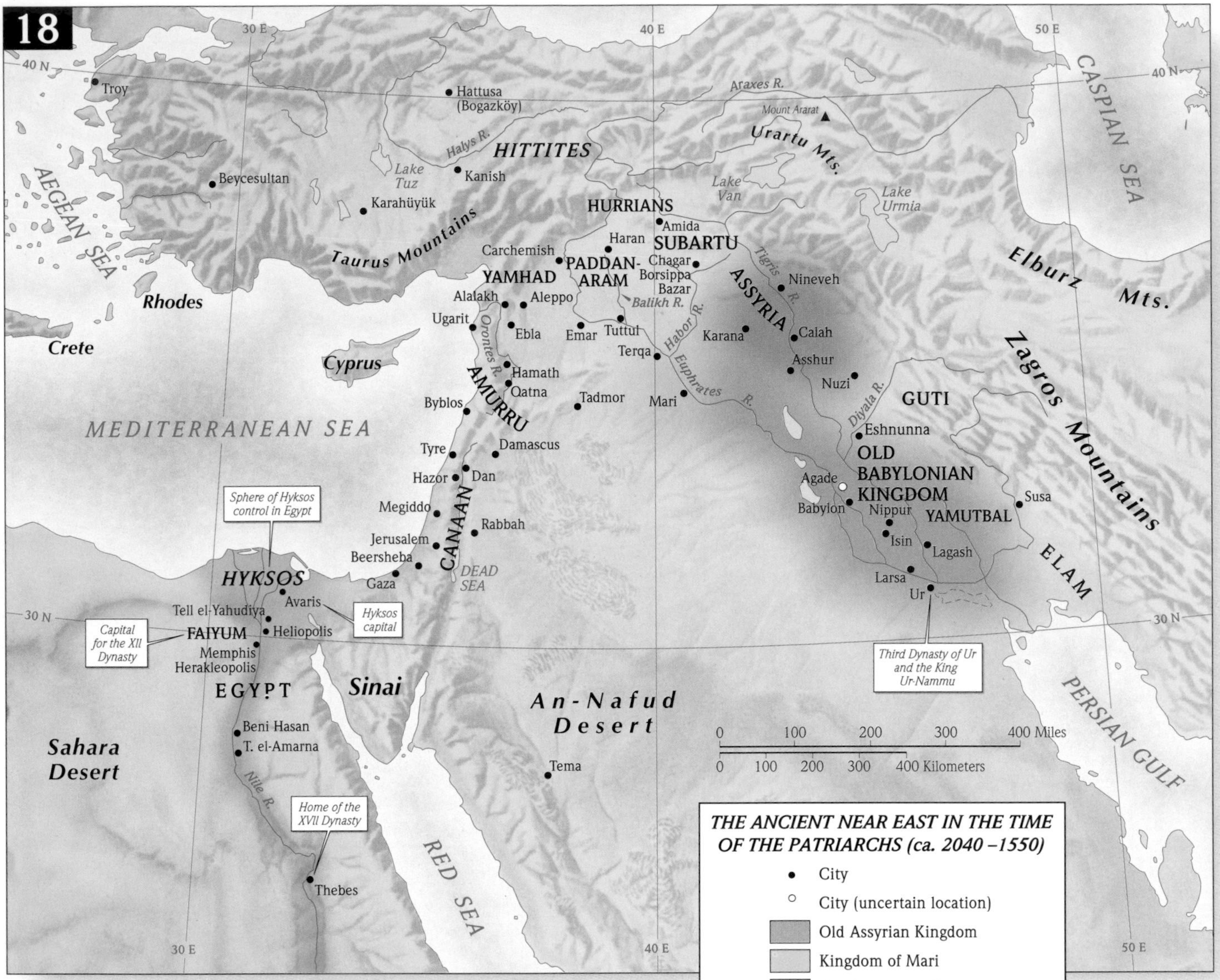

18

THE ANCIENT NEAR EAST IN THE TIME OF THE PATRIARCHS (ca. 2040 –1550)

- City
- City (uncertain location)
- Old Assyrian Kingdom
- Kingdom of Mari
- Old Babylonian Kingdom
- Egpyt
- Egyptian influence

By 1800 B.C. two powerful Amorite states—Mari and Babylon—controlled affairs along the Euphrates River. Zimri-lim, king of Mari, built a palace comprised of 260 rooms covering an area 200 x 120 meters. Within this palace archaeologists discovered twenty-five thousand clay tablets inscribed in Akkadian. These tablets contain valuable information on social customs of the Middle Bronze Age and give some indications of how prophets functioned outside Israel.

Babylon. By the 1700s B.C. Babylon became the center of a kingdom that controlled most of central and southern Mesopotamia. Hammurabi, sixth king of the First Amorite Dynasty of Babylon (1792–1750), was the most important ruler of the Old Babylonian Kingdom. He conquered Mari and established a modest empire that included southern and central Mesopotamia. His famous law code, now in the Louvre Museum in Paris, indicates high levels of social and cultural refinement.

The court at Babylon fostered the writing of great epics adapted from earlier Sumerian prototypes. The Gilgamesh Epic, or "Babylonian Flood Story," has been especially intriguing to biblical scholars because of its literary parallels with the flood recorded in Genesis 7–8. The Enuma Elish recounts the exploits of the great Babylonian god Marduk who prevailed over the primordial monster Tiamat and created the world. Although in its present form the Enuma Elish probably dates to the later second millennium, elements of the epic may go back to the old Babylonian period. The Epic of Atrahasis recounts the creation of human beings to carry out the tiresome toil upon earth assigned to the lesser gods by the greater gods. Noting the rapid increase of the human population whose noise disturbed the sleep of the gods, the epic next describes a terrible flood dispatched by the gods that destroys humankind except for Atrahasis who was spared because of his piety. After the flood the gods reestablished humankind and maintained greater control over their population. The Atrahasis Epic is the only Mesopotamian account that connects aspects of creation and a flood in a continuous narrative. The epic draws from earlier Sumerian themes but dates in its present form to the Old Babylonian period. The literature and archaeological remains of this period testify to the vitality and strength of the Mesopotamian states in the Middle Bronze Age.

After Hammurabi, the power of Babylon gradually ebbed. Nippur and Isin were lost to Babylonian control shortly after Hammurabi's death. A Hittite raid by Mursilis I about 1595 B.C. brought an end to the First Amorite Dynasty of Babylon. Babylon entered a dark age for the next four hundred years, during which the Kassites dominated southern Mesopotamia.

EGYPT

Twelfth Dynasty. Egypt, too, recovered from a period of weakness that gripped her from 2200 to 1991 B.C. The powerful Twelfth Dynasty finished the process of unification begun by the kings of the Eleventh Dynasty who came from Thebes far to the south. Moving their capital to Itjowy near the Faiyum region, the Twelfth Dynasty rulers extended their control south into Nubia and northeast into the Sinai.

The Tale of Sinuhe from about 1950 B.C. records the journey of a high Twelfth Dynasty official, Sinuhe, who was forced to flee Egypt. Sinuhe's route took him across Sinai into Palestine and southern Syria, where he lived among Asiatic tribes. Descriptions of the land in which Sinuhe sojourned bear striking similarities to biblical descriptions of the promised land: "It was a good land, named Yaa. Figs were in it, and grapes. It had more wine than water. Plentiful was its honey, abundant olives. Every (kind of) fruit was on its trees. Barley was there and emmer. There was not limit to any (kind of) cattle" (Pritchard, *ANET*, p. 21).

The Stele of Hammurabi containing the famous Law Code of Hammurabi (about 1750 B.C.).

Such contact between Egypt and various groups from Palestine was normal throughout historical times, but the Egyptians sought to regulate the traffic from the Twelfth Dynasty onward. Egypt served not only as an important outlet for trade for these seminomadic groups, but also as a place of refuge during times of drought that frequently afflicted portions of the Levant. Famine drove the patriarchs from Palestine into Egypt on several occasions (Gen. 12:10; 41:57–42:1).

Second Intermediate Period. With the decline of the Twelfth Dynasty about 1780 B.C., Egypt entered a period of political instability called the Second Intermediate Period (ca. 1780–1550 B.C. if one includes the Thirteenth and Fourteenth Dynasties). No single line of kings ruled all of Egypt. Native dynasties controlled much of southern and central Egypt, while the Delta in the north increasingly came under the influence of non-Egyptians called "Hyksos." These Hyksos infiltrated the Delta from Palestine and gradually established themselves as legitimate kings (see below).

A reproduction of tablet eleven of the Gilgamesh Epic describing the Babylonian account of a great flood.

Palestine in the Time of the Patriarchs

After more than two centuries of decline, urban life returned to Canaan in the Middle Bronze Age (ca. 2000–1550 B.C.) as classical Canaanite culture reached its zenith. Cities and villages sprang up, especially in the coastal plains and the great fertile valleys of Jezreel and the northern Jordan Valley. Over five hundred Middle Bronze Age sites have now been identified in Canaan. The urban character of Canaanite society is clear; perhaps as much as 65 percent of the population of Canaan dwelt in the numerous heavily fortified towns that dotted the land. Most towns were small, however, less than twenty acres in

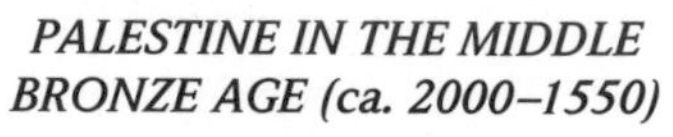

size. About 5 percent of the settlements were large cities by standards of the region—up to two hundred acres in size.

Several major Canaanite cities of this period have been excavated. Gezer, Megiddo, Aphek, Shechem, Jericho, Dan (Laish), and Hazor are among many sites yielding evidence of a sophisticated urban society. The most characteristic feature of these cities was an extensive fortification system. Each site was heavily fortified with thick walls made of mud brick set on a stone foundation. Builders utilized huge stones, quarried locally, some weighing more than a ton each. Some walls consisted of boulders roughly fitted together called "Cyclopean Masonry." Often these walls stood on massive ramparts made of local soils and debris.

Inside the walls, the Canaanites erected temples, palaces, administrative and judicial buildings, industrial facilities, along with more modest domestic houses. Many of the cities bear clear evidence of town planning. Certain crafts, such as metalworking and pottery manufacturing, reached high levels of achievement. The beautiful pottery of this period attained technical standards seldom surpassed in later times. By adding tin to copper, Middle Bronze Age metalsmiths developed a true bronze, allowing the production of new, often better and stronger, tools and weapons.

Politically, Canaan was a land of city-states. Each larger Canaanite city functioned independently and was headed by a king who controlled the surrounding villages and territory. Security must have been a prime concern judging from the large fortifications; likely, the various kings feared the ambition of other city-states.

The Canaanites basically were agricultural in their economy, although trade played an important role also. Surpluses of grain, olive oil, wine, and possibly timber and cattle were exchanged for luxury goods. Trade with Egypt, Mesopotamia, and Cyprus flourished. Contemporary economic documents found at Mari mention both Hazor, the largest of the Canaanite city-states, and Laish (Dan) in connection with the international metal trade vital to all Middle Bronze Age kingdoms. The Bible recalls that "Hazor formerly was the head of all those [Canaanite] kingdoms" (Josh. 11:10), a recognition of the political and economic importance of that great city.

Relatively few kings or cities are mentioned in the biblical accounts of the patriarchal journeys in Canaan, leading to the impression that the land was sparsely inhabited. In light of the previous description of Canaan in the Middle Bronze Age, how are we to explain this? First, the patriarchs migrated through portions of Canaan less densely inhabited at this time, primarily the Negeb and the Western Mountains. Second, the patriarchal lifestyle essentially was pastoral, avoiding the larger cities in preference for grazing land, though their travels occasionally brought them into contact with their urban neighbors. Many of the cities mentioned in Genesis in connection with the patriarchs—Shechem, Bethel, Salem (Jerusalem)—were in fact inhabited at this time. By and large the patriarchal lifestyle portrayed in Genesis is pastoral rather than urban (see the following section).

The Middle Bronze Age gate discovered in the earth rampart at Dan.

The Patriarchal Journeys

The family of Abraham (Abram) began their migration to Canaan from Ur, the ancient Sumerian city in southern Mesopotamia. Genesis offers few details of either the route or time involved in the journey. Some scholars have connected the patriarchal journeys with the larger movements of peoples between 2000 and 1700 B.C., particularly the Amorite migrations. However, the patriarchs likely were not part of any mass movement of peoples. The Bible depicts smaller units involving families or clans, possibly of Amorite stock, who carried with them herds of goats and sheep with a few cattle (Gen. 13:2–18:7). They lived in tents (Gen. 12:8; 13:18) pitched in regions with adequate water and forage for their animals.

The lifestyle of the patriarchs portrayed in Genesis is essentially pastoral and nomadic. Although they periodically settled in a particular area from time to time, perhaps growing an occasional crop of wheat or barley (Gen. 26:12), the family moved as the change of seasons and the needs of their animals dictated. A similar lifestyle appears in the Mari Texts (1900–1700 B.C.) among tribal peoples who were essentially nomadic breeders of small cattle. These groups accommodated themselves to certain features of settled life and maintained various types of contacts with villages and towns, yet still maintained tribal and pastoral ways.

THE MIGRATIONS OF ABRAHAM

According to the traditional view, Abraham began his migration from Ur in the southern Mesopotamian plain. Some scholars, however, prefer an Ur located in northwestern Mesopotamia, noting that all other references to the patriarchal homeland point to that direction. Yet the evidence for a northern Ur is meager. Leaving Ur, Abraham and his kin probably traveled up the Euphrates River to Haran. An alternate route followed the Tigris River north to the Assyrian city Asshur and thence westward across the steppes. Like Ur, a center of trade and worship of the moon god Sin, Haran lay in the region of the Habor and Balikh Rivers, a steppe land that afforded pastures and water. Genesis 11:31 implies an extended stay in the Haran region, where Abraham's father, Terah, died.

Documents from the Middle Bronze Age refer to towns near Haran bearing names similar to Abraham's kinsmen: Serug, Pethor, and Nahor. The biblical terms *Paddan-aram* (Gen. 28:2) and *Aram-naharaim* (Gen. 24:10; usually translated "Mesopotamia") apparently refer to the region of the Balikh and Habor

A row of ten monolithic upright stones (*masseboth* in Hebrew) known as the Gezer "High Place" dating from the Middle Bronze Age. The upright stones perhaps symbolized some sort of covenant ceremony in the life of the city.

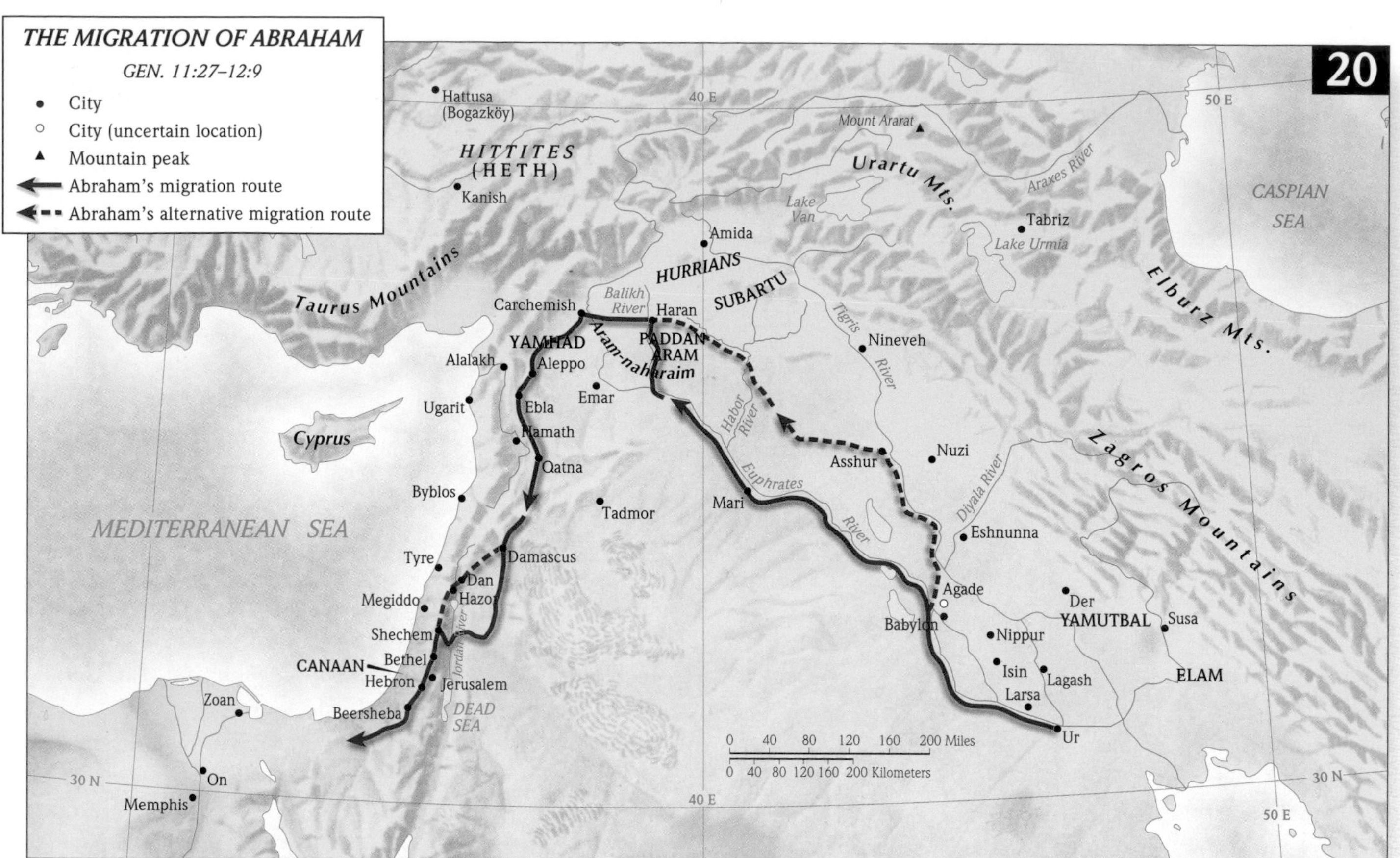

Rivers surrounding Haran. The patriarchs maintained close ties with this area; both Abraham and Isaac sought wives for their sons from kindred people who lived near Haran (Gen. 24, 28).

Entering Canaan. The route Abraham's clan took from Haran to Canaan is uncertain, although it seems logical they took one of several available trade routes. The most direct led across the desert to Damascus by way of the Tadmor Oasis. A less dangerous but longer route followed the main branch of the International Coastal Highway through Carchemish past Aleppo and Qatna to Damascus. From Damascus, the King's Highway led southward into Transjordan.

Abraham and his clan entered Canaan from the east, descending from the Transjordan Plateau via the Jabbok River. An alternative crossing near Hazor on the Upper Jordan also was possible, though less likely. Across the way, the Wadi Farah invited the group upward to Shechem in the mountains of western Palestine. Following the watershed road southward, Abraham encamped in the gentle hills between Bethel and Ai before proceeding farther south into the Negeb (Gen. 12:5–9). Eventually, a famine forced the clan to seek relief in Egypt, although the stay was temporary (Gen. 12:10–20).

Abraham in the Promised Land. Abraham's movements in Palestine were typical of the migrations of the later patriarchs, as an examination of Genesis 12–50 makes clear. The locations mentioned cluster in two basic areas: (1) the central mountains of western Palestine (Shechem, Ai, Bethel), and (2) the Negeb and the desert lands farther south (Beer-sheba, Beer-lahai-roi, Hebron [Kiriath-arba], Mamre, and Kadesh). These regions offered good grazing areas for the clan's herds and flocks. The oscillation between the mountains and the Negeb is best explained as seasonal migrations required by climatic changes, a process known as *transhumance*. During the winter the clan moved the animals south into the Negeb and the marginal wilderness areas where winter rains provided grass for grazing. During the hot summer months the patriarchs sought relief from the heat as well as grazing lands in the higher elevation of the mountains. The periodic migrations of the patriarchal clan match the pattern of small herdsman moving their encampments seeking seasonal grazing lands.

Genesis 12–50 mentions a few sites beyond the limits of these seasonal migrations (see maps 19 and 20). Abraham's nephew Lot settled in Sodom, one of five "cities of the plain" destroyed in a cataclysmic destruction brought on by the depth of their sin (Gen. 13; 19). These cities—Sodom, Gomorrah, Admah, Zeboiim, and Zoar—along with other peoples living in the southern Transjordan were the target of a military venture led by four kings from the north. It was during this onslaught that Abraham rescued Lot and received the blessing of

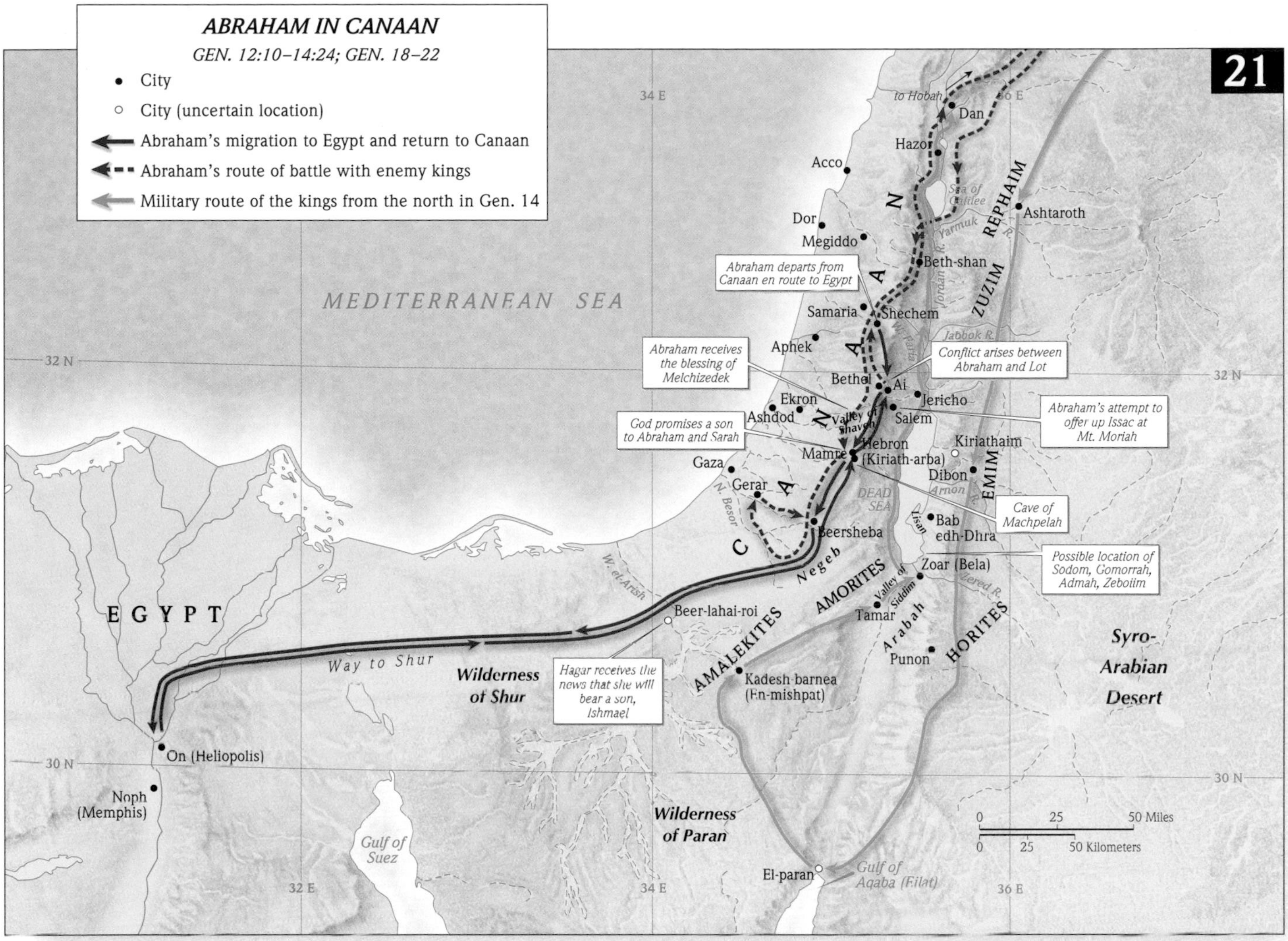

ABRAHAM IN CANAAN

GEN. 12:10–14:24; GEN. 18–22

- • City
- ○ City (uncertain location)
- Abraham's migration to Egypt and return to Canaan
- Abraham's route of battle with enemy kings
- Military route of the kings from the north in Gen. 14

21

Abraham departs from Canaan en route to Egypt

Abraham receives the blessing of Melchizedek

Conflict arises between Abraham and Lot

God promises a son to Abraham and Sarah

Abraham's attempt to offer up Issac at Mt. Moriah

Cave of Machpelah

Possible location of Sodom, Gomorrah, Admah, Zeboiim

Hagar receives the news that she will bear a son, Ishmael

Melchizedek, king of Salem (Jerusalem) and priest of the Most High God. (Gen. 14).

The precise location of these "cities of the plain" remains a mystery, although several suggestions have been made. A few scholars believe the cities lie beneath the shallow waters of the southern end of the Dead Sea, though no evidence has been found. Possibly the Early Bronze Age ruins located along the small wadis in the Arabah south of the Dead Sea are the remains of these infamous towns. A large Early Bronze Age cemetery at Bab ed-Dhra on the Lisan

The southern end of the Dead Sea. The cities of Sodom and Gomorrah as well as the other three cities of the plain destroyed by fire (Gen. 19:23–29) may have been located in this region. Notice the salt incrustations typical of the shallow southern end of the sea.

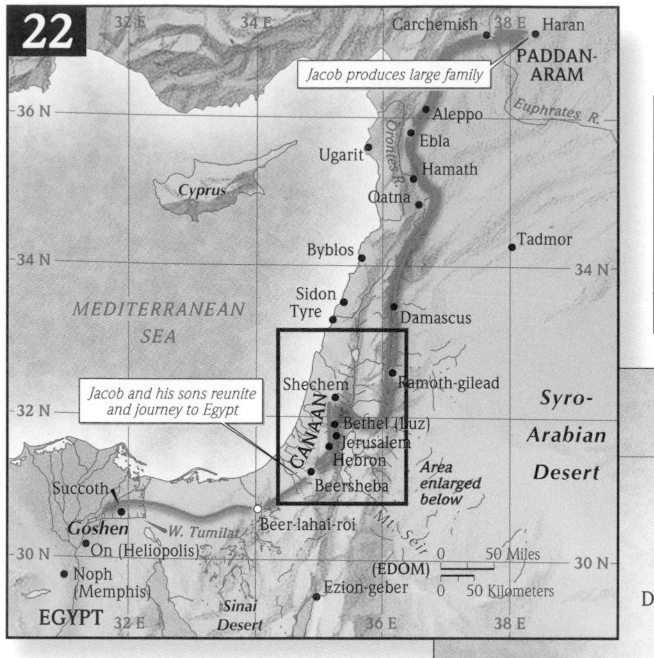

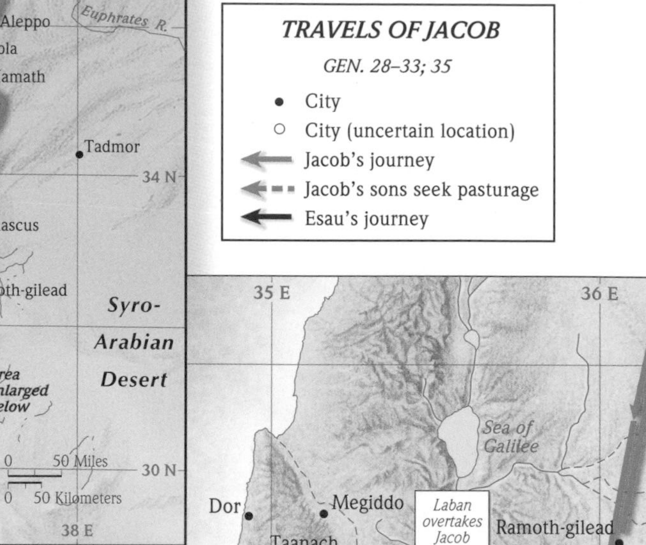

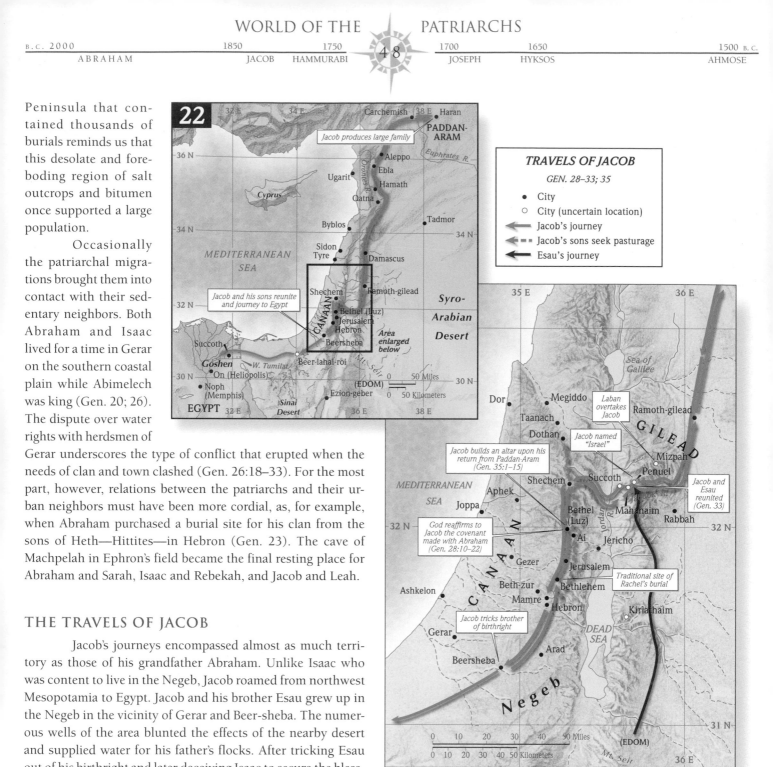

Peninsula that contained thousands of burials reminds us that this desolate and foreboding region of salt outcrops and bitumen once supported a large population.

Occasionally the patriarchal migrations brought them into contact with their sedentary neighbors. Both Abraham and Isaac lived for a time in Gerar on the southern coastal plain while Abimelech was king (Gen. 20; 26). The dispute over water rights with herdsmen of Gerar underscores the type of conflict that erupted when the needs of clan and town clashed (Gen. 26:18–33). For the most part, however, relations between the patriarchs and their urban neighbors must have been more cordial, as, for example, when Abraham purchased a burial site for his clan from the sons of Heth—Hittites—in Hebron (Gen. 23). The cave of Machpelah in Ephron's field became the final resting place for Abraham and Sarah, Isaac and Rebekah, and Jacob and Leah.

THE TRAVELS OF JACOB

Jacob's journeys encompassed almost as much territory as those of his grandfather Abraham. Unlike Isaac who was content to live in the Negeb, Jacob roamed from northwest Mesopotamia to Egypt. Jacob and his brother Esau grew up in the Negeb in the vicinity of Gerar and Beer-sheba. The numerous wells of the area blunted the effects of the nearby desert and supplied water for his father's flocks. After tricking Esau out of his birthright and later deceiving Isaac to secure the blessing of the firstborn, Jacob traveled north to his ancestral home, Paddan-aram, to find a wife. His route took him to Luz where, in a dream, God reaffirmed His covenant made with Abraham and extended it to Jacob. In gratitude Jacob renamed the place "Bethel"—"House of God"—and vowed to return with God's help (Gen. 28:10–12). He then departed for his ancestral homeland beyond the Euphrates River, probably following the same route previously taken by Abraham.

Jacob's Family Rivalries. After arrival in the Haran area, Jacob met his uncle Laban with his two daughters, Rachel and Leah. Jacob loved the comely Rachel, but Laban's trickery forced him into a marriage with Leah as well. Nevertheless, the years spent in Paddan-aram were prosperous for Jacob. Leah bore him six sons and a daughter, while her handmaiden, Zilpah, gave Jacob two more. Rachel's handmaiden, Bilhah, also bore Jacob two sons before Rachel, previously barren, gave birth to Joseph. Moreover, Laban's flocks multiplied under Jacob's supervision, creating a status of prestige and wealth for Jacob's family.

Laban's sons grew wise to Jacob's schemes and turned their father against Jacob. Secretly fleeing with his family and herds, Jacob traveled south along the King's Highway through Gilead, a distance of over three hundred miles. Laban overtook

Jacob near Mizpah in Gilead (cf. Judg. 10:17), where the two worked out a covenant of peace (Gen. 31:43–55). Jacob still had to face his brother Esau, whom he had cheated out of his birthright (Gen. 27:30–45).

Return to the Land of Promise. At Mahanaim, near the top of the Jabbok Valley, Jacob sent presents ahead to Esau in an attempted appeasement before crossing the Jabbok Ford. That night Jacob wrestled with an angel, resulting in God changing his name to Israel. Subsequently, Jacob called that place Peniel (Penuel), "face of God," in recognition of his personal encounter with Yahweh.

Jacob settled at Succoth before returning to the mountains to live, first near Shechem and then at Bethel (Gen. 33:17; 35:6). Resuming the old pattern of migrating south, Jacob was reunited with his father, Isaac, at Mamre near Hebron. Rachel died and was buried near Bethlehem along the way (Gen. 35:16–27; but cf. 1 Sam. 10:2 which implies Rachel was buried in Benjamin near Bethel). Jacob and his sons remained at Mamre, but in the summertime the sons took the herds north to the mountains near Shechem seeking pasturage.

JOSEPH AND THE ENTRY INTO EGYPT

For centuries Asiatics crossed the Sinai into Egypt seeking trade opportunities and refuge from the frequent famines that plagued the Levant. An Egyptian inscription from 1750 records the passage of one group of small livestock breeders who came to Egypt "begging a home in the domain of pharaoh . . . after the manner of your father's father (that is pharaoh) since the beginning." The Egyptians viewed these migrating peoples with contempt, calling them "wretched Asiatics" and "sand crossers." Pharaoh Amenemhet I gave orders to construct a line of fortified garrisons along the border with Sinai to guard key points of access into Egypt. This "wall of the Ruler," as it was called, allowed Egyptian frontier officials to keep check on migrations of nomadic peoples from the east.

Entry into Egypt. The story of Joseph answers the question of how Israel's ancestors arrived in Egypt. Joseph's brothers sold him to a passing Ishmaelite caravan bound for Egypt (Gen. 37:25–28). Such caravans between Palestine and Egypt must have been frequent. An Egyptian tomb painting from about 1750 B.C. at Beni-Hasan depicts a small group of Asiatics entering Egypt with their goods for trading purposes (see photo on p. 51). Joseph's odyssey in Egypt began when Potiphar, a high-ranking military officer in Pharaoh's court, bought him for a house slave.

Thirteen years later, after suffering an unjust imprisonment, Joseph rose to a position of authority second only to the king himself. His divinely bestowed ability to interpret dreams allowed him to foresee a coming famine and earned an appointment to the position of vizir. As vizir, Joseph had control of a large bureaucracy created to oversee the land and carry out the wishes of the king. The office acquired increased power from 1750 B.C. onward. Eventually two vizirs served the crown, one each for Upper (south) Egypt and Lower (north) Egypt.

Joseph's Authority. An Eighteenth Dynasty text entitled *The Duties of the Vizir* emphasized the responsibilities inherent in the office: to hear petitions, to exercise justice impartially, to mobilize troops for travel with the pharaoh, to oversee assessment and collection of taxes, to appoint and supervise officials, and to inspect and maintain royal property, among other matters. Virtually every aspect of civil government came under the vizir's oversight, with the notable exception of foreign affairs.

Joseph's primary concern was preparing Egypt to withstand the coming drought. Interestingly, Rekhmire, vizir for Thutmose III, bore the title "he who fills the storerooms and enriches the granaries," a close parallel to the duties

The Jabbok River.

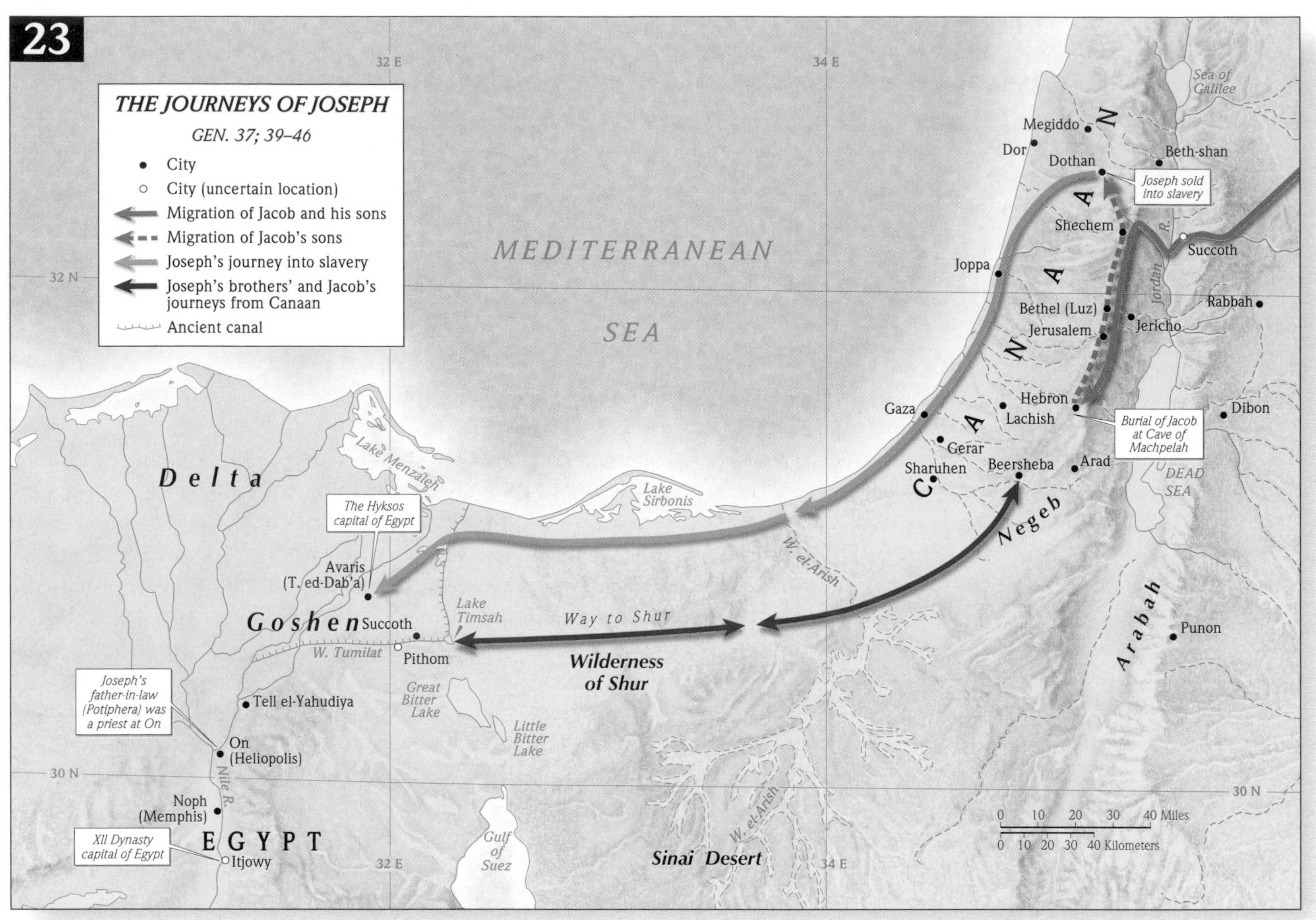

Joseph assumed. Joseph received an Egyptian name. He also married Asenath, daughter of one of the powerful priests of On (later Heliopolis, located on the northeast outskirts of Cairo) who served the sun god.

Famine in Egypt, though not as common as in Palestine, was not unknown. An early Egyptian text entitled *The Tradition of Seven Lean Years in Egypt* describes one of those occasions when the Nile River failed on successive years to rise adequately and renew the land: "Grain was scant, fruits were dried up, and everything which they eat was short. Every man robbed his companion. They moved without going (ahead). The infant was wailing; the youth was waiting; the heart of the old men was in sorrow; their legs were bent, crouching on the ground, . . . the temples were shut up; the sanctuaries held [nothing but] air. Everything was found empty" (Pritchard, *ANET*, p. 31). Other texts tell how local officials doled out stored grain to the people to fend off starvation. Just such a prolonged drought prompted Jacob to send his sons to Egypt in search of grain. Joseph's brothers made two trips to Egypt, one without Benjamin and another with their youngest sibling (Gen. 42–45). During the last journey Joseph revealed his true identity to his brothers and urged that Jacob and his clan move to Egypt to escape the drought. Overjoyed at the news that his favorite son was alive, Jacob quickly complied with Joseph's invitation.

Family Reunion. Leaving the Negeb at Beer-sheba (Gen. 46:1), Jacob and his sons journeyed across the Sinai by the "Way to Shur," entering Egypt near Succoth in the Wadi Tumilat. Asiatic shepherds and merchants coming from southern Canaan and Transjordan used this route extensively. The family entered the "land of Goshen" (Gen. 46:28; 47:6), once anachronistically called the "land of Rameses" (Gen. 47:11), located in the northeastern Delta of Egypt. Some scholars have identified Goshen more specifically with the Wadi Tumilat, a fertile finger of the Delta jutting out into the Sinai Desert.

In an audience before Pharaoh, Jacob and his sons insisted that they came as shepherds seeking relief from famine in Canaan; they posed no threat to Egypt and had no ambitions to use the influence of Joseph to acquire status themselves. In gratitude to Joseph, Pharaoh permitted the family to settle in a choice portion of the eastern Delta that provided ample pastures for their herds. Recognizing their skill with livestock, the king sought out members of Jacob's family to oversee the royal herds

Paintings from the tomb of Knum-hotep found in noblemen cemetery of Beni-Hasan. The paintings, dating from the Middle Kingdom of Egypt (ca. 1900 B.C.) shows a group of thirty-seven Asiatics as they enter Egypt.

that grazed in the region (Gen. 47:1–11). Thus began a sojourn that would last four hundred years.

Sojourn in Egypt. When did Joseph and his brothers enter Egypt? An attractive, but by no means universally held, hypothesis places the entry of Israel's ancestor into Egypt during the Second Intermediate Period—the Hyksos Period. "Hyksos" is a corrupted form of the Egyptian term meaning "foreign rulers." A people of primarily Semitic origin, the Hyksos infiltrated the eastern Delta of Egypt by the end of the Twelfth Dynasty (1780 B.C.).

Eventually Hyksos established themselves as rulers over much of the Delta, building a capital at Avaris, recently identified as Tell ed Dab'a. Sharing a culture common to the population of Palestine and southern Syria, Hyksos kings portrayed themselves as Egyptian pharaohs. The kings of the Fifteenth and Sixteenth Dynasties (1674–1567 B.C.) were Hyksos. Some scholars argue that Joseph's rise to a position of prominence could be achieved more easily under Semitic rulers. Such a scenario cannot be proven since native Egyptian rulers also employed foreigners like Joseph in both high and low governmental positions. It is also possible that Jacob's clan came to Egypt during the Twelfth Dynasty (1991–1786 B.C.). Although the precise timetable escapes us, the details of the Joseph narrative fit well in the Middle Bronze Age.

Chapter Six

THE EGYPTIAN EXPERIENCE

The Israelites were keenly aware that their ancestors suffered a lengthy period of bondage in Egypt. Four hundred years passed between the time Jacob's sons entered Egypt until the great miracle of God's deliverance of His people recorded in Exodus (Exod. 12:40; Gen. 15:13; Gal. 3:17). Yet the Bible says remarkably little about these four centuries, passing over them in a few brief verses. Only the cryptic reference, "There arose a new king over Egypt, who did not know Joseph" (Exod. 1:8) explains the change from the peaceful conditions of the last chapters of Genesis to the hardships described in the first chapters of Exodus.

Historical Background: The Eighteenth and Nineteenth Dynasties of Egypt

The historical setting for the period of bondage was the Late Bronze Age, the period from 1550 to 1200 B.C. Fortunately, we have detailed knowledge of this era from extensive Egyptian records. Egyptologists describe this era as the "New Kingdom," which included the Eighteenth through Twentieth Dynasties (1567–1085 B.C.), although the last of these capable rulers was Ramesses III who reigned about 1175 B.C. During this time the kings of Egypt established an empire whose reach stretched north to the Euphrates River.

An Egyptian text dated about 1230 B.C., often called the Merneptah Stele, mentions Israel—the first occurrence of the term outside the Bible. Although Egyptian records contain no mention of the Exodus, at some point in this period Moses, under God's direction, led the Hebrews out of Egypt toward the promised land. Whether this momentous event took place in the fifteenth century (1440 B.C.) as some scholars think or the thirteenth century (1250 B.C.) as others believe (see chart on p. 64 presenting two different views of the dating of the Exodus), the pharaohs mentioned in Exodus ruled Egypt at the height of Egyptian power and influence. Yet their power paled before the majesty of Yahweh, who spoke to Moses from the burning bush at Mount Sinai.

Hyksos control of the Delta came to an end between 1570 and 1550 when powerful native Egyptian kings arose from the city of Thebes. Seqenenre and Kamose, kings of the late Seventeenth Dynasty, attacked Hyksos strongholds in a series of

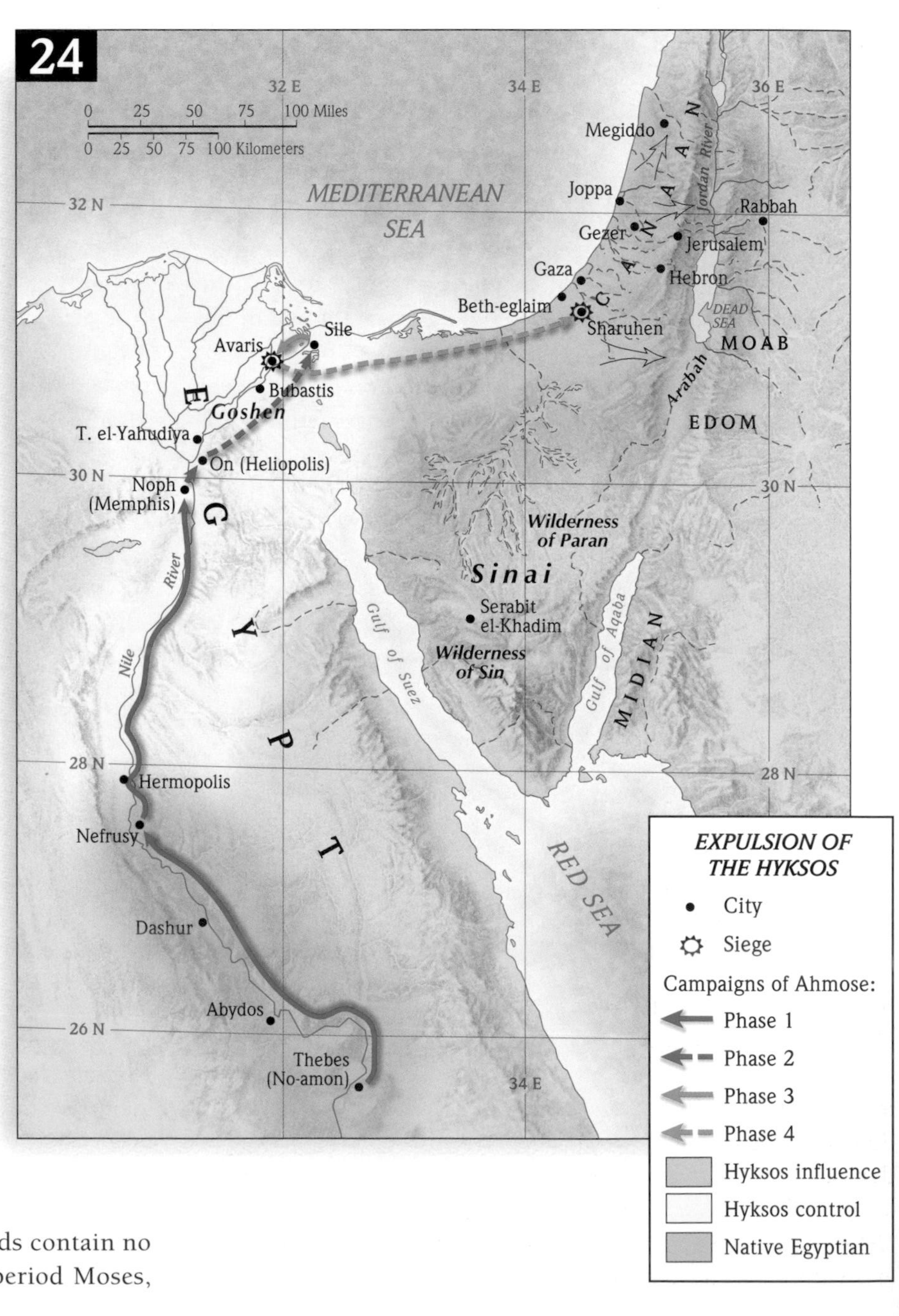

CHART 4: PERIOD AT A GLANCE: THE LATE BRONZE AGE: 1550–1200 B.C.

DATE	EGYPT	PALESTINE	MESOPOTAMIA	ASIA MINOR
1570	*The New Kingdom:* Eighteenth through Twentieth Dynasties. Ahmose expels Hyksos and establishes the Eighteenth Dynasty (1570–1320); Thebes (No-amon) rises to prominence.	Egyptian influence and interest in Palestine increasing after expulsion of Hyksos	Kingdom of Mitanni encroaches from northwest Mesopotamia into north Syria.	Hittites
1550			Nuzi Texts	
1500	Thutmose III and Amenhotep II campaign in Palestine and Syria (Exodus from Egypt?). Egypt established an empire from the central Levant south into Nubia.	Thutmose III campaigns sixteen times in the Southern Levant; Egyptian bases established in the Levant; many Canaanite cities show multiple destructions throughout Late Bronze Age.	Thutmose III and Amenhotep II defeat Mitanni; peace with Egypt	
1450	Amenhotep III; zenith of Egyptian Empire; Akhenaten "Heretic King"; Amarna Period	Numerous rulers and cities of Palestine mentioned in Tell el-Amarna Tablets; Habiru in Palestine		Hittite Empire Era
1400				
1350	Temporary loss of Egyptian power in Levant Nineteenth Dynasty (1320–1200); rise of powerful new rulers in the Delta, Ramesses II (1304–1237); battle of Kadesh on the Orontes; Egypt against the Hittites; peace with Hittites			Shuppiluliuma
1300		Seti I campaigns in Palestine; stele left at Beth-shan.	Assyria's Middle Kingdom	Muwattalis
		Ramesses II campaigns in southern Levant.	Adad-nirari I Shalmaneser I	Battle of Kadesh on the Orontes
1250	Exodus from Egypt (?)		Tukulti-ninurta I	Hattusilis III Peace with Egypt
	Merneptah campaigns in Palestine; claims to defeat Israel Twentieth Dynasty (1200–1085)	Merneptah campaigns in Palestine; first mention of Israel outside the Bible		
1200				Sudden end of Hittite Empire
1175	Ramesses III repulses Sea Peoples			

bloody battles. But it was Ahmose who finally expelled the Hyksos from Egypt, pursuing them as far as southern Palestine. Ahmose not only broke the power of the Hyksos, but also founded the Eighteenth Dynasty, inaugurating the New Kingdom. Once again, all of Egypt came under the control of a single dynasty. Some scholars identify the pharaoh who "knew not Joseph" with Ahmose. Perhaps the favored status enjoyed by the Hebrews under the predominantly Semitic Hyksos came to an end with the victorious native dynasty.

THE EIGHTEENTH DYNASTY AND PALESTINE

The Eighteenth Dynasty pharaohs carved out an empire by repeated military campaigns. Eventually the borders of their domain stretched from the Sudan (Nubia) in the south to Syria in the north. Thutmose III (1504–1450 B.C.) and Amenhotep II (1450–1425 B.C.) were especially active in the Levant, recording their exploits on temple walls at Thebes and Memphis. Thutmose III boasted he led sixteen campaigns beyond the Sinai into Canaan. Some of these expeditions took him as far north as the Euphrates River, where he checked aggression by the kingdom of Mitanni. According to his annals (ca. 1468 B.C.), he defeated a coalition of Canaanite kings at Megiddo. Amenhotep II brought back inhabitants of Canaan as prisoners during the course of his two recorded military ventures, undoubtedly utilizing them as slaves.

The Jezreel Valley seen through the Canaanite gate at Megiddo. Thutmose III defeated a Canaanite coalition in this valley, marking an era of greater Egyptian authority in the region.

DECLINE OF CANAANITE CITY-STATES

Intent on controlling the international highways that ran through Palestine, Egyptian kings reduced the petty kings of Canaan and Syria to the status of vassals and imposed heavy tribute on them. Egyptian bases were established in the Levant at Gaza, Sumer, and Kumidi with additional garrisons scattered in strategic sites like Beth-shan. At times the Canaanite kings resisted, typically with disastrous consequences. Many cities of Canaan show evidence of multiple destructions during the Late Bronze Age; some of these surely represent Egyptian reprisals for disloyalty. The constant campaigning and oppressive demands for tribute exhausted the Canaanite city-states. Archaeology bears silent witness to an erosion of Canaanite culture in the Late Bronze Age, as technological and living standards declined.

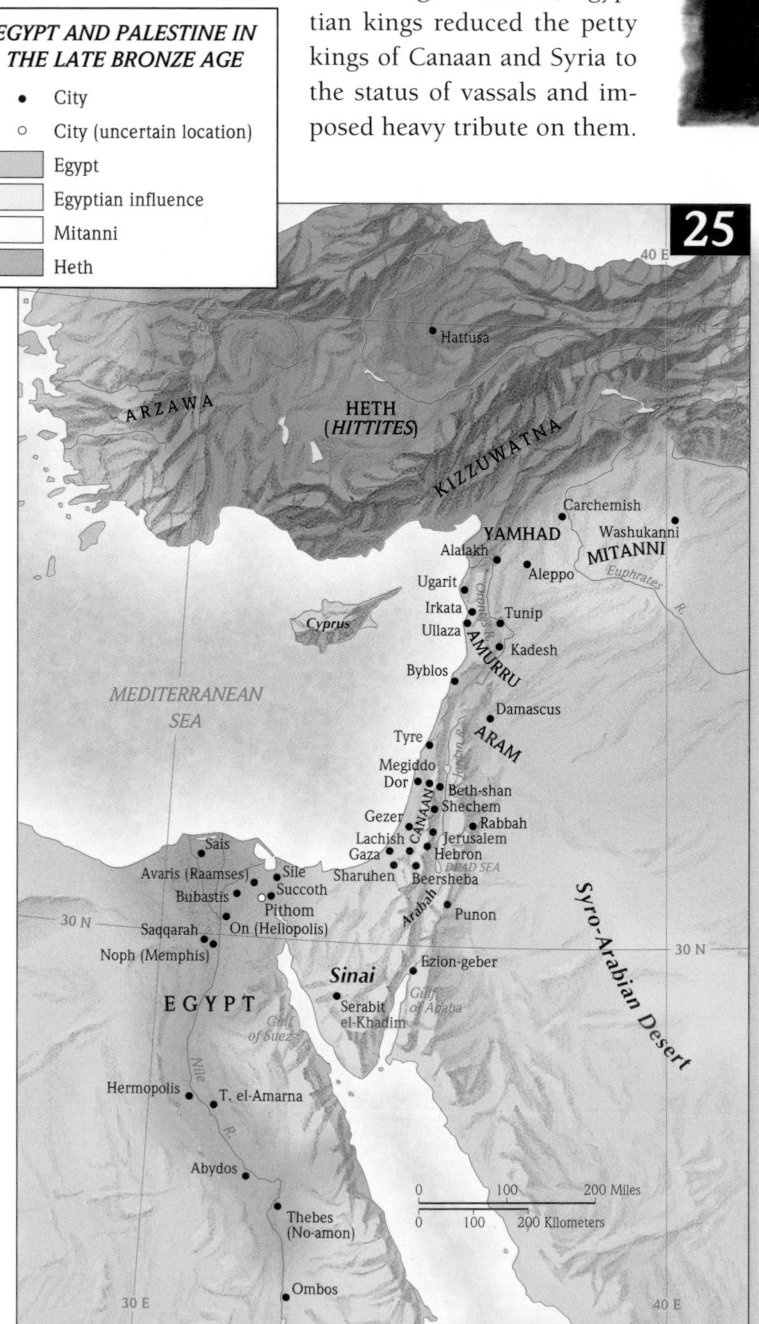

By contrast, Thebes (biblical No-amon) was the capital of the world's most powerful empire during the Late Bronze Age. The kings of the Eighteenth and Nineteenth Dynasties adorned the city with magnificent temples dedicated to Amon-Re, patron god of the New Kingdom. The temples of Luxor and Karnak at

The temple of Amon-Re at Karnak.

26

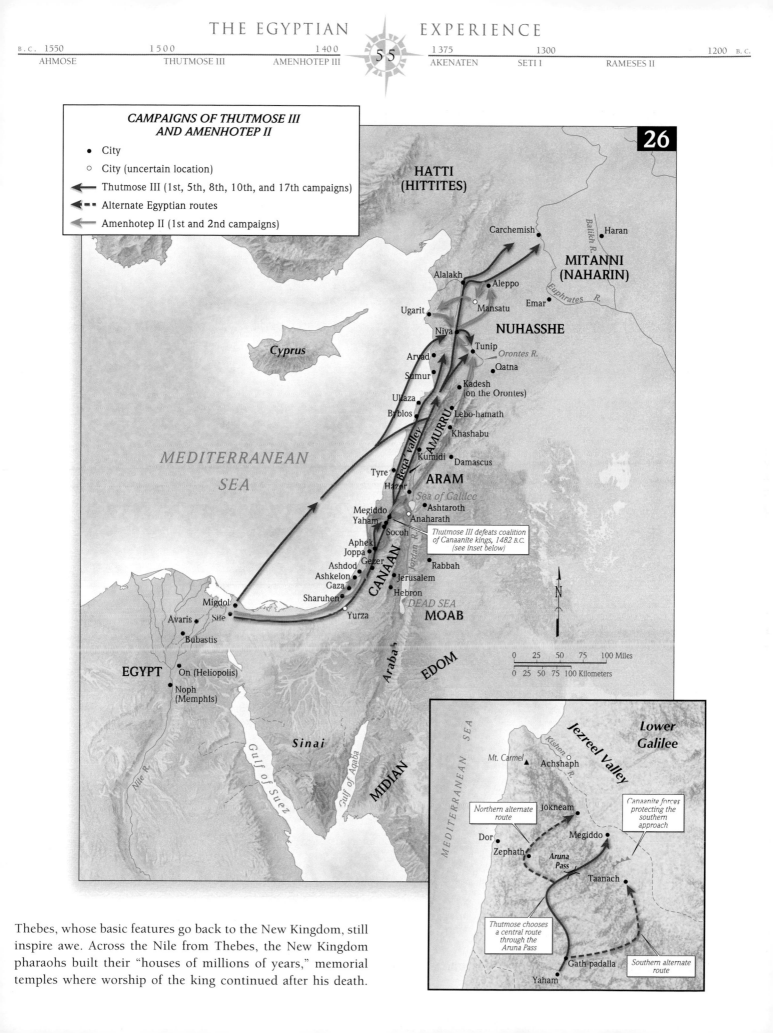

CAMPAIGNS OF THUTMOSE III AND AMENHOTEP II

- City
- City (uncertain location)
- Thutmose III (1st, 5th, 8th, 10th, and 17th campaigns)
- Alternate Egyptian routes
- Amenhotep II (1st and 2nd campaigns)

Thutmose III defeats coalition of Canaanite kings, 1482 B.C. (see inset below)

Northern alternate route

Canaanite forces protecting the southern approach

Thutmose chooses a central route through the Aruna Pass

Southern alternate route

Thebes, whose basic features go back to the New Kingdom, still inspire awe. Across the Nile from Thebes, the New Kingdom pharaohs built their "houses of millions of years," memorial temples where worship of the king continued after his death.

CHART 5: EGYPTIAN KINGS OF THE NEW KINGDOM		
EIGHTEENTH DYNASTY		
KINGS	DATES* (B.C.)	KEY EVENTS
Ahmose (Amosis)	1570–1546	Expelled Hyksos from the Delta; attacked Hyksos fortifications in Palestine; began the conquest of Nubia
Amenhotep I (Amenophis)	1546–1526	Extended Egyptian control over Nubia to the south
Thutmose I (Thutmosis)	1525–1512	Strong military leader who led Egyptian armies as far as the Euphrates River; first king to build his tomb in the Valley of the Kings west of Thebes
Thutmose II (Thutmosis)	1512–1504	Poor health limited his reign and accomplishments
Hatshepsut	1503–1482†	Queen who ruled in her own right briefly upon the death of her husband Thutmose II
Thutmose III (Thutmosis)	1504–1450	Made at least sixteen campaigns into Palestine and Syria to fend off Mitanni encroachments; left a list of 119 cities in the Levant; fought a Canaanite coalition at Megiddo
Amenhotep II (Amenophis)	1450–1425	Made at least two campaigns into the Levant to quell revolts in Palestine and beyond
Thutmose IV (Thutmosis)	1425–1417	
Amenhoptep III (Amenophis)	1417–1379	Great builder at the zenith of the Eighteenth Dynasty
Amenhotep IV = Akhenaten (Amenophis)	1379–1362	"Heretic pharaoh" who worshiped the Aten; Tell el-Amarna Tablets come largely from this period; built new capitol called Akhetaten
Smenkhare	1364–1361†	Shadowy successor of Akhenaten
Tutankhamun ("King Tut")	1361–1352	Abandoned worship of Aten and return to the worship of Amun; abandoned Akhetaten and returned to Thebes
Ay	1352–1348	Older noble who held throne only briefly
Horemhab	1348–1320	Military leader and chief advisor to Tutankhamun; secured Egypt's internal security; made transition to new dynasty
NINETEENTH DYNASTY		
Ramesses I	1320–1318	Founded Nineteenth Dynasty; established capital at Rameses (Qantir in the Northeastern Delta)
Seti I (Sethos)	1318–1304	Reestablished Egyptian Empire in southern Levant; left stele at Beth-shan giving an account of a campaign south of the Sea of Galilee
Ramesses II	1304–1237	Fought Hittites at Kadesh on the Orontes; made peace with the Hittites; monumental builder
Merneptah	1236–1223	His victory stele mentions Israel for the first time
Amenmesses	1222–1217	
Seti II (Sethos)	1216–1210	

*Chronology based on (CAH, 3rd ed.) †Presumes a coregency

The Ramesseum honoring Ramesses II and Hatshepsut's magnificent temple at Deir el-Bahri survive as testaments to the divine status accorded the pharaoh.

Farther to the west, in a remote valley, tombs carved in the Valley of the Kings held the mortal remains of these great rulers in gilded splendor. The tomb of Tutankhamun, a relatively insignificant king of the late Eighteenth Dynasty, hints at the wealth of his more powerful contemporaries.

AKHENATEN: EGYPT'S HERETIC KING

One Egyptian king deviated from accepted religious practice. Akhenaten (1379–1362) refused homage to Amon-Re and the multitude of other Egyptian deities. He concentrated his worship on the Aten, a sun god whose symbol was a solar disc. Moving his capital from Thebes, Akhenaten established a new residence he called Akhetaten, the "city of the Horizon of Aten." Today known as Tell el-Amarna, Akhenaten's capital has yielded more than 350 clay tablets inscribed in Akkadian, representing a portion of the royal correspondence. The letters came from Canaanite kings in Palestine and Syria and contain petitions for Egyptian help.

The Amarna letters reveal important information as to the overall picture of Canaan about 1350 B.C. Canaan was a land of fragmented loyalties and ambitious petty tyrants. Wary kings, suspicious of both Canaanite neighbors and Egyptian intentions, struggled to maintain control of territory surrounding their cities. Their primary concern was the advancement of their own status. These tablets shed valuable light on Canaan very near the time of the Exodus.

The Amarna tablets also mention a people called Habiru, mercenaries in league with the king of Shechem, who harassed other Canaanite kings. Noting the similarity between Hebrew and Habiru, earlier scholars tried to equate the Habiru with the biblical Hebrews; however, such a simple equation is not possible. The term *Habiru* appears in several documents from diverse geographical areas over the span of several hundred years (see article "The Elusive Habiru," p. 60). The term described a type of people who lived on the fringes of society. Possibly some of Israel's ancestors could be classified as Habiru since they had few ties to the established urban social order of the day.

Relief of Akhenaten and his queen offering sacrifices to the Aten symbolized by the sun disk extending hands to the royal family.

NINETEENTH DYNASTY AND THE HITTITES

In 1320 B.C. a new line of rulers came to power as the strength of the Eighteenth Dynasty ebbed away. In the face of a Hittite threat, centered in Asia Minor, the Ninteenth Dynasty kings vigorously reasserted Egyptian claims over Palestine after neglecting the region during the reigns of Akhenaten and his successors. For centuries the Hittites held central Asia Minor. By about 1350 B.C., Hittite king Shuppiluliuma began to encroach on territory previously under Egyptian control.

Moving their administrative center from Thebes to the north, the Nineteenth Dynasty pharaohs established a new capital on the ruins of Avaris, the old Hyksos stronghold, renaming the city Rameses. Seti I (1318–1304 B.C.), Ramesses II (1304–1237 B.C.), and Merneptah (1236–1223 B.C.) campaigned northward through Palestine, again leading military forays as far north as the Euphrates River. A stele (inscribed stone) found at Beth-shan tells of Seti I's victory over Habiru just southwest of the Sea of Galilee. In his fifth year Ramesses II, perhaps the greatest builder of monuments in Egyptian history, battled the Hittites led by Muwattalis to a draw at Kadesh on the Orontes. Later, he concluded a peace treaty with the Hittite king Hattusilis, guaranteeing Egyptian sovereignty in Canaan. Ramesses' numerous monuments adorn the Nile from Abu Simbel to Memphis.

Ramesses' son Merneptah listed Israel among several groups in Canaan he claimed to have defeated about 1230 B.C. This "Israel Stele" is noteworthy because it contains the earliest nonbiblical reference to Israel. The relevant part of the text states: "Carried off is Ashkelon; seized upon is Gezer; Yanoam is made as that which does not exist; Israel is laid waste, his seed is not" (Pritchard, *ANET*, p. 378). Unfortunately the reference is vague; we do not know if the term refers to a nation or simply a group of people present in the land. Yet the stele tells us that at least before 1200 B.C. a people known as Israel occupied a part of the promised land.

Life in Egypt

The ancestors of Israel found in Egypt a way of life very different from Canaan. Egypt belonged to the pharaoh, who ruled the land as a divine king. As the son of Re and the incarnation of the falcon god Horus, the pharaoh exercised complete authority

"Asiatic Tribute Bearers." Egyptian tomb painting from Thebes dating to approximately 1450 B.C. depicting Canaanites bringing tribute to Egypt. (Courtesy of the British Museum.)

The Merneptah Stele that contains the first mention of Israel.

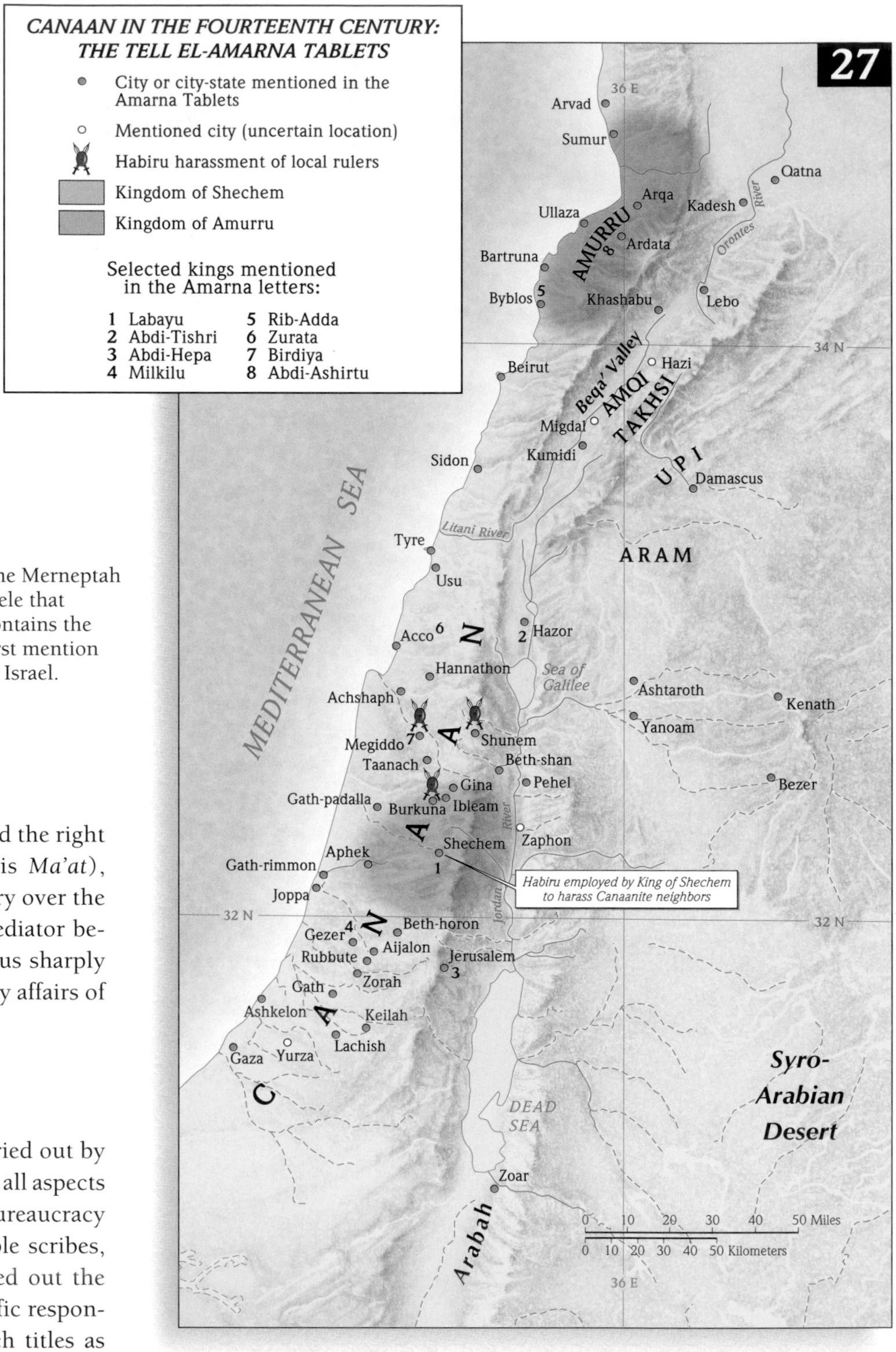

CANAAN IN THE FOURTEENTH CENTURY: THE TELL EL-AMARNA TABLETS

27

- City or city-state mentioned in the Amarna Tablets
- Mentioned city (uncertain location)
- Habiru harassment of local rulers
- Kingdom of Shechem
- Kingdom of Amurru

Selected kings mentioned in the Amarna letters:

1 Labayu
2 Abdi-Tishri
3 Abdi-Hepa
4 Milkilu
5 Rib-Adda
6 Zurata
7 Birdiya
8 Abdi-Ashirtu

Arvad, Sumur, Qatna, Ullaza, Arqa, Kadesh, AMURRU, Ardata, Bartruna, Byblos, Khashabu, Lebo, Beirut, Hazi, Beqa' Valley, AMQI, TAKHSI, Migdal, Kumidi, Sidon, UPI, Damascus, MEDITERRANEAN SEA, Litani River, Tyre, Usu, ARAM, Hazor, Acco, CANAAN, Hannathon, Sea of Galilee, Achshaph, Ashtaroth, Kenath, Megiddo, Shunem, Yanoam, Taanach, Beth-shan, Gina, Pehel, Bezer, Gath-padalla, Burkuna, Ibleam, Zaphon, Aphek, Shechem, Gath-rimmon, Joppa, Jordan River, Beth-horon, Gezer, Aijalon, Rubbute, Jerusalem, Gath, Zorah, Ashkelon, Keilah, Lachish, Gaza, Yurza, Syro-Arabian Desert, DEAD SEA, Zoar, Arabah

Habiru employed by King of Shechem to harass Canaanite neighbors

36 E · 34 N · 32 N · 0 10 20 30 40 50 Miles · 0 10 20 30 40 50 Kilometers

over all aspects of life. His power established the right order of all things (the Egyptian term is *Ma'at*), brought fertility to the land, and gave victory over the enemies of Egypt. He functioned as the mediator between the gods and men. This exalted status sharply distinguished the pharaoh from the ordinary affairs of life.

EGYPTIAN ADMINISTRATION

Details of administration were carried out by a vast bureaucracy of officials who pervaded all aspects of Egyptian society. At the head of this bureaucracy was the vizir, who directed the innumerable scribes, overseers, mayors, and officers who carried out the wishes of the court. Each official had specific responsibilities over a very defined concern. Such titles as "Overseer of the Granaries of Upper and Lower Egypt" and "Scribe of the Recruits" describe clearly the duties of each office. In early Egyptian history, members of the royal family held many of the higher offices, but from the Middle Kingdom (ca. 2050 B.C.–1786 B.C.) onward a professional class of governmental servants appeared.

Many offices became virtually hereditary, with sons following the footsteps of their fathers in a specific office. The basic requirement for high service was writing, an art learned in scribal schools. Egyptian texts emphasized the preferred life of the scribe over more menial and burdensome tasks.

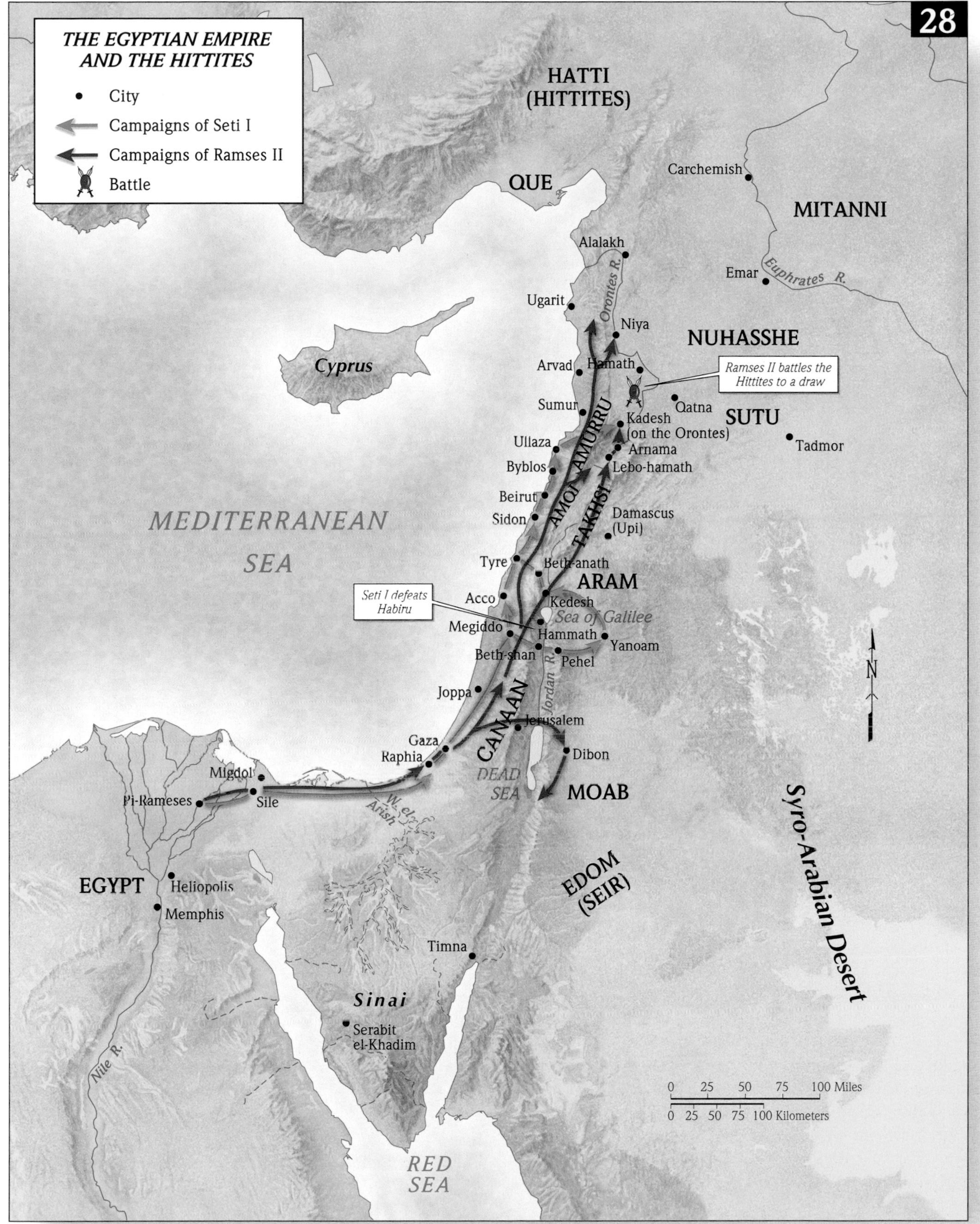
28
THE EGYPTIAN EMPIRE AND THE HITTITES
City
Campaigns of Seti I
Campaigns of Ramses II
Battle
HATTI (HITTITES)
QUE
Carchemish
MITANNI
Alalakh
Emar
Euphrates R.
Orontes R.
Ugarit
Niya
NUHASSHE
Cyprus
Arvad
Hamath
Ramses II battles the Hittites to a draw
Sumur
Qatna
AMURRU
Kadesh (on the Orontes)
SUTU
Tadmor
Ullaza
Arnama
Byblos
Lebo-hamath
AMQI
TAKHSI
Beirut
Damascus (Upi)
Sidon
MEDITERRANEAN SEA
Tyre
Beth-anath
ARAM
Seti I defeats Habiru
Acco
Kedesh
Sea of Galilee
Megiddo
Hammath
Yanoam
Beth-shan
Pehel
Jordan R.
Joppa
CANAAN
Jerusalem
Gaza
Dibon
Raphia
Migdol
DEAD SEA
MOAB
Pi-Rameses
Sile
W. el-Arish
Syro-Arabian Desert
EGYPT
Heliopolis
Memphis
EDOM (SEIR)
Timna
Sinai
Serabit el-Khadim
Nile R.
0 25 50 75 100 Miles
0 25 50 75 100 Kilometers
RED SEA
N

A RURAL SOCIETY

Egypt essentially was a rural land with few large cities. The average Egyptian peasant farmer lived in one of the numerous villages or crowded towns scattered along the Nile. Unbaked mud brick furnished the building materials for both peasant house and palace alike.

The rhythm of the great river that flowed through the land determined the pace of daily life (see chap. 1, "Egypt: Land of Bondage," pp. 6-8). The Egyptians divided the year into three seasons of four months each, with specific tasks associated with each season. During the season of "inundation" (June to September) waters progressively flooded the land allowing little agricultural work. The time of inundation provided opportunity to employ workers on the building projects of the king.

The demanding labor in the fields began in October as the receding waters signaled the season of "coming forth" (October to mid-February). Surveyors reestablished field boundaries, while workers with mattocks and hoes tackled the difficult jobs of clearing irriga-

The temple of Luxor at Thebes. This view of the first pylon shows several statues of Ramesses II whose battles against the Hittites are recorded on the walls.

THE ELUSIVE HABIRU (HAPIRU?)

Ancient Near Eastern documents from the second millennium contain over 250 references to the Habiru or Hapiru. Since the late nineteenth century when the term was first noticed in Egyptian texts called the "Tell el-Amarna Letters," scholars have puzzled over the identity of the Habiru and what relationship, if any, they might have with Israel's ancestors. Even the correct vocalization of the term—Habiru? Hapiru? 'apiru?—cannot be determined, although Habiru seems most reasonable. Recent scholarly reflection has yielded further insight about these elusive people.

The term *Habiru* first appears shortly after 1900 B.C. in documents from Assyrian trading stations in Anatolia. Subsequently, the term occurs with increasing frequency in the Mari Texts (ca. 1750 B.C.), the Nuzi Texts (ca. 1500 B.C.), texts from Alalakh and Ugarit on the Syrian coast (ca. 1350 B.C.), Hittite texts from Hattusas (Bogazkoy), and the Egyptian Tell el-Amarna texts (1400–1350 B.C.). The last known historical reference to Habiru occurs during the reign of Ramesses IV (ca. 1160 B.C.). The geographical distribution of Habiru ranged from Anatolia to Egypt, eastward to southern Mesopotamia and Elam. Egyptian sources of the Late Bronze Age (1550–1200 B.C.) frequently mention Habiru in Palestine and Lebanon. Amenhotep II (1450–1425 B.C.) and Seti I (1318–1304 B.C.) brought back captive Habiru from Palestine and put them to work on state projects.

The name *Habiru* designated a social status, not an ethnic identity. Habiru were people who, for whatever reason, had left their homeland to make their way as foreigners in another land. As outsiders, Habiru had limited rights and opportunities. They were used as state servants in royal administrations and as unskilled laborers. Other Habiru were mercenaries who sold their services to the highest bidder or lived as outlaws on the margin of society. According to the Amarna letters, the king of Shechem and his son employed Habiru to harass their Canaanite neighbors.

In Egyptian documents the Habiru frequently are found in mountainous regions outside the normal sphere of Egyptian authority. Although not all Habiru were outlaws or mercenaries, the term designated groups who held little social prestige because of their refugee status. Habiru lived by whatever means available to them given their "outcast" status. We cannot equate Habiru with Hebrews, the word used by Egyptians to designate Israel's ancestors. The term *Habiru* designated a wide-ranging phenomena in the Near East, much larger than Israel's forebearers. However, perhaps some of Israel's ancestors included elements who would have been classified as Habiru in the second millennium B.C.

A painting from the Eighteenth Dynasty at Thebes showing agricultural activities.

tion canals and preparing the fields for planting. Sowing was relatively easy in the freshly deposited silt.

More burdensome was the unending task of irrigating the crops with water drawn from catch basins. Elementary water devices similar to the modern *shaduf* (essentially a bucket attached to a lifting arm with a counterweight) and powered by feet or hands brought the water to thirsty crops (cf. Deut. 11:10). As harvesttime approached in the season of "drought" (mid-February to May), all available help took to the fields and gathered the crops. The watchful eyes of tax officials carefully noted the produce of each field, while governmental overseers saw to the collection and storage of the land's bounty.

All people were expected to participate in the agricultural work so vital to Egypt's well-being. The Egyptians employed conscripted labor to work in the fields or occasionally on royal building projects. More affluent Egyptians called up for work could pay someone to take their place or bribe an official to keep their name off the list. Because Egyptians conceived of life after death as a continuation of their present existence, small models of servants were often placed in tombs along with the deceased. These models are called *shwabti* figures and were designed to take the owner's place in the agricultural enterprise assumed to be a part of the next life. Excavators have found thousands of these figures in the tombs of the more affluent Egyptians.

An additional source of labor came from the slave population. Like all ancient societies, the Egyptians used slaves in many ways: as domestic servants and field workers, in the army, for government service, and on building projects. Some slaves were Egyptian criminals drawn from prisons, but the majority of slaves were foreigners captured in the numerous wars or purchased as slaves from merchants. Many were Asiatics from Palestine and Syria. The lot of slaves in Egypt varied, but overall they were treated humanely. The life of a slave often differed little from

A painting from the tomb of Rekhmire at Thebes (ca. 1450 B.C.) depicting the making of bricks in Egypt.

that of an Egyptian peasant farmer, and could be far better if the slave belonged to a wealthy master.

EGYPT'S DARK SIDE

Life in Egypt offered security, freedom from extended famine, and an agricultural bounty often lacking in other countries. However, the Hebrews discovered the darker side of Egyptian life when a pharaoh unsympathetic to their kind reversed their favored status. Conscripted as common field laborers and forced to construct the store cities of Pithom and Rameses (Exod. 1:11, 14), the ancestors of Israel found themselves despised foreigners in Egypt, their house of bondage. Seemingly forgotten by the God of their forefathers, the Hebrews groaned under the excessive burden imposed on them by Egyptian taskmasters (Exod. 2:23).

EMAR: AN ECONOMIC CROSSROADS IN NORTHERN SYRIA

The excavation at Tell Meskene has shed new light on northern Syria during the Late Bronze Age (1550–1200 B.C.). Located on the Euphrates River where the great river bends eastward, Tell Meskene has been identified as Emar, a modest city strategically placed on the trade routes linking the western territories with the great centers of the Euphrates Valley. Texts from Ebla and Mari mention Emar during the third and early second millennia, but the existing remains reflect only the Late Bronze Age city (fourteenth to early twelfth centuries). Presumably the site of the earlier city was abandoned, perhaps due to the shifting course of the Euphrates River, and now lies below the newly formed Lake El Assad.

The new city built under Hittite influence covered about 175 acres, a size comparable to Hazor in Canaan—the largest city in Palestine during the Middle and Late Bronze Ages (2000–1200 B.C.). Emar had little political independence and functioned as a dependent of the great Hittite empire carved out by Shuppiluliuma (1375–1335 B.C.). Emar and her sister site, Tell Faq'ous, served as trade centers and bastions on the southeastern edge of the Hittite empire, giving protection from the declining Mitanni kingdom and the more potent threat arising in Assyria. Although not as important as other north Syrian centers like Aleppo and Carchemish, Emar provided an important and ancient economic link in the region. Moreover, unlike its more politically powerful neighbors, the king of Emar apparently played a more modest role in the life of the city. Elders functioned in a prominent capacity alongside the king at Emar. This suggests that Emar represents a political-social combination of older tribal elements and an emerging monarchy that could provide clues to understanding the later emerging Israelite monarchy also marked by such combined elements.

Excavations at Emar uncovered four temples, a royal palace, and over thirty houses all dating within the period from about 1350 to the destruction of the city shortly after 1200 B.C. Two of the temples standing side by side were dedicated to the worship of Baal and Astart. Located in a sacred enclosure *(temenos)*, an altar and processional way served both temples. Both temples were built on a long axis with one main room containing an offering table and a podium for the divine image. Another temple yielded a large cache of tablets dubbed the "Diviner's Archives" since they mention an official called "the diviner of the gods of Emar." This official probably supervised a scribal school responsible for the numerous texts dealing with ritual matters found in the archive.

The royal palace is of the "bit-hilani" type typical of north-Syrian cities of a later era. This is the earliest hilani palace yet discovered and suggests Hittite influence. This style of palace—multiple rooms built around two larger halls separated by a colonnaded portico—has been suggested as a prototype for Solomon's palace in Jerusalem.

The cache of cuneiform documents written in Akkadian has provided legal documents, administrative texts, temple lists, ritual texts, and medical and divination texts. The ritual texts are especially interesting and give detailed instructions for anointing priests and priestesses, festival procedures, and matters pertaining to the calendar. Also of interest are references to a group called Nabu, people who made inquiries into divine matters. This word is related to the basic Hebrew word for "prophet"—*nabi*—and may shed light on the meaning of the term.

The excavations of Emar shed light on the complex political, social, and economic world of northern Syria in the Late Bronze Age. It adds one more dimension to our understanding of the larger world out of which Israel evolved.

Chapter Seven

THE EXODUS

Introduction

"Let my people go" proclaimed Moses to Pharaoh. No event in Israel's history was more central to Israel's faith than the Exodus, God's miraculous deliverance of the Hebrew people out of their bondage. The songs of Moses and Miriam exulted in the power of Israel's God whose strength defied the might of Egypt on Israel's behalf (Exod. 15). Later prophets recalled in tender terms God's gracious act of liberation and His sustaining hand throughout the long years of wandering in the wilderness (Hos. 11:1; Jer. 2:2–6). In the midst of the Sinai, God called the tribes of Israel into a covenant relationship with Him, giving birth to a nation (Exod. 19:3–6; 20).

Date of the Exodus

Few questions of Old Testament history present more problems than the date of the Exodus. Competent scholars debate whether the event occurred in the fifteenth century (1440 B.C.) or the thirteenth century (1250 B.C.). The former is the traditional date and is based largely on 1 Kgs. 6:1, which says that Israel left Egypt 480 years before Solomon built the temple at Jerusalem. Since the building of the temple can be dated to about 960 B.C., the addition of 480 years appears to place the Exodus in 1440 B.C. Other biblical chronological notes also seem to support a fifteenth-century date. Judges 11:26 implies the presence of Israel in the Transjordan for three hundred years preceding the time of Jephthah who lived about 1100 B.C.

References to the Habiru in the Tell el-Amarna Letters are sometimes used to support a fifteenth-century date (see "The Elusive Habiru," p. 60). Dating from the fourteenth century, these letters mention a group of social outcasts called "Habiru" who plagued certain Canaanite kings. Often the Habiru were employed by other Canaanite kings. Some scholars associate the Habiru with Hebrews, which then requires a fifteenth-century date for the Exodus.

A fifteenth-century date better accommodates an extended era for the period of the judges. The total of the years given in Judges is over 400 years. Even granting some overlap among the judges of Israel, a fifteenth-century date would accommodate the lengthy era implied in the Book of Judges.

If the Exodus occurred in the fifteenth century, Thutmose III and Amenhotep II are the most likely candidates for the pharaohs mentioned in the Book of Exodus, although a case can be made for other kings of the early Eighteenth Dynasty from Thutmose I to Thutmose IV.

The temple of Ramesses II at Abu-Simbel. The four seated colossal statues depict the king wearing the double crown signifying his role as ruler over all of Egypt.

Other lines of evidence suggest that the Exodus took place about 1250 B.C. Exodus 1:11 mentions the two store-cities—Pithom and Rameses—built by the Hebrews. Rameses has been positively identified with the sprawling site of Qantir in the northeastern Delta and may have included Tell ed Dab'a, the site of the old Hyksos capital, Avaris, in its suburbs. Excavations indicate a major rebuilding of this city took place during the thirteenth century under Ramesses II. The kings of the Nineteenth Dynasty moved their capitol north to Rameses to check Hittite encroachments on Egypt's territorial claim in Canaan and southern Syria (see chap. 6, pp. 55–57). Scholars who hold this date often point to the Merneptah Stele, dated 1230 B.C., which mentions Israel for the first time in Egyptian records (see p. 57). In stylized language, Merneptah claims to have defeated Israel

CHART 6: COMPARATIVE CHRONOLOGIES FOR THE TWO PROPOSED DATES FOR THE EXODUS

Dates (B.C.)	13th-Century Date for Exodus	Egyptian History	15th-Century Date for Exodus
2100			Abraham
			Isaac
2000		Middle Kingdom of Egypt: Twelfth Dynasty (1991–1786)	Jacob
1900	Abraham		Joseph and his brothers enter Egypt
	Isaac		
1800	Jacob	Second Intermediate Period	E G Y P T I A N S O J O U R N
1700	Joseph and his brothers enter Egypt	Hyksos Era: Fifteenth through Sixteenth Dynasties New Kingdom: Eighteenth through Twentieth Dynasties	
1600	E G Y P T I A N S O J O U R N	Ahmose	
1500		Thutmose III	
		Amenhotep II	Exodus from Egypt about 1440
1400		Amenhotep III	Conquest of Joshua
1370		Akhenaten	
		Tutankhamun	Period of the Judges
		Seti I	
1300		Ramesses II	
	Exodus from Egypt about 1250		Othniel
		Merneptah	
1200	Conquest of Joshua		Ehud
	Period of the Judges	Ramesses III	
	Othniel		Deborah and Barak
	Ehud		Gideon
1100	Deborah and Barak		Jephtah
	Gideon		
	Jephtah		Samson
	Samson		
			Samuel
	Samuel		
	Saul (ca. 1020–1000)		Saul
1000	David (ca. 1000–960)		David

along with other foes of Egypt in the southern Levant. That the Egyptians first mention Israel in the late thirteenth century can be taken as support for a thirteenth-century Exodus.

Moreover, some Canaanite cities destroyed in the 1200s B.C. may have fallen to Joshua's Israelite forces. The case of Hazor is particularly striking. The reference in Joshua 11:10 ascribes Hazor's destruction to Israel. According to Yigael Yadin, who excavated the city, Hazor came to a violent end late in the thirteenth century. Recent excavations at Hazor by Ammon Ben Tor confirm Yadin's conclusions. Admittedly, other sites mentioned in Joshua present difficult problems. No easy correlation between destruction levels at sites in Canaan and the date of the Exodus can be given. Still, the evidence of Hazor strongly suggests a date for the Exodus in the late thirteenth century.

Finally, recent surveys in the highlands of Galilee, Samaria, and Judah show evidence of an upsurge in occupation shortly after 1200 B.C., precisely where one would expect to find the earliest Israelite settlements. New villages, generally small and poorly constructed, appear in these regions at sites not previously occupied. We cannot say for certain who built these new settlements, but if they are Israelite remains, they argue strongly for an Exodus dated about 1250 B.C.

Scholars dating the Exodus to about 1250 B.C. usually propose that 1 Kgs. 6:1 refers to twelve generations that have passed (12 generations x 40 years [the symbol of a generation] = 480 years), but the actual years elapsed from one generation to the next would be less than 40 years; for example, the actual calendar years between generations—that is from birth to marriage and children—is much less than 40 years, perhaps closer to 25 years or less. Thus if the biblical writer is asserting that 12 generations elapsed between the Exodus and the building of Solomon's temple, the calendar years would be about 300 years (12 generations x 25 = 300 years; add 300 years to the 960 B.C. date of Solomon's temple = 1260 B.C. as the date for the Exodus). This interpretation lowers the date for the Exodus into the thirteenth century. If the Exodus took place in the 1200s B.C., Seti I, Ramesses II, or possibly Merneptah would be the pharaohs who spoke to Moses face to face.

Because both the biblical and archaeological data bearing on the date of the Exodus are susceptible to different interpretations, dogmatism about the precise date should be avoided. Conclusions must be held tentatively until further evidence or fresh insight provides a clearer picture. The accompanying chart shows the effect of the two proposed dates on early biblical chronology.

Geography of the Sinai

Few areas on earth offer the splendor and beauty of the Sinai. Yet the harsh living conditions that prevail in the Sinai have prevented all but bedouin tribesmen and a few hardy monks

The temple of Hathor at the Egyptian mining center of Serabit el-Khadim.

in search of solitude from investigating its secrets. Only recently has the Sinai begun to yield its treasures to explorers and archaeologists alike.

The Sinai Peninsula is a triangle of land measuring 150 miles across the top and 260 miles along the sides. Two arms of the Red Sea,—the Gulfs of Suez and Aqabah,—flank it on the west and east, respectively. Most people visualize the Sinai as a flat, sandy desert and are unprepared for the rich geological diversity nature has granted to this land. True, the Sinai is a desert with little rain and harsh climatic extremes. Vegetation is scarce except for the occasional oasis that lends a splash of green to an otherwise barren landscape. Fantastic displays of multicolored sandstone, deep wadis enclosed by towering cliffs, and majestic pink granite peaks of southern Sinai provide a feast for the eyes. Geographically, this area covering 23,220 square miles can be divided into three zones: (1) a northern coastal plain, (2) a central limestone and sandstone plateau, and (3) a southern mass of granite mountains.

NORTHERN COASTAL PLAIN

The northern section of the Sinai consists of a sandy coastal plain averaging twenty miles in width. Near the coast, sand dunes, some towering over sixty feet high, create a striking contrast to the deep blue waters of the Mediterranean Sea.

In the west the plain opens out in the Desert of al-Jifar, probably the ancient "wilderness of Shur" (Exod. 15:22). A series of lakes—Lake Timsah, Lake Balah, and the Bitter Lakes—mark the western boundary of Sinai with Egypt. Today, the Suez Canal links these lakes, forging a connection between the Gulf of Suez and the Mediterranean. These lakes figure into the discussion about the Yam Suph, or "Sea of Reeds," scene of God's deliverance by means of a strong east wind.

In the extreme north, a narrow spit of land juts out from the coasts encompassing Lake Sirbonis, actually a lagoon about forty-five miles long and thirteen miles wide. Major C. S. Jarvis characterized the lake as a vast clay pan that floods when seawater driven by winds periodically spills over the coast. Some Israeli scholars locate the miracle of the Yam Suph at this body of water.

CENTRAL PLATEAU

South of the coastal plain a central plateau composed primarily of limestone and sandstone covers more than half of the Sinai. The plateau rises slowly toward the south. A series of low mountains, including Jebel (Arabic for "mountain") Halal, Jebel Maghara, and Jebel Yeleq mark the northern limit. The central plateau terminates in the heights of Jebel et-Tih and Jebel el-Egma, whose tops reach five thousand feet. A barren, virtually waterless wilderness known to local bedouins as Badiyat et-Tih, "the Desert of the Wanderings," stretches across the center of the plateau. The Egyptians mined turquoise along the southwest edge of this plateau at Serabit el-Khadim. Inscriptions found in the mines indicate the pharaohs employed Semitic slave laborers to retrieve this valued stone.

SOUTHERN GRANITE MOUNTAINS

The southern region of the Sinai is by far the most impressive. Great pink granite mountains rise like sentinels

An early morning view of the majestic granite mountains of the southern Sinai.

to heights in excess of eight thousand feet. Almost in the middle of the region is Jebel Musa (7,482 feet)—"Mount of Moses"—the mountain traditionally identified as Mount Sinai since about A.D. 350. Here rugged peaks (Jebel umm-Shomar [8,482 feet], Jebel Katarina [8,651 feet]) divided by deep wadis endow this majestic region with strength and beauty. The Wadi Feiran, the major approach route to these great granite massifs, contains a major oasis dominated by Jebel Serbal (6,825 feet). If the Israelites came to southern Sinai, they surely traveled in part along this wadi.

Route of the Exodus

The Bible contains many geographical notations in Deuteronomy, Numbers, and Exodus about the route of the Exodus. Numbers 33 gives a comprehensive listing of all the encampments, from Egypt to the Plains of Moab opposite Jericho. Yet the information provided can be interpreted in several ways, leading to different ideas about the route. Scholars have proposed three basic routes—the northern, central, and southern route theories—each based on the biblical text. Over a dozen

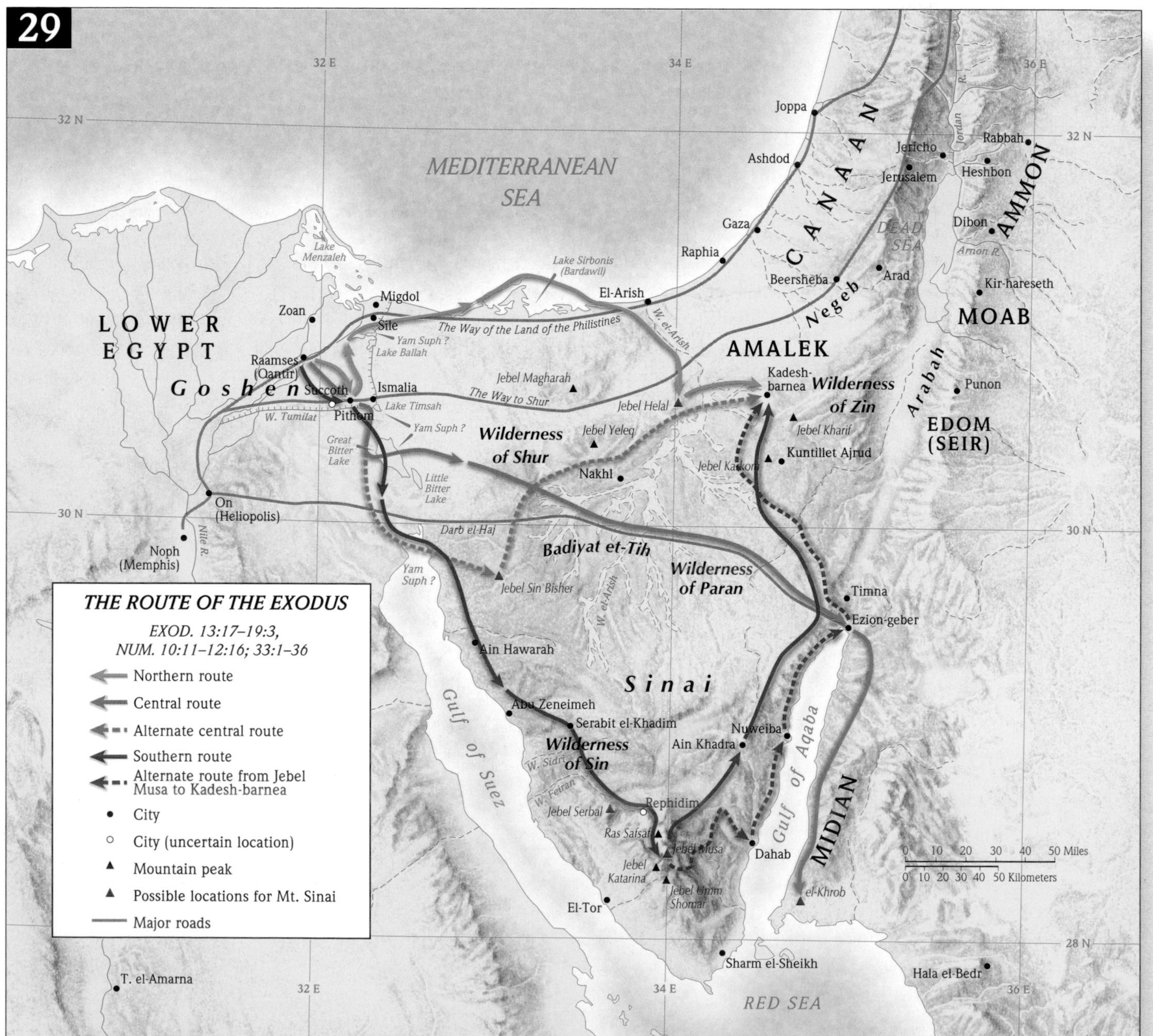

mountains have been identified by different scholars as suitable candidates for Mount Sinai, where Moses received the Ten Commandments. Only a few sites mentioned in the Exodus have been identified with some certainty. Raamses, the point of origin, has been conclusively identified with Qantir, while the central rallying point of Kadesh-barnea seems plausibly located at Ain el-Qudeirat or one of several nearby springs. Most other identifications remain tentative.

LOCATION OF MOUNT SINAI AND POSSIBLE ROUTE THEORIES

An extended discussion of the location of Mount Sinai lies beyond the scope of this work. Obviously the location of the sacred mount depends on what route the Israelites took. Several arguments have been made for a northern route theory. Moses' request to make a three-day journey into the desert to offer sacrifice to God implies a mountain close to Goshen, the eastern Nile Delta (Exod. 5:3). The encounter with the Amalekites at Rephidim (Exod. 17:8–16), a seminomadic people who appear elsewhere as inhabitants of the northern Sinai and the southern wildernesses of Palestine, suggests a northern locale for Mount Sinai. Finally, a few poetic passages (Deut. 33:2; Hab. 3:3) associate Mount Sinai with Paran, an ill-defined term used to describe the wilderness south and southwest of Palestine, perhaps implying a northern crossing. A northern route would take the Israelites toward Lake Menzaleh, perhaps along the narrow spit of land encompassing Lake Sirbonis, and then to Kadesh-barnea. In this scenario Mount Sinai could be identified with Jebel Magharah, Jebel Halal, or Jebel Yeleq. An alternative would locate Mount Sinai at Jebel Sinn Bishr southeast of the Bitter Lakes. Such an identification satisfies the "three day" request of Moses and fits well with the statement that Kadesh-barnea was an eleven-day journey from Mount Sinai (Deut. 1:2).

A canal in the Wadi Tumilat. Thought by some scholars to be the land of Goshen, the fleeing Israelites likely passed through this region on their way past nearby Succoth.

A few scholars locate Mount Sinai in Saudi Arabia, perhaps near Petra or further south in the Arabian peninsula at el-Khrob or Hala el-Bedr. Moses' flight to the land of Midian (Exod. 2:15; 18:1), normally identified with portions of the Arabian Peninsula, lend some support to this hypothesis. Yet it is readily admitted that the Midianites' migratory range took them beyond the Arabian peninsula (cf. 1 Kgs. 11:18; Judg. 6:1–6; Num. 13:29; 25:6–7). Supporters of an Arabian Mount Sinai also point to the description of God's appearance on Mount Sinai (Exod. 19:18), suggesting that earthquakes and volcanic activity are implied. Evidence of volcanic activity in historical times has been noted along the western Arabian coast. However, the language of Exodus 19 may be better understood as the language of theophany—that is, language used to describe the awesome appearance of God rather than descriptions of volcanic or earthquake activity (cf. Mic. 1:24; Ps. 18:7–15). If the Israelites journeyed to an Arabian Mount Sinai, presumably they would traverse the center of the Sinai peninsula, likely along the Moslem pilgrimage route from Africa to Mecca known as the Darb el-Hajj. However, in this writer's view, an Arabian Mount Sinai seems unlikely.

Several factors suggest the Israelites fled southward into Sinai and that Mount Sinai should be located in the southern sector of the peninsula. First, Exodus 13:17 warned against travel by the "way of the land of the Philistines." This route, which hugged the northern coast, was the major military route used by the pharaohs and was heavily garrisoned. As part of the great trunk route—the International Coastal Highway—this road would be watched closely by the Egyptians. Second, Deuteronomy 1:2 locates Mount Sinai as an eleven-day journey from Kadesh-barnea, a note that fits best with a Mount Sinai located somewhere in the southern peninsula. Third, the Israelites lost the exact location of Mount Sinai after 850 B.C. when Elijah fled to the holy mountain. Had the holy mountain been located in the more frequented regions of the north, surely its location would be remembered. Finally, a few sites mentioned on the journey from Mount Sinai to Kadesh-barnea suggest a southern route if the several tentative identifications are plausible. For example, Dizahab (Deut. 1:1) arguably is modern Dahab located on the southeastern coast of the Sinai. Jotbathah (Num. 33:33) may be identified with the Oasis of Taba a few miles south of Ezion-geber (Tell el-Kheleifeh). The following

Lake Timsah, one of the possible locations for Yam Suph, "Sea of Reeds."

discussion presumes a location for Mount Sinai somewhere in the southern part of the peninsula.

THE EXODUS ROUTE DESCRIBED

The Exodus began at Raamses, the administrative center of the Nineteenth Dynasty (Exod. 12:37). Known to the Egyptians as "House of Rameses," this sprawling capital included royal palaces and houses for high Egyptian officials who served the court. The Hebrews knew the buildings well because their labor had supplied the bricks for construction. Moving southeast to Succoth, the multitude avoided the more heavily traveled "way of the land of the Philistines" at God's command (Exod. 13:17). Succoth has been identified with Tell el-Maskhutah at the eastern end of the Wadi Tumilat, conceded to be the *TKW* (an Egyptian vocalization of an ancient place name) mentioned in Egyptian records. Succoth was a border town where frontier officials kept check on migrating tribes as they entered Egypt from Sinai.

Approaching the Sea. After Succoth, Exodus mentions four sites in connection with two encampments before the deliverance of the Sea: Etham, Pi-hahiroth, Migdol, and Baal-zephon (Exod. 13:20; 14:2). Despite this geographic detail, the direction of the march is uncertain; several alternatives are possible. The Hebrews could have continued eastward following the "way to Shur," or they could have "turned back" north, becoming trapped in the area around Lake Menzaleh. The latter was a saltwater marsh region known in Egyptian records for the papypus reeds that grew in the area.

More likely, Moses took a southeast track toward the wilderness. An Egyptian document relates the story of two fugitive slaves tracked by officials south of Succoth (Papyrus Anastasis I in Pritchard, *ANET*, p. 259). The story mentions two sites with names very similar if not identical to Etham and Migdol. This suggests that the Hebrews followed a route used by slaves that led them away from authorities.

Deliverance at the Sea. Encamped at Pi-hahiroth, the Israelites found themselves caught between the sea before them and the pursuing Egyptians. In a great miracle, God parted the waters by sending a strong east wind, allowing the children of Israel to escape. Several passages call this body of water *Yam Suph,* sometimes translated "Red Sea" but more properly "Sea of Reeds" (Exod. 13:18; 15:4). Traditionally, the north end of the Gulf of Suez has been identified with the *Yam Suph,* but the head of the Gulf is located a considerable distance south of Succoth. Likely, the chariots of pharaoh would have overtaken the fleeing Israelites sooner than the time required to reach the Gulf of Suez. One of the lakes bordering Egypt and the Sinai (Lake Timsah or one of the Bitter Lakes) seems a more likely scene of this mighty act of God.

Entering the Wilderness. After the miraculous sea crossing, Moses led the Israelites for three days into the wilderness of Shur (Exod. 15:22). The harsh reality of life in the Sinai quickly

Jebel Sin-Bishr, one of several proposed locations for Mount Sinai.

Lightning strikes over the traditional location for Mt. Sinai, Jebal Musa. The monastery of St. Catherine, built on the traditional spot where Moses saw the burning bush, is in the center of the photograph.

gripped the tribes in this arid, desolate land. The contrast with the fleshpots of Egypt could not have been more dramatic. A few scrub trees in this region are the only sign of life in an otherwise barren landscape. Little wonder that the Israelites raised a cry for water, which God answered at Marah, a Hebrew word meaning "bitter," by turning the bitter waters of an oasis sweet. Continuing down the coast of Sinai, the next encampment at Elim (Wadi Gharandel?) afforded abundant springs and date groves.

Some scholars identify Jebel Sin-Bishr, about fifty miles south of Suez, with Mount Sinai. Convenient desert tracks lead from this mountain northeastward to Kadesh-barnea. The reference to a three-day journey requested by Moses to go and worship God (Exod. 5:3) admittedly fits Jebel Sin-Bishr better than other candidates for Mount Sinai, but possibly the route of Exodus led further south away from the arm of pharaoh.

Approaching Sinai. Moses led the children of Israel beyond Elim into the Wilderness of Zin, where the divine provision of manna and quail began (Exod. 16:1). Perhaps their route took them near the Egyptian turquoise mines at Serabit el-Khadim. In this region the mountains begin to reach higher into the sky, and twisting wadis radiate off in many directions. The Israelites must have experienced a sense of alienation and fear as they pressed deeper into the wilderness, where only the sustaining and guiding hand of Yahweh prevented utter disaster.

Multicolored sandstone gave way to pink-hued granite as the tribes made their way perhaps along the Wadi Feiran leading to the heart of the southern peninsula. An attack by the Amalekites at Rephidim was successfully repelled (Exod. 17). Rephidim has been traditionally identified with Oasis Feiran, although the identification seems unlikely. Perhaps the Wadi Refayid is a better candidate. The Amalekites did not normally range this far south, possibly another argument for a northern crossing.

Mount Sinai. Finally, after three months, the Israelites arrived within a plain below the massive peaks of southern Sinai and encamped before the mountain appointed by God (Exod. 19:1; 3:12). At Mount Sinai, Yahweh made a covenant with Israel, giving to Moses the Ten Commandments (Exod. 19–20). Tradition long has identified Mount Sinai with Jebel Musa (7,482 feet), although other higher peaks like Jebel Katerin (8,651 feet) and Jebel Umm Shomar (8,482 feet) rise above the traditional site. Below Jebel Musa, the Greek Orthodox Monastery of Saint Catherine, built by Justinian about A.D. 550, marks the traditional spot where early Christians believed Moses met God at the burning bush (Exod. 3). Springs in the immediate vicinity still supply water for both bedouin flocks and monks alike.

On to Kadesh-barnea. After a year's stay at Mount Sinai, the Israelites commenced their journey again, traveling northeastward toward Kadesh-barnea about 150 miles away. The main narrative in Numbers 10–13 mentions only three stopping places, although Numbers 33 lists twenty encampments. None can be identified with certainty. Most likely the route followed a series of wadis slightly inland from the Gulf of Aqabah. Their route took them through the Wilderness of Paran (Num. 10:12; 12:16), apparently an ancient term used to describe large portions of Sinai. Along the way, Miriam and Aaron futilely challenged Moses' leadership (Num. 12), and the people continued to complain about their provisions (Num. 11). After an indeterminate time, the tribes finally arrived at Kadesh-barnea on the border between Sinai and Canaan.

The Sojourn at Kadesh

Kadesh-barnea became a gathering place for the tribes during an extended stay of thirty-eight years, occasioned by their unfaithfulness to God. Kadesh-barnea has been located on the northern edge of the Sinai, either at Ain el-Qudeirat or Ain Qedis, both sites having important springs. The Israelites likely utilized all available water sources during their prolonged stay. Although the immediate surroundings were inviting, the broader environs of Kadesh-barnea were harsher. The Bible associates Kadesh-barnea with the Wilderness of Zin, a land contorted by geology and practically devoid of vegetation and water. The Wilderness of Zin stretched northeastward from Kadesh, which itself lay in the Wilderness of Paran (Num. 13:26).

Kadesh-barnea stood at the junction of two important roads; one linked Egypt with Edom, and the other extended from the Gulf of Aqabah northward through the Negeb in the hill country of Canaan. The following is an outline of the major events centered upon Kadesh-barnea.

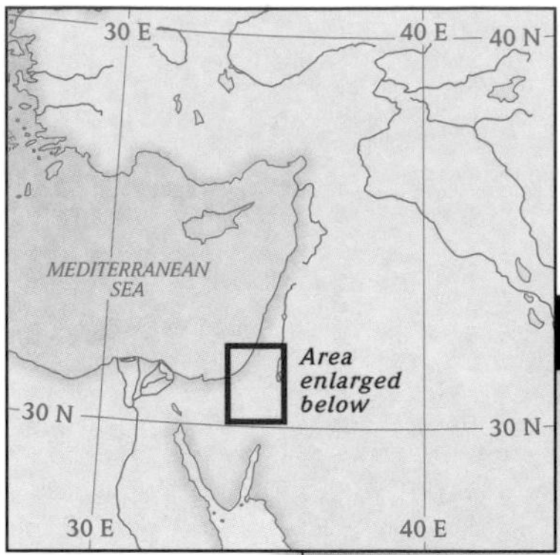

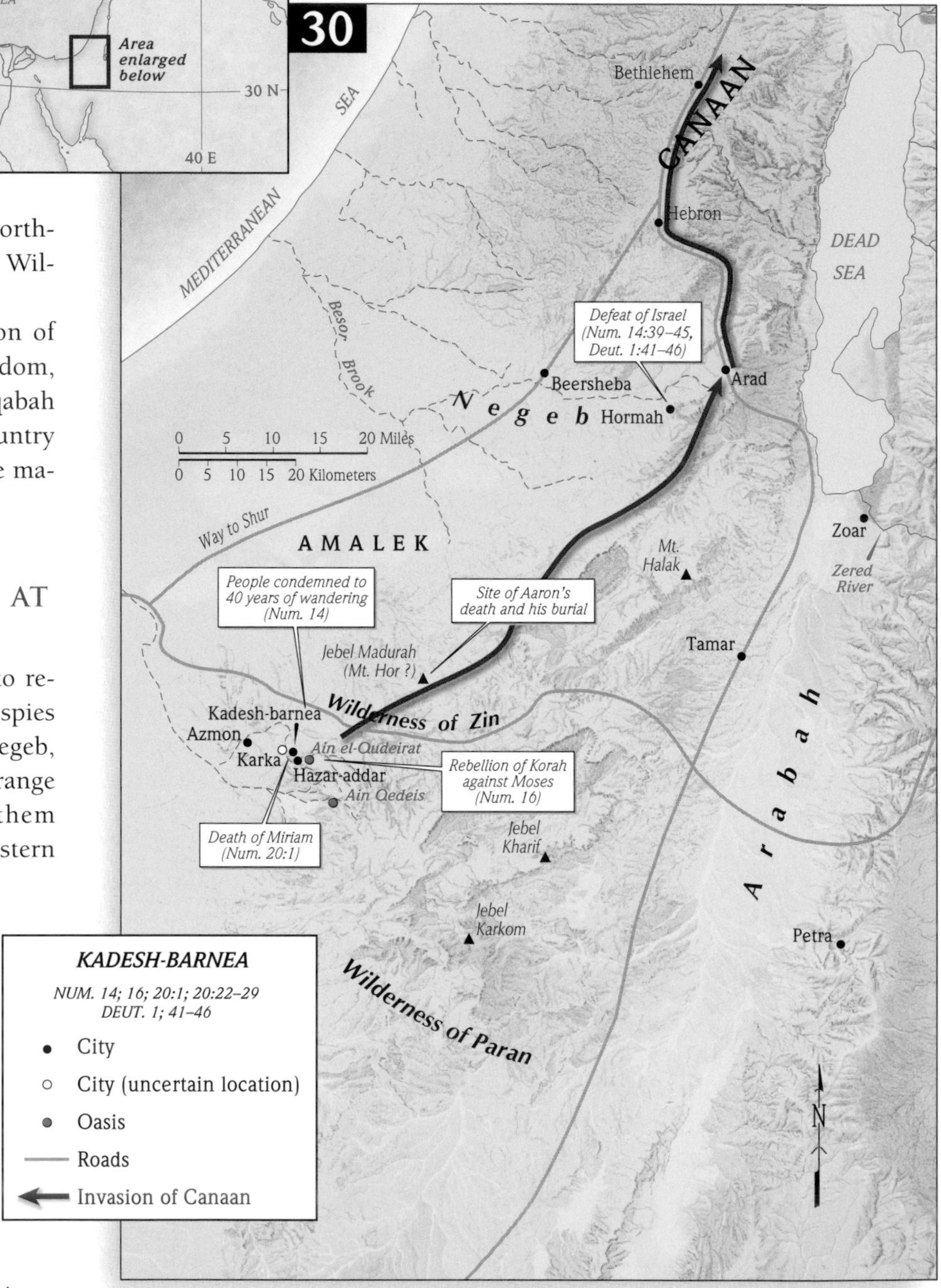

EVENTS DURING THE SOJOURN AT KADESH-BARNEA

I. Moses sent out the twelve spies to reconnoiter the promised land (Num. 13). The spies left the Wilderness of Paran, entered the Negeb, and traveled through the central mountain range of western Palestine. Their route took them through the Negeb and the mountains of western Palestine as far north as Lebo-hamath. Grapes retrieved from the Valley of Eschol indicate their journey took place in summer. The spies brought back a divided report. The majority reported that the land was well fortified and could not be conquered, but Caleb and Joshua urged the people to seize the promised land (Num. 13:25–33).

II. The people, alarmed by the report of the spies, made plans to return to Egypt despite the pleas of Joshua and Caleb that the land could be taken. Moses' intervention for Israel's rebellion against God spared the people, but God decreed a punishment of forty years of wandering that would eliminate the unbelieving generation (Num. 14:1–35).

III. Unwilling to accept God's verdict, the men of Israel attempted to storm the land of Canaan from the south, but were repulsed by a combination of Amalekites and Canaanites at Hormah in the vicinity of Beer-sheba (Num. 14:39–45; Deut. 1:41–46).

IV. Further rebellion led by Korah, Dathan, and Abiram only confirmed the faithlessness that infected the tribes (Num. 16).

V. Miriam, Moses' sister and a prophetess, died at Kadesh-barnea (Num. 20:1).

VI. Moses provided water for the complaining Israelites at Kadesh-barnea (Num. 20:2–13; cf. Exod. 17:1–7). At Kadesh, God punished both Moses and Aaron for their arrogant actions by forbidding them entrance into the promised land.

VII. Shortly after leaving Kadesh-barnea, on the way to Edom, Aaron died and was buried at Mount Hor (Num. 20:22–29). Moses consecrated Aaron's son Eleazer in the place of his father. The location of Mount Hor cannot be established with certainty, but likely it lay northeast of Kadesh-barnea on the way to Edom; one suggestion is that Mount Hor should be identified with Jebel Madurah.

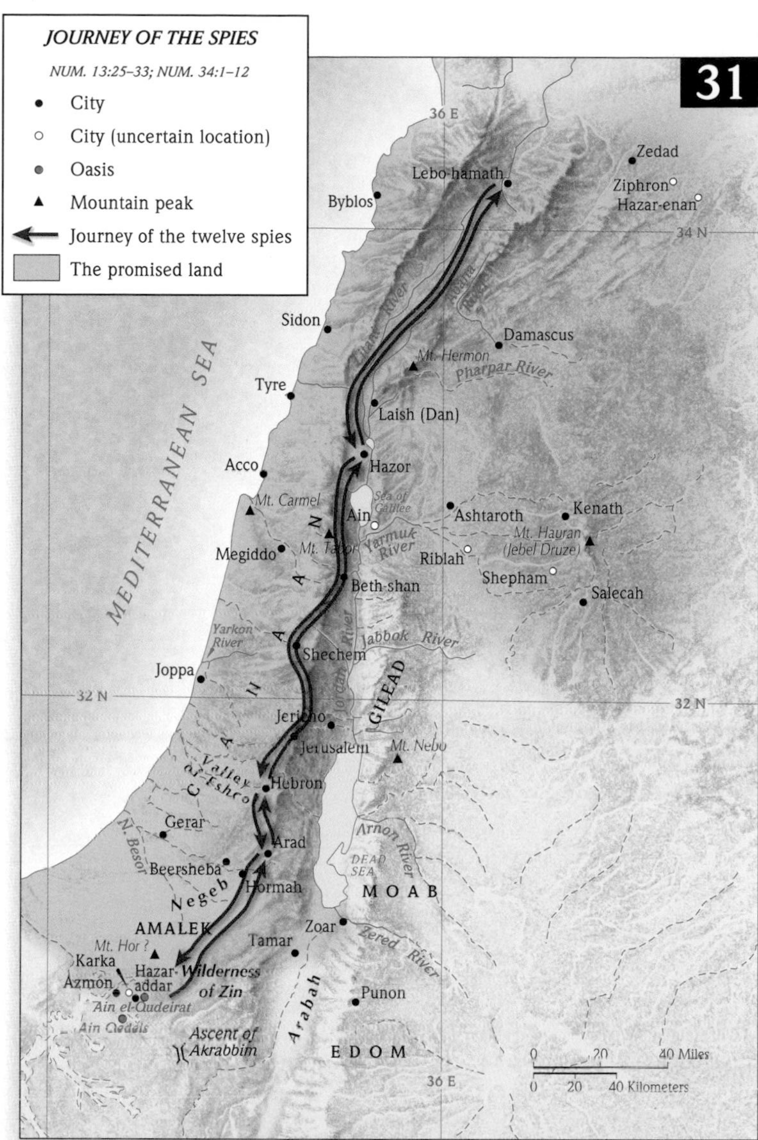

From Kadesh-barnea to the Plains of Moab

The journey from Kadesh-barnea to the Plains of Moab, narrated in Numbers 20–21; 33; Deuteronomy 1–2; and Judges 11:12–28, presents numerous geographical problems. Numbers 20, 21:4, and Deuteronomy 2 describe a detour to the east forced upon Israel when the kings of Edom and Moab refused a request by Moses to cross their kingdoms (Num. 20:14–21). However, Numbers 33 and Numbers 21:10–20 seem to suggest a route that leads across the Arabah to the King's Highway. The difference in the accounts are not easily harmonized, but a major detour best satisfies the main narrative. Perhaps the movements of more than one group of Israelites are reflected in these accounts, a hypothesis that is attractive if we consider the movements up to the crossing of the Zered as part of the wanderings.

The Kadesh-barnea region viewed from the ancient tell.

Israel initially moved northeast into the Wilderness of Zin, where Aaron died and was buried on Mount Hor (Num. 20:24–29). The Israelites may have traveled as far as the Arabah before it became clear that the kings of Edom and Moab would not let them pass. Turning south, the tribes followed the "way of the Red (Reed) Sea," arriving at Ezion-geber at the top of the Gulf of Aqabah (Num. 14:25; Deut. 2:1).

At Ezion-geber another command to turn north and bypass their distant kinsmen, the Edomites and Moabites, can be interpreted in two ways (Deut. 2:3–12). Perhaps Moses selected a desert track along the edge of the desert that skirted Edom and Moab to the east. This route, the "way of the wilderness of Moab," certainly was used at some point. Another possibility is that the tribes moved north along the eastern edge of the Arabah to Punon, a site known for its copper deposits. The bronze serpent episode fits well in this region (Num. 21:6–9). Continuing up the Zered River through difficult terrain, the Israelites skirted Moab by taking the desert road around Moab (Deut. 2:8). Finally, Moses led Israel down and across the great gorge of the Arnon and intersected the King's Highway. Amorite kings controlled much of the Transjordan Plateau stretching beyond them to the north. The days of battle had come.

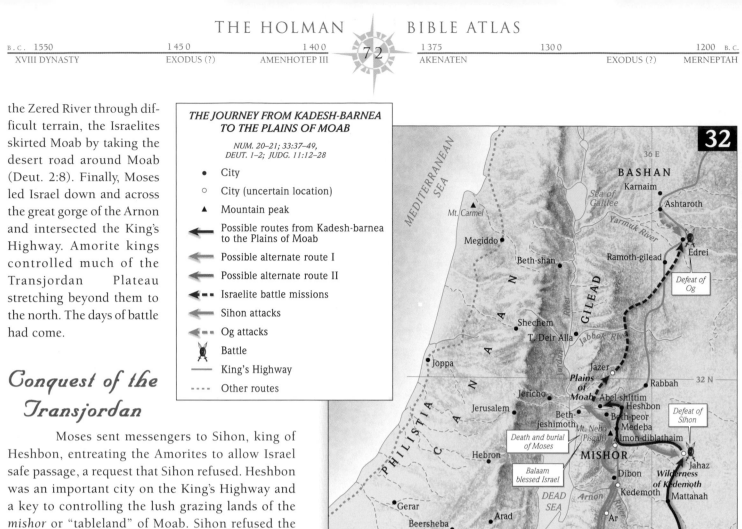

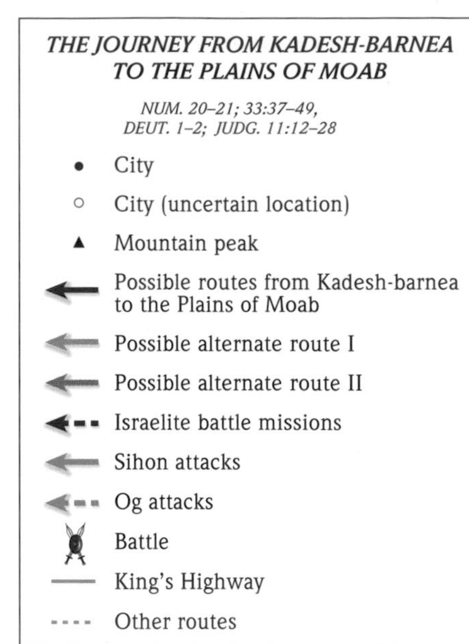

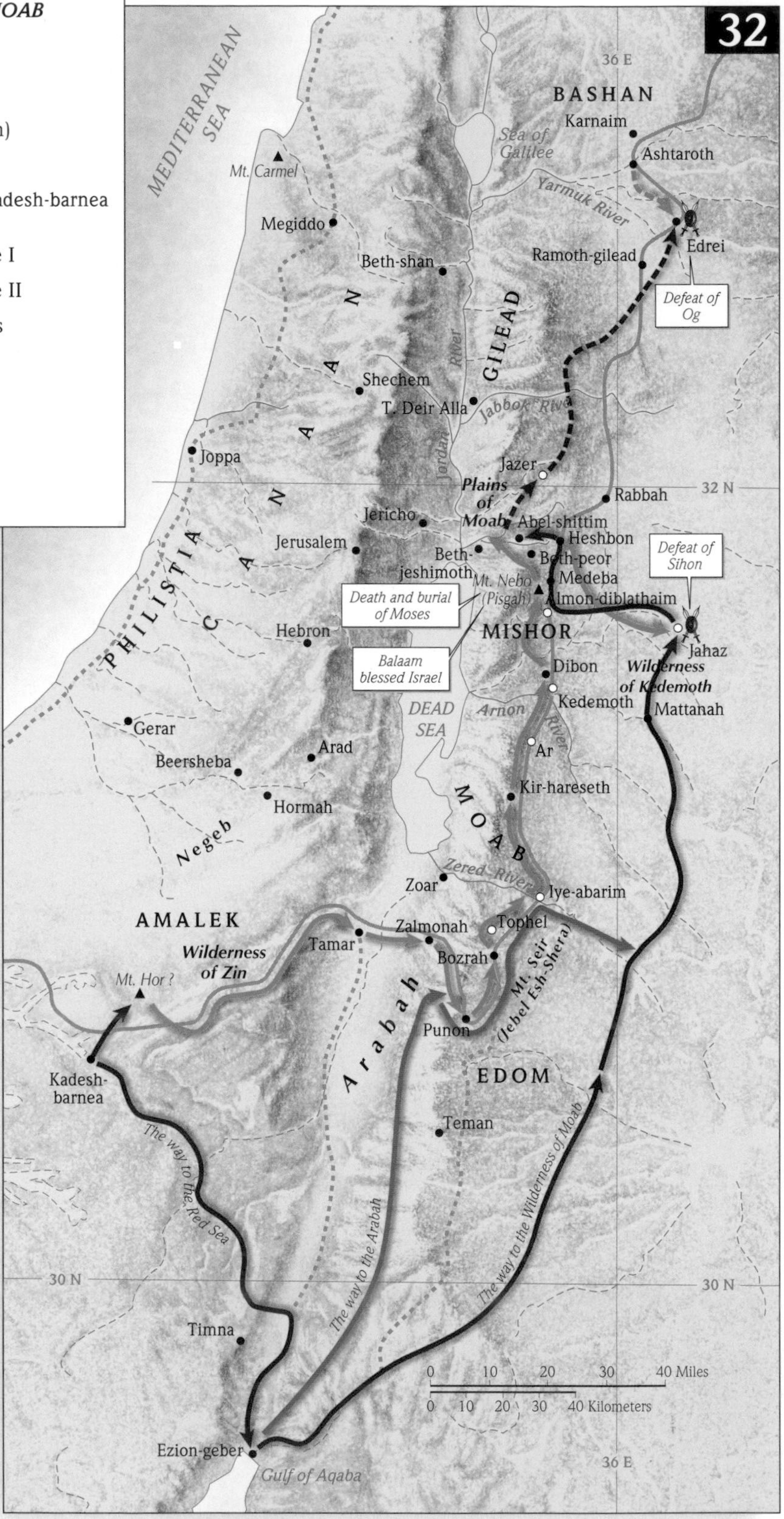

Conquest of the Transjordan

Moses sent messengers to Sihon, king of Heshbon, entreating the Amorites to allow Israel safe passage, a request that Sihon refused. Heshbon was an important city on the King's Highway and a key to controlling the lush grazing lands of the *mishor* or "tableland" of Moab. Sihon refused the request and gathered his force for attack. At Jahaz, the tribes defeated Sihon's army and subsequently conquered Amorite villages scattered between the Arnon and southern Gilead (Deut. 2:24–37; Num. 21:21–32). Next, Israel attacked Og, king of Bashan, seizing the towns and villages of his kingdom (Num. 21:33–35; Deut. 3:1–11). These victories brought much of the territory from the Arnon to Mount Hermon in the north under Israel's control, land eventually divided among the tribes of Reuben, Gad, and East Manasseh.

The victorious Israelites made camp in the Plains of Moab at Shittim, opposite Jericho beyond the Jordan. Their successes brought fear to other kings in the region. Balak, king of Moab, sought the service of Baalam, son of Beor, to place a curse on Israel in an effort to forestall further victories (Num. 22–24). Aramaic texts found at Tell Deir Alla in the Jordan Valley included prophecies of this same Baalam, whose fame as a seer continued for generations. God caused Baalam to bless Israel, although the people of Israel joined themselves to the pagan god Baal of Peor, resulting in twenty-four thousand deaths (Num. 25).

ISRAEL'S TRANSJORDANIAN NEIGHBORS

Egyptian records from at least 1250 B.C. refer to both Edom and Moab, mentioning bedouin who lived in the Transjordan. How long these groups had been in the area and their precise origins are difficult to determine. Recent archaeological surveys of the central and southern Transjordan suggests that there was no occupational gap in these areas between 2000 and 1200 B.C. as formerly thought. Israel claimed kinship with these Transjordanian kingdoms through the family of Abraham. According to Genesis, Esau was the brother of Jacob, while Moab and Ammon were descended from Lot's incestuous relationship with his daughters (Gen. 19:30–38).

EDOM

The Edomites lived south of the Wadi al-Hesa (the Zered) in the mountains east of the Arabah. The name *Edom* comes from the Hebrew word meaning "red," a reference to the red Nubian sandstone constituting the mountainous region occupied by Edom. The Bible at times equates Edom with "Seir" or "Mount Seir" (Gen. 32:3; Num. 24:18). Mount Seir traditionally has been identified with Jebel esh-Shera east of the Arabah, but some scholars locate Seir in the wilderness south of Judah.

From their mountain strongholds Teman and Bozrah, the Edomites threatened Judah's control of the Arabah and the routes that led to Ezion-geber, Solomon's port on the Gulf of Aqabah. David conquered Edom and garrisoned the land with his troops (2 Sam. 8:14). Solomon maintained control over Edom, but Edom successfully revolted during the reign of Jehoram (2 Kgs. 8:20). The next 150 years brought repeated hostilities between Judah and Edom over control of lucrative trade routes. Edom seized Ezion-geber (Elath) in the reign of Ahaz and later gradually infiltrated the Negeb south of Judah. An Edomite shrine found at Horvat Qitmit dedicated to Qaus (Qos), the national god of Edom, indicates the encroachment of Edom into Judean lands. Later, pressure from the Nabateans would increase the Edomite presence west of the Arabah, the new migrants known then as Idumeans.

No nation received more vehement condemnation from Israel than Edom. Edom appears prominently in a series of prophetic oracles against the nations (Amos 1:11–12; Isa. 34; Jer. 49:7–22) and receives singular attention in Obadiah and other oracles of judgment (Isa. 34; Mal. 1:2–5). The Edomites were implicated in the fall of Jerusalem to Nebuchadnezzar in 587/86 (Obad. 10–14; Ps. 137:7; Lam. 4:22). This activity, combined with Edom's brotherly status to Israel and Edomite encroachment upon land promised to Israel, created a deeply rooted hatred between the two nations.

MOAB

The Moabites occupied the territory east of the Dead Sea. Their traditional stronghold was the land between the Zered and Arnon Rivers. The major Moabite cities, Kir-hareseth and Ar, lay in Moab's heartland south of the Arnon. The Moabites, however, coveted the fertile "tableland" (Heb. *mishor*) north of the Arnon allotted to the tribe of Reuben. Heshbon and Medeba were important cities of the tableland with commercial appeal. Moabites, Ammonites, and Israelites often fought over this disputed land. The story of Ehud's deliverance of Israel from the Moabite king Eglon illustrates the point well. The land of Moab provided fertile fields for grain crops with adequate rains and a narrow band of cultivatable land lying in gentle rolling hills. In the story of Ruth, Moab was a refuge for Israelites who suffered drought in their land. Moab was especially noted for sheep raising and wool. When the Dynasty of Omri ruled Israel, Mesha, the most well-known Moabite king, paid to Israel a yearly tribute of one hundred thousand lambs and the wool of one hundred thousand rams (2 Kgs. 3:4). This same Mesha appears on a famous stele called the Moabite Stone, where he boasts that he led Moab in a successful revolt against Israel after the death of Omri's son, Ahab, and reclaimed the land north of the Arnon. Mesha came from Dibon, a city north of the Arnon. He attributed his success to the national god of Moab, Chemosh.

AMMON

The Ammonites were descendants of Ben Ammi, Lot's son, who carved out for themselves a small city-state between Gilead and the Syrian desert. The Ammonite capital, Rabbah (modern Amman—the capital of Jordan), was located at the headwaters of the Jabbok River. Conflict with Israel over control of the Gilead was inevitable as the Ammonites scrapped to maintain a kingdom. Jephthah deflected Ammonite encroachments into Gilead about 1100 B.C. (Judg. 11). Later, Saul secured his kingship by delivering the citizens of Jabesh-gilead from the oppression of the Ammonite king Nahash (1 Sam. 11). David conquered Ammon and made it a tribute-paying vassal, a status that held throughout Solomon's reign.

Solomon numbered Ammonites among his wives, and the Israelite king built shrines in Jerusalem dedicated to Milcom, the national deity of Ammon. The mother of Rehoboam, Solomon's son and successor, was an Ammonite (1 Kgs. 14:21). We have much less information about Ammon during the divided monarchy, although an Ammonite king paid tribute to Uzziah and Jotham (2 Chr. 26:8; 27:5). The Ammonite king Baasha fought in the anti-Assyrian coalition at the Battle of Qarqar in 853 B.C. Between 725 and 625 the Ammonite kingdom prospered under Assyrian domination. Jeremiah indicted Ammon for her pride and confidence during this era, and he also implicated Ammon's King Baalis in the murder of the Babylonian-appointed governor of Judah, Gedeliah (Jer. 40:14). Ultimately, Ammon's rebellion against Babylon led to her downfall along with many other small Levantine kingdoms.

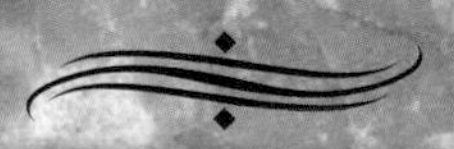

Moses delivered his final address to Israel in the Plains of Moab. Because of his disobedience in the wilderness, Moses would be permitted only to view the promised land from the heights of nearby Mount Nebo (Pisgah, Num. 20:8–13). Yet he had accomplished his purpose; Israel was now poised to strike across the Jordan and claim the land promised to her forefathers. With the death of Moses and his burial on nearby Mount Nebo, the tribes looked to a new leader—Joshua the son of Nun—as Yahweh's appointed instrument to lead Israel to future victories.

A stele found at Balua in Moab showing two Moabite rulers standing before an Egyptian deity.

The Plains of Moab at the northern end of the Dead Sea. The flanks of Mt. Nebo are on the left.

Chapter Eight

CONQUEST AND SETTLEMENT

The death of Moses closed an important chapter in the life of Israel, but a new challenge lay before the people. Poised beyond the Jordan in the Plains of Moab, the tribes of Israel beheld the land promised to Abraham. To claim their inheritance would not be an easy task; Canaan had a large, mixed population who would not yield territory willingly. The Canaanites lived in fortified cities along the coast and in the great valleys. Amorites dwelt in the hill country, while the Amalekites roamed the Negeb (Num. 13:29). Other groups—

33

ANCIENT NEAR EAST FROM 1200–1000 B.C.
THE IRON I PERIOD

- ● City
- ○ City (uncertain location)
- ▲ Mountain peak
- Neo-Hittite states
- Emerging Aramean states
- Phoenicia

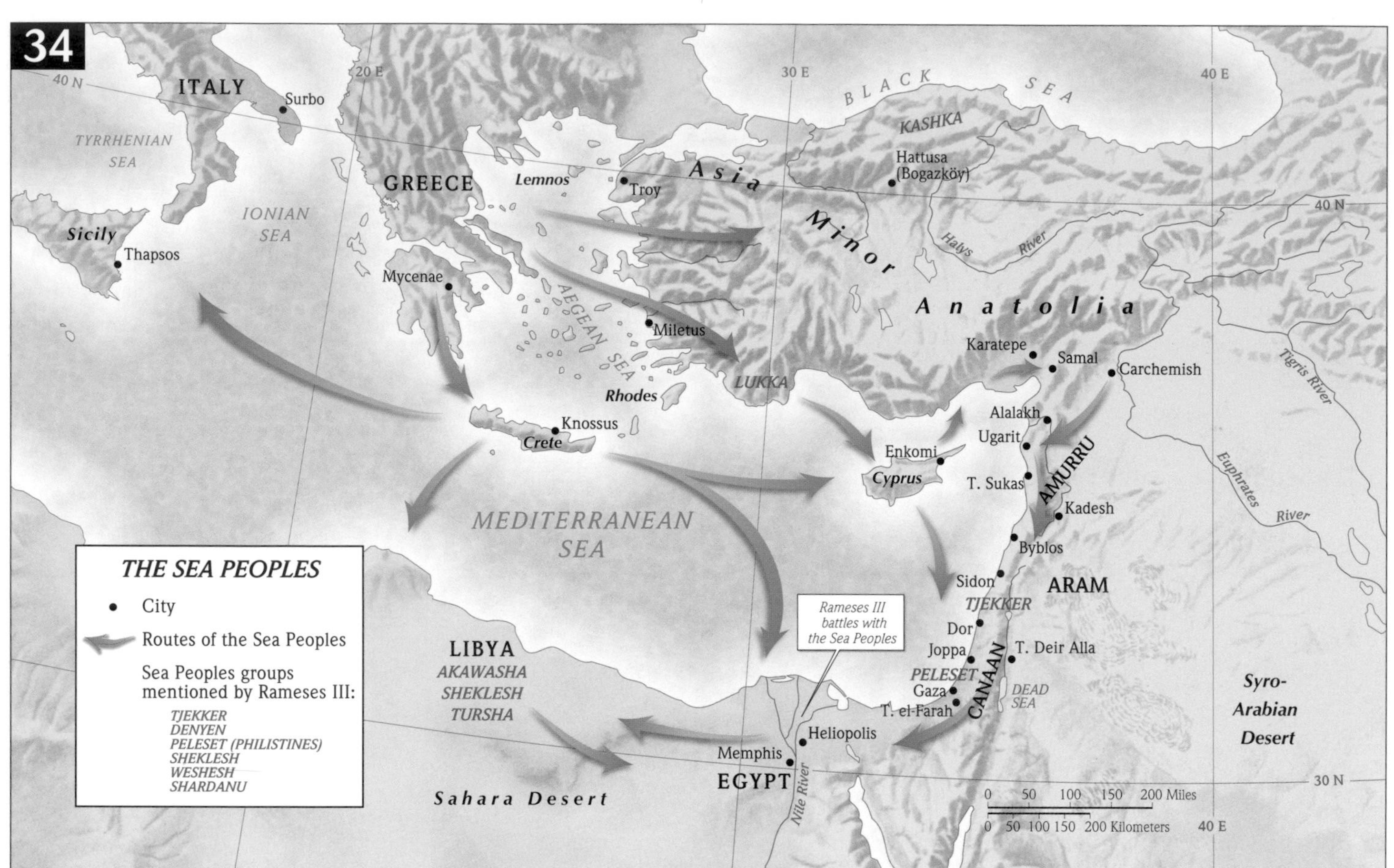

Jebusites, Hivites, Perizzites, and (Neo)Hittites—occupied the villages and towns of the land (Josh. 3:10; 9:1; Deut. 7:1). As Joshua assumed the mantle of leadership from Moses and prepared the tribes for battle, he knew only the power of God could grant the fulfillment of the ancient promise to his forefathers.

The books of Joshua and Judges tell the story of conquest and settlement. Joshua concentrates on the initial phase of the process, while Judges describes the struggle of the tribes to possess the land in the face of pressure from neighboring people. A careful reading of both books make two things clear. First, the conquest of the land was not accomplished in one generation. The conquest was a process that extended over many generations and was not completed fully until the time of David and Solomon (1000–922 B.C.). David was the first king who ruled over a territory that included all the lands allotted to the tribes. For this reason it is best to regard the period of the judges as an extension of the settlement process. Second, the Israelites had a very difficult time extending the limits of their control out of the mountains into the plains and valleys. Chariots gave the Canaanites a distinct advantage on flat lands (Josh. 17:16–18). Moreover, Israel faced threats from other peoples, like the Philistines and Moabites, as they attempted to expand their territorial limits.

Historical Background

From 1200 to 1000 B.C. the Ancient Near East experienced a time of change as the traditional powers of the Late Bronze Age, Egypt and the Hittite Empire, collapsed and new groups emerged. Destruction debris found at numerous sites throughout the Near East as well as contemporary documents testify to the turmoil attending the changes. Archaeologists call the era from 1200 to 1000 B.C. "Iron Age I," but the real changes that heralded a new era had little to do with the rapid introduction of iron. The distinguishing characteristic of Iron Age I was the appearance of new peoples in the Levant, including Israel.

THE SEA PEOPLES

No event symbolized the new era better than the migrations of the Sea Peoples as they swept across the Near East in search of new lands. Coming by both land and sea, the Sea Peoples represented several different groups who came in several waves out of the lands adjacent to the Aegean Sea, the Balkans, and the southern coast of the Black Sea in search of new territory. They overran a Hittite Empire already seriously weakened by harass-

The mortuary temple of Rameses III, Medinet Habu, inscribed with scenes of Rameses' victories over the Sea Peoples. The inset shows Philistine captives of war.

ment from Assyria and Mitanni on the east, and they destroyed important cities on the coasts of Syria (Ugarit) and Lebanon. Two different groups of Sea Peoples attacked Egypt during the reigns of Merneptah and Rameses III (ca. 1175 B.C.). Among the invaders were Philistines who later settled the southern coast of Canaan.

Scenes in the mortuary temple of Rameses III at Medinet Habu record his victories over the Sea Peoples and provide valuable information about these raiders. The Sea Peoples brought their families and belongings, often traveling in ox carts. Graphic scenes portray the fierce fighting between Egyptian and Sea Peoples' naval contingents as they clashed somewhere in the Delta of Egypt or perhaps off the coast of Palestine. These attacks, combined with other internal problems, caused Egypt to enter a long period of decline after the death of Rameses III.

THE POWER VACUUM

The political vacuum created with the collapse of the Hittite Empire and the decline of Egypt left Palestine and Syria vulnerable, but no immediate rival appeared to fill the void. Assyria, the most likely benefactor of Egypt's weakness, was in no position to take advantage of the situation. Consequently, less powerful peoples seized the opportunity, gradually creating new political bases in the Levant. Aramean groups, mentioned in records since about 1200 B.C., established kingdoms centered on key cities in Syria and northwest Mesopotamia. Aram-Damascus, Aram-zobah, and Hamath all were Aramean kingdoms mentioned from the time of David onward. The Philistines settled along the southern coast of Canaan by 1150 B.C. In the Transjordan the kingdoms of Moab, Edom, and Ammon tightened their grip on the land they had occupied for some time. Small Neo-Hittite states (Carchemish, Samal, Arpad, Aleppo) appeared in southeast Asia Minor in the aftermath of the Sea Peoples' devastation.

The political complexion of the Levant was transformed in the period from 1200 to 1000 B.C. As the tribes of Israel appeared in the mountains of western Palestine seeking to drive out the native population and possess the land, they were but one of many restless peoples on the move seeking new territory. Without interference from a traditional great power, this period indeed was a time when "every man did what was right in his own eyes" (Judg. 17:6; 21:25).

Joshua's Conquests

Joshua 1–11 narrates a series of campaigns Joshua led against selected sites in the mountains of western Palestine. At first glance these familiar stories give the impression of a single unified conquest of Canaan. A comparison with Judges 1 and Joshua 13:1–6 shows that Joshua's death left Israel with much territory still to conquer. The extensive list of conquered kings in Joshua 13:7–24 suggests that military engagements other than those described in Joshua 3–11 were part of this initial phase. The victories did give Israel a foothold in Canaan, a base from which additional expansion could proceed.

CAMPAIGNS IN CENTRAL PALESTINE

From Shittim in the Plains of Moab, Joshua sent spies ahead to Jericho before crossing the Jordan and establishing a camp at Gilgal. Jericho was a strategic oasis located near an important ford of the Jordan River. Three routes led from Jericho up into the central highlands. If Jericho could be taken, the way into the mountains of Canaan lay open. The story of Joshua's victory (Josh. 6) and the antiquity of the site has prompted three major excavations at Tell es-Sultan, the mound of ancient Jericho. Unfortunately, the archaeological evidence from the Late Bronze Age (1550 to 1200 B.C.)—the general period of the Exodus—is meager; erosion has swept away much of the remains from this era. The evidence indicates a small city (about ten acres) existed, probably defended by walls from a previous era, the Middle Bronze Age.

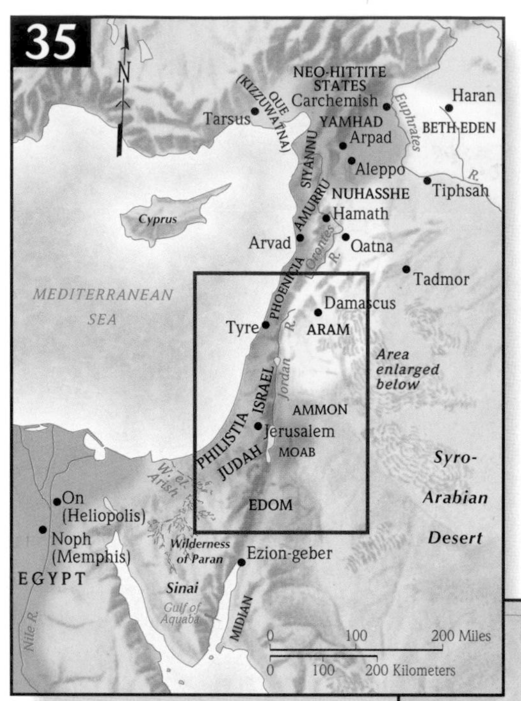

With the important oasis at Jericho in hand, Joshua faced the question of which of the several available routes leading up into the mountains should Israel take? The more heavily traveled but dangerous route to Jerusalem? Southwestward to Bethlehem? Joshua chose the Wadi Makkuk, a route that led into the heart of the hill country near Bethel. With a small force he attacked nearby Ai. Although the initial attack failed due to the sin of Achan, the tribes overcame the defenders of Ai in a cleverly laid ambush (Josh. 7–8).

Again, unfortunately, the archaeological evidence from Ai presents difficulties. Ai has been identified with et-Tell, one and a half miles southeast of Bethel. According to the excavators, et-Tell was not inhabited from 2350 to 1150 B.C. This perplexing circumstance has provided several theories that seek to harmonize the archaeological and biblical data. One suggestion is that Ai was a military outpost of nearby Bethel and therefore not an occupied site. Yet another idea questions whether et-Tell is really Ai. This suggestion has been taken seriously, but a suitable alternate site has not been located. In fact, the biblical descriptions fit the theory that Ai is et-Tell. A clear answer to this issue eludes our grasp at this time, and we must await further insight. Archaeological data from Bethel, however, confirms it was destroyed in the thirteenth century (Judg. 1:22–26). These victories gave Israel access to the heart of Canaan.

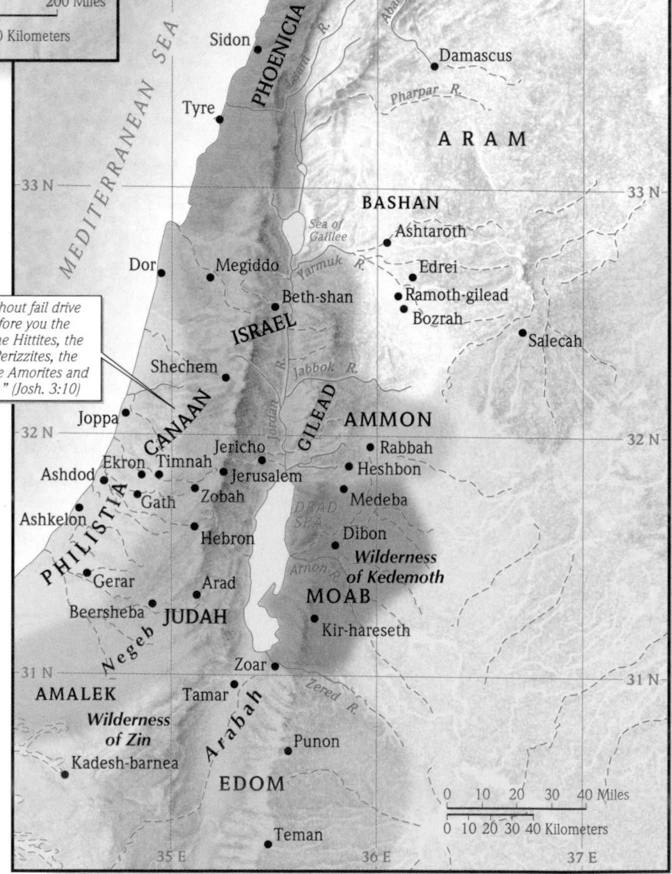

Tell es-Sultan identified as Old Testament Jericho.

CAMPAIGNS IN THE SOUTH

Joshua next engaged a coalition of five Amorite kings in a series of battles that took place in southern Canaan. Led by Adoni-zedek (the king of Jerusalem), the kings of Hebron, Jarmuth, Lachish, and Eglon threatened the Hivite villages north-

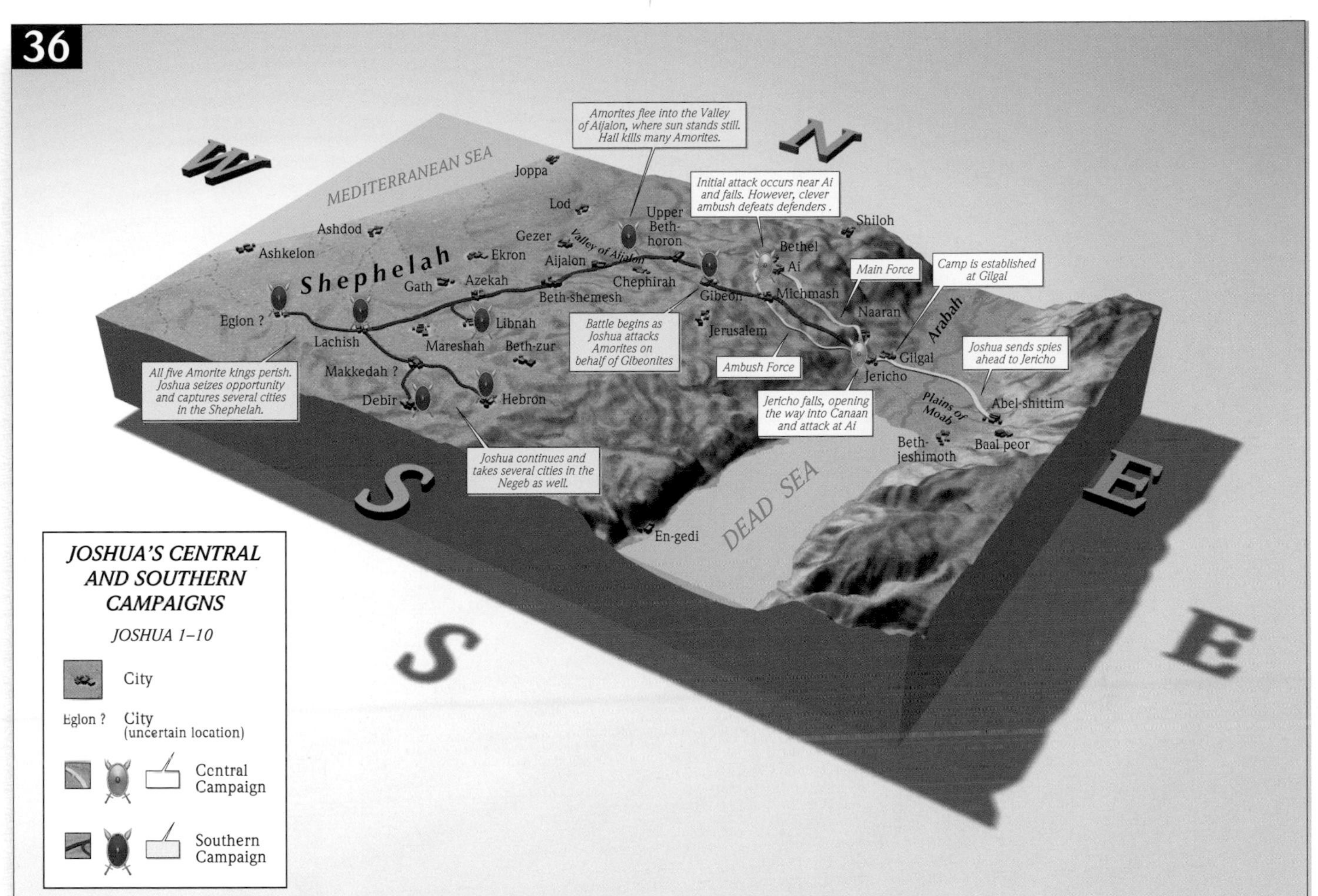
36
W
N
S
E
MEDITERRANEAN SEA
DEAD SEA
Amorites flee into the Valley of Aijalon, where sun stands still. Hail kills many Amorites.
Initial attack occurs near Ai and fails. However, clever ambush defeats defenders.
Main Force
Camp is established at Gilgal
Battle begins as Joshua attacks Amorites on behalf of Gibeonites
Ambush Force
Joshua sends spies ahead to Jericho
Jericho falls, opening the way into Canaan and attack at Ai
All five Amorite kings perish. Joshua seizes opportunity and captures several cities in the Shephelah.
Joshua continues and takes several cities in the Negeb as well.
Joppa
Lod
Ashdod
Ashkelon
Shephelah
Gezer
Ekron
Aijalon
Valley of Aijalon
Upper Beth-horon
Gath
Azekah
Chephirah
Beth-shemesh
Gibeon
Bethel
Ai
Michmash
Shiloh
Naaran
Arabah
Eglon ?
Lachish
Libnah
Mareshah
Beth-zur
Jerusalem
Gilgal
Jericho
Makkedah ?
Debir
Hebron
Plains of Moab
Abel-shittim
Beth-jeshimoth
Baal-peor
En-gedi
JOSHUA'S CENTRAL AND SOUTHERN CAMPAIGNS
JOSHUA 1–10
City
Eglon ? City (uncertain location)
Central Campaign
Southern Campaign

west of Jerusalem (Gibeon, Chephirah, Beeroth, and Kiriath-jearim) who had made a covenant with Israel.

Joshua interceded on behalf of the Gibeonites and attacked the Amorite coalition in the Valley of Aijalon, where the sun stood still (Josh. 10). A violent hailstorm killed more Amorites than did Israelite swords on that day as Israel's enemies fled southwest into the hills and valleys of the Shephelah. All five Amorite kings perished. Seizing the opportunity opened by this great victory, Joshua captured several cities in the Shephelah (Libnah, Lachish, and Eglon) before continuing against Hebron, Debir, and villages in the Negeb (Josh. 10:29–43).

THE NORTHERN CAMPAIGNS

A final thrust to the north against a Canaanite coalition headed by Jabin, king of Hazor, concluded the campaigns of Joshua. Hazor formally had been the greatest of Canaanite city-states and still possessed formidable strength with a population estimated at forty thousand. Her huge defensive earth embankments crowned with high walls defied attack.

Joshua surprised the larger Canaanite force in the highlands of Upper Galilee by the waters of Merom. Caught where chariots gave them no advantage, the Canaanite army was routed. Survivors fled northward toward Sidon, but Israelite contingents overtook them (Josh. 11:1–9). Returning to Hazor, Joshua attacked the city and burned it. Signs of a great conflagration dated to the late thirteenth century at Hazor apparently mark the victory.

JOSHUA'S ACCOMPLISHMENTS (SEE MAP 38)

How are we to understand these battles? Certainly these campaigns did not remove the Canaanite menace from the land. Deborah (Judg. 5) and others struggled against the Canaanites in years following. Not all the cities found in the Western Mountains came under Israelite control as the result of Joshua's victories. Jerusalem remained a pagan enclave until the time of David. Joshua 13:1–6 provides a description of the land yet to be conquered at the end of Joshua's campaigns. The fertile fields of the coastal plain, the Jezreel Valley, the Beth-shan region, as well as other pockets of land remained in non-Israelite hands. Yet God

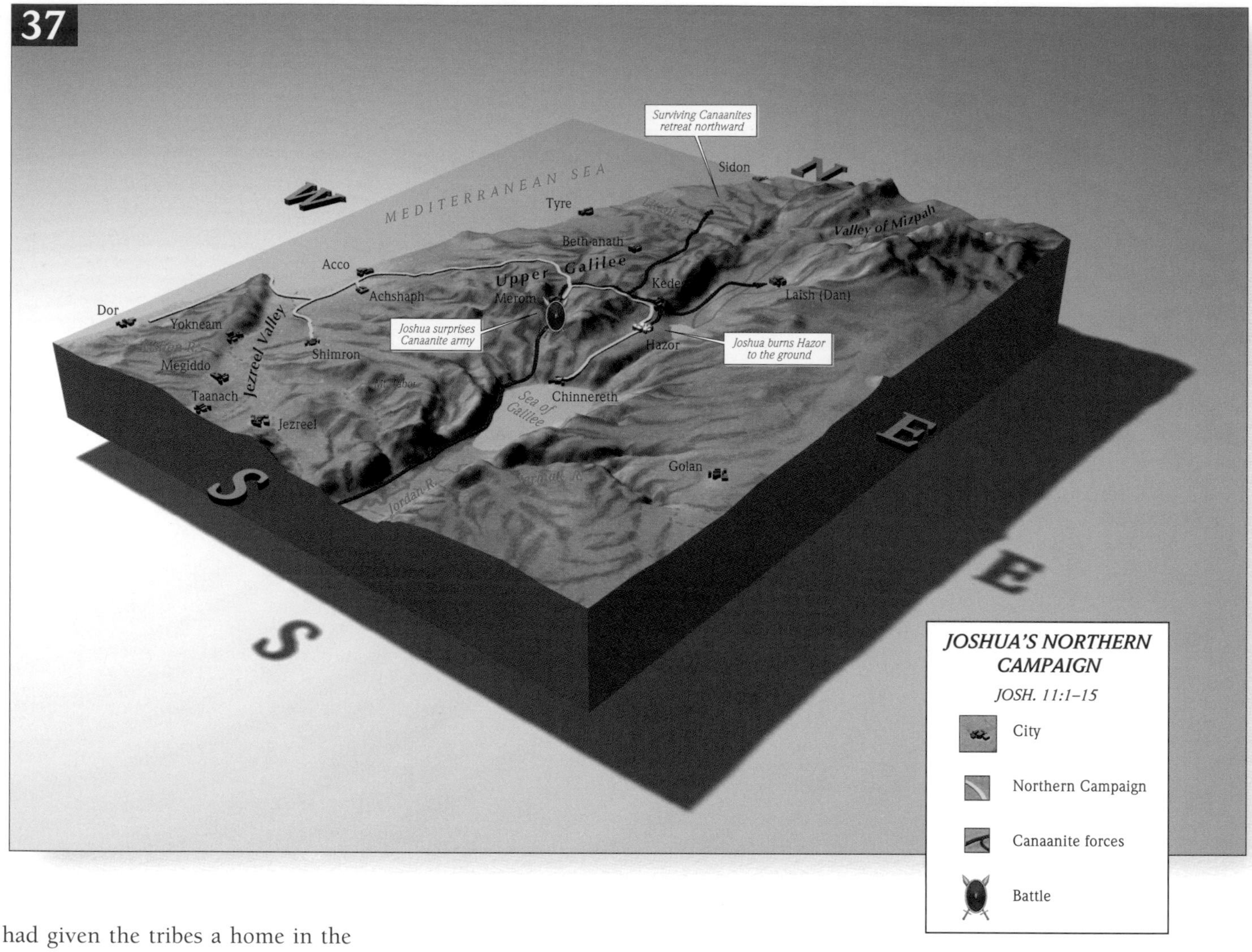

37

JOSHUA'S NORTHERN CAMPAIGN

JOSH. 11:1–15

City

Northern Campaign

Canaanite forces

Battle

had given the tribes a home in the mountains of western Palestine through Joshua's leadership. The tribes settled, for the most part, on sparsely settled lands lying between the population centers.

Israeli scholars have noted a marked increase in population density corresponding to the land controlled by Israel according to the Book of Joshua. New settlements appear in the hills of Galilee, Ephraim, and Judah. These settlements are often crudely constructed and probably represent villages of small-scale herdsmen and agriculturalists, to judge by their architecture. Perhaps sites like Giloh and Khirbet Raddana represent evidence of Israel's earliest hold on the promised land. A recent study suggests that the absence of pig bones in several highland sites could be the surest marker of Israelite settlements.

The Tell of Hazor.

HAZOR: HEAD OF ALL THOSE KINGDOMS

Hazor was the largest and one of the most important Canaanite city-states before Joshua's destruction of the city (Josh. 11:1–10). Located nine miles north of the Sea of Galilee at the point where the international trade route crossed the Jordan on the way to Damascus, Hazor dominated the Huleh Basin and controlled a key commercial route. Documents from Mari written about 1850 B.C. mention Hazor as a major commercial center involved in the vital tin trade used in making bronze. Egyptian sources often refer to Hazor, starting with its first appearance in the Execration Texts (2000–1800 B.C.) down to the reign of Seti I (1304–1290 B.C.). We are especially well informed about Hazor during the 1300s, when the city reached its zenith. The Amarna Texts mention Hazor's king, 'Abdi-tirshi. Few Canaanite rulers used the title "king" during this period, another indication of Hazor's importance. After Joshua conquered Hazor, the Bible rightly recalls that Hazor "formerly was the head of all those [Canaanite] kingdoms"(Josh. 11:10).

The massive tell of Hazor looms 130 feet above the surrounding plain. To the north, a large earthen rampart built by Canaanites in the Middle Bronze Age (ca. 1750 B.C.) enclosed a "Lower City" inhabited until its final destruction in approximately 1220 B.C. After 1200 B.C. the people who inhabited Hazor occupied only the high mound. Together, the tell and Lower City cover an area of over two hundred acres, making Hazor the largest city in Palestine prior to the Hellenistic era.

Yigael Yadin conducted excavations at Hazor from 1955 to 1958 and again in 1968. Excavations have recently resumed under the supervision of Ammon Ben-Tor. Although inhabited before 2000 B.C., Hazor achieved prominence in the Middle Bronze Age when the tell was resettled and the city greatly enlarged to the north. A massive rampart constructed of earth layered against an inner core enclosed an area one thousand yards long and seven hundred yards wide. Excavations within the enclosure revealed a substantial city complete with public buildings, domestic structures, and an unprecedented array of temples.

A major destruction occurred about 1550 B.C. Yadin attributed this to the Egyptian pharaoh Ahmose, who expelled the Hyksos from Egypt. The destruction marks the transition into the Late Bronze Age (1550–1200 B.C.).

Late Bronze Age Hazor has yielded archaeological evidence illustrating the religious life of the city. Several temples and a wealth of objects used in worship have enriched our knowledge of the period. One temple displays a plan similar to Solomon's temple of a later day. The layout of the building consists of a porch with two pillars (reminiscent of "Jachin" and "Boaz" of Solomon's temple [1 Kgs. 7:15–22]), a slightly wider hall, and an inner "holy of holies." This structure, one of a series of temples erected on the same spot, still contained the furniture used in worship when the temple was destroyed about 1220 B.C.

The objects found in the holy of holies included libation tables, two large kraters, an offering table, and a basalt incense altar decorated with an emblem associated with the storm god Hadad. The temple immediately below contained a beautiful lion orthostat in the doorway. The term *orthostat* refers to well-worked stone slabs often used as panels along the lower parts of interior walls. Similar orthostats were found in other areas and point to Hittite influence at Hazor. An inscribed clay model of a cow's liver used in divination was found nearby.

A small rectangular temple located on the inner slope of the western rampart yielded several small stele (upright stones called *mazzeboth* in Hebrew, cf. Deut. 12:3) and a seated statue of a god or king. A relief on the central stele depicted two hands extended upwards toward a crescent containing a disk. These emblems have been associated with the moon god Sin and his consort. Nearby, a potter's workshop contained small clay masks and a silver-plated bronze standard showing a goddess holding two snakes. The cult standard suggests the "Stele Temple" was dedicated to the consort of the moon god.

A Late Bronze Age Canaanite shrine termed the "Stele Temple" found at Hazor. Notice the seated figure to the left and the line of sacred stones (Hebrew *mazzeboth*).

Late Bronze Age Hazor was a truly cosmopolitan city. In addition to the Hittite influence noted above, cylinder seals of Mitannian influence and large quantities of Mycenaean pottery indicate wide-ranging international relations. However, the Late Bronze Age in Palestine was not peaceful; a major destruction of Hazor about 1450 B.C. probably was the result of an Egyptian raid during the reign of Thutmose III or Amenhotep II. Shortly before 1200 B.C. both the Upper and Lower cities were violently destroyed in a great conflagration, bringing to an end Canaanite Hazor. Many scholars connect this destruction with Joshua and the Israelite who "burned Hazor with fire" (Josh. 11:11).

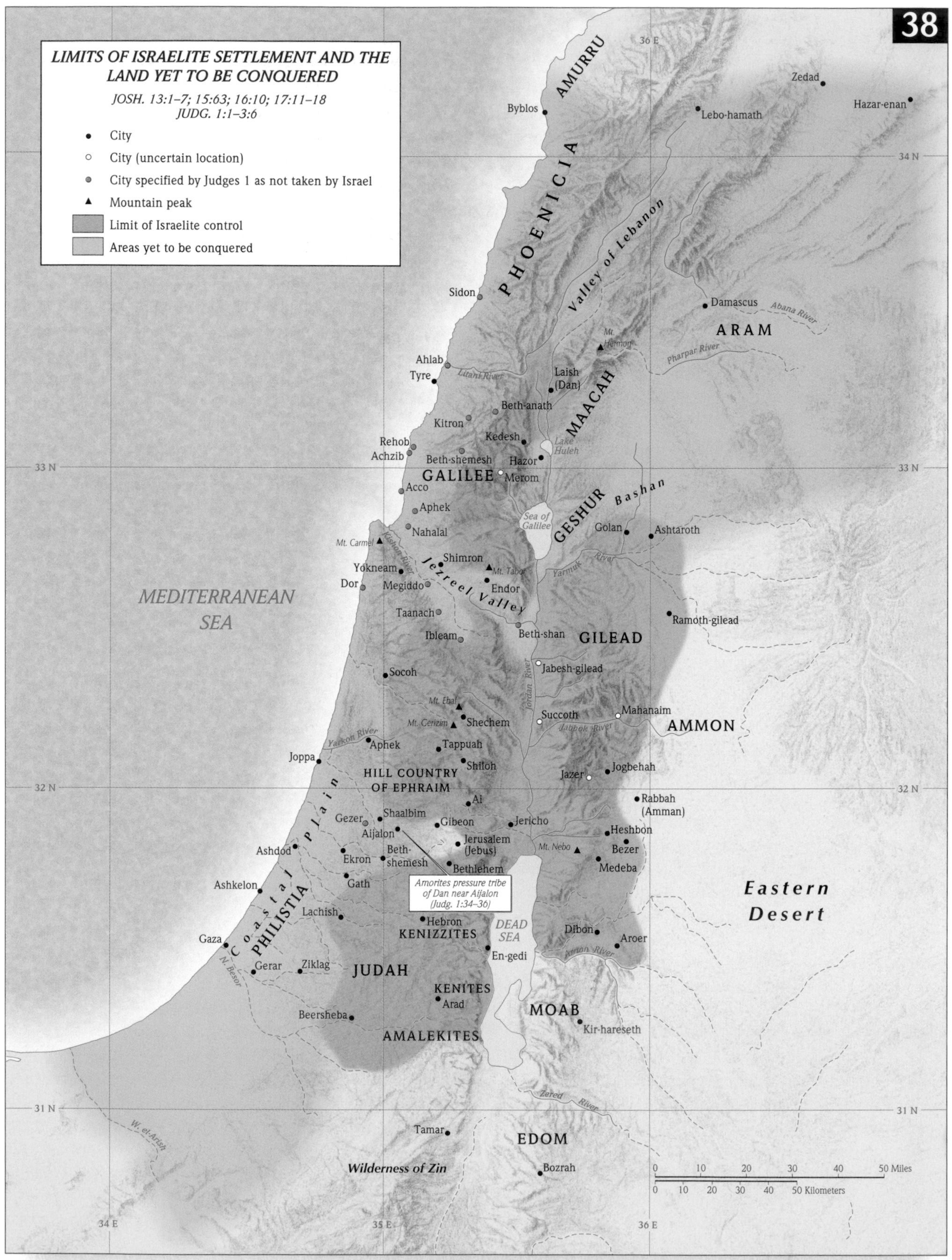
38
LIMITS OF ISRAELITE SETTLEMENT AND THE LAND YET TO BE CONQUERED
JOSH. 13:1–7; 15:63; 16:10; 17:11–18
JUDG. 1:1–3:6
City
City (uncertain location)
City specified by Judges 1 as not taken by Israel
Mountain peak
Limit of Israelite control
Areas yet to be conquered
AMURRU
PHOENICIA
Byblos
Zedad
Lebo-hamath
Hazar-enan
Valley of Lebanon
Sidon
Damascus
Abana River
ARAM
Pharpar River
Mt. Hermon
Ahlab
Tyre
Litani River
Laish (Dan)
MAACAH
Beth-anath
Kitron
Kedesh
Lake Huleh
Rehob
Achzib
Beth-shemesh
Hazor
GALILEE
Merom
GESHUR
Bashan
Acco
Aphek
Sea of Galilee
Golan
Ashtaroth
Nahalal
Mt. Carmel
Kishon River
Shimron
Jezreel Valley
Mt. Tabor
Yarmuk River
Yokneam
Dor
Megiddo
Endor
MEDITERRANEAN SEA
Taanach
Ramoth-gilead
Ibleam
Beth-shan
GILEAD
Jabesh-gilead
Jordan River
Socoh
Mt. Ebal
Mt. Gerizim
Shechem
Succoth
Mahanaim
Jabbok River
AMMON
Yarkon River
Aphek
Tappuah
Joppa
Shiloh
Jogbehah
HILL COUNTRY OF EPHRAIM
Jazer
Coastal Plain
Ai
Rabbah (Amman)
Gezer
Shaalbim
Gibeon
Jericho
Aijalon
Jerusalem (Jebus)
Heshbon
Ashdod
Mt. Nebo
Bezer
Ekron
Beth-shemesh
Bethlehem
Medeba
Ashkelon
Gath
Amorites pressure tribe of Dan near Aijalon (Judg. 1:34–36)
Eastern Desert
PHILISTIA
Lachish
Hebron
DEAD SEA
KENIZZITES
Dibon
Aroer
Gaza
En-gedi
Arnon River
N. Besor
Gerar
Ziklag
JUDAH
KENITES
Arad
MOAB
Beersheba
Kir-hareseth
AMALEKITES
Zered River
W. el-Arish
Tamar
EDOM
Wilderness of Zin
Bozrah
0 10 20 30 40 50 Miles
0 10 20 30 40 50 Kilometers
34 N
33 N
32 N
31 N
34 E
35 E
36 E

The Tribes of Israel

Earliest Israel consisted of tribes who traced their ancestry to the sons and grandsons of Jacob (Gen. 35:22–27). The number "twelve" predominates even though the names of the tribes mentioned in any given list varied slightly. For example, lists that name Levi as one of the twelve tribes also count Joseph as one of the tribes (Gen. 46:8–25; 49:1–27). Lists that omit Levi count the sons of Joseph (Ephraim and Manasseh) as separate tribes to maintain the number "twelve" (Num. 1, 26). Collectively, the tribes were called the "sons of Israel."

The "sons of Israel" shared important religious traditions and social structures that united the tribes, but tribal loyalties and a belief that only Yahweh could be king of Israel led the tribes to resist the concept of kingship until the time of Saul and David. Initially each tribe exercised a great deal of individual political and military autonomy.

Each tribe was composed of clans and families united by kinship or other social ties. The clan was the basic subunit of a tribe and consisted of several families sharing a recognizable lineage. Joshua allotted the land "according to their clans" (Josh. 15:1). The military requirement for soldiers during times of war came from the clans (see Num. 1, 26).

Each clan consisted of several extended families called in Hebrew *Beth-ab*—"Father's House"—that included all the family members of a single living male (excluding married daughters). The *Beth-ab* normally included three or more generations and could number many people. This tribal structure is seen clearly in the story of the sin of Achan, where God identified the offending culprit first by tribe, then by clan, and finally by household (Josh. 7:14–19). The clan and "Father's House" gave protection to the individual as well as identity. Land was held as a sacred trust by the family and had to be redeemed by a kinsmen from the *Beth-ab* or the clan in cases where debt threatened the loss of land (Lev. 25:23–55; cf. Jer. 32:6–15).

DISTRIBUTION OF THE LAND

The Book of Joshua recounts the division of the land of Canaan among the tribes of Israel as they settled into the land. The descriptions of the tribal allotments contain two types of information: (1) boundary descriptions and (2) lists of cities. The boundary descriptions give points of reference between landmarks and/or cities that define the borders of a tribe. These boundary descriptions vary in the amount of detail supplied; some, like that of Judah, contain considerable detail with numerous points spaced closely together. Other descriptions are abbreviated, vague, or virtually nonexistent, for example, Issachar, East Manasseh, Gad, and Naphtali. These border descriptions were important to the life of early Israel, establishing tribal claims and settling disputes. A comparison of these allotments with the description of Canaan's borders given in Numbers 34:1–12 reveals that Judah's southern border and the southern border of Canaan were identical, while the western limits defined by the Mediterranean and the eastern border are the same. Only in the north do the two descriptions differ; neither Asher nor Naphtali claimed the more extensive lands to the north roughly defined by a line from Gebal (Byblos) through Lebo-hamath to Zedad on the desert edge north of Damascus.

Town lists provide additional information. Simeon, for example, is defined by a list of towns from within Judah. Most scholars think Simeon was soon absorbed by the stronger tribe of Judah, but others believe Simeon retained its identity into the Divided Monarchy (see 1 Chr. 4:24–41). The Transjordan tribes (Reuben, Gad, East Manasseh) are defined primarily by town lists (Josh. 13:8–33; cf. Num. 32:28–42). The town lists as we have them probably were updated periodically by royal scribes and thus reflect later administrative divisions.

LEVITICAL CITIES (SEE MAP 40)

The tribe of Levi did not receive an allotment; rather, Moses commanded that the Levites be given cities and pastureland surrounding the cities from the tribal allotments (Num. 35:2). Joshua 21 contains a list of forty-eight cities given as the inheritance of the Levites, apportioned among the three Levitical clans—the Kohathites, Gershonites, and Merarites (Josh. 21; cf. 1 Chr. 6:54–81). The cities were not exclusive to the Levites, but soon became religious and administrative centers. Several of the cities were located in regions controlled by Canaanites until the time of David. Very few Levitical cities were in the heartland of Israel—the regions of Judah, Ephraim, and Manasseh.

CITIES OF REFUGE (SEE MAP 40)

Joshua 20 designates six Levitical cities as cities of refuge. People who had unwittingly committed a homicide could flee to these cities to escape the blood avenger—a relative of the victim seeking blood vengeance (see Num. 35:9–34; the Hebrew word for blood avenger is *go'el*). The accused received asylum until a proper hearing determined his innocence of premeditated murder, but the slayer was required to remain in the city of refuge until the death of the high priest. The cities of refuge were easily accessible throughout Israel: Kedesh, Shechem, and Hebron were located west of the Jordan River, while Golan, Ramoth-gilead, and Bezer were scattered along the Transjordan.

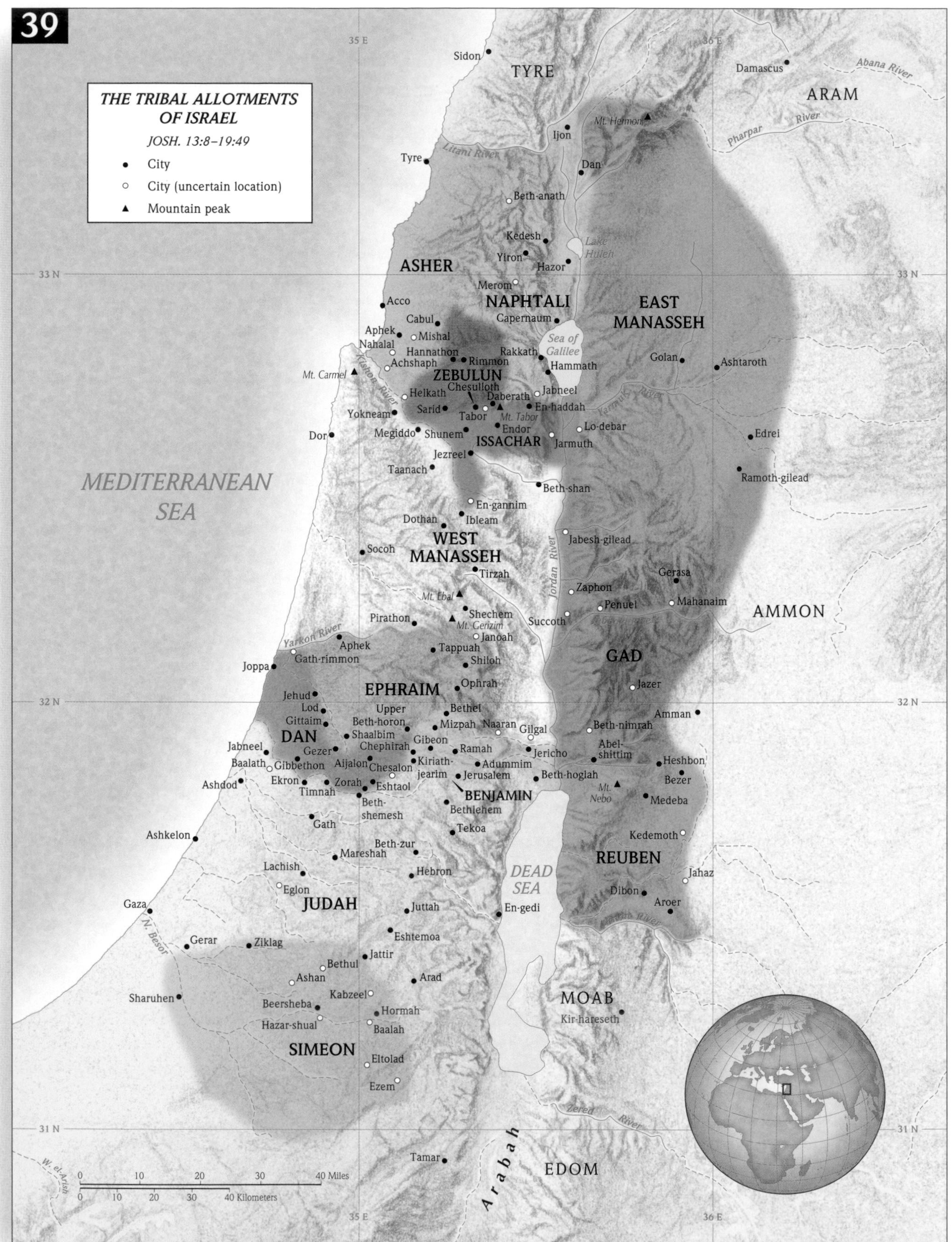
39
THE TRIBAL ALLOTMENTS OF ISRAEL
JOSH. 13:8–19:49
City
City (uncertain location)
Mountain peak
MEDITERRANEAN SEA
Sidon
TYRE
Damascus
Abana River
ARAM
Mt. Hermon
Pharpar River
Ijon
Litani River
Tyre
Dan
Beth-anath
Kedesh
Lake Huleh
Yiron
Hazor
ASHER
Merom
NAPHTALI
EAST MANASSEH
Acco
Capernaum
Cabul
Aphek
Mishal
Nahalal
Sea of Galilee
Hannathon
Rimmon
Rakkath
Golan
Ashtaroth
Achshaph
Hammath
Mt. Carmel
ZEBULUN
Kishon River
Chesulloth
Helkath
Jabneel
Daberath
Yarmuk River
Sarid
En-haddah
Yokneam
Tabor
Mt. Tabor
Lo-debar
Endor
Dor
Megiddo
Shunem
Edrei
ISSACHAR
Jarmuth
Jezreel
Taanach
Ramoth-gilead
Beth-shan
En-gannim
Ibleam
Dothan
WEST MANASSEH
Jabesh-gilead
Socoh
Jordan River
Tirzah
Gerasa
Zaphon
Mt. Ebal
Penuel
Mahanaim
Shechem
AMMON
Pirathon
Mt. Gerizim
Succoth
Janoah
Yarkon River
Aphek
Tappuah
Gath-rimmon
Shiloh
GAD
Joppa
Ophrah
EPHRAIM
Jazer
Jehud
Upper Beth-horon
Bethel
Lod
Amman
Gittaim
Mizpah
Naaran
Gilgal
Beth-nimrah
DAN
Shaalbim
Gibeon
Jabneel
Chephirah
Ramah
Abel-shittim
Gezer
Jericho
Heshbon
Baalath
Gibbethon
Aijalon
Chesalon
Kiriath-jearim
Adummim
Jerusalem
Beth-hoglah
Bezer
Ekron
Zorah
Eshtaol
Ashdod
Timnah
Mt. Nebo
BENJAMIN
Medeba
Beth-shemesh
Bethlehem
Gath
Tekoa
Ashkelon
Kedemoth
Beth-zur
Mareshah
REUBEN
DEAD SEA
Lachish
Hebron
Jahaz
Eglon
Dibon
Aroer
Gaza
JUDAH
Juttah
En-gedi
N. Besor
Eshtemoa
Gerar
Ziklag
Jattir
Bethul
Ashan
Arad
Sharuhen
Kabzeel
MOAB
Beersheba
Hormah
Kir-hareseth
Hazar-shual
Baalah
SIMEON
Eltolad
Ezem
Zered River
Tamar
Arabah
EDOM
W. el-Arish
0 10 20 30 40 Miles
0 10 20 30 40 Kilometers
35 E
36 E
33 N
32 N
31 N

THE TRIBAL ALLOTMENTS OF ISRAEL

THE TRIBES OF GALILEE: ASHER, ISSACHAR, NAPHTALI, AND ZEBULUN

ASHER (JOSH. 19:24–31)

Asher received the coastal plain north of Mount Carmel (the Plain of Acco) and the western hills of Galilee. The land was fertile, suitable to olive orchards and other agricultural products (cf. Gen. 49:20). A brief reference in Judges 5:17 associates Asher with seafaring, but the Asherites had difficulty controlling the Acco Plain. Judges 1:31 indicates that at least seven cities remained in the Canaanites' hands and the Asherites "dwelt among the Canaanites." During David's reign, Israel controlled the plain briefly, but Solomon ceded twenty cities of the plain to Hiram, king of Tyre, as payment for Tyrian craftsmen and materials used to build the temple (1 Kgs. 9:10–14).

ISSACHAR (JOSH. 19:17–23)

Issachar received as an allotment the rugged basaltic slopes of eastern Lower Galilee and a segment of the eastern Jezreel Valley. The southern border likely touched the Gilboan Mountains, while the western border extended to the Kishon River. Canaanite enclaves like Beth-shan undoubtedly were barriers to Issachar's control of the valley. The difficult terrain and lack of water sources characteristic of the high hills and descending plateaus of eastern Lower Galilee stymied settlement. This is revealed in the lack of archaeological remains in this area dating from the Late Bronze and Early Iron Ages. Issachar did contribute to Israel one judge, Tola, and two kings, Baasha and Elah (1 Kgs. 15:27; 16:8).

Mt. Tabor, in the Jezreel Valley, located where the tribal territories of Zebulun, Issachar, and Naphtali converged.

NAPHTALI (JOSH. 19:32–39)

Naphtali settled most of the mountainous, forested terrain of Galilee adjoining Asher on the west with Zebulun and Issachar to the south. Naphtali reached Mount Tabor on the edge of the Jezreel Valley. The Sea of Chinnereth and the Jordan River marked Naphtali's eastern border, but the northern boundary is not given. Perhaps the Litani River marked Naphtali's settlement northward.

The relatively unsettled uplands of Galilee and the rugged area of the Meron Mountains must have invited early Israelite settlement, although a few Canaanite cities (Beth-shemesh, Beth-anath) successfully resisted Israel's incursions in the region (Judg. 1:31).

ZEBULUN (JOSH. 19:10–16; JUDG. 1:30; DEUT. 33:18–19)

Zebulun received a small allotment located in the southwest hills of Lower Galilee that extended into the western Jezreel Valley. This land was diverse, ranging from the poorer southern flanks of the Galilean hills to the fertile expanses of the Jezreel. Most of the cities of Zebulun were located in the hills rather than the valley. Zebulun was unable to drive out the Canaanites, especially in the valley, choosing to dwell among the indigenous population and serve them (Judg. 1:30). The men of Zebulun fought valiantly alongside Issachar and Naphtali the day Deborah and Barak won a great victory at the Kishon River against the Canaanites (Judg. 4:6, 10; 5:15–18). Mount Tabor stood at the juncture of Zebulun, Issachar, and Naphtali; the three tribes probably shared a common worship place on the mountain (Deut. 33:18–19). Zebulun may have been involved in intermittent maritime trade based on the close proximity of the Plain of Acco (Gen. 49:13).

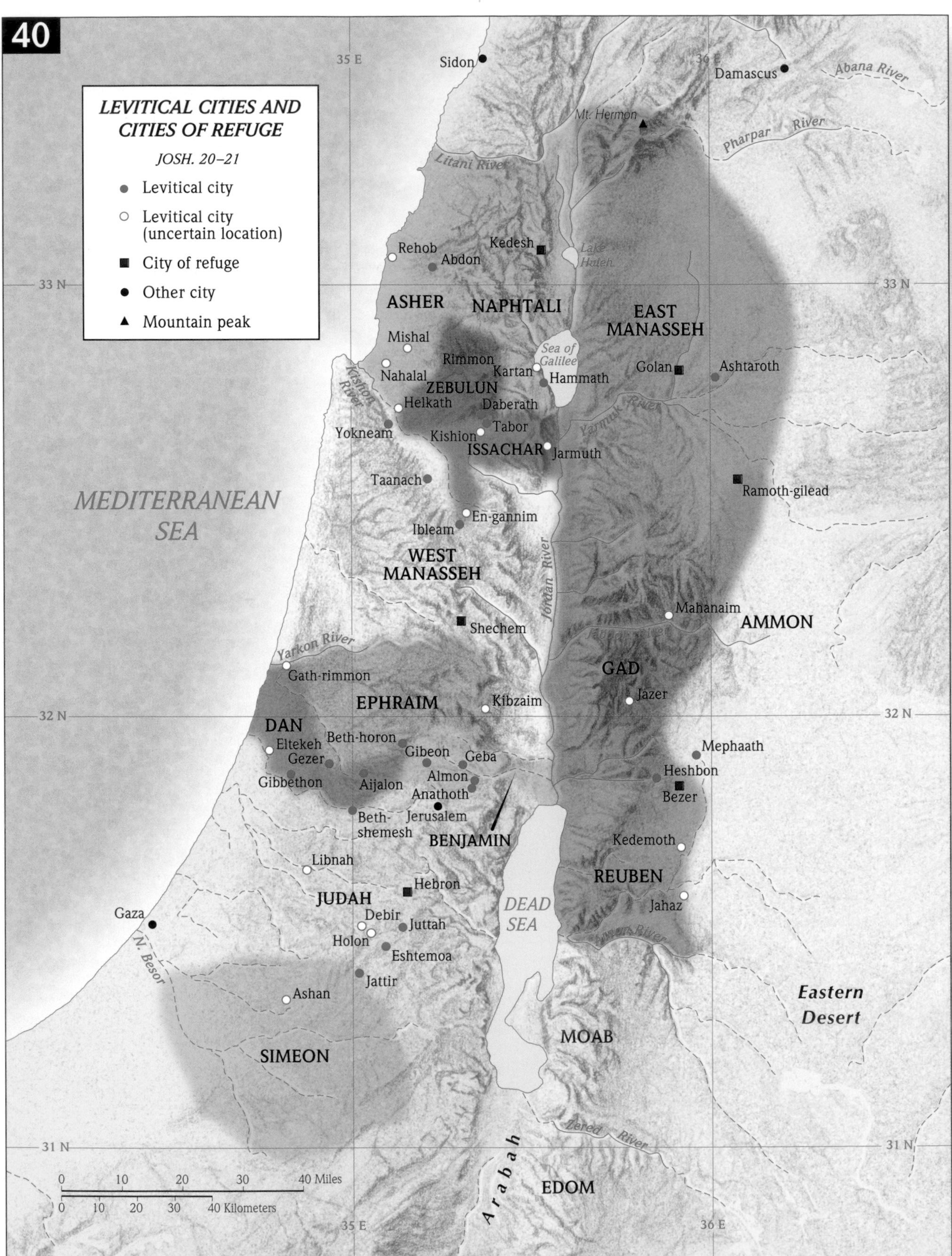
40
LEVITICAL CITIES AND CITIES OF REFUGE
JOSH. 20–21
Levitical city
Levitical city (uncertain location)
City of refuge
Other city
Mountain peak
Sidon
Damascus
Abana River
Mt. Hermon
Pharpar River
Litani River
Kedesh
Rehob
Abdon
Lake Huleh
ASHER
NAPHTALI
EAST MANASSEH
Mishal
Rimmon
Sea of Galilee
Kartan
Hammath
Golan
Ashtaroth
Nahalal
ZEBULUN
Kishon River
Helkath
Daberath
Yarmuk River
Yokneam
Kishion
Tabor
ISSACHAR
Jarmuth
Taanach
Ramoth-gilead
MEDITERRANEAN SEA
En-gannim
Ibleam
WEST MANASSEH
Jordan River
Mahanaim
AMMON
Shechem
Yarkon River
Gath-rimmon
GAD
Jazer
EPHRAIM
Kibzaim
DAN
Eltekeh
Beth-horon
Gezer
Gibeon
Geba
Mephaath
Heshbon
Gibbethon
Almon
Aijalon
Anathoth
Bezer
Beth-shemesh
Jerusalem
BENJAMIN
Kedemoth
Libnah
REUBEN
Hebron
JUDAH
DEAD SEA
Jahaz
Gaza
Debir
Juttah
Holon
Eshtemoa
N. Besor
Jattir
Ashan
Eastern Desert
MOAB
SIMEON
Zered River
Arabah
EDOM
35 E
36 E
33 N
32 N
31 N
0 10 20 30 40 Miles
0 10 20 30 40 Kilometers

THE TRANSJORDAN TRIBES: REUBEN, GAD, AND EAST MANASSEH

Israel won victories in the Transjordan over Sihon of Heshbon and Og of Bashan before crossing the Jordan River. Observing that these lands were well suited for grazing, representatives from the tribes of Gad, Reuben, and a part of Manasseh asked Moses to apportion among them the newly conquered land. Moses complied with their request, but only after receiving a promise that men from the three tribes would assist in the conquest of the lands west of the Jordan (Num. 32). Joshua 13:8–13 and Numbers 32:33–42 give brief descriptions of allotments to the Transjordan tribes. The Geshurites and Maacathites, two Aramean groups living east-northeast of the Sea of Chinnereth, were not dislodged by the tribes.

REUBEN (NUM. 32:27–38; JOSH. 13:15–23)

Reuben took the "tableland" (Heb. *mishor*) that stretched northward from the Arnon Gorge to the vicinity of Heshbon. The land was more fertile and less rugged than the territory south of the Arnon. The Moabites, who lived south of the Arnon, coveted the *mishor* and often clashed with Israel over territorial rights in the region. The fertile tableland was suitable to sheep grazing and wheat and barley crops. Heshbon, Dibon, and Medeba were the chief cities of this region. According to lists in Numbers and Joshua, the Gadites built (and presumably lived in) several cities in the allotment of Reuben (Num. 32:34–35).

GAD (NUM. 32:34–36; JOSH. 13:24–28)

The tribe of Gad occupied choice pastoral lands in Gilead east of the Jordan (cf. Deut. 33:20–21). Gad's borders are difficult to define precisely; the majority of her territory extended from near Heshbon northward to the Jabbok River. The Ammonite kingdom adjoined Gad on the east. The boundary descriptions indicate Gad controlled a narrow corridor of land extending northward from the Jabbok to the Sea of Chinnereth. The rugged western slopes of the Transjordan Plateau were densely forested, especially north of the Jabbok. Gad was subject to frequent raids from the Ammonites, Moabites, and several desert tribes, a fact echoed in "The Blessing of Jacob" (Gen. 49:19). Mahanaim, located on the northern bank of the Jabbok, was a key Gadite city on the border with East Manasseh (Josh. 13:26; 21:38). Along with the other Transjordan tribes, the Gadites were noted warriors (Deut. 33:20; 1 Chr. 5:18; 12:8).

EAST MANASSEH (NUM. 32:39–42; JOSH. 13:29–32)

The half-tribe of Manasseh settled the Gilead mountains north of the Jabbok River. Machir, eldest son of Manasseh, described as the "father of Gilead" (Num. 26:29), dispersed the Amorites living in the region (Num. 32:39). East Manasseh included parts of the Bashan north of the Yarmuk and east of the Sea of Chinnereth, but the precise limits of the northern and eastern boundaries of the tribe's holdings are not known. East Manasseh was exposed to intense Aramean pressure, especially from Damascus.

THE JOSEPH TRIBES: EPHRAIM AND WEST MANASSEH

The blessings of Jacob and Moses indicate the privileged positions and strength of the two most important northern tribes, Ephraim and Manasseh (Gen. 49:22–26; Deut. 33:13–17). Descended from the two sons of Joseph, Ephraim and Manasseh settled the central mountains south of the Jezreel Valley to the "Saddle of Benjamin," a region sparsely populated in the Late Bronze Age (1550–1200 B.C.). This territory was heavily forested when the tribes entered the land (Josh. 17:14–18). The allotments included sections of the coastal plain south of Mount Carmel, but neither Ephraim nor Manasseh successfully controlled the coastal regions for lengthy periods.

EPHRAIM (JOSH. 16:5–10)

Jacob favored the younger Ephraim over the elder Manasseh, foreshadowing the eventual prominence of the tribe of Ephraim (Gen. 48:8–20). Joshua allotted Ephraim the isolated, higher mountain plateau south of Shechem reaching to Bethel. Unlike Judah, Ephraim has no clear watershed; the land broadens in a rugged mountainous plateau not easily accessible from either east or west. However, Ephraim was an agriculturally fertile region known for its vineyards and orchards (Deut. 33:13–17; Gen. 49:22–26). Bethel and Shiloh were two of the significant towns of Ephraim.

WEST MANASSEH (JOSH. 17:1–13)

The half-tribe of Manasseh settled the densely forested land north of Ephraim up to the Jezreel Valley. Initially, Manasseh could not dislodge the Canaanites from the valley and the coasts, leaving such key cities as Beth-shan, Taanach, Dor, and Megiddo in Canaanite hands until the time of David (Judg. 1:27–28). The core of Manasseh was in the hills of the highlands south of the Jezreel Valley. Important wadis (e.g., Wadi Farah) from the west and east made access easy into Manasseh's heartland, which included such cities as Shechem, Dothan, and Bezek. The capital cities of the Northern Kingdom Israel (Shechem, Tirzah, and Samaria) all were located in Manasseh. The International Coastal Highway passed along Manasseh's western edge. Like Ephraim, this region was fertile, blessed with agricultural abundance.

THE SOUTHERN TRIBES: BENJAMIN, JUDAH, AND SIMEON

BENJAMIN (JOSH. 18:11–28 [CF. JOSH. 15:5–11; 16:1–3, 5])

Benjamin received a small, but strategic, allotment located between two powerful neighboring tribes, Ephraim and Judah. Benjamin's territory centered on a depression or "saddle" that begins south of Bethel and continues to Jerusalem. The land is fertile and reasonably well watered except along the eastern edge.

The region of Benjamin viewed from Gibeon.

Benjamin controlled important routes. The main north-south route of the Western Highlands—the "Ridge Road" that ran along the crest of the mountains—ran through Benjamin. A major east-west route connecting the coastal plain with the Transjordan crossed Benjamite territory. Gibeon, Bethel, Mizpah, and Jericho were Benjamite towns. Jerusalem is included in the city list of Benjamin, although later the city became the captial of Judah. The Benjamites were renown warriors, noted for their abilities with a sling (Judg. 20:15–17; Gen. 49:27). Benjamin's tribal sympathies lay with her northern neighbors, Ephraim and Manasseh. Saul, the first king, came from Benjamin, and Benjamin followed the leadership of Saul's son Ish-Bosheth (Esh-Baal) rather than David, the southerner from Judah (2 Sam. 2:8–10).

JUDAH (JOSH. 15:1–63; JUDG. 1:8–18)

Joshua 15 gives an extensive list of Judah's allotment, perhaps hinting at the author's interest in this important tribe that formed the nucleus of the southern kingdom and produced the Davidic dynasty. Judah occupied the southern part of the western highlands. Protected on all sides except the north by major geographical obstacles, Judah was isolated from international connections. To the west, the Shephelah guarded the main approaches to Judah's key cities. Judah at times controlled the Shephelah, but seldom held sway over the coastal plains. Wilderness regions gave Judah protection from the east and south. The numerous cities listed for Judah are divided into four groups: the Negeb, the Shephelah, the central ridge, and the eastern desert. These divisions and other subdivisions in the list may reflect administrative alignments from later periods. Lachish, Hebron, Bethlehem, and En-gedi are among the towns and villages of Judah that play key historical roles. "The Blessing of Jacob" foreshadows the Davidic kings that would come from Judah. The blessing also emphasizes the importance of herds and vineyards in this rugged region (Gen. 49:10–12). Judges 1:3–18 narrates the struggles of Judah and Simeon to take this territory, including an abortive attempt to gain control of Jerusalem. Several portions of southern Judah were assigned to various clans including the Kenites (the area around Arad), Calebites (the region of Hebron), and Kenazzites (the area around Debir).

SIMEON (JOSH. 19:1–9)

Simeon and Levi are paired in "The Blessings of Jacob" where they are condemned for their violent ways (Gen. 49:5–7), including a probable allusion to an attack on Shechem avenging the rape of Dinah (Gen. 34). A list of seventeen cities, mostly clustering in the western Negeb, defines Simeon's allotment within the territory of Judah. Many scholars suggest that the tribe of Simeon lost its identity, perhaps because of violent tendencies, and was absorbed by Judah. Simeon is not mentioned in other important blessings or lists, including "The Blessings of Moses" in Deuteronomy 33.

THE MIGRANT TRIBE: DAN (JOSH. 19:40–48; JUDG. 17–18)

Dan's original allotment touched the western slopes of the central mountains down through the Shephelah along the Sorek Valley and turned northward to the Kanah River (Yarkon River) along the coast. An enigmatic reference to Dan in the Song of Deborah may recall an earlier period when the tribe of Dan occupied at least some of their allotted territory along the coast (Judg. 5:17). Other villages and towns of this original allotment include Zorah, Timnah, and Ekron—all towns mentioned in the Samson stories.

However, Amorite and Philistine pressure eventually forced the Danites to seek new territory. Judges 17–18 narrates the migration of Dan northward where a small contingent of men captured Laish (Leshem), an ancient Canaanite city on the northern edge of the Huleh Basin. Renaming the city in honor of their eponymous ancestor, the Danites established a place of worship supervised by a Levitical priesthood at Dan.

"The Blessings of Moses" recognized the military abilities of Dan (Deut. 33:22), a characteristic perhaps reflected in "The Blessings of Jacob" as well (Gen. 49:16–17). But the latter text hints at treachery on the part of Dan: "Dan shall be a serpent in the way, a viper by the path, that bites the horse's heels so that his rider falls backward" (Gen. 49:17). Later, Dan became the center of pagan worship when Jeroboam II erected a golden bull in his new national shrine.

The Days of the Judges

The foothold gained by Israel through Joshua's victories was tested in the period of the Judges. The tribes of Israel faced pressure from various groups competing for a share of Canaan. Canaanite city-states tenaciously clung to their territories and were a constant threat to Israel. The Philistines arrived in the southern coastal plain by 1150 B.C. and quickly established themselves in five cities—Gaza, Ashdod, Gath, Ashkelon, and Ekron. Ammon, Moab, and Edom continued to press their claims to the Transjordan. Moreover, desert marauders like the Amalekites and Midianites periodically harassed the settled population, striking unsuspecting villages and towns quickly using the camel. Israel found herself surrounded by peoples seeking to expand their territorial advantage. With no king to lead them, the tribes were hard-pressed to match the strength of their more established neighbors.

But an even greater threat to Israel than hostile neighbors emerged: Canaanite religion. Despite Yahweh's command to drive out the Canaanites, Israel settled among them, adopting

CHART 7: THE JUDGES OF ISRAEL

JUDGE	YEARS OF SERVICE	OPPRESSOR	YEARS OF OPPRESSION	YEARS OF PEACE	BIBLICAL REFERENCE IN JUDGES	PROVINCE OR TRIBAL AFFILIATION
Othniel		Cushan-rishathaim (King of Aram naharim?) Aramean King?	8	40	3:8–11	Judah
Ehud		Eglon, King of Moab	18	80	3:12–30	Benjamin
Shamgar		Philistines			3:31	Son of Anath; possibly a non-Israelite
Deborah with Barak		Canaanites led by Jabin and Sisera	20		4:1–5:31	Issachar? Ephraim? Barak came from Naphtali
Gideon		Midianites and Amalekites	7	40	6:1–8:27	Manasseh
Tola	23				10:1–2	Issachar
Jair				22	10:3–5	Gileadite; East Manasseh?
Jephthah	6	Ammonites and Philistines	18		10:6–12:7	Gileadite; East Manasseh?
Ibzan	7				12:8–10	From Bethlehem: most likely in Judah, but possibly in Zebulun
Elon	10				12:11–12	Zebulun
Abdon	8				12:13–15	Pirathonite (Ephraim)
Samson	20	Philistines	40		13–16	Dan

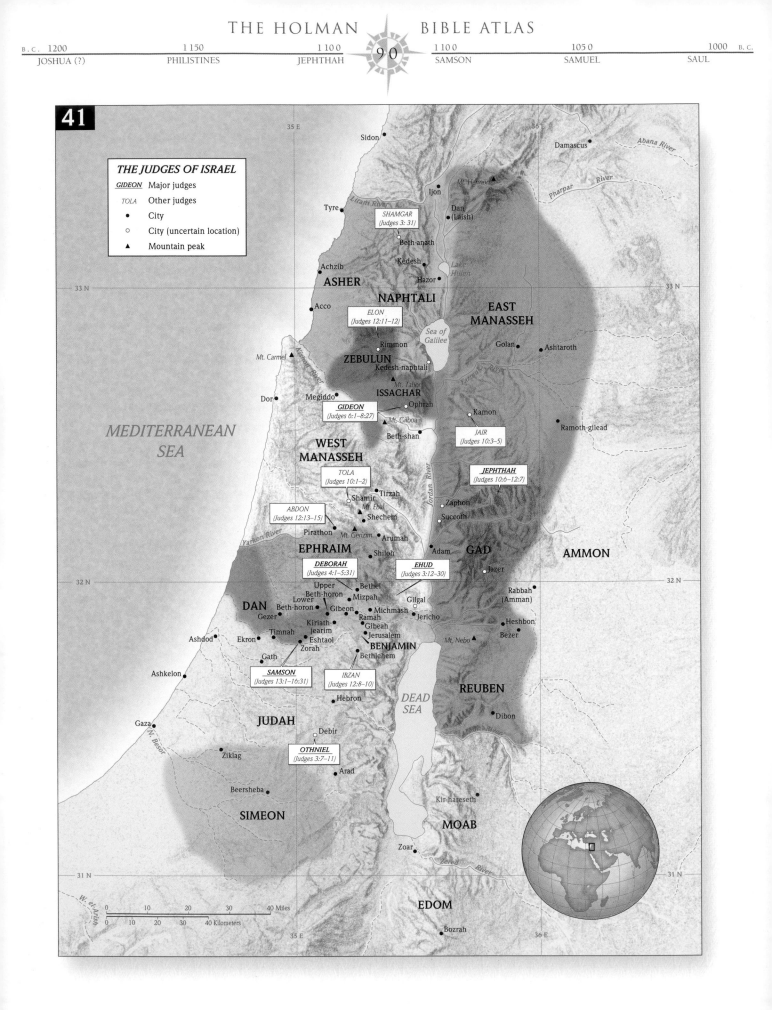

41
THE JUDGES OF ISRAEL
GIDEON Major judges
TOLA Other judges
City
City (uncertain location)
Mountain peak
MEDITERRANEAN SEA
ASHER
NAPHTALI
EAST MANASSEH
ZEBULUN
ISSACHAR
WEST MANASSEH
EPHRAIM
DAN
BENJAMIN
JUDAH
SIMEON
GAD
AMMON
REUBEN
MOAB
EDOM
DEAD SEA
Sea of Galilee
Lake Huleh
SHAMGAR (Judges 3:31)
ELON (Judges 12:11–12)
GIDEON (Judges 6:1–8:27)
JAIR (Judges 10:3–5)
TOLA (Judges 10:1–2)
JEPHTHAH (Judges 10:6–12:7)
ABDON (Judges 12:13–15)
DEBORAH (Judges 4:1–5:31)
EHUD (Judges 3:12–30)
SAMSON (Judges 13:1–16:31)
IBZAN (Judges 12:8–10)
OTHNIEL (Judges 3:7–11)
Sidon
Damascus
Abana River
Pharpar River
Mt. Hermon
Ijon
Tyre
Litani River
Dan (Laish)
Beth-anath
Kedesh
Achzib
Hazor
Acco
Rimmon
Golan
Ashtaroth
Mt. Carmel
Kishon River
Kedesh-naphtali
Mt. Tabor
Yarmuk River
Dor
Megiddo
Ophrah
Kamon
Mt. Gilboa
Beth-shan
Ramoth-gilead
Jordan River
Tirzah
Shamir
Mt. Ebal
Zaphon
Shechem
Succoth
Yarkon River
Pirathon
Mt. Gerizim
Arumah
Adam
Shiloh
Jazer
Upper Beth-horon
Bethel
Rabbah (Amman)
Lower Beth-horon
Mizpah
Gilgal
Gezer
Gibeon
Michmash
Ramah
Jericho
Kiriath-jearim
Gibeah
Heshbon
Ashdod
Ekron
Timnah
Eshtaol
Jerusalem
Bezer
Zorah
Mt. Nebo
Gath
Bethlehem
Ashkelon
Hebron
Dibon
Gaza
N. Besor
Debir
Ziklag
Arad
Beersheba
Kir-hareseth
Zoar
Zered River
Bozrah
W. el-Arish
35 E
36 E
33 N
32 N
31 N
0 10 20 30 40 Miles
0 10 20 30 40 Kilometers

CANAANITE RELIGION

Israel faced a constant battle with Canaanite religion from the time she entered the promised land until the Exile (ca. 586 B.C.). Canaanite polytheism contrasted sharply with the austere monotheism demanded by the Hebrew prophets. Baalism, the religion of Canaan, appealed to the Israelites as they settled into Canaan partly because the Canaanite religious tradition shared several features in common with Israelite worship practices, including a sacrificial system, the celebration of certain agricultural and pastoral feasts, and several similar religious motifs. The "Baal Epics" found in the Late Bronze Age city of Ugarit (Ras Shamrah on the Syrian coast) have greatly increased our understanding of Baalism.

Baalism flourished in the Levant where life depended upon the rains that nourished land, crops, and herds. Unlike Egypt and Mesopotamia, people living in the Levant had no large rivers to irrigate the land in the absence of adequate rainfall. The Canaanites worshiped many gods and goddesses upon whose powers life was thought to depend. From the vast number of names of Canaanite deities known to us, a few stand out. El, a name that means "god," was the head of the Canaanite pantheon. His home was on Mount Zaphon. As the creator god, El fathered seventy deities by his wife Asherah, who bore the title "mother of the gods." The plural of El is Elohim, one of the two names used in the Old Testament for the God of Israel.

The most important god worshiped in Canaan, however, was Baal, a title originally meaning "Lord" or "Master." Baal was the lord of the earth whose powers gave life to the earth. Frequently identified with the West Semitic storm god Hadad, Baal brought the rains that revitalized the land parched by the long summer drought. Baal's symbol was the bull, but he could also be depicted in human form standing on a cloud holding an object (perhaps a club or a thunderbolt) in his upraised hand.

The bull symbolized strength, power, and fertility. Several bull figurines have been recovered from Iron Age sites in Palestine, including a small bronze figure from the hills of Samaria and a silver calf from Ashkelon. Although the bull stood for El as well as Baal, these figurines likely indicate the prevalence of Baal's cult throughout Palestine. The Bible uses the plural form of Baal—Baalim—to identify the numerous local manifestations of this Canaanite god. A city, village, hill, or valley might have its own "Baal." For example, Baal Melqart was the chief god of Tyre, imported into Israel by Jezebel.

A representation of the god Baal on a relief from Ugarit.

The Ugaritic Texts describe Baal's battles with Yamm and Mot. Yamm, "Prince of the Sea," represented the chaotic forces that threatened to overwhelm life or disrupt the order upon which life depends. Mot ruled the underworld and sought to destroy Baal. Mot, whose name means "death" in Hebrew, captured and slew Baal. Baal's consort Anath fought Mot on behalf of Baal and secured Baal's return from the powerful clutches of Mot. This struggle between Baal and Mot has been variously interpreted, but the main point illustrates the delicate balance between feast and famine, life and death, found in cultures where life depends on rainfall. In the contest between Elijah and the prophets of Baal, the question was: Who brings the rain that gives life to the land? (1 Kgs. 18).

Asherah, a goddess widely worshiped in Palestine, plays a prominent role in the Bible. Texts refer to shrines and altars dedicated to Asherah at Samaria, Bethel, and Jerusalem (1 Kgs. 14:23; 16:33; 2 Kings 23:4). Asherah was symbolized at high places by a wooden cultic object, possibly a carved wood pole. The Old Testament repeatedly condemns these Asherim (plural of Asherah), which were cut down and burned in periods of religious reform (2 Kgs. 18:4; 2 Chr. 31:1; 34:3).

Fertility aspects of Canaanite religion appealed to Israel also. The Canaanites practiced both male and female sacred prostitution, a rite adopted also by Israel (Hos. 4:10–14; 2 Kings 23:7). Figurines of nude females, often accentuating the breasts, are frequently found in excavations in Israel. They may represent Asherah or Astarte, two well-known manifestations of fertility goddesses. The function of the figurines has been debated; perhaps they functioned as amulets used by women during times of childbearing or lactation, or, alternatively, the eroticism of the images suggests the fertility cult.

Popular religion in Israel "Baalized" the worship of Yahweh by combining elements of pagan worship with the worship of Yahweh. The prophets of Israel repeatedly condemned both the theology and practice associated with the worship of Baal in Israel and Judah (Hos. 4:11–19; 9:10–14; Jer. 7:8–9; 11:13; 19:1–9; cf. 1 Kgs. 18; 2 Kgs. 10:18–31). Hosea directly challenged the popular belief among Israelites that Baal provided the food, drink, and clothing upon which life depended (Hos. 2:5–13). How far this popular religion went in syncretizing the worship of Yahweh and Baal may be suggested by inscriptions from Kuntillet ʻAjrud near Kadesh-barnea. The inscriptions mention Yahweh, Baal, El, and Asherah. One inscription uses the phrase "Yahweh of Samaria and his Asherah." Although the interpretation of this inscription is controversial, the phrase "his Asherah" could refer either to the goddess herself or to a wooden carved pole representing Asherah. We cannot determine who wrote these inscriptions—Phoenicians, Judeans, Israelites, or some other group—but they clearly reflect the syncretistic religious environment of southern Palestine between 900 and 700 B.C.

At times the battle between Baalism and the worship of Yahweh was sharply pitched. Jezebel tried to root out the worship of Yahweh in favor of the Tyrian Baal Melqart. The prophet Elijah strongly opposed these efforts, ultimately challenging the prophets of Baal to a contest on Mount Carmel: "How long will you go limping with two different opinions? If the LORD is God, follow him; but if Baal, then follow him" (1 Kgs. 18:21).

pagan ideas and customs (Judg.3:5–6). Canaanite worship practices proliferated as Israel adapted to a more settled life and "served the Baals" (Judg. 2:11; 6:25–32; see p. 91 "Canaanite Religion"). The rape of the Levite's concubine recorded in Judges 19 epitomized the moral decay of this dark and dangerous era.

THE JUDGES AND THE OPPRESSORS OF ISRAEL (SEE MAP 41)

According to the Book of Judges, God sent oppressors against Israel to punish the people's sin and correct their behavior. Drawn from the peoples surrounding Israel, these oppressors represented three distinct groups: (1) the native population of Canaan (Canaanites), (2) recently settled peoples (the Philistines, Moabites, and Ammonites), and (3) seminomadic tribal groups who inhabited the desert fringe (Midianites and Amalekites). Generally, the oppressors afflicted tribes living in close proximity, rather than all of Israel.

God raised up judges to deliver the repentant tribes from the oppressors. Othniel, Ehud, Deborah, Gideon, Jephthah, and Samson were the major judges, although the Bible contains brief mention of six other "minor" judges (see chart "The Judges of Israel" p. 89). Empowered by the Spirit of Yahweh that descended upon them, the judges furnished military leadership against Israel's enemies. The judges came from different tribes and possessed diverse backgrounds. Normally the individual judge came from the area of each local oppression.

Ehud. The Benjamite Ehud foiled an eighteen-year oppression imposed by Eglon, king of Moab (Judg. 3:12–30). Assisted by Amalekites and Ammonites, the Moabites exerted pressure against Israel, reclaiming the territory north of the Arnon and extending their control across the Jordan. They captured Jericho, "the city of the Palms" (cf. Deut. 34:3) and collected taxes from the citizens of Benjamin. In a daring move, Ehud assassinated Eglon and rallied the Benjamites, who drove the Moabites back beyond the Jordan.

Deborah and Barak. In the period of the judges, the Canaanites maintained control of the valleys and plains

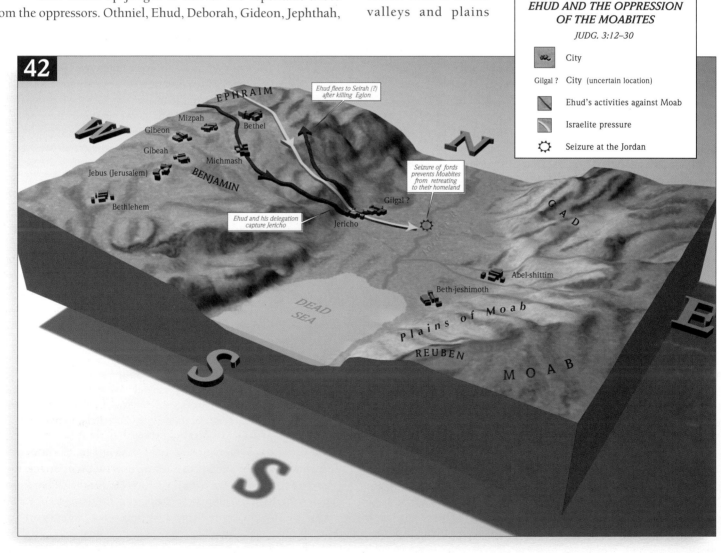

EHUD AND THE OPPRESSION OF THE MOABITES
JUDG. 3:12–30

City
Gilgal ? City (uncertain location)
Ehud's activities against Moab
Israelite pressure
Seizure at the Jordan

42

EPHRAIM
Ehud flees to Seirah (?) after killing Eglon
Mizpah
Gibeon
Bethel
Gibeah
Michmash
Jebus (Jerusalem)
BENJAMIN
Bethlehem
Seizure of fords prevents Moabites from retreating to their homeland
Gilgal ?
Ehud and his delegation capture Jericho
Jericho
GAD
Abel-shittim
Beth-jeshimoth
DEAD SEA
Plains of Moab
REUBEN
MOAB

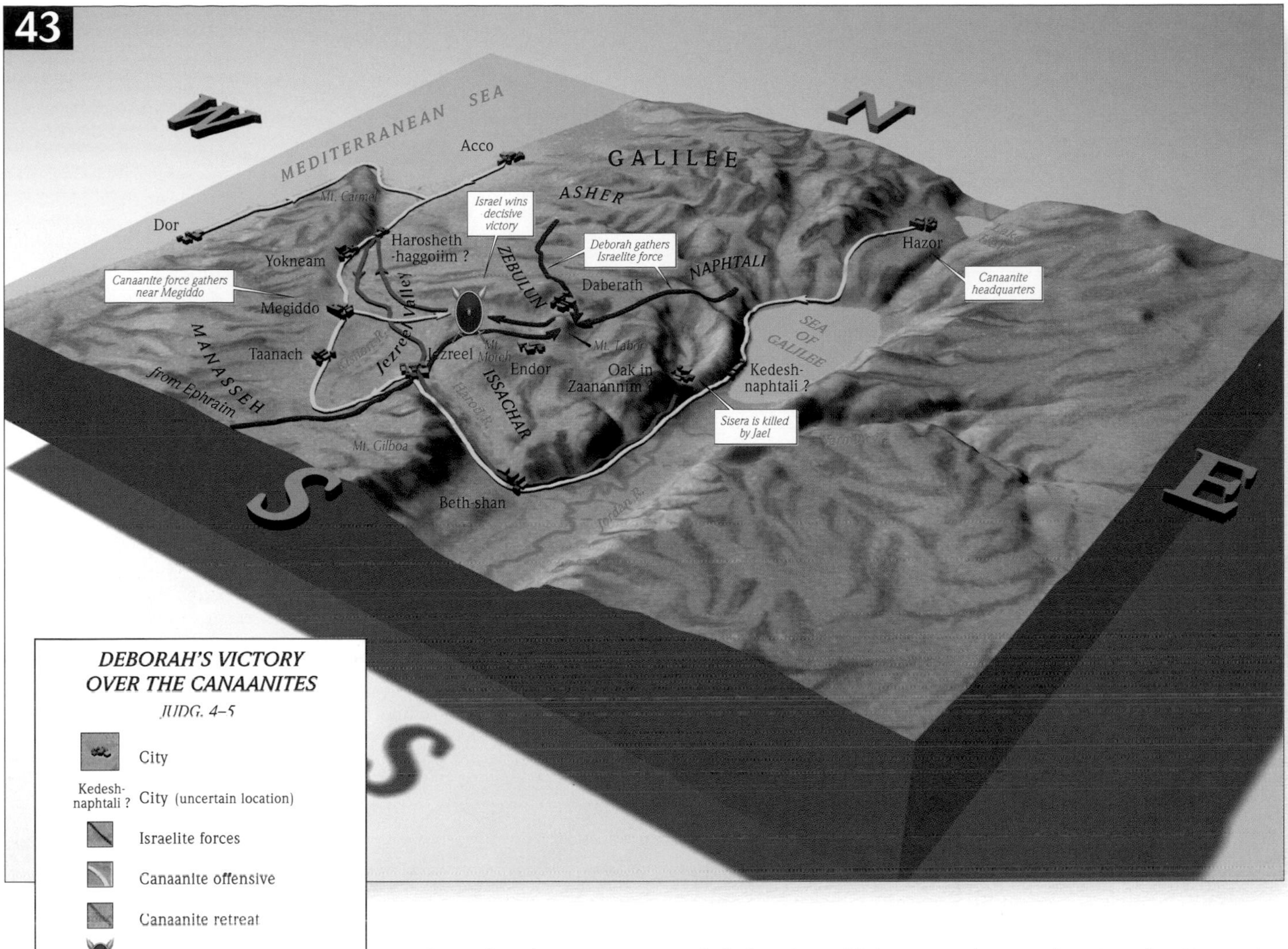

43

DEBORAH'S VICTORY OVER THE CANAANITES

JUDG. 4–5

City

Kedesh-naphtali ? City (uncertain location)

Israelite forces

Canaanite offensive

Canaanite retreat

Battle

where the chariot gave them a decisive advantage against Israel. Canaanite pressure thwarted Israel's attempt to expand beyond the hills into the lowlands. On one occasion, however, Israel won a great victory in the Jezreel Valley against Canaanite forces led by Sisera, the commander of the army of Jabin, king of Hazor. The prophetess Deborah, who judged Israel under a palm tree near Bethel, summoned Barak from Kadesh in Naphtali and charged him to gather the men of Naphtali and Zebulun on Mount Tabor. Contingents from Issachar, Ephraim, Benjamin, and Machir also rallied to Deborah's call.

To meet this provocation, Sisera moved his chariot corps from his base at Harosheth ha-goiim to the Wadi Kishon below Mount Tabor where the chariots would be most effective. At Deborah's command Barak attacked, routing the Canaanites below. Swollen by recent rains, the Kishon River rendered the chariots useless (Judg. 5:20–21). The Canaanite army perished in retreat, while Sisera escaped to the camp of Heber the Kenite at Elon-bezaananim (oak in Zaanannim) east of Mount Tabor. Jael, Heber's wife, killed Sisera by driving a tent-peg through his head while he slept. This great victory—beating the Canaanites on their own turf—was celebrated in an early Israelite poem, "The Song of Deborah" (Judg. 5).

Gideon. Gideon delivered the tribes of Israel from the scourge of seminomadic raiders who pillaged the land at harvesttime (Judg. 6–8). The Midianites and Amalekites appeared out of the deserts like a plague of locusts, encamping in the fields of ripening grain and devouring the land's produce. Using the camel, these invaders moved quickly and retreated into the deserts before organized pursuit could follow. Seven years of oppression left the tribes in the area destitute.

To relieve the oppression, God selected Gideon, a man of the Abiezerite clan from the village of Ophrah. Gideon's army came from the tribes of Asher, Manasseh, Zebulun, and Naphtali. With three hundred men selected at the Spring of Harod in the Jezreel Valley, Gideon carried out a surprise night attack on the Midianites camped near Endor (cf. Ps. 83:9–11). Blaring trumpets and lighted torches struck fear in the hearts of the invaders who fled southeastward, seeking the safety of the desert. Ephraimites cut off their escape route by seizing the Jordan Fords at Beth-barah, where Oreb and Zeeb, two Midianite chieftains,

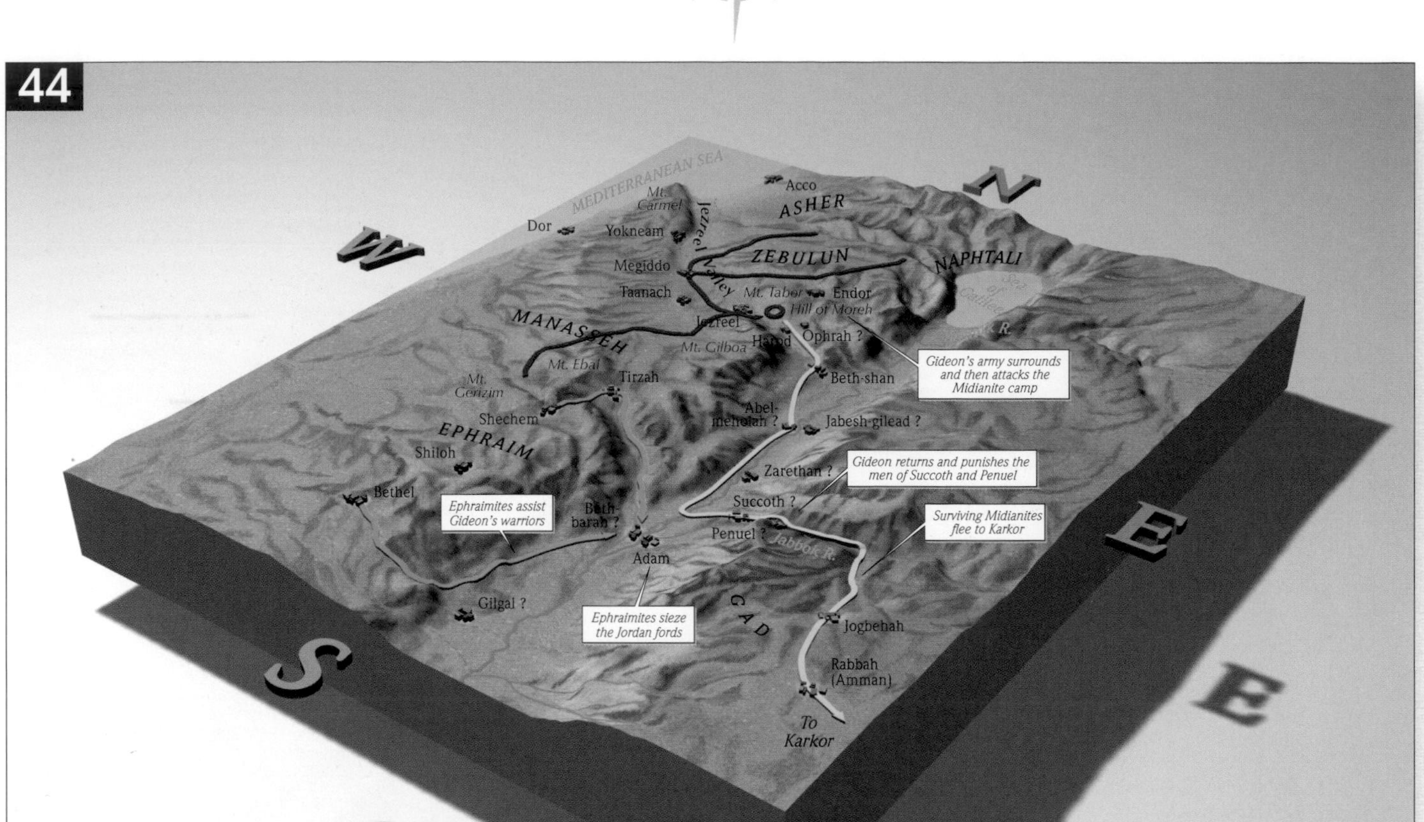

GIDEON'S BATTLES WITH THE AMALEKITES

JUDG. 6–8

City

Penuel ? City (uncertain location)

The gathering of Gideon's army

Midianite retreat

Ephraimite assistance

were captured. Gideon and his men pursued their foe across the Jordan River, passing through Succoth and Penuel along the Wadi Jabbok. Taking a caravan route eastward into the desert, Gideon surprised the Midianites again at the Oasis of Karkor in the Wadi Sirhan. After the victories, the grateful tribal elders asked Gideon to be their king, but Gideon refused, believing that only Yahweh had the right to rule Israel (Judg. 8:22–23).

Jephthah (see map 45). The Ammonites oppressed the tribes of Gilead for eighteen years before Jephthah defeated them (Judg. 10:6–12:7). Like Moab, the Ammonites contested Israel's claims in the Transjordan. From their stronghold Rabbah (modern Amman, Jordan), the Ammonites harassed the tribes of Gilead and periodically raided across the Jordan into Judah, Benjamin, and Ephraim. The elders of Gilead turned to Jephthah, a rogue outcast, for help. Jephthah defeated the Ammonites at Mizpah in Gilead; subsequently he conquered twenty towns from Aroer to Abel-keramim, west and south of Rabbah (Judg. 11:32–33). When the men of Ephraim protested Gilead's leadership in the war against Ammon, Jephthah fought and defeated the Ephraimites near Adam at the fords of the Jordan (Judg. 12:1–6).

The Philistine Menace

The Philistines posed the most persistent threat to Israel throughout the period of the judges. These fierce warriors first appeared among the Sea Peoples who attempted to invade Egypt during the reign of Rameses III. Thwarted in their assault upon the Egyptian Delta, the Philistines retreated to the southern coast of Canaan where they settled.

By the early twelfth century, 1175 to 1150 B.C., the Philistines had staked their claim in Canaan by occupying Gaza, Ashdod, and Askelon—key cities along the International Coastal Highway. They rapidly pressed inland, establishing themselves at Ekron (Tell Miqneh) and Gath (Tell es-Safi?) on the edge of the Shephelah. These five cities comprised the Philistine Pentapolis ("five city-states") that represented the core of Philistine power. Each city-state was ruled by a "Lord" (1 Sam. 5:8).

Other smaller towns and villages of the southern coastal

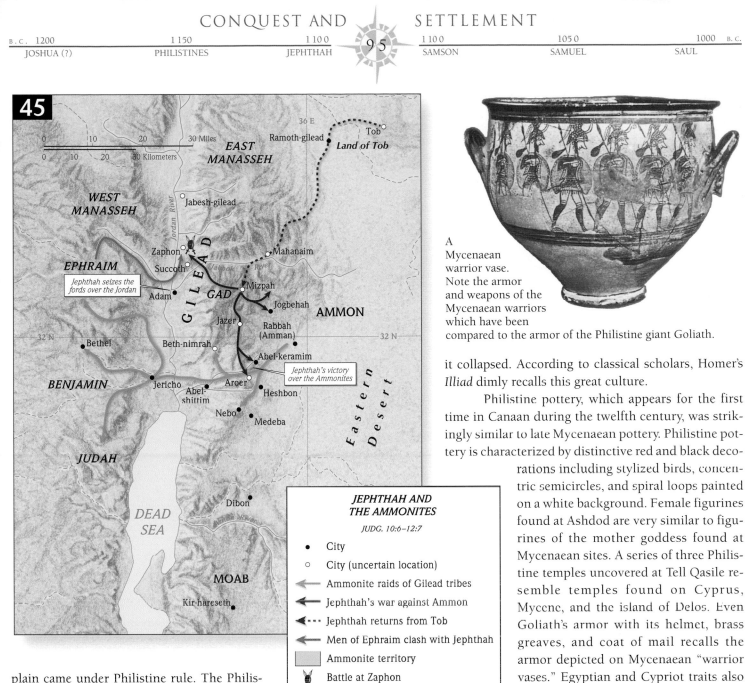

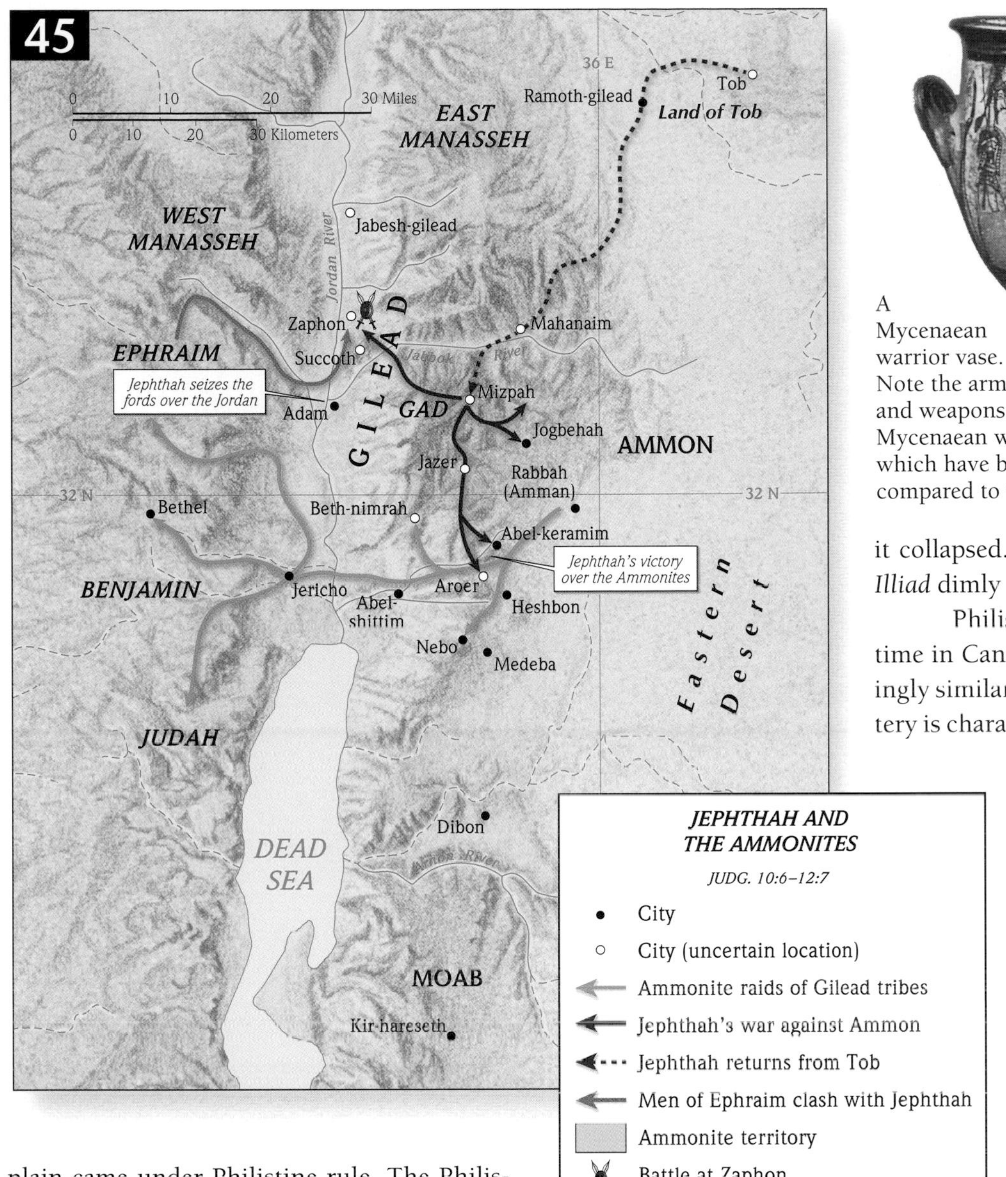

A Mycenaean warrior vase. Note the armor and weapons of the Mycenaean warriors which have been compared to the armor of the Philistine giant Goliath.

plain came under Philistine rule. The Philistines built a few new cities such as Tell Qasile, a port located on the Yarkon River founded in the early twelfth century, whose Philistine name remains unknown. From their base in the southern coastal plain, the Philistines threatened the tribal allotments of Judah and Dan.

PHILISTINE ORIGINS AND CULTURE

The Bible traces the Philistines to Caphtor, plausibly identified with the island of Crete. The term *Cherethites*, or "Cretans," is used synonymously with Philistines in a few passages (Zeph. 2:5; Ezek. 25:16). The Sea People reliefs at Medinet Habu and recent archaeological excavations have provided a clearer picture of the Philistines than ever before. Several elements of their material culture strongly suggest Aegean influence, specifically the Mycenaean culture. The Mycenaean civilization flourished on mainland Greece until shortly after 1200 B.C. when it collapsed. According to classical scholars, Homer's *Illiad* dimly recalls this great culture.

Philistine pottery, which appears for the first time in Canaan during the twelfth century, was strikingly similar to late Mycenaean pottery. Philistine pottery is characterized by distinctive red and black decorations including stylized birds, concentric semicircles, and spiral loops painted on a white background. Female figurines found at Ashdod are very similar to figurines of the mother goddess found at Mycenaean sites. A series of three Philistine temples uncovered at Tell Qasile resemble temples found on Cyprus, Mycene, and the island of Delos. Even Goliath's armor with its helmet, brass greaves, and coat of mail recalls the armor depicted on Mycenaean "warrior vases." Egyptian and Cypriot traits also appear in early Philistine material remains.

However, the Philistines rapidly assimilated the Canaanite culture of Palestine. Their distinctive pottery gradually becomes indistinguishable from Canaanite pottery. The Philistine gods and goddesses known to us in the Bible are Canaanite. Dagon, the principal Philistine deity, had temples at Gaza and Ashdod; Ekron boasted of a temple dedicated to Baal-zebub (2 Kgs. 1:2). The goddess Ashtoreth was worshiped at Beth-shan (1 Sam. 31:10).

SAMSON AND THE PHILISTINES

As the Philistines expanded their territory into the Shephelah, conflict with Israel was inevitable. The tribes of Dan and Judah claimed portions of these rolling hills and the strategic wadis that led up into the heart of Judah. The Samson stories

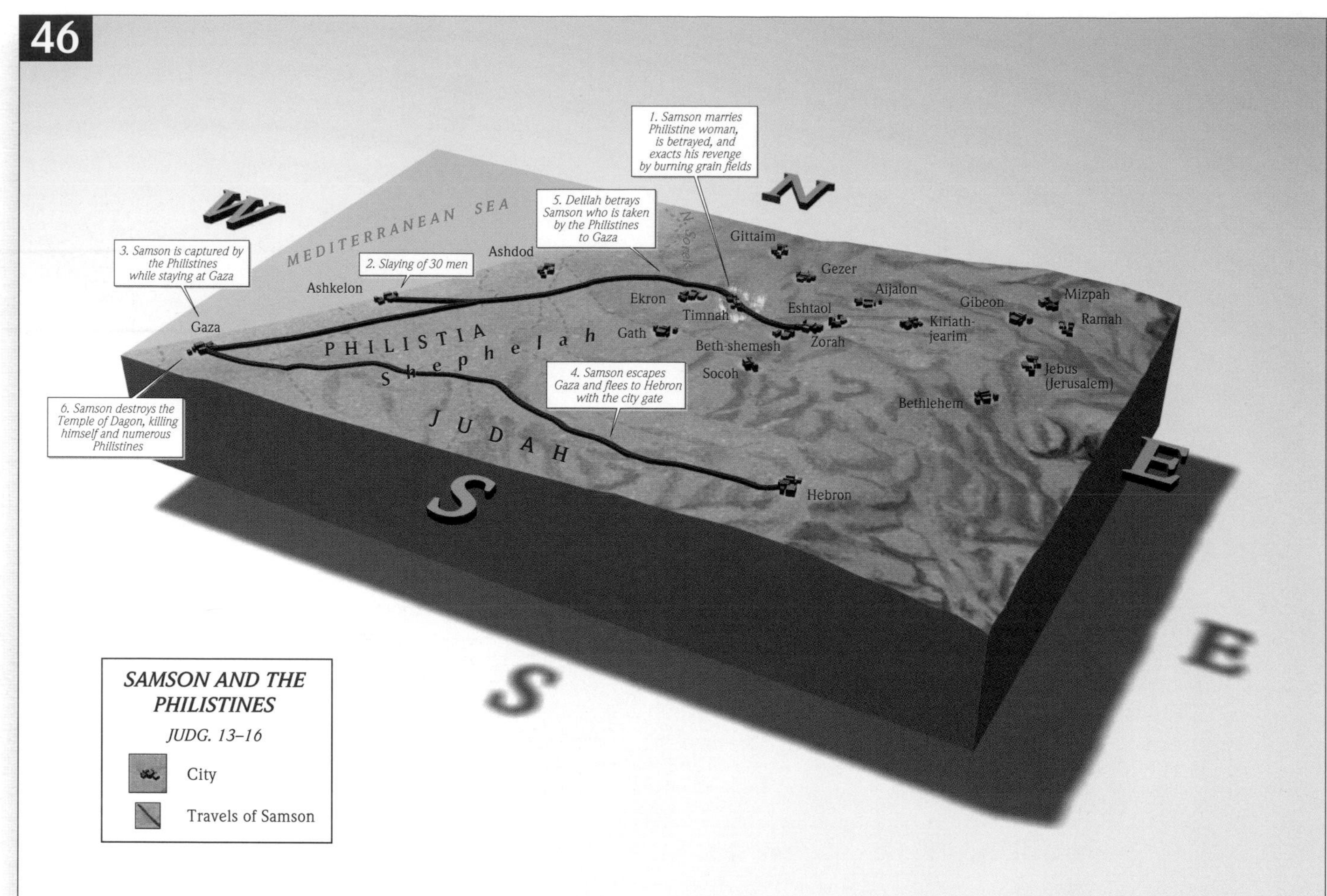
46
1. Samson marries Philistine woman, is betrayed, and exacts his revenge by burning grain fields
5. Delilah betrays Samson who is taken by the Philistines to Gaza
3. Samson is captured by the Philistines while staying at Gaza
2. Slaying of 30 men
4. Samson escapes Gaza and flees to Hebron with the city gate
6. Samson destroys the Temple of Dagon, killing himself and numerous Philistines
MEDITERRANEAN SEA
N. Sorek
W
N
E
S
Gittaim
Gezer
Ashdod
Ashkelon
Ekron
Timnah
Eshtaol
Aijalon
Gibeon
Mizpah
Ramah
Kiriath-jearim
Gaza
Gath
Beth-shemesh
Zorah
Socoh
Jebus (Jerusalem)
Bethlehem
Hebron
PHILISTIA
Shephelah
JUDAH
SAMSON AND THE PHILISTINES
JUDG. 13–16
City
Travels of Samson

portray the struggles between Philistines and Israelites for control of the Shephelah.

Samson was a Danite born at Zorah in the hills flanking the eastern Sorek Valley. He married a Philistine woman from nearby Timnah and later fell in love with Delilah, who came from the same area. Betrayed in love, Samson exacted his revenge against the Philistines by slaying thirty men of Ashkelon and setting afire the grain fields surrounding Timnah. Although the treachery of Delilah brought him into the hands of his enemies, his famous strength returned a final time to bring the walls of Dagon's temple crashing down upon the citizens of Gaza. But Samson's deeds failed to relieve Philistine pressure upon Dan. The tribe abandoned its original allotment and migrated north in search of new land (Judg. 18).

Philistine power reached its peak in the mid-eleventh century as they continued to oppress Israel. Philistine remains at Tell Zeror, Megiddo, Beth-shan, and numerous sites in the Shephelah (Timnah, Lachish, and Beth-shemesh) indicate the scope of the threat posed to Israel. The Philistine lords were capable military rulers who coordinated their strategy carefully. The Philistine army with its chariots, archers, horsemen, and infantry was superior to Israel's military forces. First Samuel 13:19–20 implies that the Philistines maintained a monopoly on sharpening metal tools, thereby hindering the Israelites from obtaining weapons.

THE ARK OF THE COVENANT (SEE MAP 47)

By 1050 B.C. the Philistines occupied the strategic city of Aphek located on the International Coastal Highway. From Aphek the Philistines threatened the central mountain cities including Shiloh where the Ark of the Covenant was kept. The Israelites responded by moving forces to Ebenezer near Aphek. In the ensuing battle the Philistines inflicted a crushing defeat on the tribes at Ebenezer and captured the Ark of the Covenant. The Philistines carried the Ark to Ashdod and placed it in the temple of Dagon. When plagues of tumors broke out in Ashdod, the Ark was sent to Gath where a similar experience prompted another transfer to Ekron. The calamities convinced the Philistines that the Ark must be returned in order to placate Israel's God. Subsequently the Philistines placed the Ark on a cart and sent it with a guilt offering to Beth-shemesh by way of the Sorek Valley (1 Sam. 5–6).

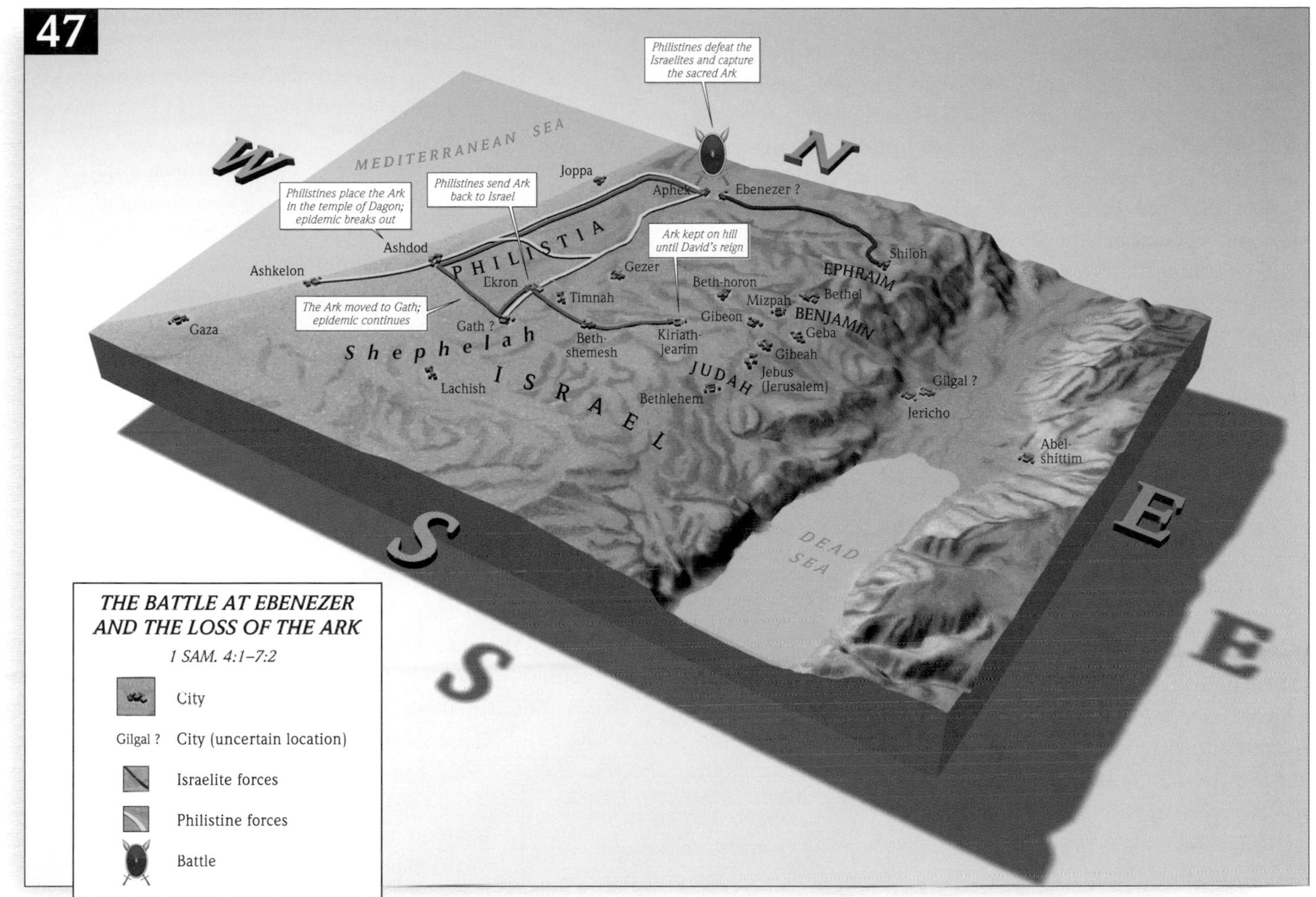

Saul: King of Israel

THE RISE OF SAUL (SEE MAPS 48 AND 49)

After the defeat at Aphek in 1050 B.C., Philistine pressure intensified despite an occasional respite brought about by Israel's sporadic fits of repentance (1 Sam. 7). Corruption of tribal leaders posed further dangers to the tribes. Samuel's sons perverted the legal system and accepted bribes in their capacity as judges at Beer-sheba (1 Sam. 8). As the situation deteriorated, the tribal elders met with Samuel at Ramah, demanding a king to "govern us and go out before us and fight our battles" (1 Sam. 8:19–20). A crucial turning point in the history of Israel had been reached.

Samuel, the aged seer from Ramah in Benjamin, played the key role in the transition from tribal confederacy to monarchy. Samuel served the tribes well as a judge, dispensing justice on his annual circuit from Ramah through Bethel, Gilgal, and Mizpah. He regarded the elders' request for a king as a personal rejection of his leadership as well as rebellion against Yahweh. At God's command, however, Samuel sought out the Benjamite Saul, the son of Kish, and at Ramah anointed him prince over Israel (1 Sam. 9:15–10:1). About 1020 B.C. tribal elders acclaimed Saul as their king in a public assembly at Mizpah (1 Sam. 10:17–27).

Saul established his capital at Gibeah, a Benjamite town a few miles north of Jerusalem. Saul's mandate was to free Israel from the Philistine yoke, but many Israelites suspected that the Philistines would prove too great a match for this untested king. The opportunity for Saul to prove himself came when the citizens of Jabesh-gilead appealed for help against the Ammonite king Nahash. While besieging Jabesh-gilead, Nahash demanded the right eye of each male as his price for lifting the siege.

Moved by the Spirit of Yahweh, Saul summoned the armies of Israel to battle. In a bold move, Saul led the combined forces across the Jordan, defeated Nahash, and relieved the siege of Jabesh-gilead (1 Sam. 11). This military victory confirmed God's choice of Saul among the people of Israel, who affirmed their allegiance to the new king at Gilgal.

SAUL AND THE PHILISTINES (SEE MAP 49)

Saul faced a more formidable threat from the Philistines who established a garrison at Geba in Benjamin, evidently located at Jaba overlooking the Wadi Suweinit. Saul and his son Jonathan gathered Israel's forces at Michmash and Gibeah—presumably the Gibeah of Saul generally located at Tell el-Ful. The precise locations of various Benjamite towns—Gibeah, Geba, Gibeon—are notoriously difficult. The terms come from Hebrew words meaning "hill" or "height" and were used to describe many points in this mountainous region. Jonathan attacked Geba, forcing the withdrawal of the Philistines.

The Philistines responded by moving a larger force to Michmash across the Wadi Suweinit from Geba. The move provoked fear in the Israelites, who abandoned Geba and fled. Some hid in the caves of the rugged wadi while others sought refuge across the Jordan in Gilead. In maneuvers designed to scatter any remaining Israelite forces, Philistine troops raided north, east, and west from Michmash. Saul retreated to Gilgal, well away from the fighting.

Again the valor of Jonathan turned the tide against the Philistines. Jonathan and his armor bearer slipped across the wadi and scaled the jagged cliffs named Bozez and Seneh. The attack caught the Philistines by surprise and set the Philistine camp in confusion. Saul, alerted by the commotion, rallied the Israelites at Gibeah and rushed to Jonathan's aid. Together Saul and Jonathan routed the Philistines at Michmash, sending them in a disorderly westward retreat. For the moment, the Philistine threat was averted.

The ensuing years of Saul's reign brought conflict both on and off the battlefield. Saul won victories over Moab, Edom, the Aramean kingdom of Zobah, and the Amalekites (1 Sam. 14:47–48), but he could never end the crucial conflict with the Philistines. As the Bible puts it, "There was hard fighting against the Philistines all the days of Saul" (1 Sam. 14:52). Moreover, Saul lost the support of Samuel when he usurped the functions of a priest in an ill-advised sacrifice offered at Gilgal. He angered Samuel further when he kept spoils of war taken from the Amalekites in defiance of God's command to destroy everything (1 Sam. 13:11–14; 15:1–35). Ultimately, God rejected Saul as an unfit king and commanded Samuel to anoint David as Israel's next king (1 Sam. 16).

SAUL AND DAVID (SEE MAP 50)

The tragic story of Saul's relationship with David unfolds in several episodes. The young shepherd from Bethlehem became a threat to Saul after his victory over the Philistine giant Goliath in the Valley of Elah (1 Sam. 17). David's fame as a warrior eclipsed that of Saul, and the women of Israel celebrated David's deeds in a refrain that tormented Saul's soul: "Saul has slain his thousands, and David his ten thousands" (1 Sam. 18:7). Finally, in a fit of jealous rage Saul forced David to flee the royal court. Henceforth, David lived the life of a fugitive until Saul died.

First Samuel 19–30 records the movements of David as he maneuvered to avoid the reach of Saul. His odyssey led first to Ramah, where Samuel afforded him temporary shelter (1 Sam. 19:18). Next, David went to Nob, where Ahimelech the priest provided food and armament as David fled westward to Gath (1 Sam. 21:1–9). Achish, the Philistine king of Gath, recognized the threat posed by David and denied him sanctuary (1 Sam. 21:12–15). David finally found refuge in the rugged hills northwest of Hebron, where he collected his family at the cave of Adullam (1 Sam. 22:1). A band of men discontented with Saul's rule gathered about David, providing him a small army. From this stronghold David rescued the village of Keilah from Philistine attack. At some point David moved his family to Moab for safety (1 Sam. 22:3).

Saul's pursuit forced David to seek refuge in the remote desert regions east of Jerusalem. Three wilderness areas—Ziph, Maon, and

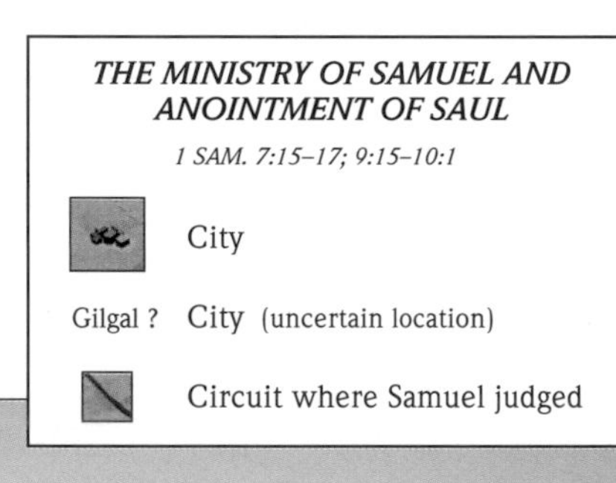

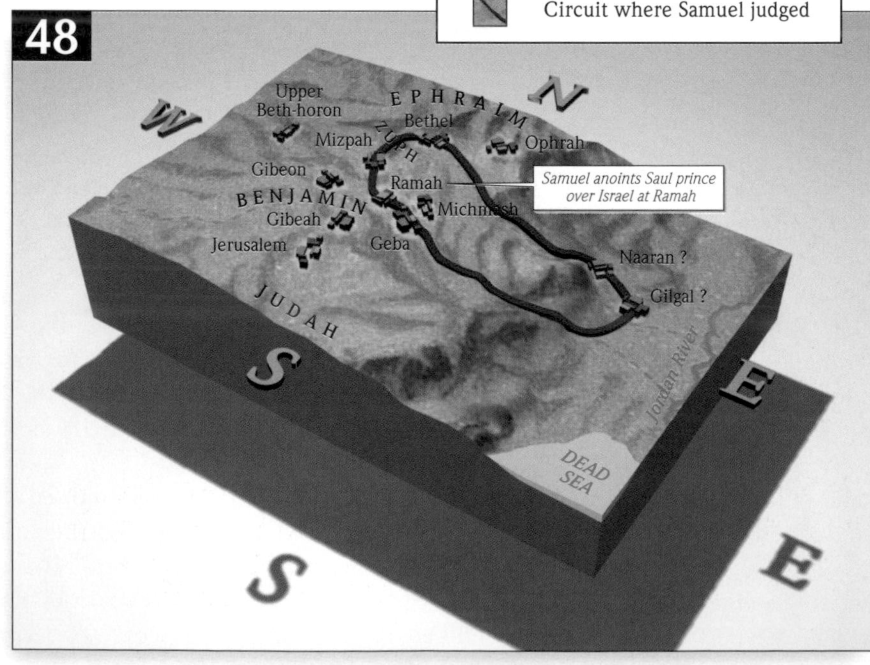

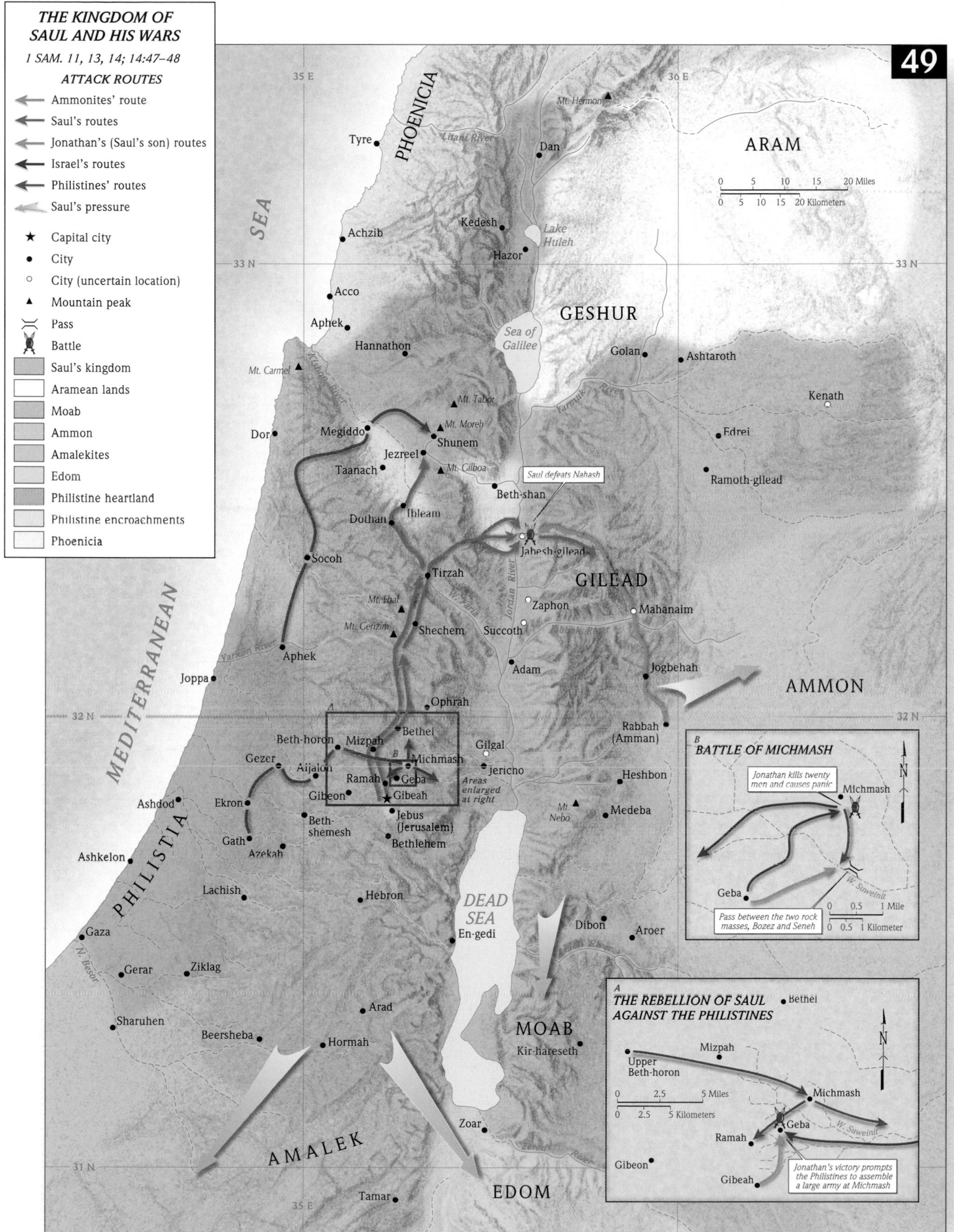
THE KINGDOM OF SAUL AND HIS WARS
1 SAM. 11, 13, 14; 14:47–48
ATTACK ROUTES
Ammonites' route
Saul's routes
Jonathan's (Saul's son) routes
Israel's routes
Philistines' routes
Saul's pressure
Capital city
City
City (uncertain location)
Mountain peak
Pass
Battle
Saul's kingdom
Aramean lands
Moab
Ammon
Amalekites
Edom
Philistine heartland
Philistine encroachments
Phoenicia
49
35 E
36 E
33 N
32 N
31 N
PHOENICIA
ARAM
GESHUR
GILEAD
AMMON
MOAB
EDOM
AMALEK
PHILISTIA
MEDITERRANEAN SEA
DEAD SEA
Sea of Galilee
Lake Huleh
Litani River
Kishon River
Yarmuk River
Jordan River
Jabbok River
Yarkon River
W. Fara
Arnon River
Zered River
N. Besor
Mt. Hermon
Mt. Carmel
Mt. Tabor
Mt. Moreh
Mt. Gilboa
Mt. Ebal
Mt. Gerizim
Mt. Nebo
0 5 10 15 20 Miles
0 5 10 15 20 Kilometers
Tyre
Dan
Achzib
Kedesh
Hazor
Acco
Aphek
Hannathon
Golan
Ashtaroth
Kenath
Edrei
Ramoth-gilead
Dor
Megiddo
Shunem
Jezreel
Taanach
Beth-shan
Saul defeats Nahash
Dothan
Ibleam
Jabesh-gilead
Socoh
Tirzah
Zaphon
Mahanaim
Shechem
Succoth
Aphek
Adam
Jogbehah
Joppa
Ophrah
Bethel
Rabbah (Amman)
Gilgal
Beth-horon
Mizpah
Michmash
Gezer
Aijalon
Jericho
Ramah
Geba
Heshbon
Gibeon
Gibeah
Areas enlarged at right
Ashdod
Ekron
Beth-shemesh
Jebus (Jerusalem)
Medeba
Bethlehem
Gath
Azekah
Ashkelon
Lachish
Hebron
Gaza
Dibon
Aroer
En-gedi
Gerar
Ziklag
Arad
Sharuhen
Beersheba
Hormah
Kir-hareseth
Zoar
Tamar
B BATTLE OF MICHMASH
Jonathan kills twenty men and causes panic
Michmash
Geba
W. Suweinit
Pass between the two rock masses, Bozez and Seneh
0 0.5 1 Mile
0 0.5 1 Kilometer
N
A THE REBELLION OF SAUL AGAINST THE PHILISTINES
Bethel
Mizpah
Upper Beth-horon
Michmash
0 2.5 5 Miles
0 2.5 5 Kilometers
Geba
Ramah
W. Suweinit
Gibeon
Gibeah
Jonathan's victory prompts the Philistines to assemble a large army at Michmash

En-gedi—are mentioned in the narrative (1 Sam. 23:14–26:25). The Ziphites betrayed David to Saul, but David escaped to the Wilderness of Maon, where a report of Philistine activity caused Saul to break off his pursuit (1 Sam. 23:14–29). David retreated to the Oasis of En-gedi located in the desolate Judean wilderness (1 Sam. 25:1). While at En-gedi, David spared Saul's life, refusing to harm God's anointed. While staying in the Wilderness of Maon, David met and eventually married Abigal, the beautiful wife of Nabal from the village of Carmel (1 Sam. 25:1–44). David eventually sought the protection of Achish, the Philistine king of Gath. Offering his men and services to Achish, David received the town of Ziklag. As a vassal of the Philistines, David was expected to plunder the surrounding territory, but David protected the villages of the area by attacking the Geshurites, Gizites, and Amalekites—seminomadic raiders who harassed the villages of Judah (1 Sam. 27). By such actions David gained the support of the people of Judah, who soon would acknowledge David as their king.

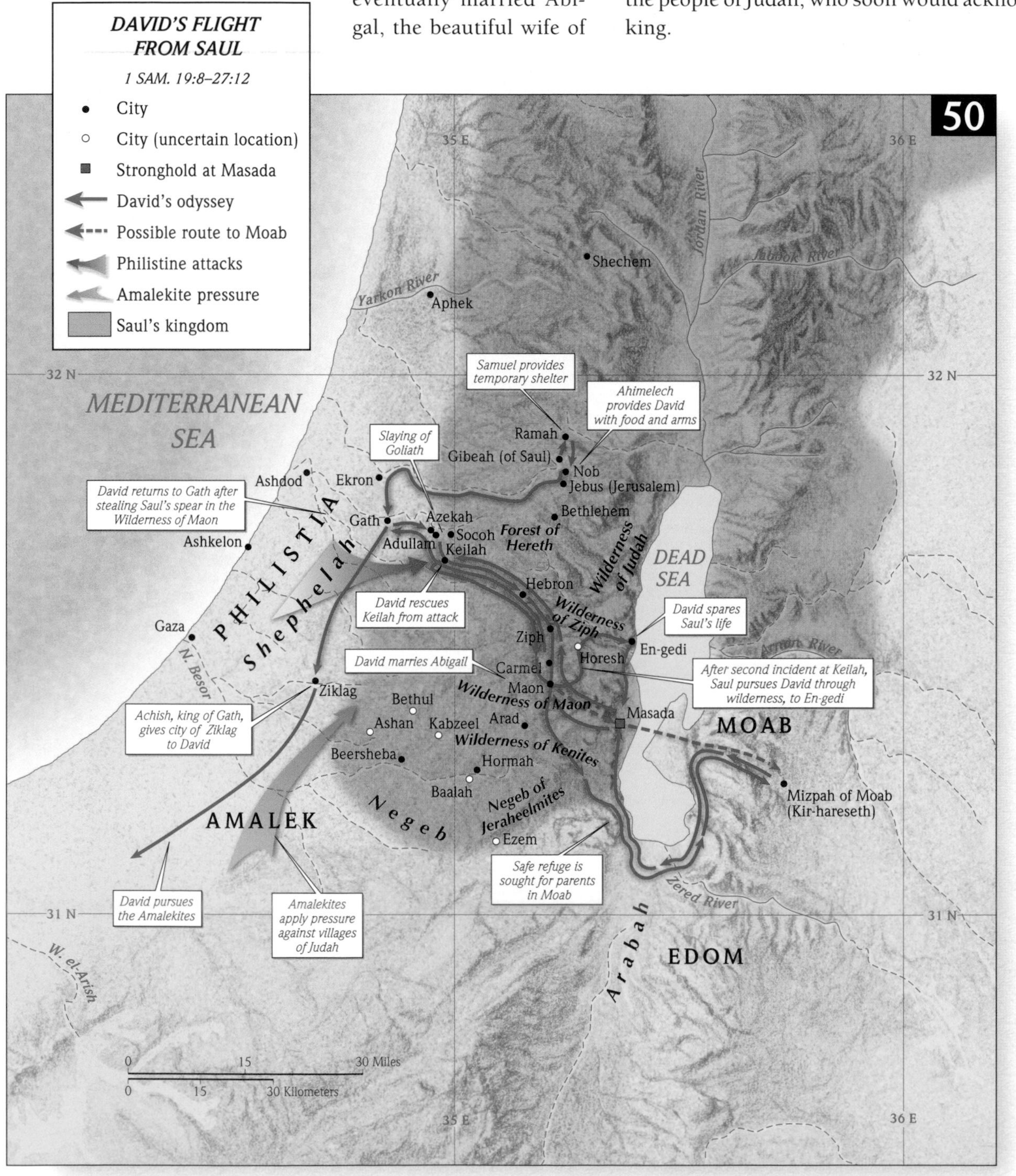

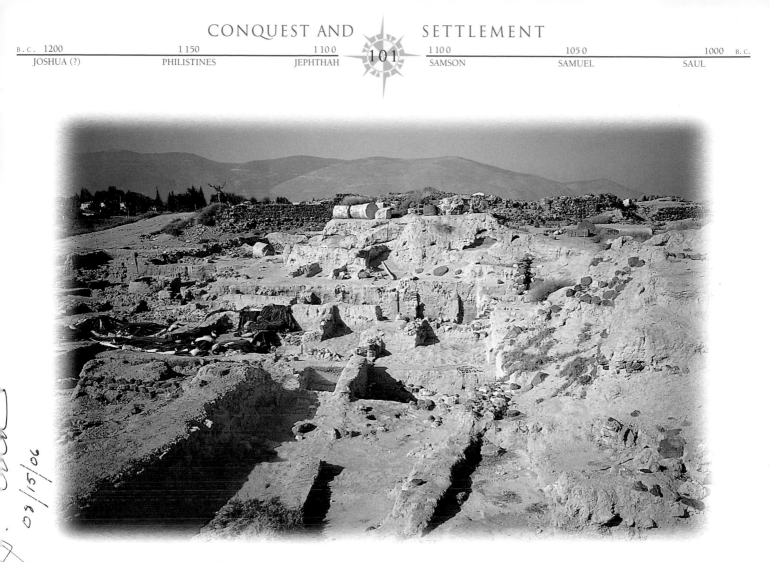

The Old Testament site of Beth-shan where the bodies of Saul and his sons were hung upon a Canaanite temple. In the background is Mount Gilboa where Saul died fighting the Philistines.

THE DEATH OF SAUL

Although preoccupied with his jealousy of David, Saul's real enemy was the Philistines. The Philistines tightened their grip on vital arteries throughout the Jezreel Valley, threatening to cut off communications with the northern Israelite tribes. Gathering their forces at Aphek, the Philistines prepared to move into the Jezreel Valley in a bid to control the vital arteries of that region (1 Sam. 29:1). Providentially, the Philistine commanders distrusted David's loyalty to their cause and refused to allow him to participate in the campaign that ultimately claimed Saul's life (1 Sam. 29:2–11). Moving into the Jezreel Valley, the Philistine force encamped at Shunem, beneath the slopes of the Hill of Moreh. Saul gathered his forces on Mount Gilboa in a futile bid to stave off disaster (1 Sam. 28:4). Desperate for help, Saul sought out the services of a medium from Endor, who conjured up the departed spirit of Samuel, whose words foretold disaster for Saul and his sons (1 Sam. 28:7–24).

Saul attempted to take away the enemy's advantage by defending the slopes of Mount Gilboa, where the chariot might not be so effective. Still, the Philistine attack overran the Israelite positions. Many of Saul's sons, including the valiant Jonathan, died on Mount Gilboa. Saul, wounded by a Philistine archer, took his own life. The Philistines found the bodies of Saul and his sons and took them to Beth-shan, where they were displayed on the walls of the city. Only the actions of the grateful citizens of Jabesh-gilead, who recovered the bodies and gave them a proper burial, saved the memory of Saul from further disgrace (1 Sam. 31).

Chapter Nine

THE KINGDOM OF DAVID AND SOLOMON

Introduction

The death of Saul about 1000 B.C. threatened to end Israel's experiment with a monarchy. The tribes were no better off with a king than they had been under the judges. Still plagued by the Philistines and surrounded by other hostile peoples, Israel could easily have been destroyed or simply absorbed among the many peoples that formed the melting pot of Palestine. Extraordinary leadership provided by David and his son Solomon led to a remarkable transformation of Israel's fortunes.

Within the space of two generations these two kings vanquished Israel's foes and created a kingdom whose influence spanned from the Sinai Desert to the Euphrates River. Under David and Solomon, Israel played a major political and economic role in the affairs of the Near East. Moreover, the tribes of Israel experienced unity, however fragile, for the first time, due in large measure to the strength of David's and Solomon's character. The material accomplishments of the period from 1000 to 922 B.C. are impressive. The royal court, established at Jerusalem, sponsored large-scale building projects, developed the economic potential of the land, and patronized the literary activities of poets and historians. Several of the Psalms are credited to David, while the incomplete "Court History" recorded in 2 Samuel 9–20 and 2 Kings 1–2 illustrates the skill of court historians during this first flowering of Israelite culture.

The Reign of David (1000–960 B.C.)

DAVID'S CONSOLIDATION OF POWER

David faced serious opposition to his rule after the death of Saul in 1000 B.C. Although the tribal elders of Judah proclaimed David king at Hebron, the northern tribes rallied around Saul's son Ish-bosheth, who escaped the massacre on Mount Gilboa. Backed by Abner, Saul's powerful commander of troops, Ish-bosheth established a capital at Mahanaim in the Transjordan from which he opposed the leadership of David (2 Sam. 2:1–11). Abner clearly was the greater threat since he had the loyalty of his army to use as a tool for furthering his ambitions.

Civil War. The deep divisions and divided loyalties manifest among the tribes threatened political chaos, but the resulting civil war lasted only two years. The only known battle was fought between the troops of Abner and Joab at the Pool of Gibeon. The bloody skirmish was inconclusive, although Joab lost his brother Asahel (2 Sam. 2:12–32). Later, after Ish-bosheth rebuffed his attempt to take one of Saul's concubines, Abner sought a rapprochement with David. Joab, wary of his rival's ambition, killed Abner in an act of revenge at Hebron before a treaty could be concluded. Within days Ish-bosheth was murdered by his own men. The

The Great Pool at Gibeon where Abner's and Joab's men fought a bloody battle after Saul's death (2 Sam. 2:12–17).

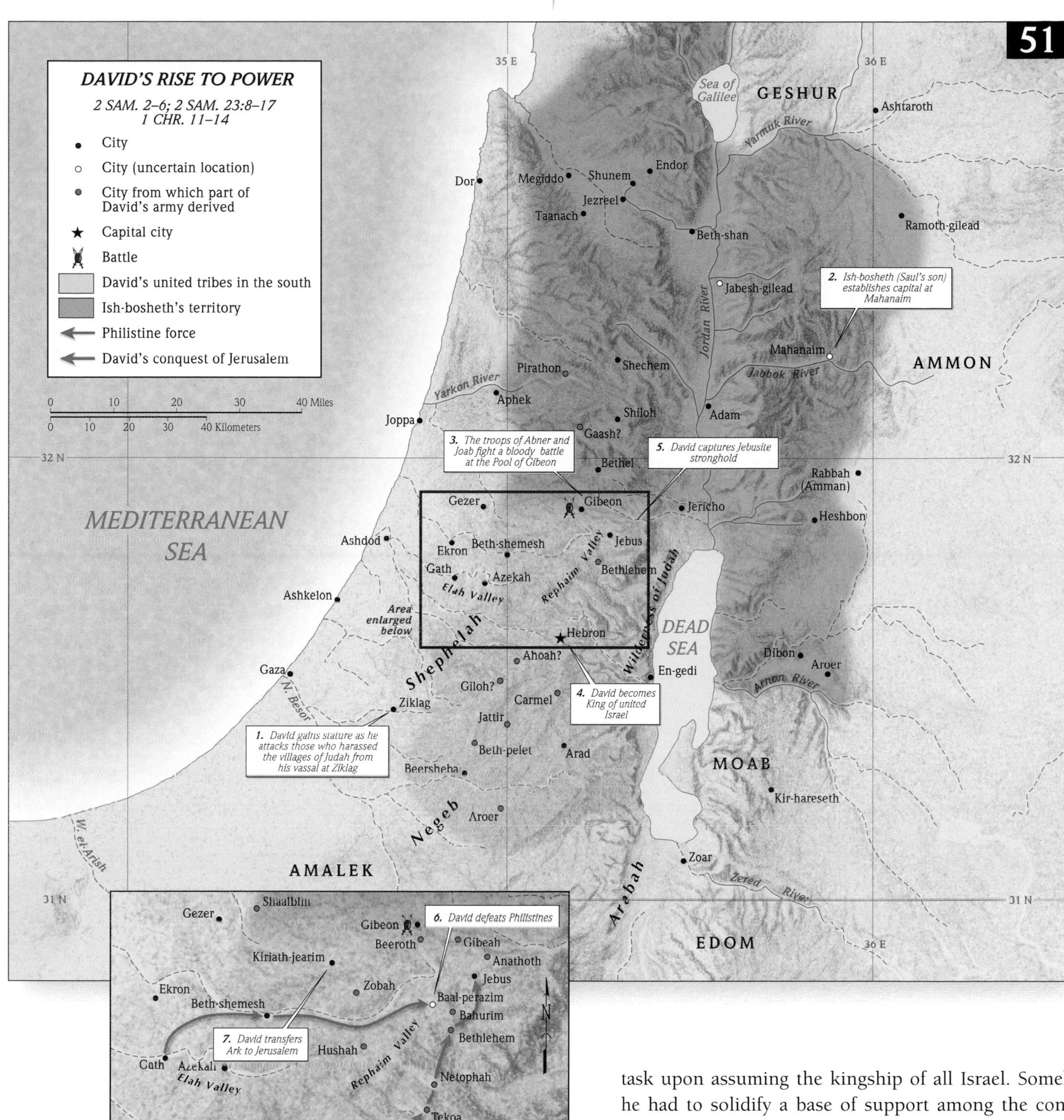
51
DAVID'S RISE TO POWER
2 SAM. 2–6; 2 SAM. 23:8–17
1 CHR. 11–14
City
City (uncertain location)
City from which part of David's army derived
Capital city
Battle
David's united tribes in the south
Ish-bosheth's territory
Philistine force
David's conquest of Jerusalem
MEDITERRANEAN SEA
GESHUR
AMMON
MOAB
EDOM
AMALEK
DEAD SEA
Sea of Galilee
1. David gains stature as he attacks those who harassed the villages of Judah from his vassal at Ziklag
2. Ish-bosheth (Saul's son) establishes capital at Mahanaim
3. The troops of Abner and Joab fight a bloody battle at the Pool of Gibeon
4. David becomes King of united Israel
5. David captures Jebusite stronghold
6. David defeats Philistines
7. David transfers Ark to Jerusalem
Area enlarged below

deaths of Ish-bosheth and Abner forced the leaders of the northern tribes to turn to David for leadership. At the age of thirty, David was proclaimed king by all the elders at Hebron. From there he ruled a united Israel for seven years (2 Sam. 5:1–5).

King over All Israel. David faced a delicate and difficult task upon assuming the kingship of all Israel. Somehow he had to solidify a base of support among the contentious tribes, gaining their loyalties while abstaining from every appearance of tribal favoritism. In a stroke of political wisdom, David captured the Jebusite stronghold of Jerusalem and made it his capital. Since no tribe had occupied the city, Jerusalem was a "neutral" site with no previous tribal associations. Perhaps David's men gained access inside the walls of the well-defended city by scurrying up a water tunnel linked to the Gihon Spring (2 Sam. 5:6–11), although recent studies of this tunnel indicate climbing up the vertical shaft

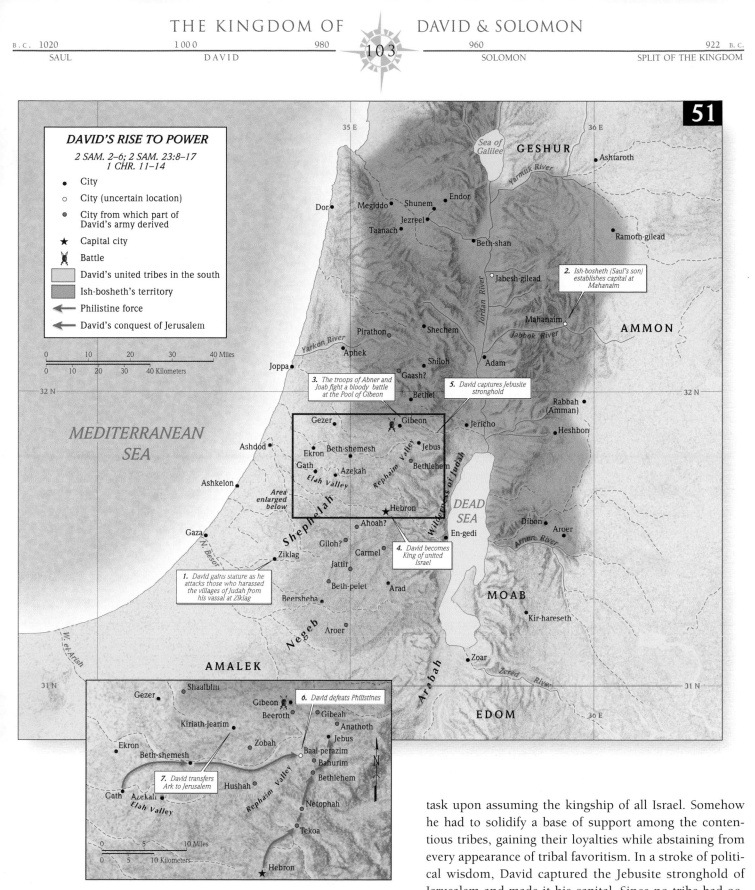

52

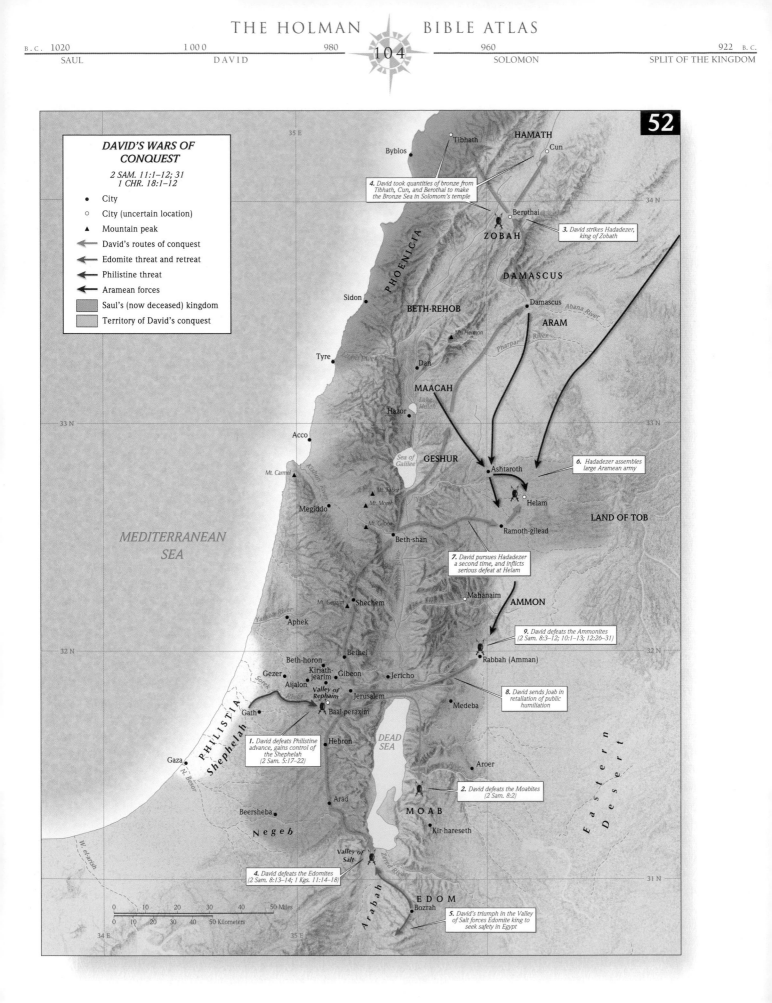

DAVID'S WARS OF CONQUEST

2 SAM. 11:1–12; 31
1 CHR. 18:1–12

- ● City
- ○ City (uncertain location)
- ▲ Mountain peak
- David's routes of conquest
- Edomite threat and retreat
- Philistine threat
- Aramean forces
- Saul's (now deceased) kingdom
- Territory of David's conquest

1. David defeats Philistine advance, gains control of the Shephelah (2 Sam. 5:17–22)

2. David defeats the Moabites (2 Sam. 8:2)

3. David strikes Hadadezer, king of Zobath

4. David took quantities of bronze from Tibhath, Cun, and Berothai to make the Bronze Sea in Solomom's temple

4. David defeats the Edomites (2 Sam. 8:13–14; 1 Kgs. 11:14–18)

5. David's triumph in the Valley of Salt forces Edomite king to seek safety in Egypt

6. Hadadezer assembles large Aramean army

7. David pursues Hadadezer a second time, and inflicts serious defeat at Helam

8. David sends Joab in retaliation of public humiliation

9. David defeats the Ammonites (2 Sam. 8:3–12; 10:1–13; 12:26–31)

HAMATH
Tibhath
Cun
Byblos
Berothai
ZOBAH
DAMASCUS
PHOENICIA
Sidon
BETH-REHOB
Damascus
Abana River
ARAM
Mt. Hermon
Pharpar River
Tyre
Litani River
Dan
MAACAH
Lake Huleh
Hazor
Acco
Sea of Galilee
GESHUR
Ashtaroth
Mt. Carmel
Kishon River
Mt. Tabor
Mt. Moreh
Helam
Megiddo
Yarmuk River
Mt. Gilboa
Ramoth-gilead
LAND OF TOB
Beth-shan
MEDITERRANEAN SEA
Jordan River
Mahanaim
AMMON
Mt. Gerizim
Shechem
Yarkon River
Aphek
Bethel
Rabbah (Amman)
Beth-horon
Gezer
Kiriath-jearim
Gibeon
Jericho
Aijalon
Sorek River
Valley of Rephaim
Jerusalem
Gath
Baal-perazim
Medeba
PHILISTIA
Shephelah
Hebron
DEAD SEA
Gaza
Aroer
Arnon River
N. Besor
Arad
MOAB
Beersheba
Kir-hareseth
Negeb
Eastern Desert
W. el-arish
Valley of Salt
Zered River
Arabah
EDOM
Bozrah

35 E | 34 N | 33 N | 32 N | 31 N | 34 E

0 10 20 30 40 50 Miles
0 10 20 30 40 50 Kilometers

would indeed be a prodigious feat (see further "Jerusalem: City of David and Solomon," pp. 110–114).

David quickly established his official residence in Jerusalem, building a palace with the aid of Hiram, king of Tyre. Moreover, recognizing that Israel's real unity resided in her faith in Yahweh, David transported the Ark of the Covenant from Kiriath-jearim to Jerusalem and built a tent shrine to house the sacred chest (2 Sam. 6). In one stroke David united both the political and religious loyalties of the tribes and paved the way for a royal theology centered on Jerusalem, David, and his descendants. Yahweh's covenant with David confirmed the divine choice of David and his descendants to rule Israel (2 Sam. 7), David's city of Jerusalem became the spiritual and political heart of Israel—the Zion of Yahweh.

THE WARS OF DAVID (SEE MAP 52)

Throughout his reign David fought a series of both defensive and offensive wars against surrounding peoples who threatened his kingdom. In the process, not only did more land allotted to the tribes come into the possession of Israel, but David extended Jerusalem's influence and control beyond Palestine into Syria. To accomplish this considerable feat, David employed a professional army composed of mercenaries drawn from various backgrounds, including Hittites, Philistines, and Ammonites, as well as Israelites. The "Thirty," an inner circle of fighting men of unquestioned loyalty to David, spearheaded his elite troops (2 Sam. 23:8–39). The sequence of David's wars, especially the conflicts in the Transjordan and Syria, can be interpreted in different ways.

David and the Philistines. Early in David's reign he moved quickly to neutralize the Philistines, who threatened Jerusalem by moving up the Sorek to the Valley of Rephaim. On two occasions David drove the Philistine advance back and, in the process, gained control of the Shephelah (2 Sam. 5:17–25; 23:9–19; 1 Chr. 14:8–17). Although David apparently did not annex the Philistine cities of the southern coastal plain, perhaps in deference to his earlier relationship with Achish of Gath, nonetheless, his victories thwarted further Philistine expansion. Henceforth, the Philistines ceased to be a major threat to Israel.

David in the Transjordan. David fought more protracted wars in the Transjordan as he sought to establish firm Israelite control over that vital region. The Bible briefly mentions campaigns against Moab and Edom (2 Sam. 8:2, 12–14; 1 Kgs. 11:14–17). A Moabite foray cemented control over the fertile tableland north of the Arnon. Later, Abishai, under Joab's command, defeated the Edomites; the key battle occurred in the Valley of Salt, south of the Dead Sea. According to 1 Kings 11:14–17, the young prince of Edom, Hadad, escaped to Egypt. David placed garrisons in Edom and collected tribute from Moab (2 Sam. 8:2, 14).

David and the Arameans. Conflict with certain Aramean kingdoms occupied David throughout much of his reign (2 Sam. 8:3–12; 10:6–19; 1 Kgs. 11:23–25; 1 Chr. 18–19). By 1100 B.C. several Aramean kingdoms had emerged in interior Lebanon and Syria. Chief among them were Zobah, Damascus, Hamath, and Beth-rehob. David's principal opposition came from Hadadezer, king of Zobah. From his stronghold in Zobah, Hadadezer controlled Damascus and harassed King Toi of Hamath. He probably considered northern Palestine and the Transjordan as territories belonging to him.

The war with Ammon precipitated further conflict with Hadadezer. The new Ammonite king, Hanun, humiliated a delegation David sent to Rabbah to express sympathy upon the death of Nahash, Hanun's father. David retaliated by sending Joab against Rabbah (2 Sam. 10). Hanun anticipated this act and enlisted the aid of Hadadezer, who organized a large army drawn from various Aramean kingdoms (Beth-rehob, Zobah, Maacah, the men of Tob) to assist the Ammonites. Joab routed the Aramean force at Medeba (1 Chr. 19:7). Hadadezer retreated and assembled an even larger force drawn from Aramean states as far north as the Euphrates. David met Hadadezer at Helam, east of the Sea of Galilee, where he inflicted a serious defeat. Hadadezer's allies sued for peace with Israel (2 Sam. 10:19).

The Israelites eventually prevailed over the Ammonites as Rabbah fell, but during the prolonged siege David committed his great sins against Bathsheba and her husband, Uriah (2 Sam. 11–12).

David invaded the territory of Hadadezer, destroyed the Aramean army, and took quantities of bronze from Betan (Tibhath?), Berothai, and Cun in the Lebanese Beqa. David placed a garrison in Damascus and established a treaty with Toi, king of Hamath, who had defected from the Aramean coalition (2 Sam. 8:3–10).

David's Accomplishments. David's prowess as a military leader greatly enlarged the territory under Israel's control. Many of the strong cities of Palestine previously unconquered, such as Beth-shan and Jerusalem, now were in Israelite hands. The Jezreel Valley, the Shephelah, all of Galilee, as well as the Transjordan with its vital trade route were a part of David's kingdom. Ammon, Moab, Edom, and certain Aramean kingdoms paid homage to David by sending tribute to the court at Jerusalem. David confined the Philistines to the southern coast and maintained friendly relations with Phoenicia.

By the time of his death about 960 B.C., David had carved out a kingdom of considerable proportions and placed Israel on the political map. Equally important, David created the machinery that carried out the day-to-day administration of his kingdom. Several lists of officials found in the biblical record provide a glimpse of the inner working of David's kingdom (2 Sam. 8:16–18; 1 Chr. 18:15–17; 27:32–34). Given the circumstances he inherited, David's accomplishments were enormous. He gave Israel a stable political foundation upon which his son Solomon would build.

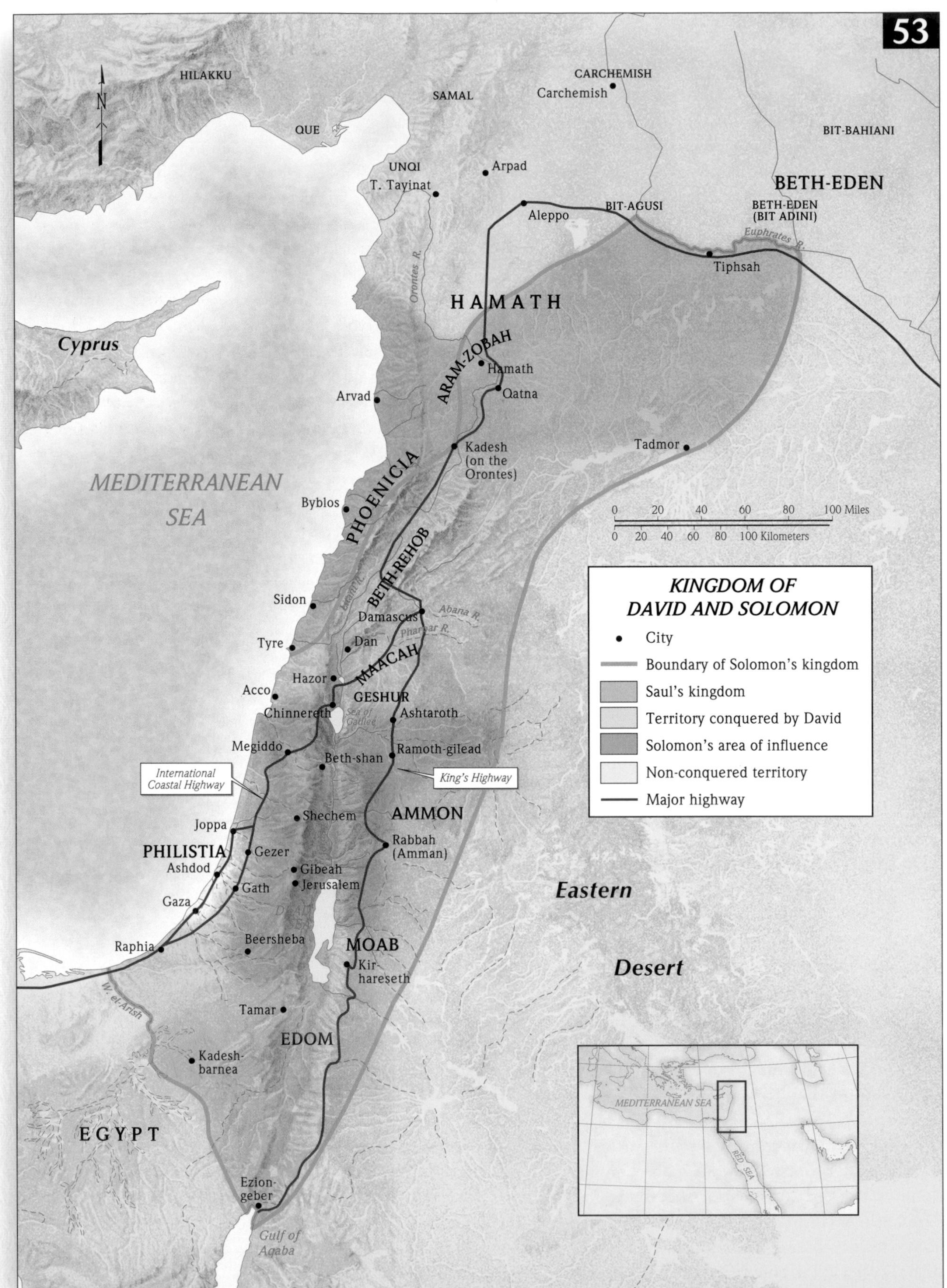
53
KINGDOM OF DAVID AND SOLOMON
City
Boundary of Solomon's kingdom
Saul's kingdom
Territory conquered by David
Solomon's area of influence
Non-conquered territory
Major highway
HILAKKU
QUE
SAMAL
CARCHEMISH
Carchemish
BIT-BAHIANI
UNQI
T. Tayinat
Arpad
BETH-EDEN
Aleppo
BIT-AGUSI
BETH-EDEN (BIT ADINI)
Euphrates R.
Tiphsah
Orontes R.
HAMATH
Cyprus
ARAM-ZOBAH
Hamath
Qatna
Arvad
Kadesh (on the Orontes)
Tadmor
MEDITERRANEAN SEA
PHOENICIA
Byblos
BETH-REHOB
Sidon
Damascus
Abana R.
Pharpar R.
Tyre
Dan
MAACAH
Hazor
Acco
GESHUR
Chinnereth
Sea of Galilee
Ashtaroth
Megiddo
Beth-shan
Ramoth-gilead
International Coastal Highway
King's Highway
Shechem
AMMON
Joppa
PHILISTIA
Gezer
Rabbah (Amman)
Ashdod
Gibeah
Jerusalem
Gath
Eastern
Gaza
Raphia
Beersheba
MOAB
Kir-hareseth
Desert
W. el-Arish
Tamar
EDOM
Kadesh-barnea
EGYPT
Ezion-geber
Gulf of Aqaba
0 20 40 60 80 100 Miles
0 20 40 60 80 100 Kilometers
MEDITERRANEAN SEA
RED SEA

The Reign Of Solomon (960–922 B.C.)

The golden era of Solomon's reign brought Israel four decades of peace and prosperity, built upon David's military success. Solomon inherited a kingdom whose borders stretched from Gaza into central Syria. This mastery gave him control of important segments of the major trade routes, the International Coastal Highway and the King's Highway. Solomon used these vital arteries, ultimately touching all the Near East, to create a network of trade relationships that funneled enormous wealth through his kingdom. Solomon expended his new wealth on an ambitious building program that gave Israel the outward trappings of an important political power. Our major sources for this period include 1 Kgs. 3–11 and 2 Chronicles 1–9, but archaeology has also cast light on the material culture Solomon fashioned.

SOLOMON'S ECONOMIC POLICIES

Solomon treaded out into international waters through his economic policies. The extent of his international contacts is suggested by the seven hundred wives and three hundred concubines found in his royal harem. Kings customarily sealed political alliances by accepting in marriage a member of the other royal household. Solomon numbered Ammonite, Edomite, Moabite, Hittite, and Phoenician women within his care (1 Kgs. 11:1). An unnamed Egyptian king of the weak Twenty-first Dynasty also sent a daughter to the court at Jerusalem, presenting Solomon the city of Gezer as her dowry (1 Kgs. 9:16). These wide-ranging alliances provided many economic opportunities for an entrepreneur like Solomon.

First Kings 3–11 hints at several trade relationships Solomon established. Undoubtedly, Solomon's most lucrative commercial ventures came through his Phoenician connection. Following David's lead, Solomon maintained strong ties with the Phoenician king of Tyre, Hiram. The Phoenicians were among the ancient world's most able seamen and merchants. From 1000 B.C. onward, Phoenician ships sailed out of their ports on the modern Lebanese coast in search of trade goods. The Phoenicians established coastal trading colonies throughout the Mediterranean basin, some as far away as Spain. The principal Phoenician

54

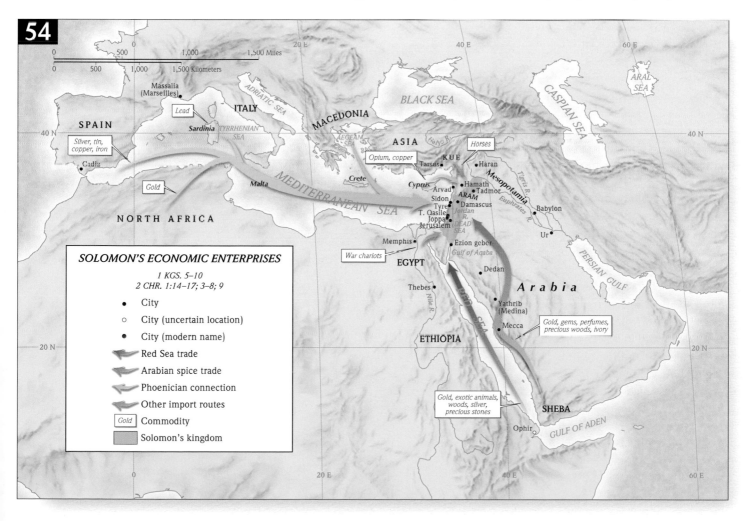

SOLOMON'S ECONOMIC ENTERPRISES

1 KGS. 5–10
2 CHR. 1:14–17; 3–8; 9

- City
- City (uncertain location)
- City (modern name)
- Red Sea trade
- Arabian spice trade
- Phoenician connection
- Other import routes
- Gold Commodity
- Solomon's kingdom

0 500 1,000 1,500 Miles
0 500 1,000 1,500 Kilometers

Massalia (Marseilles)
Lead
Sardinia
ITALY
SPAIN
Silver, tin, copper, iron
Cadiz
Gold
NORTH AFRICA
Malta
MEDITERRANEAN SEA
TYRRHENIAN SEA
ADRIATIC SEA
MACEDONIA
AEGEAN SEA
Crete
BLACK SEA
ASIA
Opium, copper
Horses
KUE
Tarsus
Haran
Cyprus
Arvad
Hamath
Tadmor
ARAM
Sidon
Tyre
Damascus
T. Qasile
Joppa
Jerusalem
Jordan R.
DEAD SEA
Mesopotamia
Tigris R.
Euphrates R.
Babylon
Ur
Memphis
War chariots
EGYPT
Ezion geber
Gulf of Aqaba
Dedan
Thebes
Nile R.
RED SEA
Arabia
Yathrib (Medina)
Mecca
Gold, gems, perfumes, precious woods, ivory
ETHIOPIA
Gold, exotic animals, woods, silver, precious stones
SHEBA
Ophir
GULF OF ADEN
PERSIAN GULF
CASPIAN SEA
ARAL SEA
40 N
20 N
0
20 E
40 E
60 E

home ports—Tyre, Sidon, Byblos, and Arvad—served as clearinghouses for the world's commodities (see "The Phoenician Culture," p. 127).

Solomon wisely entered a joint trading venture with Hiram that became mutually beneficial for both parties. With Hiram's help Solomon built a new port facility and stationed a fleet at Ezion-geber on the Gulf of Aqabah. Since Israel had no previous seafaring experience, Hiram provided the skilled craftsmen and experienced sailors necessary to maintain and operate the fleet (1 Kgs. 9:26–28; 10:11–12, 22). The ships plied the Red Sea, sailing to Ophir and returning with enormous quantities of gold along with exotic animals, woods, silver, and precious stones.

An inscription from Tell Qasile mentions the gold of Ophir, although the exact location of the land remains uncertain. Some scholars locate Ophir on the east African coast, Somaliland, while others place the legendary land of gold in Saudi Arabia. Judging from the list of goods brought back by Solomon's ships, the fleet touched several ports along both the coast of Africa and the Arabian Peninsula. The Phoenicians gained access to new markets and the land routes Solomon controlled, while Solomon added sea trade to his economic activities.

The famous visit of the queen of Sheba also undoubtedly had trade overtones. Sheba was one of several small kingdoms located in the Arabian Peninsula known for their spices, perfumes, precious stones, and gold. These isolated principalities needed market outlets for their goods. Solomon's control of the trade routes offered the camel caravans of Sheba access to the opulent courts of the Levant and beyond. Solomon also became a "broker," handling military hardware. According to 1 Kgs., Solomon imported horses from Kue (Que, later called Cilicia) in southeastern Turkey, a region noted for its fine steeds. Egypt supplied Solomon with war chariots. Solomon deployed 1,400 chariots throughout his kingdom for national defense, but evidently sold the surplus to Aramean and Hittite kings (1 Kgs. 10:26–29).

SOLOMON'S BUILDING PROGRAM

With his newfound wealth Solomon sponsored a building program designed to strengthen his kingdom and provide the outward trappings of a royal court suitable to Israel's new status. The Bible contains frequent references to his extensive constructions, while archaeology has provided additional evidence illuminating Israel's earliest attempts at monumental architecture. Excavations have revealed a burst of building activity in the 900s, most likely attributable to Solomon. The

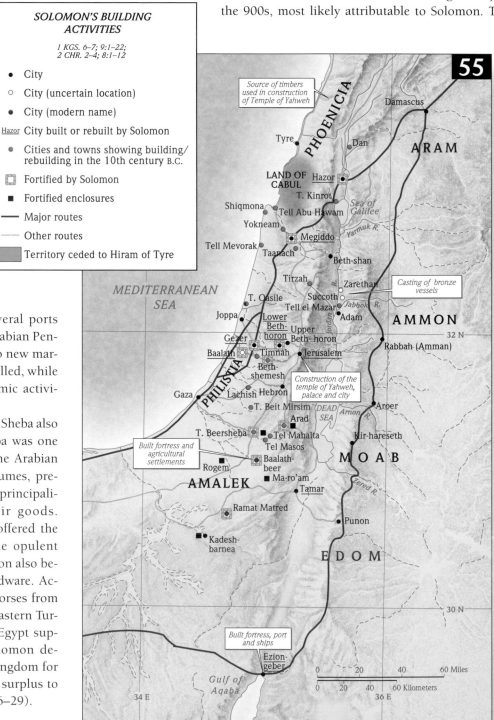

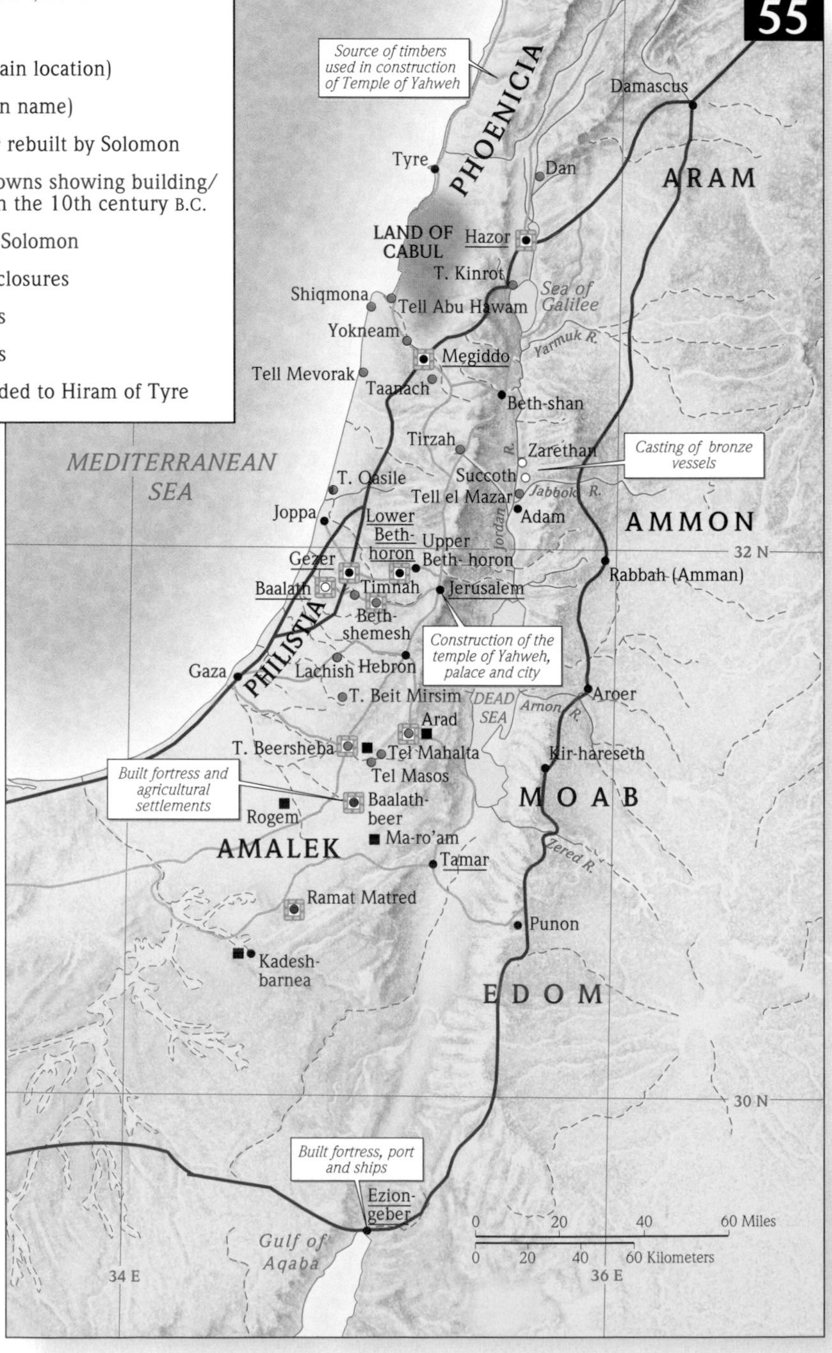

A casemate wall at Hazor dated to the time of Solomon.

evidence suggests that Solomon drew freely upon foreign architectural traditions, especially Phoenician and Aramean, and may have employed a royal architect to execute his plans.

Solomon rebuilt several strategic strongholds that guarded the major routes and functioned as key administrative centers. First Kgs. 9:15 gives special prominence to Hazor, Megiddo, and Gezer. All three were ancient Canaanite cities located at strategic points on the International Coastal Highway. Each had suffered serious decline prior to Solomon's reign. Solomon's architects encircled each city with a new casemate wall entered by an imposing six-chambered gate (see photographs). Both features appear to be typical of a Solomonic city. Casemate walls consist of double encircling walls joined periodically through perpendicular walls to form rooms or "casemates." This type of wall provided space for storage or living, was easily constructed, and provided enough security in the peaceful period of Solomon's rule. After 900 B.C. they were quickly abandoned due to the development of more formidable siege techniques.

Excavation of Megiddo so far has yielded the most information about the public buildings of those "royal cities." Two buildings, labeled "palaces," may have served to house the local governor or the king himself on an official visit. One structure, consisting of a colonnaded portico and two main rooms, was located in a large courtyard accessible only through a separate gate. At the southeastern edge of the city, a covered gallery led from inside the city to an outside spring, giving the inhabitants a secure water supply in case of siege. The so-called "Stables of Solomon" identified by earlier excavators probably were store facilities built by Omri or Ahab after 900 B.C.

First Kgs. 9:17–18 refers to other sites refortified during Solomon's reign. Baalah and Lower Beth-horon guarded passes leading from the coastal plain into the heart of Judah. Tadmor may refer to the important caravan city 120 miles north of Damascus, but many scholars believe the Hebrew original read "Tamar in the wilderness of Judah." Solomon did build in the region of Syria at Hamath and Tadmor according to 2 Chronicles 8:3–4, but the text in 1 Kgs. 9:18 seems best understood as a reference to the southern border of Judah.

Archaeology has revealed a string of small fortresses and agricultural settlements (Ramat Matred, Baalath-beer) built in the tenth century to protect the caravan routes and secure the southern limits of Solomon's kingdom. Substantial building took place at Arad and Beer-sheba also. Particularly interesting is the small temple at Arad constructed in the tenth century. These excavated

Remains of the Solomonic gateway at Megiddo. Notice the ashlar masonry laid in "headers and stretchers" fashion.

The Israelite temple at Tell Arad. Note the sacrificial altar in the forecourt on the right and the inner shrine at the back containing reproductions of two altars and two sacred stones originally found in the shrine.

materials indicate that Solomon's building program outside of Jerusalem was more extensive than even the Bible records.

The Bible gives considerable attention to the building activities of David and especially Solomon in Jerusalem (1 Kgs. 5–9; 2 Chr. 2–4; 8). Within their lifetimes the old Jebusite city became a national capital complete with all the trappings of a royal court. Although Solomon's crowning achievement was the construction of a temple to house the Ark of the Covenant, the biblical text describes other structures completed by the two kings. (See "Jerusalem: City of David and Solomon", pp. 110–114).

SOLOMON'S POLICIES AND TRIBAL JEALOUSY

Despite the great accomplishments of Solomon's reign, cracks soon appeared in the unity of his kingdom. Some policies the king pursued fanned the latent jealousies of the tribes and invited rebellion. Building on a census taken by David, Solomon divided his kingdom into twelve districts to facilitate administrative matters, especially the collection of taxes (1 Kgs. 4:7–19). The descriptions of these districts suggest that Solomon ignored some of the old tribal boundaries, and, perhaps, favored his own tribe, Judah, by treating it separately. Furthermore, Solomon used the forced labor gangs, or corvée, in his building projects. Initially these laborers were conscripts from among the non-Israelite population. However, as his needs increased, Solomon conscripted Israelites to supplement the work. Jeroboam, chief administrative officer over the corvée, rebelled against these oppressive policies and fled to Egypt (1 Kgs. 11:26–40). Finally, Solomon's lavish state policies outstripped the income brought in from his economic empire. To make up the shortfall, Solomon resorted to an increasingly burdensome taxation scheme. As the demands of the king increased, so did the complaints of the tribal leaders.

The religious permissiveness of Solomon must have been particularly odious to those Israelites loyal to Yahweh. Solomon built shrines to many of the pagan gods and goddesses worshiped by members of his harem. Altars to Chemosh, the god of Moab, to the Ammonite god Milcom, and to the Sidonian goddess Ashtoreth appeared on the hills surrounding Jerusalem (1 Kgs. 11:1–13). Soon many of Israel's old foes again rose against the kingdom. The Edomite king, Hadad, returned from Egypt to his homeland from where he could threaten the vital commercial link between Jerusalem and the Red Sea port Ezion-geber. Rezon, king of Damascus, led that Aramean principality away from Solomon's control (1 Kgs. 11:14–23).

Gradually, outlying kingdoms once loyal to Jerusalem sought their independence as the aging king, preoccupied with internal matters, proved ineffective in maintaining his control. Solomon's empire plunged towards crisis and collapse just as Ahijah the prophet had predicted (1 Kgs. 11:29–39). With Solomon's death in 922 B.C., the united kingdom collapsed.

Jerusalem: City of David & Solomon

When David captured Jerusalem and made it his capital, Jerusalem acquired an unprecedented position among biblical cities. Over the span of the previous two decades, archaeologists have increased our knowledge of Jerusalem dramatically. Excavations conducted by Benjamin Mazar, Nahman Avigad, Yigael Shiloh, Kathleen Kenyon, Magen Broshi, and many others have disclosed new information, settling old questions and raising new ones.

Excavating Jerusalem has not been an easy task; many gaps in our knowledge of the city's history remain. The numerous destructions of the city, rebuilding and reuse of material, quarrying activities, and erosion throughout the ages have disturbed or destroyed the evidence sought by archaeologists. The fact that Jerusalem was built on ridges, unlike most ancient cities, and the fact that Jerusalem is still an occupied city further complicates the task of reconstructing history through archaeology. Nonetheless, we now have a much better understanding of how Jerusalem developed.

THE TOPOGRAPHY OF JERUSALEM

Jerusalem developed along two spurs known as the western and eastern ridges. These ridges, or hills, extend from north to south and are protected by deep valleys on all sides. The Kidron Valley separates the eastern ridge from the higher elevations of Mount Scopus and the Mount of Olives (2,684 feet). The Hinnom Valley descends alongside the western ridge, encircling the two ridges to the south before joining the Kidron Valley. A central valley—called by Josephus the Tyropoeon Valley or "Valley of the Cheesemakers" (Josephus, *JW*, 5:4:1)—divides the two ridges.

Jerusalem's earliest inhabitants settled on the southern end of the eastern spur. The area was easily defended and located near the principal water source of the region—the Gihon Spring. Canaanite and Jebusite Jerusalem developed along the southern tip in an area covering about ten acres. This area was the city captured by David about 1000 B.C.; subsequently the southeastern hill has been known as "the City of David" (2 Sam. 5.9).

David expanded Jerusalem northward upon the northern part of the eastern ridge known as Mount Moriah (2 Chr. 3:1). Because the eastern ridge slopes away southward, the northern part of the ridge is 250 feet higher than the southeastern hill. Solomon built the temple upon this higher elevation, called today the Temple Mount.

The western ridge was much broader and higher than the eastern ridge, but the western ridge had no adequate water supply like the Gihon Spring. Consequently, settlement on the western ridge began about 710 B.C. when Hezekiah built a new wall enclosing the southern portions of the ridge. A valley (the "Transversal Valley") divided the western ridge into two parts and provided a natural boundary for a northern defense line. The southwest hill south of the Transversal Valley was higher than the Temple Mount. Josephus calls the southern hill the "Upper City". Wealthy Jerusalemites, including Herod the Great, built their palatial villas and palaces in the Upper City during Roman times. By the time of Jesus, Jerusalem spilled over into northern suburbs (e.g., the district of Bezetha) on both the western and eastern ridges.

56

JERUSALEM IN THE TIME OF DAVID AND SOLOMON

2 SAM. 5:6–12; 24:18–25
1 CHR. 11:4–9
1 KGS. 5–7; 9:15
2 CHR. 3–4

- ▲ Mountain peak
- Gate
- City walls
- "City of David" The Old Jebusite/Canaanite City
- Possible addition by David
- Temple Mount
- x Spot elevation
- 2400 Contour interval = 33ft. (10m)

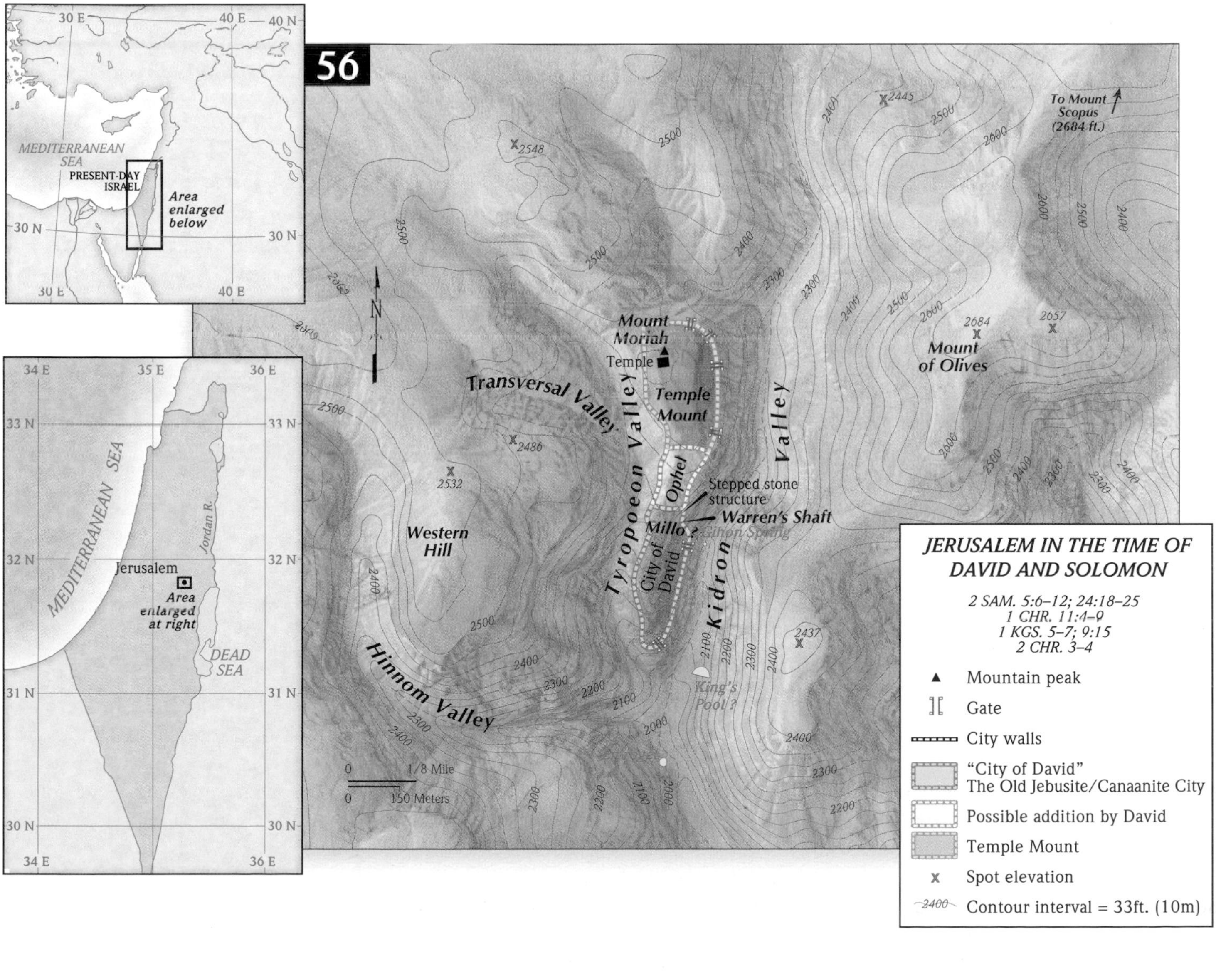

An overview of Canaanite/Jebusite Jerusalem.
Notice the "stepped-stone structure" in the center of the photograph.

CANAANITE AND JEBUSITE JERUSALEM

Pottery evidence suggests that people were first drawn to the Gihon Spring about 3500 B.C.—the Chalcolithic Period. The earliest structures date from the first part of the Early Bronze Age (3100–2800 B.C.). By the Middle Bronze Age, Jerusalem appears by name in Egyptian documents, the Execration Texts. Substantial segments of fortification walls and fragmentary buildings and floors come from this period. Genesis 14:18 mentions Melchizedek as a "priest of God Most High" and "king of Salem", possibly a reference to Jerusalem.

Jerusalem appears more frequently in Egyptian records of the Late Bronze Age (1550–1200 B.C.). The king of Jerusalem, Abdi-hepa, wrote six letters preserved in the Amarna Archive. Abdi-hepa appealed for Egyptian help against his enemies, including the Habiru (see "The Elusive Habiru," p. 60). Archaeological remains from this era are few, consisting of fragmentary structural remains on the crest of the eastern ridge. Tombs on the Mount of Olives contained pottery and other objects, including pieces imported from Cyprus.

The transition from the Late Bronze Age to the Iron Age, about 1200 B.C., is not yet well understood. At the time of Joshua the inhabitants of Jerusalem and its king, Adoni-zedek, are described as Amorites (Josh. 10:1–5). Judges 1:8 records that Judah temporarily captured Jerusalem, but the city remained in non-Israelite hands until the time of David. Several passages call Jerusalem the city of Jebus and describe the inhabitants as Jebusites, a people possibly related to the Hittites (Josh. 15:8; Judg. 19:10; 1 Chr. 11:4–5).

One interesting structure uncovered on the upper slope of the southeast side of the eastern ridge dates from this transitional period. A massive "stepped-stone structure" (eighteen meters high, thirteen meters wide) resting on and incorporating a series of terraces dates from shortly before or after 1200 B.C. The function of this structure is debated.

The stepped-stone structure may have served as a foundation for a citadel or perhaps was part of a massive buttress that expanded available building space on the crest of the ridge. Could this be part of, or related to, the "stronghold of Zion" mentioned in 2 Samuel 5:7? Or does the "stronghold of Zion" refer to the fortification that encircled the eastern ridge? These questions remain without clear answers, but the stepped-stone structure demonstrates an impressive architectural tradition during this era preceding David's conquest.

DAVID AND SOLOMON'S JERUSALEM

David's dramatic capture of Jebusite Jerusalem about 993 B.C. was the decisive event in the city's history (2 Sam. 5:6–9; 1 Chr. 11:4–7). David made Jerusalem his capital and soon

A closeup of the stepped-stone structure dating from the thirteenth/twelfth century.
Along the sides are remains of several houses dating to the later
period of the Divided Monarchy.

after transferred the Ark of the Covenant to Jerusalem. Jerusalem became Israel's national sanctuary as well as its royal capital.

The Jebusite city David conquered was about ten acres in size, concentrated on the southeastern hill above the Gihon Spring (2 Sam. 5). The water supply system of this era has been thoroughly explored. From inside the city's fortifications on the east, an entrance chamber and tunnel led down to a vertical shaft thirteen meters deep (known today as Warren's Shaft) directly over another horizonal tunnel that brought water from the Gihon

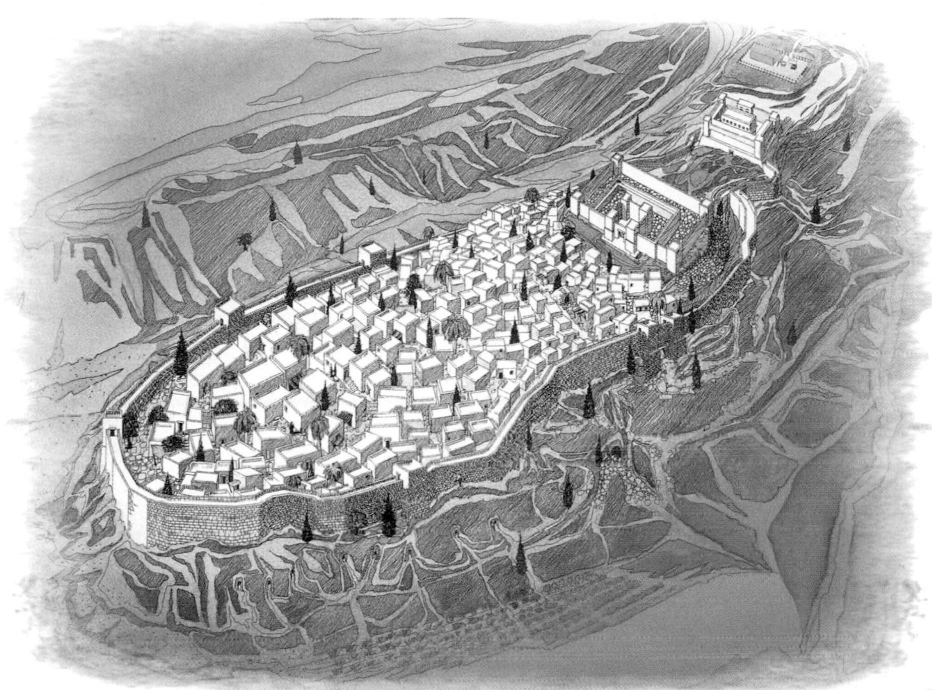

Reconstruction of David's Jerusalem.

Spring. People of Jerusalem could lower containers down the shaft to get water without leaving the protection of the walls. Speculation that David's men surprised the Jebusites by climbing up the vertical shaft cannot be proven (cf. 2 Sam. 5). Recent studies have pointed out the difficulty of scaling the shaft.

David's building operations in Jerusalem are briefly recounted: "And he built the city all around, from the millo even to the surrounding area" (1 Chr. 11:8; cf. 2 Sam. 5:9). The term *millo* has been much discussed. The Hebrew term means "fill" or "filling." Some scholars believe *millo* refers to terraces built along the eastern slope of Jerusalem that supported other structures. According to this theory, that would explain why the millo periodically had to be maintained (see 1 Kgs. 9:15; 2 Chr. 32:5). Others suggest that the millo was a filling of a narrow neck of the eastern ridge north of the City of David that joined the Temple Mount. Perhaps the "stepped-stone structure" from the earlier Jebusite era was part of the millo—possibly a stone platform that supported larger public buildings. None of these ideas commands general assent; however, the eastern slope required terracing to support buildings and expanded the usable space.

David also built the house of cedar with the assistance of Hiram, king of Tyre (2 Sam. 5:11). Although clearly a palace, David's "house" undoubtedly was much less impressive than the luxurious palace complex built by Solomon. Several indications suggest that David began the expansion of Jerusalem northward. He built an altar to God upon a higher northern elevation on a threshing floor purchased from Araunah the Jebusite (2 Sam. 24:18–25). Eventually Solomon built the temple upon this land procured by David (2 Chr. 3:1).

Solomon commenced his grand design for Jerusalem by incorporating the land purchased by David within the city walls (1 Kgs. 11:27). This action enclosed the slightly higher rise to the north of the citadel identified as Mount Moriah and provided space for the temple and palace complex. Solomon depended heavily upon Phoenician craftsmen and materials supplied by Hiram. He employed conscripted labor for his building projects, both in Jerusalem and throughout his kingdom.

Workmen labored seven years to complete the temple, while the palace required thirteen years. First Kgs. 7:1–8 mentions several components of the palace, including the House of the Forest of Lebanon, the Hall of Pillars, a Hall of Judgement, and the House of Pharaoh's daughter. Whether these represented separate buildings grouped around a common courtyard or were parts of a large ceremonial palace (*Bit Hilani* type) found in northern Syria and southern Turkey remains uncertain. In either case Solomon's official residence reflected an opulence and prestige befitting his kingdom.

SOLOMON'S TEMPLE

Solomon's most celebrated accomplishment was the construction of a temple for Yahweh. This beautiful building on the eminence north of David's city crowned the capital city until the temple was destroyed by the armies of Nebuchadnezzar more than 330 years later. Again, Phoenician influence predominated in the seven-year project. Hiram, king of Tyre, furnished timber and skilled craftsmen to assist Solomon. Men from the Phoenician city Gebal (Byblos) joined Solomon's laborers as well. Since Israel had little experience in metalworking, Solomon imported a Phoenician metalsmith, also named Hiram. He fashioned the bronze pillars and decorations, the great basin or "the molten sea," the bronze altar, and other vessels and tools used in the temple (1 Kgs. 6).

The temple of Yahweh was a rectangular structure composed of three main parts oriented on an east-west axis. A per-

Sunrise over the Temple Mount area of Jerusalem viewed from the Mount of Olives.

son entered the temple from the east through a porch flanked on both sides by two bronze pillars, Jachin and Boaz.

The porch led to the main hall of the temple, or "Holy Place," where three pieces of furniture used in worship were located: the golden lampstand (Menorah), the altar of incense, and the table of shewbread. Beyond the main room at the western end of the structure, a cubical room known as the "Holy of Holies" housed the Ark of the Covenant. Two gilded olivewood cherubim kept silent watch over the sacred chest. The architectural scheme of a three-part temple is known from a few earlier Canaanite temples found at Hazor and Lachish. A more contemporary parallel is the small "royal chapel" found at Tell Tainet in Syria, which is dated to the ninth century. The temple of Tell Tainet not only bears an architectural plan similar to Solomon's temple at Jerusalem, but was also located in close proximity to the palace, as was the Jerusalem temple.

The outer walls of Solomon's temple were made of fine white limestone that was locally quarried. The interior walls were covered by cedar planks, while cypress and olivewood provided floor coverings, doors and door frames, and other furnishings. Ornate carvings, precious stones, and gold overlay adorned the interior walls and equipment. Multilevel storage facilities surrounded the temple on all sides except the entrance. The great bronze laver and sacrificial altar stood in the forecourt east of the porch. Estimates of the size of the temple depend on the size of the cubit and one's interpretation of the measurements given in several texts (1 Kgs. 6; 2 Chr. 3; Ezek. 40–42). The length of a cubit varied historically between 17.5 and 21 inches. If the measurements in 1 Kgs. 6 refer to the interior dimensions, the interior space, counting the porch, totaled 70 cubits (115 feet) in length and 20 cubits (33 feet) in width. Ezekiel's dimensions presume the ancillary storage facilities, giving a larger total—perhaps 180 feet long and 85 feet wide. Altogether, the temple must have been an impressive structure. Its memory still stirred the hearts of faithful Jews even after its destruction (Ezra 3:12–13; Hag. 2:1–3).

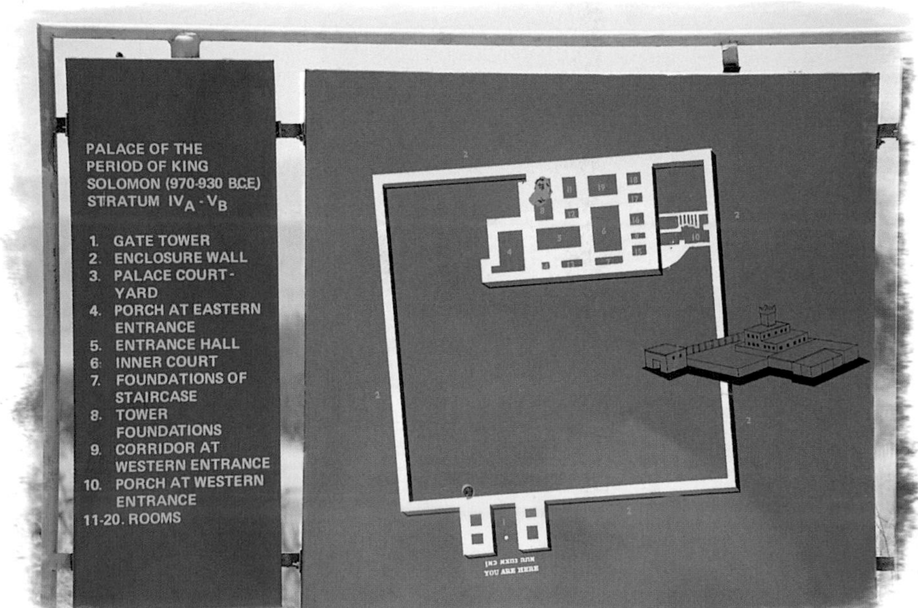

A diagram of a governor's palace surrounded by a defensive wall and gate at Megiddo. The palace takes the form of a "Bit-Hilani" structure in which several courtyards and rooms are gathered together in one structure. Solomon's palace at Jerusalem likely followed this style.

Chapter Ten

THE KINGDOMS OF ISRAEL AND JUDAH

Introduction

The death of Solomon in 922 B.C. marked the end of an era in which one king exercised authority over all the tribes of Israel. Henceforth, two independent nations emerged: Judah in the south and Israel in the north, each with distinct governments and national character. Israel survived the complex international changes of the Iron Age for two hundred years (922–722 B.C.), while Judah managed to maintain her identity until 586 B.C. In the end both Israel and Judah succumbed to the great powers of Mesopotamia—Assyria and Babylon—whose spreading tentacles engulfed the smaller states of the Levant.

This period from 922 to 586 B.C., often called the Divided Monarchy, forms the background of much of the Old Testament. Many of Israel's writing prophets—Amos, Isaiah, Hosea, Micah, Jeremiah, and others—preached in these crucial times. First Kings 12 to 2 Kings 25, complemented by 2 Chronicles 10–36, covers events of this era. Several of the Psalms and perhaps other portions of the Wisdom Literature reflect this period. All in all, the Divided Kingdom represents a complex but crucial background for understanding much of the Old Testament.

Israel, the Northern Kingdom

The two kingdoms of Israel and Judah, though originating in the empire of David and Solomon, were fundamentally different in character. Israel, also called Ephraim by the prophets, normally was the wealthier, more powerful, and larger of the two. Her borders extended from Bethel northward to Dan, encompassing the Galilee, the hills of Samaria, and portions of the Transjordan, including Gilead and northern Moab. Portions of the two major international highways—the International Coastal Highway and the King's Highway—transversed Israel's territories. Control of these trade routes meant commercial wealth and access to luxury items.

The wealthy Phoenician cities on the northwestern border provided powerful commercial allies to boost the economy. Israel's geographical openness to other cultures fostered a cosmopolitanism in her cities and villages, not only in material culture and social customs, but even in religion. The Phoenician connection stirred the epidemic of Baalism that Elijah and Elisha so bitterly opposed about 850 B.C. Politically, Israel centered on the old tribal territories of Ephraim and Manasseh.

Shechem, Tirzah, and finally Samaria—all located close together in Manasseh—served as capitals. From about 850 B.C. onward, Samaria became the nerve center of Israel until its fall to Assyria in 722 B.C. The kings of Israel came from nine different families (see chart), only two of which survived beyond the second generation. Kings were selected by prophetic designation and popular assent, but could be removed violently when popular support waned. This political instability coupled with the Northern Kingdom's vulnerability to attack were key factors in Israel's downfall.

Judah, the Southern Kingdom

Judah, on the other hand, was much more geographically isolated than Israel. Her borders stretched from the territory of Benjamin southward to Kadesh-barnea, although she often controlled much less territory. No international route crossed her borders, and natural barriers gave Judah a measure of protection lacking in Israel. This isolation meant that Judah's commercial ties were more limited than Israel's. The most important commercial ties led southward to the Red Sea port of Ezion-geber and important caravan links through the Negeb. Only when Judah was strong could these routes be exploited. The Edomites persistently battled Judah for these trade opportunities. Still, the relative isolation of Judah had the important benefit of a more homogeneous population less susceptible to outside influences.

The kingdom of Judah was founded on Jerusalem and the royal house of David. Jerusalem was both the religious and political center of the nation; the temple housing the Ark of the Covenant was the most prestigious shrine in all the land. Every king of Judah, except the usurper Athaliah, came from the line of David, giving Judah a political stability that was the envy of other states. Thus, although militarily and economically weaker than Israel, Judah possessed an innate stability based on her tribal traditions and loyalties, which permitted her to survive more than 130 years longer than her powerful northern rival.

The Division of the Kingdom

When Solomon died in 922 B.C., the tribe of Judah readily accepted his son Rehoboam as heir to the Davidic throne.

CHART 8. PERIOD AT A GLANCE: THE DIVIDED MONARCHY 922–722 B.C.

Dates	Judah	Israel	Prophets	Aram-Damascus	Assyria
922	Split of Solomon's kingdom				
	Rehoboam II (922–915)	Jeroboam I (922–901)			
	Campaign of Shishak (918)				
900	Asa appealed to Ben-hadad I			Ben-hadad I attacked Judah	
		Omri (876–869)			Ashurnasirpal II (883–859)
875			Elijah	Ben-hadad II (Hadad-ezer) besieged Samaria, fought Ahab; joined coalition at Qarqar	
		Ahab (869–850)			Shalmaneser III (859–824)
					Battle of Qarqar (853)
850			Elisha		
		Jehu paid tribute to Shalmaneser III		Hazael: frequently oppressed Israel from ca. 843–806	Received tribute from Israel (841)
825					Assyrian weakness (824–745)
				Ben-hadad III oppressed Israel, but was attacked by Adad-nirari III	Adad-nirari III (810–783) attacked Damascus; relieved pressure on Israel
		Jehoash (802–786)			
800	Amaziah (800–783)				
	Uzziah (783–742)	Jeroboam II (786–746)			
	Period of prosperity for both Judah and Israel				
775					
			Amos		
750					
			Isaiah		
			Hosea		Tiglath-pileser III (Assyrian Empire) took tribute from Menachen (738); attacked Israel (733)
735	Ahaz (735–715)	Pekah (736–732)		Rezin: with Pekah tried to force Judah to join anti-Assyrian coalition	
	Syro-Ephraimite War (735)				
		Israel attacked by Tiglath-pileser. Hoshea rebelled against Assyria			
					Shalmaneser V (727–722) Siege of Samaria
722		Destruction of Israel	Micah		Sargon II (722/1–705) Deported 27,000 Israelites

CHART 9. KINGS OF THE DIVIDED MONARCHY

Judah	(Bright)[1]	(Miller/Hays)[2]
Rehoboam	922–915	924–907
Abijam	915–913	907–906
Asa	913–873	905–874
Jehoshaphat	873–849	874–850
Jehoram	849–843	850–843
Ahaziah	843–842	843
Athaliah (usurper)	842–837	843–837
Joash	837–800	837–?
Amaziah	800–783	?–?
Uzziah (Azariah)	783–742	?–?
Jotham	742–735	?–742
Ahaz	735–715	742–727
Hezekiah	715–687/6	727–698
Manasseh	687/6–642	697–642
Amon	642–640	642–640
Josiah	640–609	639–609
Jehoahaz	609	609
Jehoiakim	609–598	608–598
Jehoiachin	598/7	598/7
Zedekiah	597–587	597–586
Destruction of Jerusalem and the temple: 586		

Israel	(Bright)[1]	(Miller/Hays)[2]
[Jeroboam I	922–901	924–903
*Nadab	901–900	903–902
[Baasha	900–877	902–886
*Elah	877–876	886–885
[Zimri (suicide)	876	
The Omrides	876–842	885–843
[Omri	876–869	885–873
Ahab	869–850	873–851
Ahaziah	850–849	851–849
*Jehoram	849–842	849–843
Dynasty of Jehu	842–746	843–745
[Jehu	843/2–815	843–816
Jehoahaz	815–801	816–800
Jehoash (Joash)	801–786	800–785
Jeroboam II	786–746	785–745
*Zechriah	746–745	745
[*Shallum	745	745
[Menahem	745–737	745–736
*Pekahiah	737–736	736–735
[*Pekah	736–732	735–732
[Hoshea	732–724	732–723
Fall of Samaria	722	

Asterisk (*) indicates assassination
[1] Dates preferred by John Bright, *A History of Israel.*3rd ed.
[2] Dates preferred by J. Maxwell Miller and John H. Hayes, *A History of Ancient Israel and Judah.*
Brackets ([) indicate dynasties

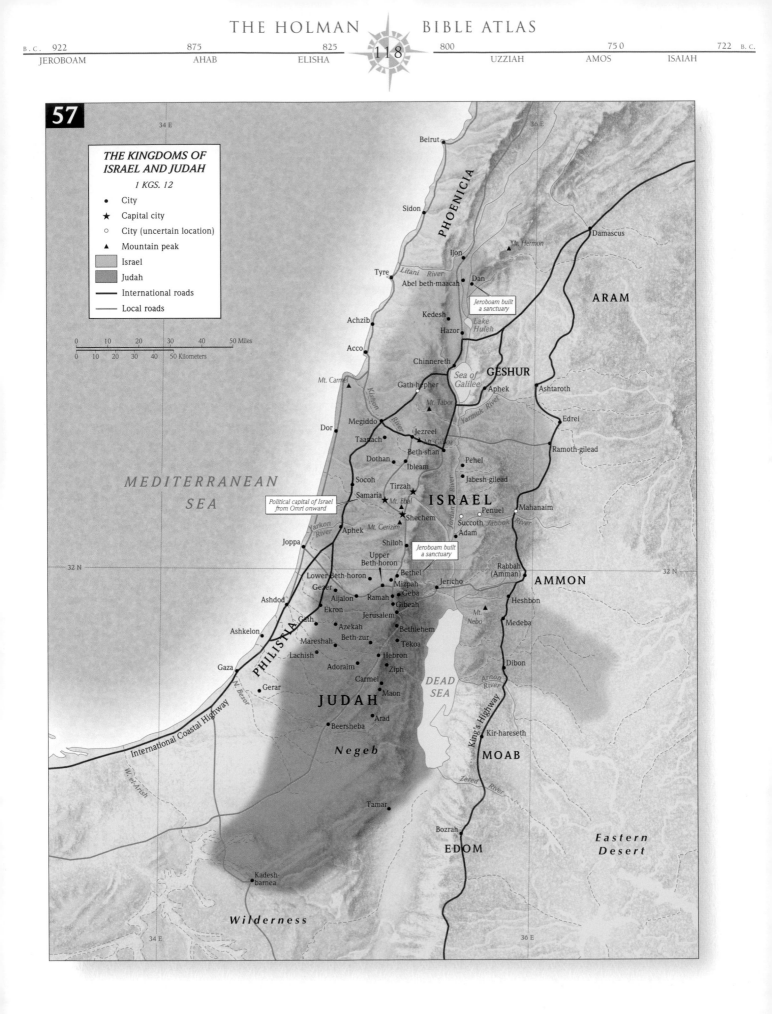

57
THE KINGDOMS OF ISRAEL AND JUDAH
1 KGS. 12
City
Capital city
City (uncertain location)
Mountain peak
Israel
Judah
International roads
Local roads
0 10 20 30 40 50 Miles
0 10 20 30 40 50 Kilometers
MEDITERRANEAN SEA
PHOENICIA
ARAM
GESHUR
ISRAEL
AMMON
JUDAH
PHILISTIA
MOAB
EDOM
Negeb
Wilderness
Eastern Desert
DEAD SEA
Sea of Galilee
Lake Huleh
Jeroboam built a sanctuary
Political capital of Israel from Omri onward
Jeroboam built a sanctuary
Beirut
Sidon
Tyre
Achzib
Acco
Mt. Carmel
Dor
Joppa
Ashdod
Ashkelon
Gaza
Gerar
Kadesh-barnea
Damascus
Mt. Hermon
Ijon
Dan
Abel beth-maacah
Kedesh
Hazor
Chinnereth
Gath-hepher
Mt. Tabor
Aphek
Ashtaroth
Edrei
Ramoth-gilead
Megiddo
Taanach
Jezreel
Mt. Gilboa
Beth-shan
Dothan
Ibleam
Pehel
Jabesh-gilead
Socoh
Tirzah
Samaria
Mt. Ebal
Shechem
Mt. Gerizim
Penuel
Mahanaim
Succoth
Adam
Aphek
Shiloh
Upper Beth-horon
Lower Beth-horon
Bethel
Mizpah
Jericho
Rabbah (Amman)
Gezer
Aijalon
Ramah
Geba
Gibeah
Ekron
Jerusalem
Heshbon
Mt. Nebo
Medeba
Gath
Azekah
Bethlehem
Beth-zur
Mareshah
Tekoa
Lachish
Hebron
Adoraim
Ziph
Dibon
Carmel
Maon
Arad
Beersheba
Kir-hareseth
Tamar
Bozrah
Litani River
Kishon River
Yarmuk River
Jordan River
Jabbok River
Yarkon River
Arnon River
Zered River
N. Besor
W. el-Arish
International Coastal Highway
King's Highway
34 E
36 E
32 N

Leaders of the northern tribes balked at the prospects of a new king who would follow the social and economic policies of the old regime, policies that they believed favored Judah and placed a heavy burden on their own tribes. Provisioning the lavish court in Jerusalem with their taxes and providing laborers for Solomon's building projects sapped the strength of the northern tribes. The result was deep dissatisfaction toward the leadership in Jerusalem. The emergence of older tribal allegiances compounded the problem. Both of these troubling issues fanned rebellious sentiment.

A fateful meeting between Rehoboam and the elders of the tribes occurred at Shechem. As a condition of their allegiance (1 Kgs. 12), the elders demanded concessions on the part of Rehoboam—relief from what they regarded as the harsh excesses of Solomon. The volatile situation deteriorated rapidly when Rehoboam rejected outright the elders' request and threatened stricter measures as a fitting antidote to sedition. Like a flash of lightning, Rehoboam's foolish response struck the heart of the northern tribal elders, who in turn voiced a cry of rebellion against the house of David.

A disgruntled Ephramite named Jeroboam, a former overseer of Solomon's forced labor gangs recently returned from exile in Egypt, emerged as the leader of the northern tribes. The point of no return had been reached; the kingdom of Solomon vanished, conquered not from without but from within by the passions of older, deeper tribal loyalties. In its place two weaker kingdoms struggled for survival.

Jeroboam quickly consolidated his control over the northern tribes, establishing a capital at Shechem. However, religious loyalties of his subjects presented a difficult dilemma. His rival Rehoboam controlled Jerusalem and along with it the temple of Yahweh, which housed the most sacred object of ancient Israel, the Ark of the Covenant. Jeroboam ordered the building of two temples—one at Dan and the other at Bethel—in which golden bulls were erected, apparently to offset the place of Jerusalem (1 Kgs. 12:25–33). Both sites were centers of ancient Israelite tradition and marked the limits of the new kingdom's borders. (See "Jeroboam's New Worship Centers," below.)

Jeroboam's new temples seemed well suited to rival the temple of Jerusalem. The choice of the bull images, however, had fatal consequences. The bull had long been associated with pagan gods, especially the Canaanite deities El and Baal. A recently discovered bronze bull figurine from Askelon (from ca. 1400 B.C.) and another found near Shechem (from ca. 1100 B.C.) confirm the idolatrous associations of the image. Probably Jeroboam intended only to offer Israel a visible alternative to the Ark—upon which the invisible presence of Yahweh was enthroned when he erected the golden bulls. Regardless of motives, the effect was disastrous: the golden calves became a focus for idolatry and pagan religion.

JEROBOAM'S NEW WORSHIP CENTERS

Jeroboam I selected two important border cities, Dan and Bethel, in which to build temples, and in them he placed the infamous golden calves (1 Kgs. 12:25–33). Dan and Bethel both had ancient cultic traditions associated with Israel's past and quickly became national shrines intended to rival the temple of Solomon at Jerusalem.

DAN

The fifty-acre site of ancient Dan (Tell el-Qadi, "the mound of the judge") lies beneath the slopes of Mount Hermon, along important caravan routes. Copious springs welling up along the edge of the mound are a major source for the Jordan River. The surrounding fertile plains attracted Early Bronze Age settlers and the city flourished throughout the Middle and Late Bronze Ages (ca. 2000–1200 B.C.). The Mari Texts and Egyptian Execration Texts mention Laish (Dan) in the Middle Bronze Age, while the Bible first mentions Dan in Abraham's time (Gen. 14:14). A remarkably preserved brick gate dating to this period was discovered encased in a slightly later earth rampart (see photograph, p. 120). At a much later time, the tribe of Dan, forced to migrate northward in search of new lands, conquered Laish and renamed the city Dan. The Danites brought with them a graven image obtained along the way and established a line of priests to serve the cult at Dan (Judg. 18).

Jeroboam I established a religious center at Dan. Israeli archaeologist Avraham Biran excavated Dan and uncovered a large podium nineteen meters long built of ashlar stones, which he identified as part of Jeroboam's cultic structure. The podium was destroyed and rebuilt sometime in the 800s, perhaps in connection with the raid of Ben-hadad mentioned in 1 Kings 15:16–20. Biran first interpreted the structure as an open-air high place, but more recently scholars believe the podium was a foundation for a temple.

A flight of five stone steps leading from a square enclosure approached the temple from the south. The enclosure contained a sacrificial altar (5 x 5 meters) made of ashlars. A small, square, horned altar and fragments of a larger horned altar were found nearby. Ancillary buildings on the west provided space for priests, storage, and minor acts of sacrifice. This temple complex must be the one described in 1 Kings 12:25–34.

Biran made an exceptionally exciting find at Dan in the form of a fragmentary stele that mentions "the house of David," the first extrabiblical reference to David and his dynasty. Recently, two other pieces of the same stele have been found. The stele likely was left at Dan by an Aramean king who took the city during the intermittent wars between Israel and Damascus throughout the ninth century (see further "The Arameans and the Kingdom of Aram-Damascus" pp.124–25).

Biran also discovered a well-preserved gate complex at Dan consisting of an outer and inner gate. The gate had two flanking towers and four guard rooms typical of the ninth and eighth centuries. Dan's forward position along Israel's northern borders required heavy fortification. Outside the northern tower of the gate, Biran discovered a benchlike installation built of ashlars with stone bases that may have supported a canopy. The function of the installation is not clear; it may have provided a place for the king to sit (cf. 2 Sam. 19:9) or perhaps it was a high place that stood near the gate (cf. 2 Kgs. 23:8).

Dan maintained its status as a major religious center into the eighth century (Amos 8:14). Although the Bible does not mention it, Dan must have fallen prey to the raid of Tiglath-pileser III in 733 B.C. Thereafter, the Bible rarely mentions Dan (see 2 Chr. 30:5; Jer. 4:15; 8:16), although the city remained an important cultic center into the Hellenistic and Roman periods. A late Greek and Aramaic bilingual inscription from the Hellenistic era is dedicated "To the God who is in Dan."

The temple of Dan built by Jeroboam I.
The steps lead up to a large platform made of ashlar masonry.

BETHEL

Traditions going back to the days of the patriarchs connected Bethel ("House of God") with Israel's past. Abraham built an altar near Bethel (Gen. 12:8), and Jacob spent the night at Bethel, formerly called Luz, where God in a dream reaffirmed the Abrahamic covenant (Gen. 28:10–22; see also Gen. 35:1–16).

Substantial temples from the Canaanite period have been uncovered at Bethel, whose ruins lie partly under the modern village of Beitin. Israel briefly kept the Ark of the Covenant at Bethel (Judg. 20:26–27), an important city during the period of the judges.

These traditions and Bethel's strategic position on the southern extremity of Israel's border prompted Jeroboam I to choose Bethel as a national shrine. As in Dan, Jeroboam erected a temple and placed within it a golden calf (1 Kgs. 12:29–33). Unfortunately, no trace of this structure has been located. Jeroboam instituted festivals and sacrifices at Bethel on an unprecedented scale. Bethel's proximity to Jerusalem (eleven miles north of Jerusalem) made it a natural rival to Solomon's temple. Prophets, both true and false, often preached at Bethel (1 Kgs. 13:1–10). In his travels Elijah encountered a group of prophets at Bethel (2 Kgs. 2:2–4), while Amos' fiery words drew the rebuke of Amaziah, the priest at Bethel (Amos 7:10–13). True prophets often condemned Bethel as the center of idolatry (Amos 3:14; 5:5–6; Hos. 10:15). Amos sarcastically parodied the corrupt worship practices at Bethel (Amos 4:4), and Hosea substituted the name Beth-aven, "House of evil," for Bethel in his scathing denunciations of religion gone terribly wrong (Hos. 5:8–9; 10:5).

The Assyrians destroyed Bethel shortly after 722 B.C., but it retained its religious significance when the new masters appointed a priest there (2 Kgs. 17:28–41). Josiah dismantled the altar and high place at Bethel during the course of his reforms in the late seventh century (2 Kgs. 23:15), yet the city survived down through the Byzantine period before succumbing to the Arab conquest.

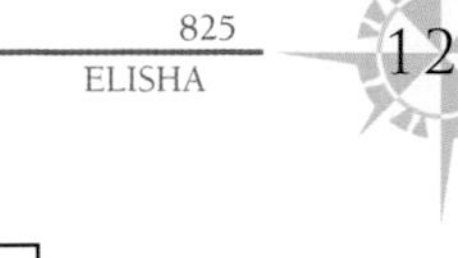

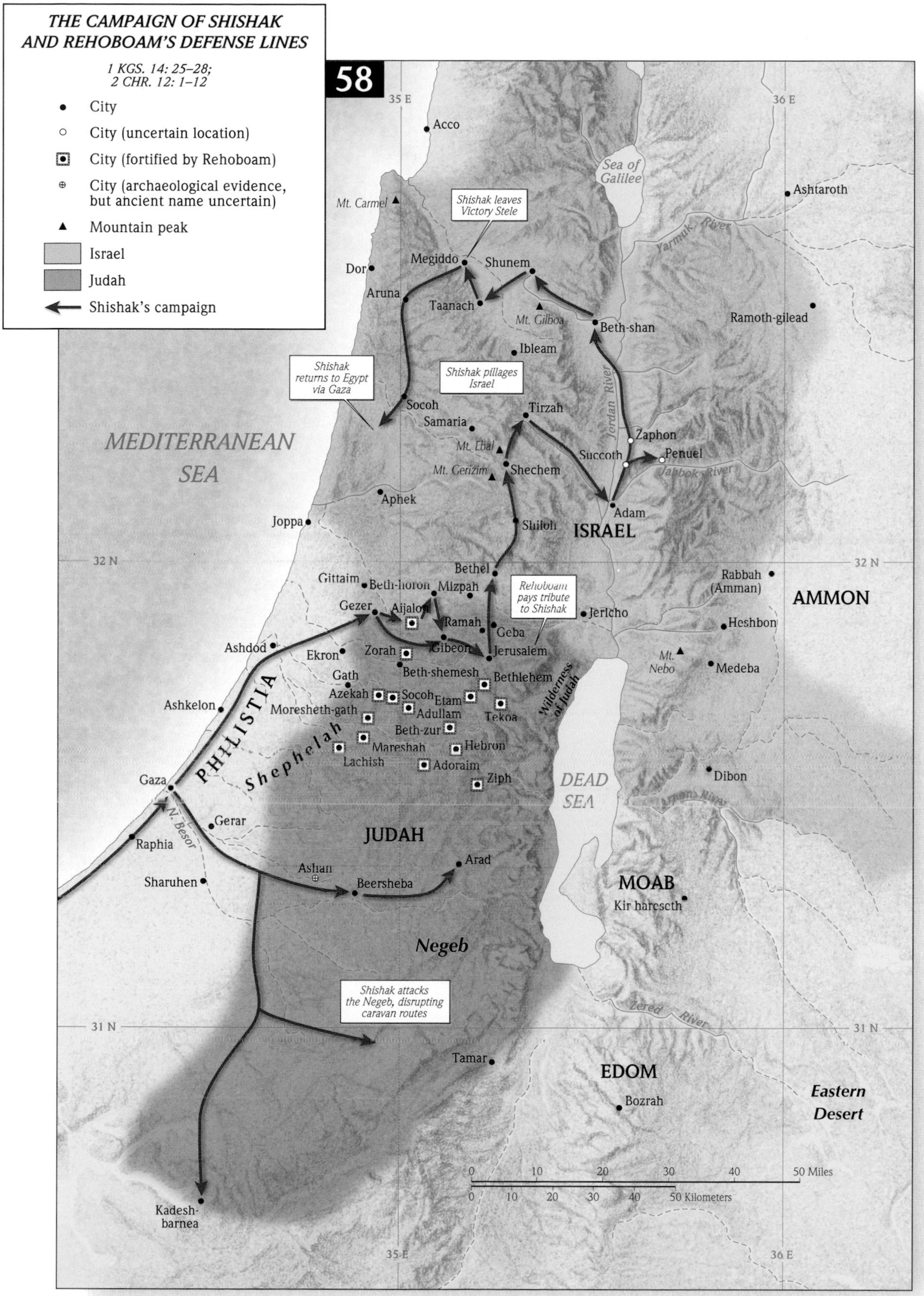

THE CAMPAIGN OF SHISHAK AND REHOBOAM'S DEFENSE LINES
1 KGS. 14: 25–28; 2 CHR. 12: 1–12
58
City
City (uncertain location)
City (fortified by Rehoboam)
City (archaeological evidence, but ancient name uncertain)
Mountain peak
Israel
Judah
Shishak's campaign
35 E
36 E
32 N
31 N
Acco
Sea of Galilee
Ashtaroth
Mt. Carmel
Shishak leaves Victory Stele
Yarmuk River
Megiddo
Shunem
Dor
Aruna
Taanach
Mt. Gilboa
Beth-shan
Ramoth-gilead
Ibleam
Shishak returns to Egypt via Gaza
Shishak pillages Israel
Socoh
Tirzah
Samaria
Jordan River
MEDITERRANEAN SEA
Zaphon
Mt. Ebal
Succoth
Penuel
Jabbok River
Mt. Gerizim
Shechem
Aphek
Adam
Joppa
Shiloh
ISRAEL
Bethel
Rabbah (Amman)
Gittaim
Beth-horon
Mizpah
Rehoboam pays tribute to Shishak
AMMON
Gezer
Aijalon
Jericho
Ramah
Heshbon
Geba
Ashdod
Gibeon
Jerusalem
Ekron
Zorah
Mt. Nebo
Medeba
Beth-shemesh
Bethlehem
Gath
Wilderness of Judah
Azekah
Socoh
Etam
Ashkelon
Moresheth-gath
Adullam
Tekoa
PHILISTIA
Beth-zur
Shephelah
Mareshah
Hebron
Lachish
Adoraim
Ziph
Dibon
DEAD SEA
Gaza
Arnon River
N. Besor
Gerar
JUDAH
Raphia
Arad
Ashan
Sharuhen
Beersheba
MOAB
Kir hareseth
Negeb
Shishak attacks the Negeb, disrupting caravan routes
Zered River
Tamar
EDOM
Eastern Desert
Bozrah
0 10 20 30 40 50 Miles
0 10 20 30 40 50 Kilometers
Kadesh-barnea

Early Conflicts and Invasions

The division of the kingdom produced immediate problems for both Israel and Judah. Both kingdoms were now considerably smaller and weaker than the kingdom of David and Solomon. Conflict broke out in the area of Benjamin as the two nations struggled to establish new borders. Benjamin had greater tribal ties with Israel, but its proximity to Jerusalem made control of Benjamin vital to Judah's interest. Skirmishes between Israelite and Judean troops continued intermittently shortly before and after 900 B.C. Ramah, Geba, and Mizpah were key fortified points, alternately won or lost in the attempt to define the limits of the two kingdoms (1 Kgs. 15).

THE EGYPTIAN THREAT

The campaign of the Egyptian pharaoh Shishak I in the fifth year of Rehoboam (918 B.C.) reveals the relative weakness of both Israel and Judah. The Egyptians had been nonaggressive in the Levant for several centuries, partly due to their own weakness, but also in response to the strength of the United Monarchy. Shishak, founder of the Twenty-second Libyan Dynasty, attacked Judah first and then pillaged Israel according to 1 Kings 14:25–26 and his own inscription carved on a doorway of the temple of Amon at Thebes.

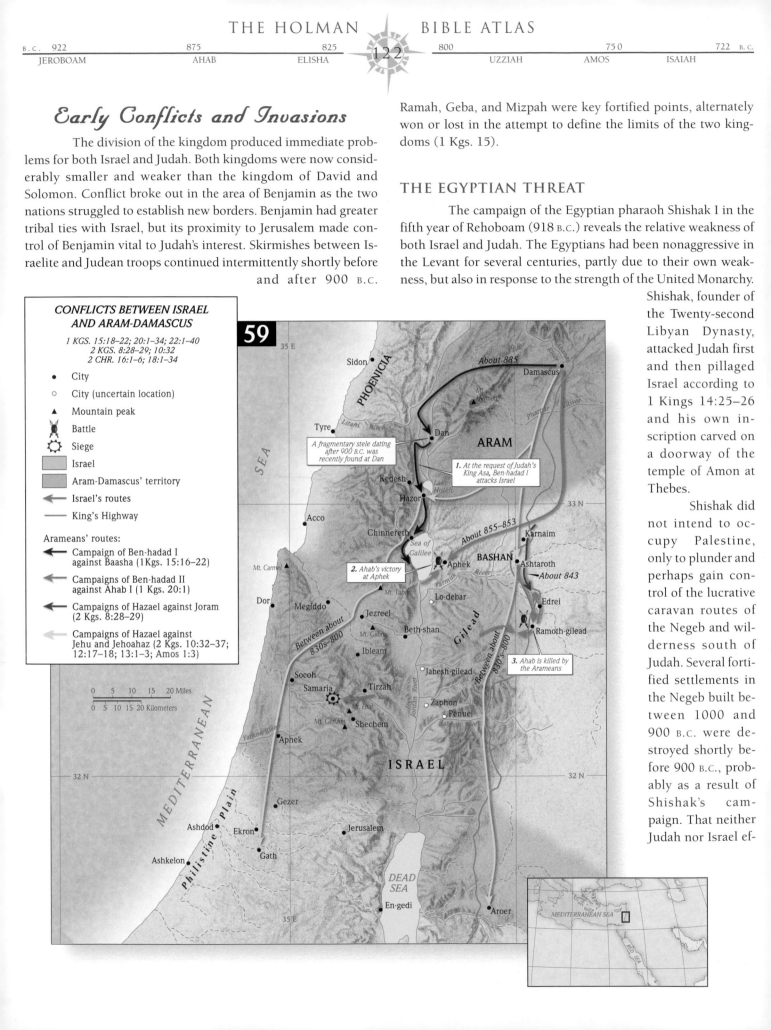

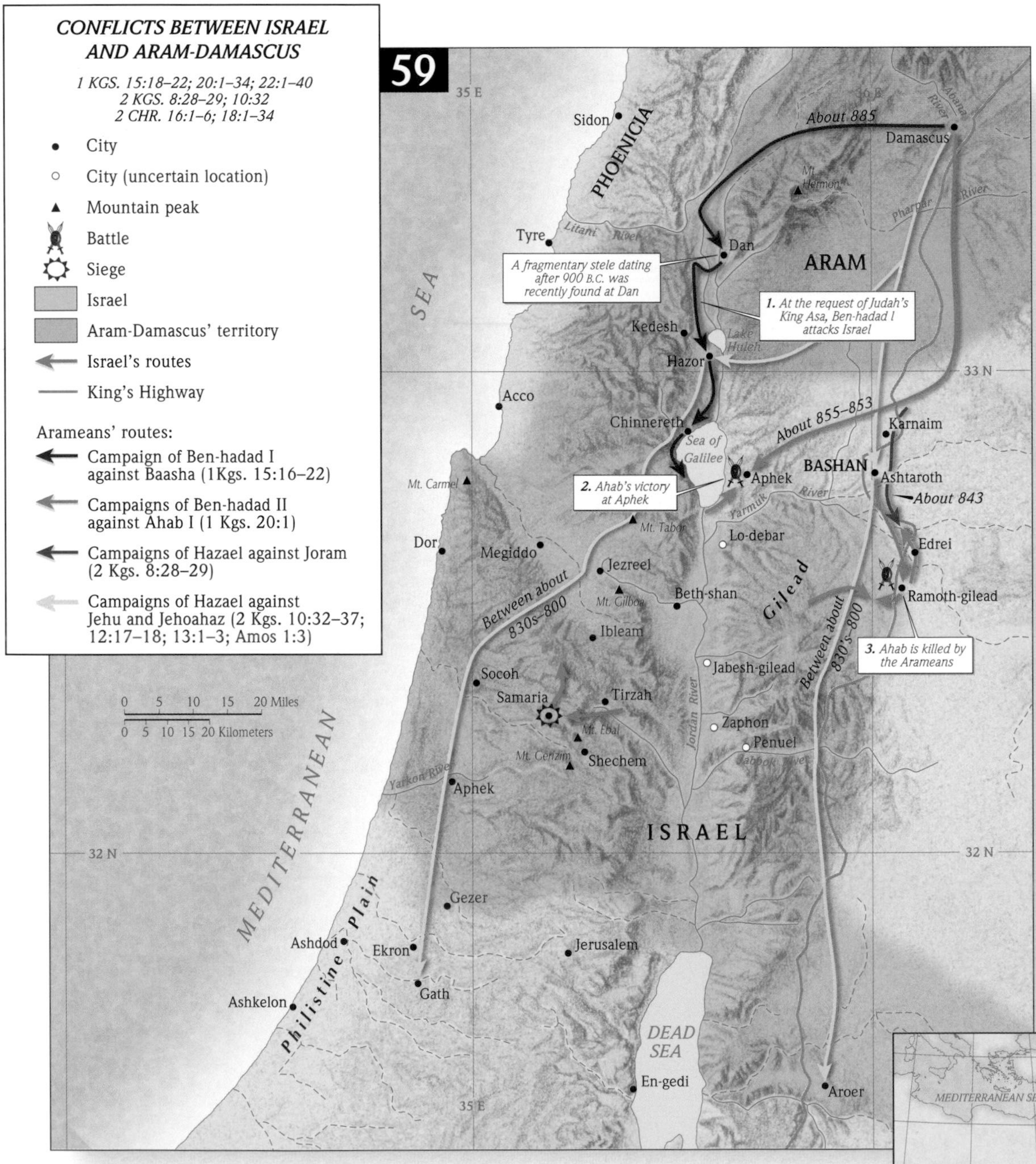

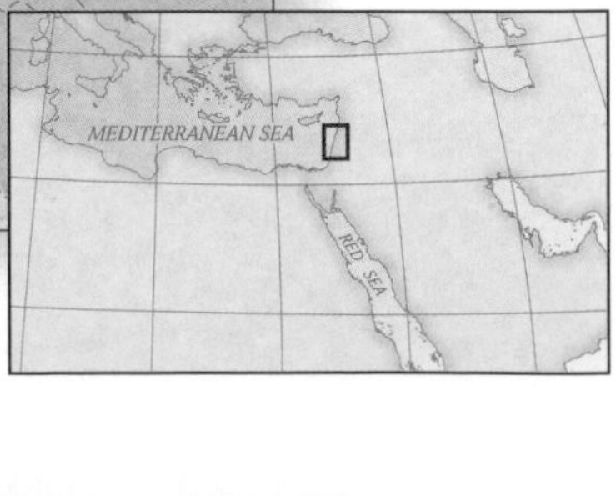

Shishak did not intend to occupy Palestine, only to plunder and perhaps gain control of the lucrative caravan routes of the Negeb and wilderness south of Judah. Several fortified settlements in the Negeb built between 1000 and 900 B.C. were destroyed shortly before 900 B.C., probably as a result of Shishak's campaign. That neither Judah nor Israel effectively resisted Shishak underscores their weakness. Moreover, when Rehoboam fortified his kingdom either shortly before or after the attack by Shishak, his lines of fortification covered a much-reduced territory when compared to the area controlled by Judah during Solomon's kingdom (2 Chr. 11:5–12). A later Egyptian campaign led by the obscure Zerah (perhaps an officer in Shishak's army) was beaten back (2 Chr. 14:9–15).

Israel fared little better in the aftermath of the division of the kingdom. Much of Israel's territorial holdings in the Transjordan melted away. Moab, Ammon, and likely Edom gained their independence. We are especially well informed about Israel's relationship to Moab through the famous Moabite Stone found at Dibon in 1868, now in the Louvre in Paris. Mesha, king of Moab (2 Kgs. 1:1; 3:4–27), described how his ancestors struggled against Israel, at times gaining their freedom, at other periods remaining under an Israelite yoke.

The Moabite Stone found at Dibon. In the inscription, Mesha, king of Moab, gives thanks to Chemosh for delivering Moab out of the hands of Israel.

THE ARAMEAN THREAT

More menacing were the Aramean states northeast of Israel, especially Aram-Damascus, whose kings coveted the King's Highway that crossed the Transjordan. Whatever authority Solomon had exercised over these kingdoms now was gone. Asa, king of Judah, appealed to Ben-hadad I for help in his border war with his Israelite rival, Baasha (1 Kgs. 15:16–21). Ben-hadad's attack on Israel relieved the pressure on Judah's northern border and initiated conflict between Israel and Damascus. Wars between Israel and Damascus continued throughout the ninth century with only

CHART 10. KINGS OF ARAM-DAMASCUS

Name	Old Testament Reference	Key Old Testament Passage
Rezon	Contemporary of Solomon; seized Damascus and became an adversary of Israel. Some scholars identify Rezon with Hezion (1 Kgs. 15:18)	1 Kgs. 11:23–25
Tabrimmon	Father of Ben-hadad I	1 Kgs. 15:18
Ben-hadad I	Son of Tabrimmon. Attacked Israel at Asa's request in the reign of Baasha	1 Kgs. 15:18–22; 2 Chr. 16:1–6
Ben-hadad II Known as Hadad-ezer in Assyrian sources	Contemporary of Ahab. Besieged Samaria. Fought Ahab at Aphek east of the Sea of Chinnereth. Fought Israel at Ramoth-gilead. Joined Ahab in an anti-Assyrian coalition that fought Shalmaneser III at Qarqar in 853 B.C.	1 Kgs. 20:1–34; 22:1–40; 2 Kgs. 6:24–7:20, 8:7–15; 2 Chr. 18:1–34
Hazael	Usurper who seized the throne of Damascus ca. 843 B.C. Assyrian records call him "a son of a nobody," i.e., a commoner. Besieged Ramoth-gilead in the days of Joram. During the late ninth century in the reigns of Jehu and Jehoahaz, Hazael frequently oppressed Israel, Judah, and the Philistine cities as well. Most able of kings of Damascus.	1 Kgs. 19:15; 2 Kgs. 8:7–15; 8:28–29; 10:32; 12:17–18; 13:1–9; 13:25
Ben-hadad III (?)*	Son of Hazael. Contemporary of Jehoahaz. Continued to oppress Israel. Joash fought Ben-hadad, temporarily throwing off the Aramean yoke; Adad-nirari III attacked Damascus (either in 805 or 796). Ben-hadad lost much of the kingdom built by his father, Hazael.	2 Kgs. 13:3–8
Rezin	Probably a usurper; led an anti-Assyrian coalition, including Israel, Philistia, and Phoenician cities ca. 737–735. With Israel, attacked Judah to force Ahaz to join coalition ca. 735 (Syro-Ephraimite War). Last king of an independent Aram-Damascus. Killed by the Assyrians ca. 732 B.C.	2 Kgs. 15–16; Isa. 7

*The number of Damascus kings bearing the name Ben-hadad is disputed.

THE ARAMEANS AND THE KINGDOM OF ARAM-DAMASCUS

Israel's northern neighbors were the various Aramean kingdoms that emerged about the same time Israel settled in Canaan. The Arameans occupied Syria and the regions of the Habor and Balikh Rivers in northwest Mesopotamia, the areas from which Abraham migrated. Israel recalled an ancestral connection with the Arameans: "a wandering Aramean was my father" (Deut. 26:5). In the biblical genealogies the Arameans are described as descendants of Aram, grandson of Abraham's brother Nahor (Gen. 22:20–21; cf. 25:20; 31:24).

THE ARAMEANS

The Arameans first appear in Egyptian records about 1200 B.C. as tribal pastoral nomads. Their language was a West Semitic dialect similar to Hebrew. Adopted later by other groups, Aramaic became the major language of the western Persian Empire. Although some scholars believe the Arameans invaded Upper Mesopotamia and Syria from the desert fringes, more recent research suggests they may have been part of the general West Semitic population of these areas who took advantage of the collapse of the great powers about 1200 B.C. to establish themselves more firmly. For the next two hundred years the Arameans consolidated their claims on tribally held lands.

By 1000 B.C. the Arameans, like Israel, formed kingdoms—some large, many others small—often bearing the name *Bit* ("House") and the name of the chief tribe (Bit-Zamani, Bit-Adini [the Beth-eden of Amos 1:5]) or *Aram* plus the major city of the region (Aram-Zobah, Aram-Damascus). In northern Syria and Upper Mesopotamia, the Aramean states competed with Neo-Hittite states such as Que, Kummuhu, and Carchemish. Because of their proximity to Israel, the Aramean states of central and southern Syria appear most prominently in the Bible. Hamath, the most northerly of the Aramean cities mentioned frequently in the Bible, was located on the Orontes River more than one hundred miles north of Damascus (2 Sam. 8:9–10). The Bible uses the phrase "entrance to Lebo-hamath" to describe the northern limits of Israel (Num. 34:8; 1 Kgs. 8:65; 2 Kgs. 14:25–28).

Aram-Zobah stretched across central Lebanon (the Beqa Valley) into the Plain of Homs. Saul and David fought the kings of Aram-Zobah (1 Sam. 14:47; 2 Sam. 8:3). Other Aramean kingdoms close to Israel included Beth-rehob, Maacah, and Geshur. However, by far the most important Aramean state for Israel was her powerful near neighbor, Aram-Damascus.

ARAM-DAMASCUS

Damascus is an oasis city on the edge of the desert watered by two rivers, the Abana and Pharpar. A great caravan center, Damascus was located at the intersection of two international trade routes, the International Coastal Highway and the King's Highway. The King's Highway brought the riches of the Arabian Peninsula northward to Damascus, while the International Coastal Highway connected with traffic flowing from Egypt and Mesopotamia. Because Damascus has been continuously inhabited over the millennia, no thorough investigation of earlier remains has been possible. However, the Ebla Texts (2000 B.C.) mention Damascus. Assyrian sources and the Bible provide considerable information on the relationship between Israel and Aram-Damascus during the pivotal era between 1000 and 700 B.C.

Israel and Damascus were natural rivals due to their proximity to one another and their mutual desire to control the King's Highway. David defeated the king of Aram-Damascus and garrisoned the city (2 Sam. 8:5–6), but Solomon lost Damascus when the Aramean upstart Rezon seized the city (1 Kgs. 11:23–24). Following the death of Solomon and the division of his kingdom, the interplay between Damascus and Israel became more complex. Several Damascus kings are mentioned in the Bible, some of whom bore the title "Ben-hadad"—"son of the storm god Hadad."

Ben-hadad I attacked Israel on behalf of Asa, king of Judah, who was pressured by Baasha of Israel (1 Kgs. 15:16–22). Ahab fought Ben-hadad (II?), according to the Bible (1 Kgs. 20; 22), but joined with his enemy in 853 in a coalition opposing the Assyrian king Shalmaneser III at Qarqar. Assyrian records name the king of Damascus "Hadad-iri." Damascus was the most powerful state of the southern Levant between 850 and 800 B.C. and became a formidable threat to Israel's security. Israel suffered greatly under Aramean domination when Hazael and a later Ben-hadad ruled Damascus (2 Kgs. 10:32–33; 13:1–5). Jehoash (Joash) paid Hazael tribute to save his kingdom when the Aramean king threatened Judah while conquering Gath (2 Kgs. 12:17–18).

New light on the relations between Israel and Damascus comes from a fragmentary stele recently found at Dan. Dating about 830 B.C., the partial inscription seems to suggest Aramean control of northern Israel and mentions the "House of David," an apparent reference to the dynastic line of Judah. The stele illustrates the changing fortunes in the relations between Israel and Damascus throughout the 800s.

Jehoash broke the grip of Ben-hadad over Israel and regained several Israelite cities (2 Kgs. 13:22–25). After the power of Damascus waned temporarily following a defeat inflicted by Adad-nirari III, Jeroboam took advantage of the situation by extending Israelite control northward to Damascus and Hamath, matching David's previous exploits (2 Kgs. 14:28).

Tiglath-pileser III renewed Assyrian expansion in 745 B.C. at the expense of the small states of the Levant. Damascus may have recovered some of its former power since it led a coalition aimed at stopping the Assyrian advance. Rezin, king of Damascus, allied with the Israelite king

Pekah and others, but Judah refused to cooperate with the anti-Assyrian conspiracy. The Syro-Ephraimite War (see pp.136–138) brought the wrath of the Assyrians down upon the conspirators. Tiglath-pileser attacked Israel in 733 B.C. and followed in 732 B.C. with a devastating blow directed at Damascus.

Aram-Damascus ceased to exist as an independent kingdom; instead her territories were incorporated into an Assyrian province. Despite this disaster, Damascus endured as a major caravan center throughout the Roman period, when the city appears in some lists of the Decapolis on the border of the Nabatean kingdom. Aretas IV, king of Nabatea, apparently controlled Damascus at the time of Saul's conversion (2 Cor. 11:32).

occasional respites. (See "The Arameans and the Kingdom of Aram-Damascus", pp. 124–125).

The House of Omri

By about 860 B.C., during the reigns of Omri and his son Ahab, Israel emerged as a leader among the small states of the Levant. The Omride Dynasty brought political stability to the nation for four decades (ca. 876–842 B.C.) before coming to an end in the bloody coup led by Jehu in 842 B.C. Omri and his successors pursued policies that brought material prosperity, military strength, and international stature to the nation. Assyrian records referred to Israel as the "House of Omri" even after the fall of the dynasty.

Yet the policies that produced the wealth and power also deeply divided Israelite society. The new wealth benefited the privileged few, creating tensions between the court at Samaria and ordinary citizens. Ahab and Jezebel's plot to seize Naboth's vineyard that resulted in his murder illustrates the corruption of the aristocracy (1 Kgs. 21). Moreover, Baalism reared its ugly head once again, this time under official patronage of Ahab's wife, Jezebel.

The Bible says remarkably little about Omri; we are dependent upon Assyrian sources and archaeology to evaluate his reign. Omri came to power in a military coup, occupying Tirzah as a temporary "capital" for six years. Later, he purchased a hill from Shemer and, along with his son Ahab, built a magnificent new capital named Samaria from which he guided Israel's fortune.

POLICIES OF OMRI AND AHAB

Three distinct policies pursued by Omri and his successors brought Israel to her zenith. First, Omri renewed a close alliance with the Phoenicians, sealed by the marriage of his son Ahab to Jezebel, the daughter of Ethbaal (Itto-baal), king of Tyre. Second, he sought peace with Judah. Third, he exercised a strong hand in the Transjordan.

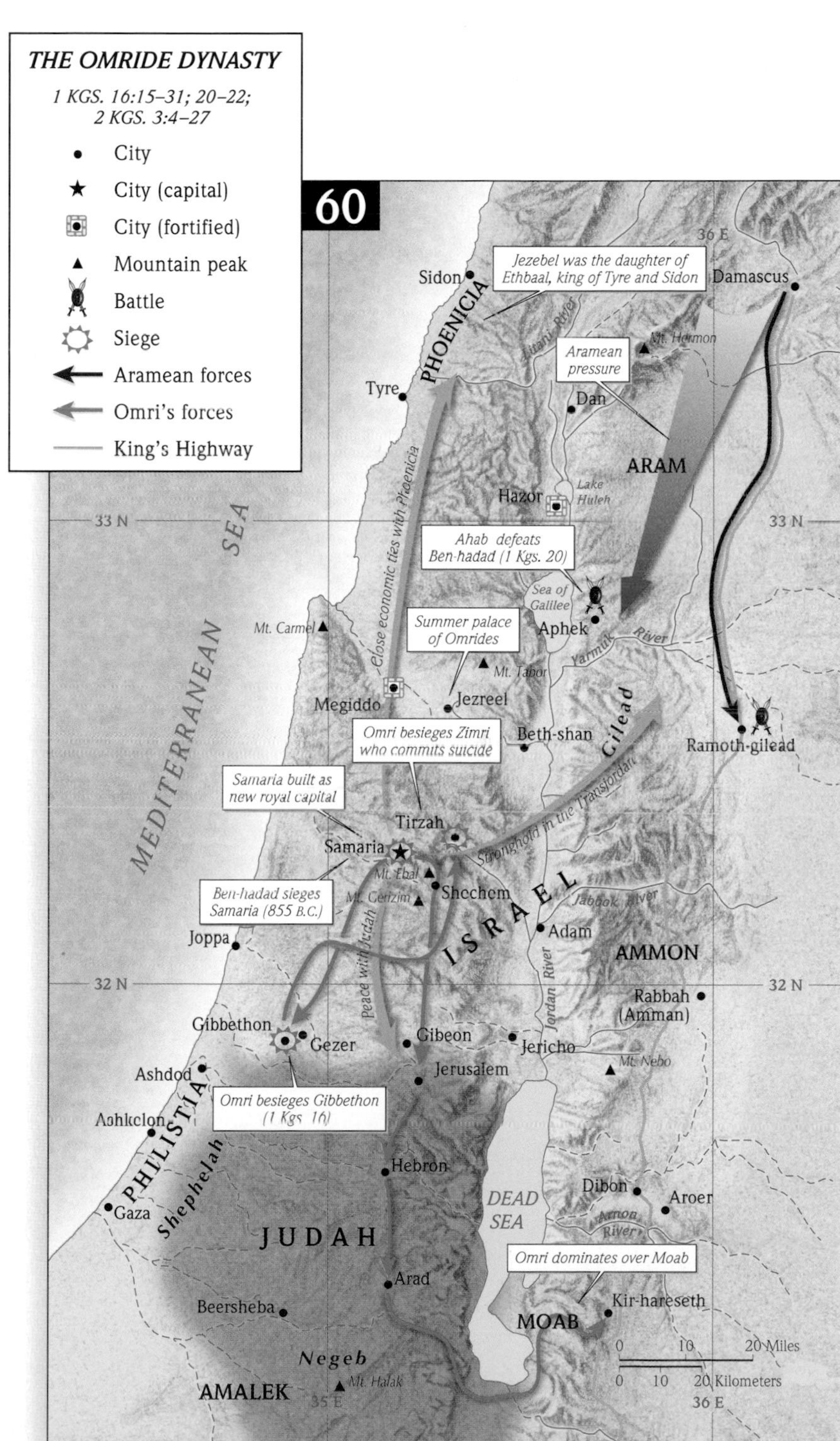

OMRI AND THE PHOENICIANS

Economic cooperation between Israel and Phoenicia can be traced from the time of David and Solomon. During the United Monarchy, Israel was a source for agricultural products and controlled the major trade routes that flowed through the southern Levant, both of which appealed to the Phoenicians. In addition, Solomon jointly sponsored with the Phoenicians a Red Sea fleet based at Ezion-geber. The fleet plied both the Arabian and African coasts, bringing back exotic woods and other luxury goods, including gold from the land of Ophir (the Somalian Coast? southern Arabian Peninsula?). Omri and Ahab continued this close economic cooperation with Phoenicia. They sealed this by a marriage between Omri's son Ahab and Jezebel, a daughter of the Sidonian king Ethbaal (1 Kgs. 16:31). This alliance provided Israel with an outlet for her agricultural surplus and gave the Phoenicians access to key trade routes and, quite possibly, the Red Sea trade initiated in the days of Solomon. However, the alliance introduced a militant Baalism promoted by Jezebel with her husband's support.

OMRI AND JUDAH

Omri sought peace with Judah, ending the border conflict that sapped the resources of both kingdoms. Eventually, the two royal families of Israel and Judah were united in marriage. Athaliah, a daughter of Ahab, married Jehoram of Judah. The alliance likely favored Israel as the stronger partner. On two occasions Judean kings committed their troops to Israel, once to repulse an Aramean threat and again to quell a Moabite rebellion (1 Kgs. 22:4; 2 Kgs. 3:7). Yet, Judah surely benefited economically. The godly Jehoshaphat of Judah sought peace with Israel and controlled the port of Ezion-geber. This fact implies that the troublesome Edomites were temporarily held in check, although Jehoshaphat's attempt to open the route to the gold mines of Ophir was thwarted (1 Kgs. 22:44–48; 2 Chr. 20:25–37). However, the alliance injected Baalism into the court at Jerusalem, fostered by Athaliah and her husband. Paganism, intrigue, and murder dogged both royal houses in this unhappy period.

OMRI AND THE TRANSJORDAN

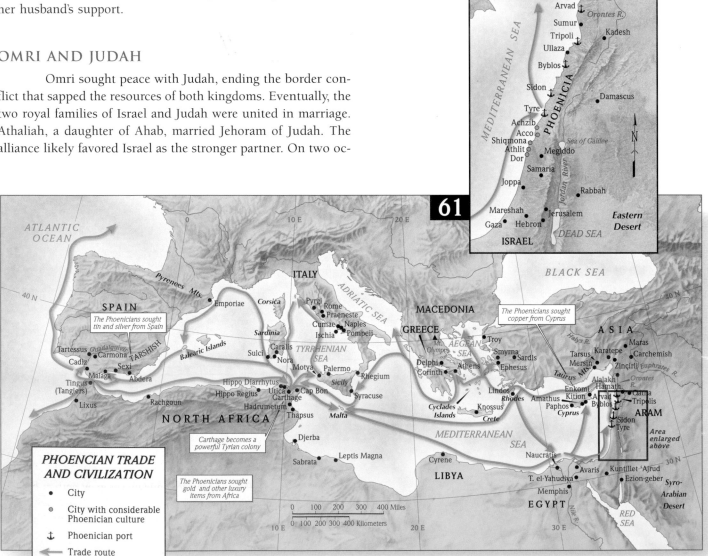

The Omrides attempted to maintain a strong hand in the Transjordan. We learned from the Mesha Stele that Omri con-

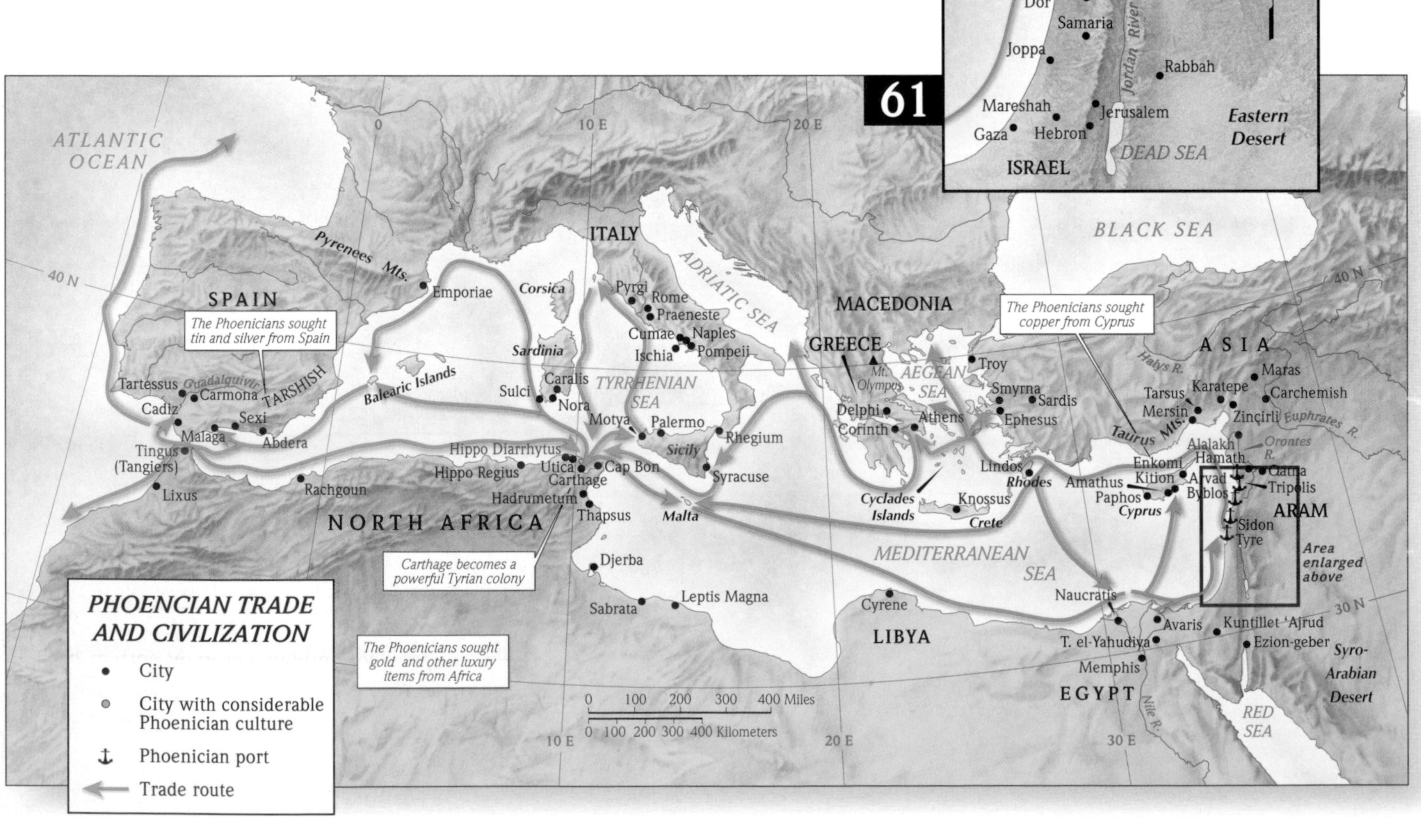

Phoenician warship depicted upon reliefs in the palace of Sennacherib.

quered Moab, although Mesha regained Moabite independence shortly after the death of Ahab. For at least part of the time Edom was held in check, possibly through Judean rule (1 Kgs. 22:47), although later the Edomites rebelled (2 Chr. 21:8–10).

The most serious threat came from the kings of Damascus, who, during the reign of Baasha, attacked Israel's northern border at the request of Asa (1 Kgs. 15:18–20). At stake was control of lucrative trade routes, principally the King's Highway and subsidiary caravan routes. Ahab fought several battles against Ben-hadad II (the Hadad-ezer of Assyrian records). Ahab repelled an Aramean invasion aimed at Samaria (1 Kgs. 20:1–25) and engaged Aramean forces several times near the strategic Transjordan fortress Ramoth-gilead (1 Kgs. 20:26–43; 22:1–40). Neither Ben-hadad nor Ahab could deliver a final blow, and the war between Israel and Damascus ebbed and flowed during the Omride era (see "The Arameans and the Kingdom of Aram-Damascus," pp 124–25).

THE OMRIDES' BUILDING ACHIEVEMENTS

Recent excavations now yield an impressive picture of the material culture created by Omri and Ahab. These two kings of Israel engaged in massive building projects throughout the

THE PHOENICIAN CULTURE

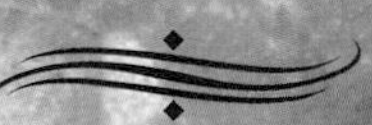

The Phoenicians were the heirs of the culture and seafaring traditions of the Bronze Age Canaanites. From their home ports scattered along the narrow coastal plain of Lebanon, the Phoenicians sent ships across the Mediterranean and became the greatest sea merchants of the first millennium. The Phoenician coast, while fertile, was too narrow to support an agricultural-based economy, but numerous natural harbors turned Phoenician merchants to the sea. Arvad, Byblos, Tyre, and Sidon were the most important Phoenician ports, each retaining its own autonomy in the city-state political structure typical of the classical Canaanites.

The Phoenicians exported cedar harvested from the Lebanon mountains; oils, wine, and grain secured from the agricultural hinterland; and a highly prized purple dye extracted from the murex shellfish found along their coast. They sought metals—copper from Cyprus, tin and silver from Spain, gold from Africa—slaves, ivory, faience and glass objects, and other luxury items. Phoenician craftsmen were skilled in ivory carving, precious metal jewelry, and the manufacture of glass vessels that reflected a distinct Phoenician style that combined elements from the various cultures with which they traded. Ezekiel 27 describes the vast trading empire the Phoenicians established.

Phoenician cities established permanent colonies throughout the Mediterranean basin as far west as Spain. Tyre and Sidon led this western extension that included the powerful Tyrian colony Carthage. The Phoenicians carried with them their alphabet, which was adapted by the Greeks and further disseminated through the Etruscans to Rome. They also exported Phoenician religion, a mixture of various gods and local goddesses from the earlier Canaanite culture that included several Baals—Baal-Melqart of Tyre, Baal-zebub, and Baal-zephon among others. Astarte and "the Lady of Byblos" (Baalat Gubla) were among the important goddesses worshiped by the Phoenicians.

Phoenician craftsmen assisted in the construction of the temple at Jerusalem and other royal buildings. A distinct Phoenician architectural style found in Israelite cities used ashlar masonry (large carved stones) laid as headers and stretchers, and Proto-Aeolic capitals.

Like the other smaller powers in the Levant, the Phoenicians had to deal with the new empires of the Iron Age. They offered tribute to Assyria repeatedly until the reign of Sennacherib (705–681 B.C.), when Sidon came under Assyrian siege. Throughout the 600s various Phoenician cities suffered similar fates, a pattern that persisted under the Neo-Babylonians. Under the Persians, Phoenician economic power grew both at home and in the western colonies. Excavations at Dor indicate Phoenician control of the coasts of Palestine north of the Yarkon throughout much of the first millennium.

kingdom, improving defenses, creating royal administrative centers, and ornamenting buildings both public and private with luxury items. Phoenician and older Canaanite craftsmanship can be detected in architectural and ornamental styles from this period. The archaeological evidence suggests that the building program sponsored by Omri and Ahab surpassed that of Solomon.

Omri and his son Ahab built a new capital six miles northwest of Shechem on a hill purchased from Shemer (1 Kgs. 16:23–24). Omri selected the site because it was easily defended and stood near a junction of roads that radiated out in all directions. The new city, Samaria, stood on top of a hill 430 meters above sea level. Crowning the hill was a royal acropolis built by Omri and Ahab covering four acres, an area that was as large as an average village of that time. The acropolis consisted of a large rectangular platform (89 x 178 meters) defended by two types of walls; a palace, storage facilities, and administrative buildings stood inside the walls.

The construction techniques used at Samaria show Phoenician influence, not surprising given the close ties the House of Omri maintained with Phoenicia—Ahab's wife Jezebel was a Phoenician princess. The stonecutting and craftsmanship at Samaria were exceptional. Walls were set in rock-cut trenches, with each stone dressed at the site to ensure a precise fit. Little remains of the palace, but scattered fragments of Proto-Aeolic capitals preserve a glimpse of the royal splendor of Samaria. A hoard of ivories recovered from the citadel are the finest surviving examples of art from the Iron II era. The ivories display Phoenician, Syrian, and Egyptian motifs and demonstrate both the cosmopolitan society and luxury of the royal court. The Bible mentions "the ivory house" built by Ahab (1 Kgs. 22:39); Amos condemned the ivory beds of luxury-loving Israelite kings (Amos 6:4). Excavators also recovered from an administrative building sixty-three ostraca (inscribed broken potsherds) containing records of shipments of oil and wine. These shipments probably record taxes paid in kind to support the royal court.

The city of Samaria spread out below the royal acropolis, but little is known of this lower city during the Iron Age. The location of the temple of Baal and an altar of Asherah ascribed to Ahab are not known (1 Kgs. 16:32–33; 2 Kgs. 10:21), although Samaria certainly was the center of a militant Baalism in the time of Elijah. A pool (10 x 5 meters), thought to be the one where Ahab's bloody chariot was cleaned—at his death—has been located inside the casemate walls of the acropolis (1 Kgs. 22:34–38).

Samaria's most prosperous era came during the long rule of Jeroboam II when Israel reconquered Aramean territories to the north in the absence of any Assyrian threat (2 Kgs. 14:25–27). During these years Amos condemned the rich aristocratic bureaucrats and royal family members for their opulent lifestyle supported by oppressing the poor (Amos 4:1–3; 5:10–13). However, Samaria's glory faded quickly when Assyria conquered the city in 722 B.C. and made it the district capital in a new Assyrian province.

Hazor and Megiddo underwent transformations during the Omride era. The Omrides doubled the size of Hazor and strongly fortified the site. Fortifications and water supplies were a major concern as threats from Assyria and Damascus increased.

An overview of the water system at Hazor.

Solid walls, often with offsets and insets, replaced the older casemate walls built during Solomon's reign. The new walls ranged from two to seven meters thick and were composed of stone foundations supporting a brick superstructure. Strong gates with four or more chambers protected the cities. Occasionally the gate complex included a second outer gate built at right angles to the inner gate, making an attack on this vulnerable spot even more difficult. Megiddo provides examples of this fortification technique.

Water supplies always were of concern, especially as armies became more adept at siege warfare (see "Assyrian Warfare," pp. 148–49). Engineers devised ingenious means to protect the water supply of large cities. At Megiddo, workmen constructed a tunnel from inside the city to a spring lying outside the city walls. A vertical shaft lined with steps, dug inside the city, provided access to the tunnel. Citizens of Hazor did not

A Proto-Aeolic capital recovered from the excavations at Ramat Rahel.

have to leave their city to get water. Engineers cut a huge vertical shaft down to the water table inside the city walls. Similar systems are known from other sites—Gezer and Gibeon—in both Israel and Judah (see "Jerusalem from Hezekiah to the Destruction in 586 B.C.," pp. 145–46).

Substantial buildings inside the fortifications housed local governors and other governmental officials. Some of these complexes were, in effect, well-defended small palaces. Numerous fragments of Proto-Aeolic capitals demonstrate that the skilled craftsmanship found in the capital—Samaria—spilled over into other major administrative centers. Open courtyards providing space for convocations and troop formations are characteristic of larger cities. The Dan temple, almost certainly the one built by Jeroboam I, was rebuilt on an enlarged scale, probably by Ahab after its destruction shortly after 900 B.C. To judge from the Israelite temple at Dan, major buildings also stood in large open spaces.

Several pillared buildings found at many sites, including Megiddo and Hazor, have been variously interpreted as storage facilities or perhaps stables that housed chariots and horses. Undoubtedly, the cities served as collection and distribution points for the royal administration; many of these pillared structures served to store food surpluses and other materials. The possibility that some of these buildings were used to support the large chariot corp of Ahab's army cannot be dismissed.

OMRI AND ASSYRIA

A sinister menace threatened Israel around 850 B.C. Under the energetic kings Ashurnasirpal II (883–859 B.C.) and Shalmaneser III (859–824 B.C.), Assyria awakened, casting her shadow westward from her homeland in annual tribute-collecting campaigns. Ashurnasirpal II rebuilt Calah (Nimrud), making it the staging center for his ambitious military expeditions that would soon gain control of northwestern Mesopotamia and northern Syria.

His son and successor, Shalmaneser III, probed southward along the Mediterranean coast six times between 853 and 838 B.C. Assyrian records inform us that the campaign of 853 B.C. encountered a coalition of Levantine kings led by Hadad-ezer of Damascus, Irhuleni of Hamath, and Ahab the Israelite at Qarqar (see below, pp. 132–134).

The Assyrian threat forced the cessation of local squabbles, causing Israel and Damascus to join forces for mutual protection. Though Shalmaneser III claimed a victory, the battle at Qarqar temporarily stalled the Assyrian advance. Interestingly, Judah is not listed among the coalition members; perhaps Judean troops fought under the leadership of Ahab, whose forces included two thousand chariots and ten thousand soldiers. The respite was temporary, though, and the kings of Israel and Judah would be forced to deal with Assyria.

THE MINISTRIES OF ELIJAH AND ELISHA

The considerable power and wealth the Omride Dynasty brought to Israel also rent the fabric of Israelite society. Phoenician influence at the court in Samaria proved troubling. This was best symbolized by the marriage of Ahab to Jezebel, a Phoenician princess of Tyre. Social and economic tensions built up within Israelite society between the privileged classes favored by the royal court, mostly city dwellers whose lifestyles grew increasingly luxurious, and those distrustful of foreign influences, mainly rural elements isolated from political and perhaps economic power.

An additional source of tension was the official patronage of Baal worship by the royal court (for more information on Baalism see chap. 8, "Canaanite Religion," p. 91). Ahab built a temple of Baal at Samaria (1 Kgs. 16:32) in addition to, or perhaps in place of, a temple of Yahweh. Jezebel promoted the worship of Baal-Melqart by supporting 450 prophets of Baal and 400 prophets of Asherah at Samaria (1 Kgs. 18:19). In addition, Jezebel ruthlessly suppressed the prophets of Yahweh in Israel. These policies prompted a major crisis of the soul for Israel. In response, God sent two unique prophetic figures—Elijah and Elisha—to minister to the nation. Both prophets remain enigmatic due to the paucity and nature of our resources, yet each guided Israel at critical junctions.

Elijah was a dour, solitary figure who hailed from Tishbe in Gilead (the major references to Elijah are found in 1 Kgs. 17–19, 21; 2 Kgs. 1–2). He appeared suddenly and mysteriously when least expected. An implacable foe of Baalism, Elijah opposed both Ahab and Jezebel publicly as the "troubler of Israel." He announced God was sending a drought upon the land, a tactic aimed at the heart of Baalism, whose chief deity brought the rain. Having made the announcement, Elijah retreated to the brook Cherith, east of the Jordan (1 Kgs. 17:1–7). Next he traveled to Zarephath near Sidon, where he stayed with a widow and raised her son from death (1 Kgs. 17:8–24).

Although the chronology is not clear, at one point Elijah confronted Ahab, announcing God's judgment for Ahab's murder of Naboth and for his confiscation of Naboth's vineyard adjacent to the royal estate at Jezreel (1 Kgs. 21). He also pronounced a deadly curse upon the house of Ahab and his wife Jezebel. The crowning event of Elijah's ministry took place on Mount Carmel. Elijah challenged the prophets of Baal to a contest to determine whether Yahweh or Baal was truly God (1 Kgs. 18). The dramatic climax of heavenly fire consuming Elijah's altar confirmed the verdict. A bloody purge of Baal's priests followed.

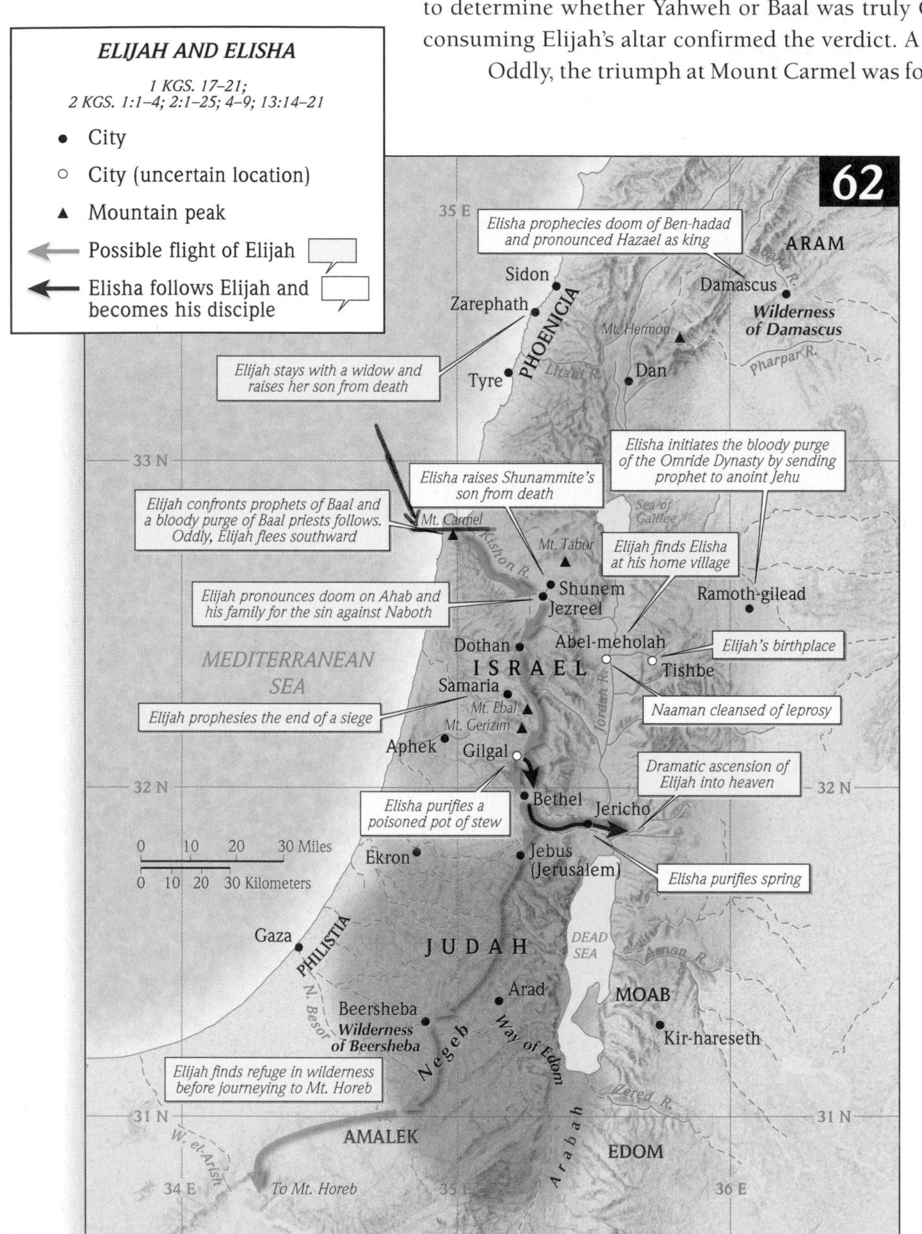
ELIJAH AND ELISHA
1 KGS. 17–21; 2 KGS. 1:1–4; 2:1–25; 4–9; 13:14–21
City
City (uncertain location)
Mountain peak
Possible flight of Elijah
Elisha follows Elijah and becomes his disciple
62
Elisha prophecies doom of Ben-hadad and pronounced Hazael as king
ARAM
Sidon
Damascus
Zarephath
PHOENICIA
Wilderness of Damascus
Mt. Hermon
Pharpar R.
Elijah stays with a widow and raises her son from death
Tyre
Dan
Elisha initiates the bloody purge of the Omride Dynasty by sending prophet to anoint Jehu
Elisha raises Shunammite's son from death
Elijah confronts prophets of Baal and a bloody purge of Baal priests follows. Oddly, Elijah flees southward
Mt. Carmel
Sea of Galilee
Kishon R.
Mt. Tabor
Elijah finds Elisha at his home village
Shunem
Elijah pronounces doom on Ahab and his family for the sin against Naboth
Jezreel
Ramoth-gilead
Dothan
Abel-meholah
Elijah's birthplace
MEDITERRANEAN SEA
ISRAEL
Tishbe
Samaria
Mt. Ebal
Mt. Gerizim
Jordan R.
Naaman cleansed of leprosy
Elijah prophesies the end of a siege
Aphek
Gilgal
Dramatic ascension of Elijah into heaven
Bethel
Elisha purifies a poisoned pot of stew
Jericho
0 10 20 30 Miles
0 10 20 30 Kilometers
Ekron
Jebus (Jerusalem)
Elisha purifies spring
Gaza
PHILISTIA
JUDAH
DEAD SEA
Arnon R.
Arad
MOAB
N. Besor
Beersheba
Wilderness of Beersheba
Negeb
Way of Edom
Kir-hareseth
Elijah finds refuge in wilderness before journeying to Mt. Horeb
Zered R.
AMALEK
Arabah
EDOM
W. el-Arish
To Mt. Horeb
33 N
32 N
31 N
34 E
35 E
36 E

Oddly, the triumph at Mount Carmel was followed by Elijah's flight southward, fleeing the wrath of Jezebel. In the vicinity of Beer-sheba, Elijah found refuge and angelic sustenance in the wilderness before continuing on to Mount Horeb, traditionally located in the southern Sinai at Jebel Musa (1 Kgs. 19; but see comments on the Exodus route, pp. 66–69 for alternative locations). At Horeb, God charged Elijah with (1) anointing Hazael king of Damascus, (2) anointing Jehu as king of Israel, and (3) designating Elisha as successor to himself.

Subsequently, Elijah found Elisha, presumably at his home village, Abel-meholah. The exact location of Abel-meholah is uncertain, but it seems to have been west of the Jordan River, perhaps near the eastern part of the Jezreel Valley.

Elisha left his fields to become the devoted disciple of Elijah. Sometime after the death of Ahaziah (850 B.C.), Elisha followed Elijah from Gilgal through Bethel and Jericho to the Jordan River. Crossing over by means of a miracle, Elisha witnessed the dramatic ascension of Elijah into heaven by a chariot of fire (2 Kgs. 2:9–12). Then Elisha took up the prophetic mantle.

Elisha differed in some respects from his predecessor. He appeared frequently in the company of the "sons of the prophets" and functioned more often as a counselor to kings. The Bible records numerous miracles Elisha performed, among them: the purification of a spring at Jericho (2 Kgs. 2:19–22), the raising of a Shunammite's son from death (2 Kgs. 4:8–37), the purification of a poisoned pot of stew at Gilgal (2 Kgs. 4:38–41), and the cleansing of an Aramean army commander, Naaman, from leprosy (2 Kgs. 5). Like Elijah, it is difficult to plot the movements of Elisha, though he often appeared at Mount Carmel and Samaria. He predicted the end of a desperate siege of Samaria by the Aramean king, Ben-hadad (2 Kgs. 6:24–7:20).

The most prominent role Elisha played was kingmaker. He was the instrument of political revolution in Damascus and Israel. Elisha went to Damascus as Ben-hadad lay ill and pronounced Hazael, viewed as a usurper in Assyrian records, as the next king. Soon after, Hazael suffocated Ben-hadad and ascended the throne of Damascus (2 Kgs. 8:7–15).

Elisha initiated the bloody purge of the Omride Dynasty when he sent a young prophet to Ramoth-gilead, a city that had been the focus of Aramean attacks led by Hazael of Damascus. Joram, king of Israel, already had been wounded and had been taken to Jezreel for recovery. Jehu was a commander in Joram's army. The young prophet sent by Elijah not only anointed Jehu, but charged him with the task of eliminating the House of Omri.

Jehu set about that task by racing in his chariot to Jezreel, where he killed Joram on the former property of Naboth in fulfillment of Elijah's prophetic word. Ahaziah, the king of Judah who had been visiting his cousin Joram, fled in his chariot toward Beth-haggan, but Jehu's warriors mortally wounded Ahaziah, who died at Megiddo. Subsequently, Jehu orchestrated the death of the Queen Mother, Jezebel, at Jezreel and the massacre of seventy sons of Ahab and numerous worshipers of Baal in Samaria (2 Kgs. 9:30–10:31). Thus ended the powerful but corrupt House of Omri.

The dynasty founded by Jehu faced immediate threats from the Aramean kingdoms in the Transjordan. Hazael attacked Israel on several occasions, severely reducing Israel's territories (2 Kgs. 10:32–33; 13:1–5)(see also "The Arameans and the Kingdom of Aram-Damascus," pp. 124–25). However, the rapidly emerging Assyrian Empire posed a much greater problem for Israel. Jehu was forced to pay tribute to Shalmaneser III in 841 B.C. (see below).

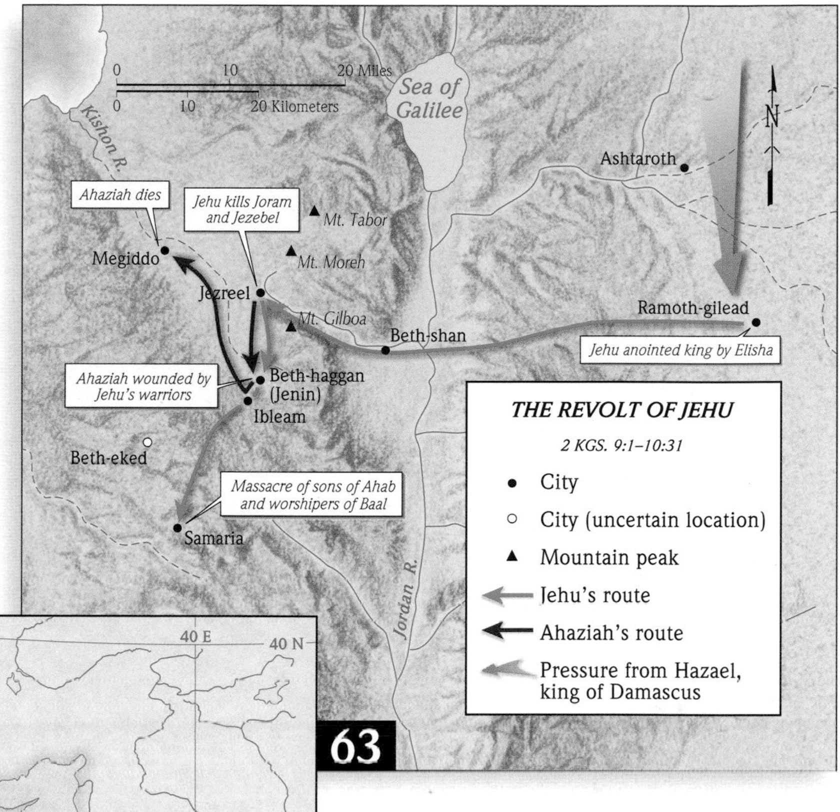

The Rise of the Neo-Assyrian Empire

Isaiah described Assyria as the "rod of God's wrath" (Isa. 10:5). These prophetic words not only warned of impending judgment on Israel's and Judah's sinful ways, but they underscored the dramatic changes occurring in the power structure of the Near East. For more than three centuries (1200–900 B.C.) no superpower meddled in the affairs of the small states of the Levant. The collapse of Egypt's Levantine empire shortly after 1200 B.C. was not matched by the intrusion of any Mesopotamian empire to fill the void. Subsequently, the numerous emerging states of the Levant—the Aramean states (Damascus, Hamath, Beth-eden), Phoenician and Philistine cities, the Transjordanian kingdoms (Moab, Edom, and Ammon), and Israel—scrapped for power and land relatively free from outside interference. Around 900 B.C. a series of strong Assyrian kings threatened the uneasy balance of power.

ASSYRIAN MILITARY OBJECTIVES

Assyrian kings faced three long-term obstacles to expansion: (1) To the west, strong Aramean states sat astride important trade routes and blocked access to the Mediterranean coast. (2) Mountain tribes to the north (the "Nairi Lands") threatened major cities in the Assyrian plain as well as vital trade links to Anatolia, the major source for horses and metals upon which Assyria was dependent. These mountain tribes eventually coalesced into the kingdom of Urartu located in the region between Lake Van and Lake Urmia. Frequently, Assyrian kings were forced to campaign deep in the mountains against Urartian forces. (3) Control of Babylonia to the south presented considerable challenges to Assyrian kings as well. This was especially true from 800 B.C. onward, when Chaldean and Elamite forces tried to use Babylon as a power base from which to attack Assyria.

MEDITERRANEAN SEA
Area enlarged above

The Assyrian kings pursued three military objectives in their campaigns: (1) to establish a security zone protecting the Assyrian heartland; (2) to gain and maintain control of vital trade routes; and (3) to ensure access to necessary raw resources (timber, metals, and horses). In addition, Assyrian kings fought for the glory and prestige of Ashur, the national Assyrian god, whose rightful domain was all the earth.

The first phase of Assyrian expansion began with Ashurdan (934–912 B.C.). He consolidated his authority and began to establish control over the Assyrian plain. His successors, Adad-nirari II (911–891 B.C.) and Tukulti-ninurta II (890–884 B.C.), campaigned against Aramean states in the west and mountain

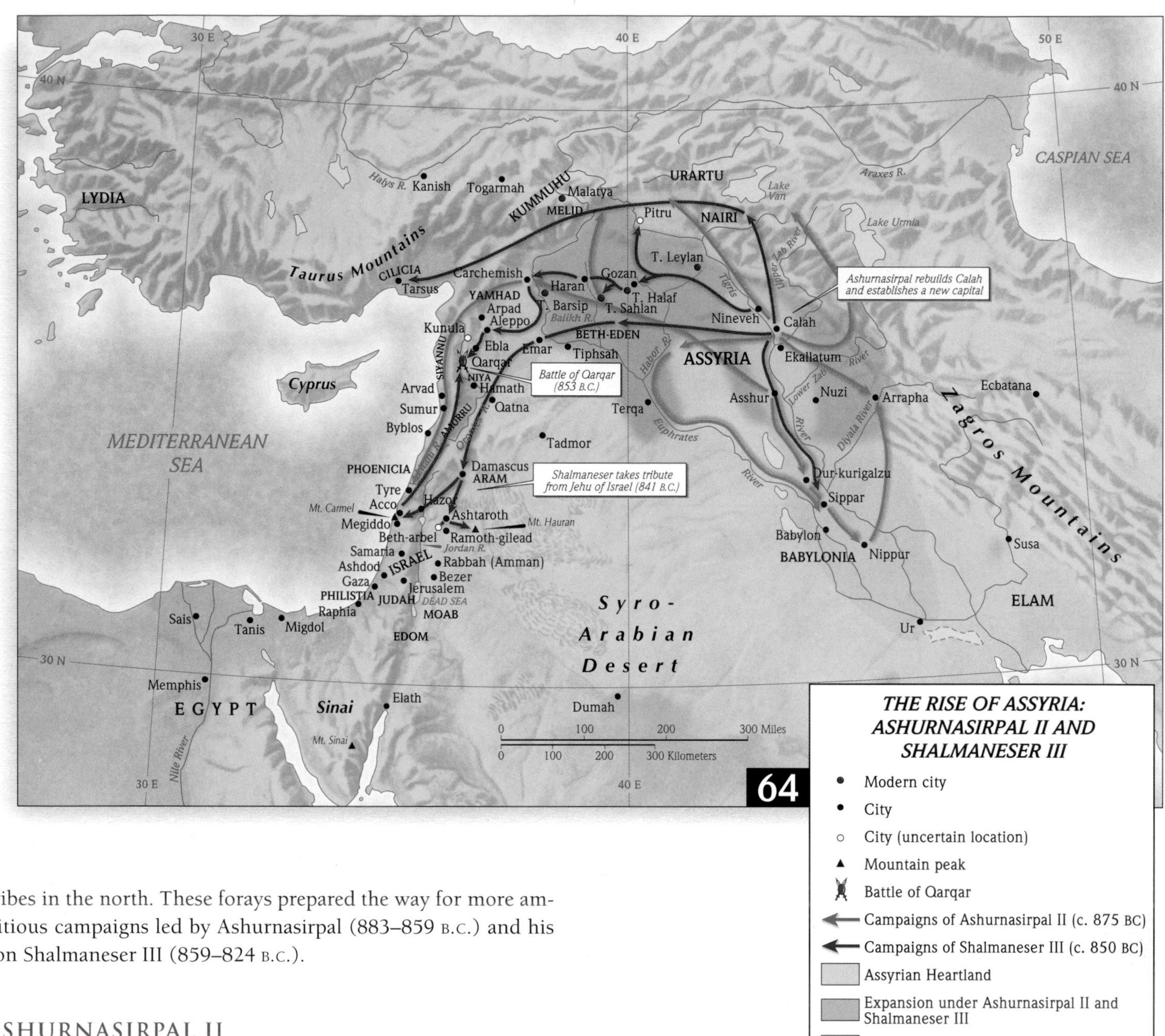

tribes in the north. These forays prepared the way for more ambitious campaigns led by Ashurnasirpal (883–859 B.C.) and his son Shalmaneser III (859–824 B.C.).

ASHURNASIRPAL II

Ashurnasirpal campaigned vigorously to the east, north, and west, establishing a large security zone for Assyria. He employed brutal tactics against rebellious leaders, setting a pattern of psychological warfare that was followed by succeeding kings of Assyria. His subjugation of the powerful Aramean state Bit-adini (the Beth-eden of Amos 1:5) paved the way for a victorious march to the Mediterranean Sea by way of Carchemish into Syria, where he received tribute from cities as far south as Tyre. Ashurnasirpal rebuilt Calah (Nimrud) on a massive scale, complete with his personal palace. From here Assyrian armies marched out in a great arc westward through the Habor region to the Euphrates River and then along the Euphrates to the border of Babylon, collecting tribute and punishing rebellious vassals, a pattern repeated many times in the next two hundred years.

SHALMANESER III

Shalmaneser III continued his father's policy of expansion. His annals record six campaigns in the west between 853 and 838 B.C. Though unmentioned in the Bible, Shalmaneser's first western campaign in 853 B.C. brought him to battle with Ahab of Israel. Ahab was part of a large coalition of Levantine states formed to oppose Assyrian expansion. According to an Assyrian inscription (the Monolith Inscription) now in the British Museum, Shalmaneser engaged the coalition in battle at Qarqar in northern Syria. Though he claimed a great victory, Shalmaneser may have suffered sufficient losses to prevent any immediate expansion southward. Later campaigns, however,

CHART 11. THE NEO-ASSYRIAN EMPIRE			
STATE OF ASSYRIAN POWER	**KINGS OF ASSYRIA**	**DATES RULED**	**ACTIVITIES AND ACCOMPLISHMENTS**
Initial phase of expansion	Ashurnasirpal II	(883–859 B.C.)	Utilized tactics of terror to achieve Assyrian goals; rebuilt Calah (Nimrud) and made it his capital; collected tribute from states as far south as Tyre, Sidon, and Byblos
	Shalmaneser III	(859–824 B.C.)	Campaigned six times in the Levant; fought a coalition that included Ahab, king of Israel, at Qarqar in 853 B.C.; took tribute from Jehu, king of Israel in 841 (Black Obelisk of Shalmaneser)
Period of weakness 823-745 B.C. Reasons for period of weakness: 1. Problems with the kingdom of Urartu 2. Internal unrest 3. Weak central government	Shamshi-adad V	(823–811 B.C.)	
	Adad-nirari III	(810–783 B.C.)	Campaigned in Syria in late ninth and early eighth centuries (805–796?); Rimnah Stele records an attack on Damascus and tribute collected from Joash "of Samaria"; perhaps the "savior" of 2 Kgs. 13:5
	Shalmaneser IV	(782–772 B.C.)	
	Ashur-dan III	(771–754 B.C.)	
	Ashur-nirari V	(753–746 B.C.)	
Period of imperial expansion	Tiglath-pileser III (Pul)	(745–727 B.C.)	Dealt with Urartu; centralized the power of the kings; developed policies to expand Assyrian territory west and south of the Euphrates; took tribute from Menahem of Israel in 738 B.C. (2 Kgs. 15:19–20); conquered Babylon. Ahaz of Judah appealed to Tiglath-pileser for help during the Syro-Ephraimite War (735 B.C.; 2 Kgs. 16:7–9). Tiglath-pileser attacked Israel and Damascus (733–732 B.C.), significantly reducing Israel's territory (2 Kgs. 15:29)
	Shalmaneser V	(727–722 B.C.)	Hoshea, king of Israel, initially paid tribute to Shalmaneser V, but finally rebelled with the promise of Egyptian help (2 Kgs. 17:1–5). Shalmaneser V besieged Samaria for three years, with the city falling in 722 B.C.)
	Sargon II	(722–705 B.C.)	Established a new capital, Dur-Sharrukin (Khorsabad); claimed to be the conqueror of Samaria; converted Samaria into an Assyrian province after putting down additional rebellions backed by Egypt and key Philistine cities in 720 B.C.; exiled 27,000 Israelites and settled them on the Habor River near Nineveh and settled them in region of Samaria (2 Kgs. 17:24); further revolts in 713/712 B.C. sponsored by Egypt (Shabaku of Twenty-fifth Dynasty) involving Ashdod, Judah, Edom, and Moab provoked additional campaigns in the Levant (see Isa. 20); faced sustained opposition from a Chaldean Elamite coalition led by Merodoch-baladan; led campaigns into Urartu, finally subduing the country; died in battle fighting the Cimmerians in 705.
	Sennacherib	(705–681 B.C.)	Rebuilt Nineveh for use as the Assyrian capital; subdued further Chaldean troubles in Babylon; led an attack on Judah in 701 B.C. in which forty-six Judean cities were destroyed; Jerusalem, though besieged, escaped destruction (2 Kgs. 18–19; Isa. 36–37; 2 Chr. 32); important archaelogical evidence: the Lachish Frieze, the Siloam Inscription, the Prism of Sennacherib
	Esarhaddon	(681–669 B.C.)	Attacked Egypt in 669 B.C.
	Ashurbanipal II	(669–627 B.C.)	Conquered Thebes in 663 B.C.; zenith of the Neo-Assyrian Empire; put down revolt in Babylon in 652 led by his brother Shamash-shum-ukin

Details of the Black Obelisk of Shalmanezzar III that records his campaign into the southern Levant in 841 B.C. Jehu or one of his representatives appears prostrated before the Assyrian king in this register. (Courtesy of the British Museum.)

took him as far south as Mount Carmel. In 841 B.C. he took tribute from Jehu and other kings of the southern Levant. The Black Obelisk of Shalmaneser shows Jehu prostrate before the Assyrian king. Shalmaneser also campaigned northwest into the Nairi lands, maintaining control of routes leading into Cilicia with its rich iron deposits.

ASSYRIA'S TEMPORARY DECLINE

Assyria reached unprecedented heights during the reign of Shalmaneser III. However, his death in 824 B.C. led to a prolonged period of Assyrian weakness that lasted until 745 B.C. Several factors caused this decline in Assyrian power. The successors of Shalmaneser III were quarrelsome and not particularly effective. Local governors assumed more power, provoking social unrest. Moreover, the kingdom of Urartu contested Assyrian control of the northwest regions, including the Upper Euphrates, thus threatening key trade routes. Consequently, Assyrian power waned as did the frequency of Assyrian campaigns in the west.

The exception to this rule was Adad-nirari III (810–783 B.C.). He led campaigns westward against Arapad in northern Syria and later against Damascus. The later campaign may have relieved Aramean pressure upon Israel. The Bible describes a "savior" who delivered Israel from Damascus in the reign of Jehoahaz (2 Kgs. 13:5). Perhaps this "savior" was Adad-nirari III.

Recovery of Israel and Judah

Shortly after 800 B.C. Israel and Judah enjoyed a lengthy period of prosperity and peace. With little Assyrian interference and the stable reigns of Jeroboam II (786–746 B.C.) and Uzziah (783–742 B.C.), both countries expanded their influence and benefited materially. Jeroboam "restored the border of Israel from the entance of Hamath as far as the Sea of the Arabah" (2 Kgs. 14:25), apparently recovering influence northward at the expense of the Aramean states of Damascus and Hamath. Likewise, in Judah, Uzziah (Azariah) recovered control of the Red Sea port of Elath against Edomite pressure, received tribute from Ammon, and captured cities in Philistia—Gath, Ashdod, and Jabneh (2 Chr. 26).

Renewed Assyrian Expansion

TIGLATH-PILESER III

The accession of Tiglath-pileser III (745–727 B.C.) to the Assyrian throne in 745 B.C. marked a new, more aggressive phase of Assyrian expansion. Tiglath-pileser, or "Pul" as he also

A relief from the palace of Ashurbanipal at Nineveh showing Assyrian soldiers subjecting captives to a series of tortures.

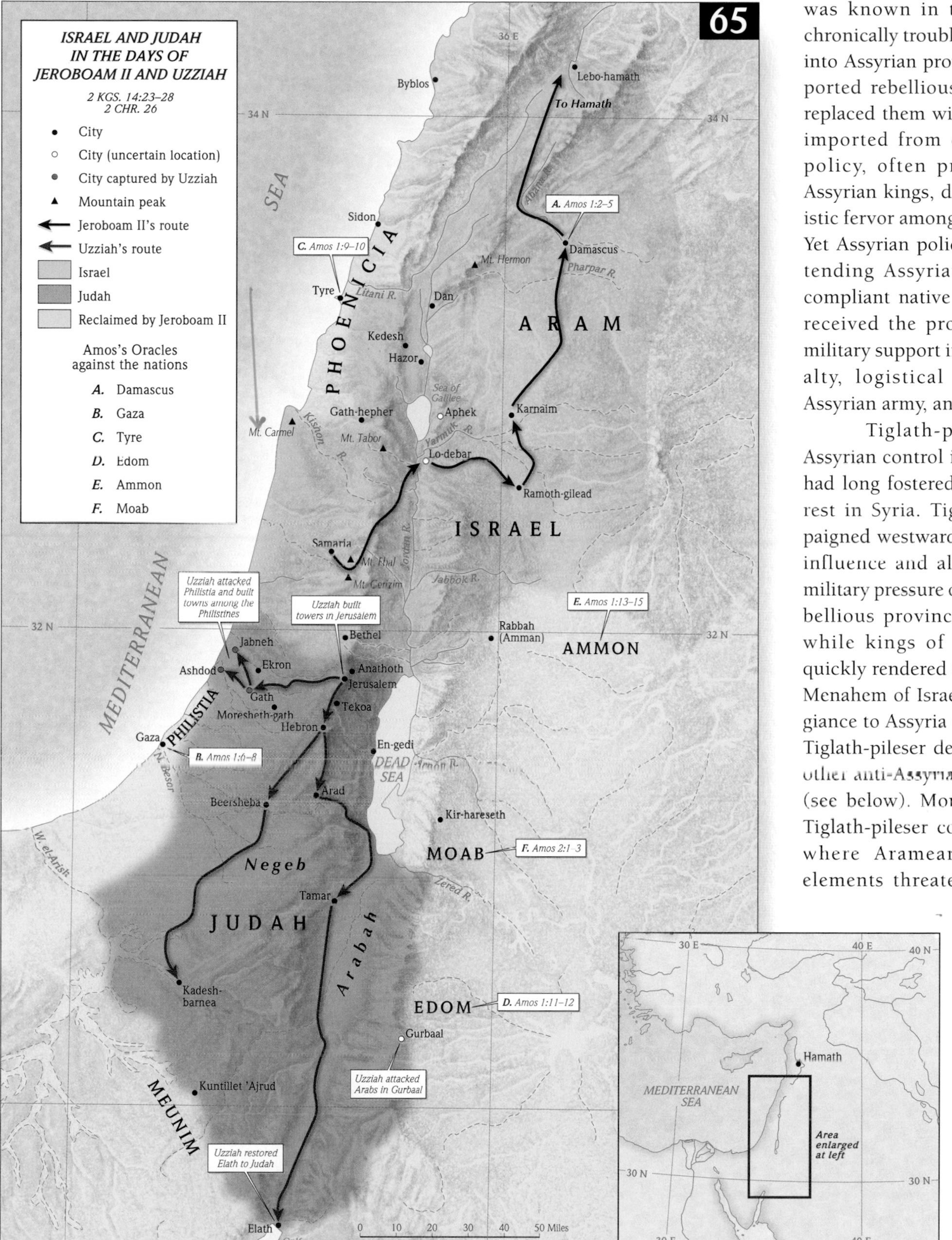

was known in the Bible, turned chronically troublesome vassal states into Assyrian provinces. He also deported rebellious populations and replaced them with foreign captives imported from other areas. This policy, often practiced by later Assyrian kings, dampened nationalistic fervor among Assyria's enemies. Yet Assyrian policy still favored extending Assyrian power through compliant native vassal rulers who received the promise of Assyrian military support in exchange for loyalty, logistical support for the Assyrian army, and yearly tribute.

Tiglath-pileser reasserted Assyrian control in the west. Urartu had long fostered anti-Assyrian unrest in Syria. Tiglath-pileser campaigned westward to break Urartian influence and also brought direct military pressure on Urartu itself. Rebellious provinces were annexed, while kings of vacillating areas quickly rendered tribute. By 738 B.C. Menahem of Israel had yielded allegiance to Assyria (2 Kgs. 15:18–20). Tiglath-pileser dealt ruthlessly with other anti-Assyrian plots in the west (see below). Moreover, in 729 B.C. Tiglath-pileser conquered Babylon, where Aramean and Chaldean elements threatened to create an

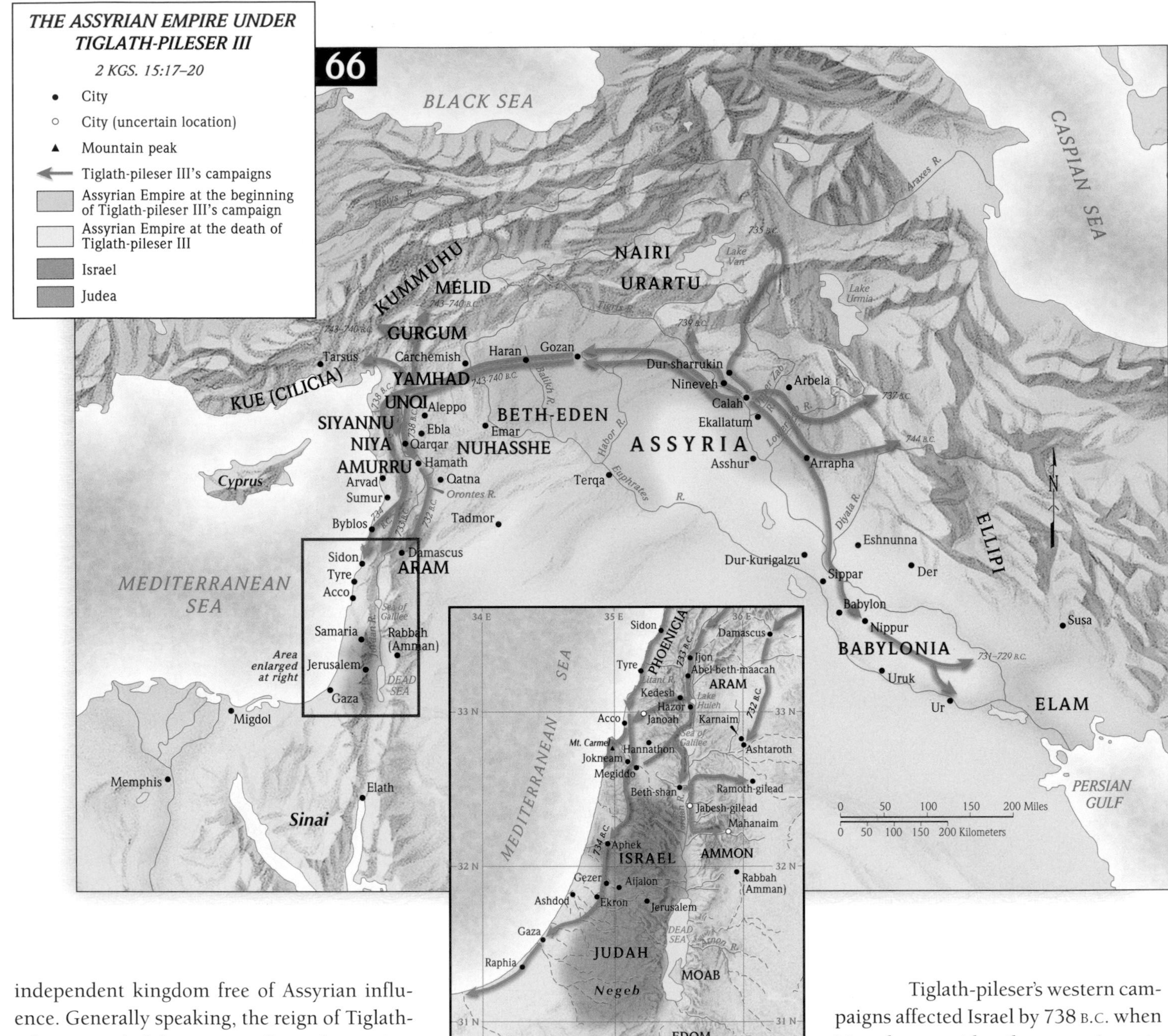

independent kingdom free of Assyrian influence. Generally speaking, the reign of Tiglath-pileser signaled the coming of age of a new imperial power whose tentacles none of the Near East could escape.

A resurgent Assyria led by Tiglath-pileser III soon threatened Israel and Judah. With the deaths of Jeroboam II and Uzziah, neither Judah nor Israel possessed the leadership to negotiate successfully the troubled waters ahead. Six kings from five different families ruled Israel from 746–722 B.C. after the death of Jeroboam; most were assassinated in office. Faithless Ahaz (735–715 B.C.) brought Judah into Assyrian vassalage. Only Hezekiah steered a course of independence, although he and his Judean citizens paid a great price for their action.

Tiglath-pileser's western campaigns affected Israel by 738 B.C. when Menahem paid tribute to Assyria (2 Kgs. 15:19–20). Perhaps Menahem displayed anti-Assyrian tendencies that caught Tiglath-pileser's attention. Assyrian inscriptions also mention an Azariah—perhaps Uzziah of Judah, but this is debated—who resisted the Assyrian advance and, likewise, paid the consequences. By 738 B.C. all of Syria and Palestine felt the Assyrian yoke.

SYRO-EPHRAIMITE WAR

Anti-Assyrian sentiment flared again, apparently fanned by Rezin, king of Damascus. Rezin organized an anti-Assyrian coalition that included Pekah of Israel, certain Phi-

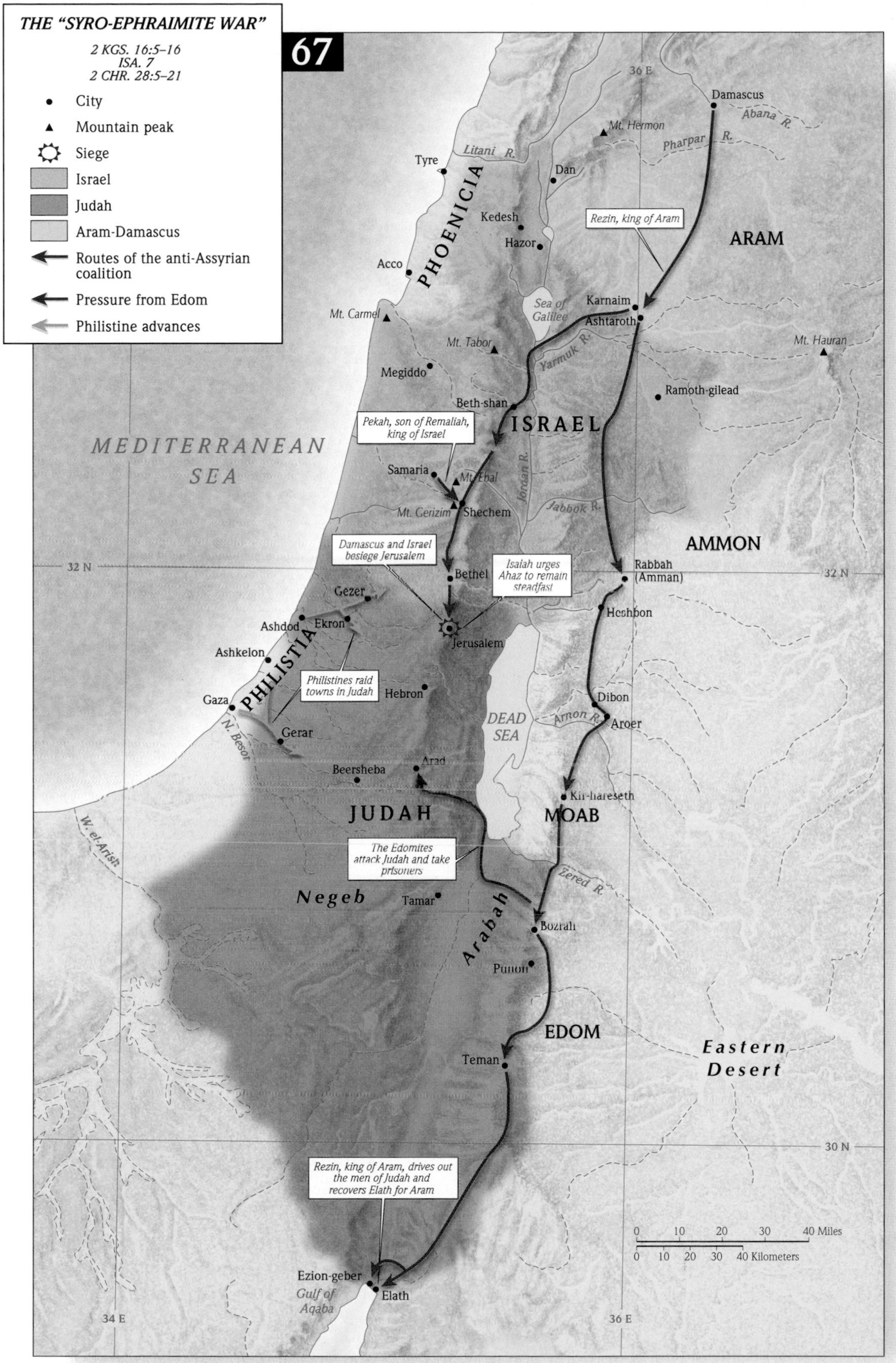

B.C. 922 | 875 | 825 | 800 | 750 | 722 B.C.

JEROBOAM | AHAB | ELISHA | UZZIAH | AMOS | ISAIAH

THE "SYRO-EPHRAIMITE WAR"

2 KGS. 16:5–16
ISA. 7
2 CHR. 28:5–21

67

- City
- Mountain peak
- Siege
- Israel
- Judah
- Aram-Damascus
- Routes of the anti-Assyrian coalition
- Pressure from Edom
- Philistine advances

36 E
Damascus
Abana R.
Mt. Hermon
Pharpar R.
Litani R.
Tyre
Dan
PHOENICIA
Kedesh
Hazor
Rezin, king of Aram
ARAM
Acco
Sea of Galilee
Karnaim
Ashtaroth
Mt. Carmel
Mt. Tabor
Yarmuk R.
Mt. Hauran
Megiddo
Ramoth-gilead
Beth-shan
Pekah, son of Remaliah, king of Israel
ISRAEL
MEDITERRANEAN SEA
Samaria
Mt. Ebal
Jordan R.
Mt. Gerizim
Shechem
Jabbok R.
Damascus and Israel besiege Jerusalem
Isaiah urges Ahaz to remain steadfast
AMMON
32 N
Bethel
Rabbah (Amman)
Gezer
Ashdod
Ekron
Heshbon
Jerusalem
PHILISTIA
Ashkelon
Philistines raid towns in Judah
Hebron
Gaza
Dibon
DEAD SEA
Arnon R.
Aroer
N. Besor
Gerar
Arad
Beersheba
Kir-hareseth
JUDAH
MOAB
W. el-Arish
The Edomites attack Judah and take prisoners
Zered R.
Negeb
Tamar
Arabah
Bozrah
Punon
EDOM
Teman
Eastern Desert
30 N
Rezin, king of Aram, drives out the men of Judah and recovers Elath for Aram
0 10 20 30 40 Miles
0 10 20 30 40 Kilometers
Ezion-geber
Elath
Gulf of Aqaba
34 E
36 E

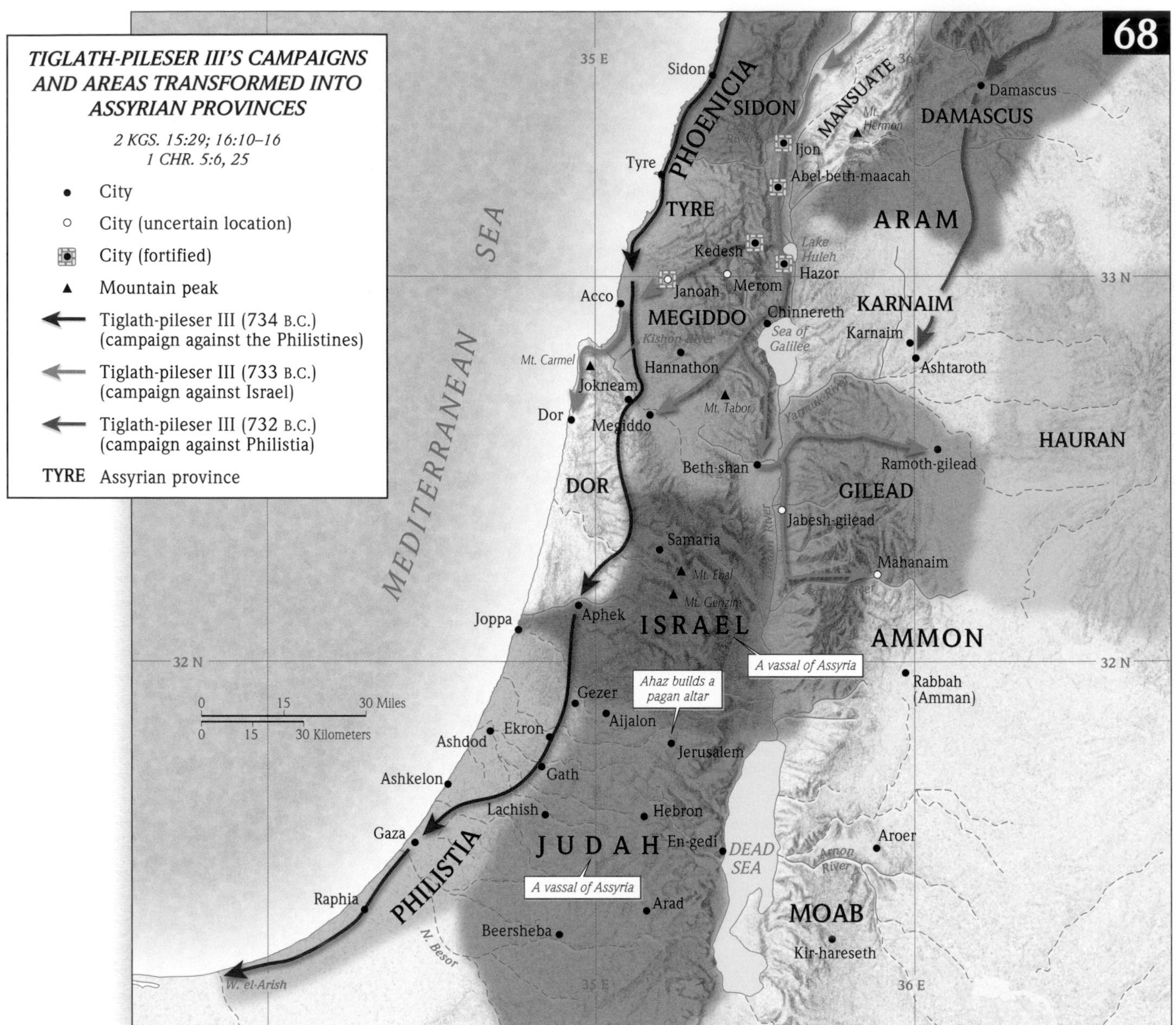

listine city-states, and perhaps Edom. Judah, first under Jotham and then Ahaz, refused to join the coalition even in the face of military pressure. Damascus and Israel besieged Jerusalem (the "Syro-Ephraimite War") in 735 B.C. with the intent of replacing Ahaz with a king willing to join the coalition (2 Kgs. 16:5; Isa. 7:1–14).

Ahaz, an Assyrian vassal, appealed to Tiglath-pileser for help, resulting in a three-pronged Assyrian attack against the coalition. In 734 B.C. Tiglath-pileser campaigned along the Mediterranean coast as far south as Gaza. This move punished the rebellious Philistine states and checked any support Egypt might give to the coalition. Then in 733 B.C. the Assyrian armies marched against Israel, moving down the Huleh Basin taking key cities and fortifying the northern approaches: Ijon, Abel-beth-maacah, Janoah, Kedesh, and Hazor (2 Kgs. 15:29).

Assyrian forces ranged throughout Israel taking many captives for deportation. About 80 percent of Israel was divided into four new Assyrian provinces (Dor, Megiddo, Gilead, and Karnaim). Pekah was killed by Hoshea, who subsequently became king of a much-reduced Israel centered on Samaria. In 732 B.C. Tiglath-pileser attacked Damascus and converted the conquered kingdom to an Assyrian province. These campaigns greatly reduced Israel and plunged Judah deeper into Assyrian bondage (2 Kgs. 16:10–19; 2 Chr. 28).

FALL OF SAMARIA

Shalmaneser V (727–722 B.C.) reigned only briefly upon the death of Tiglath-pileser III; he left very few remains. During Shalmaneser V's reign, Hoshea rebelled against Assyria with the expectation of Egyptian aid (2 Kgs. 17:1–4). Perhaps Tefnakhte, the founder of the Twenty-fourth Egyptian Dynasty, stirred up the revolt in fear of Assyrian incursions further south. The rebellion probably was more widespread and may have involved Phoenician and Philistine cities.

Shalmaneser responded by besieging Samaria for three years until the city fell in 722 B.C. (2 Kgs. 17:5–6). Though Sargon II (722–705 B.C.), successor to Shalmaneser V, claims credit for the capture of Samaria, the Bible implies that Shalmaneser was primarily responsible for the final destruction of the Northern Kingdom Israel (2 Kings 17:5).

During Sargon's early reign many Israelites were deported and resettled in the upper Habor Valley (Gozan), near Nineveh at Halah, and as far away as Media (2 Kgs. 17:6; 1 Chr. 5:26). Sargon's inscriptions mention 27,290 captives taken from Israel. Captive peoples from the area of Babylon (Cutah) and Syria (Hamath and Sepharvaim) were resettled in Samaria (2 Kgs. 17:24). Some Israelites fled southward, seeking refuge in Jerusalem, but most had to suffer the indignity of Assyrian occupation in the newly formed Assyrian province of Samaria.

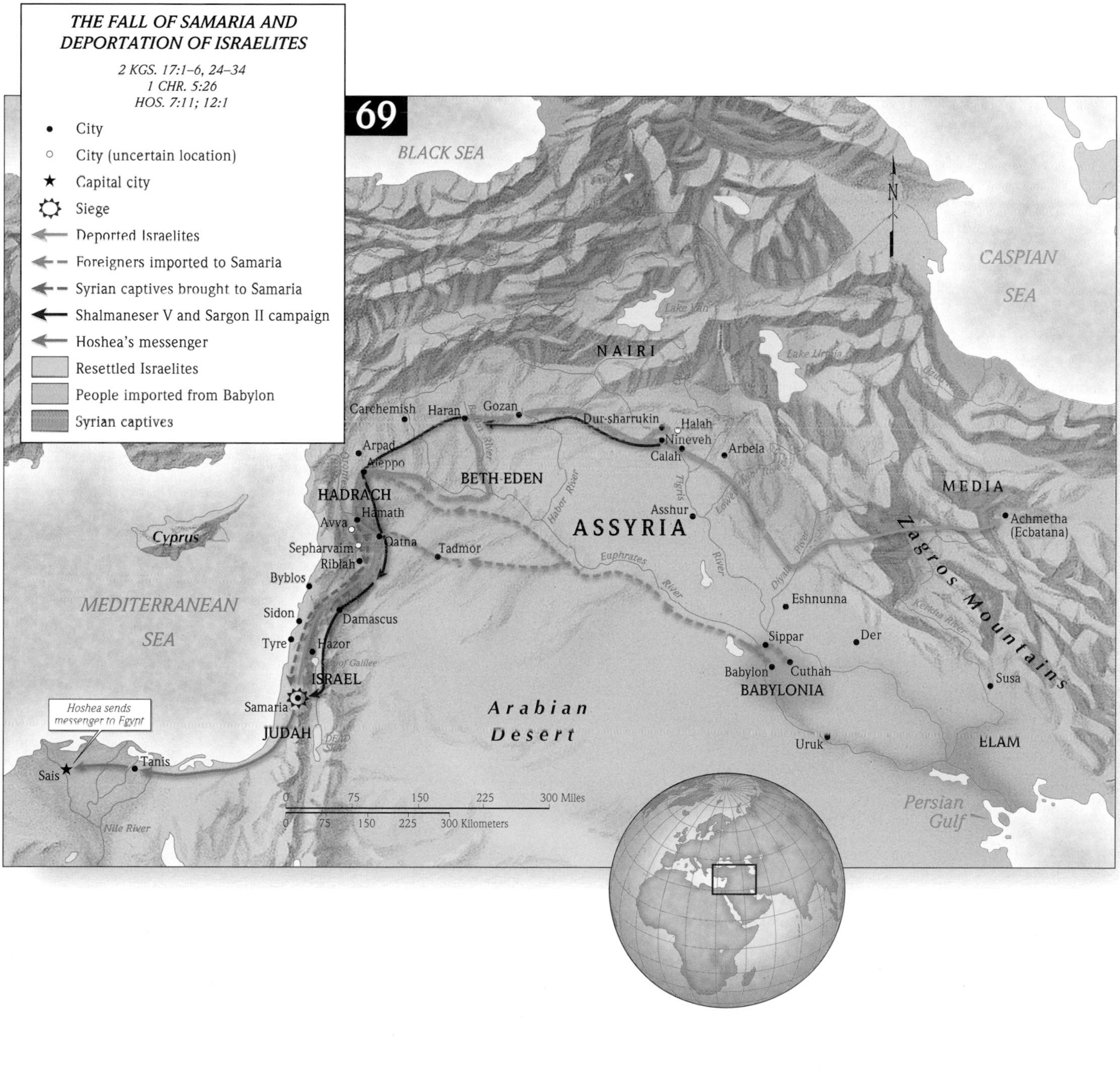

THE FALL OF SAMARIA AND DEPORTATION OF ISRAELITES

2 KGS. 17:1–6, 24–34
1 CHR. 5:26
HOS. 7:11; 12:1

- City
- City (uncertain location)
- Capital city
- Siege
- Deported Israelites
- Foreigners imported to Samaria
- Syrian captives brought to Samaria
- Shalmaneser V and Sargon II campaign
- Hoshea's messenger
- Resettled Israelites
- People imported from Babylon
- Syrian captives

69

BLACK SEA
CASPIAN SEA
MEDITERRANEAN SEA
Cyprus
NAIRI
Carchemish
Haran
Gozan
Dur-sharrukin
Halah
Nineveh
Calah
Arbela
Arpad
Aleppo
HADRACH
BETH-EDEN
Hamath
Avva
Qatna
Sepharvaim
Riblah
Tadmor
ASSYRIA
Asshur
MEDIA
Achmetha (Ecbatana)
Zagros Mountains
Byblos
Sidon
Tyre
Damascus
Hazor
ISRAEL
Samaria
JUDAH
Arabian Desert
Eshnunna
Sippar
Der
Babylon
Cuthah
BABYLONIA
Susa
Uruk
ELAM
Persian Gulf
Hoshea sends messenger to Egypt
Sais
Tanis
Nile River
0 75 150 225 300 Miles
0 75 150 225 300 Kilometers

THE EIGHTH CENTURY PROPHETS: AMOS, HOSEA, MICAH, AND ISAIAH

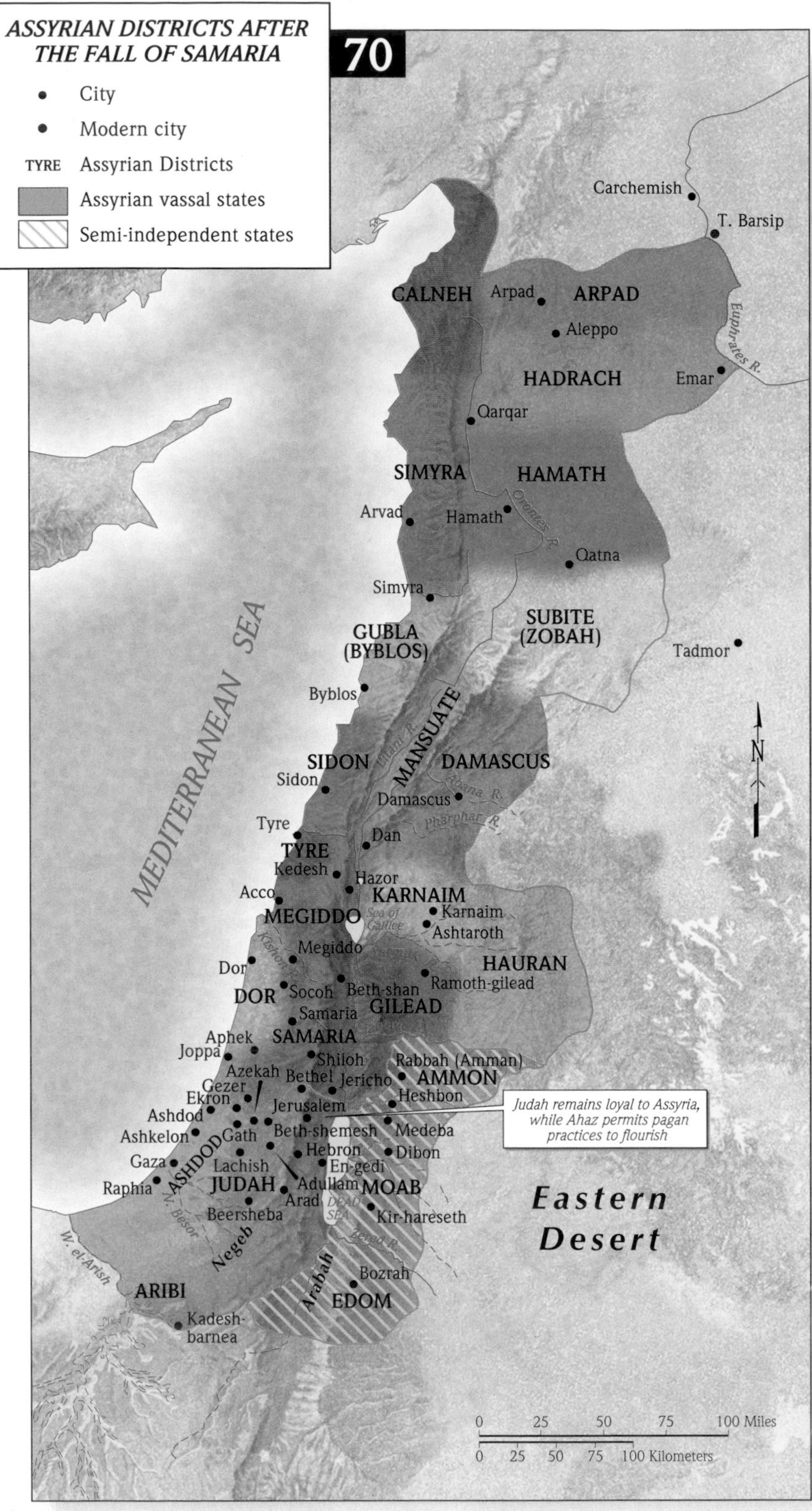

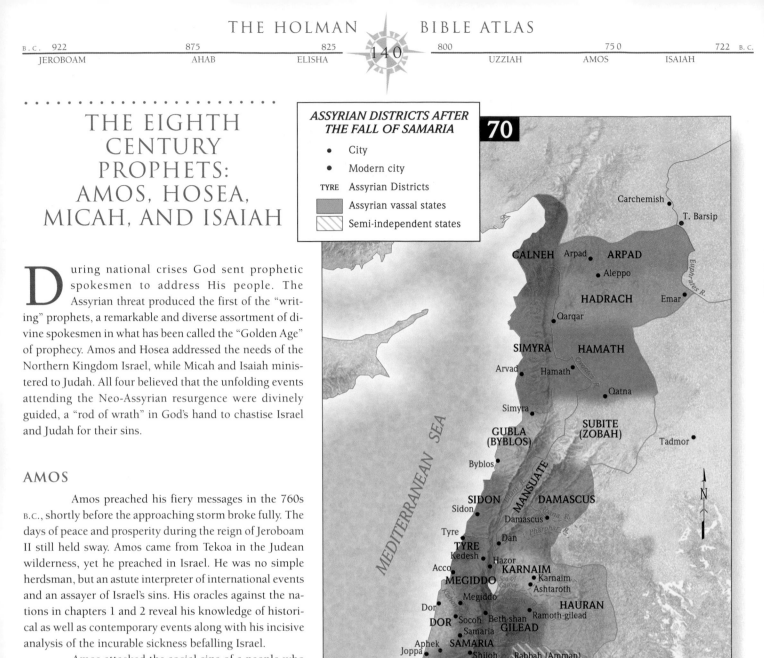

During national crises God sent prophetic spokesmen to address His people. The Assyrian threat produced the first of the "writing" prophets, a remarkable and diverse assortment of divine spokesmen in what has been called the "Golden Age" of prophecy. Amos and Hosea addressed the needs of the Northern Kingdom Israel, while Micah and Isaiah ministered to Judah. All four believed that the unfolding events attending the Neo-Assyrian resurgence were divinely guided, a "rod of wrath" in God's hand to chastise Israel and Judah for their sins.

AMOS

Amos preached his fiery messages in the 760s B.C., shortly before the approaching storm broke fully. The days of peace and prosperity during the reign of Jeroboam II still held sway. Amos came from Tekoa in the Judean wilderness, yet he preached in Israel. He was no simple herdsman, but an astute interpreter of international events and an assayer of Israel's sins. His oracles against the nations in chapters 1 and 2 reveal his knowledge of historical as well as contemporary events along with his incisive analysis of the incurable sickness befalling Israel.

Amos attacked the social sins of a people who derived their wealth from the oppression of their countrymen (Amos 4:1; 5:10–13; 6:4–7). He contrasted the luxury of the royal court at Samaria and the homes of the aristocracy with the plight of the poor who had been robbed of their land and livelihood by unscrupulous tactics sanctioned at the highest levels. Some of Amos' most thunderous denunciations were delivered at the royal sanctuary at Bethel and in Samaria. Although his ministry did not last long, his dire predictions of impending judgment must have been unsettling to many Israelites (Amos 3:11–15; 6:8–11; 8:7–14; 9:1–4).

HOSEA

Hosea may have been the only "writing" prophet who came from Israel. He delivered his oracles to Israel in the chaotic final decades of the nation's existence (740s–720s B.C.). Hosea's tragic marriage to Gomer became the vehicle through which he understood the depth of both God's love and Israel's unfaithfulness. His marriage became a paradigm, expressing the spiritual adultery of Israel against God, the despicable rejection of Yahweh by Israel for Baal, the pagan god of bounty and blessing (Hos. 4:11–14; 10:1–2; 11:1–4). He foresaw national disaster for Israel (Hos. 5:8–9; 8:1–7; 10:14–15) unless Israel returned to her God. He warned against trying to fend off God's just punishment by reliance upon military strength or political and military alliances (Hos. 7:11; 8:8–10; 14:1–3). Hosea, unfortunately, lived to see his prophecies of destruction fulfilled by Tiglath-pileser III, who devastated northern Israel, deporting citizens and incorporating much of Israel into Assyrian provinces. He probably also witnessed the capture of Samaria in 722 B.C. as well.

MICAH

Micah came from Moresheth, most likely Moresheth-gath, a small town located in the Shephelah about twenty-five miles southwest of Jerusalem. Along with its nearby neighbors—Lachish and Azekah—Moresheth-gath lay in harm's way for any army seeking to capture Jerusalem. Micah seems to have spent much time in Jerusalem, perhaps as an elder representing his village's interests before the corrupt national bureaucracy. He aimed much of his message toward the same kind of social abuses that provoked Amos a few decades earlier (Mic. 2:1–5; 3:1–3). He was the first prophet to predict the destruction of Jerusalem (Mic. 3:12). Like the other eighth-century prophets, Micah was much interested in the nature of true religion, which he believed required justice, kindness, and humility—qualities he found altogether lacking in too many of Judah's citizens (Mic. 6:1–8; cf. Amos 5:21–24; Hos. 6:4–6; Isa. 1:10–17). Micah identified closely with those who were powerless and at the mercy of corrupt powermongers.

Dating the ministry of Micah is difficult. Some of his oracles require a dating before the destruction of Samaria in 722 B.C., while others suggest the campaign of Sennacherib in 701 B.C.

ISAIAH

Isaiah received his prophetic call about 742 B.C. in the turbulent days following the death of king Uzziah (Isa. 6). His ministry coincided with the advent of the powerful Assyrian king Tiglath-pileser III (745–727 B.C.) and continued throughout the siege of Jerusalem by Sennacherib in 701 B.C. (cf. Isa. 36–39). As a confidant of kings, Isaiah provided counsel for Ahaz and Hezekiah at a time when Judah faced serious external and internal threats. Isaiah may have been a member of the Judean royal family; according to tradition, Isaiah's father, Amoz, was the brother of Amaziah, thus making Isaiah and Uzziah cousins. Although the tradition cannot be verified, it would explain Isaiah's ease of access to the kings of Judah.

Isaiah married a woman described as a "prophetess" (Isa. 8:3) who bore him two sons, symbolic of themes in the prophet's message. Maher-shalal-hash-baz means "hasten booty, speed the spoil," a reference to the impending destruction of Judah's enemies, Damascus and Israel, by the Assyrians. Shear-jashub—"a remnant shall return"—foreshadows either a promise or warning that a remnant of Judah would survive God's judgment meted out by the Assyrians.

Isaiah's ministry spanned at least five decades, from 742 B.C. to after 701 B.C. His message addressed the social evils of his nation (Isa. 1:21–22; 3:1–26; 5:1–30), the nature of true religion (Isa. 1:12–17), and the coming of an ideal Davidic king (Isa. 9; 11). Isaiah advised Ahaz in the Syro-Ephraimite War (Isa. 7) and stood by the side of Hezekiah when Sennacherib invaded Judah, destroying forty-six Judean cities, and besieged Jerusalem. How long Isaiah lived and preached beyond this event the Bible does not say. Tradition says that Isaiah was killed early in the reign of Manasseh.

Chapter Eleven

JUDAH ALONE AMID INTERNATIONAL POWERS

The Assyrian Threat

The century following the fall of Israel in 722 B.C. was the high-water mark for the Assyrian Empire. Assyria reached the zenith of power during the reigns of Esarhaddon (681–669 B.C.) and Ashurbanipal (669–627 B.C.) before experiencing a rapid collapse in the late seventh century. On their own, the vassal states of Syria and Palestine were ill-equipped to resist Assyrian might during this era; however, Egypt, under the new, more aggressive Twenty-fifth Dynasty (725–664 B.C.) of Nubian origin, promised aid. Chaldean and Elamite elements created unrest in Babylonia. These actions prompted rebellions against Assyria among certain kings of Palestine and Syria, usually with predictably calamitous results.

In the days of Ahaz (735–715 B.C.) Judah remained a loyal Assyrian vassal. Judah paid a terrible price for Assyrian overlordship, since Ahaz permitted pagan practices to flourish in Jerusalem (2 Kgs. 16:10–18). The same social evils characteristic of Israel's final days crept into Judean life as well (Mic. 2:1–5; 3:1–3; Isa. 5:8–23).

Sargon II (722–705 B.C.), the conqueror of Samaria, encountered rebellion in various parts of the empire throughout much of his reign. The pesky Chaldean chieftain Merodach-baladan, in alliance with Elam, claimed the throne in Babylon in 721 B.C., a military threat to Assyria requiring Sargon's immediate attention. These events sparked rebellion against Assyria in Syria and Gaza, the latter inspired by Egyptian promises of aid. Assyrian forces crushed both uprisings. Samaria, too, was implicated in the disorders, prompting the Assyrians to deport inhabitants of Samaria to cities in Gozan in northwest Mesopotamia, the area around Nineveh, and as far east as Media (see above, p. 139). In 714 B.C. Urartian pressure on Assyrian supply lines forced Sargon to lead a major northern campaign against the main Urartian army. Chronic Chaldean and Elamite pressure on Babylon combined with the Urartian problem gave vassals in the west opportunity to seek independence from Assyria, especially with the possibility of Egyptian assistance.

A jar handle bearing the Hebrew inscription *l'melek* ("belonging to the king").

Hezekiah's Independence Movement

HEZEKIAH'S REFORM

Hezekiah came to the throne of Judah in these turbulent times. The date Hezekiah became king is disputed; certain biblical statements permit a date as early as 729 or as late as 715 B.C.; the later date is traditionally preferred (715–687 B.C.). Unlike his father, Ahaz, Hezekiah steered a course of religious reform and political freedom (2 Chr. 29–31). As early as 712 B.C., he contemplated joining a revolt against Assyria led by Ashdod and supported by Shabako of Egypt; however, along with Edom and Moab, Hezekiah pulled back, perhaps cautioned by Isaiah's warnings against depending upon Egyptian help (Isa. 20).

Gradually Hezekiah strengthened his position by extending his control over cities in the Philistine Plain (2 Kgs. 18:8). Next, he carried out a series of religious reforms that eliminated the pagan practices permitted by Ahaz. Hezekiah ordered the destruction of high places with their idolatrous symbols (sacred pillars and Asherim [wooden objects sacred to Asherah]), cleansed the Jerusalem temple, and celebrated a great Passover (2 Chr. 29–31). Under Hezekiah, Judah became the strongest state in the southern Levant.

HEZEKIAH'S OPPORTUNITY FOR REVOLT

When Sargon II died in 705 B.C., his successor, Sennacherib (705–681 B.C.), faced revolt in Babylon, once again led by Merodach-baladan. At some point Hezekiah received in Jerusalem envoys sent from Merodach-baladan, an act intimating an anti-Assyrian conspiracy (2 Kgs. 20:12–15). That Hezekiah intended rebellion seems clear from the biblical descriptions of the strengthening of his country's defenses.

HEZEKIAH'S PREPARATION FOR WAR

In Jerusalem, Hezekiah built a massive new wall to fortify the western suburbs of the city, and he secured the city's water supply by diverting the waters of the Gihon Spring through a 1,700-foot tunnel that led to a pool within the city fortifications (Isa. 22:8–11; 2 Kgs. 20:20; 2 Chr. 32:30). Hezekiah strength-

CHART 12. JUDAH ALONE 722–586 B.C.						
Date (B.C.)	Judah	Prophets	Egypt	Assyria	Medes	Babylon
722	Ahaz (735–715): Vassal of Assyria	Isaiah Micah		Sargon II (722–705)		
715	Hezekiah (715–687) Hezekiah's rebellion against Assyria			Sennacherib (705–681) Campaign against Judah		Chaldean chieftain Merodach-baladan
700	Sennacherib's campaign (701) Manasseh (687–642)		Tirhakah (690–664)	Sennacherib destroys Babylon Esarhaddon (681–669) attacks Egypt		
675	Corruption and pagan practices promoted by Manasseh grip Judah		Psammeticus (664–610)	Ashurbanipal II (669–627); sack of Thebes (663)		
650	Josiah (640–609)	Jeremiah (627–582)		Death of Ashurbanipal II (627)		Nabopolassar seized throne of Babylon (626)
625	Josianic reform "Book of the Law" (621)	Nahum		Sin-shar-ushkun	Cyaxares (623–584)	
615	Death of Josiah (609) Jehoiakim (609–598)	Zephaniah Habbakuk	Neco II (610–594)	Asshur sacked (614) Ashur-uballit II; Nineveh destroyed (612) Haran falls (610)		Nebuchadnezzar (605–562) Battle of Carchemish
605	Rebellion against Babylon					
600						
598/97	1st siege of Jerusalem and deportation (Jehoiachin 598–597)	Ezekiel	Apries (Hophra) (589–570)			1st campaign against Judah
587/86	2nd siege of Jerusalem; destruction of temple					2nd campaign against Judah; destruction of Jerusalem and the temple

ened the army and apparently provided a supply system of stored goods designed to withstand Assyrian siege.

Numerous storage-jar fragments stamped with a royal seal, inscribed "belonging (or for) the king" (*L'melek* in Hebrew), found in excavations in Judah bear four names: Ziph, Socoh, Hebron, and the enigmatic *mmsht*. The first three are Judean towns, while the latter may refer to the governmental offices at Jerusalem. Perhaps these four names designated regional collection-distribution centers of essential goods—oil, wine, etc. Goods would be collected in the form of taxes in kind, stored, and then redistributed as needed (see photo on p. 142).

HEZEKIAH'S REBELLION

With his kingdom properly prepared, Hezekiah rebelled against Sennacherib, provoking an Assyrian response in 701 B.C. Hezekiah's actions were part of a larger anti-Assyrian insurrection that included Sidon, Ashkelon, and the citizens of Ekron, who turned their king, Padi, over to Hezekiah. Sennacherib's campaign to crush the rebellious vassals is well documented both in biblical and Assyrian texts (2 Kgs. 18:13–19:35; Isa. 36–37; 2 Chr. 32:1–23; five whole or fragmentary copies of Sennacherib's Annals mention the campaign).

ASSYRIAN ATTACKS ON JUDAH

First, Sennacherib moved against Sidon, replacing its rebellious kings and receiving tribute from subjugated Phoenician cities. Next, Sennacherib moved south against Ashkelon and removed its king, Sidqia. He subdued cities in the northern Philistine Plain (Joppa, Bene-berak, Azor, and Beth-dagon) formerly controlled by Sidqia and then proceeded into the Shephelah. Sennacherib's annals mention the capture of Ekron and Timnah, both located in the strategic Sorek Valley. Assyrian pressure forced Hezekiah to release Padi, who was reinstated as king of Ekron.

The villages and towns of the Shephelah were particularly hard hit by the Assyrian invasion. Friezes from Sennacherib's palace at Nineveh depict in graphic detail the siege of Lachish, a key Judean fortress in the Shephelah protecting the approaches to Jerusalem. Micah 1:10–16 undoubtedly refers to other towns that suffered a similar fate (Moresheth-gath, Achzib, Gath, and Adullam); Libnah is mentioned in the account of the Rabshakeh's warnings to the citizens of Jerusalem (2 Kgs. 19:8). An oracle of Isaiah suggests a northern approach to Jerusalem by elements of the Assyrian army, which threatened the towns and villages of Benjamin (Isa. 10:28–34). Altogether, Sennacherib claims to have destroyed forty-six Judean cities, a boast adequately supported by the numerous destruction levels found in the excavation of Judean sites datable close to 700 B.C. (see also "Assyrian Warfare," pp. 148–49).

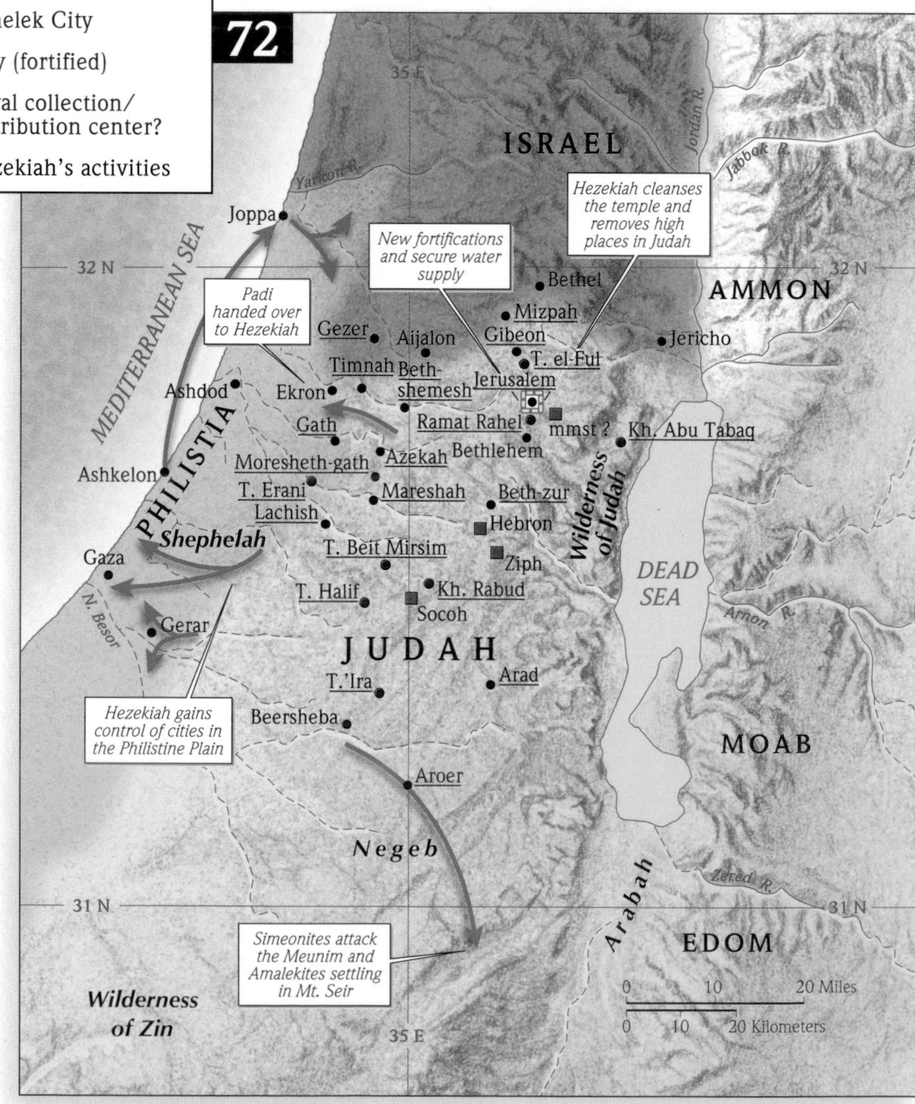

JERUSALEM FROM HEZEKIAH TO THE DESTRUCTION IN 586 B.C.

Recent archaeological excavations have confirmed a western expansion of Jerusalem dating from the reign of Hezekiah (715–687 B.C). Archaeologists speculate that a population influx, in part of Israelite refugees fleeing the Assyrian invasions, made the expansion necessary. Clear evidence indicates the southwestern hill was now incorporated into Jerusalem's defenses. A segment of a "broad wall" sixty-five meters long and seven meters wide, south of the Transversal Valley, has been unearthed by Nahman Avigad. Avigad attributed the wall to Hezekiah, who "counted the houses of Jerusalem, and . . . broke down the houses to fortify the wall" (Isa. 22:10). Indeed, Hezekiah's wall was built on top of the foundations of houses visible under the outer edge of Avigad's wall. This massive wall, made to withstand

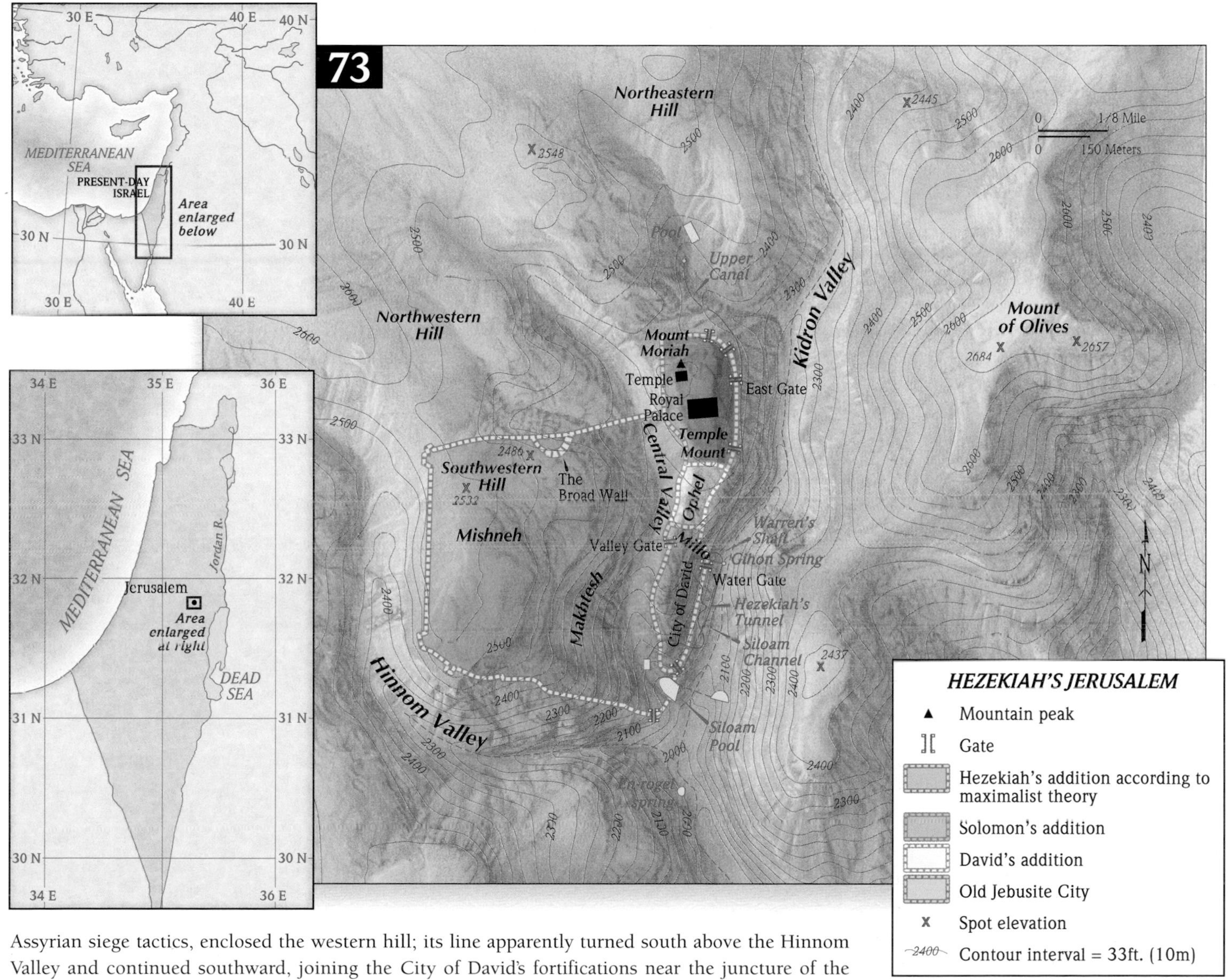

Assyrian siege tactics, enclosed the western hill; its line apparently turned south above the Hinnom Valley and continued southward, joining the City of David's fortifications near the juncture of the Hinnom and Kidron Valleys.

The "broad wall" enclosed an additional ninety acres of land, making the total fortified area of Jerusalem approximately one hundred and fifty acres. The area taken in included the *mishneh*—"Second Quarter," where the prophet Huldah lived (2 Kgs. 22:14)—and the *maktesh* (the Mortar), probably a reference to the depression between the western and eastern slope (Zech. 1:11). Population estimates for the city at this time range from fifteen to twenty-five thousand.

THE WATER SYSTEMS

By about 700 B.C. Jerusalem benefited from three water systems. In addition to Warren's Shaft, which gave vertical access to the Gihon Spring, two other systems channeled the water of the spring to various parts of the city. The Siloam Channel extends four hundred meters from the Gihon Spring southward to a pool at the southern end of the eastern ridge. The channel lies outside the protective walls of the city. It was composed of both a narrow tunnel and a covered channel capped by stone. The channel not only brought water to a reservoir, but was used as an irrigation system as well. Apertures in the east side of the channel could be opened to water fields located in the Kidron Valley.

Hezekiah's most impressive engineering feat was a tunnel excavated through the eastern ridge and was used to bring the waters of the Gihon Spring inside Jerusalem. Two teams of workmen starting from opposite sides carved a 533-meter-long tunnel through the southeastern hill. The tunnel emerges in the southern Tyropoeon Valley and empties into the Pool of Siloam. An overflow channel continues southward from the pool. This system gave Jerusalem a protected water supply in times of siege, an expedient measure taken by Hezekiah as he steered Judah along a course of independence against Assyrian control (Isa. 22:10–11; 2 Kgs. 20:20; 2 Chr. 32:34).

The foundations of the Broad Wall in Jerusalem attributed to the building activities of Hezekiah as he prepared his city for revolt against the Assyrians.

JERUSALEM IN THE LAST YEARS OF THE MONARCHY

Remarkable finds illuminating Jerusalem between about 700 to 587 B.C. come from the east slope of the southeastern ridge. A series of terraces descending along the slope supported numerous public and domestic structures clinging to the slope. Some are large stone buildings (ashlar masonry) that probably served some public function. Other structures were more modest private dwellings patterned after a typical four-room plan known from other sites. The "House of Ahiel," so-called because of a name found in the ruins, is more typical of these dwellings. Narrow alleyways and steps interconnected the various units along the slope. One partially excavated building yielded fifty-one clay sealings called *bullae* used as seals on documents. The bullae mention names including two that may have biblical connections. One bulla mentions Gemariah ben Shaphan, possibly the royal official mentioned several times in Jeremiah (36:9–12, 25–26). Azariah ben Hilkiah is mentioned on another bulla, likely a priest named in priestly genealogical lists (1 Chr. 9:10–11; cf. Ezra 7:1).

The tunnel of Hezekiah that leads from the Gihon Spring to the safety of a pool within the city's defenses.

Additional finds from the houses of the eastern slope include weights, zoomorphic figurines, fragments of carved wood, and fertility figurines. The latter testify to the pagan worship practices tolerated and promoted by Manasseh and other Judean kings. Prophetic warnings failed to root out these practices that brought God's judgment upon the city when Nebuchadnezzar, king of Babylon, sacked Jerusalem in 586 B.C. Archaeologists have found abundant evidence in many excavated areas of the city of the final assault inflicted upon Jerusalem and the conflagration that consumed parts of the city. After 586 B.C. Jerusalem languished in ruins until exiles began the long process of rebuilding in the post-exilic period.

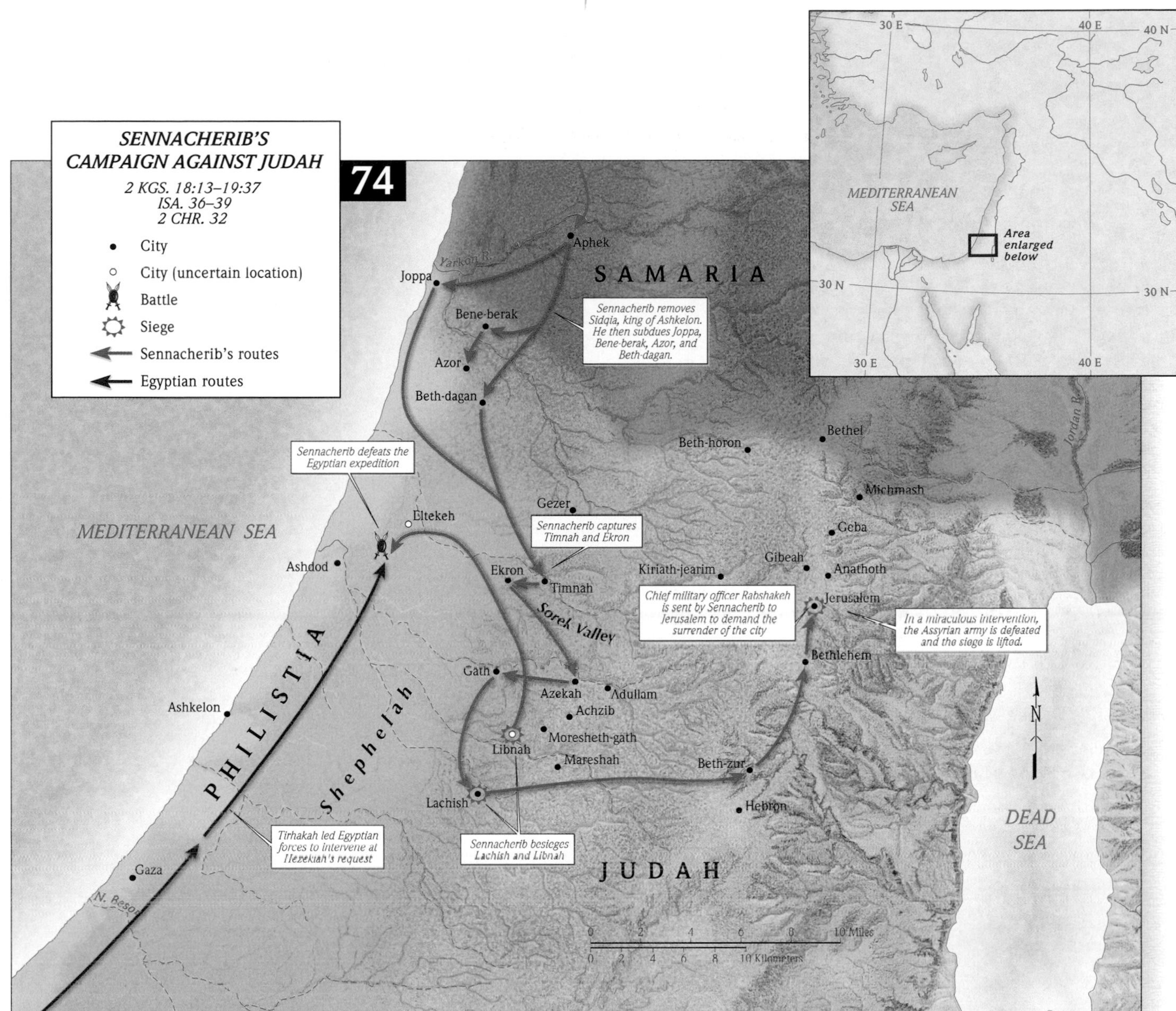

THE SIEGE OF JERUSALEM

While besieging Libnah and Lachish, Sennacherib sent a high military officer—the Rabshakeh—to Jerusalem to demand the surrender of the city. The Assyrian forces surrounded the city and built an earthen embankment around it to prevent any escape. Sennacherib boasted that he made Hezekiah a prisoner in Jerusalem "like a bird in a cage." At some point, an Egyptian force led by Tirhakah intervened in response to Hezekiah's desperate appeals, but Sennacherib defeated the expedition near Eltekeh.

The Rabshakeh taunted the Jerusalem citizenry for relying on Egypt, "that broken reed of a staff, which will pierce the hand of any man who leans on it" (2 Kgs. 18:21). The situation appeared hopeless, and Hezekiah, cut off from all help, despaired for the city. Isaiah encouraged the king and gave assurance to Hezekiah that Jerusalem would not fall. Subsequently, in a miraculous intervention, the besieging Assyrian army lost 185,000 men, and the siege was lifted (2 Kgs. 19:35–36).

An interesting incident reported by the Greek historian Herodotus recalls that the Assyrian army met defeat near Pelusium when a plague of mice stripped the weapons of the Assyrian troops. What, if any, relationship exists between the two accounts of an Assyrian defeat in the southern Levant cannot be determined for certain. Nonetheless, Jerusalem was spared destruction, although Hezekiah paid a great price for his rebellion. In addition to the destruction of numerous Judean cities, Hezekiah paid a large tribute to Sennacherib and lost control of Philistine territory previously under his control.

ASSYRIAN WARFARE

The Assyrian army marched with a reputation for unbridled cruelty and professional efficiency. Nahum's graphic descriptions of Assyrian chariotry capture the chaotic terror the Assyrian military could inflict (Nah. 3:1–3). Indeed, the Neo-Assyrian Empire gathered together a finely tuned military machine and employed it judiciously to maintain and expand Assyrian economic and political objectives. Far from being sadistic brutes, the Assyrians used cruelty selectively against chronically rebellious peoples to prevent further sedition. In effect, Assyrian battle tactics served propaganda purposes by clearly demonstrating the consequences of rebellion. The numerous reliefs in Assyrian palaces depicting torture and mutilations of captured leaders were grim reminders to visiting provincial officials of the penalties for rebellion.

Assyrian kings commanded armies that could number in the hundreds of thousands. The nature of the terrain and the military objectives determined the size of the force. A standing army provided protection for the king, permanent garrison personnel, and immediately available troops. These men were professionals, conscripted from both native Assyrian and provincial territories. Provinces were required to provide a certain levy of troops for the army. Other troops could be conscripted quickly in time of national need. Major Assyrian cities—Nineveh, Calah, and Khorsabad—had large royal arsenals where troops could be marshaled, equipped, reviewed, and dispatched. These arsenals consisted of storage facilities, workshops, and official accommodations surrounding large courtyards. "Fort Shalmaneser" at Calah is a good example of these military bases.

An Assyrian relief from the palace of Tiglath-pileser III at Nineveh showing an Assyrian battering ram at work.

A grain storage silo at Megiddo.

The Assyrian army consisted of many different kinds of troops. The infantry contained slingmen, spearmen, and archers. They were used both in pitched battles in open terrain as well as in siege warfare. The archers, with their strong and accurate composite bows, were the backbone of the infantry. From the eighth century onward the Assyrians used slingmen, whose deadly projectiles proved especially useful in providing cover fire when besieging fortified cities. The cavalry consisted of mounted archers and spearmen, valuable in open terrain but seldom used in siege warfare.

The Assyrian chariot corps was among the most feared elements in the army. Reliefs depict chariots pulled by two or four horses manned by two, three, and even four crewmen. The two-man crew consisted of a driver and an archer. Later, one and then two shield bearers were added. The driver also wielded a spear in battle, and all crewmen possessed swords. In addition to these battle troops, the army carried transport wagons and supply personnel; engineers who cut roads, built bridges, constructed ramps, and built siege machines; intelligence operatives (spies and interpreters); scribes who recorded the campaign and provided lists of the booty taken; and cultic personnel who offered sacrifices and divined omens. Normally, the army campaigned in the summer months, avoiding the agricultural season and the bad winter weather. In friendly territory, local vassals supplied provisions, but in hostile regions the army lived off the land.

Detail of the siege of Lachish recorded on the walls of the palace of Sennacherib at Nineveh. Assyrian battering rams attack the desperate defenders of the Judean city who attempt to counteract the assault by hurling flaming torches toward the battering rams. At the right captives stream out of the doomed city. (Courtesy of the British Museum.)

The Assyrian army engaged in guerilla warfare (especially in the northern mountain regions), pitched battles in open terrain, and siege warfare. The Battle of Qarqar in 853 B.C. between a coalition involving Ahab of Israel and Shalmaneser III is typical of pitched battles. Armies took a horrific mauling, and much loss of life could be expected, even in victory. The people of Israel and Judah were, unfortunately, more familiar with siege warfare. The Assyrians often surrounded a city with the intent of taking the city by assault or starving the city into submission.

The keys to resisting a siege successfully were threefold: (1) strong fortifications, (2) a secure water supply, and (3) adequate food supplies. The archaeology of many cities of Israel and Judah during the Assyrian period shows a preoccupation with these matters (see "The Omrides' Building Achievements" pp. 127–29).

Assyrian reliefs contain many scenes displaying their siege strategies. The "Lachish Frieze" is especially pertinent, since it depicts Sennacherib's siege of Lachish in his campaign aimed at Jerusalem in 701 B.C. Typically, the Assyrians encamped near their target and established a perimeter around the city, ensuring no escape for the defenders. Assyrian siege machinery, including battering rams with mobile siege towers, were maneuvered into position along ramparts of earth and stones constructed by engineers. The battering rams were used to attack gates and weak points in walls (see Ezek. 4:2; 21:22). Crews inside operated the ram, while from above archers gave protecting fire. Rams even carried firemen whose mission was to thwart any attempt by defenders to set the siege machines on fire. Assault troops used scaling ladders to reach the upper walls of a city, while sappers tunneled beneath the fortifications or attempted to breach walls at weak points.

Archers and slingmen provided covering fire to the assault forces from the periphery. This coordinated attack involving different elements placed maximum pressure upon the defenders, whose hopes rested on hurling projectiles at the attackers while attempting to set the siege machines on fire. If resistance proved too costly to the attackers or if the siege could be prolonged until help came or the enemy simply gave up, the city might be spared.

Often cities suffered severe famine during a siege; inhabitants occasionally resorted to cannibalism to relieve their desperate plight (2 Kgs. 6:24–30). The Assyrians employed a type of psychological warfare to break the resistance of a city. During Sennacherib's campaign against Judah, he sent military officials (the Rabshakeh, Tartan, and Rabsaris) to Jerusalem along with a military contingent to threaten Hezekiah (2 Kgs. 18–19). The Rabshakeh addressed the inhabitants of Jerusalem in the Hebrew language as he warned them of the futility of resistance. He seems to have been well informed of Hezekiah's reform efforts and used his information to suggest that Hezekiah had offended the God of Israel (2 Kgs. 18:22). The Rabshakeh also taunted Hezekiah for trusting in Egyptian help and his own military preparations. The Assyrian intelligence system provided reliable information, a fact demonstrated often in other Assyrian documents.

When the city surrendered or was taken by assault, various fates awaited the survivors. Many were killed, especially the leaders. Their mutilated bodies were often displayed on Assyrian reliefs. This was especially true of chronically rebellious territories. More often, the Assyrians gathered groups of survivors and deported them to other parts of the Assyrian Empire. The Assyrians chose areas similar to the deportee's homeland when possible. These people were important sources of labor and could be used to make agriculturally unproductive lands valuable again. Families were not broken up, and some effort was expended to make the transition successful. The experience must have been traumatic, although interestingly, the Israelite deportees must have quickly assimilated to their new surroundings and did not retain their identity as those of their later kindred in the Babylonian captivity.

Manasseh's Long Rule

The later years of Hezekiah's reign passed unnoticed by the biblical writers. Presumably, he caused no further trouble for Assyria. His son Manasseh succeeded him in 687 B.C. and ruled fifty-five years. Like his grandfather Ahaz, Manasseh returned to pagan ways, permitting idolatrous practices and abominations to flourish. Altars to astral deities appeared in the court of the temple, while the high places dedicated to Baal were rebuilt. The practice of human sacrifice returned to Jerusalem (2 Kgs. 21:1–17; 2 Chr. 33:1–21). The writer of Chronicles noted that Manasseh repented in later years and includes a description of some building activities in Jerusalem, but Manasseh had little practical political recourse other than to play the loyal vassal of Assyria.

Against the background of Assyrian dominance, Manasseh's course seemed logical. Assyrian kings reached the height of their power shortly after 700 B.C. Sennacherib dealt with perennial Babylonian rebellion by sacking the city in 689 B.C. The image of Marduk was taken to Assyria, and Sennacherib took the ancient title of "King of Sumer and Akkad." His death in 681 B.C. at the hands of one of his own sons produced a momentary shudder in the Assyrian juggernaut, but another son—Esarhaddon—quickly gained control.

Assyrian Supremacy under Esarhaddon and Ashurbanipal II

ESARHADDON

Esarhaddon (681–669 B.C.) healed the breach with Babylon by rebuilding the city. He gave the Medes military assistance in order to check Elamite advances and as a buffer against the invading Cimmerians (the Gomer of the Bible) and the Scythians (biblical Ashkenaz). In the west, Esarhaddon quelled revolts in Tyre and Sidon and received tribute from various Syro-Palestinian kings, including Manasseh, who is mentioned in a tribute list. The Egyptian king Tirhakah (690–664 B.C.) stirred up problems to the south, eventually requiring an Assyrian response. In 671 B.C. Esarhaddon attacked Tirhakah, took Memphis, and received tribute from the native princes of the Egyptian Delta. Tirhakah escaped, only to return later to retake Memphis, provoking a second Assyrian campaign. Esarhaddon died, however, before he reached his objective.

ASHURBANIPAL II

In 669 B.C. Ashurbanipal II (669–627 B.C.) succeeded Esarhaddon as king of Assyria, and his brother Shamash-shum-ukin became king of Babylon. This division of power was according to the will of Esarhaddon, who sought to ensure an orderly succession.

VICTORY OVER EGYPT

Ashurbanipal completed the conquest of Egypt by marching against Tirhakah in 667 B.C. and defeating him; Memphis again was captured, but Tirhakah escaped. His successor Tanuatamun retook the Delta, but Ashurbanipal dealt him a crushing blow and pursued his army as far south as Thebes (biblical No-amon), sacking the city in 663 B.C. (Nah. 3:8–10 mentions the sack of Thebes). Assyrian power had now reached its zenith despite the fact that Ashurbanipal was not particularly adept either as a soldier or statesman.

THREATS TO THE ASSYRIAN EMPIRE

The Assyrian Empire was already on the verge of serious trouble during the reign of Ashurbanipal. Restless tribes threatened Assyrian interests in many directions. Cimmerians and Scythians bore down in areas north and west of the Assyrian heartland, while Medes and Persians entrenched themselves in various parts of the Iranian plateau. Ashurbanipal fought a lengthy, bloody war against Elam from 655 to 642 B.C., during which the Elamite capital, Susa, was destroyed.

Babylon became a serious problem for Assyria. Ashurbanipal's brother, Shamash-shum-ukin, revolted with Elamite and Chaldean support in 652 B.C. A long and cruel Assyrian siege of Babylon ended in 648 B.C. with the suicide of Shamash-shum-ukin as the Babylonian defense failed. Egypt proved troublesome for Assyria also. Though generally on cooperative terms with Assyria, kings of the Twenty-sixth Dynasty of Sais expelled Assyrian garrisons with the help of Lydian mercenaries. During these tumultuous years, Ashurbanipal proved to be ineffective as serious cracks appeared in the Assyrian Empire.

Assyria's Fall

The death of Ashurbanipal in 627 B.C. marked the beginning of the end for Assyria. Already weakened by decades of external conflict and increasing social unrest, Assyria suffered a four-year civil war between two sons of Ashurbanipal: Ashur-etil-ilani and Sin-shar-iskin. Neither provided adequate leadership, although the latter secured the throne in 623 B.C. and ruled until 612 B.C. The domestic turmoil invited disaster since powerful enemies of Assyria waited in the wings.

THE RIVAL POWERS AND ASSYRIA'S FINAL DAYS

In 626 B.C. Nabopolassar, the last in a long line of Chaldean troublemakers for Assyria, seized the throne of Babylon.

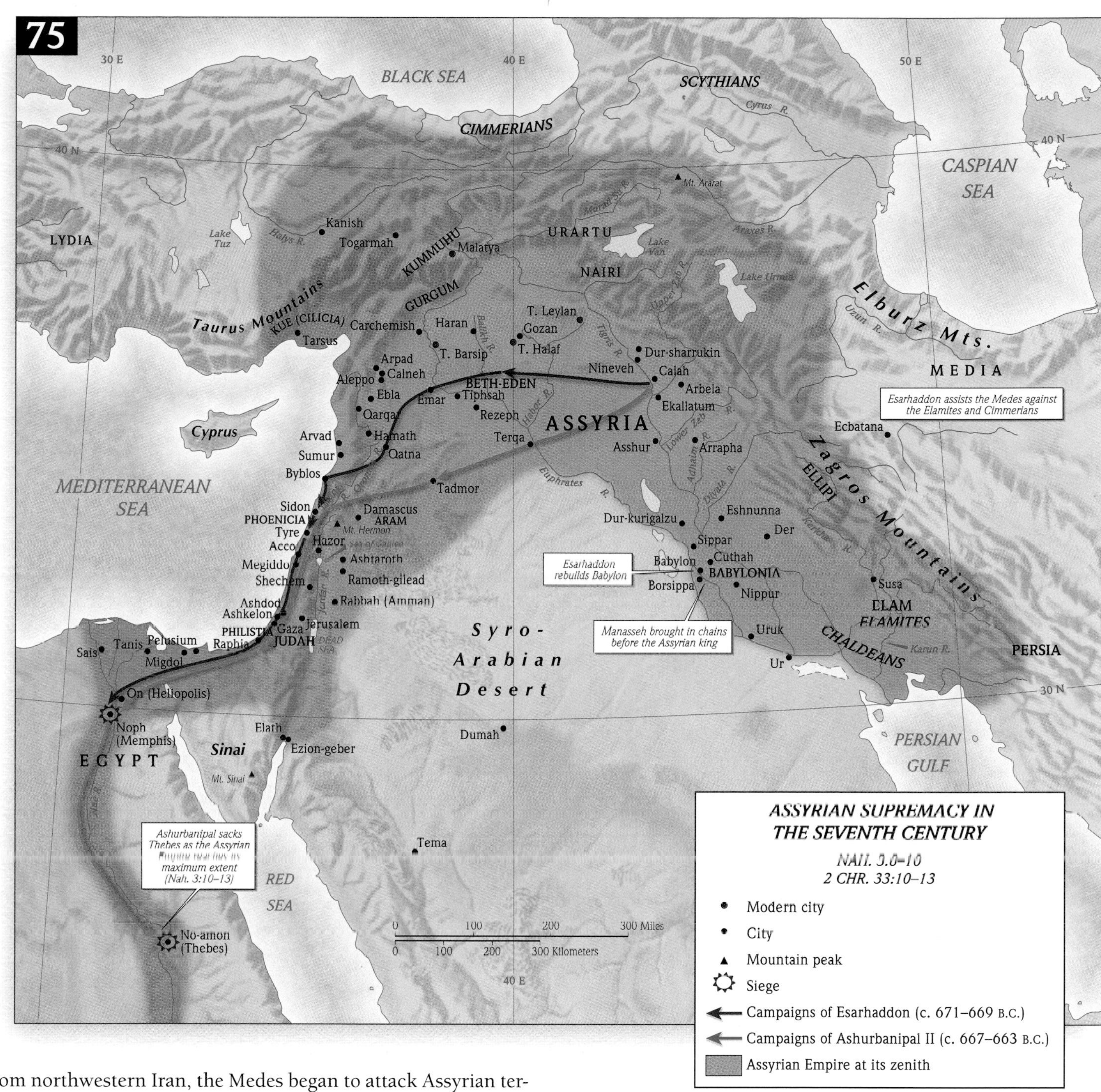

From northwestern Iran, the Medes began to attack Assyrian territories, first led by Phraortes (647–624 B.C.) and then more vigorously under Cyaxares (623–584 B.C.). Psammeticus I (664–610 B.C.) of Egypt came to the aid of Assyria, apparently more fearful of a strong Medo-Chaldean alliance controlling Mesopotamia and threatening the Levant than of the status quo with Assyria. Psammeticus also was undoubtedly reasserting traditional Egyptian claims on Syria and Palestine, seeking to control the vital trade routes of that region.

The end for Assyria came rapidly during the final two decades of the seventh century. Nabopolassar attacked Assyria from the south, while Cyaxares slashed at the Assyrian heartland from the east. In 614 B.C. Ashur, the ancient Assyrian capital and namesake of the great god of Assyria, fell to Median forces commanded by Cyaxares. Shortly thereafter, Cyaxares and Nabopolassar joined against Assyria in a formal alliance sealed by marriage. Nineveh fell in 612 B.C. to the coalition. Sin-shariskin perished, and the capital of Assyria was destroyed.

The prophet Nahum exulted in the destruction wreaked upon once-powerful Nineveh (Nah. 1:15–3:19). The remnants of the Assyrian army, led by a surviving member of the Assyrian

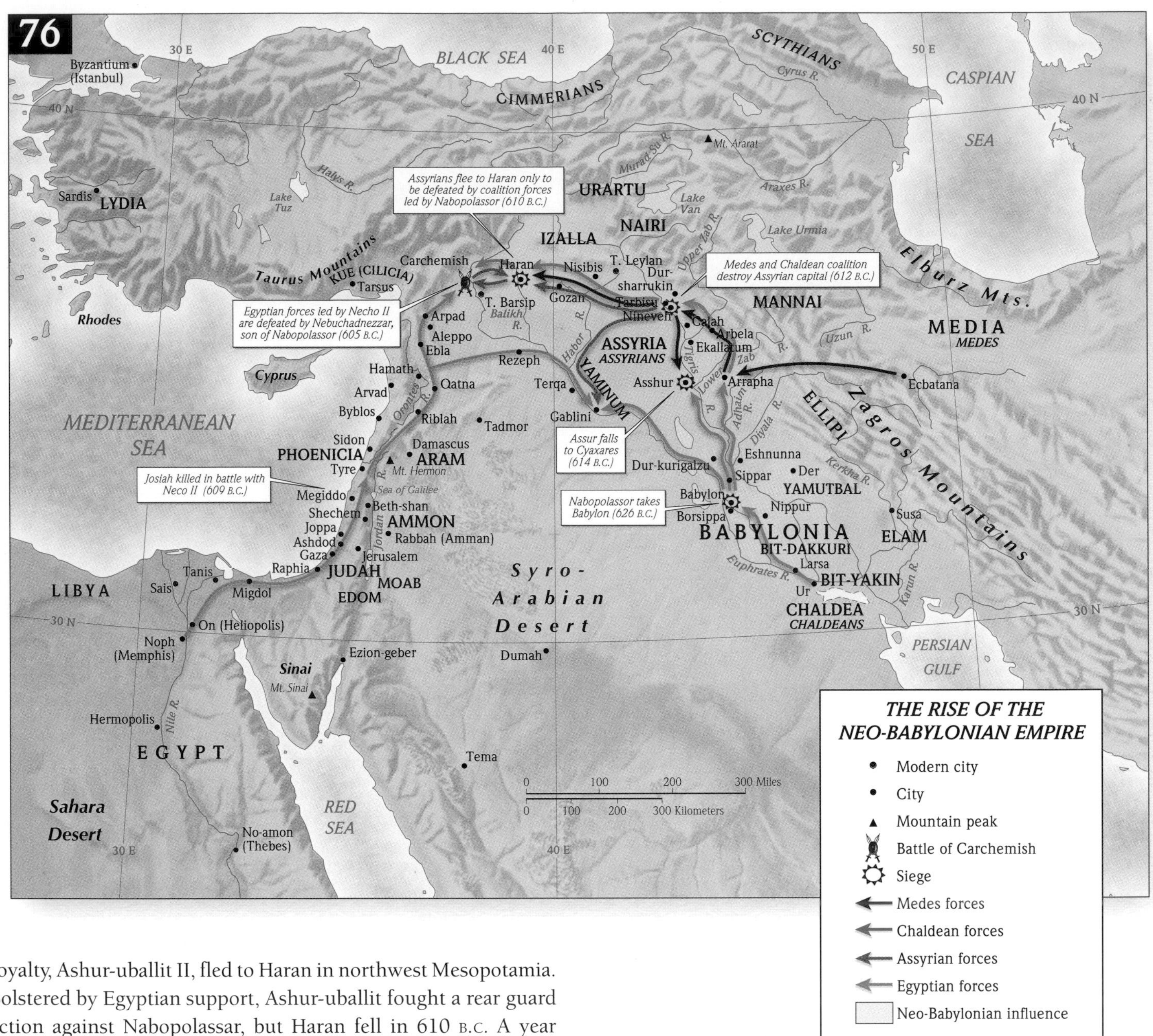

royalty, Ashur-uballit II, fled to Haran in northwest Mesopotamia. Bolstered by Egyptian support, Ashur-uballit fought a rear guard action against Nabopolassar, but Haran fell in 610 B.C. A year later the Assyrians, now vigorously supported by the new Egyptian pharaoh Neco II (610–594 B.C.), attempted to gain back Haran, but the attempt was unsuccessful. For all practical purposes, Assyria ceased to exist. The only question remaining was whether Neco II could retain any control of Syria-Palestine in the face of the Chaldean (Babylonian) advance.

Egyptian Ambitions

Egypt retained control of the International Coastal Highway and had substantial garrisons at Riblah in central Syria and Carchemish on the west bank of the Euphrates River. In addition, the Egyptians controlled the cities of the Philistine Plain (Jer. 47:1) and other key sites on the International Coastal Highway, likely including Megiddo, near where Josiah died fighting Neco in 609 B.C. (2 Kgs. 23:28–30; see Josiah's death, p. 154).

The final showdown between Egypt and Babylonia occurred in 605 B.C. at Carchemish. Nebuchadnezzar, son of Nabopolassar, led the Chaldean troops that day in a great struggle, graphically recalled by an oracle in Jeremiah (Jer. 46). Of Egypt, the prophet says:

> The swift cannot flee away,
> nor the warrior escape;
> in the north by the river Euphrates
> they have stumbled and fallen. . .

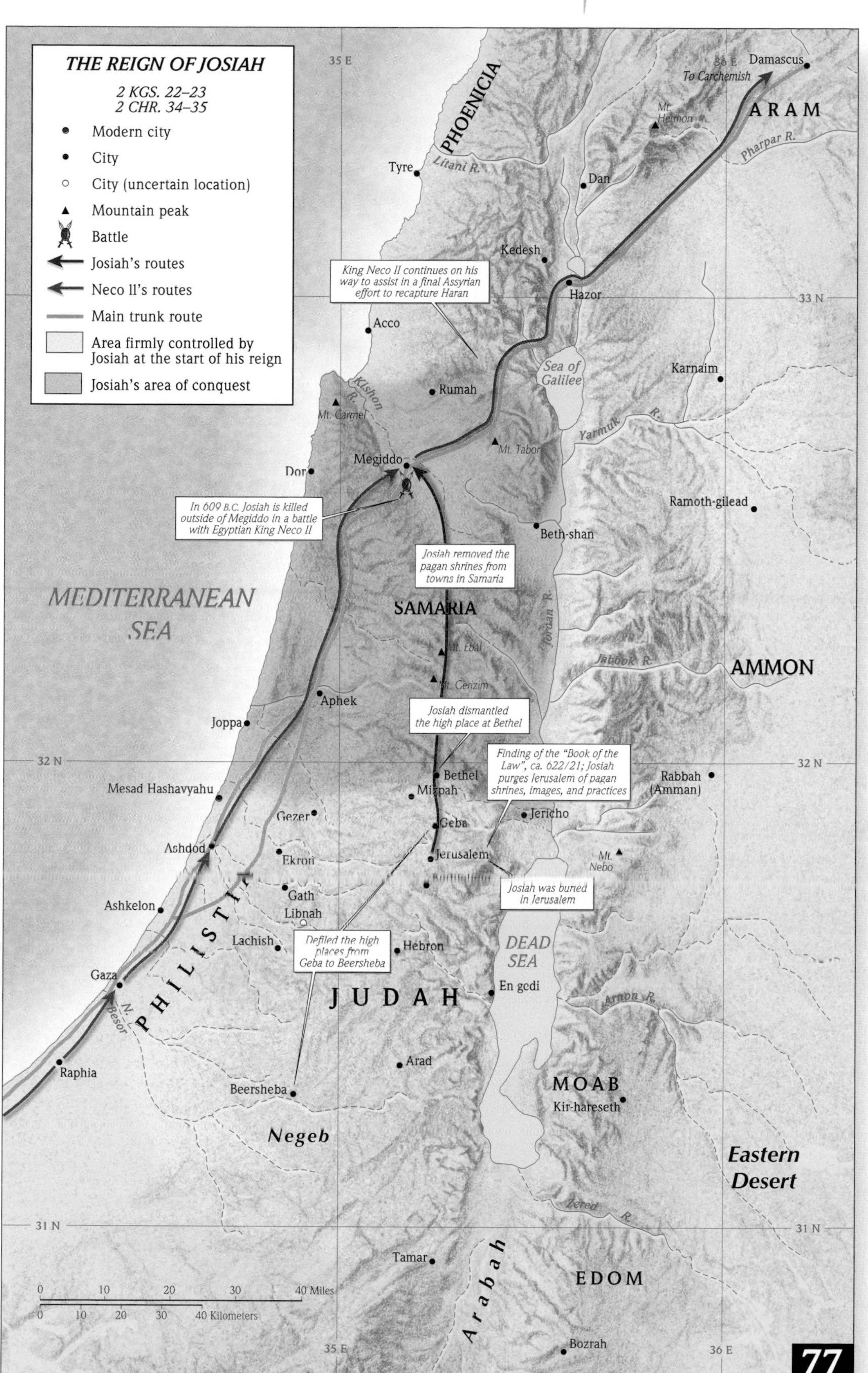

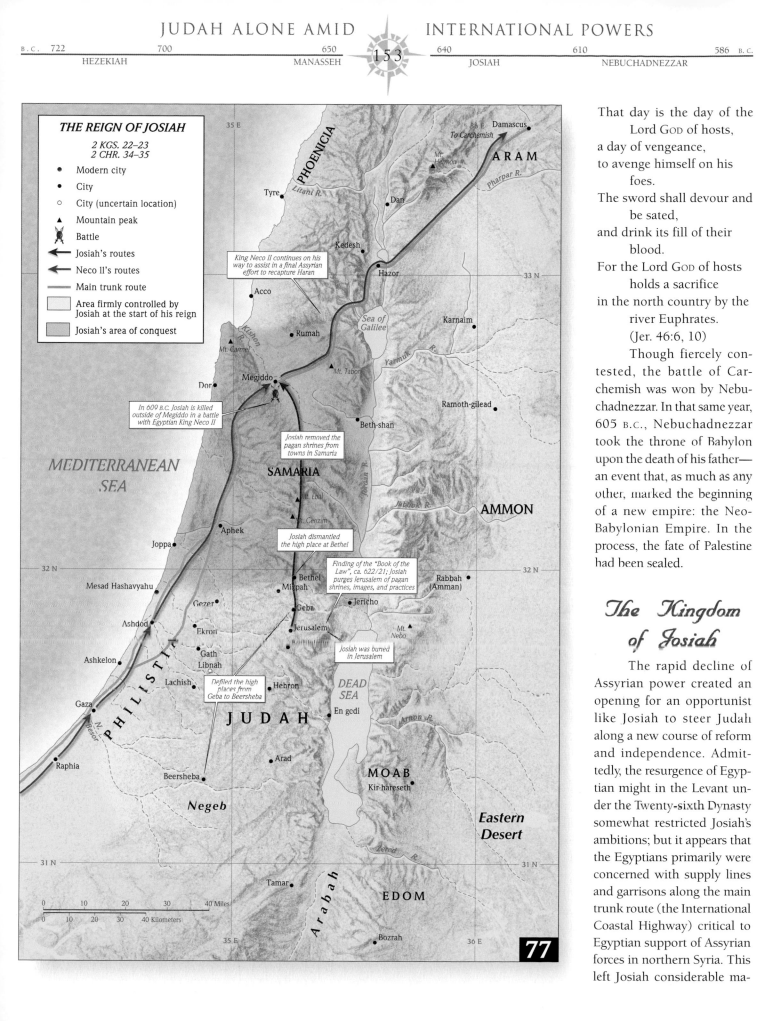

That day is the day of the
Lord God of hosts,
a day of vengeance,
to avenge himself on his
foes.
The sword shall devour and
be sated,
and drink its fill of their
blood.
For the Lord God of hosts
holds a sacrifice
in the north country by the
river Euphrates.
(Jer. 46:6, 10)

Though fiercely contested, the battle of Carchemish was won by Nebuchadnezzar. In that same year, 605 B.C., Nebuchadnezzar took the throne of Babylon upon the death of his father—an event that, as much as any other, marked the beginning of a new empire: the Neo-Babylonian Empire. In the process, the fate of Palestine had been sealed.

The Kingdom of Josiah

The rapid decline of Assyrian power created an opening for an opportunist like Josiah to steer Judah along a new course of reform and independence. Admittedly, the resurgence of Egyptian might in the Levant under the Twenty-sixth Dynasty somewhat restricted Josiah's ambitions; but it appears that the Egyptians primarily were concerned with supply lines and garrisons along the main trunk route (the International Coastal Highway) critical to Egyptian support of Assyrian forces in northern Syria. This left Josiah considerable maneuvering room, especially in the last two decades of his thirty-one-year reign.

Josiah came to the throne as an eight-year-old boy. Unlike his father and grandfather, Josiah demonstrated a godly character, and his reign was most remembered for a thorough purge of pagan practices that had proliferated under Manasseh and Amon. The precise chronology of the Josianic reform is unclear. According to Chronicles, it may have begun as early as his eighth regnal year (ca. 633/32 B.C.), but it is more likely that upon reaching manhood in his twelfth year (628/27 B.C.) Josiah began the activity of reforming the cult. If so, this would roughly correspond to the death of Ashurbanipal in 627 B.C., a momentous event in the Assyrian decline.

BOOK OF THE LAW FOUND

In 622 B.C. the recovery of "the book of the law" in the temple, generally regarded as some form of Deuteronomy, gave a great boost to Josiah's efforts (2 Kgs. 22:8–20). The Bible describes a variety of pagan elements within both Jerusalem and Judah that Josiah dismantled or destroyed: high places of Baal, symbols of Asherah, horses and chariots dedicated to the sun, vessels used in the worship of the "host of heaven" (astral deities), and the places of human sacrifice in the Valley of Ben-hinnom (2 Kgs. 23:4–20; 2 Chr. 34:1–7). He also removed idolatrous priests and attempted to centralize worship practices in Jerusalem. These actions undoubtedly isolated key elements of Judean society, especially those who favored a policy of pacification with Assyria and, of course, any displaced or banished priests. Yet Josiah's efforts had sufficient backing to last throughout his reign. Moreover, these reforms clearly signaled a new nationalistic policy designed to reestablish Judean autonomy as much as possible in the rapidly changing international scene.

JOSIAH'S ACCOMPLISHMENTS

To what degree Josiah reached his nationalistic goal is not clear. Certainly, the Egyptian king Psammeticus I was not unaware of Josiah's ambitions. However, historically the Egyptians preferred to maintain control of the coastal routes of Palestine and the major cities inland along the International Coastal Highway. What Josiah did in the mountainous hinterlands was of less concern. Certain biblical texts suggest that Josiah did quite a lot. He received moneys from towns in Manasseh and Ephraim and carried out purges in those territories and as far north as Naphtali (2 Chr. 34:6, 9). This strongly suggests that Josiah was claiming the northern territories of old Israel.

The writer of Kings records that Josiah dismantled the high place at Bethel built by Jeroboam I and carried out additional cleansings in Samaria (2 Kgs. 23:15–20). In Judah the reform effort extended from "Geba to Beer-sheba" (2 Kgs. 23:8). Taken together it is tempting to propose that Josiah had in mind nothing short of a restoration of the old Davidic kingdom. Whether Josiah pursued this goal as at least a nominal vassal of Egypt or whether he acted completely independently cannot be determined.

JOSIAH'S DEATH

What is clear is that in 609 B.C. Josiah met his death in battle with the Egyptian king Neco II (610–594 B.C.). Neco was leading an Egyptian force northward to support a final Assyrian effort to recapture Haran. Josiah intercepted Neco near Megiddo, was mortally wounded, and eventually was buried in Jerusalem (2 Kgs. 23:28–30; 2 Chr. 35:20–27). Josiah's motives for attacking Neco are unclear; perhaps he sensed the ultimate victory of Babylon over Egypt, or maybe he feared further Egyptian interference in his kingdom. The result was not only the loss of a great king, but also the end of the religious reforms and the reduction of any territories outside of Judah (except Bethel) over which Josiah had gained control.

The Neo-Babylonian Empire and the Last Kings of Judah

The consolidation of the Chaldean Dynasty at Babylon was complete by 609 B.C. The victories of Nabopolassar over

CHART 13. KINGS OF THE NEO-BABYLONIAN EMPIRE 626–539 B.C.

Name	Dates (B.C.)	Significant Events
Nabopolassar	626–605	Chaldean chieftain who seized Babylon in 626; established an alliance with Cyaxares the Mede; conquered Nineveh in 612.
Nebuchadnezzar	605–562	Defeated Egypt at Battle of Carchemish in 605; twice besieged Jerusalem (698/97; 587/86).
Evil Merodach (Amel-marduk)	562–560	Son of Nebuchadnezzar; freed Jehoiachin, king of Judah (2 Kgs. 25:27–30).
Neriglissar	560–556	Son-in-law of Nebuchadnezzar; likely the Nergal-sharezer who was present at the final siege of Jerusalem (Jer. 39:3).
Labashi-marduk	556 (3-month reign)	Son of Neriglissar; removed by Nabonidus.
Nabonidus	556–539	Spent considerable time outside of Babylon; Belshazzar served as regent in his absence; Babylon surrendered to Cyrus the Great in 539.

Assyrian and Egyptian armies made Babylon the master of Mesopotamia and placed Babylonian armies in position to thrust southward into Syria and Palestine. Only Egypt, now ruled by Neco II, could put up an effective resistance to the Babylonian advance. The prophet Habbakuk foresaw these events, declaring that God was "rousing the Chaldeans, / that bitter and hasty nation, / who march through the breadth of the earth, / to seize habitations not their own" (Hab. 1:6).

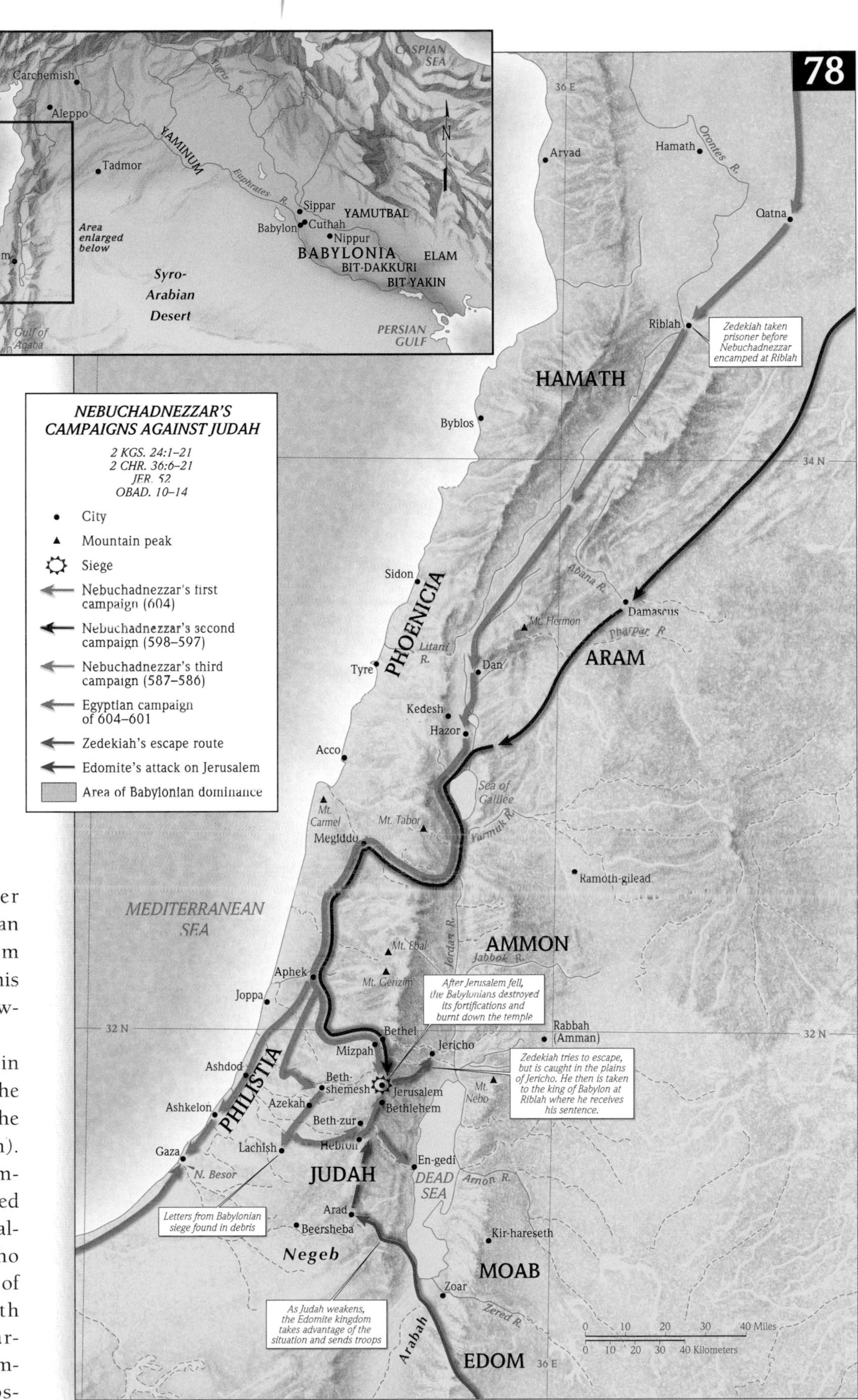

JUDAH'S DILEMMA

The power struggle between Babylonia and Egypt placed the kings of Judah in a most precarious situation. After the death of Josiah in 609 B.C., Neco removed Jehoahaz, a son of Josiah chosen by the people of Judah, and replaced him with another son whose throne name was Jehoiakim (2 Kgs. 23:30–35). Whatever independence Judah enjoyed under Josiah clearly was gone; Judah was an Egyptian vassal, and Jehoiakim reigned at the pleasure of Neco. This state of affairs did not last long however.

The Battle of Carchemish in 605 B.C. established Babylon as the dominant power all the way to the border of Egypt (the Wadi el-Arish). In 604 B.C. Nebuchadnezzar campaigned in Palestine and conquered Ashkelon. Jehoiakim quickly gave allegiance to Nebuchadnezzar, who had recently been crowned king of Babylon after his father's death shortly after the Battle of Carchemish. Perhaps during this campaign Nebuchadnezzar took hostages, including Daniel and his three companions Hananiah, Mishael, and Azariah, and carried them captive to Babylon (Dan. 1:1–7).

Judah now was caught between two unequal superpowers, Egypt and Babylon. Babylon controlled the Levant; Egypt, however, resented the loss of prestige and the loss of Phoenician ports, important links in maritime trade. Consequently, Egypt constantly promoted rebellion against Babylon among the states of the southern Levant by promising support. Moreover, Jehoiakim, who owed his throne to Neco, was pro-Egyptian in his politics. He had considerable backing for his position within the leadership of Judah, despite Jeremiah's repeated warnings that God was using Babylon to punish Judah's sins, thus making resistance to Babylon futile (see "The Prophets of the Seventh Century," p. 157). Jehoiakim paid tribute to Babylon for three years (604–601 B.C.), but then withheld his pledge late in 601 B.C. when Nebuchadnezzar suffered a temporary setback as Neco thwarted his attempt to invade Egypt. Judah, with Egyptian support, now was in open rebellion against Babylon.

One of the "Lachish Letters" found in the ruins of the city of Lachish destroyed by Nebuchadnezzar. The letter contains a report of a junior military officer to his superior indicating his compliance with orders received by means of a fire signal. The text reads: "Know that we are watching for the signals of Lachish according to all the indications that my lord has given, for we cannot see the signal of Azekah."

THE FIRST CAMPAIGN AGAINST JERUSALEM

Nebuchadnezzar delayed his response to Judah's rebellion for a short time, preferring to harass Jehoiakim with auxiliary troops (2 Kgs. 24:2). Bands of Ammonites, Moabites, and Arameans attacked Judah. Edomites took advantage of the deteriorating situation by attacking Judah from the south, pillaging as opportunity permitted (2 Kgs. 24:1–2; Ps. 137:7; Lam. 4:21–22; Obad. 10–14). In 598 B.C. Nebuchadnezzar led the Babylonian army against Jehoiakim. Jerusalem was besieged and finally surrendered on March 16, 597 B.C. Jehoiakim apparently died during the siege (see 2 Kgs. 24:6, but compare 2 Chr. 36:6) and was replaced by Jehoiachin, who surrendered the city. The Babylonians plundered Jerusalem, including the temple treasures, and deported Jehoiachin and his family to Babylon along with other Jewish leaders (2 Kgs. 24:13–16). This first deportation in 597 included the prophet Ezekiel.

THE END OF JUDAH AND JERUSALEM

After the surrender of Jerusalem in 597 B.C. Nebuchadnezzar appointed Mattaniah, the young uncle of Jehoiachin, as king of Judah and changed his name to Zedekiah. Zedekiah's reign of eleven years was marked by anti-Babylonian conspiracy despite strong condemnation of this policy by Jeremiah (Jer. 27–29). Zedekiah ignored these warnings, perhaps inspired by recent Egyptian advances against Babylon by Psammeticus II (595–589 B.C.) and Hophra (Apries, 589–570 B.C.). The latter campaigned in 588 B.C. against Tyre and Sidon.

In the same year Nebuchadnezzar attacked Judah in response to Zedekiah's rebellion. The cities of Judah suffered grievously, a fact attested by destruction levels at various sites. The evidence from Lachish is particularly gripping. Lachish again fell to foreign troops, as it had in 701 B.C. Eighteen ostraca—the "Lachish Letters"—found in the destruction of level II contain grim testimony to the hopeless circumstance. One letter mentions how officials watched for fire signals from Lachish because they no longer could see the beacons from nearby Azekah. Likely, Azekah already had fallen to Babylonian forces.

Nebuchadnezzar's army besieged Jerusalem for two years (588–586 B.C.). Cut off from any possible hope and with food supplies depleted, Jerusalem fell in July of 586 B.C. The Babylonians destroyed the city, breaking down the fortifications and burning the temple, palaces, and houses (2 Kgs. 25:8–21; Jer. 39:1–10). Burnt debris excavated in several places in Jerusalem gives evidence of the ferocity of the attack and aftermath. Zedekiah fled Jerusalem to the east but was captured near Jericho. Taken before Nebuchadnezzar, who was at Riblah in central Syria, Zedekiah was forced to witness the execution of his sons before being blinded and led away to Babylon in chains. An additional deportation of Jews further depleted the leadership of the kingdom (Jer. 52:29; 2 Kgs. 25:11). Judah and Jerusalem lay defenseless, open to attack, with few material resources and little hope for the immediate future. The days of exile predicted by Jeremiah had become reality.

THE PROPHETS OF THE SEVENTH CENTURY

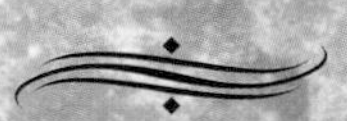

The crisis prompted by the demise of the Neo-Assyrian Empire and the rapid rise of a Neo-Babylonian Dynasty produced another series of prophetic spokesmen. These prophets addressed Judah during the dying days of the kingdom. Some of them preached only briefly, while the ministry of others extended beyond the fall of Jerusalem in 586 B.C.

NAHUM

Little is known of the prophet Nahum. Even the location of his home village, Elkosh, is uncertain. Most probably it was in Judah, but late traditions place the village in Galilee. Nahum delivered his oracles against the destruction of the Neo-Assyrian Empire. He was aware of the high tide of Assyrian supremacy in the mid-seventh century B.C. He mentioned the destruction of Thebes (No-amon) by Ashurbanipal II in 663 B.C. (Nah. 3:8), but he exulted in the impending destruction of Nineveh, finally accomplished in 612 B.C. He did not address Judah at all, but confined his oracles to the overthrow of the Assyrian Empire, whose sinful days had been completed.

ZEPHANIAH

Zephaniah reveals very little of himself in his prophecy; not even his birthplace is given. If the Hezekiah mentioned in 1:1 is a reference to the former king of Judah—an interpretation by no means certain—then Zephaniah was related to Judean royalty and presumably lived in Jerusalem. He delivered oracles of judgment against Jerusalem in the time of Josiah.

Zephaniah declared the imminent punishment of Judah and Jerusalem because of the magnitude of their sin (1:4, 12–13; 3:1–4). Echoing themes voiced by Amos and Isaiah a century earlier, Zephaniah described the "day of the Lord" as a time of divine affliction upon Judah (1:14–18), but promised new blessings for the remnant that remained after judgment (2:7, 9; 3:12–13). Zephaniah did not clearly specify the enemy of destruction. Some scholars think he meant the Scythians, who were pushing southward from the steppes of southern Russia, while others believe Zephaniah was thinking of the Assyrians or even the Chaldeans.

HABAKKUK

Habakkuk was troubled by the intriguing question of how God could use a less righteous nation to punish a more righteous people (1:12–13). His dilemma arose with his awareness that God was raising up the Chaldeans, "that bitter and hasty nation" (1:6), as a means of punishing Judah. At a deeper level, Habakkuk was troubled by the seeming inactivity of God in permitting evil to go unpunished in a time when right and wrong seemed turned upside down. Habakkuk took a position as a watchman upon a watchtower and awaited God's answer to his questions (2:1). Ultimately God answered by declaring that the righteous live by faith, that unrighteousness has within it the seed of inevitable destruction (2:2–5).

God would ensure that justice ultimately triumphed, and even though Habakkuk perhaps could not see the outcome, faith always produced life. Habakkuk faced his dilemma and delivered his messages as the Chaldean onslaught gained supremacy between 616 and 600 B.C. Perhaps the great victory of Nebuchadnezzar over Egypt at the Battle of Carchemish in 605 B.C. intensified his questions.

JEREMIAH

Jeremiah addressed his countrymen in Jerusalem throughout the final decades of Judah's existence. We know more about Jeremiah than any other Old Testament prophet since he reveals much of his personal spiritual odyssey within his oracles. Born in Anathoth, a Benjamite village two miles northeast of Jerusalem, Jeremiah was of priestly stock. He ministered in Judah from the thirteenth year of Josiah's reign (627/26 B.C.) to beyond the fall of Jerusalem in 586 B.C. He thus witnessed the great reform of Josiah, the fall of Assyria, the rise of the Neo-Babylonian Empire, the first siege of Jerusalem (598/97 B.C.) and the destruction of his nation in 586 B.C. He finally was spirited off to Egypt against his will, where he presumably died (Jer. 43:1–7).

Jeremiah's relationship to Josiah and his reform remains unclear. Relatively few of his oracles can be dated with certainty to the time of Josiah (Chapters 1–6 are best placed in the time of Josiah). Much of his preaching was directed against the disastrous policies of Jehoiakim and Zedekiah, both of whom rebelled against Nebuchadnezzar. Jeremiah believed that Babylon was the instrument of divine judgment upon Judah for her chronic sins. Resistance against Babylon was hopeless. Jeremiah counseled surrender to the Babylonian "yoke" (Jer. 27). He was branded a traitor for his words and suffered loss of face and imprisonment.

Jeremiah preached some of his harshest words against Judah's folly in the temple precincts, where he forecast the destruction of Judah and Jerusalem, and Babylonian exile (Jer. 7; 28). In the dark days of the final siege of Jerusalem, Jeremiah spoke some of his greatest words of hope and encouragement (Jer. 30–33). He envisioned a restoration of Israel (Jer. 30:18–22) and a new covenant written on the hearts of a redeemed community (Jer. 31:31–34). To symbolize his hope, Jeremiah exercised his right to redeem ancestral land in Anathoth at a time when the armies of Nebuchadnezzar besieged Jerusalem (Jer. 32). Jeremiah also believed that the exile, though longer than the false prophets expected, would nonetheless be temporary.

Jeremiah's hope was placed in a God who loves with an "everlasting love," the source of God's great faithfulness (Jer. 31:3).

Chapter Twelve

THE EXILE

Introduction

The destruction of Jerusalem in 586 B.C. marks a great watershed in Jewish history. The loss of independence, deportations of significant segments of the population, and the apparent end of the Davidic Dynasty provoked an unprecedented crisis. What now was the relationship between God and His people? What did the destruction of Jerusalem with its temple mean for the physical and spiritual destiny of the Jews? These and other profound questions necessitated a radical rethinking of God's purposes with and for the Jewish community.

We know very little about this pivotal period. Jeremiah provides some insight about the years from 586 to 582 B.C.(Jer. 39–44), while Ezekiel supplies additional information about those taken into captivity (see also Jer. 29). Many scholars believe Isaiah 40–55 reflects this same era, thus providing additional insight into the plight of those Jews taken to Babylon. Further glimpses of exilic life come from Babylonian sources. Mention is made of King Jehoiachin in exile. Aramaic legal documents from a business firm operated by the Murushu family near Nippur mentions several Jewish names, perhaps descendants of Jewish exiles. Although dating from a later period (440–416 B.C.), these materials shed valuable light on living conditions in the exilic community.

Two different Jewish communities must be considered: those who remained in the land of Judah and those who were sent or escaped from Judah—the Diaspora Jews.

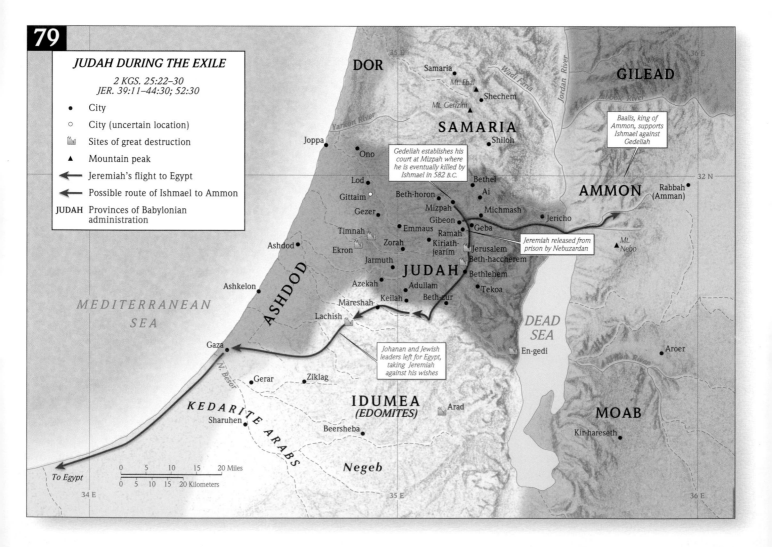

79

JUDAH DURING THE EXILE

2 KGS. 25:22–30
JER. 39:11–44:30; 52:30

- ● City
- ○ City (uncertain location)
- Sites of great destruction
- ▲ Mountain peak
- ← Jeremiah's flight to Egypt
- ← Possible route of Ishmael to Ammon
- JUDAH Provinces of Babylonian administration

Gedeliah establishes his court at Mizpah where he is eventually killed by Ishmael in 582 B.C.

Baalis, king of Ammon, supports Ishmael against Gedeliah

Jeremiah released from prison by Nebuzardan

Johanan and Jewish leaders left for Egypt, taking Jeremiah against his wishes

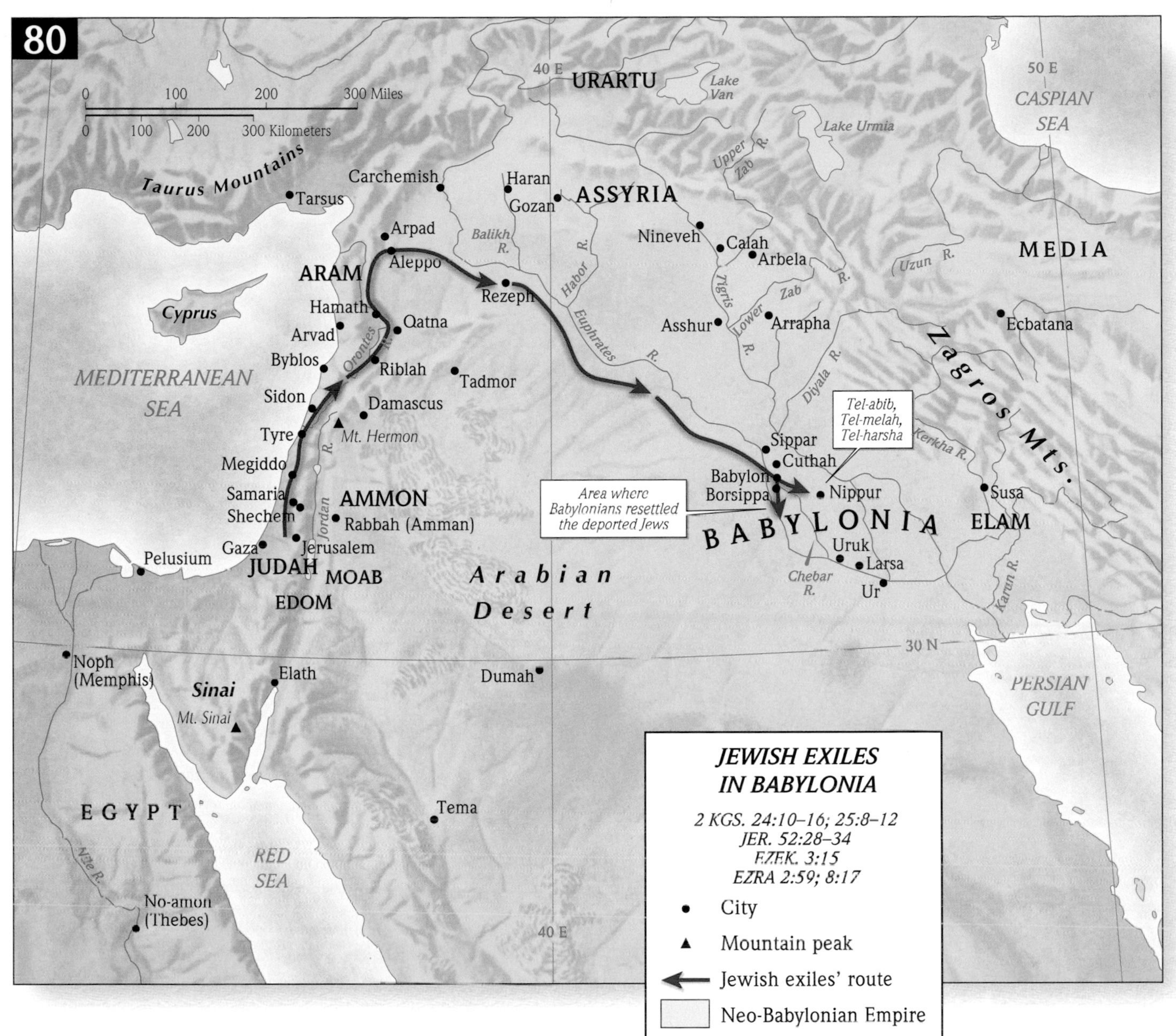

The Community in Judah

Conditions in Judah must have been severe, for many Judean cities suffered during the Babylonian invasions. Arad, Lachish, Ramat Rahel, En-gedi, Timnah, Ekron, and Jerusalem are among the excavated sites showing evidence of destruction at this time. Only the region north of Jerusalem appears to have escaped relatively unscathed.

The political status of Judah in this period remains somewhat unclear. Nebuchadnezzar appointed Gedeliah as ruler over Judah, but his title is uncertain. He may have been appointed as a king (see Jer. 41:1, 10); if so, then Judah remained separate from the Babylonian provincial system until at least 582 B.C. Perhaps Gedeliah was appointed as a governor, in which case the kingdom of Judah was converted to a Babylonian province immediately after 586 B.C.

Gedeliah, though not of royal lineage, nonetheless came from an important Jerusalemite family. His father, Ahiakim, and grandfather, Shaphan, both had served in Josiah's court (2 Kgs. 22:12–14).

Gedeliah established his court at Mizpah, a town in Benjamin with ancient tribal traditions. From Mizpah he administered the affairs of a thoroughly devastated region, devoid of adequate leadership and material resources. Babylonian officials attempted to ease the burden. Nebuzaradan, captain of the royal guard, redistributed the land among the poor who remained in the land and supplied a contingent of troops to assist Gedeliah (Jer. 39:10; 40:10–12). Some religious rituals were continued at the altar of the ruined temple at Jerusalem (Jer. 41:4–5). Overall, the situation must have been grim; the plaintive laments recorded in the Book of Lamentations present testimonies of the pain those who remained in Judah endured.

Ishmael, a military officer of royal Judean blood, backed by the Ammonite king Baalis, led a coup attempt, assassinating Gedaliah in 582 B.C. (Jer. 41:1–10). The coup failed when other military elements, led by Johanan ben Kereah, interceded. Ishmael and a handful of his supporters fled to Ammon. Fearing Babylonian reprisals, Johanan and Jewish leaders sought refuge in Egypt, taking Jeremiah with them against his wishes (Jer. 41:16–43:8). Subsequently, the Babylonians deported an additional group of Jews, perhaps as punishment for the murder of Gedaliah (Jer. 52:30).

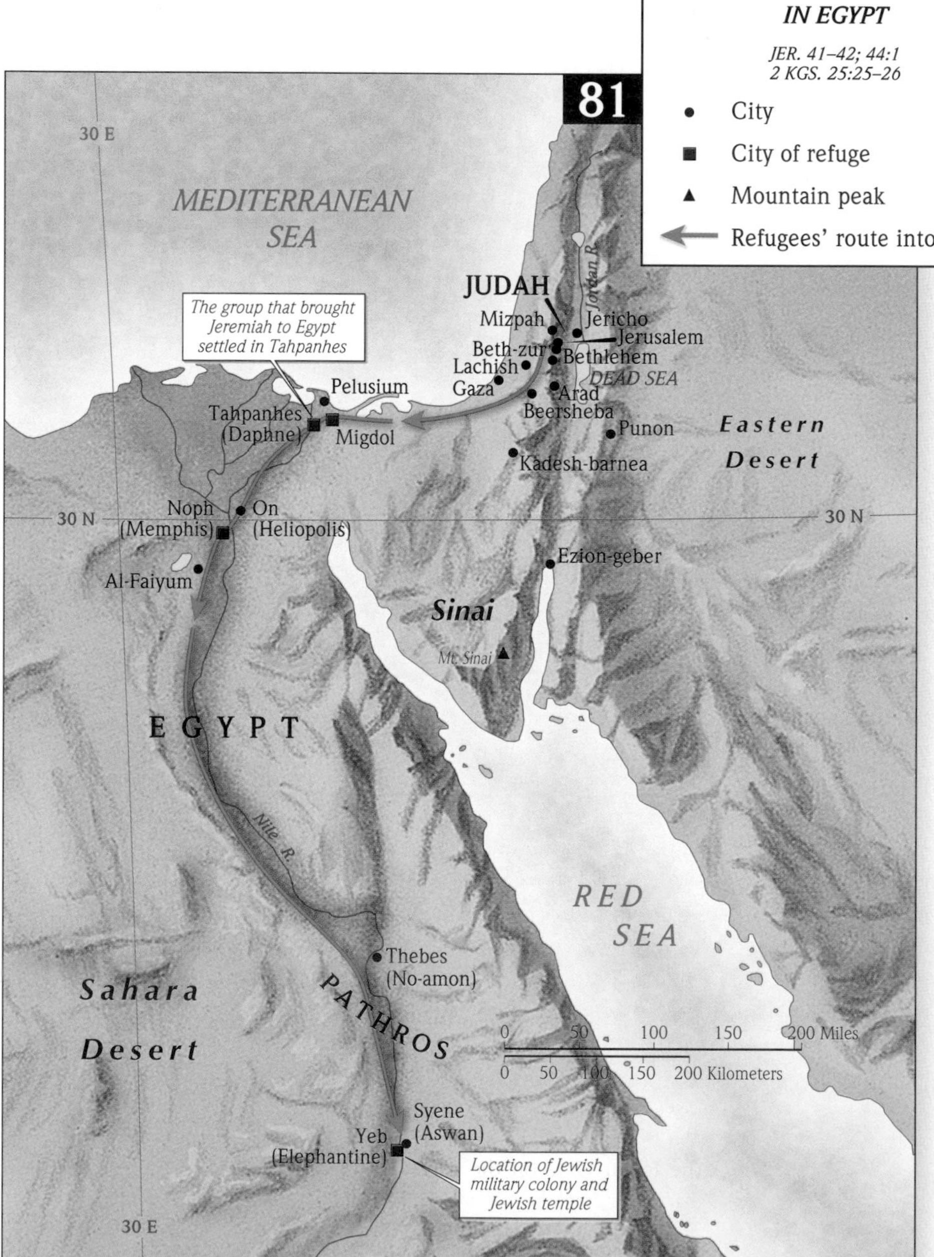

The Community in Babylon

The lot of those taken into exile was, on the whole, better than their kinsmen who remained in Judah. Jeremiah urged the exiles to build houses, plant gardens, and establish normal social relationships in their new land of residence (Jer. 29:4–7).

The Babylonians resettled their deported captives in villages and towns near Babylon and Nippur along the river Chebar (Ezek. 1:1; 3:15; Ezra 2:59). Several sites settled by the deportees bear the name "Tel" (Tel-abib, Tel-melah, Tel-harsha), a term designating an abandoned ruin. This suggests that the Babylonians may have selected abandoned villages for some of the settlements.

In administrative documents excavated at Babylon, King Jehoiachin, taken captive in 597 B.C., and his sons are mentioned. The Babylonian king, Evil-merodach (562–560 B.C.), released Jehoiachin from prison and gave him a place at the royal court (2 Kgs. 25:27–30). For the most part, the physical safety and relative security of the exiles must have been acceptable; life was not unduly harsh. However, the spiritual anguish of being separated from their homeland is clearly reflected in Psalm 137.

The Community in Egypt

Egypt became a haven for other Jewish refugees. The group that spirited Jeremiah away from Judah and settled at Tahpanhes in the Delta no doubt was representative of a steady trickle who sought sanctuary and a new life in Egypt (Jer. 43:1–7). Additional groups of Jews settled in Migdol, Memphis, and Pathros (Jer. 44:1). Later evidence of a Jewish military colony at Elephantine (Yeb), deep in the south of Egypt, demonstrates how fully some Jewish refugees adapted to their new homeland. They built a temple at Elephantine and carried on a complete system of rituals and festivals, although evidence of syncretistic worship of Yahweh and other gods betrays the impact of their new environment. These and other Jewish communities were the forerunners of the Diaspora—the widespread dispersion of Jews so important in the later spread of Christianity.

BABYLON: HEART OF AN EMPIRE

Mighty Babylon reached its zenith shortly after 600 B.C. under the generous patronage of the Neo-Babylonian kings. Having suffered devastation in 689 B.C. at the hands of Sennacherib, Babylon began to rise again. The Chaldean kings Nabopolassar and Nebuchadnezzar endowed the city with monuments worthy of the capital of a glorious empire. About 450 B.C. the Greek historian Herodotus wrote that Babylon "was adorned in a manner surpassing any city we are acquainted with" (*Histories*, Book I).

Babylon's strategic location on the Euphrates River gave the city control of important converging caravan routes as well as the river traffic. The river ran through Babylon, bisecting the city into two unequal parts. The heart of the ancient city lay on the eastern bank where the most important civic buildings were located. Nebuchadnezzar annexed the west bank, which was mostly residential. A massive bridge mounted on great boat-shaped piers spanned the Euphrates to connect the two sectors. A grid of streets and canals gave access to all parts of the city.

Herodotus was especially impressed with the fortifications of Babylon. Excavations have generally confirmed the description of Herodotus. A double wall composed of mud brick encircled the eastern and western sectors to form a rough rectangle enclosing approximately four square miles. The inner wall was 6.5 meters thick and stood higher than the outer wall, which was 3.7 meters thick. A space between the two walls perhaps could have been used to move troops and chariots as implied in Herodotus' description. Numerous towers protruded from the wall at regular intervals of sixty-five feet. Twenty meters beyond the outer wall stood a moat drawing water from the Euphrates.

Nebuchadnezzar erected another fortification on the eastern bank to give additional protection to his capital. The wall began in the north near the "Summer Palace" and extended east and south of the inner city, where it met the Euphrates. Nine gates pierced the double wall, giving access to the inner city. The gates were named after various gods and goddesses sacred to Babylon (Ishtar, Marduk, Sin, Enlil, Urash, Shamash, Adad, Zababa, and Lugalgirra). The ancient city center lay on the east bank in an area covering slightly less than a square mile. Here the venerable temples of ancient Babylon and the great palaces of her kings all were located.

An artist's reconstruction of Babylon as it would have appeared in the sixth century B.C. (Courtesy of the University of Chicago.)

Relief figure of a dragon from the facade of the Ishtar Gate at Babylon.

The famous Ishtar Gate, now reconstructed in the Berlin Museum, allowed entrance to the city from the north along the royal "Processional Street." Over sixty feet in width in some places, this street was used during the all-important New Year's festival and passed by the major civic building of the inner city. The Ishtar Gate consisted of two pairs of flanking towers covered with deep-blue glazed bricks. Brightly colored brick reliefs depicting dragons and bulls decorated the facade of the gate. In addition, the facades of the buildings fronting the "Processional Street" were similarly decorated with great lions.

The main palace of the Neo-Babylonian kings stood just inside the Ishtar Gate on the west. This sprawling complex (approximately thirteen acres) begun by Nebuchadnezzar included state rooms, royal quarters, garrisons for the royal bodyguard, storage rooms, and administrative workplaces. The palace consisted of five sections, with each section grouped around a courtyard. The third courtyard was the largest (218 x 180 feet) and stood in the center of the complex. South of this

court, the excavators discovered an adjoining throne room (170 x 56 feet) entered through three portals. Fragmentary walls and columns along with a multitude of broken tiles give glimpses of royal splendor. Glazed bricks of blues, browns, yellows, and black adorned the great hall.

The architects used many motifs—serpents, scorpions, rosettes, and lions—for decoration. This room, or possibly one of the other state rooms, perhaps was the scene where Belshazzar witnessed the mysterious writing on the wall that announced the fate of the Babylonian Empire (Dan. 5).

The Babylonians built many temples to their gods and goddesses; over forty are known from Babylonian texts, but only a few have been excavated. A temple to Ninmahk, the goddess of the underworld, stood inside the Ishtar Gate across from the palace. The temple of Ishtar of Agade and a shrine to Ninurta also have been recovered. The most important temple in Babylon was the temple of Marduk, known as Esagila ("House of the Uplifted Head"). Excavations have reached only portions of the temple, whose ruins lie buried deep within one of the mounds of the ancient city. A double wall surrounded the temple, marking off the sacred territory of the god. Ancilliary buildings for the priests and functionaries as well as smaller shrines to other deities were found within the enclosure. Nebuchadnezzar boasted that he covered the walls of Marduk's shrine with gold, inset with precious stones. Herodotus states that two golden statues of Marduk—one seated and another standing—were kept in this temple, though he did not see them.

Undoubtedly the most imposing structure in Babylon was the ziggurat known as Etemenanki—"Building of the foundation of Heaven and Earth." Ziggurats or "temple-towers" were a feature of Mesopotamian cities as far back as the third millennium. The ziggurat stood within its own large sacred enclosure north of Esagila. Virtually nothing survives of the structure made of sun-dried and baked bricks, and scholars must depend primarily on ancient descriptions to reconstruct this famous landmark. The ziggurat consisted of a square base (three hundred feet to each side) supporting a series of six levels, each level an increasingly smaller square. Each level may have been a different color.

A temple to Marduk crowned the top of the ziggurat, with at least one flight of stairs giving access to the sanctuary. The total height was slightly less than three hundred feet. Ancilliary buildings around the ziggurat provided living quarters, storage rooms, and administrative space necessary for the cult. Nothing survives of the famous "Hanging Gardens" of Babylon, one of the wonders of the ancient world.

The impressive remains excavated thus far reveal evidence of the power and opulence of Nabopolassar and his successors. The capture of Babylon by Cyrus in 539 B.C., however, began a long period of decline. Xerxes destroyed the ziggurat and removed the great statue of Marduk in response to rebellion in 482 B.C. Alexander the Great tried to restore the Esagila, but his death cut short other projects. Under the Ptolemies, Babylon's economic fortunes declined, though the city remained important as a religious center. New Testament writers use the name Babylon as a symbol for forces opposed to God's kingdom (Rev. 14:8). By the early Christian era the site of Babylon lay deserted.

PROPHETS OF THE EXILE AND RETURN TO THE LAND OF JUDAH

The spiritual crisis created by the Exile and the subsequent return to the land challenged the very core of Israel's faith. Crucial questions begged answers. Why had God sent the Jews into exile? Was God finished with the Jewish people? Was the covenant between God and Israel nullified? Would the Jews return to their homeland and, if so, what could they expect? To provide answers to these questions, encouragement to the exiles, and guidance to those exiles who returned to Judah was the mission of the exilic and post-exilic prophets who preached in the sixth and fifth centuries.

EZEKIEL

Ezekiel ("God Strengthens") was the son of Buzi, a Zadokite priest. A resident of Jerusalem, Ezekiel was married, although his wife died shortly before the final destruction of Jerusalem by Nebuchadnezzar in 586 B.C. Ezekiel was among the Jews deported from Jerusalem in 597 B.C. (2 Kgs. 24:8–17). He lived among the captives in Tel-abib (Ezek. 3:15), one of the sites assigned to the Jewish deportees near the river Chebar in Babylonia (Ezek. 1:1). Ezekiel received his prophetic commission to preach to the exiles in the fifth year of Jehoiachin's exile (593 B.C.) and continued to preach for at least twenty years thereafter (Ezek. 40:1).

Ezekiel's message of judgement and hope was delivered primarily to the exiles, but also reached out to the Jews living in Jerusalem until 586 B.C. As a watchman over Israel (Ezek. 3:17, cf. chap. 33), Ezekiel warned of Jerusalem's impending doom as God's just punishment

for the nation's sins. A complex and compelling figure, Ezekiel used several odd symbolic acts and visionary experiences to deliver his message (Ezek. 1–24). He mimicked the siege of Jerusalem utilizing a brick, and lay on his side for a specific number of days to symbolize the sin and punishment of Judah and Israel (Ezek. 4:1–8). Later he tunneled out through a city wall carrying his baggage as a sign of what soon would befall the residents of Jerusalem, especially King Zedekiah, during the final stages of Jerusalem's destruction (Ezek. 12). In a dramatic and powerful series of visions, Ezekiel saw the departure of God's glory from the Holy temple, now profaned by Israel's sins (Ezek. 8–11). By these actions Ezekiel drove home the message that God had abandoned His Holy Place and delivered a rebellious people over to the hands of Babylon.

Ezekiel 25–32 contains a series of oracles delivered against the nations that surround Judah. Egypt and the wealthy Phoenician city of Tyre are given special attention.

After the destruction of Jerusalem, God used Ezekiel to convey a message of hope and future restoration to the exiles. Ezekiel's portrayal of God as a good shepherd who would restore His flock (Ezek. 34:11–31) foreshadows the New Testament motif of Christ as the Good Shepherd (John 10). Ezekiel's famous vision of a valley filled with bones that came to life at God's command (Ezek. 37) promised restoration and life to the shattered Jewish people. Ezekiel foresaw a new day when God would again dwell among a purified remnant: "My dwelling place shall be with them; and I will be their God, and they shall be my people" (Ezek. 37:27). Ezekiel concluded his message of hope with a series of visions depicting a new temple with blessings flowing symbolically like a river that brings life into the deserts (Ezek. 40–48).

HAGGAI AND ZECHARIAH

Haggai and Zechariah preached in Jerusalem in 520 B.C., the second year of the Persian king Darius I (Hag. 1:1; Zech. 1:1). Darius secured his claim to the Persian throne in the tumult following the death of Cambyses in 522 B.C. Together the two prophets urged the Jews to rebuild the temple in Jerusalem. The Jewish exiles returning to Judah after the edict of Cyrus (538 B.C.) found Jerusalem devastated. Under the leadership first of Sheshbazzar (ca. 537 B.C.) and then Zerubbabel, attempts were made to rebuild the temple, but the task had not been finished by 520 B.C.(Ezra 5:16). Haggai and Zechariah challenged the people to complete the project as an outward sign of their commitment to God. Zerubbabel was the governor of Judah at the time, while Joshua, son of Jehozadak, served as high priest.

Haggai, whose name comes from the Hebrew word for "feast" or "festival," perhaps was an older man who may have been one of the Jews who remained in the land after the destruction of Jerusalem in 586 B.C. If so, he would have remembered the glory of Solomon's temple (cf. Hag. 2:2). Haggai preached just over three months (August to December, 520 B.C.), briefly overlapping the ministry of Zechariah (Ezra 5:1).

Haggai chastened the returning exiles for concentrating on rebuilding their own houses while neglecting to work on the temple (Hag. 1:1–15). He encouraged the people by promising that the second temple would be greater than the first, despite outward appearance (2:19), and foretold a time of blessing for the nation (2:10–19).

Zechariah ("Yahweh remembers," a very common name in the Old Testament) was from a priestly lineage, assuming that the Iddo mentioned in Zechariah 1:1 is identified with the Iddo who returned with Zerubbabel from exile (Neh. 12:4, 16). Zechariah's ministry lasted at least two years, beginning in 520 B.C. (Zech. 1:1; 7:1). Like Haggai, Zechariah urged the people to rebuild the temple (Zech. 1:16; 4:9; 6:12–15), a task that was completed by 515 B.C. (Ezra 6:16–22; cf. 5:1–5). Zechariah received a series of night visions anticipating a forgiven, restored people in a land of peace and blessing (Zech. 1–8). He believed the high priest Joshua, son of Jehozadak, was a special instrument in God's plan for a glorious future (Zech. 6:9–10). Emphasizing God's ultimate triumph over the nations that oppose His will, Zechariah envisioned the universal reign of God (Zech. 12–14).

MALACHI

Malachi—"my messenger"—was the last of the "writing" prophets. He addressed the Jews of Judah sometime between the dedication of the new temple (515 B.C.) and Ezra's return to Jerusalem in 458 B.C. During Malachi's time the people of Judah were gripped by spiritual lethargy and threatened by assimilation with pagan people. Evidently the bright future anticipated by the preaching of Haggai and Zechariah had not come about as expected, leading to careless worship practices and neglect of spiritual matters (Mal. 1:6–8; 3:8–15). Utilizing a series of six disputations, Malachi condemned the social and religious sins of the people, including divorce and marriage to pagan women (2:10–16), exploitation of the poor (3:5), and the ingratitude expressed by those who refuse God His tithe (3:6–12). Malachi predicted judgment upon an unfaithful people, but promised deliverance upon those who fear the Lord and keep His covenant. Malachi concluded his prophecy with the promise of an Elijah figure before a new day of judgement and deliverance (Mal. 4:4–6).

Chapter Thirteen

THE PERSIAN PERIOD

Introduction

The century from 600 to 500 B.C. brought tumultuous changes to the Near East. Four major powers dominated the political landscape at the beginning of the century. The Neo-Babylonian Empire extended across Mesopotamia and the Levant. Under Amasis (570–526 B.C.) Egypt prospered, while continuing to threaten Babylonian interests in the southern Levant. Increasingly, Amasis forged economic and military links with Greek traders and mercenaries who settled in the Delta.

The Medes occupied the territories north of Mesopotamia, governing their empire from their capital at Ecbatana. Median kings extended their holdings westward into the central Anatolian plateau (modern Turkey). Beyond the western limits of the Median Empire lay the kingdom of Lydia, with its capital at Sardis. The Lydian kings Gyges and Croesus built Lydia into a formidable force utilizing the gold retrieved from the Pactolus River. Within decades all four of these powers would be conquered by a new force—the Persians—resulting in the formation of the largest empire the Near East ever produced: the Persian Empire. For the Jews these changes meant an end to the Exile and restoration to their ancestral home.

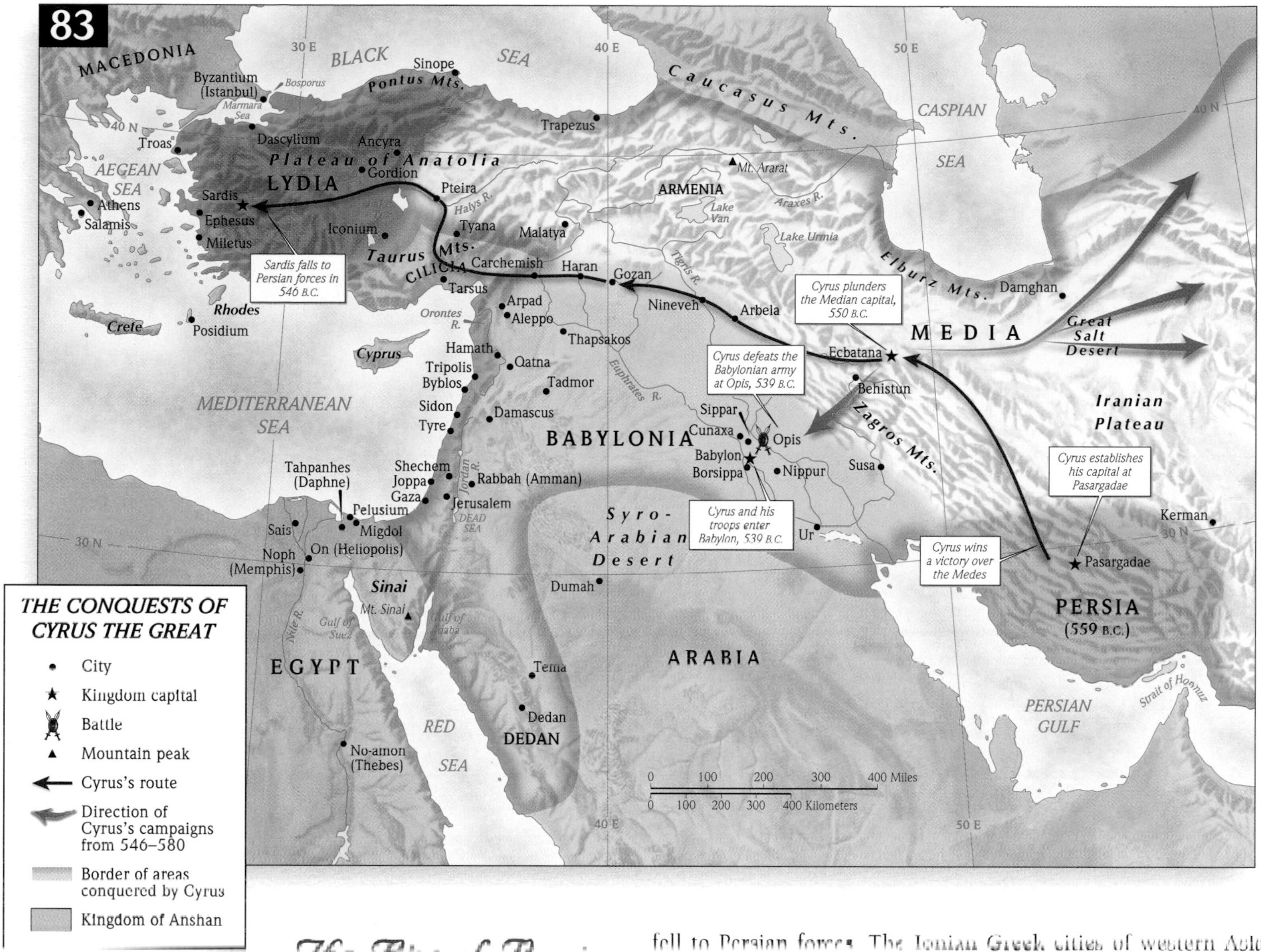

83

THE CONQUESTS OF CYRUS THE GREAT

- City
- Kingdom capital
- Battle
- Mountain peak
- Cyrus's route
- Direction of Cyrus's campaigns from 546–580
- Border of areas conquered by Cyrus
- Kingdom of Anshan

Sardis falls to Persian forces in 546 B.C.

Cyrus plunders the Median capital, 550 B.C.

Cyrus defeats the Babylonian army at Opis, 539 B.C.

Cyrus and his troops enter Babylon, 539 B.C.

Cyrus wins a victory over the Medes

Cyrus establishes his capital at Pasargadae

The Rise of Persia

The Persian peoples migrated (sometime after 900 B.C.) into southwestern Iran, settling inland from the Persian Gulf. By about 700 B.C. a line of rulers claiming descent from Achaemenes eventually governed the region of Anshan, hence the term *Achaemenids* was used to describe the later Persian royal line. Cyrus II ("the Great") was a son of Cambyses I and the Median princess Mandane, daughter of the great Median king Astyages. Thus Cyrus was born to a marriage representing both the Persian and Median royal houses.

CYRUS THE GREAT

Cyrus began his rapid rise to power as the king of Anshan. He overthrew his Median overlord, Astyages, and plundered the Median capital, Ecbatana, in 550 B.C. Cyrus established his capital at Pasargadae, perhaps to commemorate a nearby victory over Median forces. Cyrus then moved against the Lydian king, Croesus, achieving final victory in 546 B.C. when Sardis fell to Persian forces. The Ionian Greek cities of western Asia Minor also, under force of arms, came under Persian control. The subjection of the Ionian's by Cyrus began a period of great tensions between the Greeks and Persians.

THE FALL OF BABYLON

Additional conquests by Cyrus in the east further isolated Babylonia, cutting off vital supply lines. Nabonidus, the last Babylonian king, provoked an internal crisis when he left the city of Babylon for ten years, spending much of this time in the Arabian oasis of Tema. In his absence he appointed his son Belshazzar as coregent during the last few years. During this ten-year period Nabonidus did not participate in the crucial New Year's Festival designed to win the favor of the gods for the coming year. His absence occasioned unrest among the Babylonian people and offended the powerful priests of Marduk. Coupled with shrinking markets and dwindling availability of goods caused by the loss of trade routes to Cyrus, tensions between the people of Babylon and Nabonidus were high.

CHART 14. KINGS OF PERSIA (CA. 559–330 B.C.)			
Persian King	**Dates(B.C.)**	**Biblical Connections**	**Events and Accomplishments**
Cyrus II (the Great)	559–530	Permitted return of the Jews from Exile; facilitated rebuilding of the temple at Jerusalem (Ezra 1:1–4; 6:3–5); the "Anointed One" of Isa. 45:1	King of Anshan, 559 B.C., conquered kingdom of Media (550 B.C.) and Lydian kingdom (546 B.C.); conquered Babylon, 539 B.C.
Cambyses II	530–522	Not mentioned in the Bible	Son of Cyrus the Great; conquered Egypt, 525 B.C.; his death (suicide?) in 522 B.C. led to two years of fighting between rival claimants to the throne
Darius I Hystaspes	522–486	Haggai and Zechariah preached during the second year of Darius I (520 B.C.); temple rebuilt and dedicated 515 B.C., (cf. Ezra 6:13–15)	Member of a collateral royal line; secured the throne ending the unrest following the death of Cambyses; reorganized the Persian Empire into satrapies; established royal postal system; began building Persepolis; invaded Greece and was defeated at Marathon, 490 B.C.; revolt in Egypt
Xerxes I	486–465	Possibly Ahasuerus of the Book of Esther	Son of Darius I; continued building Persepolis; encountered numerous rebellions at the beginning of his reign (Egypt, Babylon); invaded Greece, sacked Athens (480 B.C.), but was defeated by the Greeks in a naval engagement (Salamis, 480 B.C.) and on land (Plataea and Mycale, 479 B.C.); killed in a palace coup in 465 B.C.
Artaxerxes I Longimanus	465–425	Nehemiah, cup bearer to Artaxerxes; came to Judah (444 B.C., compare Neh. 2:1; 13:6); traditional date of Ezra's mission in the seventh year of his reign (458 B.C., cf. Ezra 7:7)	Faced revolt in Egypt; completed major buildings at Persepolis; made peace with the Greeks (Peace of Callias, 449 B.C.); died of natural causes
Xerxes II	423	Not mentioned in the Bible	Ruled less than two months
Darius II Nothus	423–404	Not mentioned in the Bible; Jews in Egypt (Elephantine) appealed to Samaria and Jerusalem for help in rebuilding their temple about 407 B.C.	Peloponnesian War, 431–404 B.C.; Persia recovered several Greek cities in Asia Minor
Artaxerxes II Mnemon	404–359/8	Some scholars place Ezra's mission in the seventh year of Artaxerxes II, about 398 B.C.	Egypt regained freedom from Persia for a time; revolt of the Satraps, 366–360 B.C.
Artaxerxes III Ochus	359/8–338/7	Not mentioned in the Bible	Philip II of Macedon; rises to power about 359 B.C.; Alexander the Great born, 356 B.C.; Persia reclaims Egypt, 342 B.C.
Arses	338/7–336	Not mentioned in the Bible	Unknown
Darius III Codomannus	336–330	Alexander subdues the Levant; Tyre and Gaza besieged, 332 B.C.; conquest of Egypt by Alexander, 332 B.C.	Philip assassinated, 336 B.C.; Alexander the Great invades the Persian Empire, 334 B.C.; Darius III defeated by Alexander at Issus, 333 B.C., and Gaugamela, 331 B.C.; death of Darius, 330 B.C.

The end of the Babylonian Empire came quickly. The Persian army, aided by Babylonian defections, defeated the Babylonian army at Opis on the Tigris River. Although hastily fortified by Nabonidus, Babylon fell shortly thereafter. In late October, 539 B.C., Cyrus entered Babylon, according to his own accounts, as a liberator of the oppressed peoples of the city. The famous "Cyrus Cylinder," found in the ruins of the temple of Marduk, boasts that Cyrus treated the citizens with magnaminity, restored the city, and ordered the restoration of ancient temples. Such pronouncements were typical of conquering kings, who stressed their role as "restorers" of order and often spoke of the return of dispersed peoples.

Cyrus died in 530 B.C., fighting in the northeastern areas of his realm. His son Cambyses II succeeded him and ruled for eight years. Cambyses' most notable achievement was the conquest of Egypt in 525 B.C. Unfortunately, Egypt proved to be a most troublesome vassal, frequently rebelling against Persia and often in league with the Greeks. Cambyses' somewhat mysterious death in 522 B.C. left Persia in a state of turmoil for two years, during which time rival claimants fought for the throne. By 520 B.C. Darius I emerged as the victor. His famous inscription known as the Behistun Stone states his claim to be the legitimate king.

The Cyrus Cylinder. The inscription portrays Cyrus as the liberator of Babylon. Cyrus boasts that he allowed displaced peoples to return to their homes and restored the temples neglected under the Babylonians.

DARIUS I

Darius proved to be the ablest administrator of all Persian rulers. He organized the empire into twenty large regions called satrapies, each region governed by a satrap. He established a royal postal service, built a royal road connecting Susa with Sardis, exploited the Red Sea trade, and commenced the building of a new royal residence, Persepolis. However, Darius also launched a crusade against mainland Greece in reprisal for the Ionian Revolt (499 B.C.) inspired by Athens and Sparta. At Marathon, Greek warriors stopped the Persian advance in 490 B.C.; Darius retreated in defeat. At his death in 486 B.C. several provinces, including Egypt, were in revolt.

XERXES I

Xerxes I (486–465 B.C.) inherited from his father the Greek problem and various revolts. He, too, suffered defeat at the hands of the Greeks (Salamis, a naval engagement in 480 B.C. was the most crushing).

The Persian king Darius I seated upon his throne.

Xerxes is best known to Bible students as the Persian king Ahasuerus in the Book of Esther. Xerxes did not possess the abilities of his father, and his accomplishments were minimal, though he did manage to crush revolts in Babylon and Egypt. Babylon was sacked by Xerxes in 482 B.C. Although he continued construction of Persepolis, Xerxes later died in a palace coup in 465 B.C.

ARTAXERXES I

Artaxerxes I Longimanus (465–425 B.C.) succeeded his father, Xerxes, in 465 B.C. Artaxerxes faced serious threats from Athens and Egypt. The Peace of Callias (449 B.C.) temporarily ended the fighting with the Greeks by limiting the two combatants' respective spheres of influence. Artaxerxes was especially concerned with Egypt. The mission of Nehemiah authorized by the Persian king likely reflects the strategic value of southern Palestine and control of the major routes leading to Egypt. Artaxerxes needed the loyalty of the Jews in those troubled days. His death in 425 B.C. likely marked the end of the Persian kings who played roles in the biblical drama, unless the Artaxerxes named in connection with Ezra's mission (Ezra 7:7) was Artaxerxes II (404–358 B.C.). (See p. 172.)

Persepolis, the Persian royal retreat, built principally by Darius I and Xerxes I.

The Return of the Exiles to Judah

The conquest of Babylon by Cyrus the Great in 539 B.C. brought the dawn of a new day for the Jewish exiles. Isaiah called Cyrus the Lord's anointed who would be God's chosen instrument to restore the exiles to their ancestral homeland (Isa. 45:1, 13). Several times the Bible mentions an edict Cyrus issued in 538 B.C. allowing the Jews two privileges. First, those who so desired could return to Judah. Second, Cyrus commanded that the Jerusalem temple be rebuilt, and directed funds from the royal treasury be given to support the project (Ezra 1:2–4; 6:3–5; 2 Chr. 36:22–23). The stipulations of this edict reflect accurately the general policies of Cyrus known from other royal inscriptions, including the famous "Cyrus Cylinder" located in the British Museum. Cyrus pursued a more beneficent and tolerant policy toward the peoples of his empire than his Assyrian and Babylonian predecessors.

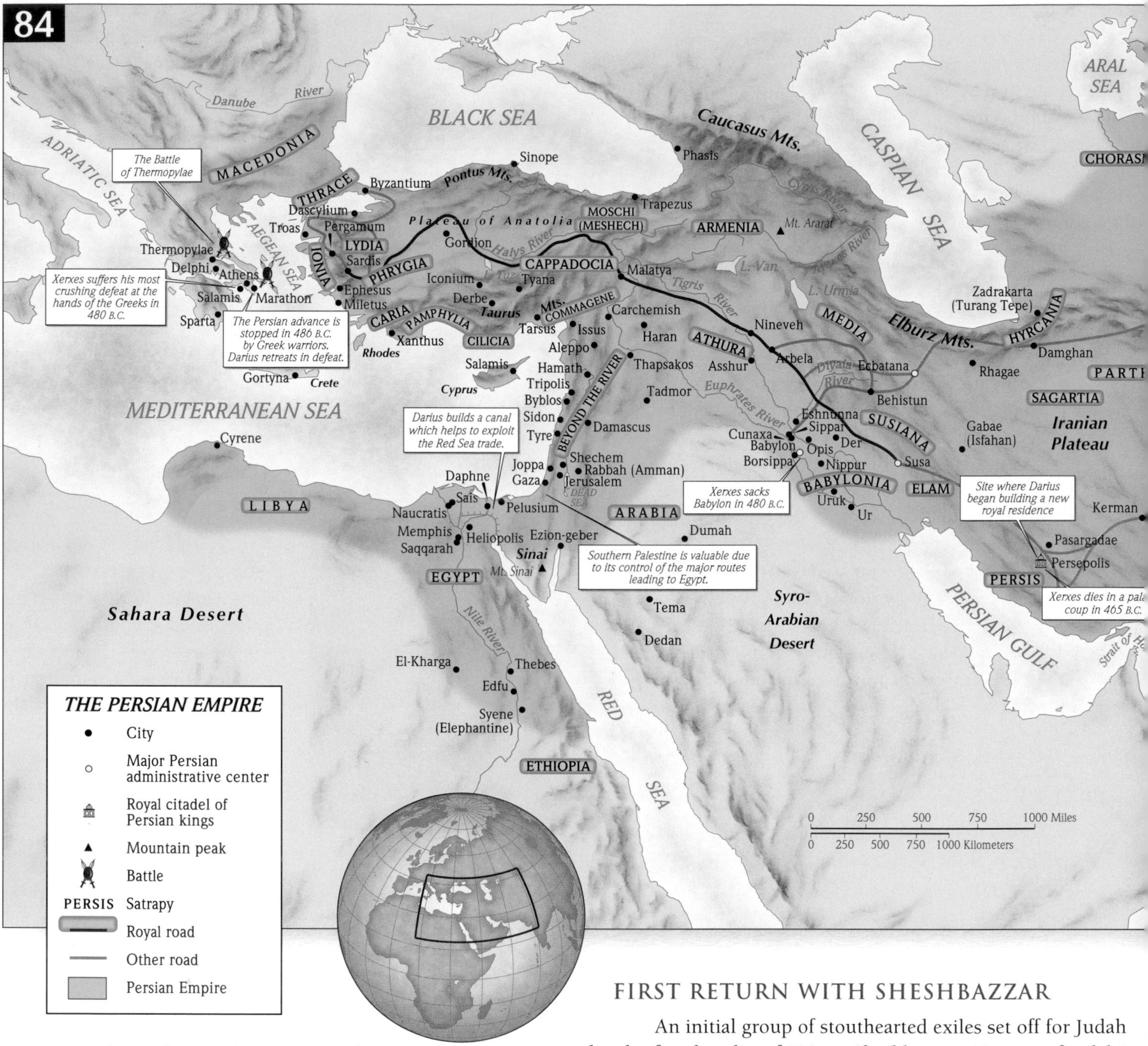

FIRST RETURN WITH SHESHBAZZAR

An initial group of stouthearted exiles set off for Judah shortly after the edict of 538 B.C. Sheshbazzar, a "prince of Judah" (Ezra 1:8), led the first returnees on the long and difficult trek homeward. The Bible does not mention the details of their route. The quickest route was the more dangerous desert road that passed through the oasis city of Tadmor. More likely, the exiles followed the trade route westward along the Euphrates River to Aleppo and then turned south along the main arteries that led to Judah. Altogether the journey would exceed one thousand miles. Ezra 2 and Nehemiah 7 list a total of 42,360 returnees. Scholars debate whether these lists refer to those returning with the first group or, more likely, those returning in several groups over an extended period of time.

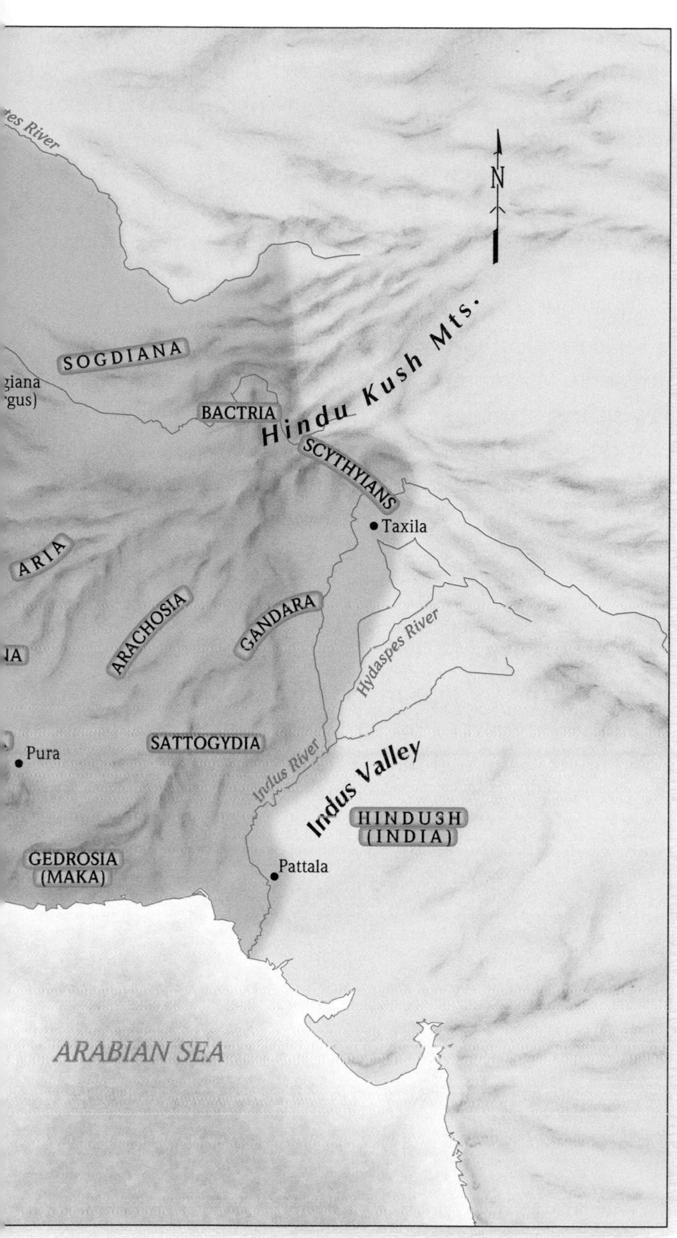

What is clear is that not all of those taken into exile chose to return. Many Jews remained in Babylon, becoming permanent residents, the core of an influential Jewish community that much later produced one of the two Talmuds.

We know little about the initial phases of the return. Sheshbazzar was of royal Davidic lineage, a son of Jehoiachin, the exiled king of Judah. Cyrus appointed him as governor and entrusted to him the return of silver vessels taken from the temple by Nebuchadnezzar (Ezra 5:13–16). Under Sheshbazzar's leadership the foundations of a new temple were laid in Jerusalem. However, biblical information about Sheshbazzar ceases at this point; his fate remains unknown.

ZERUBBABEL AND JOSHUA

Two new leaders of the Jewish community—Zerubbabel and Joshua—eventually emerged. Zerubbabel was another son of Jehoiachin and nephew of Sheshbazzar. The date of his arrival in Jerusalem and the relationship of his work to that of Sheshbazzar is much debated.

In many ways the deeds attributed to Zerubbabel and Sheshbazzar are strikingly similar: both led returnees back to Judah; both were governors of Judah; both men led the people of Judah to begin the process of rebuilding the temple. Most likely, Zerubbabel returned to Judah later than Sheshbazzar and took over leadership of the community at a time when discouragement had set in. The people of Judah met stiff opposition to their rebuilding efforts both from Persian authorities, such as Tattenai, a regional governor (Ezra 5:6), and from enemies among the local populations (Ezra 4).

Spurred on by the prophetic voices of Haggai and Zechariah in 520 B.C., Zerubbabel led the people of Judah to complete the rebuilding of the temple. The high priest Joshua gave invaluable assistance. These events took place against the backdrop of the turmoil attending the death of Cambyses II and the accession of Darius I. Perhaps the Judean community saw an opportunity to assert themselves in the hope of greater independence. In any case, in 515 B.C. the people of Judah dedicated the new temple in Jerusalem (Ezra 6:13–18). This event marked the culmination of the initial phases of the Jewish return to their homeland (see further pp. 162–63).

Persian Administration

Judah was a small province in the great behemoth of the Persian Empire. Persian kings divided the empire into satrapies, larger administrative units governed by a royal official called a satrap. Palestine was part of the fifth satrapy, known as "Beyond the River" (Aramaic *'Abar nahara*, Ezra 4:10; Hebrew *'Eber-ha-nahar*, Ezra 8:36; Neh. 2:7). "Beyond the River" referred to the lands lying west of the Euphrates River, which by 450 B.C. included Syria, Palestine, Phoenicia, and Cyprus. Under Cyrus and Cambyses, "Beyond the River" was jointly administered with Babylonia. According to Herodotus, Darius I reorganized the empire into twenty satrapies and separated "Beyond the River" from Babylonia. Some scholars believe the final separation took place during the time of Xerxes I. In any case, the fifth satrapy stretched from Poseidium in the north to the Sinai in the south.

Persian administrative policy further subdivided the satrapies into provinces administered by a governor. In turn the province could be further subdivided into districts or half-districts, each with its own leader (see Neh. 3:9, 14–15). The Persians retained many of the administrative divisions previously made by their Assyrian and Babylonian predecessors. For example, the provinces created by the Assyrians in the wake of their subjugation of Israel—Megiddo, Dor, Samaria, Karnaim, and Gilead—remained largely intact in the Persian era.

JUDAH, SAMARIA, AND THEIR NEIGHBORS

Samaria became particularly troublesome for Judah since her powerful governors, such as Nehemiah's enemy Sanballat, constantly interfered with Judean efforts to rebuild their homeland. Perhaps the Samaritan authorities feared a fully recovered Judah to their south. Ashdod (including the coastal plain south of the Sorek River to Gerar and the Shephelah) and Idumea became provinces under Babylonian control.

Phoenician influence along the Palestinian coast became pronounced as the Persians permitted Tyre and Sidon access to coastal cities. Idumea extended over the southern Judean hills. The population increasingly consisted of Edomites dislodged by Arab incursions from their ancestral home southeast of the Dead Sea. Idumeans were to play a key role in later biblical history through the powerful Herodian Dynasty. The provincial structure of Transjordan is less well known.

Ammon appears as a separate province with an important Jewish population. The powerful family headed by Tobiah the Ammonite, one of Nehemiah's foes (Neh. 2:19; 4:3), hailed from this area. The Tobiads meddled in the affairs of Judah for centuries. Their impressive palace at 'Araq el-Amir testifies to their wealth.

Moab suffered greatly under Arab pressure but maintained a separate identity unlike Edom, which collapsed under Arab intrusions. Ammonite and Moabite women were among wives Jewish men had taken in the time of Nehemiah (Neh. 13:23). To the south, the Kedarite Arabs controlled Edom and the Sinai. Another of Nehemiah's enemies was Geshem the Arab, a powerful chieftain who controlled trade routes vital to Persian interests (Neh. 6:1).

PROVINCE OF YEHUD

The province of Judah was restricted to the mountainous region in and around Jerusalem, the provincial capital. Seals and coins minted in the region give the province's official name:

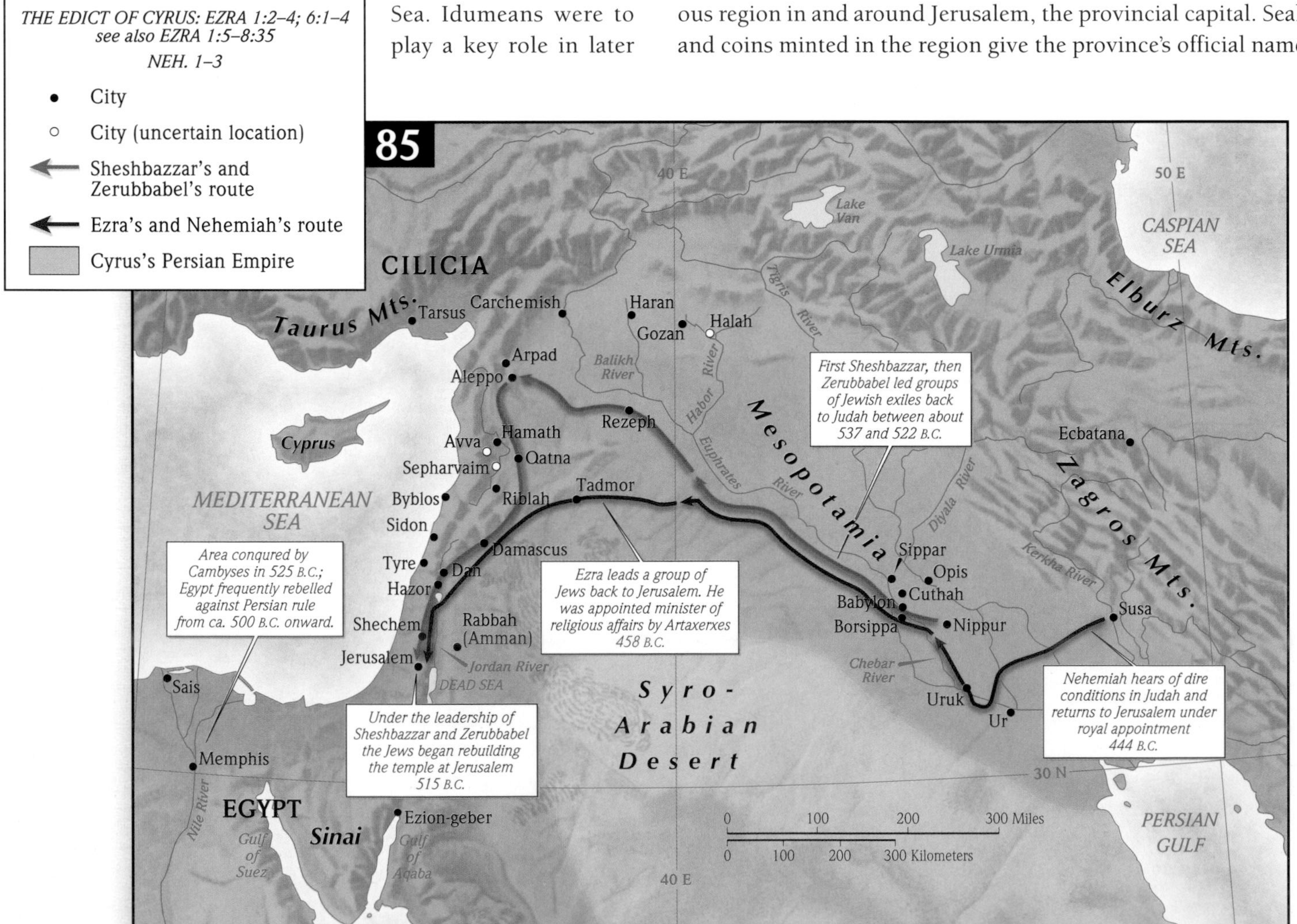

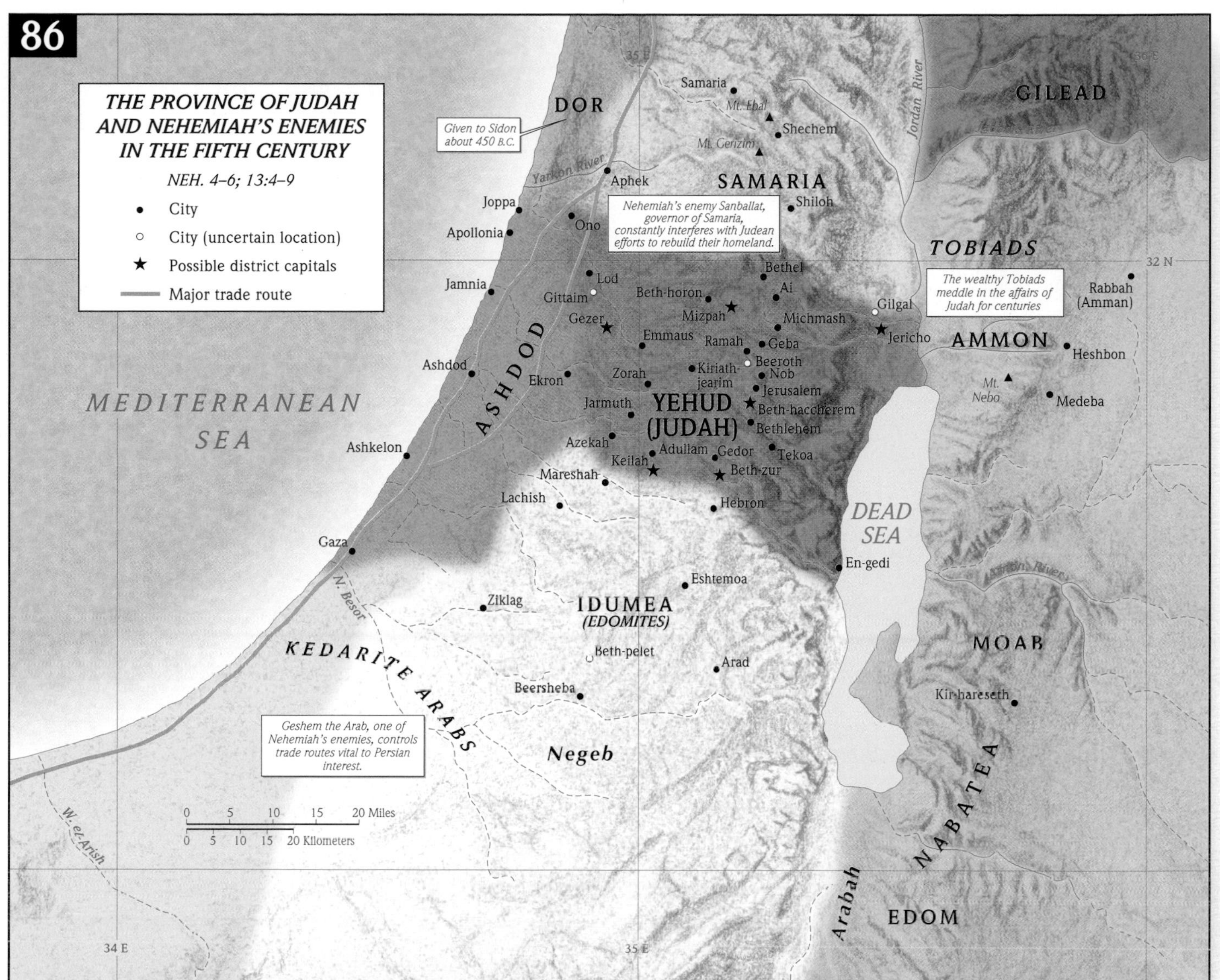

Yehud. These materials give a good approximation of the borders of the province of Judah. Plotting their distribution reveals a northern limit in the territory of Benjamin, including Mizpah; a southern boundary that extends to Beth-zur; an eastern limit including Jericho and En-gedi; and a western boundary that embraces Gezer and Azekah.

Numerous biblical lists containing information about place names and returnees (Ezra 2:21–35; Neh. 3:2–22; 7:25–38; 11:25–35; 12:28–29) agree with this distribution. Judah comprised an area covering roughly nine hundred square miles. Jerusalem was the provincial capital where the resident governor lived.

The list of builders who worked on the walls of Jerusalem under Nehemiah's direction indicates that Judah was further subdivided into districts and half-districts. Scholars debate the precise number of districts. Excluding Jerusalem, the following cities likely served as district capitals: Beth-zur, Mizpah, Beth-haccerem, and Keilah. Other scholars assume the list is incomplete and include Jericho and Gezer as well.

Archaeology indicates that Judah in the Persian period was predominantly rural; most people chose to tend their plots of land in or near their ancestral villages. Jerusalem was not especially inviting; Nehemiah had to levy the villages to repopulate the city (Neh. 11:1–2). Luxury items were limited. Moreover, Judah was increasingly culturally isolated, as Greek and Phoenician influence predominated in the coastal regions. Persian policy toward Judah on the whole was benevolent, but hostile neighbors like the governors of Samaria were zealous to see that Jerusalem did not threaten their positions.

NEHEMIAH'S JERUSALEM

When Nehemiah arrived in Jerusalem in 445/444 B.C., he found the city in ruinous condition. The temple had been rebuilt and dedicated in 515 B.C. with Persian help, despite stiff opposition from local and regional authorities (Ezra 4:11–16; 5:3–17; 6:1–18). Yet the gates and walls that gave Jerusalem protection had yet to be repaired properly following the destructions wreaked upon the city by Nebuchadnezzar (Neh. 1:3; 2:3). Unscrupulous provincial officials who had much to gain by seeing that Jerusalem remained unprotected—thus no threat to their power—thwarted attempts to repair the city.

Nehemiah faced intense opposition from Sanballat, the governor of Samaria; Tobiah the Ammonite; and Geshem the Arab (Neh. 3:17–20; 4). In a nocturnal journey, Nehemiah surveyed the damage and developed a plan to repair Jerusalem's defenses (Neh. 2:11–16). Apparently the eastern slope of the City of David was in an impassable condition due to collapsed retaining walls and ruined structures. Nehemiah assigned various sections of the fortifications to groups supervised by leaders of the Jewish community. Nehemiah 3 contains numerous references to gates and structures along Jerusalem's fortifications. Unfortunately, identifying archaeological remains with any of these structures has been difficult, yet archaeologists have provided a clearer picture of Nehemiah's Jerusalem.

After the destruction of Jerusalem in 586 B.C., settlers confined themselves to the eastern ridge, the old City of David and the Temple Mount. There is no evidence of any occupation of the western ridge during the Persian era, although parts of Hezekiah's walls must have remained in fragmentary condition. Settlement upon the City of David apparently was more constricted than ever before. Much of the eastern slope perhaps was left unprotected, as a new line of defense was established farther up the slope, perhaps built along the line of a much earlier wall. Fragments of a wall built of roughly dressed limestone near the crest have been identified by some archaeologists as "Nehemiah's Wall," but others believe the "wall" is actually a quarry line. A few of the domestic structures on the eastern slope were reused, but most buildings were located on the crest of the ridge.

The fact that Nehemiah completed his initial repairs in fifty-two days argues strongly that segments of the earlier defenses must have been still standing; presumably the western line of defense and the walls enclosing the Temple Mount were on the same lines as those prior to 586 B.C. The Valley Gate (Neh. 3:13), along the Tyropoeon Valley, has tentatively been identified by some scholars with remains dating from the Iron Age. The location of other gates in Nehemiah 3 are more speculative. It seems reasonable to locate the Water Gate (Neh. 3:26) near the Gihon Spring and the Fountain Gate at the base of the southeastern hill (Neh. 2:14; 3:15). Several towers mentioned in Nehemiah 3 (the Tower of Hananel, the Tower of the Hundred) undoubtedly lay along the north defenses where Jerusalem was most vulnerable.

Jerusalem of Nehemiah's day was slightly smaller than the city of David and Solomon, perhaps covering thirty-seven to thirty-eight acres. The initial population must have been quite small, prompting a levy upon the people of Judah to repopulate the city (Neh. 11:1–2; cf. Neh. 7:4). Pottery impressions found in the city containing the name "Yehud" proclaim the Persian domination of the Jewish people. But Nehemiah's efforts not only restored the defenses of the city, but also reasserted Jerusalem's status as a provincial capital. In time, Jerusalem would recover, expanding once again over the western ridge and northward beyond the old fortified boundaries. The process unfolded slowly in the Hellenistic and Hasmonean periods, but reached its full flower under Herod the Great and his successors.

RENEWAL UNDER EZRA AND NEHEMIAH

Soon after 500 B.C. discouragement and spiritual apathy gripped Judah. Malachi confronted the people with his penetrating oracles that sought to revitalize the spirit of the people. The Jewish community was on the verge of cultural assimilation and extinction. God sent two pivotal figures to salvage the situation: Ezra and Nehemiah. Their ministries coincided with much greater Persian interest in their southern border. Egypt, backed by Greek encouragement, revolted against Persia, first in 488 B.C., and then later in 461 B.C., during the reign of Artaxerxes I (465–425 B.C.). The Persians fortified many sites along the Palestinian coast and the Shephelah as supply stations and garrisons to maintain their hold on Egypt. Judah became strategically important in light of Egypt's obstinance. Both Ezra and Nehemiah's missions to Judah must be viewed against this backdrop.

Ezra arrived in Jerusalem during the seventh year of Artaxerxes (Ezra 7:7), traditionally taken to mean Artaxerxes I and therefore 458 B.C. However, an alternative hypothesis suggests that Ezra followed Nehemiah, arriving in the seventh year of Artaxerxes II—398 B.C. For a variety of reasons the traditional date seems preferable. Ezra was "a scribe skilled in the law of Moses" (Ezra 7:6) who called the people back to their covenant obligations. He led a group back from Babylon, carrying with him gold and silver granted by the king in addition to freewill offerings from the Jewish exiles. Apparently Artaxerxes appointed him as a "minister of religious affairs" in keeping with the general Persian policy of supporting local cults. After reading the Law to the people of Jerusalem, Ezra led the people in confession of their sin and recommitment of their lives (Neh. 8–10).

Nehemiah served as a cupbearer to Artaxerxes I (Neh. 2:1) before receiving his appointment as governor of Judah. Distressed by reports of the dire conditions of his kinspeople in Judah, he left Susa under royal appointment and journeyed to Jerusalem, arriving in 445/44 B.C. Nehemiah faced serious opposition to his effort to rebuild Jerusalem from Tobiah, Geshem the Arab, and, especially, Sanballat, governor of Samaria. Nehemiah quickly surveyed the situation and commenced rebuilding the fortifications of Jerusalem (Neh. 2:11–4:23). After securing the city walls, Nehemiah took economic measures to relieve the suffering of the poorer citizens: (1) usury was abolished, and (2) the burdensome taxation used to support governmental officials was ended (Neh. 5).

Returning to Susa after a twelve-year term, Nehemiah served his people as governor a second time, during which time he dealt with certain social and religious problems threatening Jewish identity. Mixed marriages were forbidden, commercial activities were banned on the Sabbath, and the Levites were reinstated to their rightful positions (Neh. 11–13).

In effect, the efforts of Ezra and Nehemiah saved the Jewish community from extinction. New foundations of the Jews were laid for the physical and spiritual well-being of the Jewish community. However, the threat of cultural assimilation was not over. The Greek period would present even greater challenges to Jewish identity.

Median soldiers in the service of the royal Persian guard as shown on a relief made of glazed bricks found at Susa, one of the Persian administrative centers.

Chapter Fourteen

THE HELLENISTIC PERIOD

Introduction

The conquests of Alexander the Great signaled the dawn of a new era for the Near East. The center of international power shifted from East to West, first to Greece and later to Rome. Students of world history speak of the "Hellenistic Period," since *Hellas* is the Greek word for "Greece." The Hellenistic era witnessed momentous developments that prepared the way for the Christian movement and led to far-reaching changes in Judaism.

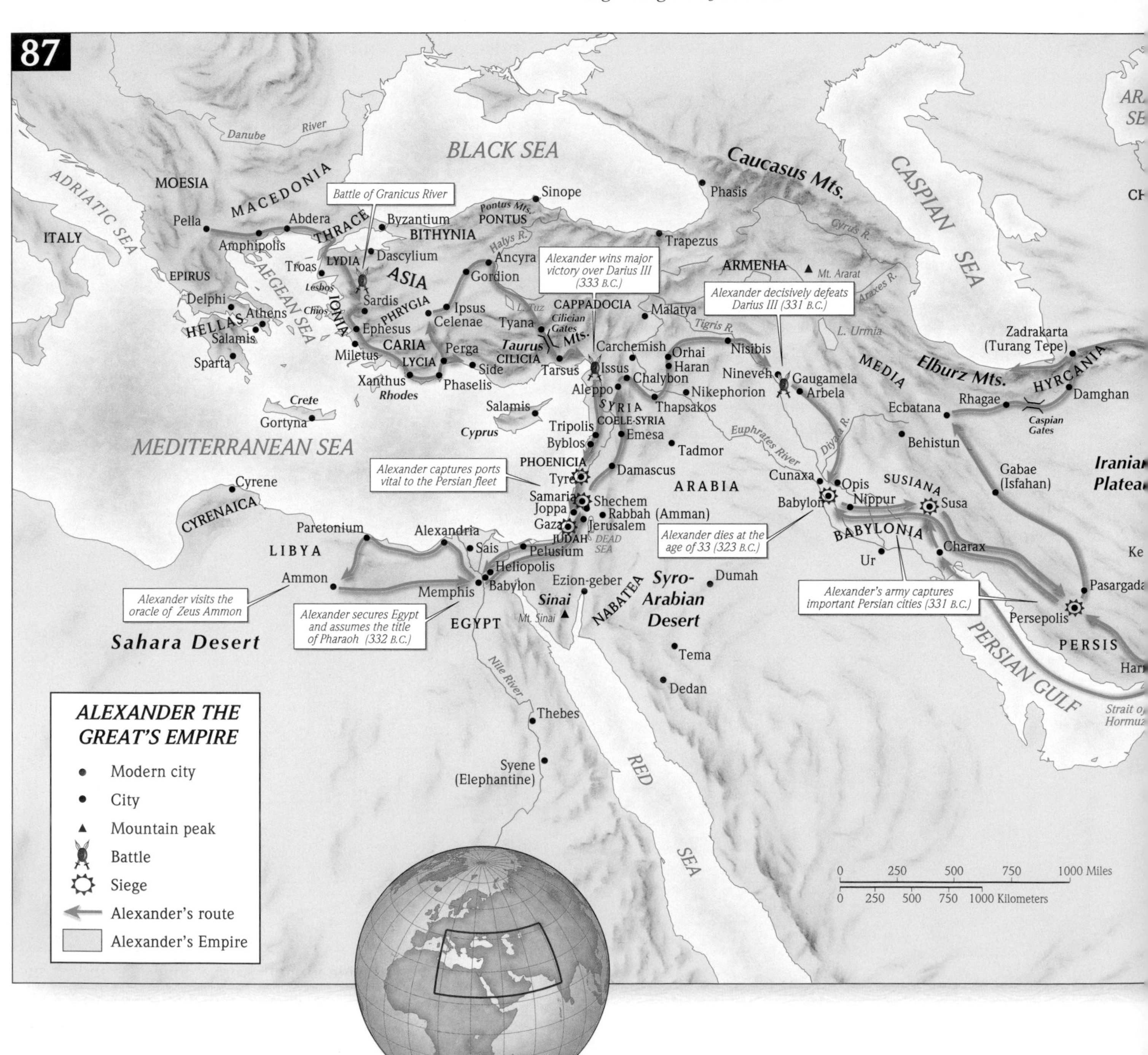

Trade between East and West had prospered for centuries. Greek merchants visited the coastal regions of the eastern Mediterranean before 1000 B.C. The military campaigns of Alexander accelerated the influx of Greek culture. He envisioned a single, unifying culture based on Greek ideals embracing all his conquered territories. Classical Greek ideas blended with local customs and concepts. The mix produced a new period of history marked by a rich and diverse blend of cultures. An international, cosmopolitan perspective began to replace the regionalism of previous historical eras.

Alexander's victories brought a culture uniting the world of his day, but he did not bring political unity. Palestine and the Near East suffered under the jealous wars of Alexander's successors. Two of Alexander's generals divided the eastern part of his empire. Ptolemy ruled from Alexandria, Egypt, while Seleucus set up his kingdom in Babylonia and Syria. They encouraged friends and leaders from Greece to join them in the East. Thus Westerners flooded the East as bureaucrats, merchants, and soldiers of war and fortune. This Greek upper class baptized the Near East with Greek customs, language, thought, and morality.

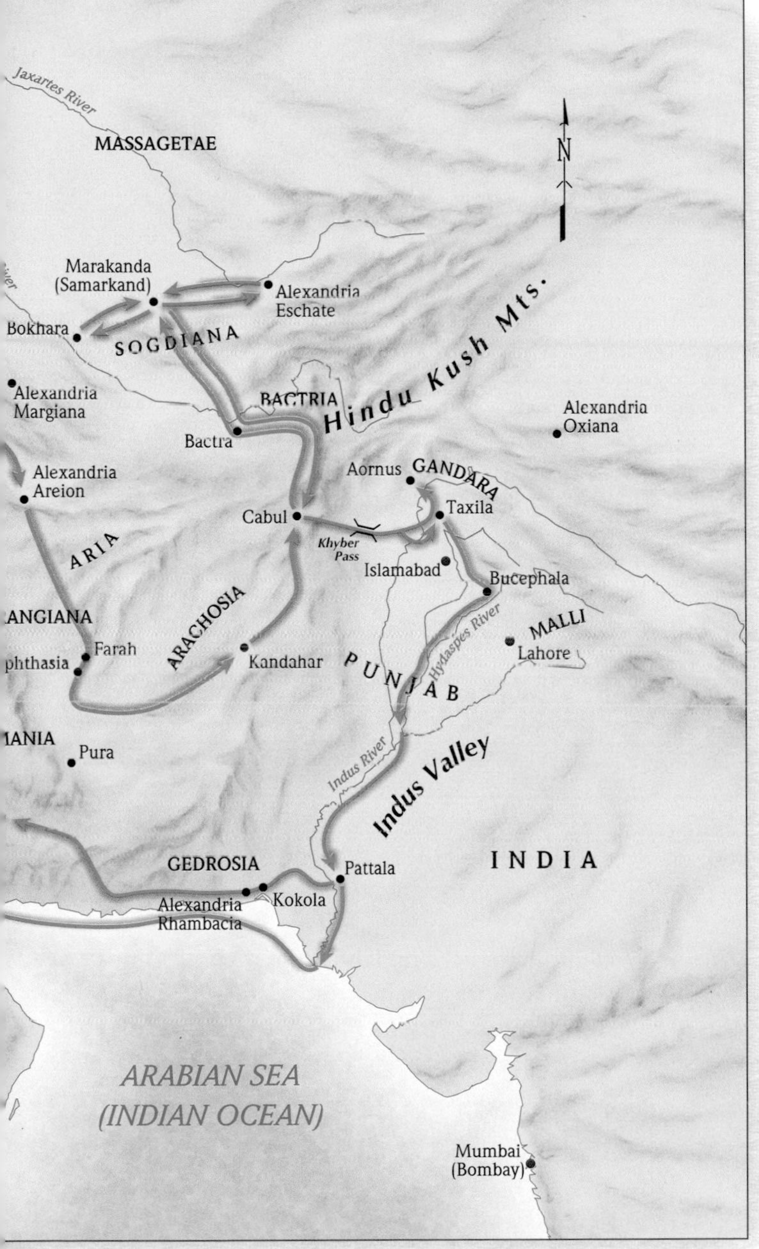

THE INFLUX AND INFLUENCE OF GREEK CULTURE

The Near East changed radically under the impact of Hellenism. The Greek language of the common people of Greece (*koine* Greek) in contrast with the Greek of the famous philosophers and poets (classical Greek) became the international language of politics, economics, and culture. Greek kings founded new cities such as Alexandria and Antioch. These cities quickly became major economic and cultural centers. The kings' massive building programs proclaimed royal power, erecting Greek temples, gymnasiums, and theaters in the major cities of the East. In the gymnasium, young men trained both body and mind in accord with classical Greek ideals. Thus Greek learning and practices spread through the Eastern world. Education levels rose rapidly throughout the area, as people sought skills to function and succeed in an increasingly complex society.

Standardized coins and easier access to larger markets caused trade to flourish. People began gradually to catch a vision of life beyond the limits of the small city-state. The rich possibilities of the inhabited, civilized world beckoned all citizens to new adventures. In many ways, these changes prepared the way for the "fullness of time" in which the gospel events unfolded.

Hellenism did not solve all problems, nor did it affect all people. Native cultures continued to flourish, especially in rural areas. The Greek ideas and way of life appealed primarily to the upper classes of the cities. The material benefits of Hellenistic life impacted the urban dwellers the most and thus also had greater allure for them.

THE CHALLENGE OF HELLENISM

Hellenism brought problems as well. Lack of political unity resulted in wide-ranging wars among Alexander's successors. This meant insecurity and economic hardship for the vast majority of the population. Slavery became a continuing characteristic of Greek society. Greek values stood in strong opposition to traditional religious and cultural

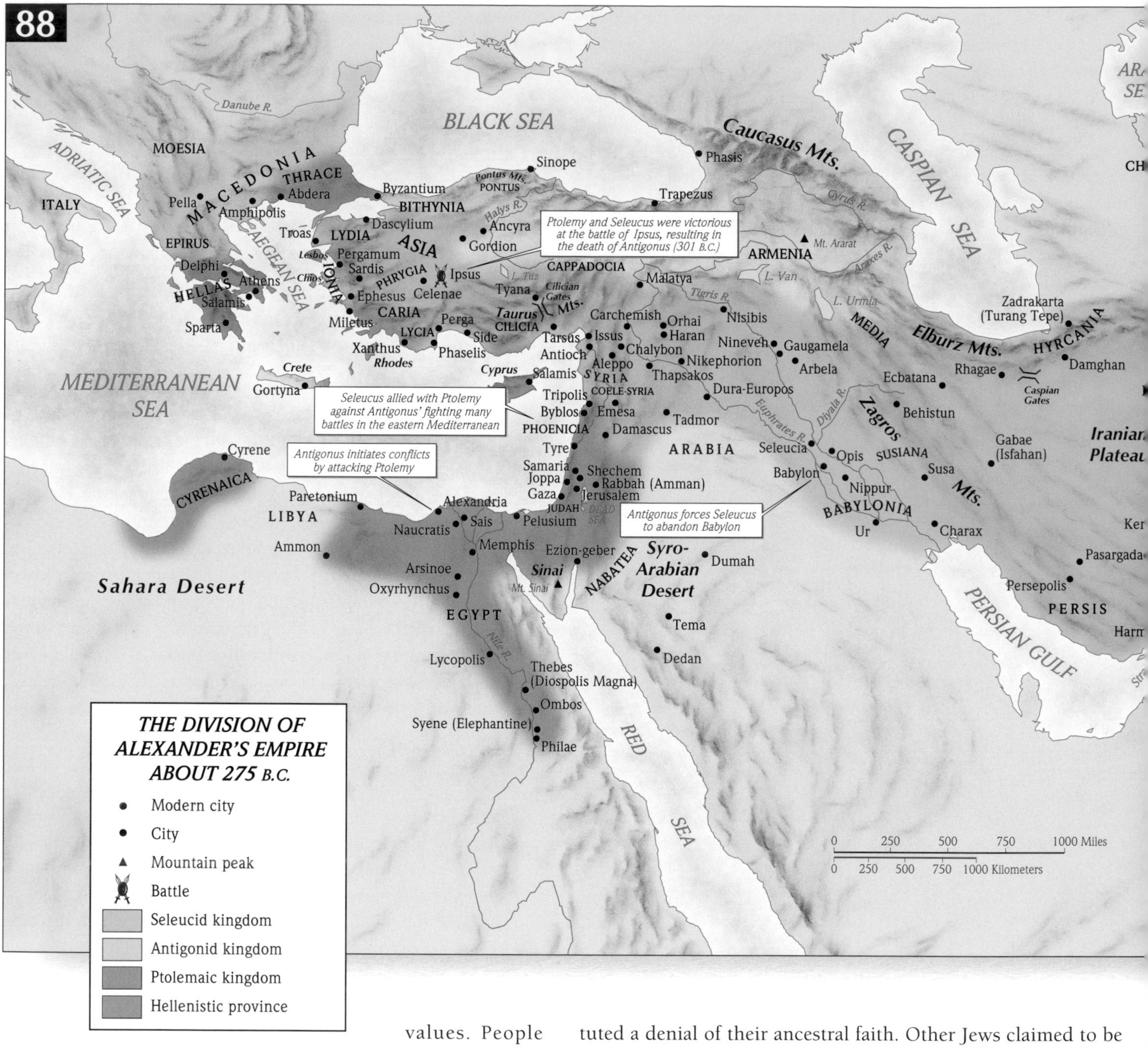

88

THE DIVISION OF ALEXANDER'S EMPIRE ABOUT 275 B.C.

- Modern city
- City
- Mountain peak
- Battle
- Seleucid kingdom
- Antigonid kingdom
- Ptolemaic kingdom
- Hellenistic province

Ptolemy and Seleucus were victorious at the battle of Ipsus, resulting in the death of Antigonus (301 B.C.)

Seleucus allied with Ptolemy against Antigonus' fighting many battles in the eastern Mediterranean

Antigonus initiates conflicts by attacking Ptolemy

Antigonus forces Seleucus to abandon Babylon

values. People lived under the tension of loyalty to the old and the hope of prosperity from the new. Jews, with their traditional worship of only one God, stood under extreme threat and tension from Hellenism. Still, the new international traffic and trade led to rapid expansion and development of Judaism outside Palestine. These new international Jews (the Diaspora) prospered in a vital, Hellenized Judaism in cities like Alexandria.

New growth and expansion brought new tensions for Jews. To what degree could a Jew adopt the new culture and still adhere to the faith? More conservative Jewish elements strenuously resisted Hellenistic ideas, believing compromise constituted a denial of their ancestral faith. Other Jews claimed to be faithful to the traditional religion while also enjoying the benefits of Hellenistic culture. Eventually this tension erupted when the Seleucid kingdom of Syria aggressively sought to force Jews to adopt Hellenistic practices. This ignited the Maccabean revolt and led to a brief period of Jewish independence.

Campaigns of Alexander the Great

In 336 B.C., at the age of twenty, Alexander (356–323 B.C.) assumed the title "King of Macedon" upon the death of his father, Philip II. He shared his father's vision of leading a united Greek army against the Persian Empire, the long-standing en-

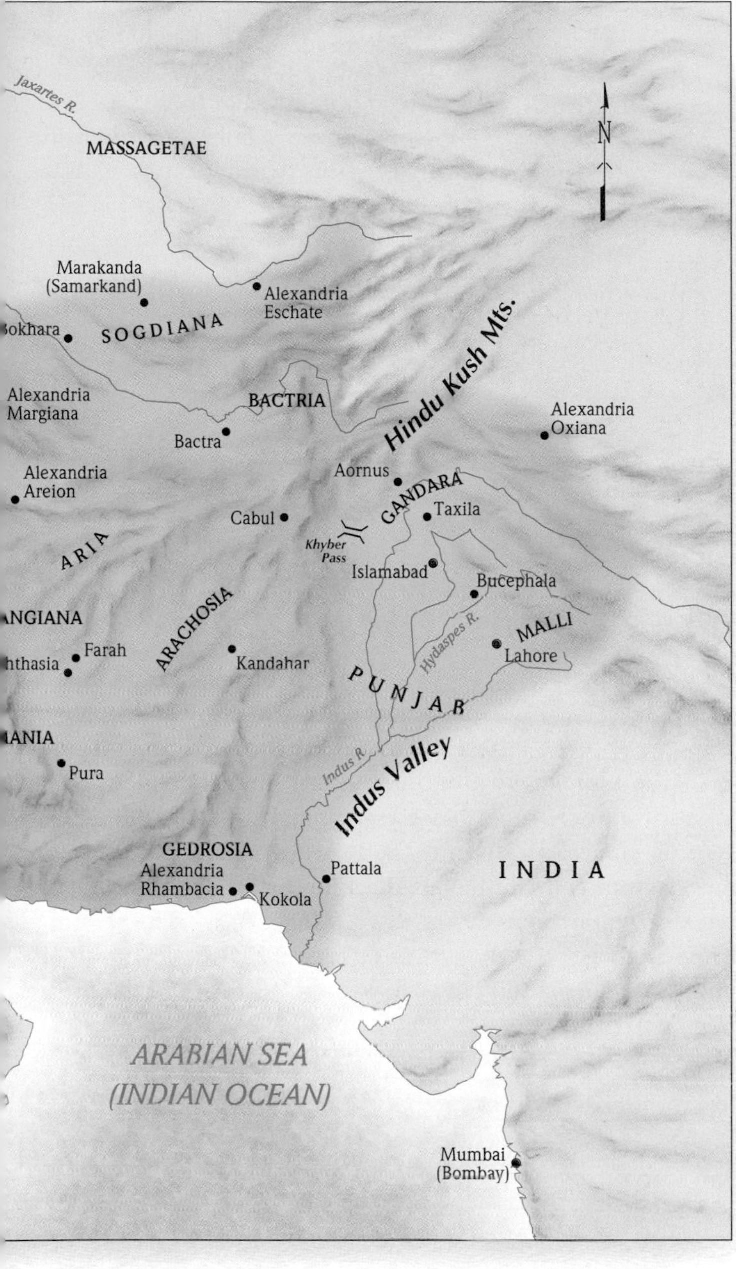

emy of the Greek city-states. To that end he assembled an army of forty thousand men composed primarily of Macedonians and Greeks. Alexander faced a much larger Persian army supported by a Persian fleet manned by Phoenicians. His opponent was Darius III, king of Persia.

Alexander crossed into Asia Minor in 334 B.C. with the immediate aim of "liberating" the Greek city-states from Persian rule. At the river Granicus he defeated a Persian force led by the local satraps (governors). Further skirmishes secured much of Asia Minor. Alexander appointed governors, mainly Macedonian or Greek, to consolidate his gains. In 333 B.C. Alexander engaged Darius III directly at the Battle of Issus and won a major victory. Darius escaped, but the Persian army was in full retreat.

THE EGYPTIAN PHASE

Alexander next moved south to capture the ports vital to the Persian fleet and to secure Egypt (332–331 B.C.). Many of the cities along the coastal regions of Syria, Phoenicia, and Palestine surrendered peacefully. Tyre, a key base for the Persian fleet, refused to surrender, forcing Alexander to besiege the island city for seven months. After sacking the city, Alexander sold much of the population into slavery. Later, Gaza also resisted for two months with the same result. Alexander used his cavalry to range inland, when necessary, to secure interior areas. Most cities, apparently including Jerusalem, submitted without conflict; others, such as Samaria, offered resistance and suffered destruction. Alexander secured Egypt in late 332 B.C. and assumed the title of "Pharaoh."

THE MESOPOTAMIAN PHASE

In 331 B.C. Alexander moved his army north into Mesopotamia in pursuit of Darius. At Gaugamela, Alexander decisively defeated the Persian army, although Darius again escaped, only to be slain later by his own men. Alexander's forces captured the main centers of Persian administration—Babylon, Susa, and Persepolis—ending Persian rule. Subsequently, Alexander campaigned farther east, eventually reaching modern Afghanistan and the Indus Valley. He established numerous cities in which he placed Macedonian and Greek troops. Because he increasingly sought to share power with native people, his own troops threatened rebellion. Exhausted by the constant campaigns, his army finally mutinied and forced Alexander to return westward. He died in Babylon in 323 B.C. at the age of thirty-three.

The Division of Alexander's Empire

Alexander's sudden, unexpected death in 323 B.C. created a crisis. Who would succeed him as master over his vast empire? Alexander left no viable heir. Several of his close advisors formed a governing council and divided the empire among themselves. These men, known as *Diadochi* or "successors," were powerful figures who each coveted more territory. For our purposes, the most important of these successors were Ptolemy I, Soter, Antigonus Monopthalmus and his son Demetrius Poliorcetes ("beseiger of cities"), and Seleucus I. Ptolemy controlled Egypt, while Antigonus was awarded Asia Minor. Seleucus, another of Alexander's generals, was granted Babylon. War was inevitable among these ambitious rulers.

Antigonus initiated the conflicts by attacking Ptolemy I

The Hellenistic city of Jerash and the temple of Zeus.

and forcing Seleucus to abandon Babylon. Seleucus quickly allied with Ptolemy against Antigonus. Beginning about 315 B.C., the two competing forces fought fierce battles, principally in Syria, Phoenicia, and Palestine. Naval battles raged in the eastern Mediterranean. The fate of Palestine and the Jewish people hung in the balance, and the people of Palestine suffered greatly in this battle-plagued era.

In 312 B.C. Ptolemy forcibly removed a large group of Jews from Jerusalem and resettled them in Alexandria. Seleucus I returned to Babylon in 312 B.C., gaining a new advantage against Antigonus. A combined sea and land assault on Egypt led by Antigonus and Demetrius failed in 306 B.C. The decisive Battle of Ipsus in 301 B.C. resulted in the death of Antigonus and victory for Ptolemy and Seleucus.

Control of the East fell to the two competing Hellenistic dynasties that survived these wars. The Ptolemaic Dynasty, descended from Ptolemy I, centered upon Egypt and gained initial control over Phoenicia and Palestine. From their capital at Alexandria, the Ptolemies ruled Palestine for the next one hundred years (301–200 B.C.). The Seleucid Dynasty, successors to Seleucus I, claimed Syria and Babylonia. In 301 B.C. Palestine became a bone of contention between the two dynasties because Seleucus claimed Palestine as the spoil of war after the Battle of Ipsus. During the next century the Ptolemies and Seleucids fought five wars over Palestine until 200 B.C. when Palestine became Seleucid territory.

Alexander the Great fighting Darius III at the battle of Issus in 333 B.C. The scene comes from a first century A.D. mosaic found at Pompeii.

Ptolemaic Rule in Palestine (301–200 B.C.)

The Ptolemaic Kingdom was among the most wealthy and stable of the Hellenistic kingdoms. From Alexandria, the Ptolemies ruled over a vast empire, which, at its greatest extent, included Cyrenacia, Palestine, Phoenicia, Cyprus, some Greek islands, and parts of western Asia Minor. Two factors contributed to the kingdom's stability: (1) the native Egyptian population was homogeneous and, therefore, more easily governed, and (2) Egypt's clearly defined borders and relative isolation lent a measure of security to the Ptolemaic heartland.

PTOLEMAIC POLICIES

Ptolemy I Soter (304–285 B.C.) and his son Ptolemy II Philadelphus (285–246 B.C.) established the basic policies that made the kingdom powerful and wealthy. The Ptolemies strictly controlled commerce, finance, and agriculture through a complex bureaucracy that furnished money to the king. Land was farmed out under state control; certain industries came under state monopoly. Taxes were heavy and numerous.

Yet the Ptolemies did not force Hellenization upon the native peoples. The average Egyptian was unaffected culturally by the new policies. The Ptolemies' concern was to maximize profit for the court at Alexandria.

ALEXANDRIA

Alexandria became a major center of Greek culture and commerce under the Ptolemies. Located on the coast of the western Delta where a major branch of the Nile reaches the sea, the city had enormous economic potential. Two harbors served a fleet that exported grains, papyrus, and glass, among other things. Imports included metals and timber. The famous lighthouse of Pharos, one of the seven wonders of the ancient world, towered over the port. The early Ptolemies fostered the development of Hellenistic culture by supporting a large group of scholars at the Museum, an academy of learning, and building a library world renowned as the greatest repository of literary works in the ancient world.

The Jewish population of Alexandria increased steadily as Jews immigrated to Alexandria in search of new opportunities, often serving as mercenaries and merchants. Many Jews adopted features of Hellenistic culture, including the Greek language, a fact seen in the need for a Greek translation of their Hebrew and Aramaic Scriptures. This translation, known as the Septuagint, probably was begun in the reign of Ptolemy II, although it was not completed until much later. This version later became the "Bible" of the earliest Christian missionaries. They preached from this Greek version of the Old Testament since Hebrew was unintelligible to the vast majority of potential converts.

PALESTINE

Our knowledge of conditions in Palestine under Ptolemaic rule is sketchy due to the paucity of archaeological and literary sources. Since security against Seleucid expansion was a major consideration, the border regions and strategic points in southern Syria and Palestine were fortified and garrisoned with Ptolemaic troops. Macedonian and Greek garrisons had been placed previously at Gaza and Samaria by Alexander or Perdiccas; the latter was a Macedonian general originally charged with the

CHART 15: THE PTOLEMIES AND THE SELEUCIDS: 323–175 B.C.

PTOLEMAIC RULERS	KEY EVENTS	SELEUCID RULERS	KEY EVENTS
Ptolemy I Soter (323–285)	Established Ptolemaic line; founded great library of Alexandria; resettled many Jews in Alexandria	Seleucid I (312–280)	Founded Seleucid line of rulers; founded Antioch in 300
Ptolemy II Philadelphus (285–246)	First and Second Wars with Seleucids; Septuagint (LXX) begun in Alexandria	Antiochus I (280–261)	
Ptolemy III Euregetes (246–221)	Third War with Seleucids	Antiochus II (261–246)	
Ptolemy IV Philopator (221–203)	Defeated Antiochus III at Raphia	Seleucus II (246–223)	
Ptolemy V Epiphanes (203–181)	Lost Palestine to Seleucids in 200	Antiochus III (223–187)	Secured Palestine for Seleucid rule at Panias in 200, defeated by Rome in Asia Minor at Magnesia in 190
Ptolemy VI Philometor (181–146)		Seleucus IV (187–175)	Heliodorus tries to plunder the temple at Jerusalem
		Antiochus IV (175–163)	Corrupted the high priesthood in Jerusalem; invaded Egypt, but was forced to withdraw by Romans; policies provoked the Maccabean Revolt; profaned the temple in Jerusalem

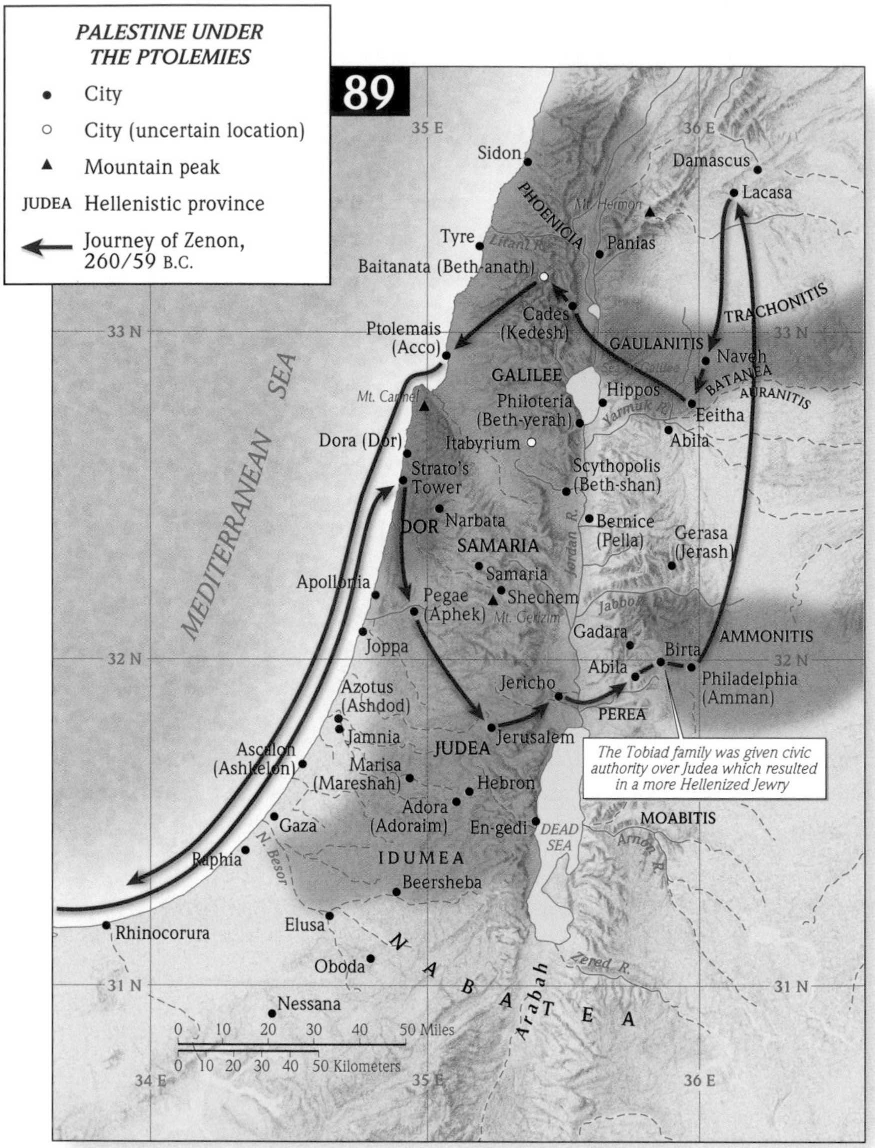

responsibility of overseeing Alexander's Empire as divided among the *Diadochi* until his death in 321 B.C. Other such garrisons emerged through allotments granted to Greek military personnel in exchange for service.

The Ptolemies also developed the economic potential of southern Syria and Palestine and imposed upon these lands the same tight bureaucratic system found in Egypt to collect taxes and control trade. Dates, olive oil, grain, fish, cheese, and fruit exported to Egypt boasted Ptolemaic wealth. The Zenon Papyri (about 259–258 B.C.) record the travel in Palestine of a representative of the Ptolemaic finance minister Apollonius. These papyri allow us a glimpse of life in Palestine under the Ptolemies and the efficient bureaucracy designed to generate revenues.

The Ptolemies treated Judea as a temple state, that is, land dedicated to a particular god. For the Ptolemies, the high priest of Jerusalem functioned as the religious and civil authority of the Jewish people. The high priest was an intermediary between the Jews and the Ptolemies. His main governmental responsibility was to collect and pay an annual tax.

When Onias II, high priest under Ptolemy III, refused to render the tax, the Ptolemies permitted the Tobiad family to assume the responsibility and the consequent civic authority. The Tobiads, a wealthy business family who can be traced back to one of Nehemiah's opponents (Neh. 2:10; 6:1–19), represented a more Hellenized Jewry who presumably saw the benefits of Ptolemaic policies. Traditional Jews became increasingly isolated, both physically and spiritually, as economic and security factors promoted Hellenization in many cities, especially along the coasts and in the Transjordan. Ptolemais (Acco), Gadara, Philadelphia (Rabbah), Philoteria (Beth-yerah), and other cities surrounded Jerusalem as something of a Hellenistic border. Traditional beliefs inevitably were challenged.

The Seleucid Dynasty

The Ptolemies' rivals for power in the East were the Seleucids, a powerful dynasty officially founded in 312 B.C. when Seleucus I became satrap of Babylonia. As one of the "successors," Seleucus I claimed the title "king" in 305 B.C. He and Antiochus I, his son, set about establishing control of vast areas of northern Syria, Mesopotamia, portions of Asia Minor, and the Iranian plateau.

SELEUCID POLICIES

The Seleucids ruled their empire from two newly founded cities located at strategic points. Antioch in Syria, founded in 300 B.C., became the most important politically. Like its counterpart Alexandria in Egypt, Antioch rapidly became a city of great size and wealth, a virtual showcase for Hellenistic culture. Seleucia on the Tigris, dominating the confluence of vital trade routes, served as a base for administering the central and eastern regions.

Seleucid rule was less centralized and less bureaucratic due in part to the sheer size of the empire, which presented serious administrative problems. Unlike the Ptolemaic Kingdom, the Seleucid Kingdom had no clear geographic borders and was not easily defended. Moreover, its population, unlike Egypt, was heterogeneous. Powerful local rulers exerted significant influence and required diplomatic tact on the part of the Seleucid kings to prevent rebellion.

To unify their diverse kingdom, the Seleucids aggressively encouraged people to adopt Greek practices and ideas. Seleucus I and Antiochus I established numerous military colo-

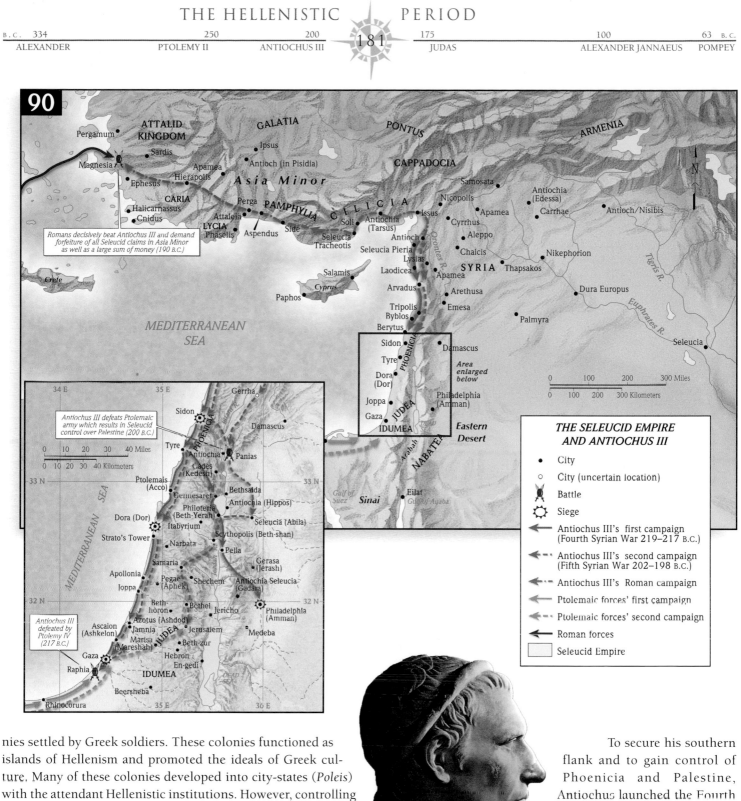

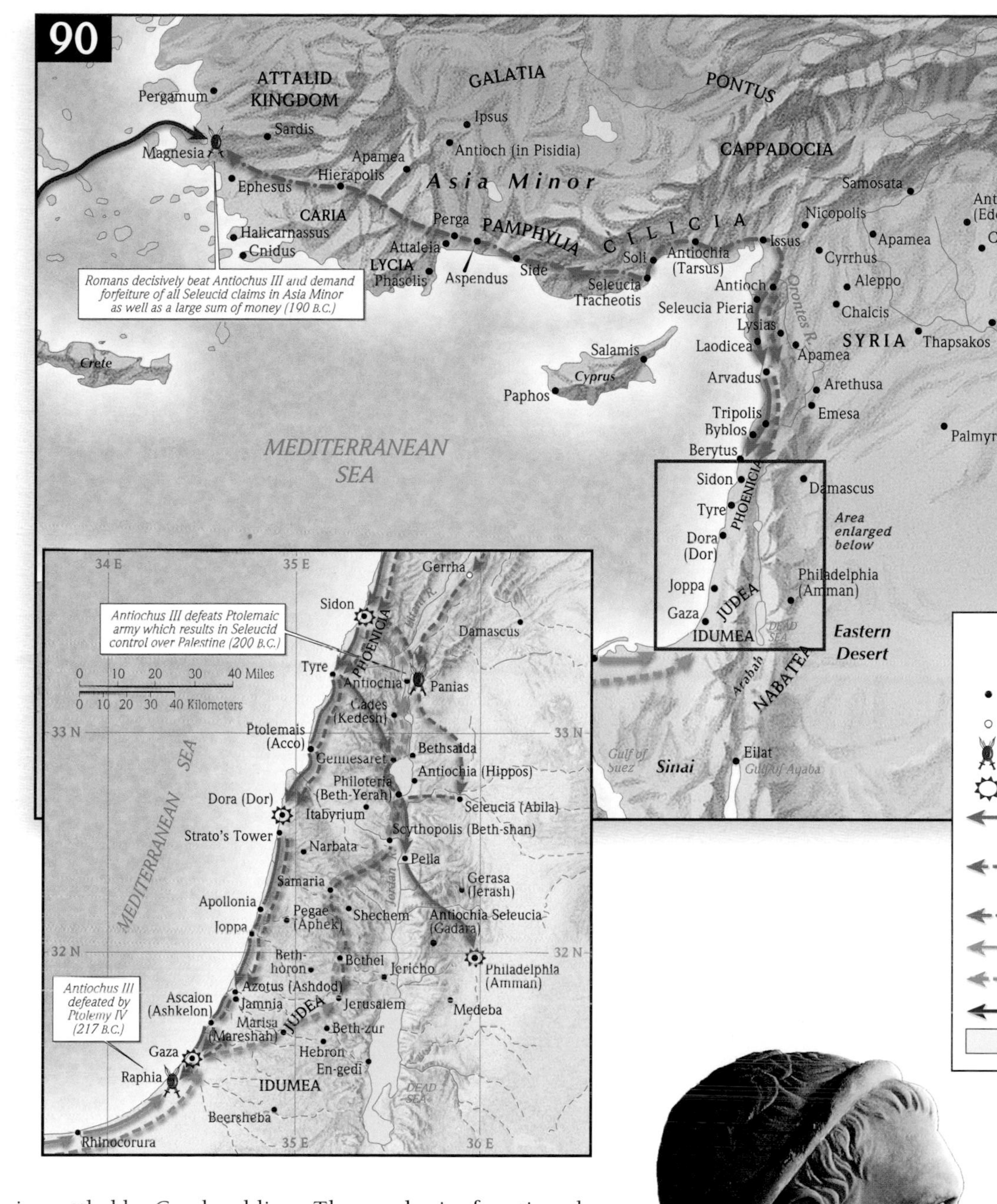

nies settled by Greek soldiers. These colonies functioned as islands of Hellenism and promoted the ideals of Greek culture. Many of these colonies developed into city-states (*Poleis*) with the attendant Hellenistic institutions. However, controlling the massive empire proved troublesome. The eastern provinces rebelled, while wars with the Ptolemies weakened both kingdoms.

ANTIOCHUS III

When Antiochus III (223–187 B.C.) came to power in 223 B.C., Seleucid fortunes revived. This energetic king pursued a policy of consolidation and expansion that ultimately earned him the title "the Great."

Antiochus III.

To secure his southern flank and to gain control of Phoenicia and Palestine, Antiochus launched the Fourth Syrian War (219–217 B.C.), but a large Ptolemaic force consisting primarily of native Egyptians stopped him at Raphia, just south of Gaza, in 217 B.C. As a result, these territories remained Ptolemaic. Antiochus was more successful in a series of campaigns in the eastern provinces, but the problem of securing his southern border remained. The Fifth Syrian War (202–198 B.C.) settled the matter with the decisive victory over the Ptolemaic

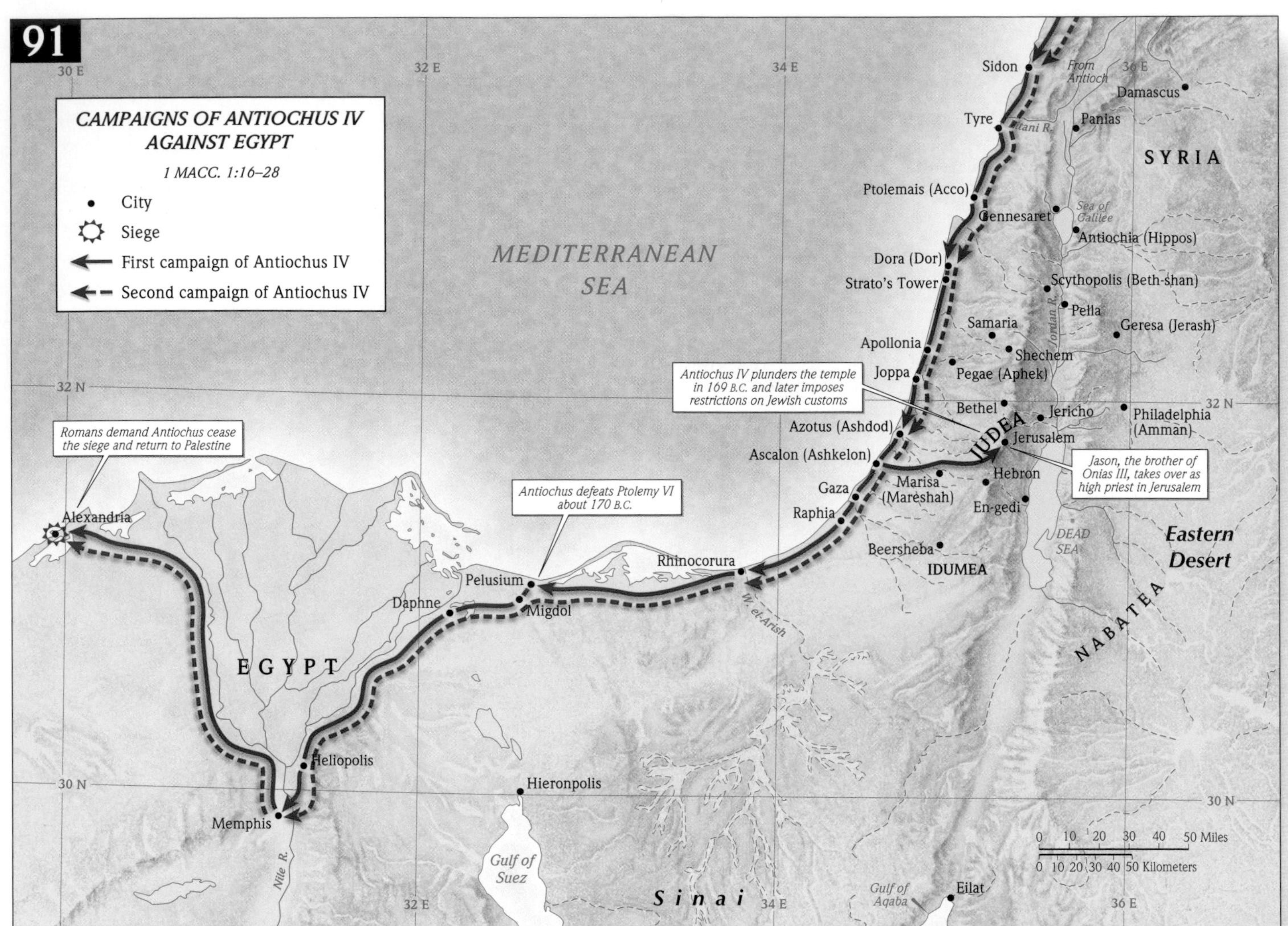

army at Panias (later Caesarea Philippi) in 200 B.C. Southern Syria and Palestine became Seleucid territories.

Palestine under Seleucid Rule

Antiochus III's victory in 200 B.C. over the Ptolemies caused most Jews to rejoice. The Jews were weary of the heavy taxes and oppressive bureaucracy of the Ptolemies. Antiochus rewarded their loyalty by granting the Jews the right to live according to their ancient traditions. He remitted several taxes and assisted in the repair of the Jerusalem temple, evidently damaged in recent fighting. The early years of Seleucid rule over Palestine were peaceful and prosperous.

WAR WITH ROME

War with Rome changed matters quickly. Antiochus expanded westward into Greece in the 190s B.C., where he caught the attention of Rome. Rome and Carthage had just finished an exhausting war (the Second Punic War) in which Hannibal rampaged across the Italian peninsula (see chap. 15 for a brief history of Roman expansion). When Antiochus invaded Greece in the company of Hannibal, Rome fought back. In western Asia Minor at Magnesia in 190 B.C., Antiochus was beaten decisively. The Romans demanded a large sum of money and the forfeiture of all Seleucid claims in Asia Minor. Antiochus III faced financial disaster and diminished power. He died in 187 B.C. while looting a temple in his eastern provinces attempting to secure money to pay his debts.

Antiochus III left two sons as potential heirs to the

Seleucid throne: the eldest, Seleucus IV, became king in 187 B.C. and ruled until his assassination in 175 B.C. Saddled with his father's debt to Rome, he increased taxes to pay the tribute and sanctioned plundering of temples in his kingdom. Seleucus sent Heliodorus to Jerusalem to confiscate the temple treasury. The attempt failed, according to a story in 2 Maccabees 3, when angelic beings intervened and forced Heliodorus to abandon his mission.

ANTIOCHUS IV

Heliodorus murdered Seleucus IV in 175 B.C. Antiochus IV, a brother of Seleucus who had been previously held as a political hostage in Rome, returned to Antioch to claim the throne. An ardent supporter of Greek culture, Antiochus took the typically Hellenistic title "Theos Epiphanes"—"god manifest." The new king also was ambitious and dreamed of restoring glory to the Seleucid kingdom through expansion. Egypt was the most promising target since any move toward the West would invite swift Roman retaliation.

Antiochus IV began an aggressive policy of Hellenization to unify his kingdom and prepare the way for an invasion of Egypt. In Jerusalem a strongly Hellenistic pro-Seleucid party emerged that Antiochus favored. The king sold the office of high priest to Jason, the brother of Onias III, who was the legitimate high priest. Jason was a thorough Hellenist who introduced Greek festivals and sporting events to Jerusalem. Young Jewish men received training in Greek ways at the gymnasia built in the city (2 Macc. 4:7–17). In 172 B.C. Menelaus outbid Jason for the high priestly office. Menelaus was from a nonhigh priestly lineage. The sacred office of high priest became a political tool and source of revenue for Antiochus while Jerusalem took on the trappings of a Greek city. These changes deeply distressed the more traditional elements of Jewish society.

Antiochus attacked Egypt on two occasions between 170 and 168 B.C. He was on the verge of complete success when Rome ordered him to withdraw from Egypt. Unwilling to risk war with Rome, Antiochus retreated. News of his failure—and a rumor that Antiochus was dead—prompted Jason to attempt to reclaim the high priesthood, a move Antiochus interpreted as rebellion against Seleucid rule.

Determined to ensure the loyalty of Palestine and secure his border with Egypt, Antiochus imposed restrictions on Jewish traditions and forced Greek customs on the Jewish population. An edict forbade the rite of circumcision and the observance of the Sabbath. A pagan altar dedicated to the worship of Zeus was built in the Jerusalem temple (the "Abomination of Desolation" in Dan. 11:31; 12:11 [NASB]). As a sign of loyalty, Jews were required to offer pagan sacrifices, including the offering of swine flesh. Antiochus placed Seleucid troops in Jerusalem at a citadel known as the Akra to ensure compliance to his edicts. On two occasions Seleucid troops plundered the temple on orders of the king.

THE MACCABEAN REVOLT

Many Jews cooperated willingly or under compulsion with the new regime. Others resisted. The catalyst that sparked the Maccabean revolt happened in Modein, a small village northwest of Jerusalem. When the king's representative came to Modein demanding a sacrifice to prove the loyalty of the village, an aged Jewish priest named Mattathias refused the demand. A fight ensued in which the king's representative and others were killed. Mattathias and his five sons—Simon, John, Judas, Eleazar, and Jonathan—fled to the Gophna Hills. The passionately orthodox followers of Jewish law, the Hasidim ("Pious Ones"), joined them in armed resistance. The Hasidim rejected any compromise with Greek culture, regarding such compromises as a betrayal of faith. The Pharisees and Essenes, who appear a little later, were spiritual kinsmen of the Hasidim.

Judas Maccabeus. After the death of the aged Mattathias, his son Judas became the leader of the revolt. Called Maccabeus, "the Hammerer," Judas fought a guerrilla war against Seleucid armies sent to crush the revolt. His success depended upon surprise and an intimate knowledge of terrain. He attacked enemy

CHART 16: THE FAMILY OF MATTATHIAS AND THE MACCABEAN REVOLT

Mattathias	167–166 B.C.	Aged priest living at Modein; died in 166 B.C.; defied the order to offer a sacrifice in homage to Antiochus IV
Judas "Maccabeus"	166–160 B.C.	Third son of Mattathias'; led revolt from 166-160 B.C.; won victories over Seleucid troops at Beth-horon, Samaria, Emmaus, and Beth-zur; reclaimed and cleansed the Temple at Jerusalem in 164B.C..; gained religious freedom for the Jews in 162 B.C.; died fighting at Elasa
Jonathan	160–142 B.C.	Youngest son of Mattathias; led a guerilla war from the Judean deserts; eventually established a base at Michmash; appointed as High Priest in 152 B.C.; taken prisoner and executed by the Seleucid Trypho in 143 B.C..
Simon	142–134 B.C.	Second eldest son of Mattathias; gained political concessions from Seleucid rulers that led to an independent Jewish state in 142 B.C.; died in a coup in 135 B.C.

forces in the narrow approaches leading to Jerusalem, arming his followers with weapons secured in his victories.

Judas won an impressive string of victories over Seleucid commanders, including the defeat of Apollonius at the Ascent of Lebonah (167 B.C.) (1 Macc. 3:10–12), Seron at the Beth-horon Pass (166 B.C.) (1 Macc. 3:13–23), and Nicanor near Emmaus (165 B.C.) (1 Macc. 3:38–4:3–5). Judas' most impressive victory occurred in December, 164 B.C., when he recaptured the Jerusalem temple, dismantled the pagan altar, and cleansed the temple (1 Macc. 4:36–5:61). The Jewish sacrificial system once again was carried out in accordance with the Law of Moses. The Festival of Hannukah was instituted to commemorate this joyous event. Jesus declared: "I and the Father are one" while He attended this festival two hundred years later (see John 10:22–30).

Judas continued the struggle until his death in battle in

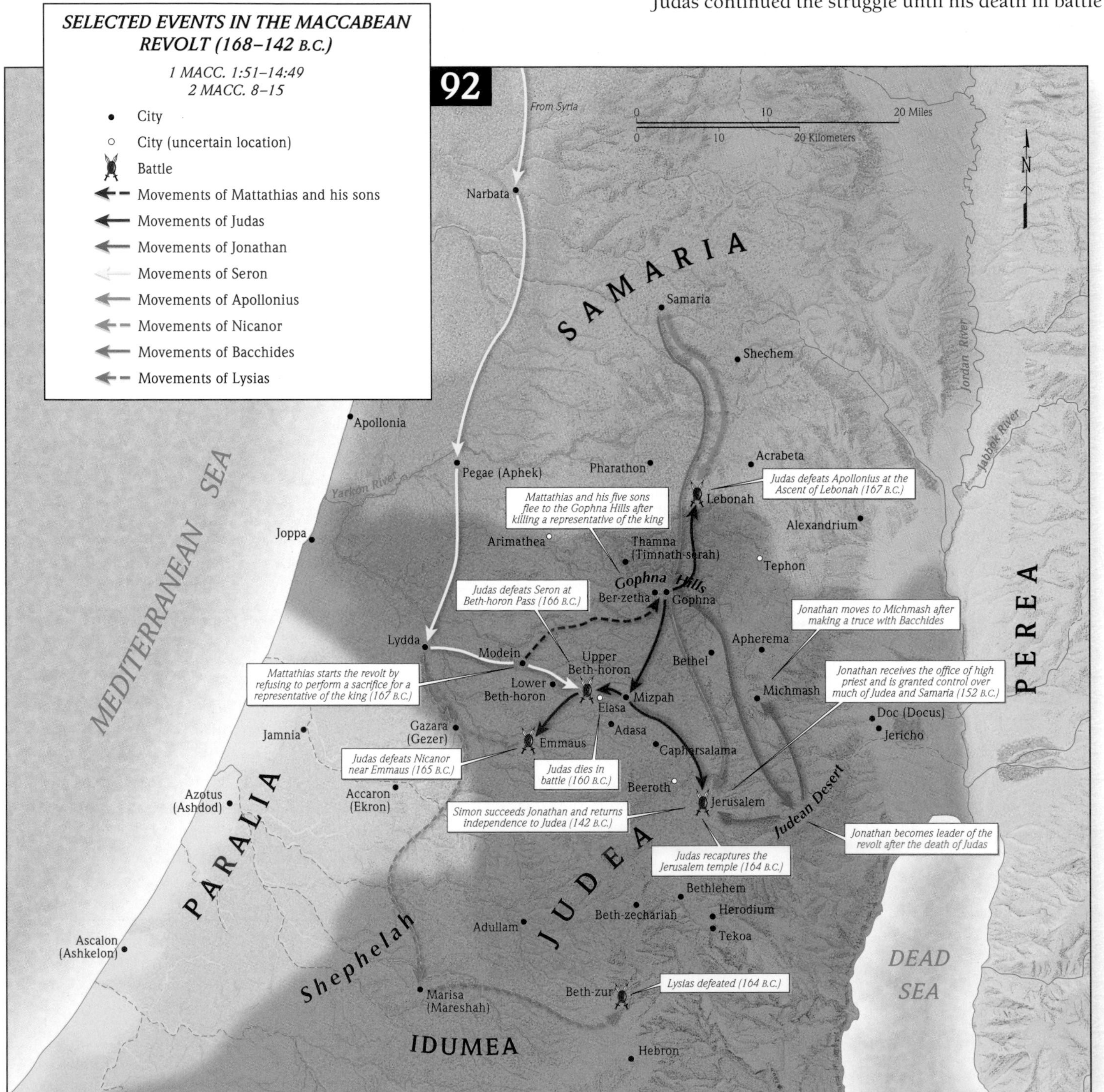

160 B.C. As his confidence increased, Judas grew bolder and suffered defeats. However, the death of Antiochus IV in 164 B.C. led to an important concession to the Jews. Several claimants to the Seleucid throne—including the son of Selecus IV, Demetrius I, and the Seleucid general Lysias—vied for power. To win Jewish support, Lysias granted religious freedom to the Jews (162 B.C.). This act overturned the oppressive edicts of Antiochus IV and satisfied the Hasidim, many of whom gave up the armed struggle. Later Jewish leaders exploited the Seleucid dynastic rivalries to gain additional concessions.

Jonathan. Jonathan became the leader of the revolt upon the death of his brother Judas in 160 B.C. His situation was desperate because many supporters had abandoned the conflict while Seleucid pressure increased. Jonathan moved to the Judean Desert and carried on a strategy of hit-and-run tactics against Bacchides, the Seleucid general sent to oppose him. Bacchides finally made a truce with Jonathan, prompting Jonathan to move to Michmash, where he "began to judge the people; and he destroyed the ungodly out of Israel" (1 Macc. 9:73). Jerusalem, however, remained in the hands of Greek sympathizers and Seleucid troops.

Jonathan skillfully exploited the rivalry between Alexander Balas and Demetrius, both aspirants to the Seleucid throne. Rome and Jonathan backed the pretender Alexander Balas, who claimed to be a son of Antiochus IV. For his support Jonathan received the office of high priest; later, he was granted control over much of Judea and Samaria. Unfortunately, Jonathan was murdered by Trypho, a Seleucid general representing yet another claimant for power—Antiochus VI.

Simon. Simon, the last surviving son of Mattathias, succeeded Jonathan in 143 B.C. During his days, two powerful rivals—Trypho and Demetrius II—fought for the right to rule the Seleucid kingdom. Simon sided with Demetrius in return for the independence of Jerusalem and Judea. In 142 B.C. Demetrius exempted all taxes upon Judea, in effect acknowledging Judean independence. Simon removed by force the despised Seleucid troops garrisoned in the Jerusalem Akra. In gratitude the Jewish people proclaimed Simon high priest and ethnarch ("ruler of a people") "forever, until a faithful prophet should arise" (1 Macc. 14:22). For the first time since 586 B.C., Judea was free.

The Hasmonean Dynasty

Simon and his descendants governed an independent Jewish state approximately eighty years until Roman intervention in 63 B.C. Historians call this line of kings "the Hasmonean Dynasty," named after an obscure ancestor of Mattathias mentioned in the works of the first-century Jewish historian Josephus (see chart of Hasmonean rulers, below). The Hasmonean rulers expanded their control to include most of Palestine. At the same time, these kings betrayed an increasing inclination toward Greek ways and the pomp of pagan royalty. Because they bore the title "high priest" even though Mattathias was not of high-priestly lineage, traditional Jews such as the Pharisees (who first appear in this era) distanced themselves from the Hasmoneans. Tensions between conservative elements and the royal court eventually led to armed conflict in the reign of Alexander Janneus.

Simon expanded the Jewish state to the coast when he seized Joppa and Gezer. He reaffirmed Judea's status as an ally of Rome. Antiochus VII Sidetes, one of the last effective Seleucid kings, tried to regain Palestine, but Simon and his sons repulsed the invasion near Modein.

In 135 B.C. Simon and most of his family were murdered in a palace coup at a banquet held at Dok near Jericho. The coup leaders intended to hand Judea over to Antiochus VII. The coup failed because Simon's son John Hyrcanus was at Gazara. John managed to reach Jerusalem, where he was proclaimed high priest.

CHART 17: HASMONEAN RULERS

Name	Dates of Rule	Significant Events
John Hyrcanus	135–104 B.C.	Son of Simon, last of the Maccabean brothers; conquered Medeba, Idumea, Samaria, and Joppa; Pharisees and Sadducees first appear in his reign
Aristobulus	104–103 B.C.	Oldest son of John Hyrcanus; eliminated all but one of his brothers in securing his rule; Upper Galilee conquered during his reign; first Hasmonean to use the title "king"
Alexander Jannaeus	103–76 B.C.	Brother of Aristobulus who married his widow, Salome Alexandra; added territories along the coast (Gaza, Dora, Anthedon, Raphia, Strato's Tower); extended Jewish rule in the Transjordan; civil war between Jannaeus and the Pharisees and their supporters
Salome Alexandra	76–67 B.C.	Widow of Alexander Jannaeus; assumed civil authority; appointed her eldest son Hyrcanus II high priest; favored the Pharisees
Hyrcanus II and Aristobulus II	67–63 B.C.	Rival sons of Salome Alexandra; Aristobulus, supported by Sadducees, seized power from Hyrcanus II; the Idumean governor Antipater used the Nabateans in an attempt to restore Hyrcanus to power; in 63 B.C. Pompey intervened in the dispute

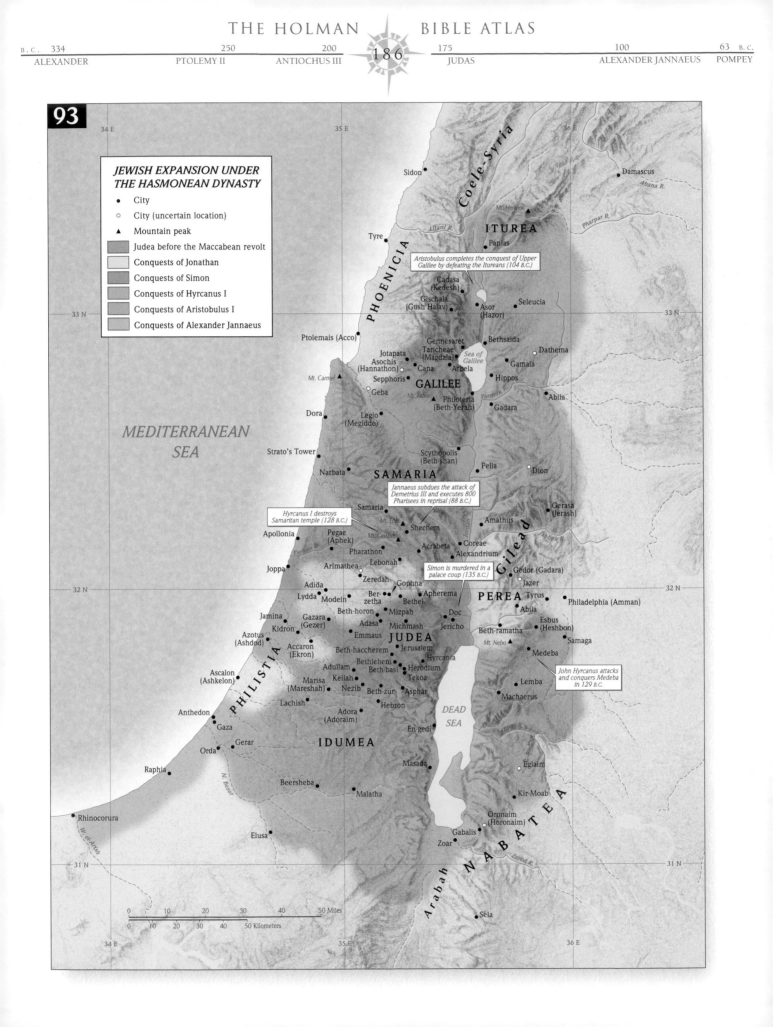

93
JEWISH EXPANSION UNDER THE HASMONEAN DYNASTY
City
City (uncertain location)
Mountain peak
Judea before the Maccabean revolt
Conquests of Jonathan
Conquests of Simon
Conquests of Hyrcanus I
Conquests of Aristobulus I
Conquests of Alexander Jannaeus
Aristobulus completes the conquest of Upper Galilee by defeating the Itureans (104 B.C.)
Jannaeus subdues the attack of Demetrius III and executes 800 Pharisees in reprisal (88 B.C.)
Hyrcanus I destroys Samaritan temple (128 B.C.)
Simon is murdered in a palace coup (135 B.C.)
John Hyrcanus attacks and conquers Medeba in 129 B.C.
MEDITERRANEAN SEA
DEAD SEA
Sea of Galilee
Coele-Syria
ITUREA
PHOENICIA
GALILEE
SAMARIA
JUDEA
PEREA
Gilead
PHILISTIA
IDUMEA
NABATEA
Arabah
Sidon
Damascus
Abana R.
Pharpar R.
Litani R.
Mt. Hermon
Tyre
Panias
Cadasa (Kedesh)
Gischala (Gush Halav)
Asor (Hazor)
Seleucia
Ptolemais (Acco)
Gennesaret
Taricheae (Magdala)
Bethsaida
Dathema
Jotapata
Asochis (Hannathon)
Cana
Arbela
Gamala
Mt. Carmel
Sepphoris
Hippos
Geba
Mt. Tabor
Philoteria (Beth-Yerah)
Yarmuk R.
Abila
Gadara
Dora
Legio (Megiddo)
Strato's Tower
Scythopolis (Beth-shan)
Pella
Dion
Narbata
Samaria
Mt. Ebal
Shechem
Mt. Gerizim
Gerasa (Jerash)
Amathus
Jordan R.
Jabbok R.
Apollonia
Pegae (Aphek)
Yarkon R.
Pharathon
Acrabeta
Coreae
Alexandrium
Joppa
Arimathea
Lebonah
Zeredah
Gophna
Gedor (Gadara)
Jazer
Adida
Lydda
Modein
Ber-zetha
Bethel
Apherema
Tyrus
Philadelphia (Amman)
Beth-horon
Mizpah
Abila
Jamina
Gazara (Gezer)
Adasa
Michmash
Doc
Jericho
Esbus (Heshbon)
Kidron
Emmaus
Beth-ramatha
Azotus (Ashdod)
Accaron (Ekron)
Beth-haccherem
Jerusalem
Mt. Nebo
Samaga
Medeba
Hyrcania
Bethlehem
Adullam
Beth-basi
Herodium
Ascalon (Ashkelon)
Keilah
Tekoa
Marisa (Mareshah)
Nezib
Beth-zur
Asphar
Lemba
Machaerus
Lachish
Hebron
Adora (Adoraim)
Anthedon
Gaza
En-gedi
Gerar
Orda
Raphia
Masada
Eglaim
N. Besor
Beersheba
Malatha
Kir-Moab
Rhinocorura
W. el-Arish
Oronaim (Horonaim)
Gabalis
Elusa
Zoar
Zered R.
Sela
34 E
35 E
36 E
33 N
32 N
31 N
0 10 20 30 40 50 Miles
0 10 20 30 40 50 Kilometers

JOHN HYRCANUS

Antiochus VII's death in 129 B.C. left John Hyrcanus in a position to extend his rule further. In that year John attacked Medeba east of the Dead Sea and added the surrounding territory. A year later, he led a campaign into Samaria, eventually destroying the Samaritan temple on Mount Gerizim. John conquered Idumea in 125 B.C., forcing the Idumeans to submit to Jewish religion or leave. A second campaign northward against the cities of Samaria and Scythopolis brought more of Samaria and the Esdraelon Valley under Jewish control.

The thirty-year rule of John Hyrcanus (135–105/4 B.C.) lifted the political and economic fortunes of the Jews, but it revealed some curious features. The Hasmonean Dynasty took on the characteristics of a Hellenistic monarchy. John employed foreign mercenaries in his army. He changed the names of his children from Hebrew into Greek. Although he avoided the title "king," his court gradually assumed the trappings of Greek culture. Religion became a tool of conquest with John and his successors, as conquered people were forcibly converted to Judaism.

The majority of Jews supported John, but such actions stirred grave concerns among orthodox groups. John favored the Sadducees over the Pharisees. The Sadducees came from the aristocratic landowners and priestly upper classes who were more comfortable with royal power and, perhaps, less offended by certain accommodations to Greek customs.

ARISTOBULUS I

The brief reign of Aristobulus I (104–103 B.C.) was marked by cruelty. The eldest son of John Hyrcanus, Aristobulus received the high priesthood, but his mother occupied the throne. In a bid for complete power, Aristobulus imprisoned his mother— who later starved to death— and all of his brothers except one. He was the first Hasmonean to claim the title "king." The one enduring accomplishment of his reign was the conquest of Upper Galilee, which he wrestled from the Itureans, an Arab tribe inhabiting lands north and east of the Sea of Galilee. Aristobulus forced the Itureans to submit to circumcision.

ALEXANDER JANNAEUS

Alexander Jannaeus succeeded his brother Aristobulus upon his death in 103 B.C. To solidify his claim to the throne, Alexander married the widow of Aristobulus, Salome Alexandra. Jannaeus pursued a policy of conquest, extending the Jewish state to its greatest extent, with victories in Transjordan, the southern coastal plain (Raphia, Gaza, Anthedon), and the Sharon Plain (Strato's Tower, Dora). Campaigns in the Transjordan increased the Jewish state from Panias to the Dead Sea, with the exception of Philadelphia.

Commercial success followed as import taxes, tariffs, and exports derived from Jannaeus' control of trade routes produced revenues for the royal coffers. However, social and religious tensions ignited a six-year civil war pitting Jannaeus and his Sadducean supporters against the Pharisees. The Pharisees appealed to the Seleucid king Demetrius III for help. Demetrius III responded by attacking and inflicting a serious defeat on Jannaeus near Shechem. The presence of a Seleucid king in Palestine caused many Jews to support the Hasmonean Dynasty. Ultimately Jannaeus triumphed, although the political cost was great. Jannaeus executed eight hundred Pharisees and their families in reprisal and thereby alienated many Jews.

THE END OF INDEPENDENCE

The widow of Jannaeus, Salome Alexandra, assumed civil authority upon her husband's death and reigned nine years (76–67 B.C.). Her eldest son, Hyrcanus II, assumed the role of high priest. Under Salome's leadership the Pharisees rose to power in the Sanhedrin. Later Jewish literature described Salome's reign as extraordinarily prosperous, reflecting the Talmud's bias toward the Pharisees. However, upon Salome's death, her younger son, Aristobulus II, with support from the Sadducees, challenged the right of Hyrcanus II to rule. The Pharisees supported Hyrcanus in the ensuing civil war.

Hyrcanus was the weaker of the two brothers, although he was High Priest. After a military defeat, he was ready to surrender his cause when an Idumean governor named Antipater intervened on his behalf. Antipater, the father of Herod (the Great), was from a line of Idumean governors who served the Hasmonean Dynasty. Antipater, recognizing the opportunity to become a power broker, backed Hyrcanus, securing the aid of the Nabatean king Aretas III. The ploy worked; Aristobulus was defeated and put on the defensive.

The Jewish civil war came at an inopportune time. In 64 B.C. the Roman general Pompey conquered Syria and threatened Palestine. Supporters of both Jewish factions appealed to Pompey for help in deciding the matter. Pompey favored Hyrcanus—to the chagrin of Aristobulus, who resisted Pompey's decision. Pompey marched on Jerusalem in 63 B.C., seized the city, and established Hyrcanus as a High Priest. The era of Roman rule over the Jews had begun.

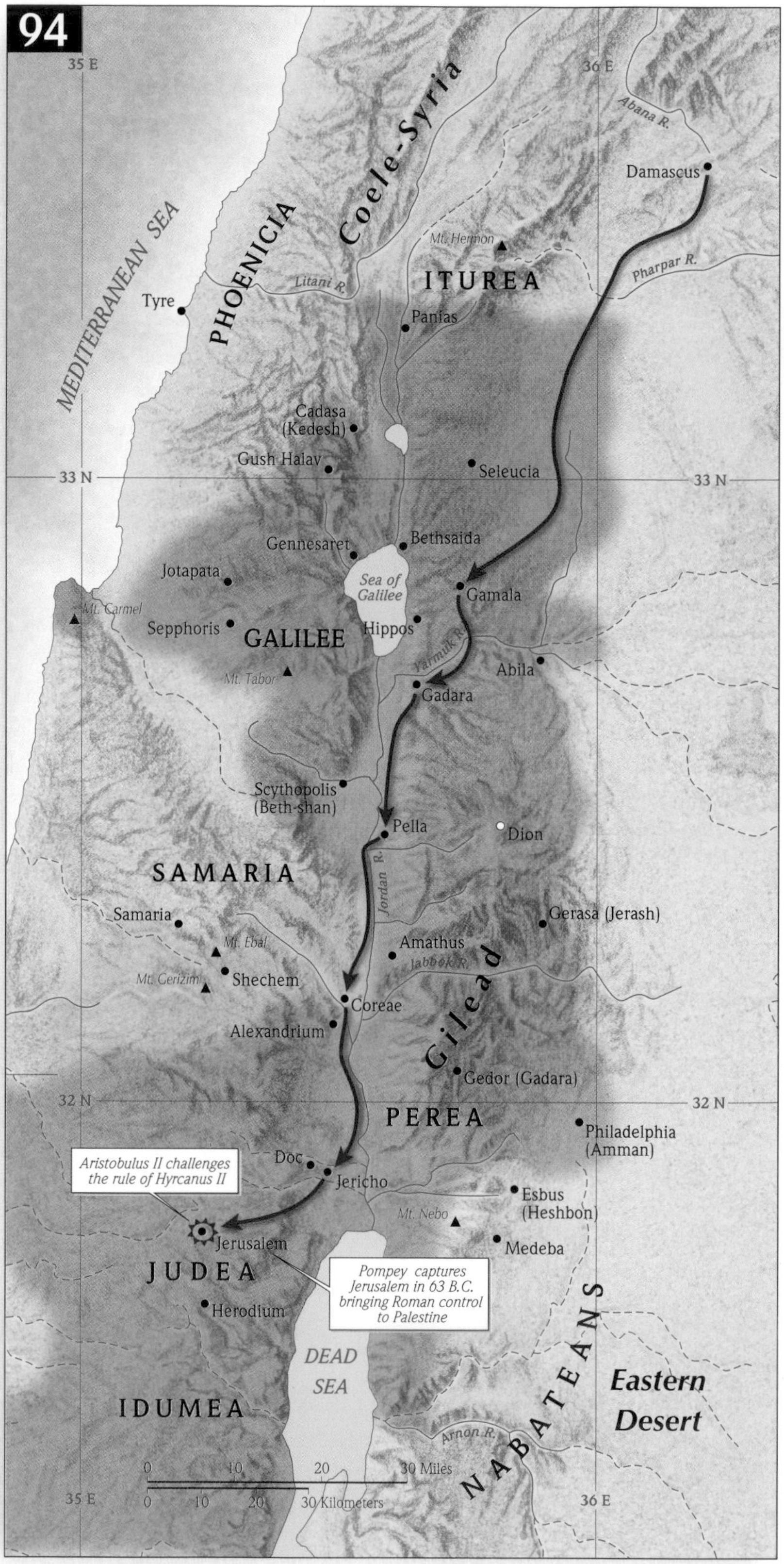

94
POMPEY'S CAMPAIGN AGAINST JERUSALEM AND THE RESULTING ROMAN SETTLEMENT 63 B.C.
City
City (uncertain location)
Mountain peak
Siege of Jerusalem
Pompey's campaign
The Romans break through the walls into Jerusalem
Aristobulus's route
Jewish state after Pompey's settlement
Jewish territories ceded to Iturea and Ptolemais
Samaritan state
Cities of the Decapolis
35 E
36 E
33 N
32 N
MEDITERRANEAN SEA
PHOENICIA
Coele-Syria
Abana R.
Damascus
Mt. Hermon
Pharpar R.
Litani R.
ITUREA
Tyre
Panias
Cadasa (Kedesh)
Gush Halav
Seleucia
Gennesaret
Bethsaida
Sea of Galilee
Jotapata
Gamala
Mt. Carmel
Sepphoris
GALILEE
Hippos
Yarmuk R.
Abila
Mt. Tabor
Gadara
Scythopolis (Beth-shan)
Pella
Dion
SAMARIA
Jordan R.
Samaria
Gerasa (Jerash)
Mt. Ebal
Amathus
Jabbok R.
Mt. Gerizim
Shechem
Coreae
Alexandrium
Gilead
Gedor (Gadara)
PEREA
Philadelphia (Amman)
Doc
Aristobulus II challenges the rule of Hyrcanus II
Jericho
Esbus (Heshbon)
Mt. Nebo
Jerusalem
Medeba
JUDEA
Pompey captures Jerusalem in 63 B.C. bringing Roman control to Palestine
Herodium
DEAD SEA
NABATEANS
Eastern Desert
IDUMEA
Arnon R.
0 10 20 30 Miles
0 10 20 30 Kilometers

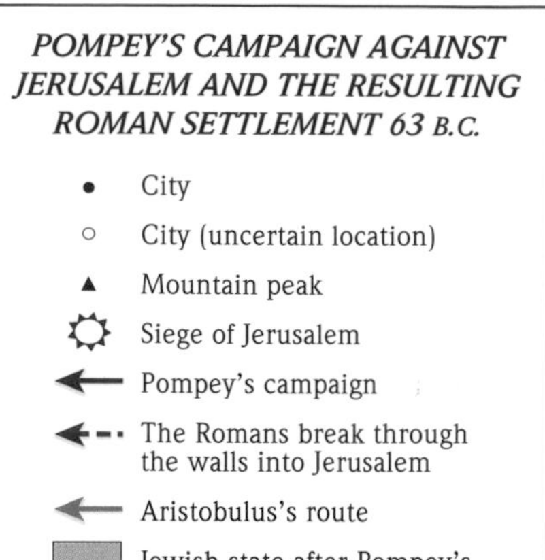

POMPEY'S SIEGE OF JERUSALEM
Spot elevation
2400 Contour interval = 33ft. (10m)
Pompey's Camp
Pool
Romans build a dike around temple fortifications
Hasmonean Baris
Tadi Gate
Northwestern Hill
Romans position ramp, catapults, and siege engines
Kiponus' Gate
Bridge
Temple
Shushan Gate
N
2480
Hasmonean Palace
2532
Southwestern Hill
Kidron Valley
2437
Hinnom Valley
Dung Gate
0 1/8 Mile
0 150 Meters

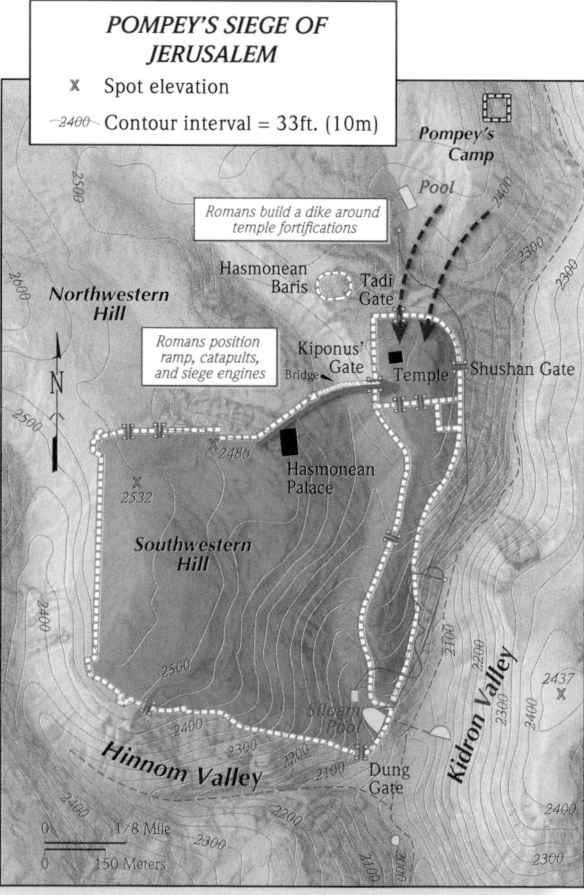

Part Three

THE NEW TESTAMENT ERA: THE WORLD OF JESUS AND THE EARLY CHURCH

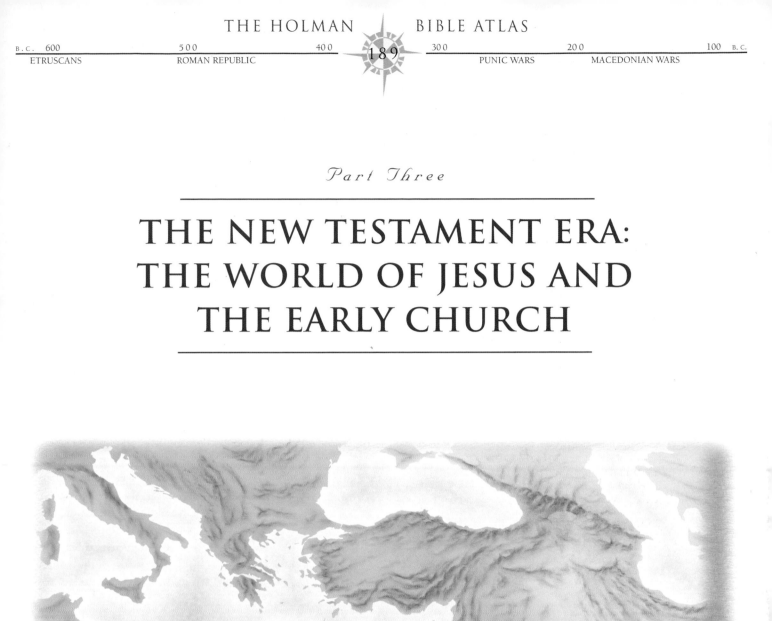

Chapter Fifteen

ROME'S EMERGENCE AS A WORLD POWER

Introduction

The gospel story begins "In those days a decree went out from Caesar Augustus" (Luke 2:1). These familiar words link the New Testament era with the most powerful state the ancient world ever produced. The Roman Empire provided the historical setting for all New Testament events and created the conditions necessary for the spread of the gospel. The Roman Peace (*Pax Romana*) established by Augustus ended centuries of bitter conflict and established safe borders within which Roman law governed. Travel and commerce flowed freely throughout the vast empire. In some sense, the political and cultural dominance of Rome over the Mediterranean basin was part of the "fulness of the time" (Gal. 4:4 KJV) God prepared for His supreme revelation through His Son.

Tombs in one of the numerous Etruscan cemeteries north of Rome.

Rise of Rome

The fascinating story of Rome's rise from a small cluster of villages to world power can only be sketched briefly here. Rome's early history is shrouded in legendary folk tales. According to late Roman tradition, Romulus founded Rome in 753 B.C. Greek and Roman historians developed the legend that Romulus came from a long line of kings descended from Aeneas, one of the Trojan War heroes. Recent evidence indicates Latin settlers inhabited the hills near a strategic island on the Tiber River shortly after 900 B.C. These rugged agriculturalists built rustic huts on the hills, often feuding with neighboring Italic and Latin tribes. Around 650 B.C. these early Romans came under the influence of the Etruscans, a more sophisticated people who lived in cities north of Rome. About 600 B.C. Etruscan kings ruled Rome. The Romans borrowed many ideas from the Etruscans, including architectural styles, writing, several religious ideas, and certain social customs. Etruscan influence changed Rome from a collection of rustic villages to an urban environment. Later, the Romans absorbed Greek ideas in the areas of literature, education, and philosophy. Part of the Roman genius was their ability to borrow ideas from other peoples and use them with a particularly Roman stamp.

The Republican Period

Tradition claimed that in 509 B.C. the Romans expelled the last of seven kings who had ruled from the time of Romulus. Henceforth, the Romans became deeply suspicious of kingship. In the newly founded Republic, two annually elected consuls governed the affairs of Rome with the advice of the Senate. A number of assemblies and civic officers assured the distribution of power. The political processes, however, were heavily weighted in favor of wealth and privilege. This created tensions that eventually flared into violence between the social classes of Roman citizens.

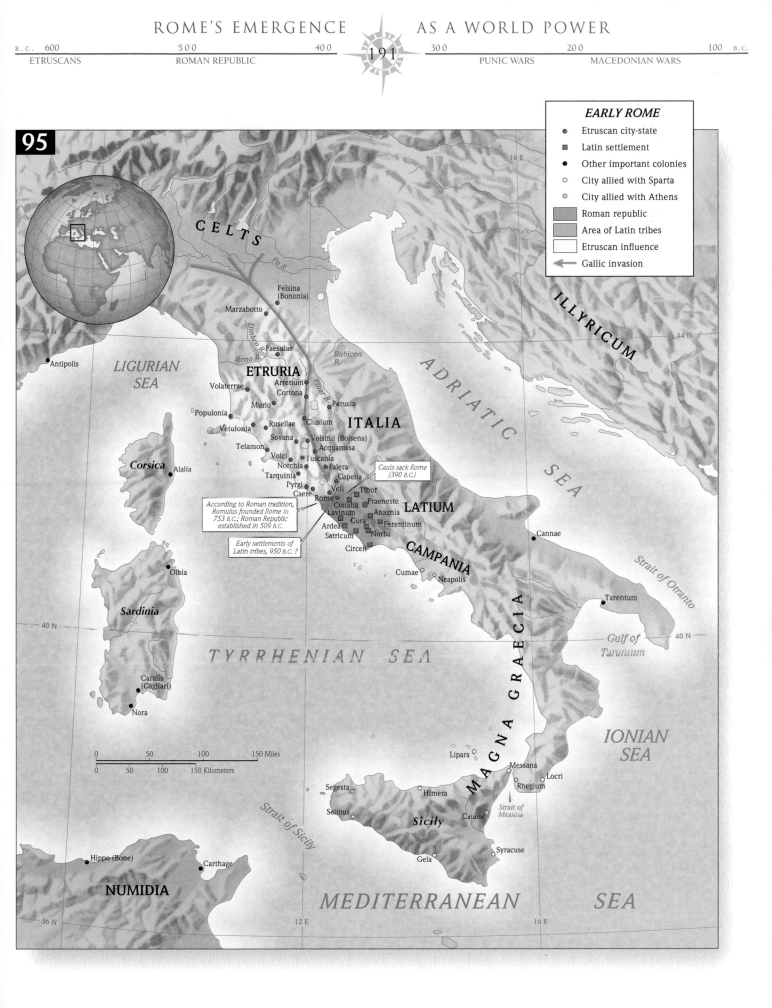

95
EARLY ROME
Etruscan city-state
Latin settlement
Other important colonies
City allied with Sparta
City allied with Athens
Roman republic
Area of Latin tribes
Etruscan influence
Gallic invasion
CELTS
Po R.
Felsina (Bononia)
Marzabotto
Umbro R.
Faesulae
Arno R.
Rubicon R.
Antipolis
LIGURIAN SEA
ETRURIA
Arretium
Cortona
Tiber R.
Volaterrae
Murlo
Perusia
Populonia
Vetulonia
Rusellae
Clusium
ITALIA
Sovana
Volsinii (Bolsena)
Telamon
Acquarossa
Volci
Tuscania
Norchia
Falera
Tarquinia
Capena
Pyrgi
Caere
Veii
Tibur
Rome
Collatia
Praeneste
Lavinum
Anagnia
Cora
Ferentinum
Ardea
Norba
Satricum
Circeii
LATIUM
Cauls sack Rome (390 B.C.)
According to Roman tradition, Romulus founded Rome in 753 B.C.; Roman Republic established in 509 B.C.
Early settlements of Latin tribes, 950 B.C. ?
Corsica
Alalia
Olbia
Sardinia
Caralis (Cagliari)
Nora
CAMPANIA
Cumae
Neapolis
Cannae
ADRIATIC SEA
ILLYRICUM
Strait of Otranto
Tarentum
Gulf of Tarentum
TYRRHENIAN SEA
MAGNA GRAECIA
IONIAN SEA
Lipara
Messana
Locri
Rhegium
Strait of Messina
Segesta
Himera
Selinus
Sicily
Catana
Syracuse
Gela
Strait of Sicily
Hippo (Bone)
Carthage
NUMIDIA
MEDITERRANEAN SEA
0 50 100 150 Miles
0 50 100 150 Kilometers
44 N
40 N
36 N
12 E
16 E

The Via Appia, the first of the great Roman roads built in 312 B.C.

defeated Carthage in the First Punic War (262–241 B.C.) and annexed Sicily, Sardinia, and Corsica.

During the Second Punic War (218–201 B.C.) the Carthaginian General Hannibal crossed the Alps and invaded Italy. Although Hannibal stayed in Italy fifteen years, he never conquered Rome. Scipio Africanus led a Roman invasion of Africa that forced Hannibal's retreat to Africa, where Scipio defeated him at Zama in 202 B.C. Carthage lost her military and economic power, while Rome acquired a navy and a taste for territorial expansion. Conquered territories produced taxes and tribute to fill the coffers of Rome.

ROME GAINS CONTROL OF THE ITALIAN PENINSULA

Rome secured control of the Italian peninsula through a lengthy series of bitter wars and shrewd treaties. The wars honed the skills of Roman soldiers and forged an indelible character upon the Roman people: tough, realistic, bound in deep loyalty to family and to Rome. When the Gauls sacked Rome in 390 B.C., Rome determined to control the Italian peninsula. In a series of wars (the Samnite Wars, the Latin Wars, and wars with other Italic tribes), Rome conquered and colonized Italy, suffering some defeats but winning more victories.

Military colonies placed at strategic points and connected by Roman roads linked the colonies with Rome. The *Via Appia* built in 312 B.C. was the first of the great highways that radiated outward, carrying Roman armies and culture.

THE WARS WITH CARTHAGE (THE PUNIC WARS)

Shortly after 300 B.C. Rome was the ruler of Italy. Conflicts with Carthage provoked Rome to expand beyond Italian shores. Founded as a Phoenician colony in 814 B.C., Carthage threatened Roman interest in Sicily. A minor incident escalated into a series of wars between Rome and Carthage known as the Punic Wars. Rome

CHART 18. THE RISE OF ROME

DATE (B.C.)	EVENTS
1000–900?	Early settlement of Latin tribes on hills near Tiber River crossing
753	Traditional date of the founding of Rome; seven kings of Rome; increasing influence and dominance of Etruscans over Rome
509	Expulsion of the Etruscan king Tarquin II (534–509 B.C.) and establishment of the Roman Republic
390	Sack of Rome by Gauls
312	Construction of the Via Appia, first of the great Roman roads
264–241	Roman colonization and conquest of Italian Peninsula (334–264 B.C.); First Punic War (Carthage); annexation of Sicily (241 B.C.), Sardinia (238 B.C.), and Corsica (238 B.C.)
218–202	Second Punic War; Hannibal's campaign in Italy; defeat of Carthage; Rome occupies Spain; First Macedonian War (214–205 B.C.)
200–197/6	Second Macedonian War; Philip V defeated; Rome invades Asia and defeats Antiochus III at Magnesia in 190 B.C.
171–168/7	Third Macedonian War; Macedonia divided up into four districts
150–148	Fourth Macedonian War; Macedonia annexed as a province
146	Rome destroys Corinth after a Greek uprising; Third Punic War (149–146 B.C.); Carthage destroyed; Rome annexes the province of Africa
133	Attalus III bequeaths the Attalid kingdom centered on Pergamum to Rome

GAUL

Rome's armies ranged westward into Spain and Gaul (France), where stiff opposition from local people resulted in a prolonged period of costly hostilities. One Roman general complained that in Spain "small armies are defeated, and large ones starve." Eventually, Spain became thoroughly Romanized, as the extensive Roman remains there still testify. Later, Julius Caesar won military glory pacifying Gaul.

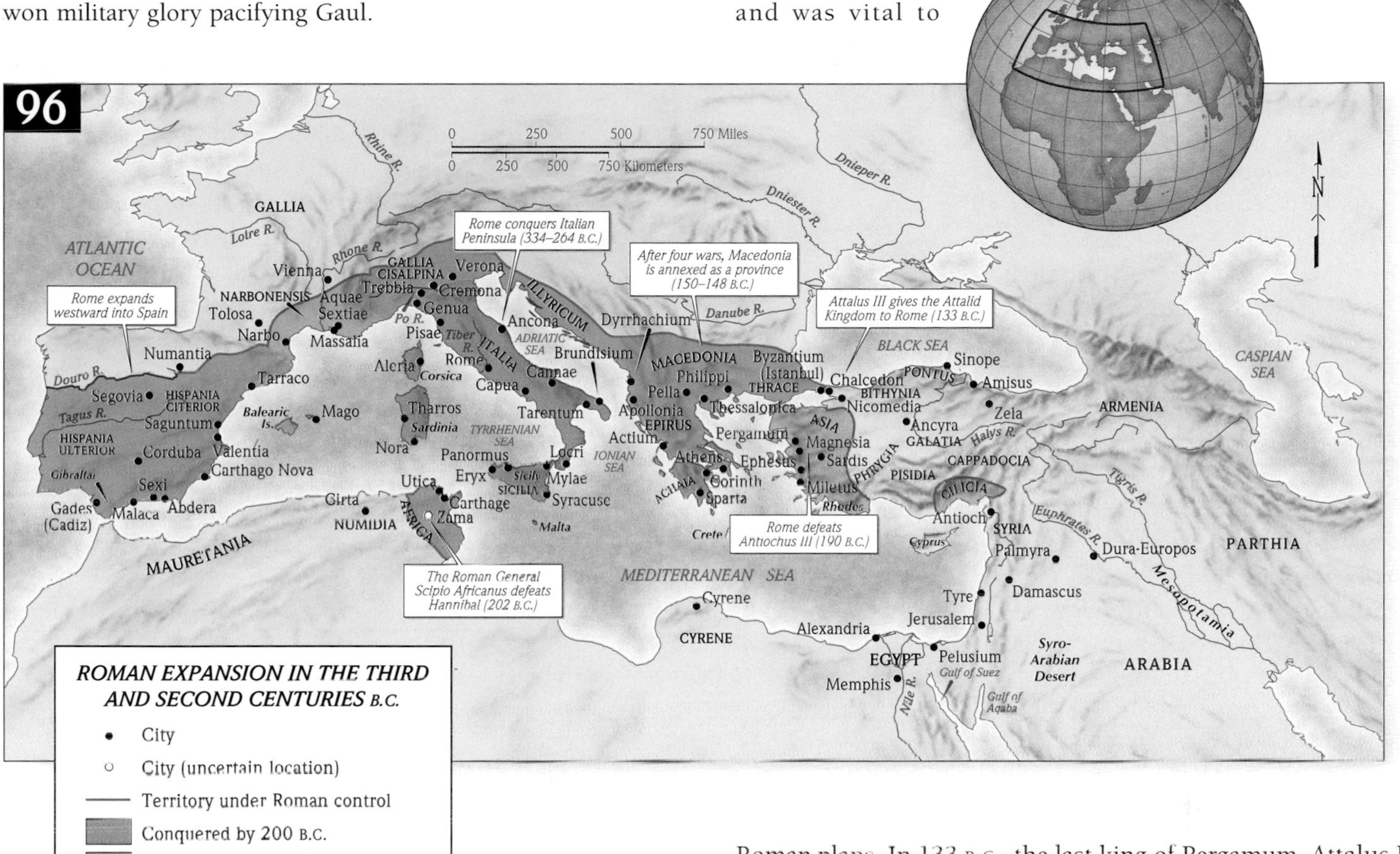

EASTWARD EXPANSION

Pacifying the East was a different matter. Roman expansion eastward encountered numerous well-entrenched powers. The Macedonian Wars (214–205, 200–196, 171–167, 150–148 B.C.) were especially difficult. In 197 B.C. Rome defeated Philip V of Macedon, and the Romans assumed the role of protector of the Greek city-states. Further resistance resulted in the partition of Macedonia into four republics (168 B.C.) and the annexation of Macedonia as a Roman province (148 B.C.). In 146 B.C. Rome destroyed Corinth to punish the Achaean League of Greek city-states for resisting Roman advances.

Roman armies advanced into Asia Minor in response to threats posed by Antiochus III. The Seleucid ruler invaded Greece in 193 B.C. The Romans reacted by driving Antiochus out of Greece into Asia Minor, where they delivered a crushing defeat to Antiochus in 190 B.C. at Magnesia (see p. 182). Rome then supported kings in Asia Minor who were sympathetic to her own interest. The Kingdom of Pergamum, ruled by a dynasty known as the Attalids, controlled western Asia Minor and was vital to Roman plans. In 133 B.C., the last king of Pergamum, Attalus III, after decades of Roman pressure, willed his kingdom to Rome. Only the remnants of the Seleucid Empire in Syria, a handful of kingdoms in eastern Asia Minor, and the waning Ptolemaic kingdom of Egypt stood in Rome's way. However, a new menace caused Rome great concern—the powerful Parthian Kingdom entrenched in Mesopotamia.

ROMAN CIVIL WARS AND THE RISE OF AUGUSTUS

The period between 133 B.C. and 27 B.C. was perhaps the most turbulent in Roman history. Deep social tensions divided the Roman people. Continual warfare exacted a terrible toll on the peasant-farmer, the backbone of the Roman army. Many died in war, while others lost their land to wealthy landowners who bought up property made available by the ravages of war. Large estates called *latifundia* worked by slave labor replaced the small farmer. Landless citizens flocked to Rome, creating a climate ripe for social revolution. Wealthy, landed aristocrats in the Senate protected their rights and privileges against any inroads gained by the lower classes.

The Gracchi Reforms. Tiberius and Gaius Gracchus developed a plan to redistribute public land among the dispossessed peasant-farmers by limiting the size of public land available to wealthy landowners. By redistributing the land, the Gracchi brothers hoped to ensure a supply of Roman recruits for the army (landholding qualified a person for military service) and to lessen the internal security threat of a massive slave population. When the wealthy aristocrats of the Senate resisted, Tiberius and Gaius paid for their efforts with their lives.

The conservative, aristocratic leaders of the Roman Senate, however, proved ineffective in the face of new threats from the Numidian king Jugurtha and pressure from uncivilized tribes along several borders. Powerful "new men" (i.e., men unconnected with Rome's aristocratic families) raised professional armies loyal to themselves. One of these, Marius, defeated Jugurtha and threatened the power of the Senate. Another military leader, Sulla, used his army to restore the traditional aristocratic senatorial faction to power, but the deep divisions between factions and social classes remained.

Julius Caesar.

Other crises emerged. In 88 B.C. Mithradates of Pontus led a bloody revolt in Asia Minor in which thousands of Roman citizens were slaughtered. Cilician- and Cretan-based pirates disrupted shipping lanes and raided coastal areas. Large-scale slave revolts, like the one led by Spartacus (73–71 B.C.), threatened Italy. Although Rome continued to annex provinces (Bithynia and Cyrene in 74 B.C.), the old political structures were breaking apart.

Julius Caesar. In those troubled years, several key leaders emerged. Pompey gained fame by suppressing revolt in Spain, clearing the Mediterranean of pirates, assisting in quelling the slave revolts, and defeating Mithradates. He conquered Syria in 64 B.C. and a year later annexed Palestine to the province of Syria. Crassus led Roman legions against Spartacus in 71 B.C. The populist Julius Caesar won his reputation in command of the Gallic Wars (58–51 B.C.). In

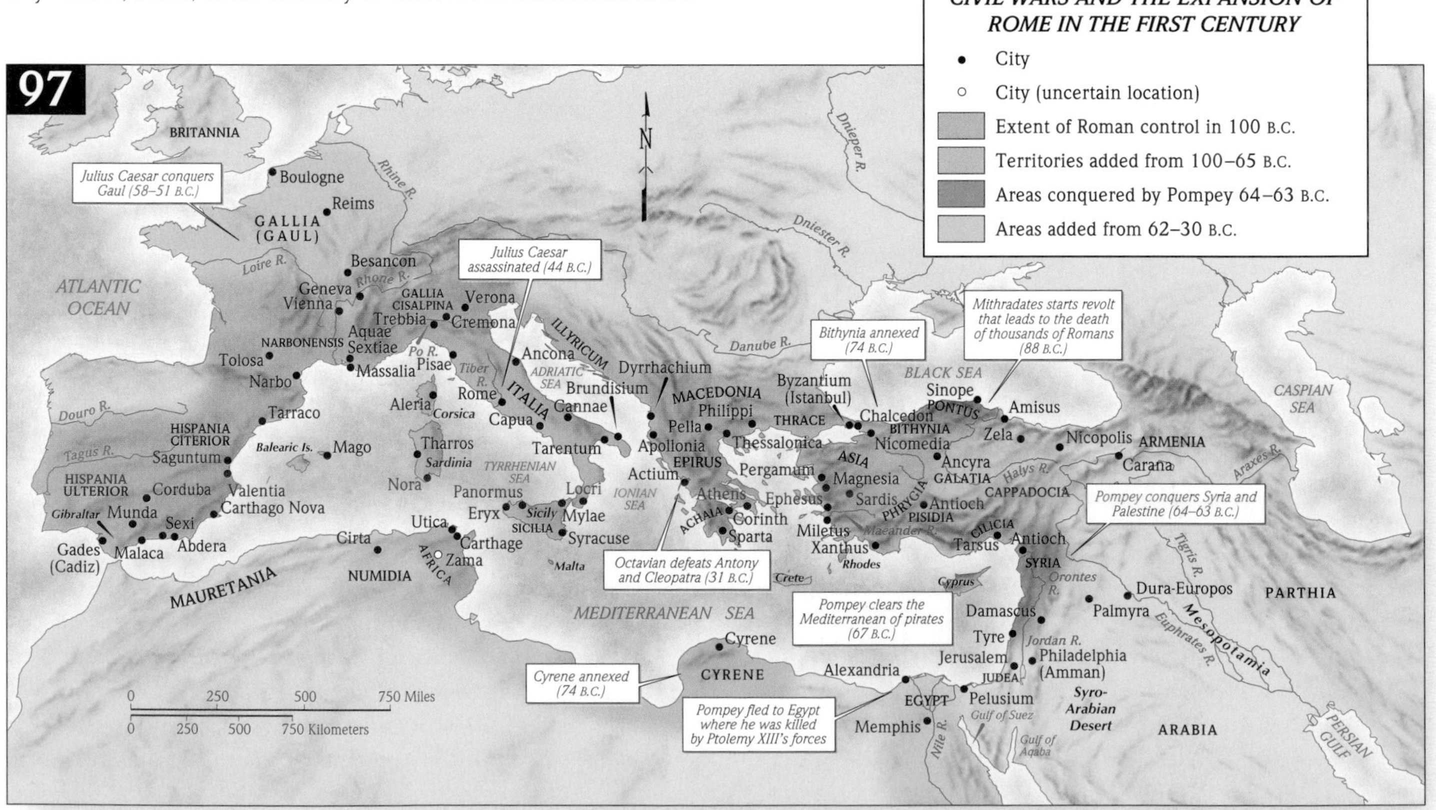

CHART 19. EVENTS AND PERSONALITIES OF ROME: 133–27 B.C.

DATES (B.C.)	EVENTS
133–122	Land reforms proposed by Gaius and Tiberias Gracchus; increasing social tensions
112–105	First war with Jugurtha, king of Numidia; Marius and his professional army threaten the power of the Roman Senate
88–84	Wars against Mithradates, king of Pontus; Sulla sent to deal with Mithradates
74	Annexation of the provinces of Bithynia and Cyrene
73–71	Slave revolt of Spartacus
66–63	Pompey conquers Syria (64 B.C.) and Palestine (63 B.C.) as part of the "Eastern Settlement"
60	First Triumvirate—60–53 B.C. (Julius Caesar, Pompey, and Crassus)
58–51	Julius Caesar conquers Gaul
49–45	Civil war between Pompey and Caesar
48	Death of Pompey
46	Julius Caesar declared dictator of Rome
44	Julius Caesar murdered by conservative elements of the Senate on March 15, 44 B.C.
42	Battle of Philippi; Mark Antony and Octavian, grandnephew of Julius Caesar, defeat Caesar's assassins
42–31	Years of conflict between Octavian and Antony for ultimate power; Octavian, with command of Italy and the West, struggled with Antony and his consort Cleopatra, with their power base in the East, for control of Rome
31	Octavian defeats Antony and Cleopatra at Actium on the coast of Greece
27	Octavian given the honorific title of "Augustus"; the beginning of the Roman Imperial Period

60 B.C. these three formed the First Triumvirate, a loose coalition of shared power. Crassus died fighting the Parthians in 53 B.C., ending the arrangement and setting up a struggle for power between Pompey and Caesar.

The Senate feared Caesar's growing popularity and power, with good reason. Caesar defeated his chief rival Pompey in 48 B.C. When Pompey fled to Egypt, Caesar pursued him to Alexandria, where Ptolemy XIII's forces killed the great Roman general. Soon Caesar arrived at Alexandria, only to fall under the spell of Ptolemy's sister Cleopatra VII, who coveted the throne of her brother. In the winter of 48/47 B.C. Caesar withstood a siege by Ptolemy's army, receiving along the way help from Antipater, the Idumean strongman who effectively ruled Judea at the time (see p. 187). Caesar remembered this act of loyalty and later rewarded the Jewish people with certain rights and privileges.

Gold coin of the young Octavian, best known to New Testament students as Caesar Augustus.

Caesar returned to Rome in 46 B.C. and was declared dictator by the Senate, a position he took for life in 44 B.C. Acting as a virtual king, Caesar appointed magistrates without consulting the Senate. These acts outraged conservative elements of the Senate, who plotted the death of the popular dictator. On the Ides of March (March 15) in 44 B.C., radical conservatives led by Brutus and Cassius assassinated Caesar.

Antony and Octavian: The Final Struggle for Power. Caesar's death brought crisis and a power struggle to Rome. Mark Antony assumed control at Rome only to learn that Caesar's will named his young grandnephew Octavian as his heir. Antony and Octavian forged an uneasy alliance against Caesar's assassins, defeating them on the Plains of Philippi in 42 B.C. After the battle, Octavian received command of Italy and the western provinces, while Antony took command of the East where the main concern was the Parthian threat. Antony eventually fell under the spell of Cleopatra in Alexandria. Conflict was inevitable as Octavian portrayed Antony as a dupe of an oriental queen. In 31 B.C., Octavian defeated Antony in the Battle of Actium on the west coast of Greece. Subsequently both Antony and Cleopatra returned to Alexandria and committed suicide. Henceforth, Octavian would determine the future of Rome.

The Age of Augustus: Foundation of an Empire (27 B.C.–A.D. 14)

Octavian's victory over Antony at the Battle of Actium gave him undisputed supremacy in Rome. However, unlike his uncle Julius Caesar, Octavian wisely allowed the Roman people to grant him the power and privileges he craved. The Senate named Octavian *Princeps Senatus* ("first in the Senate") and bestowed upon him the honorific title "Augustus" in 27 B.C. Gradually, Augustus obtained by senatorial confirmation the primary offices and powers of Rome. He commanded the legions through his *imperium* (executive power) and, in 23 B.C., was granted the greatest executive power *(maius imperium proconsulare)* giving Augustus ultimate authority over all provincial officials.

As *princeps*, Augustus determined the order of business in the Senate; his tribunician powers allowed him to approach the Roman people directly about any matter. Augustus' authority could not be exceeded, although he wisely cloaked his power in the guise of

cooperating with the Senate. Ostensibly, Augustus reformed the republic, but historians recognize his reign as the dawn of a new era—the Period of Imperial Rome.

ORGANIZATION OF AN EMPIRE

Augustus reduced the legions of Rome to twenty-six (about 150,000 men) and stationed them along strategic borders or in troublesome provinces. The empire was divided into two types of provinces: imperial and senatorial. Imperial provinces most often were sources of potential trouble or of strategic importance to the empire. Augustus controlled imperial provinces by direct appointment.

Augustus appointed a legate *(legatus)* to govern imperial provinces such as Syria where many of the legions were stationed. Legates came from the senatorial class. Prefects and procurators drawn from the equestrian ranks (nonsenatorial men of some means) oversaw the imperial interests in smaller, more troublesome regions, such as Judea. Proconsuls selected from former consuls and praetors of the Roman Senate governed senatorial provinces by the power of the Senate *(imperium)*. However, the Senate granted Augustus a greater power *(maius imperium proconsulare)*, giving the emperor the power to intervene at any time. Asia, Cyprus, and Achaea all were senatorial provinces. Augustus added many provinces to Rome during his reign (Galatia, Gallia, Narbonensis, Belgica, Baetica, and others in Spain and Gaul).

THE AUGUSTAN PEACE

The Augustan peace or *Pax Romana* established by Octavian ended the civil wars and brought security and economic prosperity to the Mediterranean basin. The reign of Augustus marked the beginning of a new era, celebrated in glowing terms in literature of the day. Augustus was hailed as a savior in the East, although he wisely encouraged divine honors only as they honored Rome. He encouraged the practice of traditional Roman religion by restoring numerous temples; he also sponsored social reforms that emphasized traditional Roman values (loyalty to family and state). In Rome, Augustus built or rebuilt numerous public buildings, boasting, "I found Rome built of sun-dried bricks; I leave her clothed in marble."

Although the powers Augustus possessed were not hereditary, the emperor tried to assure his successor. He turned first to his son-in-law Agrippa and, later, to two sons born to

Agrippa and his wife Julia. Unfortunately, all three died before Augustus. Augustus then adopted Tiberius, his stepson by his wife Livia, as his successor. The Senate conferred upon Tiberius the same powers given to Augustus, making Tiberius a virtual coregent. When Augustus died on August 19, A.D. 14., Tiberius became emperor of Rome.

CHART 20. THE EMPERORS OF ROME

NAME	DYNASTY	DATES	SIGNIFICANT NEW TESTAMENT EVENTS
Caesar Augustus (Octavian)	Julio-Claudian	27 B.C.–A.D. 14	Birth of Jesus; death of Herod the Great and division of his kingdom; first procuratorship established in A.D. 6
Tiberius	Julio-Claudian	A.D. 14–37	Public ministry of Jesus; Day of Pentecost; Paul's conversion
Gaius (Caligula)	Julio-Claudian	A.D. 37–41	Kingdom of Herod Agrippa I
Claudius	Julio-Claudian	A.D. 41–54	Agrippa I, king of all Palestine, A.D. 41–44; martyrdom of James; famine in Judea; Paul's First Missionary Journey (A.D. 46–48); the Jerusalem Conference (A.D. 49); Claudius issued an edict expelling the Jews from Rome (see Acts 18:1); Paul's Second Missionary Journey (A.D. 50–52); Zealot disturbances
Nero	Julio-Claudian	A.D. 54–68	Paul's Third Missionary Journey (ca. A.D. 53–57); increasing Zealot pressure; Paul imprisoned at Caesarea (A.D. 57–59); Paul's voyage to Rome and imprisonment (A.D. 60–62) likely setting for writing prison letters (Ephesians, Colossians, Philemon, Philippians); great fire in Rome, A.D. 64; brief, but intense, persecution of Christians in Rome; outbreak of Jewish Revolt, A.D. 66; Paul's second Roman imprisonment?, A.D. 66–67; martyrdom of Paul and Peter, A.D. 65 or 67?; Rome conquers Galilee; suicide of Nero in June, A.D. 68
"The Year of the Four Emperors": Galba, Otho, Vitellius, Vespasian		A.D. 68–69	The uncertainty about Nero's successor temporarily interrupted Rome's suppression of the Jewish Revolt
Vespasian	Flavian	A.D. 69–79	Jerusalem besieged and destroyed by Titus, April-August A.D. 70, Masada falls, A.D. 73 or 74
Titus	Flavian	A.D. 79–81	Rome again burns, A.D. 80; dedication of the Flavian Amphitheater (the Colosseum); Arch of Titus dedicated, A.D. 81
Domitian	Flavian	A.D. 81–96	Dacian Wars, A.D. 86–87, 89, 92; persecutions against leading philosophers and Roman senators, A.D. 93–94; persecution of Christians, about A.D. 95; Domitian assassinated, A.D. 96; John's Revelation
Nerva		A.D. 96–98	
Trajan		A.D. 98–117	Annexation of Nabatean kingdom, A.D. 106; persecution of Christians in Bithynia-Pontus, A.D. 113, and Syria, A.D. 114; Parthian Wars and conquests in the East, A.D. 114–117; Second Jewish Revolt in Cyrene, Egypt, and Mesopotamia, A.D. 115–117
Hadrian		A.D. 117–138	Bar Kokhbah Rebellion in Palestine, A.D. 132–135; Jerusalem rebuilt as a Roman colony, Aelia Capitolina; continuation of intermittent persecution of Christians in the province

Chapter Sixteen

THE ROMANS, PALESTINE, AND HEROD THE GREAT

Roman Intervention in Palestine 63–40 B.C.

After eighty years of Jewish independence under the Hasmonean Dynasty, Palestine came under Roman rule in 63 B.C. The Roman general Pompey annexed Syria in 64 B.C. and a year later conquered Palestine, ending a civil war between Aristobulus II and Hyrcanus II (see chap. 14, p. 188). Both moves were part of the "Eastern Settlement" designed to create a buffer of Roman client-states as a defense against the increasing Parthian threat in Mesopotamia. Palestine became a frontier state strategically important to Roman interest, but of little consequence economically.

POMPEY AND THE CONQUEST OF JERUSALEM

Pompey intervened in the Jewish civil war on the side of Hyrcanus II. Hyrcanus had the support of the Idumean governor Antipater, who proved to be doggedly loyal to Rome. When Aristobulus and his supporters objected, Pompey sent Scaurus, legate of Syria, to Palestine. But Aristobulus defeated Scaurus near the Jordan River and retreated. Pompey marched from Damascus with his army, crossed over the Jordan near Scythopolis, and advanced upon Jerusalem by way of Jericho. Upon arrival at Jerusalem, supporters of Hyrcanus surrendered the city to Pompey, but Aristobulus' supporters retreated to the Temple Mount and resisted. Pompey besieged the Temple Mount using siege dikes and ramps. After three months, the temple area fell into Roman hands. Pompey did no damage to the temple, but offended the Jews by entering the Holy of Holies.

ROMAN ADMINISTRATION OF PALESTINE

Pompey appointed Hyrcanus II high priest of the Jews, but Antipater was the unofficial ruler trusted by Rome. Pompey removed several Greek cites from Jewish control (Gaza, Azotus, Dora, Strato's Tower, and other coastal cities) and granted autonomy to several cities east of the Jordan, including Hippos, Dium, Abila, Gadara, Pella, and probably Gerasa. These cities were part of the Decapolis, a league of Hellenistic cities Rome placed under the authority of the governors of Syria. The number and names of the

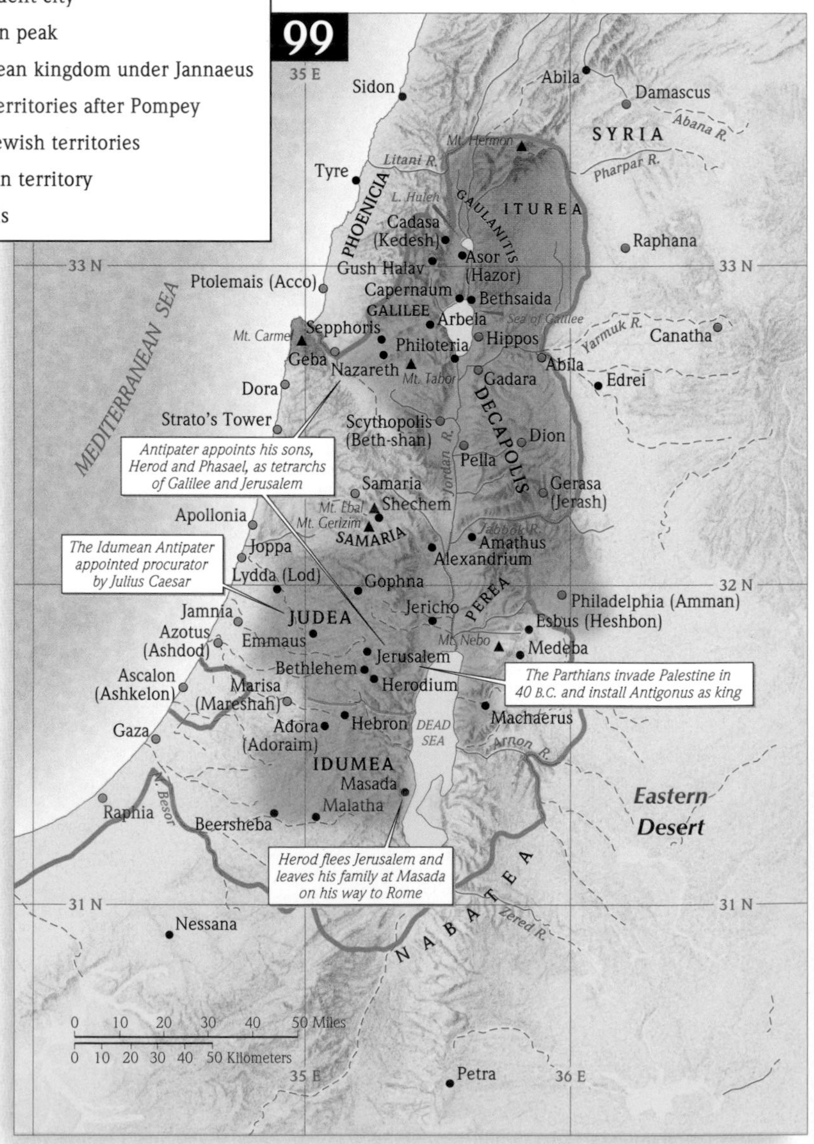

cities of the Decapolis varies in ancient sources. Only Scythopolis was located west of the Jordan. Pompey ceded the territory east of the Sea of Galilee to the Itureans, an Arab people. Samaria also was detached from Jewish control.

Hyrcanus II and Antipater faced several rebellions led by Aristobulus II and his two sons, Antigonus and Alexander. Antipater and the Romans ensured none succeeded, although thousands of Jews perished in the fighting. The fortunes of Hyrcanus and Antipater rose dramatically when the two gave military aid to Julius Caesar who was trapped in Alexandria by Ptolemaic forces. Caesar rewarded Antipater by granting him Roman citizenship and the title of "Procurator." Hyrcanus became an ethnarch, a position higher than Procurator, although Antipater clearly was in charge.

Antipater promptly installed his two sons Phasael and Herod as governors over Jerusalem and Galilee respectively. Phasael's tenure as governor of Jerusalem was uneventful. Herod, however, quickly earned a reputation for brutal conduct by suppressing a Jewish revolt in Galilee led by Hezekiah. After Antipater's assassination in 43 B.C., Mark Antony appointed Phasael and Herod tetrarchs. Jewish nationalists chafed under the rule of these two Idumean upstarts whose authority clearly exceeded that of Hyrcanus II.

THE PARTHIAN INVASION

In 40 B.C. the Parthians invaded the eastern Roman provinces, including Syria and Palestine. Antigonus, son of Aristobulus II, made a pact with the Parthians who installed him as high priest and king of the Jews. During the invasion, Phasael was taken prisoner near Ptolemais and committed suicide. Herod, besieged in Jerusalem, escaped with his family to Masada, where he left them and continued to Rome. With the support of Mark Antony and Octavian, Herod pled his case before the Roman Senate. The Senate confirmed Herod as king of the Jews and gave him the old territories of Hyrcanus—Judea, Galilee, and eastern Idumea—and added Samaria and western Idumea.

Herod the Great: Client-King of Rome

The Romanization of Palestine began in earnest during the reign of Herod the Great. Herod was Rome's choice to handle affairs in Palestine. He won the favor of successive Roman rulers by his unfailing loyalty to the interests of Rome. In return, Rome granted Herod a large territory that he ruled effectively. Rome allowed her client-kings broad powers within their territories, but placed firm restrictions upon them in matters of foreign policy and waging war.

HEROD'S STRUGGLE FOR HIS KINGDOM

With Roman support, Herod returned to Palestine to claim his kingdom. Roman armies dispatched the Parthians while Herod battled the supporters of Antigonus. Jerusalem surrendered in 37 B.C. At Herod's insistence, Antigonus and many of his Sadducean supporters were executed at Antioch. With the death of Antigonus, Herod finally possessed a kingdom that included Judea, Samaria, Idumea, Galilee, and Perea.

CONSOLIDATION OF POWER

Facing a precarious position during his first ten years, Herod ruthlessly consolidated his power. Herod was an Idumean, an Edomite half-caste; in Jewish eyes he was unfit to rule. As a client-king of Rome, Herod symbolized foreign domination to the Jews, especially supporters of the Hasmonean Dynasty. In an effort to win Jewish support, Herod divorced his Idumean wife, Doris, and married a Hasmonean princess, Mariamne. The strategy failed due in large measure to Herod's mother-in-law, Alexandra. While insisting that Herod appoint her young son, Aristobulus III, high priest, Alexandra plotted against Herod. She solicited the support of Cleopatra of Egypt and generally sowed distrust and sedition. Herod responded to these threats by ordering the murder of his chief rivals: Aristobulus (he mysteriously "drowned" at Jericho) and the aging Hyrcanus II. Mariamne and Alexandra eventually died by Herod's orders also.

The Ptolemaic queen, Cleopatra, was a serious threat to Herod's power. Cleopatra was Mark Antony's consort; together they ruled the East. Antony gave Cleopatra the valuable oasis of Jericho, some key coastal cities, and other territories east of the Jordan. Herod feared Cleopatra, but he remained loyal so long as Antony remained in power. Herod's crisis came when Octavian defeated Antony at Actium in 31 B.C. Cleopatra and Antony committed suicide shortly thereafter. Summoned to Rhodes by Octavian, Herod convinced the victor of Actium (and soon-to-be emperor) of his loyalty to Rome. Octavian rewarded Herod by confirming him as king, restoring in the process the lands taken by Cleopatra. In 23 B.C., Octavian, now known as Augustus, added Trachonitis, Batanea, and Auranitis to Herod's kingdom. Gaulanitis, Panias, and Ulatha were added in 20 B.C.

HEROD'S BUILDING PROGRAM

Herod ranks as one of the greatest builders in the ancient world, second only to Tiberius. He embarked on a grand building program during the middle years of his reign. As a Roman client-king, Herod was expected to act as a benefactor within his own kingdom and beyond. Several projects honored his patron, Augustus. Samaria was rebuilt and renamed Sebaste, the Greek equivalent of Augustus. A massive temple dedicated

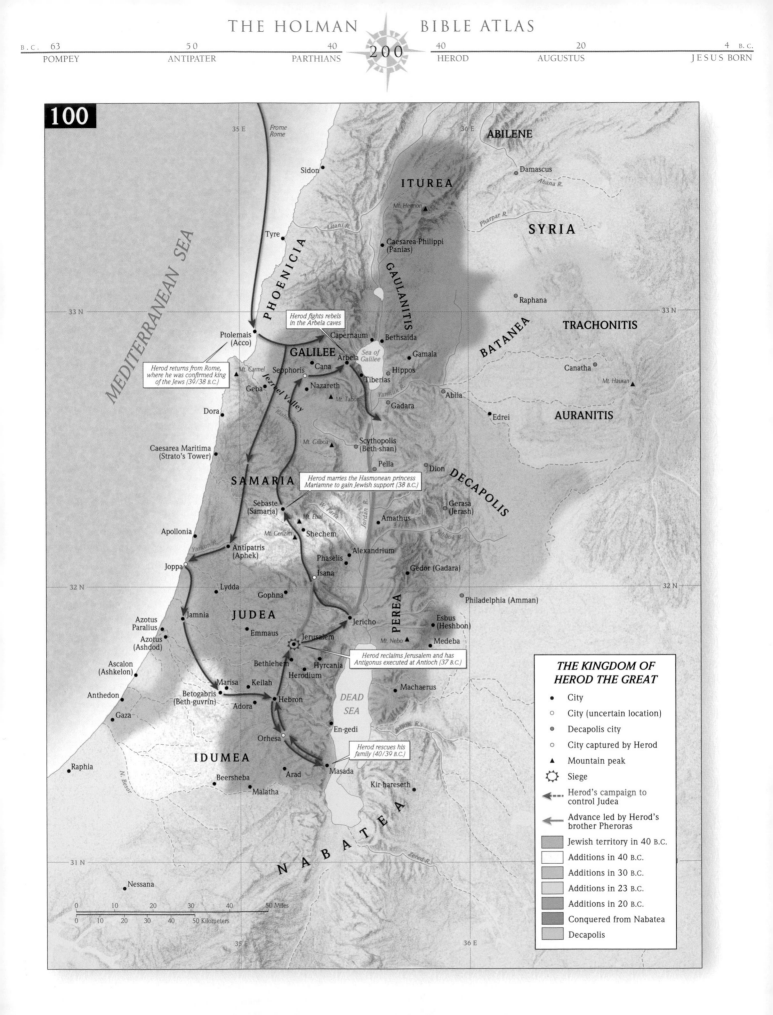

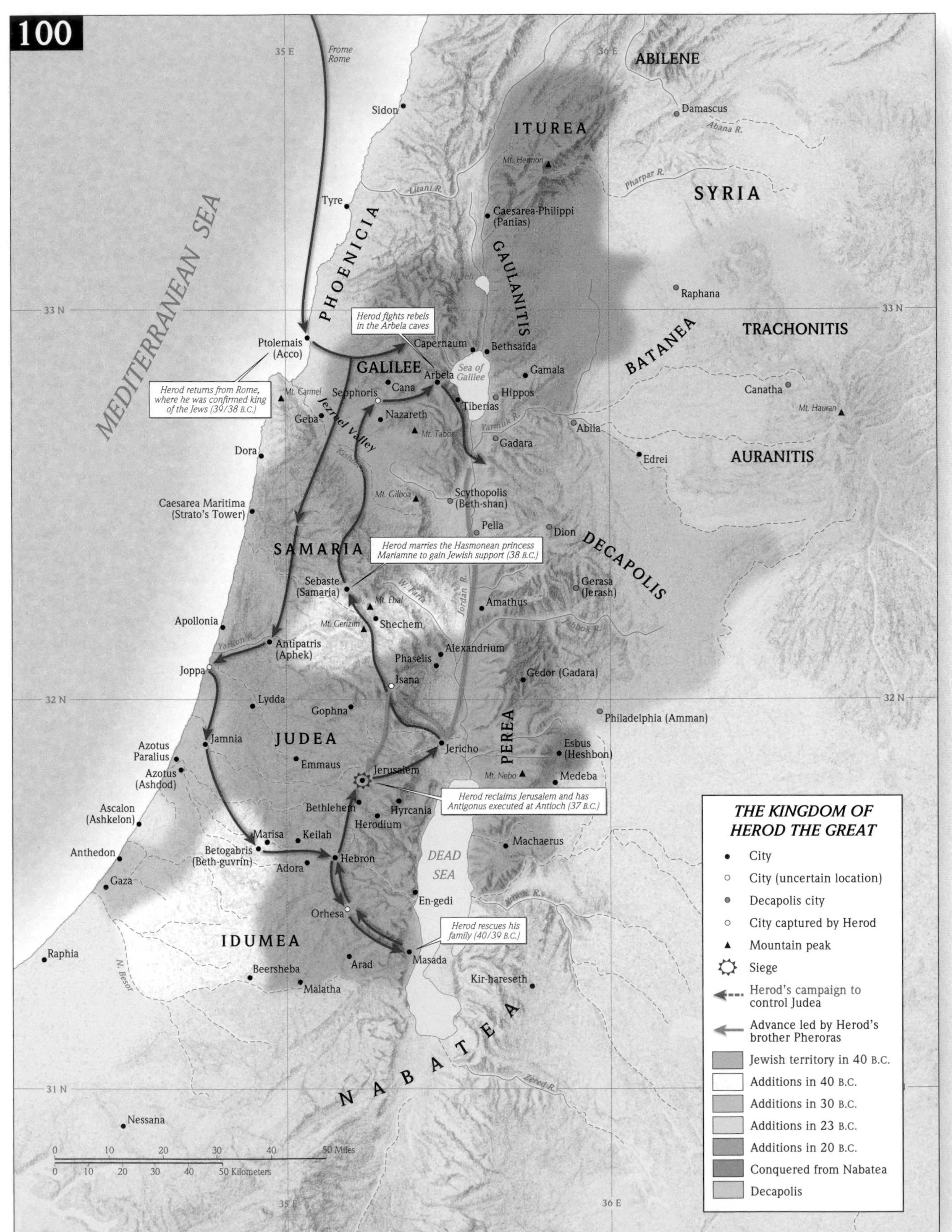
100
THE KINGDOM OF HEROD THE GREAT
City
City (uncertain location)
Decapolis city
City captured by Herod
Mountain peak
Siege
Herod's campaign to control Judea
Advance led by Herod's brother Pheroras
Jewish territory in 40 B.C.
Additions in 40 B.C.
Additions in 30 B.C.
Additions in 23 B.C.
Additions in 20 B.C.
Conquered from Nabatea
Decapolis
Herod fights rebels in the Arbela caves
Herod returns from Rome, where he was confirmed king of the Jews (39/38 B.C.)
Herod marries the Hasmonean princess Mariamne to gain Jewish support (38 B.C.)
Herod reclaims Jerusalem and has Antigonus executed at Antioch (37 B.C.)
Herod rescues his family (40/39 B.C.)
From Rome
MEDITERRANEAN SEA
PHOENICIA
GALILEE
SAMARIA
JUDEA
IDUMEA
NABATEA
PEREA
DECAPOLIS
GAULANITIS
ITUREA
ABILENE
SYRIA
BATANEA
TRACHONITIS
AURANITIS
Sidon
Tyre
Damascus
Abana R.
Pharpar R.
Litani R.
Mt. Hermon
Caesarea-Philippi (Panias)
Raphana
Ptolemais (Acco)
Capernaum
Bethsaida
Sea of Galilee
Arbela
Gamala
Cana
Sepphoris
Tiberias
Hippos
Nazareth
Mt. Carmel
Geba
Jezreel Valley
Mt. Tabor
Yarmuk R.
Abila
Gadara
Canatha
Mt. Hauran
Edrei
Dora
Mt. Gilboa
Scythopolis (Beth-shan)
Caesarea Maritima (Strato's Tower)
Pella
Dion
Sebaste (Samaria)
Mt. Ebal
Mt. Gerizim
Shechem
W. Farah
Jordan R.
Gerasa (Jerash)
Amathus
Jabbok R.
Apollonia
Yarkon R.
Antipatris (Aphek)
Joppa
Alexandrium
Phaselis
Isana
Gedor (Gadara)
Lydda
Gophna
Philadelphia (Amman)
Azotus Paralius
Jamnia
Azotus (Ashdod)
Emmaus
Jericho
Esbus (Heshbon)
Jerusalem
Mt. Nebo
Medeba
Ascalon (Ashkelon)
Bethlehem
Hyrcania
Herodium
Machaerus
Marisa
Keilah
Anthedon
Betogabris (Beth-guvrin)
Adora
Hebron
DEAD SEA
Gaza
En-gedi
Orhesa
Raphia
Arad
Masada
Beersheba
Malatha
N. Besor
Kir-hareseth
Zered R.
Nessana
33 N
32 N
31 N
35 E
36 E
0 10 20 30 40 50 Miles
0 10 20 30 40 50 Kilometers

to the emperor reflected the new city's pagan character. Herod's most ambitious project outside of Jerusalem was a new port at Caesarea Maritima (see below). Herod's engineers created a large protected harbor by utilizing quarried stone and hydraulic cement to build a massive mole. Caesarea became Herod's "window to the world," a cosmopolitan city that linked Palestine commercially and culturally to the Roman Empire.

HEROD'S BUILDING PROJECTS IN JERUSALEM

Herod transformed Jerusalem during his reign. He built a new palace on the western side of the city protected by three towers on the north named after friends and relatives: Mariamne, Hippicus, and Phasael. His architects constructed the Antonia fortress with its four distinctive towers on the north side of the temple complex. According to Josephus, Herod added a theater, hippodrome, and stadium to the city, but their locations have not been confirmed by archaeology. Herod increased Jerusalem's water supply by erecting aqueducts that brought water from the Bethlehem region into Jerusalem. Herod's crowning achievement was the building of a new temple to replace the unimpressive structure dedicated by Zerubbabel in 515 B.C. Begun in 19 B.C., the project was not completed until A.D. 64. The size of the temple complex was doubled by massive earthfills and retaining walls. The temple building was expanded, its marble facade overlaid with gold trim. Herod accomplished the task with scrupulous attention to Jewish law, including the use of priests trained as stonemasons (see further "Jerusalem in the Days of Herod and Jesus" pp. 228–33).

Herod's building program brought economic prosperity to Palestine by creating jobs and a demand for materials. However, taxation increased to support these grand schemes that transformed the face of Herod's kingdom. Social and political tensions smoldered and, occasionally, flared. Herod won some favor with his generosity. Following natural disasters (famine and earthquake), Herod supported relief efforts out of his own treasury, but the Jewish people generally despised their master. Herod also built monuments and buildings outside of Palestine (e.g., Athens, Damascus, Antioch, Rhodes, and Berytus) and sponsored lavish games as expected of a Roman client-king.

HEROD'S FINAL YEARS

Bitterness and increasing fears of those he believed coveted his throne plagued Herod in his final years. He turned on his nation and family, exacting vengeance on conspirators both real and imagined. Herod grew suspicious of his sons and changed his will several times in his last years. Prompted by his sister Salome, in 7 B.C. Herod executed two sons born to him by Mariamne—Alexander and Aristobulus—for treason. A third son, Antipater, the son of Doris, died in 4 B.C. by Herod's orders only five days before the king's death. The tragic murder of the Bethlehem babies recorded only in the New Testament (Matt. 2:16–23) fits all too well the remorseless paranoia of Herod's last years.

Herod felt the hatred of his Jewish subjects deeply in his last days and believed he would die unmourned. He suffered a chronic and painful stomach disease from which he sought relief in the hot baths at Callirrhoe. Herod's death in 4 B.C. sparked relief and joy among many Jews, who believed the agonies of his illness were a divine punishment. Herod's body was taken on a royal bier from Jericho to the Herodium for burial.

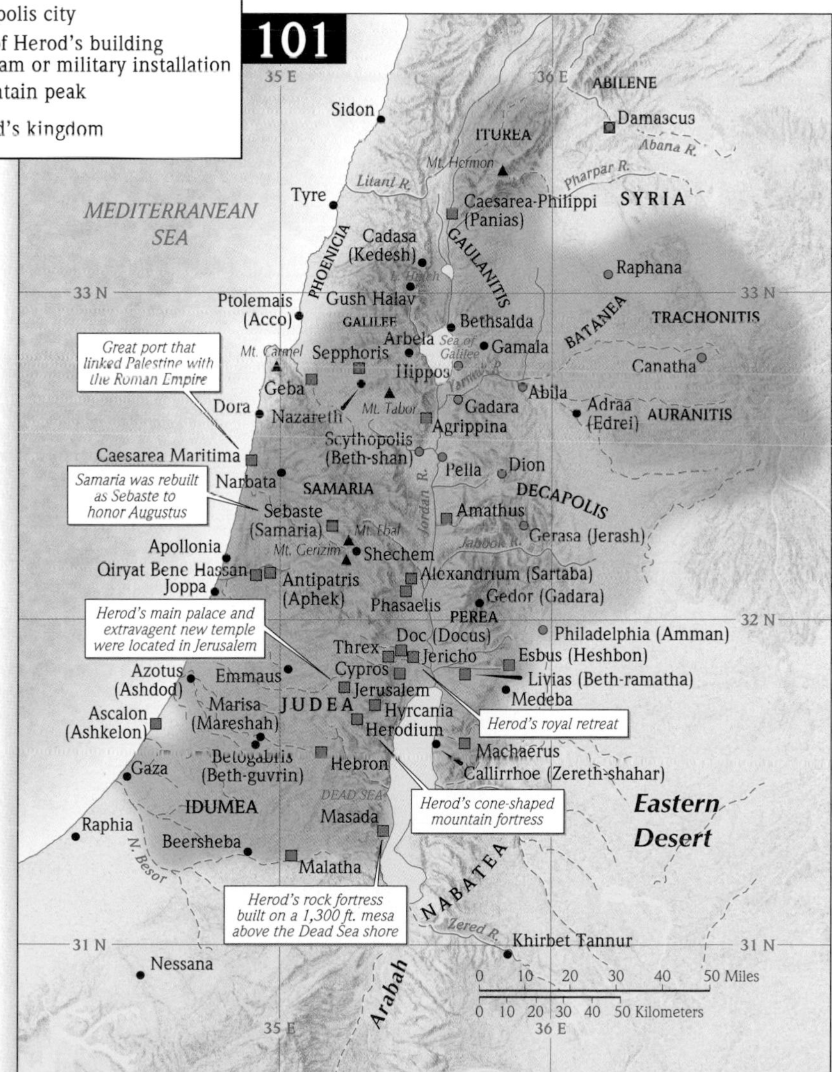

CAESAREA: HEROD'S WINDOW ON THE WORLD

The theater at Caesarea Maritima.

Herod's most ambitious project was the magnificent port facility, Caesarea. Built between 22 and 9 B.C., the new city honored Herod's patron, Caesar Augustus. Herod's engineers selected a site about twenty-two miles south of Mount Carmel, used previously by the Phoenicians as a small anchorage, known in Hellenistic times as Strato's Tower. After A.D. 6 Caesarea became the official residence of the Roman procurators and thus the center of Roman administration in Palestine. Vespasian elevated Caesarea to the status of a Roman colony as a reward for the loyalty of the city to Rome during the First Jewish Revolt.

Herod's kingdom lacked a deep-water port facility capable of accommodating the larger Roman cargo vessels. Engineers remedied the problem by greatly expanding the small Phoenician port into a large harbor facility named Sebastos. Two huge breakwaters built of ashlar stones and a conglomerate formed by pouring hydraulic cement into wooden forms enclosed twenty-five acres of open sea. The project was unprecedented in scale as was the application of poured forms to create the breakwaters. The southern breakwater extended west for 200 meters, then curved northward for another 300 meters. The inner side of the breakwater served as a quay where ships were loaded and unloaded. The northern breakwater extended westward over 180 meters. Statues on massive stone pedestals flanked the harbor entrance located in the northwest; they may have served as navigational guides steering the ships clear of sandbars that accumulated near the breakwaters. Two inner basins within the harbor provided additional port facilities, including a series of barrel-vaulted warehouses along the inner basin.

Fragments of amphorae (storage vessels) found near the warehouses testify to the lively trade in olive oil, wine, grain, and fish sauce carried out from Caesarea. In one of the warehouses, excavators discovered a Mithraeum—a place imitating a cave where the god Mithras was worshiped in secret ceremonies—complete with an altar and a medallion depicting Mithras slaying a bull. The Mithraeum dates from a period later than the New Testament times.

The high-water aquaduct bringing water to Caesarea Maritima. Inscriptions indicate that sections of the aquaduct were built by the Roman Tenth Legion Fretensis after the First Jewish Revolt that ended in A.D. 73.

Herod planned Caesarea as a Hellenistic city meant to accommodate a predominately non-Jewish population. The city was laid out in a typical Hellenistic grid plan. Aqueducts furnished Caesarea with water from springs on Mount Carmel and the Zarqa River. A temple to Roma and Augustus stood high on a raised platform east of the harbor. The most visible structure today is the restored theater, one of the earliest such structures to be introduced in the Near East. A partial inscription found in secondary use in the theater mentions Pontius Pilate, who dedicated a temple at Caesarea to the emperor Tiberias. Recent archaeological work on a promontory west of the theater revealed the remains of a palace complex with a pool or fish tank and beautiful mosaics, possibly Herod's royal palace described by Josephus. Caesarea had an amphitheater and hippodrome (circus) to entertain the population, though neither has been fully explored. The amphitheater had a spacious oval arena (95 x 62 meters) and was located in the northeast quadrant of the city. The hippodrome dates from a time later than Herod, but could accommodate upwards of thirty thousand spectators. Recently a smaller hippodrome has been uncovered west of the theater.

Caesarea was a thoroughly Hellenistic-Roman city from its inception. Although a significant Jewish community resided in the city, Caesarea served the needs of the Gentile population and Roman administrators. Peter's mission to Caesarea helped pave the way for Christian expansion among the Gentiles (Acts 10). Although the First Jewish Revolt decimated the Jewish community at Caesarea, the city thrived as a Roman colony into the Byzantine period, when Caesarea became a center of Christian learning. Origen and Eusebius taught and wrote while in residence at Caesarea.

A small hippodrome recently discovered at Caesarea.

HEROD'S FORTRESSES

Herod built a series of fortresses along the edge of the Jordan Valley and Dead Sea to provide a place of rest and refuge. These fortresses, located on top of secluded hills or mountains, were linked together with Jerusalem by means of fire signals. They afforded Herod safety in times of political unrest. Masada, Machaerus, Cypros, Alexandrium, and the Herodium are the better known of these fortresses. Herod's main palace was in Jerusalem, but he maintained other luxurious palaces and villas for his personal pleasure, including a magnificent winter palace near Jericho.

The Herodium.

HERODIUM

The distinctive cone-shaped mountain fortress, Herodium, rises 758 meters above sea level about eight miles southeast of Jerusalem. Herodium served as a fortress, district capital, and finally as Herod's burial place. The mountain fortress soars sixty meters above the surrounding landscape. Herod's engineers leveled the top of the mountain, then built a cylindrical cone consisting of four towers, three semicircular in shape and one solid tower, connected by two concentric walls. Earth and stone heaped against the walls gave the Herodium its distinctive shape. The upper section of the walls and towers contained storage facilities and apartments. The space within the cone was divided into two sections. The eastern section was a garden surrounded by columns measuring 12.5 x 77 meters. A bathhouse, triclinium (dining room), and courtyard occupied the western sector. Entrance to the fortress was gained by marble steps leading to a passage through the northeast walls. Several cisterns within the palace and others dug deeply within the mountain itself supplied water.

Lower Herodium, lying below the north side of the fortress palace, covered an additional thirty-seven acres. In addition to service and administrative structures, Lower Herodium featured a large pool (46 x 70 meters; 3 meters deep) fed by an aqueduct. A colonnaded pavilion in the middle of the pool was surrounded by gardens. A large bathhouse complex abutted the southwestern corner of the pool. An unusual feature at Lower Herodium is a long, narrow terrace (350 x 30 meters) connected on the west to a beautifully constructed structure called by the excavators the "Monumental Building." Speculation that the terrace and the Monumental Building were built for Herod's funeral procession and his burial remains unproven. Josephus, however, provides a vivid description of the funeral procession that brought Herod to his final resting place.

An overview of the interior of the Herodium. Visible in the foreground is the courtyard; a dining room and other personal facilities used by the Herodian family are visible beyond the courtyard.

MASADA

Masada was a rock fortress perched on top of a high mesa 1,300 feet above the shore of the Dead Sea. The primary access was up the eastern side along the winding "Snakepath." Herod greatly expanded the Hasmonean structures already present on the mesa and added many new buildings to suit his needs. A casemate wall encircled the top, enclosing a surface measuring 1,950 feet north to south and 1,000 feet east to west. Herod built two new palaces to accommodate the royal family. A unique three-tiered palace supported by massive terraces and revetment walls clung to the northern face of Masada. A bath complex on the lower level utilized Roman styles imitating fine marbles. Two concentric walls formed the middle level and may have served as a garden. A larger western palace contained royal apartments, a bath, a throne room, and service quarters. Beautiful mosaics found in the palace contain no images that would be offensive to Herod's Jewish subjects.

The Herodian fortress Masada on the western shore of the Dead Sea. The Roman ramp built by Jewish slave labor to break the siege of Masada is visible in the center (the lighter color).

Large storage facilities kept a ready supply of wheat, oil, and other essentials. Massive cisterns chiseled into the surface and sides of the mountain received water channeled from the surface. Archaeologist Yigael Yadin estimated that the cisterns had a capacity of 1,400,000 cubic feet of water. In addition to drinking and cooking purposes, water was needed on Masada for the bathhouses, ritual baths, and swimming pools.

Masada was the last stronghold held by the Zealots against the Romans after the fall of Jerusalem. Under the command of Flavius Silva, the Romans besieged the approximately 960 Zealots who defended the rocky fortress and chose suicide over surrender. Traces of Roman camps and a fortification wall still surround Masada. The Roman ramp thrown up along Masada's western side was used by the Romans to maneuver siege machines into position during the final assault. Yadin recovered personal belongings and skeletal remains of the valiant Zealots, mute testimony to their final grim act of defiance (see further chap. 20).

HERODIAN JERICHO

A portion of the northern palace complex built by Herod the Great at Masada.

During the Hellenistic and Roman periods, Jericho again flourished, this time on a royal scale. The Hasmonean rulers and Herod the Great recognized Jericho's healthy climate and economic potential. Both built large palaces at Tulul Abu el-`Alaiq on the southwest side of the oasis. Sometimes called "Herodian Jericho" or "New Testament Jericho," Tulul Abu el-`Alaiq more properly should be called a royal retreat—complete with palaces, swimming pools, baths, and gardens. Located on the Wadi Qelt as it begins its journey upwards toward Jerusalem, this site was but thirteen miles from the capital. The delightful winter climate and perennial beauty of its oasis gave welcome relief from the pressures and dangers of nearby Jerusalem.

A vast irrigation system constructed during this time greatly enlarged the oasis, creating lucrative royal estates. Josephus described the date palm groves that produced a rich honey and the balsam groves as "the most precious of all local products" (Josephus, *JW* 4,8.3§467–472). The Roman geographer Strabo also wrote of Jericho's famous groves. Balsam came from the sap of the shrub *commiphora opobalsamum* and was renowned for its medicinal qualities, especially for relief of eye diseases and headaches, as well as for its use in perfumes. Strabo noted that this costly substance could be found only at Jericho (Strabo, *Geography,* 16.2.41).

Herod the Great seized Jericho from his Hasmonean rival Antigonus in 37 B.C. However, Mark Antony gave the region of Jericho to Cleopatra, who controlled the oasis until the victory of Augustus over Antony at Actium in 31 B.C. Herod envisioned developing the oasis for pleasure and economic benefit. He rebuilt a fortress above Tulul Abu el-`Alaiq, naming it Cypros after his mother.

At Tulul Abu el-`Alaiq, Herod's architects built three palaces for Herod's pleasure during the course of his reign. The first lay south of Wadi Qelt and consisted of a rectangular structure (89 x 46 meters) centered around a court. Later, this building probably was converted to guest quarters. A second palace complex partially covered the remains of the earlier Hasmonean palace and was likely destroyed by an earthquake in 31 B.C. Laborers erected an artificial mound (the "northern mound") over the central building of the earlier palace, providing a platform for royal dwellings. Herod combined the two Hasmonean pools into one and added ancillary buildings to the southeast.

However, Herod's most ambitious project at Jericho was carried out in the later years of his reign. Utilizing Roman techniques and possibly Roman craftsmen, Herod built a large palace complex spanning both sides of the Wadi Qelt, extending some three hundred meters and covering over seven acres. The complex is of four distinct parts, three south of the Wadi Qelt and one to the north. South of the wadi, Herod's architects constructed an artificial mound (the "southern mound") with a rectangular building on top. Perhaps this was a reception hall, although the structure's function cannot be determined with certainty. A flight of stairs led down the mound toward the north, possibly extending across the wadi via a bridge.

A pool measuring 92 x 40 meters stood just north to the right of the mound. To the left of the mound the remains of a gigantic, formal sunken garden 150 meters in length with double colonnades at each end has been found. A grand facade forming the southern wall of this structure exhibits beautiful brickwork known as *opus reticulatum*, where square-faced stones are set diagonally in concrete at 45° angles to form a network design. A series of semicircular terraces extend southward in the middle of the facade. The effect must have been dazzling, especially when viewed from across the wadi.

The northern wing of the palace complex mirrored in part the sunken gardens south of the wadi. While the southern wing was primarily recreational, the northern portion contained two huge colonnaded courts or halls, the largest measuring 29 x 19 meters, used for receptions. Paved in marble and local stone set in *opus sectile* style with Ionic and Corinthian columns, these architectural features reflect Roman style, which Herod adapted to Jewish sensitivity. According to Josephus, Herod named two halls in his palace at Jerusalem "Caesarion" and "Agrippon" after his patron and a friend. These names appear at Jericho and may refer to these halls.

The northern wing also contains a Roman bath complete with a dressing room *(apodyterium)*, warm bathroom *(tepidarium)*, cold bathroom *(frigidarium)*, and hot bathroom *(caldarium)*. Colonnades across the southern exposure offered a magnificent view over the wadi to the gardens and pool beyond.

Recent excavations at Tell el-Sammarat, located between Tell es-Sultan and Tulul Abu el-`Alaiq, have yielded remains of a hippodrome (317 x 86 meters) and theater built by Herod. These structures attest to the vitality of the city. Unfortunately, much of the New Testament city lies buried beneath the modern town, but the excavation of a series of tombs in the hills near Jericho demonstrates the presence of a thriving Jewish community in the first century A.D.

Herodian Jericho.

Chapter Seventeen

THE WORLD OF JESUS

The Roman Empire during Jesus' Ministry: The Reign of Tiberius

The ministry of Jesus took place during the reign of Tiberius. Tiberius came to the imperial throne at age fifty-five. As the reluctant heir of Augustus, Tiberius inherited a stable empire built upon the Roman peace established by his predecessor. An accomplished military leader, Tiberius was uncomfortable with the trappings of power and the heavy administrative responsibilities of his office. An unhappy marriage to Julia, daughter of Augustus, was a constant source of misery. Julia's profligate reputation was well known in Rome.

Though Tiberius did not possess the charisma of Augustus, he proved to be a capable leader. To promote administrative stability, Tiberius extended the time provincial officials served. He was fiscally conservative and, at his death, left Rome in a solid financial position. (Many Romans, however, regarded his financial policies as miserly.) Tiberius also further stabilized the frontiers of the Roman Empire.

Despite these accomplishments, Tiberius was not well liked by either the Senate or the Roman populace. He avoided Rome and eventually established his residence on the Island of Capri, where he indulged his passion for astrology. Tiberius entrusted the administration of his government to Sejanus, prefect of the Praetorian Guard, a cruel, oppressive despot who abused his power. Perhaps an anti-Semite, Sejanus appointed Pontius Pilate as prefect over Judea. In A.D. 31 Tiberius executed Sejanus for plotting against his life. In his later years, Tiberius encouraged treason trials that further alienated him from the Senate. When Tiberius died in A.D. 37, many Romans cheered the death of this reclusive and reluctant emperor.

Politics of Palestine: 4 B.C. to A.D. 41

After the death of Herod the Great in 4 B.C., Herod's kingdom was divided among three of his surviving sons. Throughout the ministry of Jesus, two of those sons, Herod Antipas and Philip, ruled as clients of Rome. However, Archelaus, the third son, was removed in A.D. 6 for incompetence, and his territories were given over to the care of a procurator.

HEROD'S SUCCESSORS

Herod's death in 4 B.C. precipitated a crisis: who would succeed Herod as ruler of Palestine? Many Jews were violently anti-Herodian as well as anti-Roman. In Herod's last will he divided his kingdom, as stated above, among three of his surviving sons: Archelaus, Antipas, and Philip. When Jews rebelled to show their displeasure, the legate of Syria, Varus, dispatched Roman troops. Augustus might have chosen to annex Palestine to the province of Syria, but he reluctantly ratified Herod's will, with certain modifications.

CHART 21. THE HERODIAN RULERS

Ruler	Family Relationship	Realm of Responsibility	Dates of Reign	Biblical Reference
Herod I (the Great)	Son of Antipater	King of Judea	37–4 B.C.	Matt. 2:1–22; Luke 1:5
Herod Archelaus	Oldest son of Herod the Great	Ethanarch of Judea, Samaria, and Idumea	4 B.C.–A.D. 6	Matt. 2:22
Philip*	Son of Herod the Great and Cleopatra of Jerusalem	Tetrarch of territories north and east of the Sea of Galilee	4 B.C.–A.D. 34	Luke 3:1
Herod Antipas	Youngest son of Herod the Great; second husband of Herodias	Tetrarch of Galilee and Perea	4 B.C.–A.D. 39	Matt. 14:1–11; Mark 6:14–29; Luke 3:1, 19; 13:31–33; 23:7–12
Herod Agrippa I	Grandson of Herod the Great	King of Judea	A.D. 37–44	Acts 12
Herod Agrippa II	Great-grandson of Herod the Great	Tetrach and king of Chalcis	A.D. 44–100 (became king in A.D. 48)	Acts 25:13–26:32

*Not to be confused with Herod Philip also mentioned in the New Testament. Herod Philip was the son of Herod the Great and Mariamne and was the first husband of Herodias. (See Matt. 14:3; Mark 6:17; and Luke 3:19.)

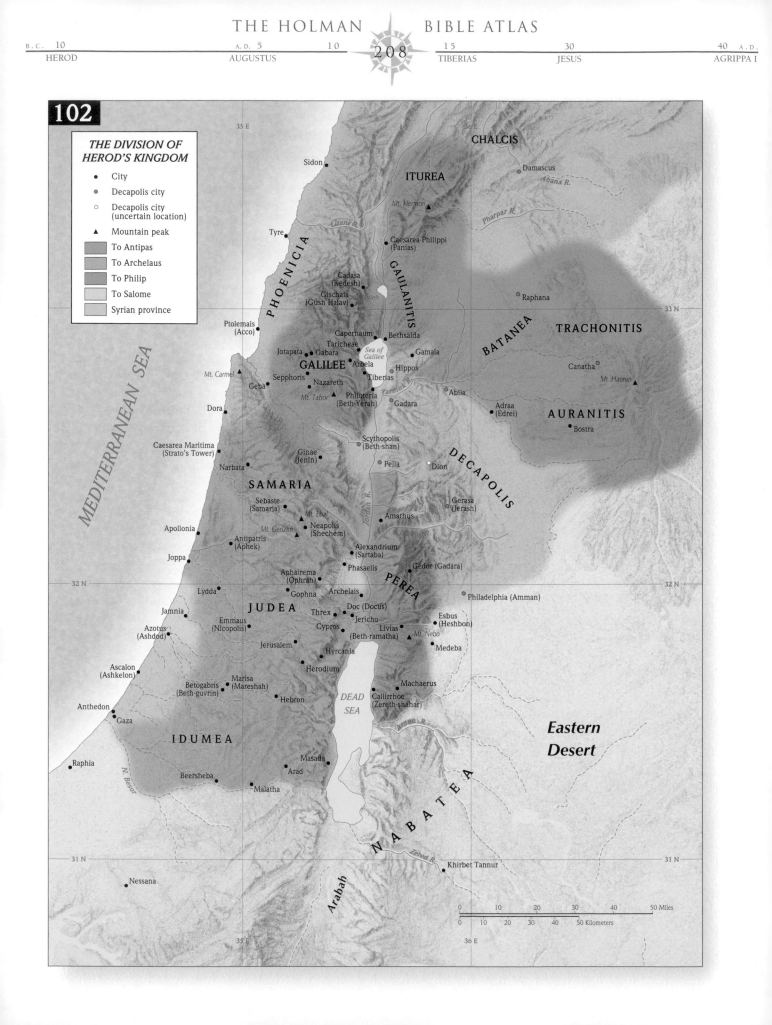

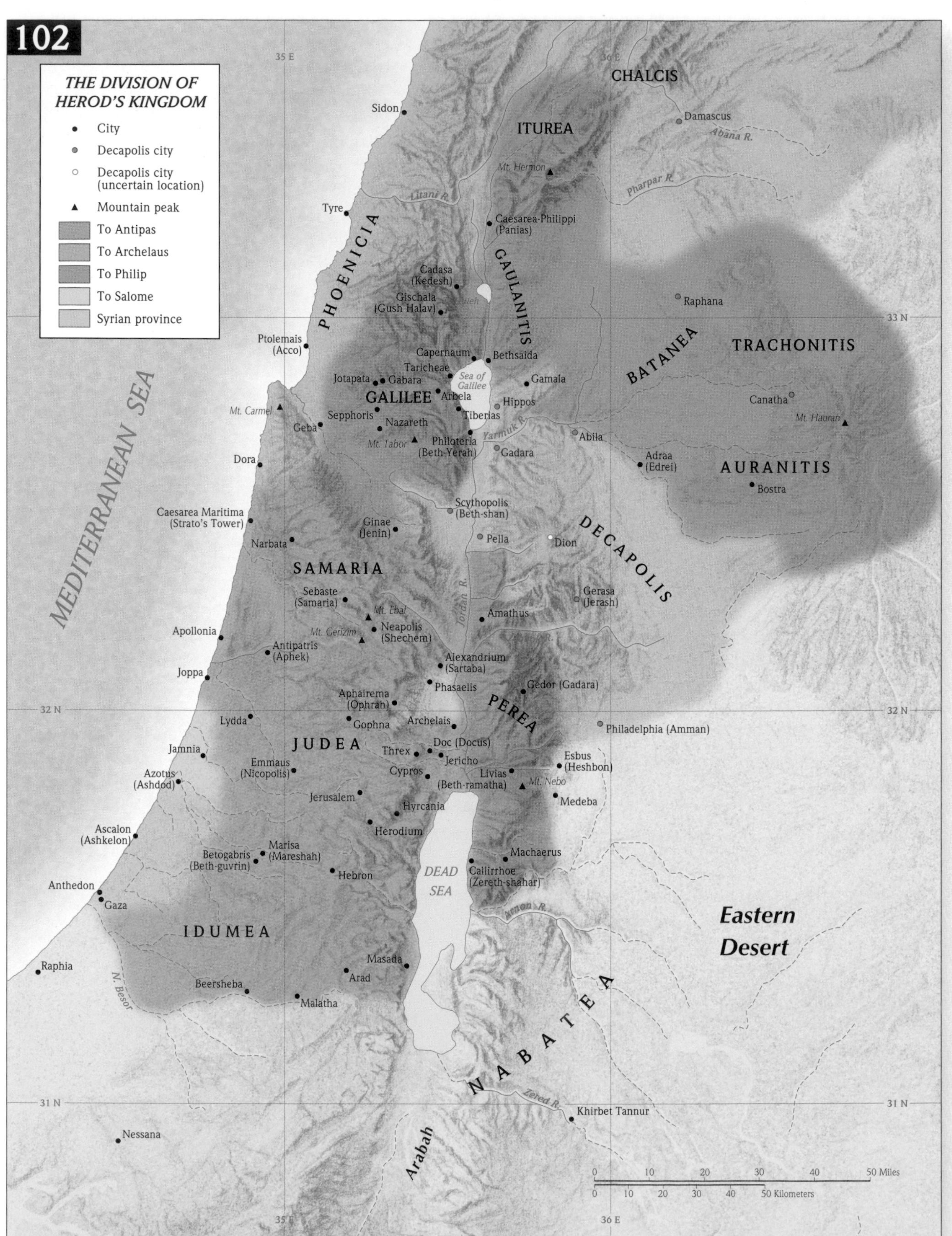
102
THE DIVISION OF HEROD'S KINGDOM
City
Decapolis city
Decapolis city (uncertain location)
Mountain peak
To Antipas
To Archelaus
To Philip
To Salome
Syrian province
MEDITERRANEAN SEA
PHOENICIA
ITUREA
CHALCIS
GAULANITIS
BATANEA
TRACHONITIS
AURANITIS
GALILEE
DECAPOLIS
SAMARIA
PEREA
JUDEA
IDUMEA
NABATEA
Eastern Desert
Sidon
Damascus
Abana R.
Mt. Hermon
Pharpar R.
Litani R.
Tyre
Caesarea-Philippi (Panias)
Cadasa (Kedesh)
Gischala (Gush Halav)
Raphana
Ptolemais (Acco)
Capernaum
Bethsaida
Taricheae
Sea of Galilee
Jotapata
Gabara
Arbela
Gamala
Hippos
Canatha
Mt. Hauran
Mt. Carmel
Sepphoris
Nazareth
Tiberias
Geba
Mt. Tabor
Philoteria (Beth-Yerah)
Yarmuk R.
Abila
Gadara
Adraa (Edrei)
Bostra
Dora
Scythopolis (Beth-shan)
Caesarea Maritima (Strato's Tower)
Ginae (Jenin)
Pella
Dion
Narbata
Sebaste (Samaria)
Mt. Ebal
Gerasa (Jerash)
Jordan R.
Amathus
Apollonia
Mt. Gerizim
Neapolis (Shechem)
Antipatris (Aphek)
Alexandrium (Sartaba)
Joppa
Phasaelis
Aphairema (Ophrah)
Gedor (Gadara)
Lydda
Gophna
Archelais
Philadelphia (Amman)
Jamnia
Threx
Doc (Docus)
Jericho
Emmaus (Nicopolis)
Cypros
Esbus (Heshbon)
Azotus (Ashdod)
Livias (Beth-ramatha)
Mt. Nebo
Jerusalem
Medeba
Hyrcania
Herodium
Ascalon (Ashkelon)
Marisa (Mareshah)
Betogabris (Beth-guvrin)
Hebron
DEAD SEA
Machaerus
Callirrhoe (Zereth-shahar)
Anthedon
Gaza
Arnon R.
Raphia
N. Besor
Masada
Arad
Beersheba
Malatha
Zered R.
Khirbet Tannur
Nessana
Arabah
35 E
36 E
33 N
32 N
31 N
0 10 20 30 40 50 Miles
0 10 20 30 40 50 Kilometers

Archelaus. Augustus appointed Archelaus ethnarch ("ruler of a people") governing Judea, Samaria, and Idumea. Archelaus, whose mother was the Samaritan Malthace, ruled with an iron fist. His wife, Glaphyra, was the widow of his stepbrother—a marriage prohibited by biblical law. Neither of these relationships endeared Archelaus to his Jewish subjects. Like his father, Archelaus sponsored building projects, including a fortress near Jericho named after himself. His oppressive and brutal policies finally provoked such opposition among the Jews that Augustus removed Archelaus in A.D. 6 and banished him to Vienne in Gaul. Augustus established direct Roman rule over Archelaus' former territories by appointing a Roman prefect to administer them (see chart 22, "The First Procuratorship" p. 210). The Bible mentions Archelaus only once (Matt. 2:19–23), explaining that Mary and Joseph would not settle in Judea while this tyrant ruled; instead they resided in Galilee, where Jesus grew to manhood.

The Roman theater at Sepphoris.

Herod Antipas. Antipas received Galilee and Perea as his share of Herod's kingdom and bore the title "tetrarch" ("ruler of a fourth"). Portions of the Decapolis separated his two territories. Antipas assumed the dynastic name *Herod* after his brother Archelaus was deposed. Because Galilee was the scene of much of Jesus' ministry, the New Testament mentions Herod Antipas twenty times. Antipas feared the growing popularity of Jesus, who on one occasion called the king "that fox" (Luke 13:31–32). Pilate sent Jesus to Herod Antipas during his trial (Luke 23:6–12). Antipas married the daughter of the Nabatean king Aretas IV, but divorced her in favor of Herodias, his half brother's wife. This marriage haunted Antipas in two ways. First, John the Baptist condemned the marriage as adulterous; ultimately, Antipas ordered John's execution in fear of the Baptizer's preaching. Second, the disgrace brought upon Aretas IV by the divorce of his daughter led to conflict between Antipas and the Nabateans. King Aretas IV defeated Herod Antipas in A.D. 36, avenging the dishonor brought upon his daughter.

Antipas was a clever and competent ruler despite his moral deficiencies. He rebuilt Sepphoris after the Romans destroyed the city in reprisal for a raid by Judas the Galilean upon the city's arsenal after Herod's death in 4 B.C. Located only a few miles north of Nazareth, Sepphoris was situated at the crossroads of two main trade routes. Recent excavations have confirmed Josephus' statement that Antipas made Sepphoris the most beautiful city of Galilee. A thriving city adorned with a colonnaded street and theater, Sepphoris functioned as the capital of Galilee until A.D. 18.

Herod Antipas supported building projects throughout much of his reign, although the cost in taxation to his subjects must have been high. He rebuilt an older settlement in the Transjordan and named it Livias after the wife of Augustus. Antipas honored his patron, Tiberius, by naming a new city after the emperor. Located on the western shore of the Sea of Galilee, Tiberius served as the capital of Galilee until Caligula deposed Antipas in A.D. 39.

The Romans valued Antipas for his arbitration skills in their conflict with the Parthians, but when Caligula succeeded Tiberius in A.D 37, Antipas lost the support of the emperor. Caligula favored Agrippa I, whom he named king over Antipas. Herodias envied the new status of her brother Agrippa I and urged her husband to seek the same high office. Antipas' enemies sabotaged this effort by charging Antipas with plotting rebellion against Rome with Parthian help. The charges were unfounded, but Caligula banished the ambitious Antipas to southern France (Lugdunum) in A.D. 39. Herodias joined her husband in exile.

Philip. Philip was the third son of Herod the Great to receive a portion of his father's kingdom. Augustus appointed him tetrarch over the areas north and east of the Sea of Galilee:

Gaulantis, Batanea, Auranitis, Panias, Trachonitis, and Iturea. Because non-Jews and Greeks predominated in these areas, Philip did not have to deal with the religious issues and Jewish nationalistic sentiments that plagued the territories of his half brothers. His marriage to Salome, daughter of Herodias, occasioned no scandal among his subjects.

The springs at Caesarea Philippi. Note the sacred cave of Pan and the niches in the cliff walls in the background.

Josephus described Philip as a capable administrator and a just ruler whose reign was peaceable and prosperous. Philip built his capital at Caesarea Philippi near one of the main sources of the Jordan River. He rebuilt the village Bethsaida and renamed the expanded city "Julia" in honor of Augustus' daughter.

Scholars differ whether there were two Bethsaidas or one; the precise location and limits of the city are also subject to debate. Current excavations at the ruins called "et-Tell" located on the east bank of the Jordan River may solve the debate. The Jordan River marked the division between Philip's tetrarchy and that of Herod Antipas; conceivably two villages bearing the same name—one in the tetrarchy of Antipas and the other in the territory of Philip—stood on either side. The ruins at et-Tell, one and a half miles north of the Sea of Galilee, have been identified as Bethsaida-Julias, or at least the acropolis of the city. The ruins at el-Araj on the shores of the lake probably represent the fishing village. Josephus mentions the fishing fleet based at Bethsaida, commandeered for use during the Jewish revolt. Jesus occasionally journeyed into Philip's tetrarchy to get away from the crowds who thronged Him in Galilee (see below, "Jesus Outside Galilee," p. 223). Philip died peacefully in A.D. 34. Rome temporarily assigned his territories to the governor of Syria before they were granted to Agrippa I.

THE FIRST PROCURATORSHIP (A.D. 6-41)

When Rome deposed Archelaus as ethnarch over Judea, Samaria, and Idumea in A.D. 6, Augustus chose to govern these areas directly through a prefect, later called a procurator. Because of Judea's relative insignificance to Rome, these officials often were drawn from less competent administrators. Coponius, the first prefect, established his residence at Caesarea Maritima, the administrative capital of the Province of Judea. The prefect commanded no legions, but had five cohorts of auxiliaries drawn from the local populations (principally from Caesarea and Sebaste) at his disposal. One cohort and a unit of cavalry were permanently stationed at Jerusalem in the Antonia Fortress. On feast days the prefect traveled to Jerusalem with additional troops to ensure the peace. As the direct representative of the emperor, the prefect oversaw financial affairs of the province, including the collection of taxes and

CHART 22. ROMAN GOVERNORS OF THE FIRST PROCURATORSHIP (A.D. 6–41)

Name	Dates (A.D.)	Appointed By	Selected References in the Works of Josephus to the Procurator
Coponius	6–9	Augustus	*ANT* 18.1.1 § 2; 18.2.2§29–31 *JW* 2.8.1§117–118
Marcus Ambibulus	9–12	Augustus	*ANT* 18.2.2§31
Annius Rufus	12–15	Augustus	*ANT* 18.2.2§32
Valerius Gratus	15–26	Tiberius	*ANT* 18.2.2§33–35
Pontius Pilate	26–36	Tiberius	*ANT* 18.3.1§55–62; 18.4.1–2 §85–89; *JW* 2.9.2–4§169–177
Marcellus	37	Vitellius, Legate of Syria	*ANT* 18.4.2§89
Marullus	37–41	Caligula	*ANT* 18.6.10§237

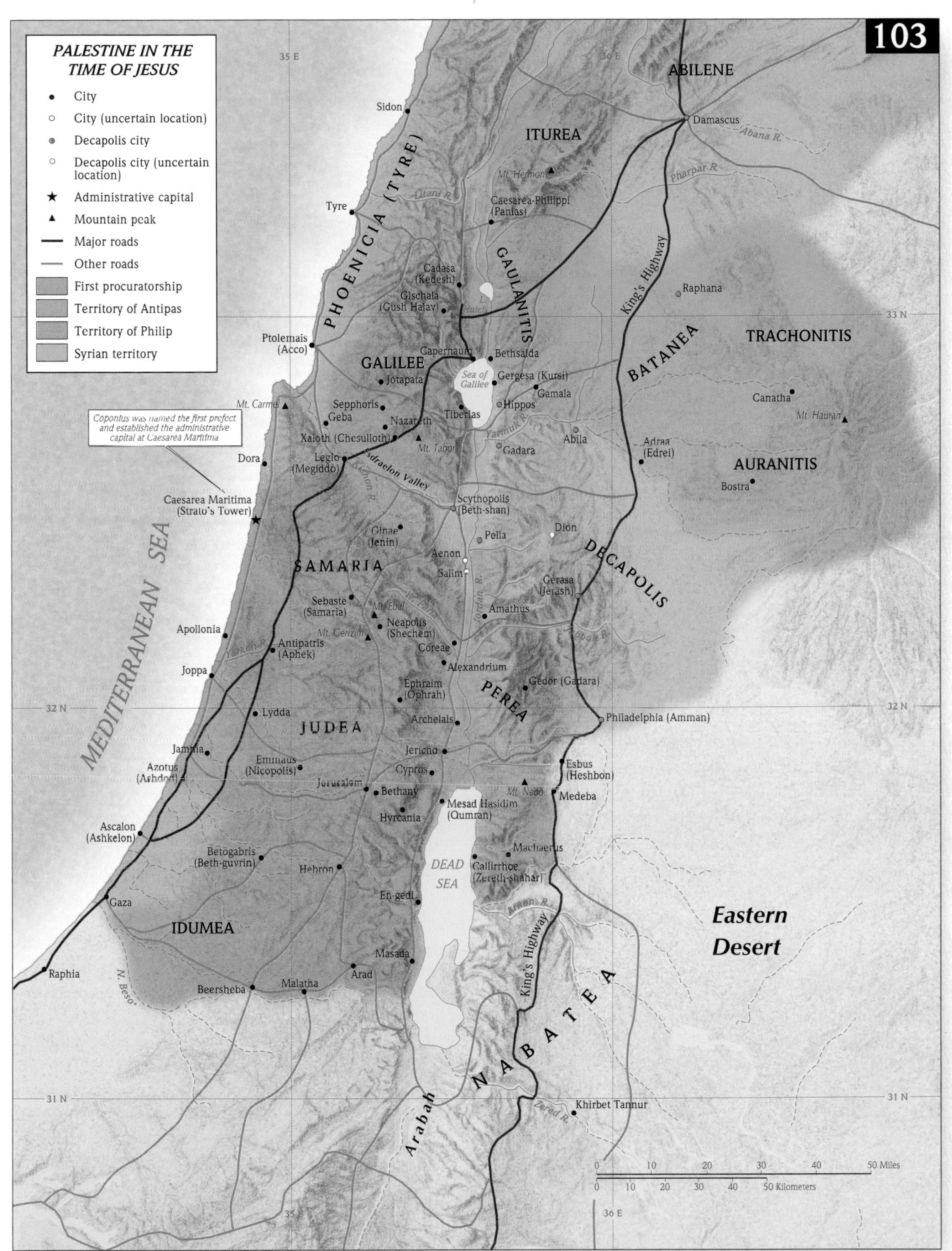
103
PALESTINE IN THE TIME OF JESUS
City
City (uncertain location)
Decapolis city
Decapolis city (uncertain location)
Administrative capital
Mountain peak
Major roads
Other roads
First procuratorship
Territory of Antipas
Territory of Philip
Syrian territory
Coponius was named the first prefect and established the administrative capital at Caesarea Maritima
ABILENE
ITUREA
PHOENICIA (TYRE)
GAULANITIS
GALILEE
BATANEA
TRACHONITIS
AURANITIS
SAMARIA
DECAPOLIS
PEREA
JUDEA
IDUMEA
NABATEA
MEDITERRANEAN SEA
DEAD SEA
Sea of Galilee
Eastern Desert
Sidon
Damascus
Tyre
Caesarea-Philippi (Panias)
Mt. Hermon
Raphana
Cadasa (Kedesh)
Gischala (Gush Halav)
Ptolemais (Acco)
Capernaum
Bethsaida
Jotapata
Gergesa (Kursi)
Gamala
Hippos
Canatha
Mt. Hauran
Mt. Carmel
Sepphoris
Geba
Nazareth
Tiberias
Xaloth (Chesulloth)
Mt. Tabor
Abila
Gadara
Adraa (Edrei)
Dora
Legio (Megiddo)
Esdraelon Valley
Bostra
Caesarea Maritima (Strato's Tower)
Scythopolis (Beth-shan)
Ginae (Jenin)
Pella
Dion
Aenon
Salim
Gerasa (Jerash)
Sebaste (Samaria)
Mt. Ebal
Neapolis (Shechem)
Mt. Gerizim
Amathus
Apollonia
Antipatris (Aphek)
Coreae
Alexandrium
Joppa
Ephraim (Ophrah)
Gedor (Gadara)
Lydda
Archelais
Philadelphia (Amman)
Jamnia
Jericho
Esbus (Heshbon)
Azotus (Ashdod)
Emmaus (Nicopolis)
Cypros
Jerusalem
Bethany
Mt. Nebo
Medeba
Hyrcania
Mesad Hasidim (Qumran)
Ascalon (Ashkelon)
Machaerus
Betogabris (Beth-guvrin)
Hebron
Callirrhoe (Zereth-shahar)
En-gedi
Gaza
Masada
Arad
Raphia
Beersheba
Malatha
Khirbet Tannur
Arabah
King's Highway
Abana R.
Pharpar R.
Litani R.
Yarmuk R.
Jordan R.
Kishon R.
Yarkon R.
Jabbok R.
Arnon R.
Zered R.
N. Besor
35 E
36 E
33 N
32 N
31 N
0 10 20 30 40 50 Miles
0 10 20 30 40 50 Kilometers

tariffs. High priestly appointments also fell under the prefect's authority.

Augustus favored short-term appointments for provincial officials; the three prefects he appointed governed three years each (see chart 22, p. 210). Tiberias preferred longer appointments for greater stability. Pontius Pilate, the most famous of these prefects, governed Judea for ten years (A.D. 26–36). Pilate's appointment probably was made by Sejanus, the ruthless (possibly anti-Semitic) Praetorian Prefect entrusted by Tiberias to manage the Roman government.

According to Josephus, Pilate antagonized the Jews on several occasions, once permitting Roman troops to enter Jerusalem bearing standards decorated with the image of the emperor (*ANT* 18.3.1§55–59), and again by turning his soldiers loose upon Jews upset that Pilate confiscated temple monies (*ANT* 18.3.2§60–62). Perhaps these incidents reflect freedom Pilate felt in dealing harshly with his subjects so long as Sejanus was in power; after the execution of Sejanus in A.D. 31, Pilate was more cautious in his dealings with the Jews. Ultimately, Pilate overstepped his bounds and was removed from office by the Syrian legate Vitellius. The next two procurators served five years before the province of Judea was given to Rome's new client-king, Agrippa I, in A.D. 41. (see pp. 237–39).

Jewish Religious Groups in the Roman Period

Josephus mentions four "philosophies" (cf. *ANT* 18.1.2§11) of the Jews in his writings addressed to a Gentile audience: Pharisees, Sadducees, Essenes, and Zealots. The first three are identifiable religious groups within Judaism, while the Zealots espoused the overthrow of Roman rule. Students of the New Testament must appreciate the differences among these diverse groups.

PHARISEES

The Pharisees are the most familiar Jewish party. They probably originated among the Hasidim ("Pious Ones") who fought the Seleucids during the Maccabean Revolt. Josephus first mentions them during the time period of Jonathan and John Hyrcanus (see above, p. 185). He states that in his day, six thousand adherents to the party of the Pharisees lived in Palestine. The Pharisees held minimal political power throughout the Hasmonean era and into the Roman period, although at times (for example, during the reign of Salome Alexandra) their influence and power in the Sanhedrin rose. Phariseeism essentially was a lay movement dedicated to obeying the Torah in daily life.

Teachings. The Pharisees valued the Torah ("law" or "instruction," a term applied to the first five books of the Old Testament) above all else. They believed the truths of the Torah were timeless, requiring only proper application in the midst of changing times. To that end the Pharisees developed a complex oral tradition designed to specify in detail how a law applied to every circumstance. A close relationship existed between scribes and Pharisees. As interpreters of the law, the scribes provided the Pharisees with authoritative pronouncements upon what the law demanded. Not all scribes were Pharisees, although many were (cf. Mark 2:16). The Pharisees regarded this oral tradition to be as fully authoritative as the written law, a belief that most distinguished them from the Sadducees. A later rabbinic tradition held that God gave Moses the oral law on Mount Sinai.

The Pharisees were progressive theologically. Josephus described the Pharisees as moderates who maintained a theological balance between God's sovereignty and human freedom. They readily accepted new theological ideas, including angelology, demonology, the concepts of heaven and hell, and the resurrection. As a former Pharisee, Paul accepted these ideas, albeit through the radical insight provided by his encounter with Christ. The Sadducees rejected these "new ideas." On one occasion Paul exploited this difference between the two parties for his benefit (Acts 23:6–10).

Organization and Practice. The name *Pharisee* probably is derived from the Hebrew word for "separate;" thus the Pharisees were the "separate ones." They organized into small groups for fellowship, eating meals together, and practicing their piety. The Pharisees were especially concerned about laws of ritual purity, Sabbath observances, and tithing. Scrupulous observance of the oral tradition regarding these areas marked the Pharisee as a separated one who endeavored to keep the whole law. "Sinners" were those Jews whose observance fell short of the standards set by the Pharisees. Ordinary Jews greatly admired the Pharisees for their piety as well as their reputation for leniency with regard to religious punishments. Hillel, Shammai, and Gamaliel—the latter the teacher of the young Saul—were among the important Pharisees in the first century.

Pharisees and Jesus. The conflicts between Jesus and the Pharisees often centered on the oral tradition because Jesus did not regard it as binding (Mark 2:23–28; 7:1–13; Luke 6:1–11). The Pharisees also practiced other forms of piety—fasting and prayer—shared by other groups, but Jesus accused some of them of nullifying these acts by improper motives (Matt. 6:5–18; 23:1–39). In turn, the Pharisees condemned Jesus because He consorted with "sinners" (Matt. 9:11; Luke 15:2). However, Jesus also maintained positive contacts with Pharisees, eating in their homes and encouraging their search for God (Mark 12:28–34; Luke 7:36–50; John 3).

The Pharisees were the only Jewish party to survive the destruction of Jerusalem in A.D. 70. The Judaism that emerged in the aftermath of that catastrophe and produced the rabbinic literature (the Mishnah, Gemara, and Talmud) essentially represented the viewpoint of the Pharisees.

SADDUCEES

Our knowledge of the Sadducees is seriously lacking. We know them only through scattered references in the writings of Josephus, the New Testament, and Rabbinic literature—all sources unsympathetic to the Sadducees. Our picture of the Sadducees, therefore, is incomplete and rather general.

Identity. The Sadducees appear in the reign of John Hyrcanus (134–105 B.C.), who favored them over the Pharisees. The name *Sadducee* probably was derived from Zadok, the high priest who served David and Solomon (1 Kgs. 1:38–48; 1 Chr. 16:39). Reflecting the religious party of the powerful and privileged, the Sadducees drew their members from wealthy aristocrats and socially prominent families in and around Jerusalem. Prominent Sadducean families included the rival high priestly clans of Boethus and Annas.

One of several caves in the Qumran area in which the Dead Sea Scrolls were found.

Though not all Sadducees were priests, wealthy priestly families comprised a major component of the Sadducean party. Their stronghold was the temple, where they dominated the Sanhedrin throughout much of the Hasmonean and Roman periods until A.D. 70. The Sadducees appear prominently in the trials of Peter and John before the Sanhedrin (Acts 4:1–4; 5:17–18).

The Sadducees were political realists who cooperated with the ruling powers to ensure national survival. The exception to this, of course, was Herod. The Sadducees supported the Hasmonean Dynasty in the struggle for power at the beginning of the Roman period, and Herod made them pay dearly. Like the later Hasmonean kings, the Sadducees developed Hellenistic tendencies. Perhaps their wealth and power both encouraged and depended upon a more cosmopolitan viewpoint. Josephus states that the Sadducees had little support among the common people, who preferred both the religious teachings and social attitudes of the Pharisees.

Teachings. We know little about Sadducean doctrine. Josephus writes that the Sadducees emphasized human freedom and responsibility before God. Other religious groups placed more emphasis on God's sovereignty (Pharisees) and determinism (Essenes). The major point of disagreement with the Pharisees was authority. The Sadducees rejected the oral tradition the Pharisees valued so highly, and they continuously battled the Pharisees over matters of interpretation.

Rabbinic literature, pronouncedly Pharisaic in its outlook, mentions disputes between Pharisees and Sadducees over laws of purity in particular. We must exercise caution here, however. Although the Sadducees may well have been more Hellenized and cosmopolitan than their Pharisee counterparts, they were quite conservative religiously. Recent excavations in Jerusalem have provided evidence that matters of purity were scrupulously observed among the wealthy class. Several aristocratic houses have one or more ritual baths *(mikvaoth)* in them (see also "Jerusalem in the Days of Herod and Jesus," pp. 228–33).

The Sadducees rejected the more progressive theological ideas embraced by the Pharisees. Believing that faithfulness to God was rewarded in this life, the Sadducees denied such concepts as eternal rewards and punishments and the idea of resurrection. The Sadducees held much less common theological ground with Christianity than did the Pharisees. Their rejection of the idea of resurrection presented an insurmountable obstacle to the new faith.

The Sadducean party collapsed in the wake of the destruction of Jerusalem in A.D. 70. Their influence dissolved when their stronghold, the temple, was lost. Henceforth, Judaism was shaped by the Pharisees, the chief rivals of this once powerful party.

DEAD SEA SCROLL COMMUNITY (ESSENES?)

The Dead Sea Scrolls, discovered since 1948, brought to life another Jewish group more sectarian than either the Pharisees or Sadducees. The scrolls, found in caves on the northwestern edge of the Dead Sea, describe the beliefs and practices of a Jewish community centered upon Qumran. Excavations at Qumran established the community's existence from about 150 B.C. to A.D. 68, with a brief period of abandonment during the reign of Herod the Great.

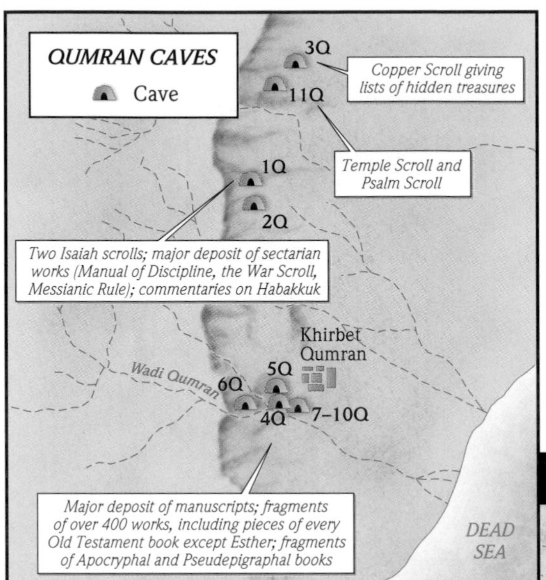

Identity. The Qumran community has been compared with the Essenes, a Jewish sect described by Josephus and other classical writers, but recent scholarship questions this identification. Josephus said the Essenes numbered about four thousand adherents in his day and lived scattered about in several towns. Some discrepancies exist between these written sources and our knowledge of the Qumran community gained by examination of the scrolls they produced and the ruins of Qumran. Recently, several scholars have urged caution when identifying the Dead Sea Scroll community with the Essenes. Perhaps the Qumran community represented a distinct sect within Judaism. Lawerence Schiffman has developed earlier insights identifying the Qumran community as an offshoot of the Sadducees. Nonetheless, the majority of scholars still believe the people who collected and wrote the Dead Sea Scrolls were Essenes.

Teachings. The people of Qumran lived communally in covenant with God and one another. Withdrawing to the desert, the members of the sect gave themselves to the study of Scripture and maintained a status of ritual and ethical purity in the belief they were the "true Israel" living in the last stage of history. Soon, they believed, God would intervene decisively against the evil that enveloped the world. They were faithful "Sons of Light" prepared to join God in His approaching victory over the "Sons of Darkness."

The Qumran covenanters expected the coming of a prophet and two messiahs, one each from the lineage of Aaron and David. This eschatological focus was given to the community by the "Teacher of Righteousness," perhaps the founder of the sect and certainly its most influential leader. Although the Teacher of Righteousness was killed by a "Wicked Priest," his interpretations of Old Testament books shaped the Qumran community's entire perspective.

Organization and Practices. Certain scrolls (for example, *The Manual of Discipline*) describe the organization and practices of the group. The community was organized in a hierarchy dominated by priests. A supreme council composed of both priests and laymen guided the life of the community. The community met in assemblies of "the many" to discuss matters of importance. Each member could speak, but only in order of rank established by the council. Discipline within the community was severe; penalties for minor and major infractions of the community's standards were clearly outlined and enforced. An overseer

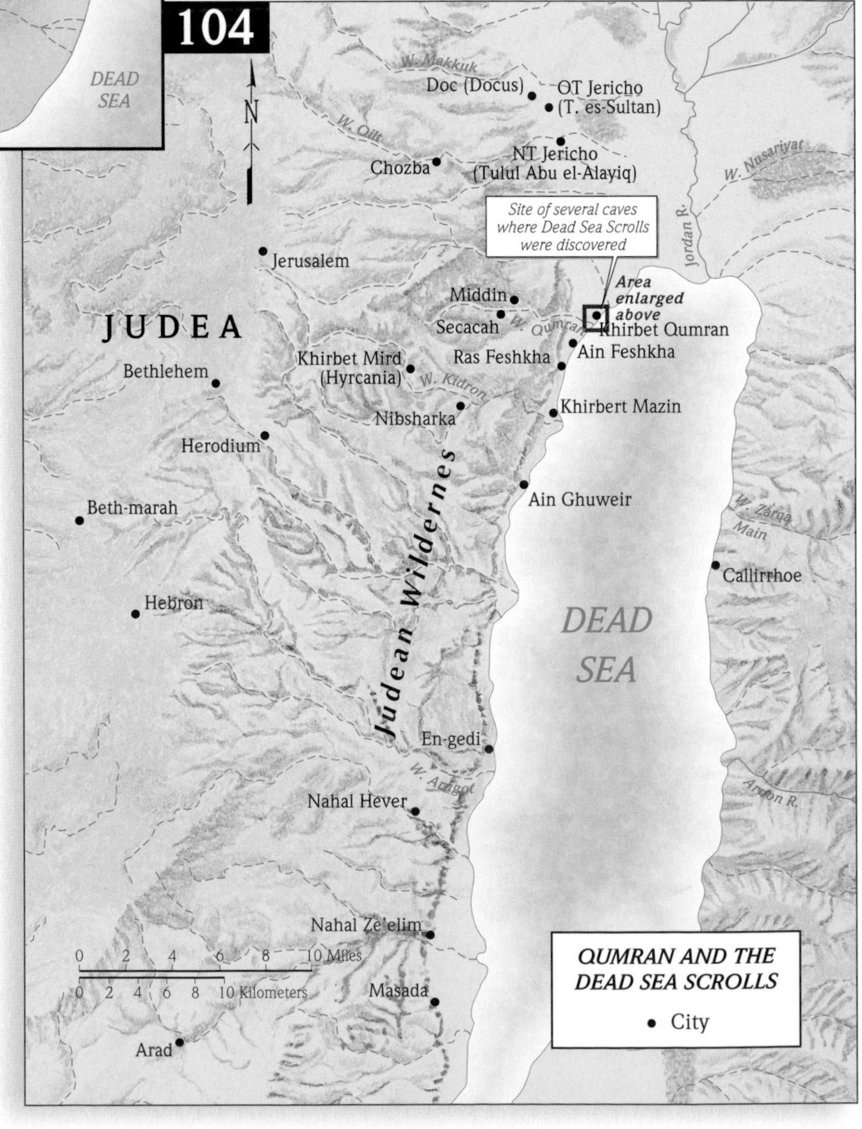

An overview of the Qumran community from the defensive tower.

directed financial matters and assigned tasks required for the daily operation of the sect. The community held property in common, disdaining personal wealth and distinctions based on riches. The community practiced two common rites: a shared meal and ritual washings.

According to several sources, the Essenes practiced celibacy, but Josephus suggests that some Essenes married. Whether or not the people at Qumran married remains unclear. Their scrolls do not forbid marriage, and a few female skeletons have been found at Qumran in the adjacent cemetery.

Candidates for admission into the Qumran community faced a two-or possibly three-year period of examinations, instruction, and discipline. The overseer examined each candidate initially. At first the candidate's possessions were strictly separated from that of the community; neither could the candidate partake of certain rites within the community. New candidates were integrated into the community in stages only after they passed muster.

The Scrolls. The scrolls copied and studied at Qumran found a haven in the numerous caves piercing the steep cliffs at the edge of the Dead Sea. Perhaps they were placed there for safekeeping upon the approach of the Roman army during the First Jewish Revolt. The numerous scrolls and scroll fragments found in a dozen caves from 1947 onward are now known as the Dead Sea Scrolls. Among them are the earliest known Hebrew texts of Old Testament books. Some manuscripts are virtually intact, such as Isaiah; many more are fragmentary. Only Esther remains unrepresented among the Old Testament materials.

Other scrolls contain interpretations of prophetic books such as Nahum and Habbakuk. Noncanonical Jewish writings are also numbered among the scrolls as well as sectarian documents ordering the life of the community at Qumran. These scrolls provide a treasure for biblical scholars that has yet to be fully explored.

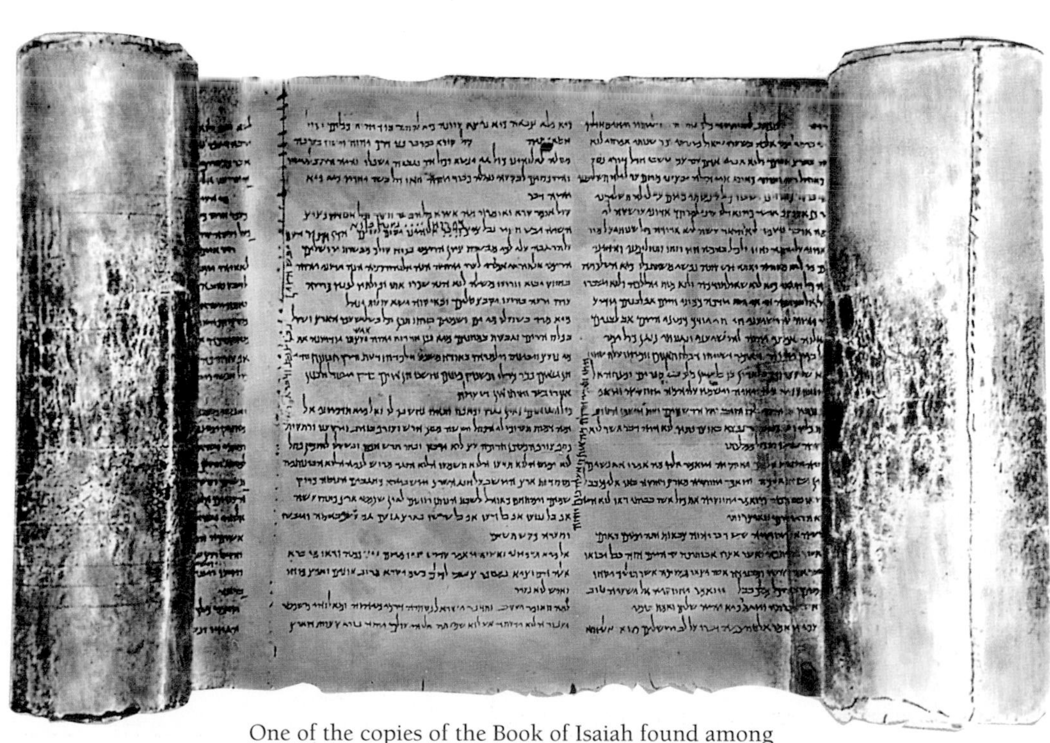

One of the copies of the Book of Isaiah found among the Dead Sea Scrolls.

Chapter Eighteen

THE LIFE AND MINISTRY OF JESUS

Introduction

The life of Jesus unfolds in four Gospels that testify to His powerful ministry. The Gospels are not biographies in the modern sense of the word, but are inspired testimonies that give us portraits of Jesus. The Synoptic Gospels—Matthew, Luke, and Mark—portray Jesus in a similar manner (*synoptic* literally means "to see together"), but each contains distinctives. Matthew and Luke include information about the birth of Jesus, while Mark begins with Jesus' public ministry. The Synoptic Gospels detail many things Jesus said and did, though each Gospel writer arranged the material to suit the overall picture he wanted to paint of Jesus.

Each writer emphasized certain aspects of Jesus' ministry and selected from the many events that transpired in the unique life of the Lord (John 21:25). The Synoptics paid special attention to the ministry in Galilee. The Gospel of John, on the other hand, paints a different portrait of Jesus' ministry. John emphasized Jesus' Jerusalem ministry and concentrated on the numerous Jewish festivals that Jesus attended in the Holy City. John's portrait centers on seven miracles that he called "signs" that disclosed the true identity of Jesus. The "I AM" sayings of John's Gospel (John 6:35; 8:12; 10:7–9; 11:25; 14:6; 15:1) likewise pointed to Jesus as God's Son. John included lengthy discourses of Jesus unparalleled in the Synoptic Gospels. Each Gospel portrait adds a dimension to our understanding of the life and ministry of Jesus without which our overall picture would be incomplete.

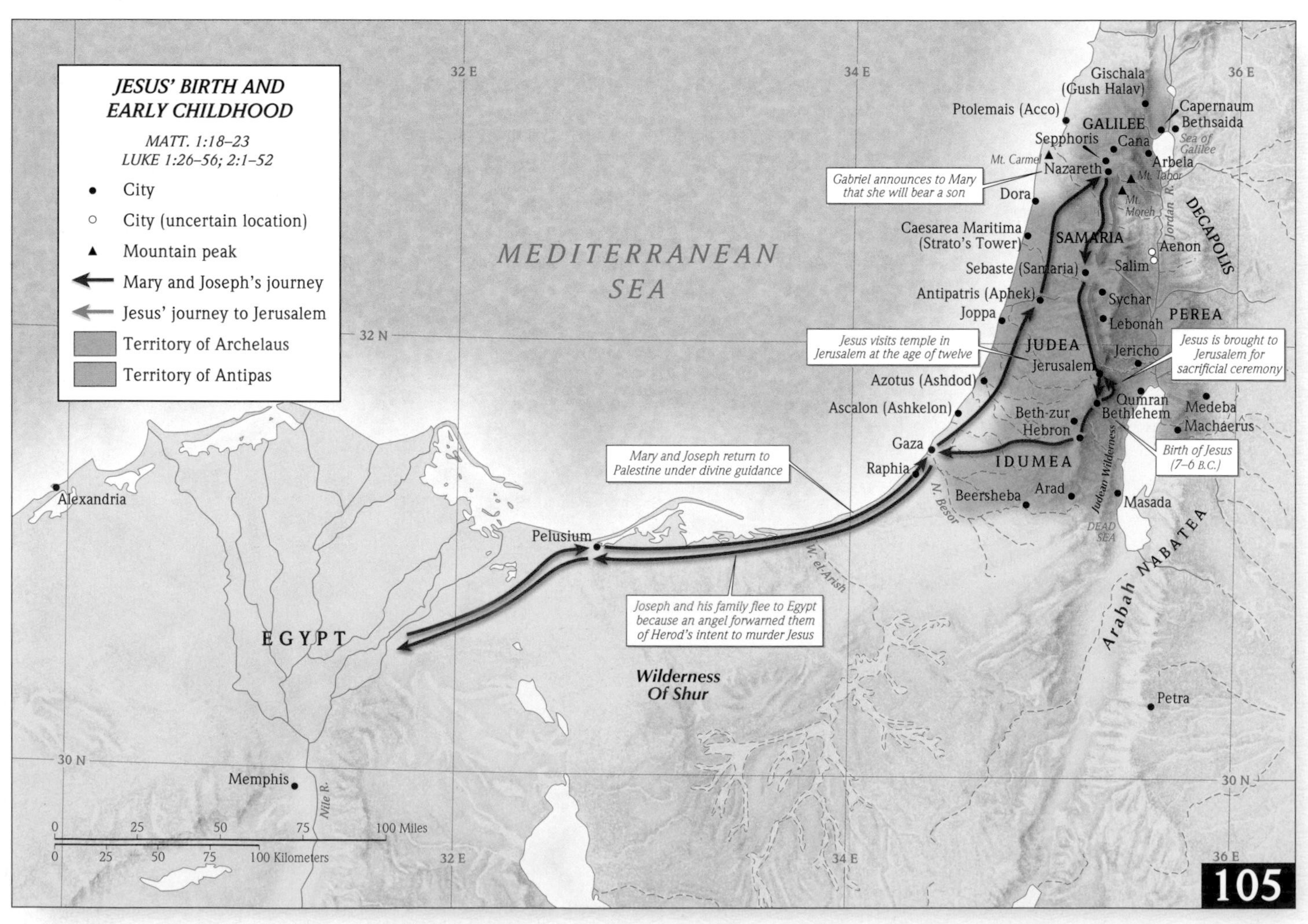

The Church of the Nativity at Bethlehem.

The nature of the Gospels, however, presents obstacles to reconstructing the life of Jesus. As testimonies rather than biographies, the Gospels are less concerned about chronological and geographical details than a biographer would be. The location of some events are given in general terms, while the chronological linkage between events often can be vague or uncertain. In what follows, we will concentrate on key geographical settings in Jesus' ministry and leave aside the more complex discussion of chronology.

The Birth of Jesus and His Childhood

The gospel story begins with the announcement of two births, each in its own way miraculous. Luke records the birth of John the Baptist to aged parents, Zechariah and Elizabeth. Tradition says that the couple lived in a small village in the hills west of Jerusalem, today called Ein Karim. Six months later, the angel Gabriel announced in Nazareth that Mary would bear a Son whose name would be called Jesus—"The Lord is salvation." The two cousins, Mary and Elizabeth, met later in Judah at the house of Zechariah, where Mary expressed her great joy for the favor granted to her by God (Luke 1:39–56).

As the day of delivery drew near, Mary and Joseph traveled to Bethlehem, the City of David. A tax census ordered when Quirinius was governor of Syria required subjects to be enrolled in their ancestral home. Because Joseph was of the lineage of David, that meant a journey to Bethlehem, a village located near the ridge road that connected Jerusalem with Hebron. Today the Church of the Nativity covers several caves that may have been used for storage and sheltering animals from the elements. Helena, the mother of the emperor Constantine, built the church in A.D. 335 to commemorate the birth of Jesus. Justinian expanded the church considerably in the sixth century to accommodate pilgrims who flocked to the site.

The date of Jesus' birth remains uncertain, although it preceded Herod's death in 4 B.C., perhaps by two or three years, making it likely that Jesus was born between 7 and 6 B.C. The angelic announcement of Jesus' birth to shepherds tending flocks in the surrounding Judean hills proclaimed joy and peace upon the earth. Matthew records the visit of the Magi—wisemen or astrologers from Mesopotamia—who came to worship the newborn Child.

Luke records the circumcision of Jesus on the eighth day and the first visit of Jesus to Jerusalem, where Mary and Joseph offered the prescribed sacrifices for a firstborn (Luke 2:21–35). Born under the Law, Jesus fulfilled all the provisions prescribed by the Law.

An angel forewarned Mary and Joseph that Herod viewed Jesus as a potential rival for his throne and intended to murder Him. The family fled to Egypt, long a place of refuge for people experiencing troubled times in Palestine. After an indefinite stay, Mary and Joseph returned to Palestine under divine

An overview of the modern city of Nazareth.

guidance. They bypassed Judea because of the turmoil attending the reign of Archelaus, choosing instead to return to Nazareth.

We know virtually nothing about Jesus during the formative years as He grew to maturity. Nazareth, His home, was a small village overlooking the fertile Jezreel Valley to the south. Three miles to the north lay the city of Sepphoris with its merchants, traders, and governmental officials. The large-scale building projects in Sepphoris supported by Herod Antipas provided jobs and an economic boost for the villages of the area.

What impact Sepphoris may have had on Jesus is debated. Perhaps Joseph found work in the building program sponsored by Herod Antipas. Jesus also may have labored in the city if He practiced the carpentry trade of His father. The proximity of Sepphoris to Nazareth provided a much more urban setting in which Jesus grew to maturity than previously suspected. However, Sepphoris was a royal city, the center of Roman domination over the villages and towns of Galilee. In the minds of the Galilean peasants, Sepphoris stood for burdensome taxes and, perhaps, Roman oppression. The nature and interaction between capitals such as Sepphoris and the typical Galilean Jewish village is debatable.

Jesus absorbed the sights and sounds of a busy city in His childhood years, but He also delighted in the beautiful grain fields, orchards, vineyards, and open meadows that surrounded Him in Galilee. Because His family were faithful Jews, Mary and Joseph often went up to Jerusalem to attend the festivals. Luke describes one of these visits when Jesus was twelve years old (Luke 2:41–51).

The journey took several days and often was made in the company of other pilgrims for safety and companionship. The gleaming white-and-gold temple must have made quite an impression on the young boy. In His dialogue with Jewish teachers of the law, His knowledge and maturity elicited amazement from them. Aside from this incident we know nothing else about the early years of Jesus. The Gospels resume their story when Jesus was about thirty years of age (Luke 3:23).

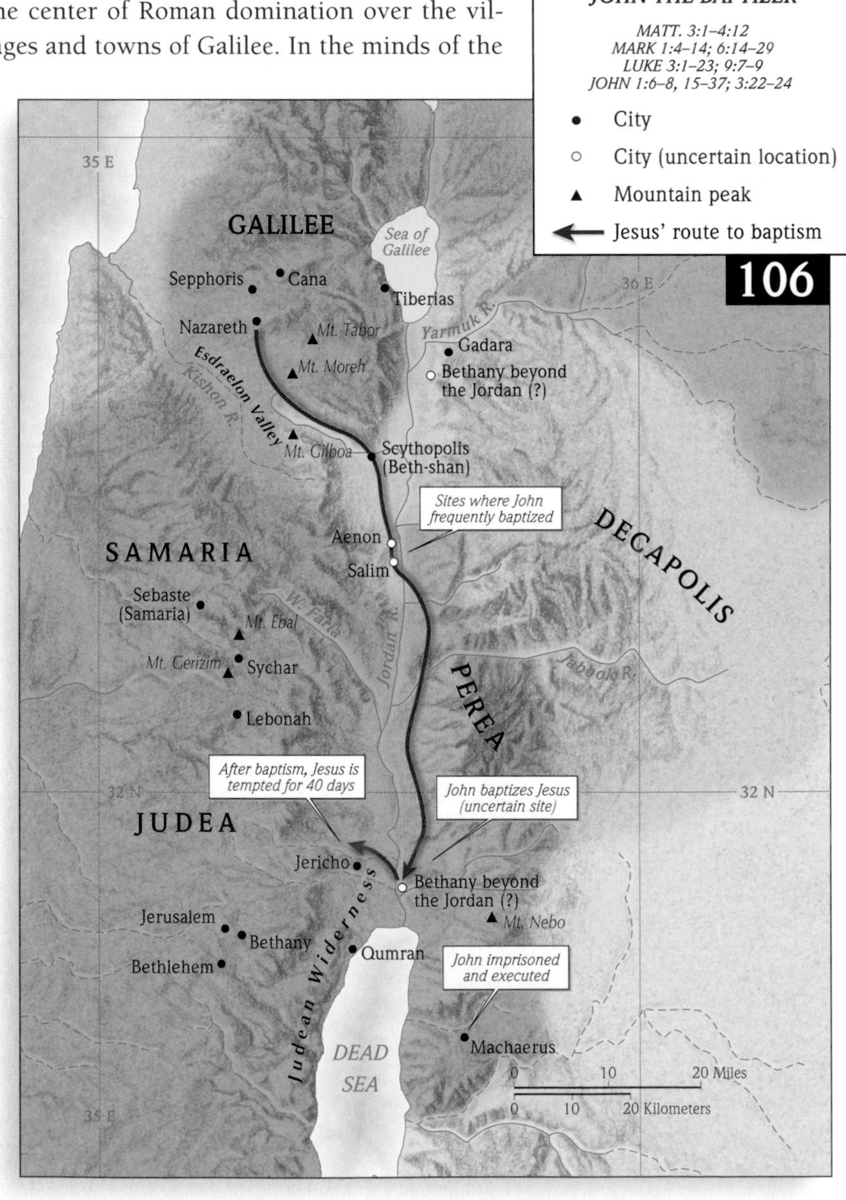

John the Baptist's Message and Ministry

John the Baptist appeared in the wilderness east of Judea in the fifteenth year of Tiberius, that is about A.D. 27–28. John preached a "baptism of repentance for the forgiveness of sins" (Mark 1:4) as a prelude to the coming of the messianic era. Making his home in the desert, John may have lived in the wilderness for a long time (see Luke 1:80). At some point John may have been associated with the Qumran community, who, likewise, believed the messianic era was about to dawn and also practiced a form of baptism. If so, John left the community to fulfill his mission.

John preached his message in the wilderness along the edge of the Jordan (Matt. 3:1; Mark 1:4). He attracted curious crowds from Jerusalem and Judea, announcing "the kingdom of God is at hand" (Mark 1:14), thus fulfilling Isaiah's prophecy (Isa. 40:3). Jews believed the wilderness was a place of preparation for the expected messianic era. A few references suggest John also preached in Perea ("Bethany beyond the Jordan" [John 1:28]) and in the region of Scythopolis, where John baptized at Aenon near Salim (John 3:23). John's attack upon the marriage between Herod Antipas and Herodias

The rugged terrain of the wilderness of Judea west of Jericho. Tradition places the temptations of Jesus in this desolate terrain.

brought the wrath of the tetrarch, a fact that may have prompted John at times to stay out of the reach of Antipas.

Jesus traveled from Galilee to be baptized by John in the Jordan. The exact location of Jesus' baptism remains unknown, but tradition located the event east of Jericho near the Hajlah Ford. Immediately after the baptism, Jesus went into the wilderness, where He was tempted for forty days. Again, the precise locale of the temptations escapes us, but tradition places the event in the rugged wilderness mountains west of Jericho at Jebel Qarantal. Here, in the desolation and isolation afforded by the wilderness, Jesus wrestled with the temptations to compromise His mission.

According to the Gospel of John, the ministries of John the Baptist and Jesus briefly overlapped (John 4:1–3), before Herod Antipas eventually ordered John's arrest. Herod feared John's preaching would lead to revolution among his subjects.

Galilee in Jesus' Days

As a native of Nazareth, Jesus was intimately acquainted with the hills, valleys, and sloping plateaus of Galilee. The Synoptic Gospels locate the majority of the public ministry of Jesus in the villages and towns of Galilee. Josephus, the first-century Jewish historian who commanded the Jewish forces of Galilee during the First Jewish Revolt (A.D. 66–70), gave first-hand descriptions of Galilee in his numerous writings. According to Josephus, Galilee was divided into two parts, Upper and Lower Galilee, with the dividing line following the Bet Kerem Valley.

Recent surveys indicate that Upper Galilee was not as isolated as formerly thought. Trade routes crisscrossed Galilee, connecting the Phoenician coastal cities (Sidon, Tyre, and Ptolemais) with the villages and towns of the hinterland, while the great trunk route commonly called the *Via Maris* crossed Galilee on the way to Damascus.

Galilee was encircled by non-Jewish populations with Greek cities along the coastal plain to the west, several Greek cities of the Decapolis to the east/southeast (Scythopolis, Hippos, Gadara, and Pella), and the tetrarchy of Philip to the northeast. Samaria and the royal Herodian estates of the Jezreel Valley bordered Galilee on the south.

Galilee supported a predominately Jewish population estimated at between 150,000 and 300,000. Josephus mentions 204 villages scattered about the hills and valleys of the region, suggesting the strong rural character of the population. The area was fertile and blessed with a good climate favorable to crops. Agriculture always was the chief base of the local economy. Grapes, olives, figs, and grains (wheat and barley) grew in abundance on the small family farms that dotted the area. Larger estates owned by wealthier landowners who might live away from Galilee also were found.

Jesus referred to such absentee landowners in His parables (Luke 20:9–18), but His stories more often portrayed the family-owned farms that predominated in Galilee (Matt. 21:28–32). Tenant farmers leased the land and sharecropped with the owner, while poorer people hired out as day laborers. Jesus' sayings and parables are filled with the images drawn from agriculture as practiced in His native land. On one occasion He observed that the "harvest is plentiful, but the laborers are few" (Matt. 9:37).

Along with its heavy agricultural basis, Galilee supported some industries. The Sea of Galilee produced an abundance of fish, especially along the lake's northern end. Fresh fish was consumed locally, but much of the catch was salted for export. Magdala, also known as Taricheae (a name suggesting a place where fish were salted), was the center of a salted-fish industry. The pottery industry also prospered, although exports of pottery were limited in the first century. Customs and taxes were collected on goods that flowed across Galilee at stations placed

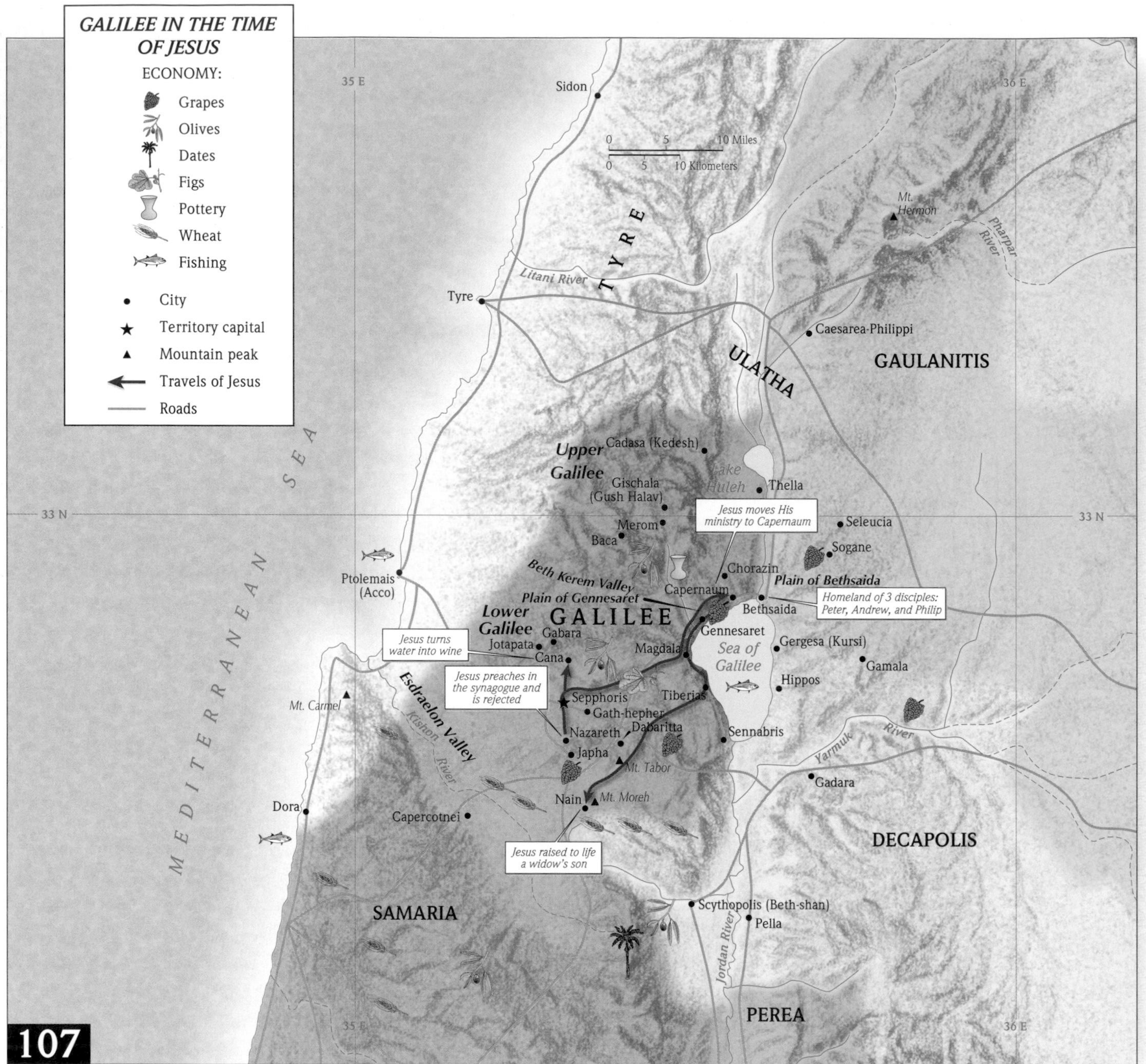

near borders. Jesus called Matthew to be His disciple from one such station located in the vicinity of Capernaum.

In addition to the numerous villages, Galilee had several cities that were the focus of administration and commerce. Sepphoris (see p. 209 under "Herod Antipas") served as the regional capital until Herod Antipas founded Tiberias about A.D. 18 or 19. These two cities along with Magdala injected a more pronounced Hellenistic/Roman element into the Galilean ethos. Theaters, palaces, and hippodromes found in larger cities added cultural spice to the mix. Greek could be heard, especially in the cities, along with the more common Aramaic. Even villages like Chorazim and Capernaum could also have non-Jews as residents, but Galilee was a predominately rural, Jewish land.

Jesus' Early Ministry

NAZARETH

Jesus' public ministry began in Galilee at Nazareth. In the local synagogue He claimed that Isaiah's ancient prophecies of good news to oppressed people were coming true (Luke 4:16–

21). Nazareth was located in the rocky limestone hills overlooking the Jezreel Valley. Although only three or four miles from Sepphoris, Nazareth was a small village from which little could be expected (note Nathanael's remark, "Can anything good come out of Nazareth?" [John 1:46]). Other villages in the area, like Japha, were more important. Nazareth, nonetheless, was interconnected by trade with the numerous villages and towns of western Galilee.

Four miles northwest of Nazareth was Cana, where Jesus performed His first miracle—changing the water into wine (John 2). Later in Cana He healed an official's son who lived in Capernaum (John 4:46–54). At least one of Jesus' disciples, Nathanael, and possibly Simon the Cananean came from Cana.

Following His rejection by His home village and kinsmen, Jesus shifted His ministry to the Sea of Galilee—the scene of some of His most memorable events. The journey from Nazareth took Jesus about twenty miles across the slopes and the expansive grain fields clustered about the Horns of Hattin, an extinct volcanic cone. The eastern sector of Lower Galilee was more sparsely settled than the western portion. Steep mountains surrounded much of the Sea of Galilee, except for the south and the northwest, where the fertile Plain of Gennesaret—extolled by Josephus for its climate and variety of fruits—provided an agricultural bounty. From the surrounding heights, one could look down upon the numerous villages and towns ringing the lake's shores.

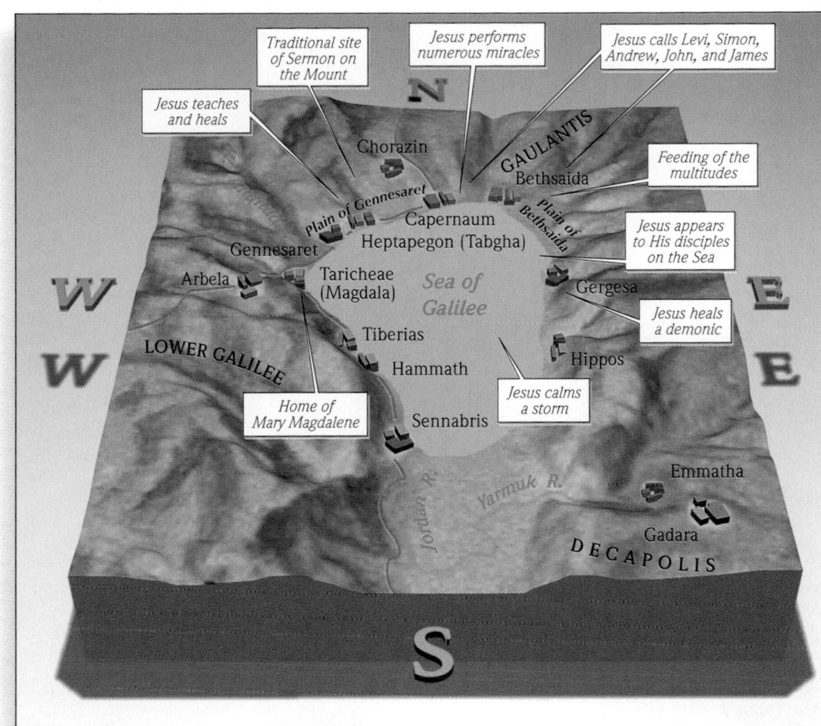

108

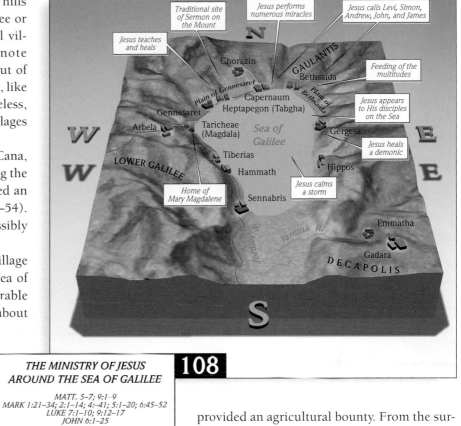

THE MINISTRY OF JESUS AROUND THE SEA OF GALILEE

MATT. 5–7; 9:1–9
MARK 1:21–34; 2:1–14; 4:–41; 5:1–20; 6:45–52
LUKE 7:1–10; 9:12–17
JOHN 6:1–25

 City

—— Road

The limestone synagogue at Capernaum. This synagogue dates from a later time than Jesus, but underlying structures perhaps dating to the first century B.C. suggest that an earlier synagogue stood at the same place. Ruins from modest houses built of the local black basalt stone dating from the first century A.D. are visible in the foreground.

CAPERNAUM AND BETHSAIDA

Jesus concentrated His ministry along the north shore of the Sea of Galilee near Capernaum and Bethsaida, both of which appear frequently in the Gospels. Matthew refers to Capernaum as Jesus' "own city" (Matt. 9:1). Jesus lived in Capernaum for a time and called His first disciples from the villagers and fishermen nearby (Matt. 4:12–22; Mark 1:16–20; Luke 5:1–11).

Capernaum was located on the main trade route that hugged the western shore of the lake before turning north along the Jordan River. The small town stretched three to four hundred yards east and west along the lake's edge. Jesus taught in the local synagogue and performed several healing miracles in Capernaum, including curing Peter's mother-in-law of a fever and healing two paralytics (Matt. 8:5–17; Mark 2:1–22). Jesus raised from the dead the daughter of Jairus, a ruler of the synagogue, at Capernaum (Luke 8:40–56). Excavations of Capernaum (Tel Hum) have yielded

An overview of the northwestern shore of the Sea of Galilee and the Plain of Gennesaret.

remains of modest houses built of the local black basalt; they are clustered in groups *(insulae)* along well-laid-out streets.

Early Christians identified one of these houses as the house of Simon Peter, and they converted it to a "house church." An octagonal church was built over the house church as a memorial to the great apostle about A.D. 450. A white limestone synagogue dated by the excavators to about A.D. 400 stood a few yards west of the church. Underneath, the synagogue excavations revealed basalt foundations, possibly part of the synagogue in which Jesus preached.

Located on the north end of the Sea of Galilee about five miles east of Capernaum, Bethsaida played a key role in Jesus' Galilean ministry (see pp. 209-10 under "Philip"). Three of Jesus' disciples—Peter, Andrew, and Philip—came from Bethsaida (John 1:44; 12:21). Jesus performed a healing miracle in Bethsaida (Mark 8:22–26) and fed the hungry multitude of five thousand nearby (Luke 9:10). Philip expanded the small fishing village of Bethsaida into a larger, more adequately adorned city to honor Augustus' daughter, Julia.

As His fame grew, people flocked to Jesus, bringing their sick and infirmed for healing (Mark 6:53–56). A crowd from Tiberias pursued Jesus across the lake to Capernaum (John 6:22–25), and on another occasion crowds gathered on the Plain of Gennesaret seeking the healing touch of Jesus (Matt. 14:34–36). Tradition locates the Sermon on the Mount on the grassy slopes of a hill overlooking the sea near Tabgha on the northern edge of Gennesaret. Tabgha, a corruption of *Heptapegon*—"place of the seven springs"—was identified by early pilgrims as the place where Jesus fed the five thousand. Neither tradition can be confirmed, but the copious springs at Tabgha, located just one and a half miles from Capernaum and the surrounding hills, surely were the backdrop of events in the ministry of Jesus.

VILLAGES BEYOND THE SEA OF GALILEE

Several Gospel incidents took place on the Sea of Galilee. On one occasion Jesus calmed one of the frequent storms

A storm breaking across the Sea of Galilee.

that afflict the lake (Matt. 8:23–27). Another time Jesus appeared on the Sea walking upon the water—to the astonishment of the disciples (Mark 6:47–52).

Jesus also traveled to the villages of Galilee beyond the lake. Beneath the slopes of Mount Moreh, Jesus raised to life a widow's son at Nain. His condemnation of Chorazin indicated He had performed mighty works in that village (Matt. 11:21). Archaeological work at Chorazin has revealed a modest village built of the local basalt and a synagogue built about A.D. 300, but few remains date from the first century.

Jesus outside Galilee

Galilee was the focus of Jesus' early ministry, but He also traveled outside of Galilee for various reasons. Jesus needed rest and a temporary respite from the crowds that thronged Him. He traveled to and from Jerusalem on journeys that took Him through the Decapolis, Perea, and Samaria. On one occasion Jesus journeyed into the region of Tyre and Sidon, where He cured the afflicted daughter of a Syro-Phoenician woman (Matt. 15:21–28; Mark 7:24–39). Jesus met the woman in one of the villages of this Hellenized region, perhaps His only journey outside the traditional borders of Israel. Both Tyre and Sidon were ancient Phoenician ports that flourished in the heyday of Phoenician expansion between 1000 and 500 B.C. (see p. 127 under "Phoenicians"). Under the Romans, Tyre was the most important commercial center on the Phoenician coast. The high uplands of Upper Galilee bordered the territory of these two cities that were interconnected by lively trade with the Galilean hinterland.

Jesus occasionally withdrew to Philip's tetrarchy northeast of the Sea of Galilee to find rest and to instruct His disciples. With a predominantly gentile population and a less volatile political environment, Philip's territories offered Jesus rest from His labors and an escape from the hand of Herod Antipas. Inviting springs at the foot of Mount Hermon offered islands of lush vegetation and natural beauty. This was especially true at Panias, an area sacred to the Graeco-Roman nature god, Pan, where Philip constructed his new capital Caesarea Philippi, complete with a temple dedicated to Caesar. (See photograph, p. 210.)

At Caesarea Philippi, Jesus queried His disciples about His true identity, eliciting Simon Peter's response, "Thou art the Christ, the Son of the Living God," still the foundational Christian confession of faith (Matt. 16:16). The transfiguration of Jesus probably took place in Philip's land also. Tradition located this event on Mount Tabor in the eastern Jezreel, but most scholars favor the slopes of Mount Hermon as the more likely setting (Matt. 17:1–8; Mark 9:2–8).

The Way to Jerusalem

Along with many other Galilean Jews, Jesus often traveled to Jerusalem to attend festivals. Pilgrims preferred a route that crossed over the Jordan near Scythopolis into Perea so as to avoid contact with the despised Samaritans. They crossed back over the Jordan at Jericho and ascended the barren eastern slopes of the Judean mountains to Jerusalem. Jesus must have taken this route on occasion. The story of the good Samaritan, perhaps Jesus' most well-known parable, is set along the dangerous and desolate road from Jericho to Jerusalem.

The synagogue at Chorazin. Though these ruins are later than the ministry of Jesus, Chorazin was an important village located not far from Capernaum, the center of Jesus' Galilean ministry.

SAMARIA

Jesus did not avoid Samaria. John described a journey Jesus and His disciples took through Samaria, highlighted by a dramatic meeting between Jesus and a Samaritan woman (John 4). The woman, from the nearby village of Sychar, encountered Jesus at the ancient watering place identified as Jacob's Well, located in a valley beneath Mounts Ebal and Gerizim. Josephus

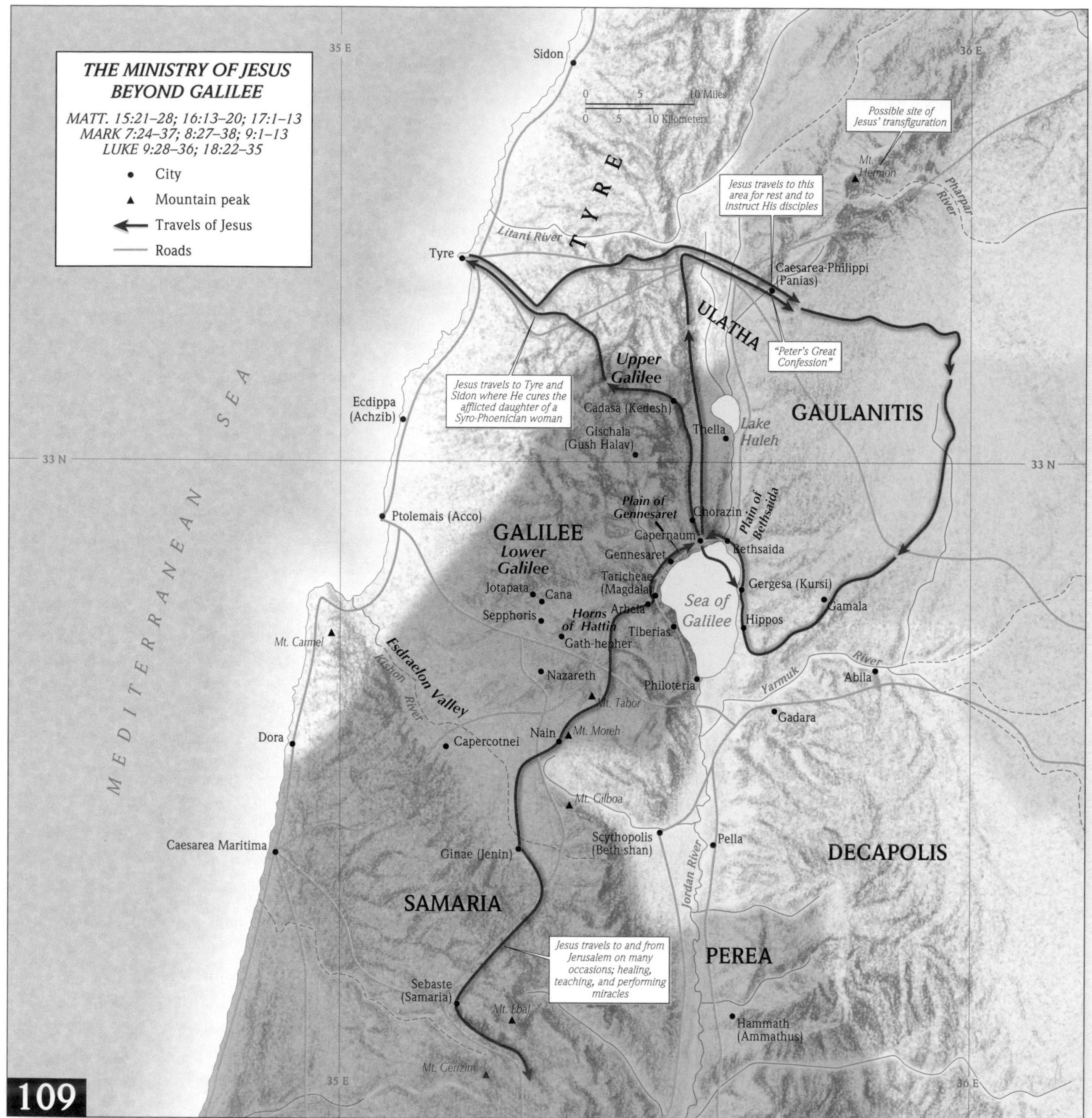

recounts a bloody conflict between Jewish pilgrims and Samaritans during the procuratorship of Cumanus (A.D. 48–52) at Ginae, only a few miles north of Jacob's Well. A Samaritan temple on Mount Gerizim was destroyed by the Hasmonean ruler John Hyrcanus about 150 years earlier.

By addressing the woman, Jesus challenged all the social, gender, and religious barriers so carefully nurtured in His day. Jesus and His disciples found food in the Samaritan villages that day, but on another occasion the villages of Samaria would not assist Him (Luke 9:52–53).

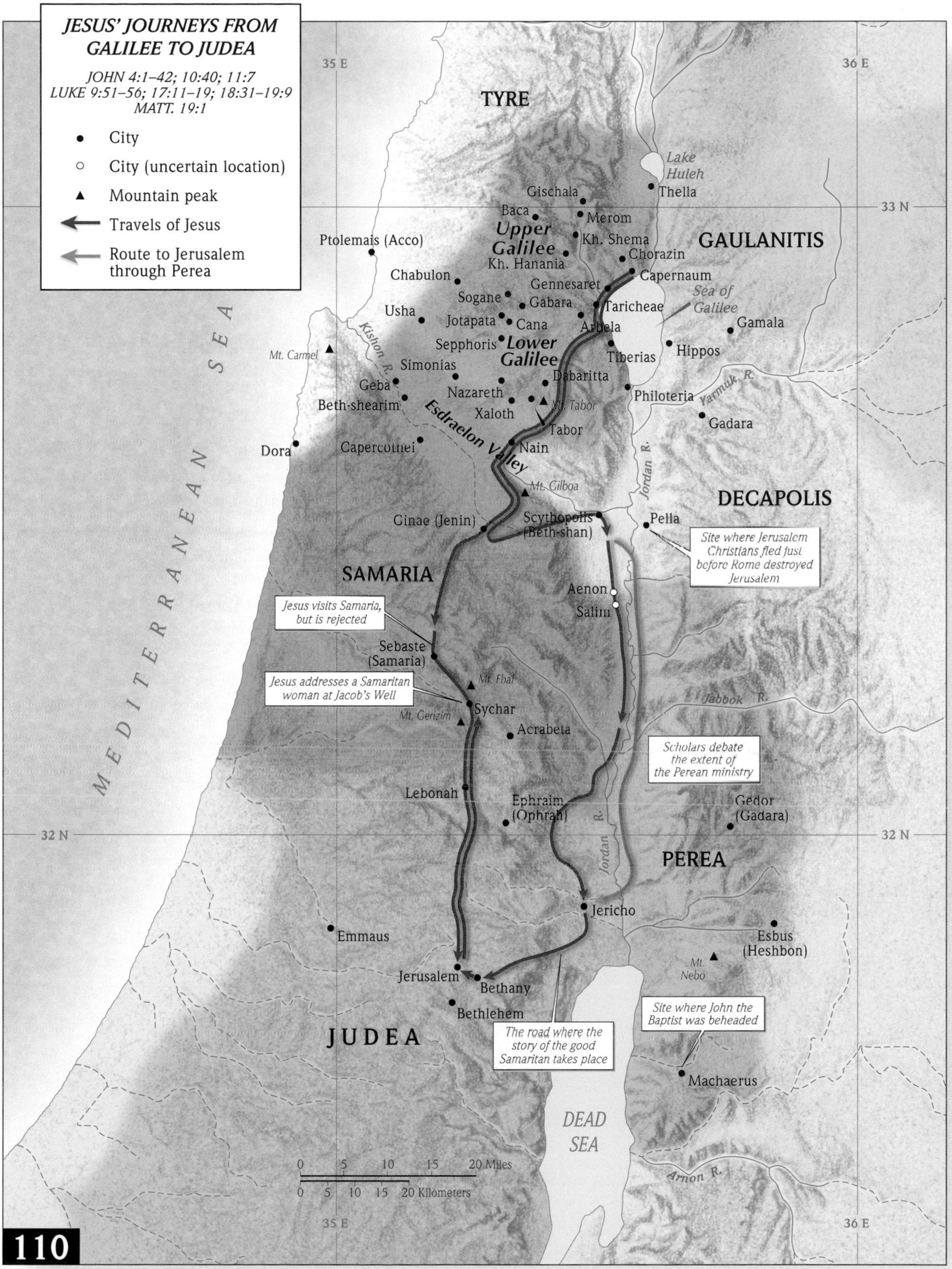

JESUS' JOURNEYS FROM GALILEE TO JUDEA

JOHN 4:1–42; 10:40; 11:7
LUKE 9:51–56; 17:11–19; 18:31–19:9
MATT. 19:1

- ● City
- ○ City (uncertain location)
- ▲ Mountain peak
- Travels of Jesus
- Route to Jerusalem through Perea

Jesus visits Samaria, but is rejected

Jesus addresses a Samaritan woman at Jacob's Well

Site where Jerusalem Christians fled just before Rome destroyed Jerusalem

Scholars debate the extent of the Perean ministry

Site where John the Baptist was beheaded

The road where the story of the good Samaritan takes place

35 E
36 E
33 N
32 N
TYRE
GAULANITIS
DECAPOLIS
SAMARIA
PEREA
JUDEA
MEDITERRANEAN SEA
Lake Huleh
Thella
Gischala
Baca
Merom
Upper Galilee
Kh. Shema
Ptolemais (Acco)
Chorazin
Kh. Hanania
Capernaum
Chabulon
Gennesaret
Sea of Galilee
Sogane
Gabara
Taricheae
Usha
Jotapata
Cana
Arbela
Gamala
Mt. Carmel
Kishon R.
Sepphoris
Lower Galilee
Hippos
Tiberias
Simonias
Dabaritta
Geba
Yarmuk R.
Nazareth
Philoteria
Beth-shearim
Mt. Tabor
Xaloth
Gadara
Esdraelon Valley
Tabor
Dora
Capercotnei
Nain
Jordan R.
Mt. Gilboa
Ginae (Jenin)
Scythopolis (Beth-shan)
Pella
Aenon
Salim
Sebaste (Samaria)
Mt. Ebal
Sychar
Jabbok R.
Mt. Gerizim
Acrabeta
Lebonah
Ephraim (Ophrah)
Gedor (Gadara)
Jericho
Emmaus
Esbus (Heshbon)
Mt. Nebo
Jerusalem
Bethany
Bethlehem
Machaerus
DEAD SEA
Arnon R.

0 5 10 15 20 Miles
0 5 10 15 20 Kilometers

110

PEREAN MINISTRY

Luke describes a "Perean ministry" that accompanied Jesus' final journey to Jerusalem (Luke 9:51–18:34). Perea was a Roman district east of the Jordan with its capital at Gadara. The Arnon River formed its southern boundary. Its eastern boundary was west of Gerasa and Philadelphia. Perea included the fortress of Machaerus, where John the Baptist was beheaded, and Pella, where Jerusalem Christians fled just before Rome destroyed Jerusalem in A.D. 70. Herod the Great and then Herod Antipas governed Perea.

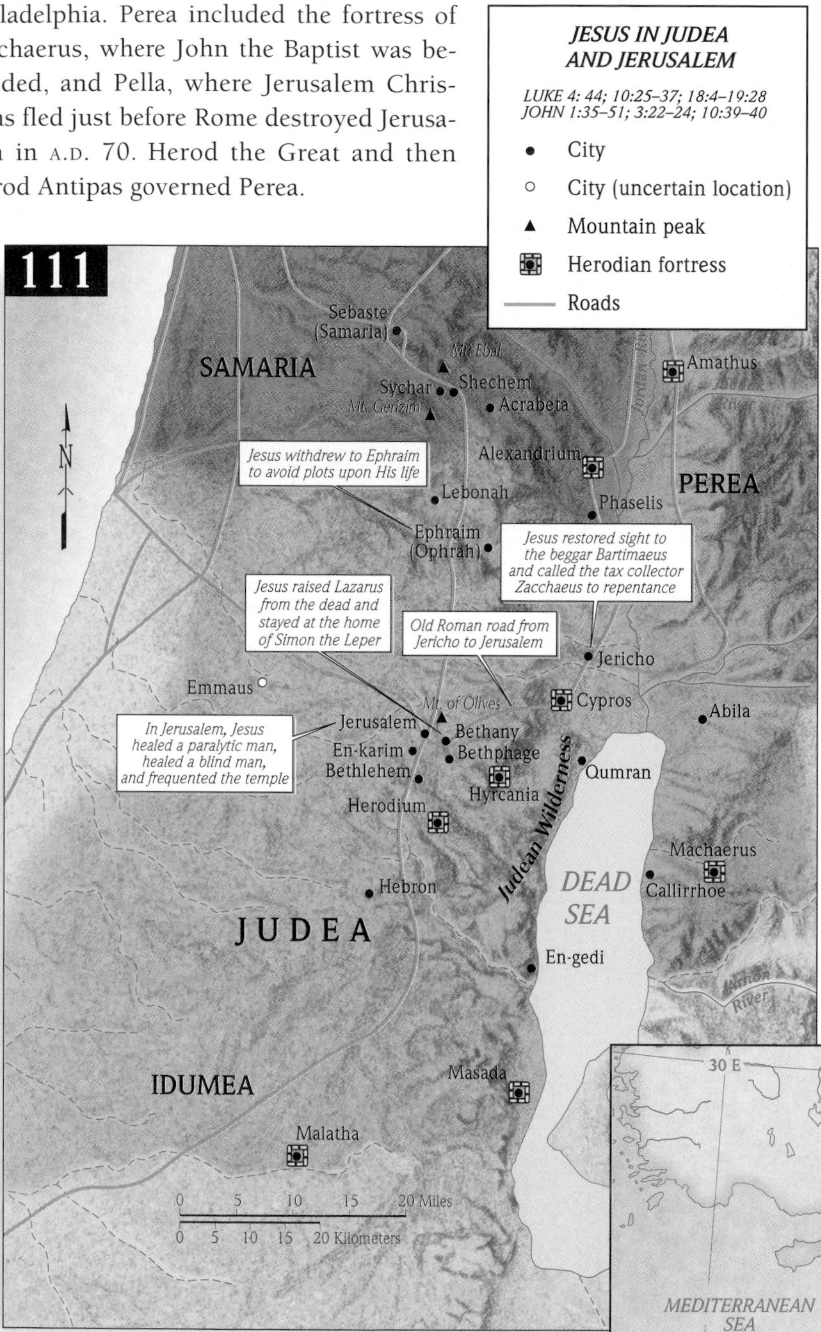

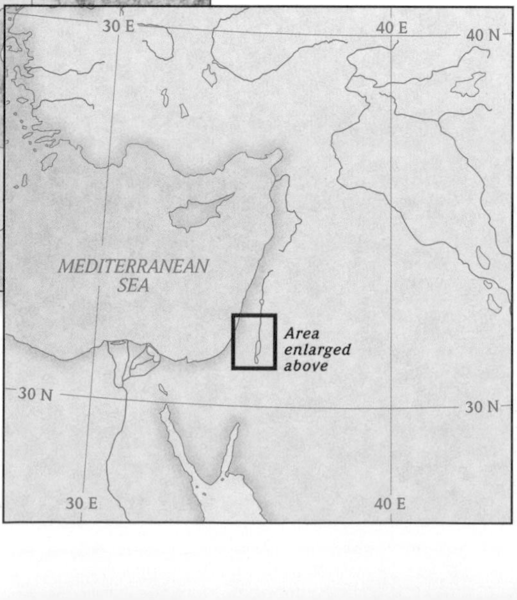

Scholars continue to debate the extent of the Perean ministry, although several passages suggest that Jesus visited Perea more than once (see John 10:40; Matt. 19:1, where "Judea beyond the Jordan" points to Perea).

111

JESUS IN JUDEA AND JERUSALEM

LUKE 4: 44; 10:25–37; 18:4–19:28
JOHN 1:35–51; 3:22–24; 10:39–40

- ● City
- ○ City (uncertain location)
- ▲ Mountain peak
- Herodian fortress
- Roads

Jesus withdrew to Ephraim to avoid plots upon His life

Jesus restored sight to the beggar Bartimaeus and called the tax collector Zacchaeus to repentance

Jesus raised Lazarus from the dead and stayed at the home of Simon the Leper

Old Roman road from Jericho to Jerusalem

In Jerusalem, Jesus healed a paralytic man, healed a blind man, and frequented the temple

Jesus in Judea and Jerusalem

The Synoptic Gospels focus on the ministry of Jesus in Galilee and only rarely allude to Judea until Jesus' final trip to Jerusalem. The Gospel of John, on the other hand, describes an extensive ministry of Jesus in the holy city. John mentions five occasions when Jesus traveled to Jerusalem, often in connection with the great pilgrim festivals—the Feast of Tabernacles (also called "Ingathering"), Passover, and the Feast of Weeks, also called Pentecost. From His childhood, Jesus customarily joined the throngs of pilgrims who converged upon Jerusalem in obedience to the Law of Moses that required all Jewish males to attend the festivals (Exod. 23:15–17; cf. Luke 2:41). John names three Passover feasts (John 2:13; 6:4; 11:55), one Feast of Tabernacles (John 7:2), an unnamed feast (John 5:1), and a festival of Dedication—"Hanukkah"—(John 10:22) that Jesus attended. The three Passovers strongly imply a public ministry for Jesus of at least two, possibly three years.

Luke records that Jesus preached in the synagogues of Judea early in His ministry (Luke 4:44). He and His disciples also baptized in the territory of Judea (John 3:22; although John 4:2 comments that Jesus did not administer baptism Himself). The Gospel of John especially links the early ministry of Jesus with the mission of John the Baptist, some of whose disciples became followers of Jesus (John 1:35ff; 3:23–30).

The Gospels mention several Judean villages and towns significant in the ministry of Jesus. At Jericho, Jesus restored sight to the beggar Bartimaeus (Luke 18:35–43) and called the tax collector Zacchaeus to repentance (Luke 19:1–10). Jericho flourished as an administrative center under the Romans, and it was a good location

The village of Bethany.

for a tax man like Zacchaeus to live. Trade routes linking Judea with the Transjordan and the northern Jordan Valley passed through the city. The winter palaces of the Herodian family stood west of the city near the road that led up to Jerusalem (see "Herodian Jericho," pp. 205-6).

Bethany, a village located 1.8 miles east of Jerusalem on the slope of the Mount of Olives, was the home of Lazarus and his sisters, Mary and Martha (John 11). Jesus was a guest in their house occasionally (Luke 10:38–42) and apparently lodged with His friends in Bethany during the week preceding His death (Matt. 21:17; Mark 11:11). Jesus raised Lazarus from the dead at Bethany (John 11). Jesus also was a guest in the home of Simon the Leper, who lived in Bethany (Mark 14:3). Ancient Bethany is identified with the modern village el-'Azariyeh.

On occasion Jesus retreated from Jerusalem to avoid plots upon His life. He withdrew to Ephraim, probably the site of ancient Ophrah (Josh. 18:23), a village often identified with et-Taiyibeh northeast of Jerusalem. To avoid arrest, Jesus crossed the Jordan to the region where John first baptized (John 10:39–40)

Jerusalem was the scene of many memorable events in the life of Jesus. He healed a paralytic man at the "Sheep's Pool," called "Beth-zatha (Bethesda)" (John 5:2–9). The pool was located north of the Temple Mount and apparently was a twin pool with a northern and southern basin. Another reservoir, the Pool

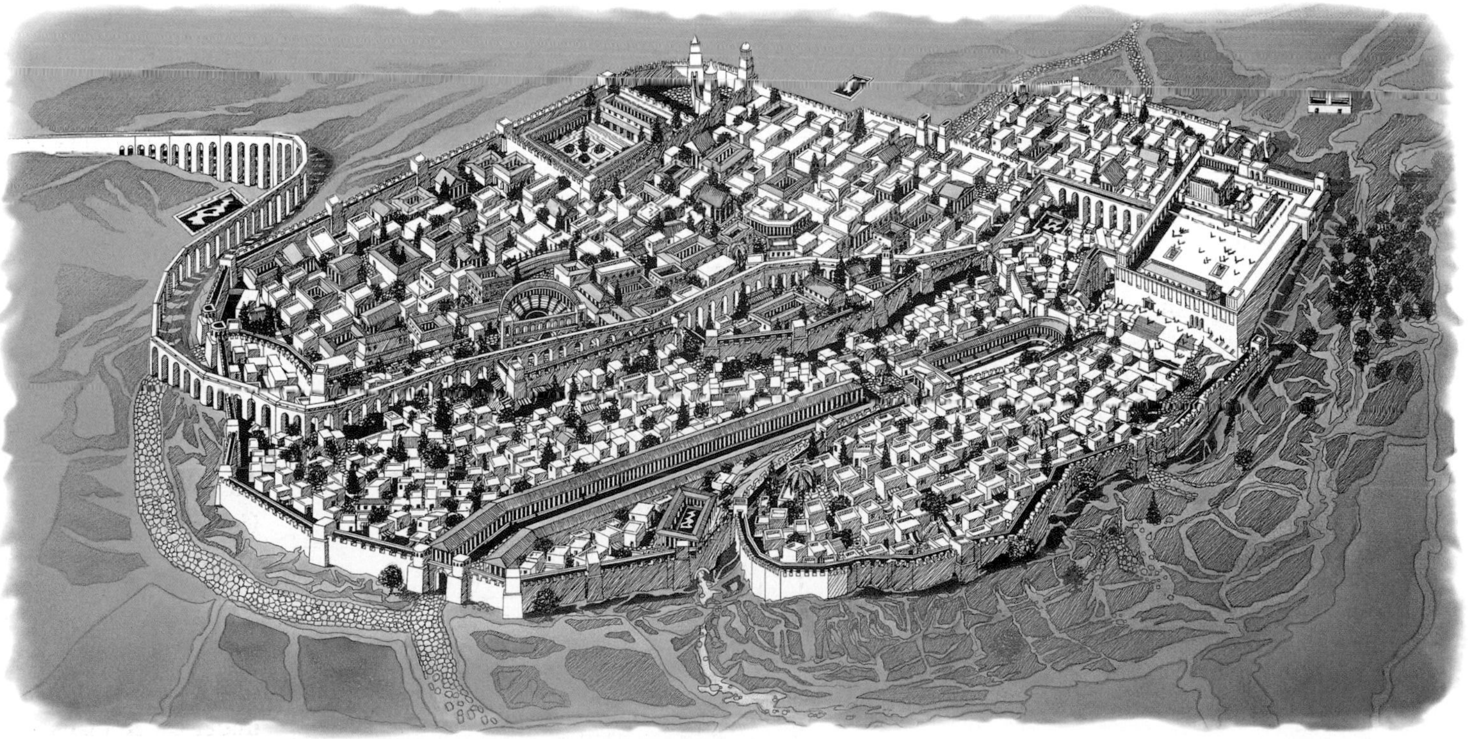

Reconstruction of Jerusalem

of Siloam, played a role in the healing of a blind man (John 9:1–12). Jesus instructed the man to wash away the clay poultice Jesus had applied to his eyes in the Pool of Siloam. The nocturnal discourse concerning a new birth between Nicodemus and Jesus also took place in Jerusalem in the course of Jesus' early Passover visit (John 3).

While in Jerusalem, Jesus frequented the temple, where He taught His disciples and the multitudes of pilgrims (John 5:14; 7:14). The colonnaded porticoes that ringed the temple courtyard provided a fine location for His teaching ministry. John 10:23 specifically mentions the Portico of Solomon on the east side of the temple, while the Royal Portico on the south end may have been the scene of the temple cleansing (John 2:13–22).

JERUSALEM IN THE DAYS OF HEROD AND JESUS

Jerusalem reached its zenith when Herod the Great transformed the Hasmonean city into a capital worthy of his kingdom. The scale of Herod's projects dwarfed those of all his predecessors and can still be seen throughout Jerusalem today. Herod's successors expanded the suburbs northward to include Bezetha, but the Jerusalem of Jesus' day essentially was that created by Herod the Great.

In addition to the vast amount of archaeological data retrieved in the last two decades, we also have the eyewitness accounts of Jerusalem in the first century A.D. written by the Jewish historian Flavius Josephus (A.D. 37 to ca. A.D. 100) and descriptions of the temple found in the Jewish Mishnah to aid in our reconstruction of the city. Josephus' *Jewish Wars* (Books V-VI) give lengthy descriptions of Jerusalem.

GENERAL DESCRIPTION

Jerusalem in the first century covered over four hundred acres and had a population that has been variously estimated to be between twenty and fifty thousand residents. Pilgrims swelled the population considerably during festivals. Josephus estimated the circumference of the city as thirty-three furlongs or about three and a half miles (Josephus, *JW,* 5§156–159). Jerusalem occupied all of both the eastern and western ridges (On the topography of Jerusalem, see "The Topography of Jerusalem," p. 111). The City of David and the Temple Mount retained their own walls, the former along the lines of Nehemiah's time while the latter was greatly expanded by Herod. The southwest hill or Upper City contained Herod's palace and numerous dwellings of wealthy Jerusalemites. The protective wall encircling the Upper City followed the line established by Hezekiah in the eighth century B.C. The increased population spilled over into northern suburbs that eventually were enclosed by two additional northern walls.

One of the most complex questions in the archaeology of Jerusalem is the course of the three northern walls described by Josephus. The first wall had fourteen towers spaced at intervals on a line from the Citadel to the Temple Mount. Scholars agree this wall followed a straight course along the Transversal Valley. However, the course and extent of the second wall described by Josephus are much debated. Josephus states this wall began at the Gennath Gate in the first wall and continued to the Antonia Fortress. The location of the Gennath Gate is disputed; a location next to the Citadel is preferred by some scholars, while others place the Gennath Gate midway along the first wall. The question of how far north the second wall extended has yet to be answered clearly. Many scholars believe the wall extended to the Damascus Gate in the present Old City wall; others believe the second wall extended no farther north than the Antonia Fortress. What is undisputed is that the second wall did not include the area surrounding the Church of the Holy Sepulcher, an area today inside the Old City walls. During this time of Jesus, this area was a quarry and was used for burials.

Likewise, the location of the third wall also is much disputed. Josephus says it began at the Citadel, went northward to Psephinus Tower, turned eastward past several landmarks to the Kidron Valley, and then proceeded south to the northeastern corner of the Temple Mount. Some four hundred

The remains of the Pool of "Bethesda" just north of the Temple Mount area in Jerusalem.

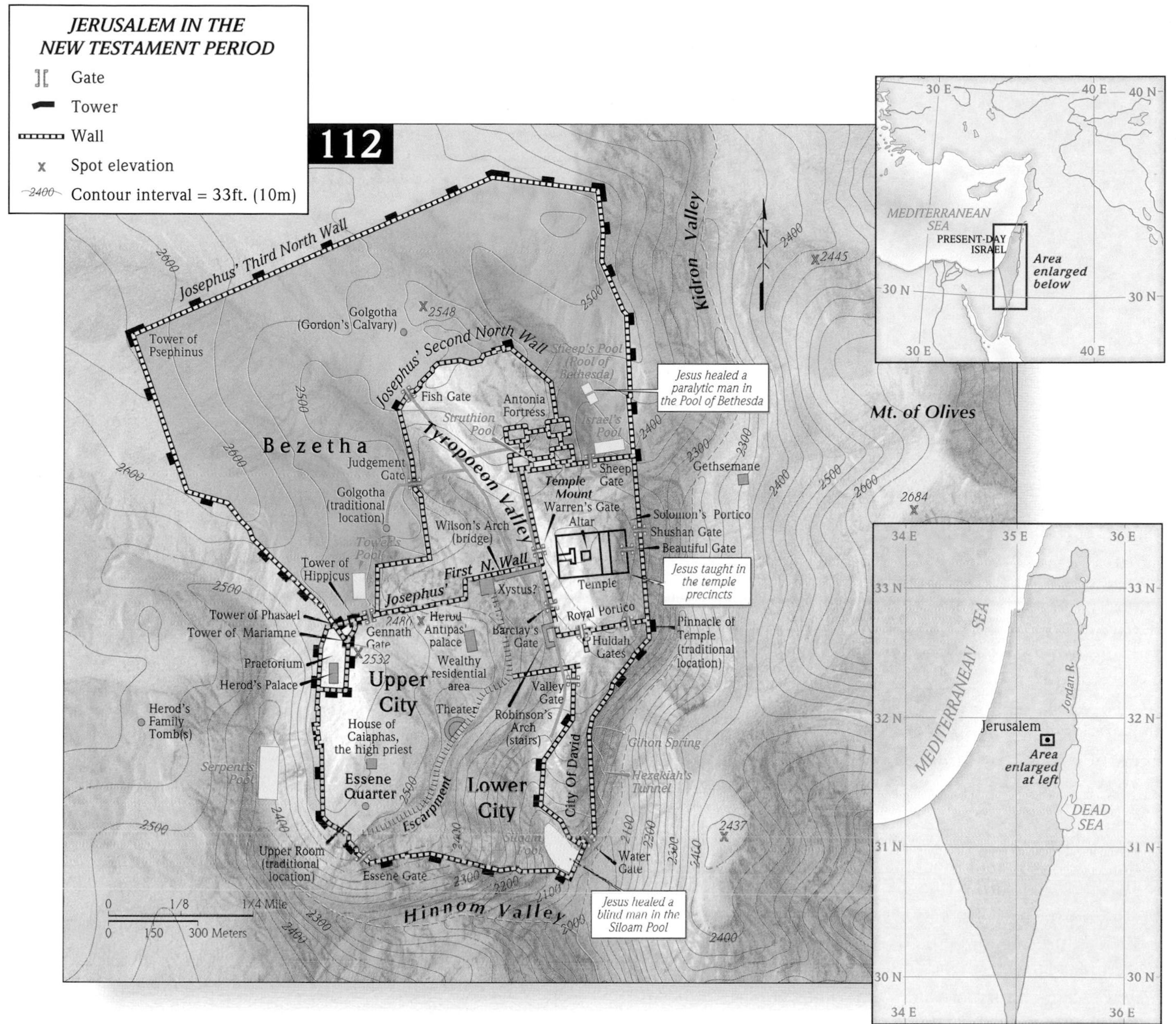

meters north of the Damascus Gate several sections of a wall have been uncovered (the so-called "Sukenik Wall," named after one of the men who first unearthed sections of the wall). Many scholars believe this is the third wall begun by Agrippa I, who was ordered to stop the project by the emperor; presumably zealots finished the project shortly before the First Jewish Revolt. Other scholars believe the "Sukenik Wall" was a Roman siege wall thrown up to keep Jewish defenders from escaping. If this is true, the third wall must have followed the northern line of the present Old City wall under the present-day Damascus Gate. Although the discussions on the third wall continue, supporters of the Sukenik Wall appear to have the better case.

WATER SUPPLY

Herod the Great and the Roman procurators constructed numerous pools, reservoirs, and cisterns to satisfy the water needs of an expanding Jerusalem and a burgeoning population. The Gihon Spring and the Pool of Siloam continued to supply water to the Lower City. Dams were built across portions of the Kidron and Tyropoeon Valleys creating reservoirs; pools were cut into bedrock with ashlar masonry walls enclosing the sides. Drainage systems channeled runoff water into these structures and the innumerable cisterns found in homes and public buildings. The Temple Mount alone had thirty-seven cisterns carved into the bedrock. The Pool of Israel, north of the Temple Mount, was the largest of the reservoirs, measuring 329 x 125 feet. Slightly north of this reservoir was the Sheep's Pool or Pool of Bethesda mentioned in John 5:2–4; this pool has been partially uncovered by excavations. Jesus healed a man, afflicted for thirty-eight years, in the twin pools. Other large pools included the Struthion Pool associated with the Antonia Fortress (169 x 46 feet), the Tower's Pool west of the Citadel (239 x 143 feet), and the Serpent's Pool in the Hinnom Valley.

A low-level aqueduct, perhaps dating to Hasmonean times, expanded by Herod and possibly Pontius Pilate, brought additional water from springs and pools in the Bethlehem region. Beginning at one of "Solomon's Pools" six miles from Jerusalem, the aqueduct wound its way through open space and tunnels, following a gradual gradient to enter Jerusalem in the south. The aqueduct ended at the Temple Mount, crossing the Tyropoeon Valley atop a bridge supported in part by Wilson's Arch.

THE UPPER CITY

The western hill looms over the eastern ridge and the Temple Mount across the Tyropoeon Valley. The higher elevation made it an attractive location for wealthy Jerusalemites and the royal family. Herod the Great's palace crowned the Upper City on the west side just inside the first north wall. The palace had two sections separated by a colonnaded courtyard and garden. Nothing remains of the complex except portions of the large podium that supported the palace. Just north of the palace, Herod built three defensive towers, naming them after a friend, Hippicus; his brother, Phasael; and his wife, Mariamne. The Herodian masonry of one of these three towers is visible in the Citadel area just inside the Jaffa Gate.

The Temple Mount area viewed from the west showing the Wailing Wall.

Nahaman Avigad's excavations in the Jewish quarter of the Old City revealed impressive remains of villas from the Herodian city. The Roman destruction of Jerusalem in A.D. 70 sealed the remains for nearly two thousand years, but today one may view them—partially reconstructed and fitted with objects from daily life—and gain a glimpse of how the Jerusalem aristocracy lived about the time of Jesus.

An exceptionally large villa dubbed the "Palatial Mansion" covered six hundred square meters. The houses had basements, a first floor, and, in some cases, an additional story. The basements contained numerous cisterns, footbaths, ritual baths (*mikvaots*), and wine and cheese storage facilities. Beautiful mosaics set into the floor and colorful frescoes on the walls suitably adorned the luxurious homes. Stone tables and vessels, imported pottery, and beautiful glass pieces attest to the wealth of the owners, some of whom probably represented important priestly families. An inscription found in one house names the priestly family Kathros. The presence of multiple ritual baths and the use of stone cups testify to the occupant's faithfulness to Jewish law. Ritual immersion was an important aspect of ritual purity. The numerous stone vessels have been explained by the Jewish legal stipulation that stone, unlike pottery, could not be ritually contaminated.

Closeup of the Wailing Wall. The lower courses of the wall date from the time of Herod the Great and are characterized by a marginal draft along the outside perimeter.

HEROD'S MAGNIFICENT TEMPLE (SEE JOSEPHUS, *ANT* 15.11.1–7 §380–425; *JW* 5.5–8 184–247 FOR DESCRIPTIONS OF THE TEMPLE MOUNT)

The crowning achievement of Herod's building plan for Jerusalem was the expansion of the Temple Mount. Zerubbabel's temple was damaged in the days of Antiochus Epiphanes IV (168 B.C.) and Pompey (63 B.C.) and suffered additional abuse in the transfer of power to Herod. Herod transformed the Temple Mount into a thing of beauty, partly hoping to win the favor of his Jewish subjects, but also to provide additional space for pilgrims and to bring honor to his own name and kingdom.

Construction on the Temple Mount began in 20/19 B.C. and continued for several years. Josephus states that the temple was built in eighteen months using priests specially trained so as not to violate laws of sanctity. The massive outer walls on the temple enclosure took eight years, with smaller additions and repairs continuing to the days of the First Jewish Revolt (cf. John 2:20). To provide the space necessary for his grand scheme, Herod enlarged the temple platform to the south, west, and north. Vaults were used in the Tyropoeon Valley to extend the platform westward. Great retaining walls built of fine ashlar masonry held the massive fill in place. Each stone was trimmed with a distinctive technique: a slightly raised boss surrounded by a narrow margin. The "Wailing Wall," venerated by Jews, is a part of the western retaining wall. The stones used to build the retaining walls average between two and five tons each, with several blocks in the southern wall weighing fifty tons. Stonecutters removed the stones from local quarries and prepared them to fit without mortar. The dimensions of the walls are as follows: north wall, 1,035 feet; south wall, 912 feet; east wall, 1,536 feet; west wall, 1,590 feet. Altogether, Herod enclosed a trapezoidal space of forty acres.

The southern Temple Mount area showing the steps that led up to the gates that led into the temple courts.

The impressive enclosure walls rose a hundred feet over the streets below. In some places the maximum height from bedrock to the top of towers exceeded 180 feet. Engaged pilasters decorated the walls, producing a beautiful effect still observable in another Herodian structure at Hebron built over the "Tomb of the Patriarchs."

A walk around the Temple Mount discloses many features recently revealed by archaeology. Pilgrims approached the Temple Mount from the south and climbed a flight of steps constructed in a manner designed to insure a slow, worshipful ascent. This flight of stairs 214 feet wide led up from a large plaza to a broad street (21.5 feet wide) along the southern wall. To the right of the stairs were buildings containing ritual baths—*mikvaoths*—where pilgrims could purify themselves before entering the sacred precincts. Two gates in the southern wall known as the Huldah Gates gave access to the courts of the temple. The Double Gate was on the west; the Triple Gate stood 211 feet east of the Double Gate. Tunnels led from the gates upward into the Temple Mount, emerging in the Court of the Gentiles. Beautifully carved decorative geometric and floral motifs preserved in domes inside the Double Gate testify to the craftsmanship Herod employed at every stage.

Josephus describes four gates in the western retaining wall leading into the temple precinct. Today the remains of these gates bear the names of the explorers who first identified them. Robinson's Arch was part of a magnificent staircase that ascended on a series of arches arising on a wide street and ascending to a gate in the southwest corner of the facade. The staircase linked a wide street that ran northward beside the western wall with the Royal Stoa at the southern end of the Temple Mount. The street split into two roads near the gate, a broad lower street running beside shops built along the western wall and a more narrow street (about ten feet wide) that ran above the shops. Barclay's Gate, thirty-three feet high and twenty-one feet wide, fronted the upper street level north of Robinson's Arch. The lintel of Barclay's Gate still can be seen near the women's court of the Wailing Wall.

Wilson's Arch in the middle of the western wall was one of a series of arches supporting a bridge spanning the Tyropoeon Valley. The bridge connected the Upper City with the Temple Mount and carried both foot traffic and water brought by means of a low-level aqueduct. A large Herodian structure associated with Wilson's Arch, formerly called the "Free Mason's Hall," is often identified as the "Council Building" or "Chamber of Hewn Stone" mentioned by Josephus. The remains of Warren's Gate have been found north of Wilson's Arch. Similar to Barclay's Gate, this gate gave access from the Tyropoeon Street through an underground staircase into the temple court.

The northern enclosure wall of the Temple Mount is less well known. The Mishnah mentions the Tadi Gate on the north, but no remains of this gate have been located. Josephus describes the Antonia Fortress (*JW*, 5.5.8§238–247) built by Herod on the site of the old Baris and named in honor of Mark Antony. This fortress was both a palace with baths and other amenities as well as a barracks housing Roman soldiers who kept watch over temple crowds.

The Antonia had four towers, with the southeastern tower rising above the others. Passageways connected the Antonia with the temple courts. Little remains of this fortress that stood beside the Struthion Pool, but the elevated bedrock upon which the fortress stood is visible today in the northwestern corner of the Haram esh-Sharif. Recent work demonstrates that the pavement and archway (the "Ecce Homo Arch") in the Sisters of Zion Convent are part of buildings associated with the Roman colony Aelia Capitolina, built by Hadrian after A.D. 135. Whether Jesus faced Pilate and a scourging in the Antonia Fortress as a part of His trial remains debatable. Many scholars believe Pilate stayed in the Herodian palace in the Upper City while in Jerusalem.

A model of Jerusalem in the first century A.D. showing the Roman fortress Antonia with its four massive towers just north of the Temple Mount. To the left of the fortress is the Pool of Bethesda where Jesus performed one of His miracles.

The eastern enclosure wall apparently followed the course of walls from previous eras. Herod extended the wall southward as he expanded the available building space. A "straight joint" 105 feet north of the southeastern corner marks this extension. The wall south of the seam differs from the masonry north of the seam, the former being distinctly Herodian. Arches scorched into the southeastern corner and remains of springers indicate a monumental staircase similar to Robinson's Arch once descended from the eastern wall.

Virtually no physical evidence has survived from the interior of the Temple Mount with its courtyards, stoas, and the temple itself. Open porticoes surrounded the temple and its courts on all sides. Especially breathtaking was the Royal Portico built by Herod at the southern end of the enclosure. Built in the form of a basilica, with a central hall flanked by two side aisles, the Royal Stoa or Portico was 620 feet long. One hundred sixty-two columns carved with Corinthian capitals divided into four rows supported the roof. Fragments of columns and capitals recovered in debris south of the Temple Mount hint at the grandeur of the Royal Stoa.

A model of the temple of Herod the Great with the surrounding courts.

The porticoes that surrounded the temple courts provided shelter from the elements for the crowds and merchants who thronged the temple. Money changers, who converted Roman coins into shekels, and sellers of doves and other items needed for sacrifice huddled in the porticoes. On occasion Jesus drove such people out of the temple precinct because of their lack of sensitivity to worshipers (Matt. 21:12–13; Luke 19:45–46; cf. John 2:13–17).

The Court of the Gentiles occupied much of the interior of the Temple Mount. A stone "fence" or balustrade (Heb. *soreg*) separated the Court of the Gentiles from the more sacred areas reserved for Jews alone. Notices engraved in Greek on stone plaques, two of which have been recovered, warned Gentiles to approach no further under penalty of death. Beyond *the soreg* was an elevated platform containing the Court of Women, the Court of Israel, the Court of the Priests, and the temple building itself.

The main entrance to the Court of Women was from the east through a gate, possibly the Beautiful Gate mentioned in Acts 3:2. At the west end of the Court of Women, fifteen steps led up to the Nicanor Gate, made of Corinthian bronze (also a possibility for the Beautiful Gate), that led to the Court of Israel, a long narrow court facing the temple. The Court of the Priests, slightly elevated, surrounded the temple on all sides. In the court stood the great altar of sacrifice, the bronze laver for washings, and places to perform sacrifices. Beyond the gleaming marble the temple itself, gilded with gold, roared like a lion—so said the rabbis because the front porch was of greater width than the tapered dimensions of the Holy Place and the Holy of Holies. The Holy Place contained the altar of incense, the golden candelabrum (menorah), and the table of shewbread. The Holy of Holies was empty.

The entire temple complex was among the largest in the Roman world and made a great impression on visitors from both near and far. The rabbis said anyone who had not seen Herod's temple had never seen a beautiful building.

The Last Week of Jesus

All four Gospels devote considerable attention to the culminating events of the last week of Jesus' earthly ministry. According to John, Jesus arrived in Bethany and the house of His friends Lazarus, Martha, and Mary six days before the Passover (John 12:1). Mary anointed Jesus with costly perfumes, a gesture of hospitality that foreshadowed the imminent death and burial awaiting Jesus in Jerusalem.

SUNDAY

The next day, Sunday, Jesus descended the Mount of Olives on a donkey, the cries of "Hosanna" ringing in His ears, and entered the temple precincts. With this "triumphal entry" Jesus acknowledged His identity as Messiah. After entering the temple, Jesus retired for the evening, returning to Bethany to lodge with His friends.

MONDAY

Having spent the night in Bethany, Jesus returned to Jerusalem on Monday. The cleansing of the temple (when Jesus drove the money changers from the temple courts) recorded by all three Synoptic Gospels (Mark 11:15–18; Luke 19:45–48; and Matt. 21:12–13) ocurred on Monday. This action signaling Jesus' sovereignty over the temple provoked the Jerusalem authorities to plot His death (Mark 11:18). On this day, John also records a delegation of Greeks who desired to see Jesus (John 12:20–50).

TUESDAY

Jesus returned to Jerusalem on Tuesday and spent much of the day in the temple precincts answering questions posed by religious authorities seeking to entrap Him (Matt. 21:15–17, 23–46; 22:15–46). The authorities baited Jesus with questions about John the Baptist, paying tribute, and the resurrection, but Jesus skillfully deflected their plots. In the midst of this hectic day, Jesus watched a widow place her small coins (Greek *lepton*, the smallest copper coin) in the temple treasury. He commended her actions to His disciples, noting that her gift was more worthy than the ostentatious offerings of the wealthy (Mark 12:41–44). Jesus also taught His disciples about "end times" while seated upon the Mount of Olives overlooking Jerusalem (Matt. 24; Mark 13).

The Mount of Olives viewed from the Temple Mount.

WEDNESDAY

According to traditional interpretations, the Gospels record no events on Wednesday of the final week. However, it is possible that Jesus received a second anointing administered by an unnamed woman at Bethany in the house of Simon the Leper (Matt. 26:6–13; Mark 14:3–9). This act, strikingly similar to the anointing administered by Mary only days before, points eminently to Jesus' impending death. Ironically, Judas Iscariot may have concluded his bargain to betray Jesus to Jewish authorities on the same day (Matt. 26:14–16).

THURSDAY

Jesus spent Thursday with His disciples anticipating sharing the Passover meal with them. Peter and John were sent ahead to make final preparations (Luke 22:8–12). In the evening Jesus observed the traditional meal with His disciples and interpreted the wine and bread in light of His impending death (Luke 22:14–20). Later in the evening, Jesus retired with His disciples to the Mount of Olives and a place called Gethsemane, where He engaged in fervent prayer (Matt. 26:36–45; Mark 14:32–42). Ancient traditions locate Gethsemane opposite the temple, across the Kidron Valley on the lower slopes of the Mount of Olives. Here Judas betrayed Jesus to temple authorities who placed Jesus under arrest (Luke 22:47–53; John 18:2–12).

The trial of Jesus unfolded in stages late Thursday night into early Friday. Jesus was taken into Jerusalem to the house of Joseph Caiaphas, the high priest, for a preliminary hearing before Caiaphas and his father-in-law, Annas, the former high priest (Matt. 26:57–75; John 18:12–

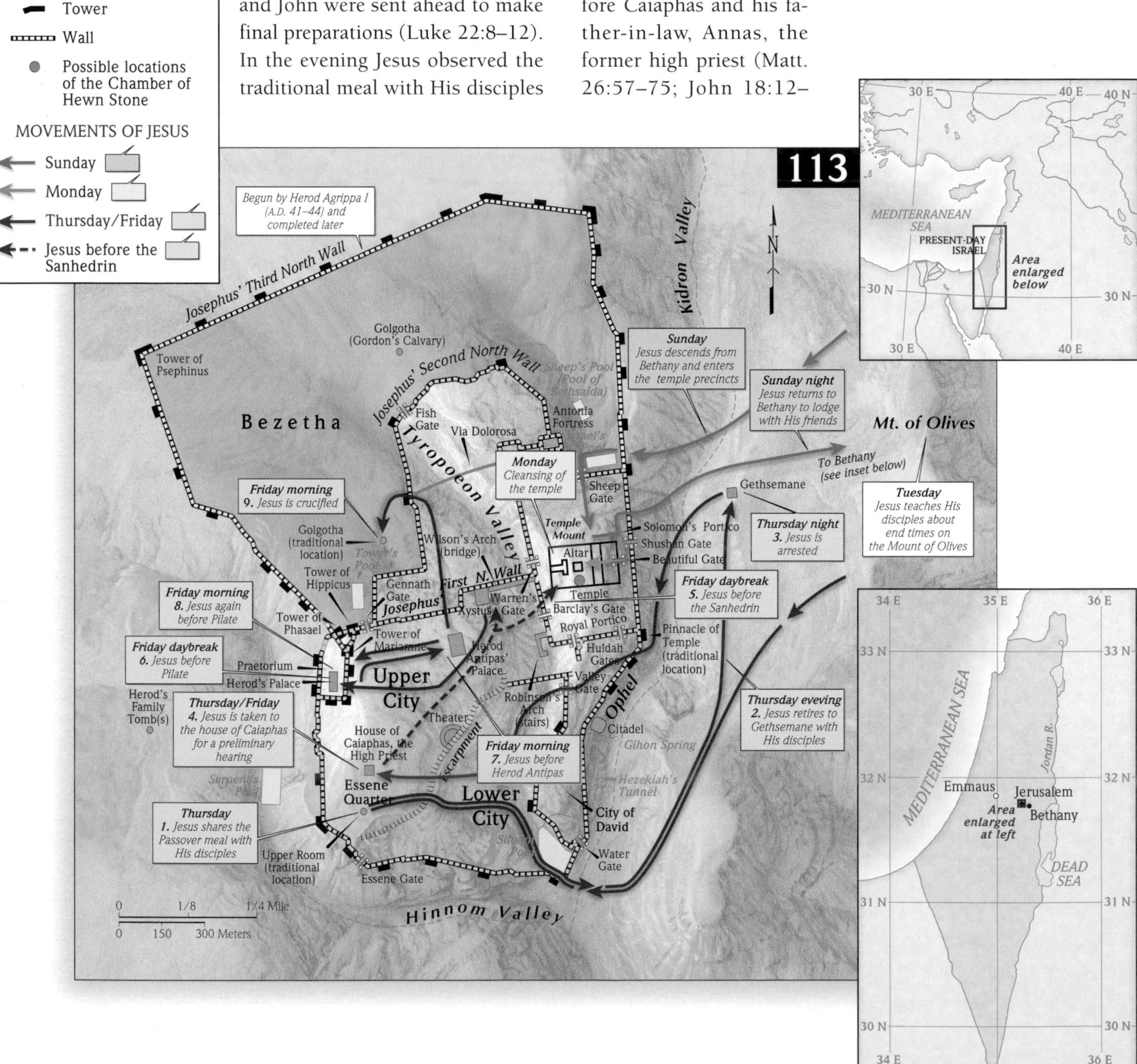

A stand of old olive trees in the traditional Garden of Gethsemane.

23). Archaeologists recently found the family tomb of Caiaphas south of Jerusalem in the Peace Forest. Caiaphas' house must have been located in the Upper City, where recent excavations have uncovered several large, palatial houses belonging to wealthy Jerusalemites from that period. These houses contain several ritual baths (*mikvaot*) used in Jewish purification rites.

FRIDAY

As dawn broke Friday, the Sanhedrin formally condemned Jesus to death for blasphemy. The high council then brought Jesus before Pilate, seeking the procurator's assent to their verdict (Mark 15:1–5; Luke 23:1–5). Before Pilate, the Jewish authorities charged Jesus with treason. The site of the interrogation before Pilate, who was in Jerusalem because of the Passover, is debated. One possibility is Herod's palace in the western part of the city. The palace would have provided suitable accommodations for the Roman procurator. Another possibility is that Pilate lodged in the Antonia Fortress while residing in Jerusalem (see further "Jerusalem in the Days of Herod and Jesus" p. 232).

Realizing that Jesus was a Galilean, Pilate shuttled Jesus off to Herod Antipas, who was also in the city observing the feast (Luke 23:6–12). The meeting between Herod and Jesus may have taken place at the Western Palace, assuming that Pilate was not there, or perhaps in the Hasmonean Palace located a little west of the Temple Mount along the first north wall. Herod returned Jesus to Pilate when he tired of Jesus' refusal to perform a miracle, but not before his soldiers mocked Jesus by clothing Him in royal apparel. Pilate gave in to Jewish demands that Jesus be executed, allowed his soldiers to scourge the prisoner, and then delivered Jesus over for crucifixion (Matt. 27:27–31; Luke 23:13–25).

Jesus was crucified Friday morning outside the city walls at a place called Golgotha, "the place of the skull." Ancient tradition places Jesus' death, burial, and resurrection on the site now covered by the Church of the Holy Sepulchre. Queen Helena, mother of Constantine, ordered the church built over the site Christians showed her when she visited Jerusalem about A.D. 335. Archaeology has demonstrated that the area under the church was outside the city walls at the time of Jesus' death and was used as a quarry with numerous tombs cut into the rock. The circumstances fit the biblical description, but the authenticity of the site cannot be established conclusively. The picturesque Garden Tomb and Gordon's Calvary north of the Old City have little historical or archaeological support as authentic sites.

SUNDAY

Sunday witnessed the resurrection of Jesus and His first appearance to His close friends and disciples. Subsequently, the Gospels describe several post-Resurrection appearances, including several in Jerusalem (Matt. 28:9–10; Mark 16:14–18; John 20:19–29), an appearance to two disciples on the road to Emmaus (Luke 24:13–35), and several appearances in Galilee (John 21; Matt. 28:16–20). His final appearance to the disciples took place near Bethany on the Mount of Olives when Jesus ascended to heaven (Luke 28:50–51; Acts 1:9–12).

The Church of the Holy Sepulchre in Jerusalem.

Chapter Nineteen

EARLY EXPANSION OF THE CHURCH

The Roman Empire during the Early Expansion of the Church

After the resurrection and ascension of Jesus, the early disciples spread the gospel story first in Palestine and then in the larger Roman world. Understanding the political backdrop of the Roman Empire—and Palestine, specifically—is essential to comprehend the story. The following focuses first on the Emperors of Rome at this period and then turns to the political situation in Palestine A.D. 37–66. Then follows the key events of the early church's expansion in Palestine and, through Paul, the Roman world. Four emperors controlled the political situation that both helped and hindered the church as it made its first steps towards growth. These emperors maintained a Roman system that allowed relatively easy access to all parts of the empire, created thriving urban populations where early missionaries had access to large crowds, and maintained peaceful conditions. The emperors did not always view the church with favor, however, and created conditions and regulations that often brought persecution on the church.

GAIUS CALIGULA (A.D. 37–41)

Gaius succeeded Tiberius as emperor in A.D. 37 with the help of the Praetorian Guard. Known by his nickname "Caligula" ("little boot") since his childhood, Gaius was the son of Germanicus and Agrippina I and a grandson of Tiberius. He enjoyed initial favor with the Senate and used the imperial treasury to provide entertainment for the citizens of Rome.

A serious illness midway through his reign left Gaius mentally unstable. Becoming unpredictable in his actions toward both the Senate and the Roman citizens, Gaius insisted that he be worshiped as a god, perhaps in imitation of Hellenistic ruler cults. Persecution against the Jews broke out in Alexandria, spawned by Hellenists who used Caligula's penchant for worship to bait the Jewish community. Later, Hellenists at Jamnia set up an altar to Caligula that incensed the Jews. Caligula responded by ordering an image of himself erected in the Jerusalem temple. Agrippa I and the Syrian legate Petronius interceded, arguing that such an action insured a Jewish rebellion. Unwilling to relent, Caligula ordered the task completed but was assassinated by members of the Praetorian Guard in A.D. 41 before his orders could be carried out.

CLAUDIUS (A.D. 41–54)

Upon the assassination of Caligula, the Roman Senate considered restoring the Republican form of government, but the Praetorian Guard acted quickly and secured an imperial successor. They chose Claudius, the uncle of Caligula and brother of the military hero Germanicus. Claudius was a most unlikely candidate for the imperial throne. Physically unattractive, he walked with a limp and stuttered in his speech. When the Praetorian Guard selected Claudius as emperor in A.D. 41, they surely could not foresee that Claudius' keen mind and abilities would make him a most capable ruler.

Claudius strengthened the provinces and annexed Britain and Mauretania. In Palestine he expanded Agrippa's lands until they rivaled those administered by Herod the Great. Upon Agrippa's death in A.D. 44, Claudius established a procuratorship over Palestine. Claudius built Ostia, a new port facility serving the needs of Rome. In general, his policies facilitated trade by expanding Roman influence into outlying regions. In Rome, Claudius utilized freedmen in his administration, a fact that perturbed the nobles in the Senate. Freedmen such as Pallas and Callistus acquired great power in the Roman bureaucracy.

Paul's first two missionary journeys were completed during the reign of Claudius. According to Suetonius (*Life of Claudius* 25.4), a disturbance among the Jews of Rome over a certain "Chrestus" (Christ?) caused Claudius to issue an edict temporarily banishing the Jews from Rome as a remedy. On his second missionary journey, Paul met Aquilla and Priscilla in Corinth. The Jewish couple had recently been expelled from Rome following Claudius' edict (Acts 18:1–2). Claudius also intervened on behalf of the Alexandrian Jewish community in their social and political struggles against the Gentile community, although he warned them to be content with their status rather than press for additional privileges.

Claudius' personal life was a source of scandal. He was dominated by his wives, Messalina and Agrippina II. The mother of Nero, Agrippina spent her time securing the selection of her son as Claudius' successor. When Claudius died in A.D. 54, Roman historians claimed Agrippina poisoned him, thus fulfilling her ambition to see her son Nero succeed her husband.

NERO (A.D. 54–68)

The transition of power from Claudius to Nero went smoothly, under the direction of the Praetorian Guard. The early years of Nero's reign were remarkably stable and free of the ex-

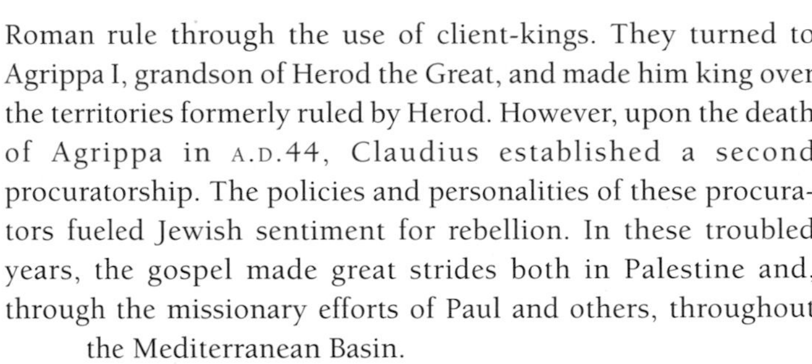

cesses characteristic of his later years. Tutored by the Stoic philosopher Seneca and ably assisted by the Praetorian prefect Burrus, the young Nero gained favor with both the Senate and Rome, despite the meddling of his dominating mother, Agrippina. Nero's Hellenism, demonstrated in his fondness for the arts and athletics, surfaced in these years.

In A.D. 59 Nero murdered his mother and began to pull away from his close advisors. He became a tyrannical despot who ruled with increasing terror. Under the sway of his mistress, Poppaea Sabina, Nero jettisoned Seneca and turned to a prefect, Tigellinus, who catered to Nero's vanity. Nero crushed opposition in the Senate while pressing his claims to divine status, yet he maintained favor with the common people by staging lavish entertainments. He frequently toured as an actor, musician, and charioteer, entering (and winning!) numerous contests.

On July 19, A.D. 64, a fire broke out in Rome that consumed much of the city and afforded Nero the opportunity to rebuild Rome on a grand scale. His new palace, the "Golden House," was the epitome of opulence. Suspicions grew, however, that Nero had purposely set the fire to carry out his grandiose scheme. In an effort to place blame elsewhere, Nero pursued a brief but intense persecution of the Christians in Rome in the aftermath of the fire (perhaps a year or more later). Christians were burned alive or savaged by animals in spectacles before a Roman audience. Tradition counts Paul and Peter among the victims.

A bust of the emperor Nero.

Nero faced a financial crisis and plots against his life as results of the fire. He ruthlessly destroyed the conspirators, but rebellions broke out in the provinces. Judea rebelled in A.D. 66 while Nero toured Greece. The governors of Africa, Spain, and Gaul rebelled in A.D. 67–68. Nero fled Rome but was condemned to death by the Senate and committed suicide June 9, A.D. 68. His death ended the Julio-Claudian line of emperors who guided Rome's fortunes the first one hundred years of the empire.

The Politics of Palestine (A.D. 41–66)

By A.D. 39 the three sons of Herod the Great who had received a portion of his kingdom were either dead or deposed. The Roman emperors Gaius and Claudius favored maintaining Roman rule through the use of client-kings. They turned to Agrippa I, grandson of Herod the Great, and made him king over the territories formerly ruled by Herod. However, upon the death of Agrippa in A.D.44, Claudius established a second procuratorship. The policies and personalities of these procurators fueled Jewish sentiment for rebellion. In these troubled years, the gospel made great strides both in Palestine and, through the missionary efforts of Paul and others, throughout the Mediterranean Basin.

THE KINGDOM OF HEROD AGRIPPA I

Claudius appointed Agrippa I king in A.D. 41, ending thirty-five years of direct Roman control through procurators. Many Jews preferred a ruler from the Herodian Dynasty after their unhappy experiences with Roman procurators. Later Jewish literature recalls the seven-year reign of Agrippa I (A.D. 37–44) with favor, but the early decades of Agrippa's life did not signal much promise for the future. Born in 10 B.C. to Bernice and Aristobulus (a son of Herod and Mariamne who was executed in 7 B.C.), Agrippa grew up in Rome, where he made his fortune. He was well connected in Roman society through relatives of Tiberius.

Agrippa Gains a Kingdom. Moving to Palestine, Agrippa never found a secure niche and once again returned to Rome. On the death of Tiberius on March 16, A.D. 37, Agrippa's friendship with Gaius (Caligula) and Claudius catapulted him to prominence. The new emperor Caligula rewarded Agrippa's loyalty by naming him ruler over the territories formerly belonging to Philip (Gaulanitis, Trachonitis, and Batanea). Caligula added Perea and Galilee to Agrippa's territories in A.D. 40 after deposing Agrippa's uncle, Herod Antipas, in the previous year. Agrippa's intervention on behalf of the Jews when Caligula foolishly ordered a statue of himself to be erected in Jerusalem earned Agrippa great respect among his subjects.

Agrippa was fortunate to be in Rome when Caligula was assassinated (Jan. 24, A.D. 41) by the Praetorian Guard. When civil war threatened Rome, Agrippa helped broker the transition of power to Claudius, an old friend. Claudius followed a policy that granted control of eastern provinces to client-kings. He increased Agrippa's holdings by adding Judea, Samaria, and Idumea in A.D. 41.

Agrippa, now bearing the title "king," ruled all the

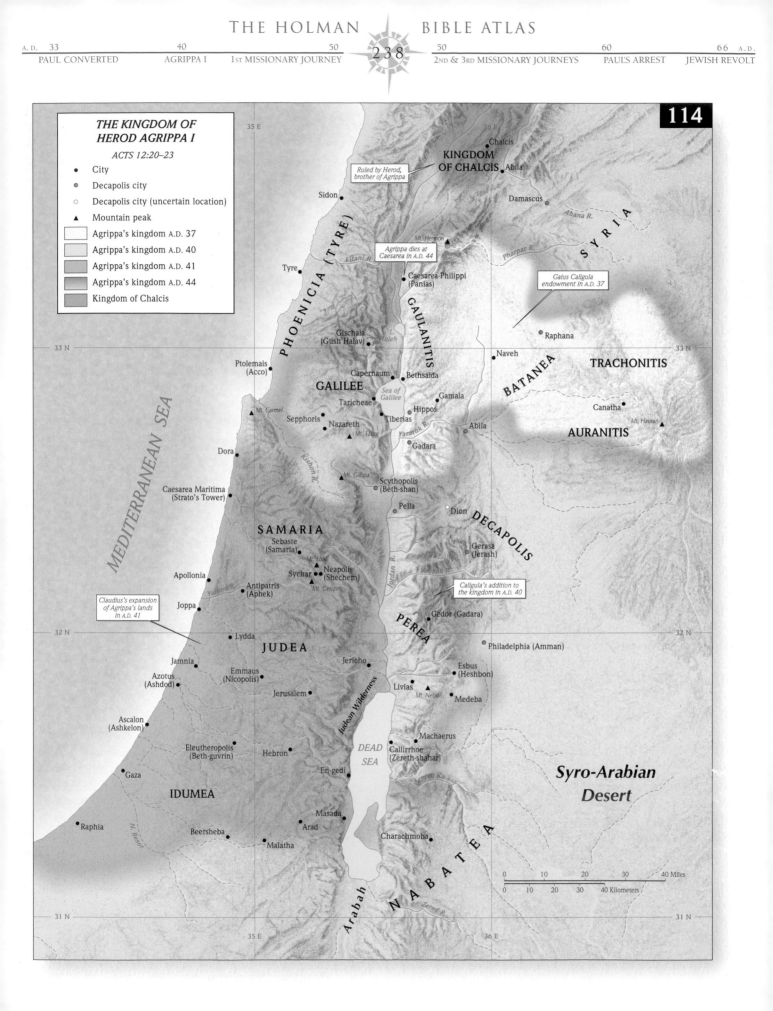

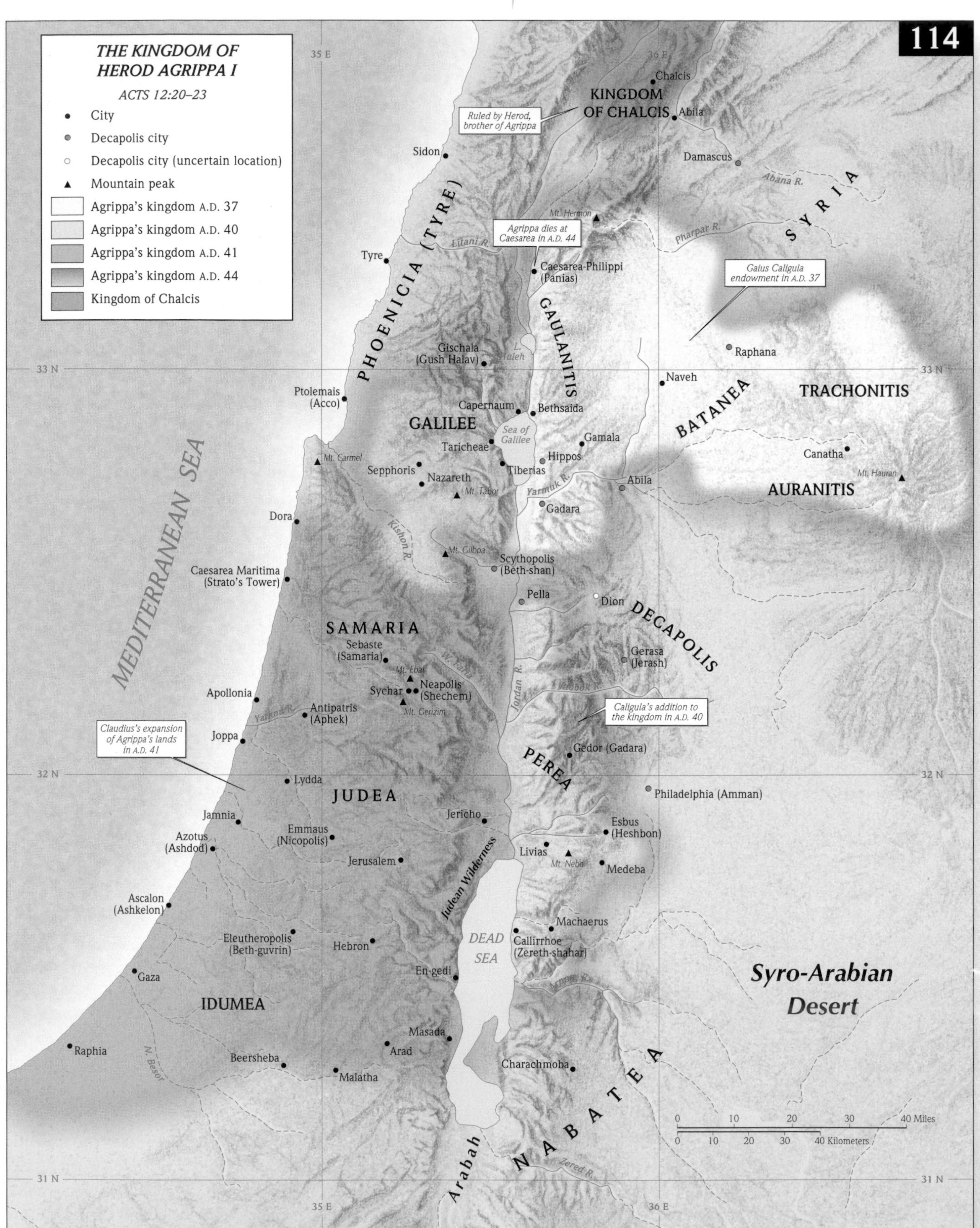
114
THE KINGDOM OF HEROD AGRIPPA I
ACTS 12:20–23
City
Decapolis city
Decapolis city (uncertain location)
Mountain peak
Agrippa's kingdom A.D. 37
Agrippa's kingdom A.D. 40
Agrippa's kingdom A.D. 41
Agrippa's kingdom A.D. 44
Kingdom of Chalcis
Ruled by Herod, brother of Agrippa
KINGDOM OF CHALCIS
Chalcis
Abila
Damascus
Sidon
Agrippa dies at Caesarea in A.D. 44
Gaius Caligula endowment in A.D. 37
SYRIA
PHOENICIA (TYRE)
Tyre
Caesarea-Philippi (Panias)
GAULANITIS
Raphana
Gischala (Gush Halav)
Naveh
TRACHONITIS
BATANEA
Ptolemais (Acco)
Capernaum
Bethsaida
GALILEE
Sea of Galilee
Gamala
Taricheae
Hippos
Canatha
Sepphoris
Tiberias
Nazareth
Abila
AURANITIS
Mt. Carmel
Mt. Tabor
Mt. Hauran
Gadara
MEDITERRANEAN SEA
Dora
Mt. Gilboa
Scythopolis (Beth-shan)
Caesarea Maritima (Strato's Tower)
Pella
Dion
DECAPOLIS
SAMARIA
Sebaste (Samaria)
Gerasa (Jerash)
Mt. Ebal
Sychar
Neapolis (Shechem)
Apollonia
Mt. Gerizim
Antipatris (Aphek)
Caligula's addition to the kingdom in A.D. 40
Claudius's expansion of Agrippa's lands in A.D. 41
Joppa
Gedor (Gadara)
PEREA
Lydda
JUDEA
Philadelphia (Amman)
Jamnia
Jericho
Esbus (Heshbon)
Azotus (Ashdod)
Emmaus (Nicopolis)
Livias
Mt. Nebo
Medeba
Jerusalem
Judean Wilderness
Ascalon (Ashkelon)
Machaerus
Eleutheropolis (Beth-guvrin)
Hebron
DEAD SEA
Callirrhoe (Zereth-shahar)
En-gedi
Gaza
Syro-Arabian Desert
IDUMEA
Masada
Arad
Raphia
Beersheba
Malatha
Charachmoba
NABATEA
Arabah
0 10 20 30 40 Miles
0 10 20 30 40 Kilometers
35 E
36 E
33 N
32 N
31 N

territories formerly governed by his uncles, the sons of Herod the Great, including the cities of Azotus, Jamnia, and possibly Apollonia and Antipatris on the coast. Hippos, Gadara, and Gaza came under the jurisdiction of Syria. Taking the dynastic name Herod, Agrippa ruled a kingdom that now rivaled that of his grandfather, and his influence and power in Rome surpassed that of any Herodian ruler.

Agrippa and the Jews. Herod Agrippa aligned himself with the Jewish religious leadership in Palestine, where he ruled with an orthodox hand. The Romans granted Agrippa the responsibility of appointing the high priest, a privilege reserved for Roman authorities since A.D. 6. Agrippa dealt with the increasing problem posed by the Christian movement by executing James the son of Zebedee and imprisoning Peter (Acts 12:1–19). However, Agrippa overreached his bounds when he attempted to build a new north wall in Jerusalem that would greatly strengthen the city's defenses. The Syrian legate Marus reported this action to Claudius, who ordered the project stopped.

Outside of Palestine, Herod Agrippa demonstrated his Roman roots and sympathies. He minted coins bearing his image and that of the emperor, constructed an amphitheater and theater at Berytus (Beirut), and sponsored gladiatorial games. Still, he did not win the favor of his non-Jewish subjects, some of whom cheered his death at Caesarea in A.D. 44.

On the death of Herod Agrippa I, Palestine reverted to direct Roman rule through a second series of procurators. Claudius preferred to allow Agrippa's young son, Agrippa II, to succeed his father, but his advisors dissuaded him. Agrippa II did receive control of several territories as he matured.

AGRIPPA II

Agrippa II extended the influence of the Herodian Dynasty in Palestinian politics during his years, though his role was of much less significance than that of his father, Agrippa I. Claudius appointed him ruler of Chalcis (ca. A.D. 50) and, later (A.D. 53), exchanged Chalcis for the region of Philip's old tetrarchy. Nero added parts of Galilee and Perea to Agrippa's realm, along with several Jewish cities including Tiberias, Taricheae, Abila, and Julius in Perea.

Agrippa II represented the Jews before the emperors of Rome and retained the right to appoint the high priest. His close relations with his eldest sister, Bernice, caused a scandal among the Jews. Paul shared his faith before Agrippa II and Bernice while imprisoned at Caesarea shortly before journeying to Rome (Acts 25:23–26:32).

CHART 23. ROMAN PROCURATORS OF THE SECOND PROCURATORSHIP (A.D. 44–66)

Name	Dates (A.D.)	Appointed by	Selected References in the Works of Josephus to the Procurator
Cuspius Fadus	44–46	Claudius	*ANT* 19.9.2§363–366; 20.1.1–2§1–10; 20.5.1§97–99
Tiberius Alexander	46–48	Claudius	*ANT* 20.5.2§100–103
Ventidius Cumanus	48–52	Claudius	*ANT* 20.5.2–6§103–136
Antonius Felix	52–60	Claudius	*ANT* 20.7.1–2§137–144; 20.8.5–6§160–172
Porcius Festus	60–62	Nero	*ANT* 20.8.9–11§182–196
Lucceius Albinus	62–64	Nero	*ANT* 20.9.1–5§197–215
Gessius Florus	64–66	Nero	*ANT* 20.9.5§215; 20.11.1§252–258

PRELUDE TO REVOLUTION: THE SECOND PROCURATORSHIP

The Role of the Procurator. Seven procurators or governors (see chart) appointed by Claudius and Nero controlled the province of Judea from their headquarters at Caesarea Maritima. The procurators were primarily financial agents drawn from circles seeking higher offices; they commanded no legions and were dependent upon the Roman legate of Syria for help in the event of serious disturbances. Auxiliary units drawn mainly from the non-Jewish populations of Sebaste and Samaria supplied troops to the procurators for local operations. Roman legions in Syria held in check the more formidable threat posed by the Parthians.

Jewish Reaction to the Procurators. Jewish desires to be free from their Roman masters greatly intensified under this second group of procurators. Messianic pretenders such as Theudas and "the Egyptian" (see Acts 21:38) periodically fanned Jewish hopes with promises of divine intervention. The oppressive policies and corrupt tendencies characteristic of several of these procurators heightened tensions between Jews and Romans. One procurator, Tiberius Alexander (A.D. 46–48), was an apostate Jew.

Josephus records a series of incidents illustrating the ethical and administrative deficiencies of these governors. The Romans removed Cumanus for bribery after he sided with Samaritans in an incident involving Jewish pilgrims. Antonius Felix (A.D. 52–60) drew the following sharp rebuke from the Roman writer Tacitus: "Practicing every kind of cruelty and lust, he wielded power with the instincts of a slave." The last two procurators, Albinus (A.D. 62–64) and Gessius Florus (A.D. 64–66), were especially corrupt and insensitive.

During these years, the Zealot party, heirs of Judas the Galilean (Acts 5:37), spearheaded opposition to Roman rule. Especially dangerous were the Sicarri, a fanatical faction of Zealots

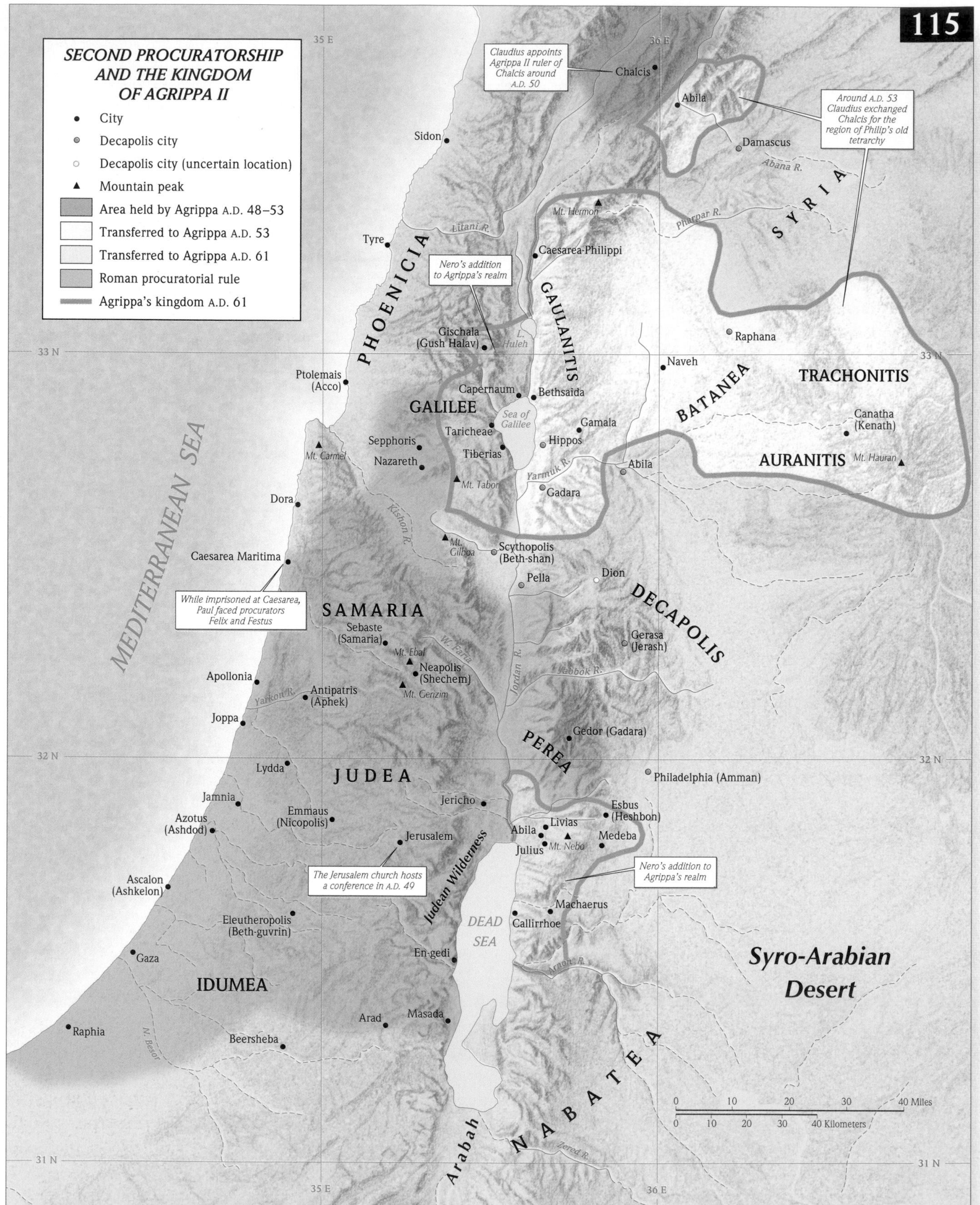
115
SECOND PROCURATORSHIP AND THE KINGDOM OF AGRIPPA II
City
Decapolis city
Decapolis city (uncertain location)
Mountain peak
Area held by Agrippa A.D. 48–53
Transferred to Agrippa A.D. 53
Transferred to Agrippa A.D. 61
Roman procuratorial rule
Agrippa's kingdom A.D. 61
Claudius appoints Agrippa II ruler of Chalcis around A.D. 50
Around A.D. 53 Claudius exchanged Chalcis for the region of Philip's old tetrarchy
Nero's addition to Agrippa's realm
While imprisoned at Caesarea, Paul faced procurators Felix and Festus
The Jerusalem church hosts a conference in A.D. 49
Nero's addition to Agrippa's realm
MEDITERRANEAN SEA
PHOENICIA
GAULANITIS
SYRIA
BATANEA
TRACHONITIS
AURANITIS
GALILEE
SAMARIA
DECAPOLIS
PEREA
JUDEA
IDUMEA
NABATEA
Syro-Arabian Desert
Judean Wilderness
Arabah
DEAD SEA
Sea of Galilee
L. Huleh
Chalcis
Abila
Damascus
Abana R.
Pharpar R.
Mt. Hermon
Sidon
Tyre
Litani R.
Caesarea-Philippi
Gischala (Gush Halav)
Raphana
Naveh
Ptolemais (Acco)
Capernaum
Bethsaida
Canatha (Kenath)
Gamala
Taricheae
Sepphoris
Hippos
Nazareth
Tiberias
Mt. Carmel
Abila
Mt. Hauran
Yarmuk R.
Mt. Tabor
Gadara
Dora
Kishon R.
Mt. Gilboa
Scythopolis (Beth-shan)
Caesarea Maritima
Dion
Pella
Sebaste (Samaria)
Mt. Ebal
W. Faria
Gerasa (Jerash)
Neapolis (Shechem)
Jordan R.
Jabbok R.
Apollonia
Mt. Gerizim
Antipatris (Aphek)
Yarkon R.
Joppa
Gedor (Gadara)
Lydda
Philadelphia (Amman)
Jamnia
Jericho
Esbus (Heshbon)
Emmaus (Nicopolis)
Azotus (Ashdod)
Livias
Abila
Jerusalem
Mt. Nebo
Medeba
Julius
Ascalon (Ashkelon)
Machaerus
Eleutheropolis (Beth-guvrin)
Callirrhoe
En-gedi
Gaza
Arnon R.
Arad
Masada
Raphia
N. Besor
Beersheba
Zered R.
0 10 20 30 40 Miles
0 10 20 30 40 Kilometers
35 E
36 E
33 N
32 N
31 N

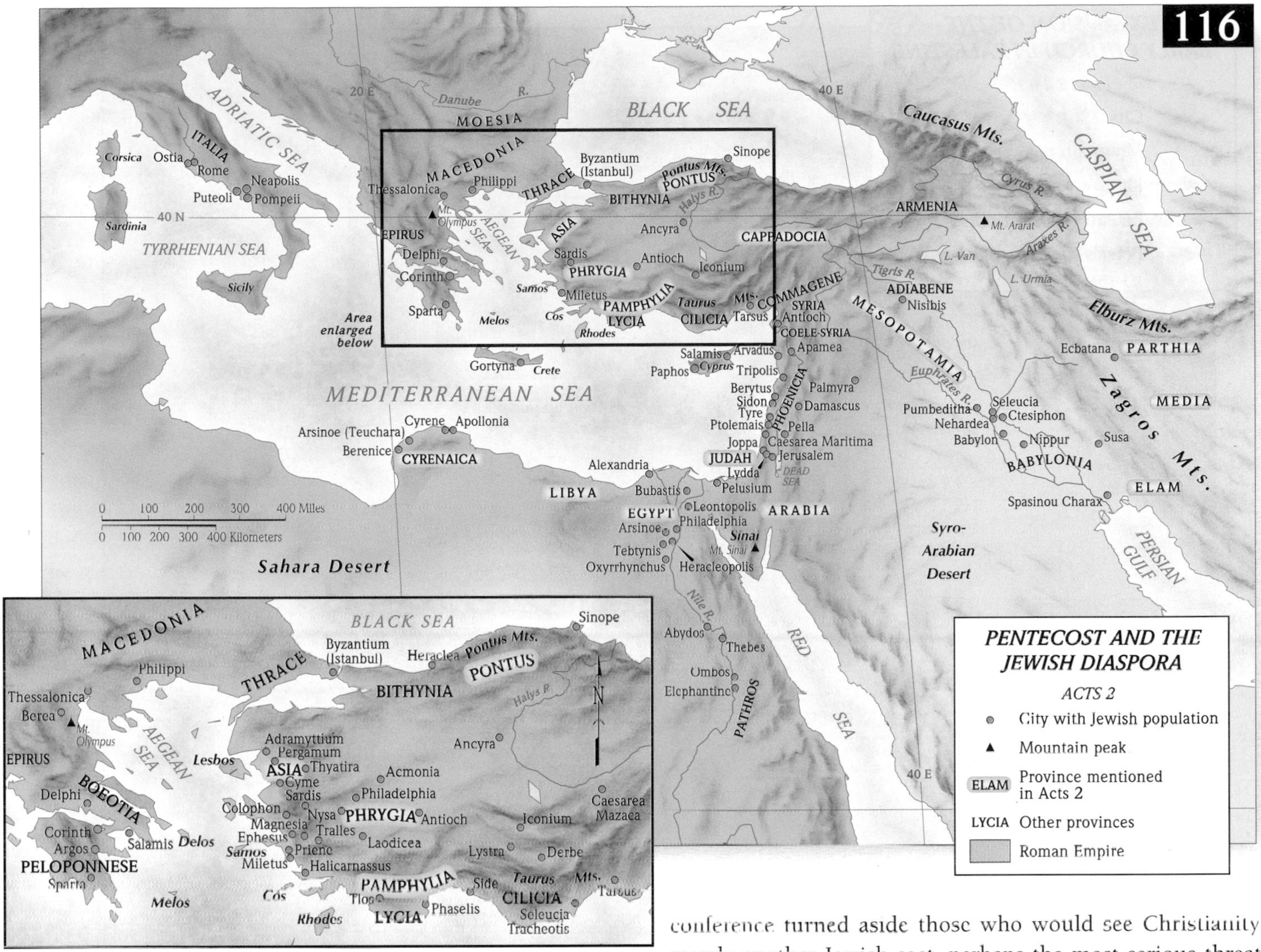

116

PENTECOST AND THE JEWISH DIASPORA

ACTS 2

- City with Jewish population
- Mountain peak
- ELAM Province mentioned in Acts 2
- LYCIA Other provinces
- Roman Empire

who resorted to acts of terror, assassination, and kidnapping to achieve political independence. As tensions mounted, armed revolt was inevitable (see chap. 20).

The Jerusalem Church under the Second Procuratorship. The Jerusalem church suffered persecution and privation during the years of the second procuratorship. Famine struck Judea during the governorship of Tiberius Alexander (Acts 11:27–30) and brought hardship upon the people. Paul organized a collection for the saints of Jerusalem during his missionary journeys to ease the suffering of needy Jewish Christians during difficult years (Acts 24:17; 1 Cor. 16:1–4).

Despite such hardships, the Jerusalem church hosted a conference in A.D. 49 prompted by the successes of Paul and others among the Gentiles. The topic of discussion was whether Gentile Christians must submit to the requirements of Jewish law to be followers of Christ. After an intense discussion, Barnabas and Paul persuaded the apostles and elders that grace alone was sufficient to make a person a Christian (Acts 15). The conference turned aside those who would see Christianity as merely another Jewish sect, perhaps the most serious threat to the life of the early church.

Later, (ca. 62), the High Priest Ananus II condemned to death James the brother of Jesus. Paul also faced two procurators, Felix and Festus, while imprisoned at Caesarea (Acts 24:1–25:22).

Acts and the Progress of the Gospel in Palestine (Acts 1–11)

The Day of Pentecost (Acts 2) empowered the early disciples and established the Christian movement. Jewish pilgrims attending the great festivals in Jerusalem became the seed-planters of early expansion. Acts mentions pilgrims from all over the Roman world and beyond who witnessed the events of Pentecost. They came from Parthia, Media, Elam, Cappadocia, Pontus, Asia, Libya, Crete, and many other places.

Converts carried the gospel back to their homelands, where the good news took root. For the most part the details of their efforts cannot be recovered, although it is probable that the

(2 Cor. 11:32). Damascus flourished as a commercial center, strategically placed at the intersection of trade routes extending southward into Arabia and northward into Mesopotamia. After his conversion, Paul began testifying to his newfound faith in the synagogues of Damascus. Soon a plot against his life forced Paul to flee the city (Acts 9:10–25).

We know few details about Paul's life over the next dozen years following his conversion. Galatians (1:11–2:14) contains a condensed autobiography that states Paul went to Arabia (probably a reference to the Nabatean Kingdom) for an unspecified time, after which he returned to Jerusalem (Gal. 1:17–19). Acts records five visits Paul made to Jerusalem (Acts 9:26; 11:30; 15:2; 18:22; 21:15). His first postconversion visit to Jerusalem mentioned in Galations 1:18 likely is the one recorded in Acts 9:26 and happened "three years" after Paul's vision of the risen Christ. Paul met with Peter and James in fellowship for fifteen days. Afterwards, Paul returned to Syria and Cilicia for an unknown period of time.

Cilicia was the province of Paul's birth. His hometown, Tarsus, was a vital military center in the strategic Cilician Plain, through which major routes connected Asia Minor to the East. The Cydnus River flowed through the city into Lake Rhegma and gave Tarsus a naval importance. According to Strabo, Tarsus also was a city of learning and culture. Paul remained in Tarsus until Barnabas sought his help to lead the church in Antioch (Acts 11:19–26). Previously Barnabas had been sent by the Jerusalem church to investigate the rumor that Gentiles in large numbers were receiving the gospel in Antioch. Together Paul and Barnabas returned to Antioch.

THE CHURCH AT ANTIOCH

Antioch was a prestigious city of the East, founded as a Hellenistic capital by Seleucus I in 300 B.C. The Romans made Antioch the provincial capital of Syria and the residence of the Roman legate. A sizable Jewish community lived among a total population that exceeded a quarter million people.

Julius Caesar, Augustus, and Tiberius adorned Antioch with temples, baths, aqueducts, and other public buildings. Herod the Great provided a two-and-a-half-mile colonnaded street paved with marble that bisected the city from north to south. Greeks, Romans, and citizens of the East gave Antioch a truly cosmopolitan image. The church in Antioch became the mother church of Gentile Christianity by sponsoring the mission endeavors of Paul and others. In this melting pot of various creeds and cults, believers in "the Way" first were called Christians (Acts 11:26–29).

Barnabas and Paul colabored perhaps for a year in Antioch, establishing a strong church. News that a widespread famine caused great suffering among the Christians in Judea prompted a second visit to Jerusalem. Paul and Barnabas carried relief funds gathered from Antioch (Acts 11:27–30). A few scholars identify this famine visit with the trip made by Paul and Barnabas to Jerusalem described in Galatians 2:1–10 when Paul presented the gospel he preached to the Jerusalem apostles. Many other scholars think Galatians 2:1–10 is a variant account of the Jerusalem conference described in Acts 15.

Through these early years of ministry, Paul won the confidence of Jewish Christians he formerly persecuted (Gal. 1:22–24). He established a great rapport with Gentiles during his ministry in Cilicia and Antioch. Not all of his labors resulted in victory; likely some of the hardships described in 2 Corinthians 11:23–28—beatings, imprisonments, physical deprivations, dangers in travel—befell Paul in these obscure years of his initial missionary labors. Still, the visionary congregation at Antioch that was nourished by Paul and Barnabas soon launched the pair on more ambitious endeavors.

THE MISSIONARY JOURNEYS

First Missionary Journey (Acts 13–14). The church at Antioch set apart Paul and Barnabas to do missionary work in the West. In the company of John Mark, the pair set forth on their first journey, leaving from Seleucia Pieria, port city of Antioch. Their destination was the island of Cyprus, home of Barnabas (Acts 4:36) and a large Jewish community.

Cyprus. Cyprus was a senatorial province located on a vital sealink in the eastern Mediterranean. Landing at Salamis, the trio proclaimed the gospel across the island on their way to Paphos, the capital of Cyprus and well known for a temple dedicated to Aphrodite. The Roman proconsul, Sergius Paulus, resided there. Acts 11:19 informs us that believers fleeing Jerusalem after the stoning of Stephen had planted the gospel in Cyprus. Barnabas and Paul evangelized the island by preaching in synagogues, but their crowning success was the conversion of Sergius Paulus (Acts 13:12).

Asia Minor. From Cyprus the three travelers set out for Asia Minor, arriving at Perga on the Pamphylian coast. The region was known for its unhealthy climate and marshes, and the trio did not tarry long. John Mark unexpectedly returned home to Jerusalem, while Barnabas and Paul pressed northward into the Pisidian highlands to Antioch. These uplands beyond the western edge of the Taurus Mountains presented considerable challenges to travelers; peaks and valleys harbored brigands, while the rough terrain required careful attention to the pathways.

Perhaps Paul had in mind segments of this journey when he wrote of personal perils he fought while traveling (for example, 2 Cor. 11:26, "danger from rivers, danger from robbers, . . . danger in the wilderness"). It is also possible that Paul detoured eastward to take advantage of better roads to reach Antioch. Despite initial success preaching in the synagogue in Antioch, Paul found such intense Jewish opposition to the gospel that he determined to turn his message toward the Gentiles (Acts 13:46).

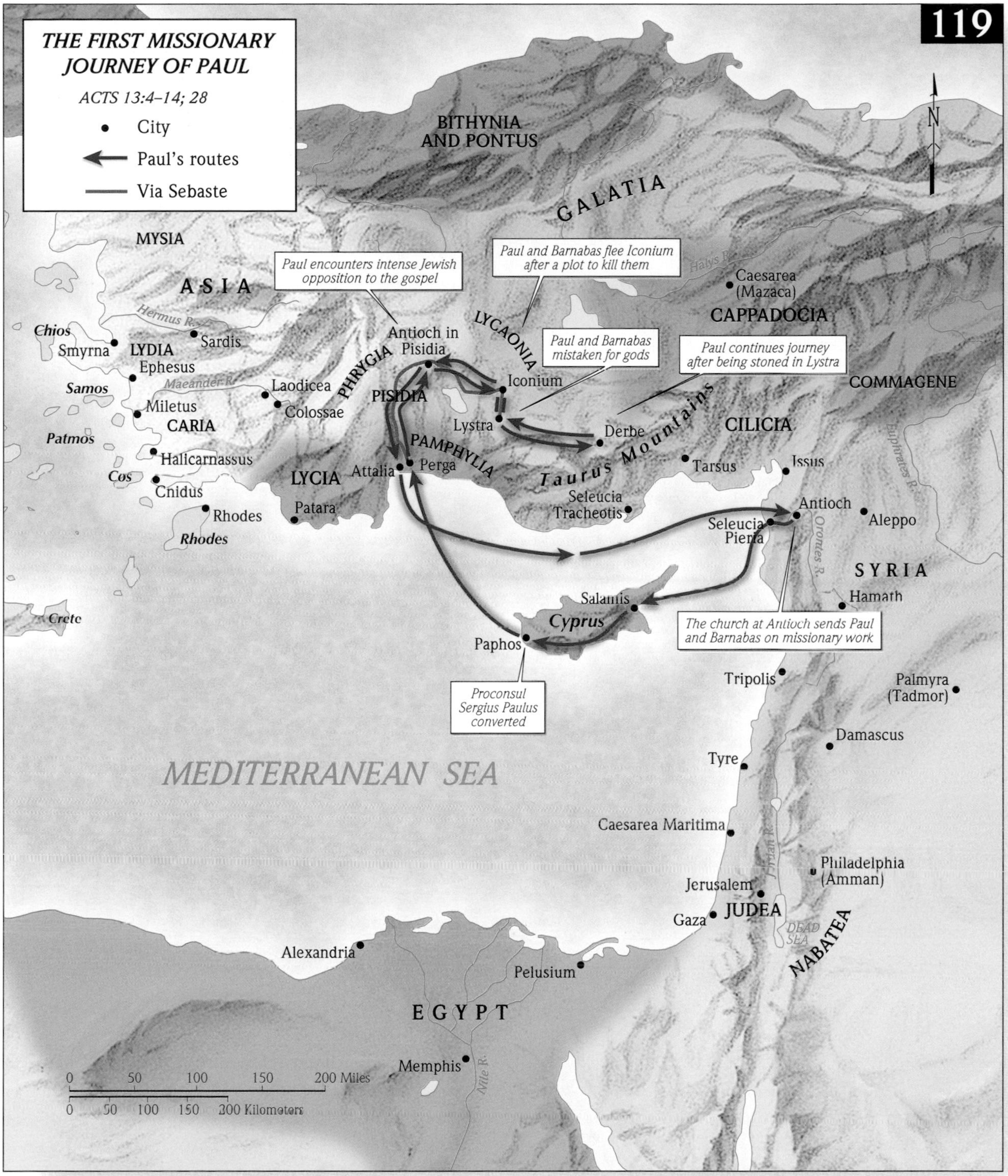

Leaving Antioch, Paul and Barnabas ventured southeast into Lycaonia. Augustus formed the province of Galatia in 25 B.C., which included Lycaonia, and established several Roman colonies—Antioch, Iconium, and Lystra—connected by the Via Sebaste. These cities were isolated and therefore less influenced by Graeco-Roman culture than the cities of the western coast. Native populations retained their customs and languages more readily in the more isolated villages and towns typical of the region. Many of the inhabitants were descendants of Gauls who invaded the region after 300 B.C. By Paul's day the province of Galatia had been expanded, stretching from Pamphylia northward to Pontius. (see map above)

At Iconium, Paul and Barnabas again found opposition

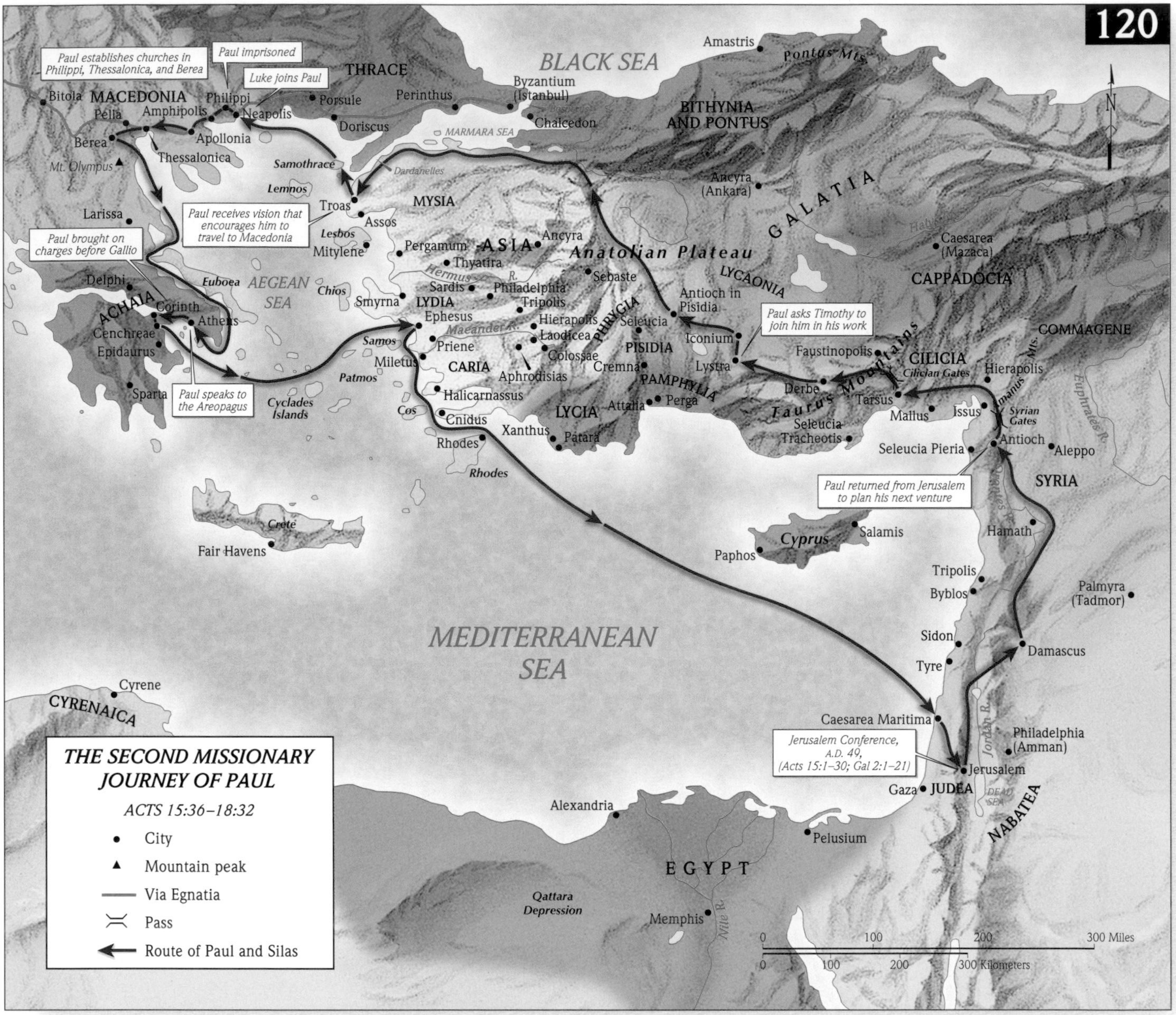

120

THE SECOND MISSIONARY JOURNEY OF PAUL

ACTS 15:36–18:32

- City
- Mountain peak
- Via Egnatia
- Pass
- Route of Paul and Silas

from both Jews and Gentiles, escaping a plot to kill them by fleeing to Lystra in the district of Lycaonia. Here, after healing a lame man, the two were mistaken for gods. Their fortunes changed quickly when Jews from Antioch and Iconium led a mob that stoned Paul and left him for dead. Undeterred, Paul went to Derbe, where he and Barnabas were received more warmly. After a brief stay, Paul retraced his steps through Lystra, Iconium, Antioch in Pisidia, and Perga, strengthening the believers along the way before returning by sea from the port of Attalia to Antioch in Syria.

The Jerusalem Conference (Acts 15). Reports of Paul and Barnabas' successes among the Gentiles reached Jerusalem and stirred a controversy: Must a Gentile convert submit to circumcision to be a Christian? The question was crucial since the issue of salvation was at stake. Paul and Barnabas led a delegation sent from Antioch to a conference convened in Jerusalem to discuss the matter. At the Jerusalem conference, Peter championed salvation by grace apart from any human works, leading the Jerusalem apostles and elders to commend the ministry to the Gentiles unfettered by Jewish legal observance. They requested only that Gentile believers be sensitive to certain Jewish customs (Acts 15:1–29).

Second Missionary Journey (Acts 15:36–18:22). Rejoicing in this victory for the gospel, Paul returned to Antioch and planned a new venture with Barnabas. Unfortunately, Paul and Barnabas quarreled over whether or not John Mark should accompany them. Barnabas took John Mark with him to Cyprus, continuing the work there, while Paul selected Silas to accompany him back to Asia Minor.

Traveling through the Amanus Mountains into the Cilician Plain and then up on the Anatolian Plateau by way of the Cilician Gates, Paul again headed into Galatia, encouraging the churches established on his previous journey. At Lystra, Paul asked Timothy to join him in his work. A son of a believing Jewish woman and a Gentile father, Timothy became one of Paul's most steadfast and trusted companions (1 Cor. 4:17; Acts 19:22; 2 Tim. 1:1–8).

Paul's initial objective for this trip was to evangelize the populous province of Asia on the west coast of Asia Minor, but the Spirit dictated a more northwesterly direction through Phrygia, south of Bithynia, into Mysia. In the port city of Troas, Paul received a vision of a Macedonian imploring him to cross over into Europe with his message (Acts 16:6–10). Boarding a ship at Troas, Paul and his companions overnighted on the island of Samothrace before arriving at Neapolis, the chief port of Macedonia. Acts 16:10 introduces the famous "we" passages of Acts, thought by many scholars to reflect the eyewitness account of one of Paul's companions—Luke—who joined the apostle at this point.

From Neapolis, Paul followed the *Via Egnatia* inland into the heart of Macedonia. This important military highway carried commercial goods across Macedonia to the Adriatic Sea, a distance of over five hundred miles. Along its length lay important cities of Macedonia: Philippi, Apollonia, Amphipolis, and Thessalonica. Rome annexed Macedonia as a province in 148 B.C. Later, Augustus refounded several cities as Roman colonies (Philippi, Pella, and Dion), where he settled Roman veterans as a reward for their service to Rome. Thessalonica and Amphipolis were free cities. At the time of Paul's visit, Macedonia was a senatorial province.

In his first visit to Macedonia, Paul established churches in Philippi, Thessalonica, and Berea. His first convert on European soil was Lydia, a dealer of purple-dyed cloth from Thyatira. Paul met her outside the city at Philippi.

Located ten miles inland from Neapolis, Philippi was named after Philip of Macedon, the father of Alexander the Great. Philippi increased in political importance when Mark Antony defeated Caesar's assassins on a nearby plain in 42 B.C., after which Augustus refounded the colony as *Colonia Iulia Augusta Philippensium.*

Paul's visit to Philippi was an eventful one. When Paul delivered a young slave woman from a Pythian spirit, local magistrates imprisoned and beat him and Silas. An earthquake provided an opportunity for the two to escape, but Paul stayed and shared his faith with the jailer. Paul's appeal to his Roman citizenship prompted fear among the magistrates and his release from prison. Shortly afterward, Paul and Silas departed for Thessalonica by way of Amphipolis and Apollonia.

Paul had a brief, contentious ministry in Thessalonica, a district capital of Macedonia and a major port. Initial success among God-fearing Gentiles and some Jews in a synagogue agitated a mob who attacked the house of Jason where the two missionaries were staying.

The mob charged Paul with proclaiming a king other than Caesar, an act of treason against the Roman Empire. Although the charge was false, Paul and Silas fled to Berea, where several prominent Greek men and women received the gospel. However, Jewish agitators arrived from Thessalonica, forcing an end to Paul's first Macedonian mission.

The mission had borne much fruit; three churches were established, two of which were strategically located on the *Via Egnatia.* The gospel would travel far along this commercial conduit. Paul developed a deep affection for the Macedonian churches, as revealed in his letters. First Thessalonians commends the church for spreading the gospel in Macedonia and Achaia (1 Thess. 1:8). Paul's love and gratitude for the Philippian Christians resonates in his warmest letter addressed to the church at Philippi, penned during a later imprisonment. (Phil. 1:3–11; 4:10–20).

Paul left Macedonia and

An overview of the Roman colony of Philippi. The great Roman road, the *Via Egnatia,* visible in the center of the photograph, brought Paul to Philippi from the nearby port of Neapolis.

journeyed on to Athens, probably by sea, leaving Silas and Timothy behind in Berea. Athens was still an intellectual center, but the city had already lost its political and commercial leadership in Greece (see "Important Cities in Paul's Ministry," pp. 251–55). Depressed by paganism's grip upon the ancient city, evidenced by a multitude of idols, Paul preached in the synagogue and daily debated Epicurean and Stoic philosophers in the marketplace. His message of the resurrected Christ attracted the attention of members of the Areopagus, a body of men concerned with investigating new ideas espoused in Athens.

The rocky outcrop known as Mars Hill in Athens seen from the Acropolis.

Originally, the Areopagus met on a hill northwest of the Acropolis (Mars Hill), but by Paul's day the members likely met in one of the stoas (colonnaded buildings open on one side) in the civic agora or marketplace. Paul invoked Greek poets as he preached before the members of the venerable council; one member of the council, Dionysius, became a believer. However, most members of the Aeropagus scoffed at the idea of a resurrection (Acts 17:22–34). Paul soon left Athens for Corinth, fifty-five miles to the southwest, whether by land or sea is not stated.

Corinth was the proconsular capital of Achaia and one of the major commercial centers of the Roman world (see "Important Cities in Paul's Ministry," pp. 251–55). Here Paul met fellow tent makers Aquila and Priscilla, recently forced to leave Rome by an edict of Claudius banishing Jews. Paul spent eighteen months in Corinth, the second-longest recorded stay of his missionary activities.

Ephesus, where Paul spent two and a half years in ministry.
The view shows Curetes Street descending down to the Library of Celsus.

Silas and Timothy rejoined Paul at Corinth just as the apostle encountered great resistance to his message in the local synagogue. Paul then moved into the home of Titius Justus and concentrated his efforts on the Gentiles. While at Corinth, Paul also penned two of his earliest New Testament epistles: 1 and 2 Thessalonians.

Near the end of Paul's stay, the Jews brought charges against him before Gallio, the proconsul, who found no merit in their claims. The Roman proconsul dismissed the charges as religious matters of no concern to Rome. An inscription found at Delphi mentions Gallio's proconsulship and provides a firm date for the Pauline chronology. According to data from the inscription, Gallio commenced his duties July 1, A.D. 51., a fact that allows us to date Paul's arrival in Corinth sometime in A.D. 50.

Paul left Corinth for the nearby port of Cenchreae accompanied by Aquila and Priscilla. There he kept a vow before sailing

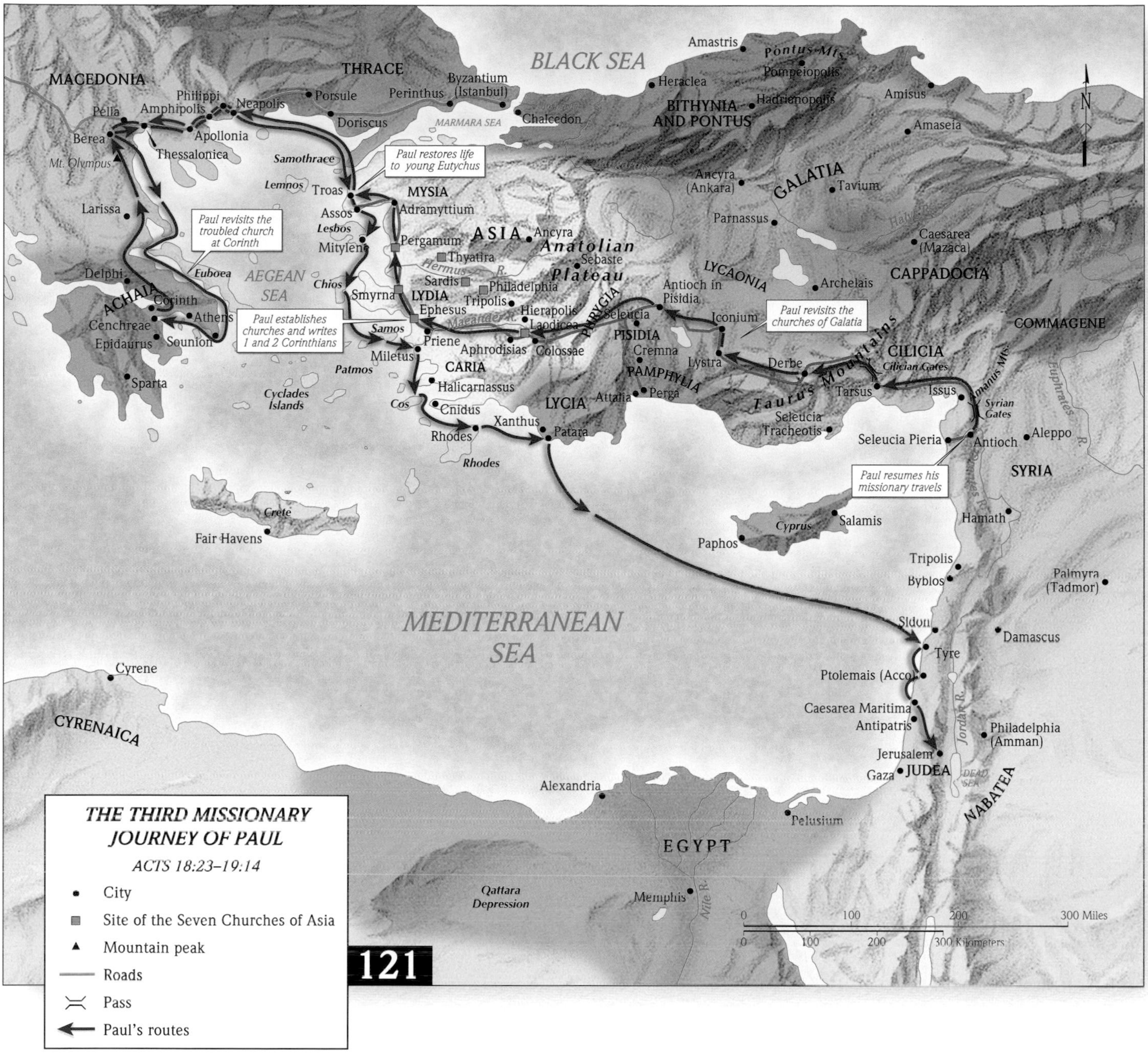

121

THE THIRD MISSIONARY JOURNEY OF PAUL

ACTS 18:23–19:14

- City
- Site of the Seven Churches of Asia
- Mountain peak
- Roads
- Pass
- Paul's routes

back to Syria. Paul stopped briefly at Ephesus, where he parted with his friends and sailed on to Caesarea.

Third Missionary Journey (Acts 18:23–21:14). After a brief stay at Antioch, Paul resumed his missionary endeavors, traveling northwest into Asia Minor. He revisited the churches of Galatia and strengthened the believers in the face of a threat posed by the Judaizers described in Galatians. Paul's destination, however, was Ephesus, the great commercial emporium located on the western coast of Asia Minor (see "Important Cities in Paul's Ministry," pp. 251–55).

This third journey actually was an extended stay of over two years in Ephesus (Acts 19:10). Paul's work in Ephesus advanced the gospel along the valleys that descended westward from the Anatolian Plateau (Hermus, Cayster, and Meander Valleys, and perhaps the Caicus Valley as well). Paul sent disciples such as Epaphras up the valleys to evangelize key cities (Col. 1:7). Many of the churches mentioned in Revelation 2–3 must have been established in these years.

Paul approached Ephesus from the east, perhaps traveling by Pisidian Antioch through Phyrgia into Asia and then down the Cayster Valley. A city of over a quarter million people, Ephesus controlled important land and sea routes. Thousands of pilgrims came to Ephesus yearly to honor the great goddess Artemis, whose temple stood in Ephesus.

Paul's stay in Ephesus was fraught with anxieties and

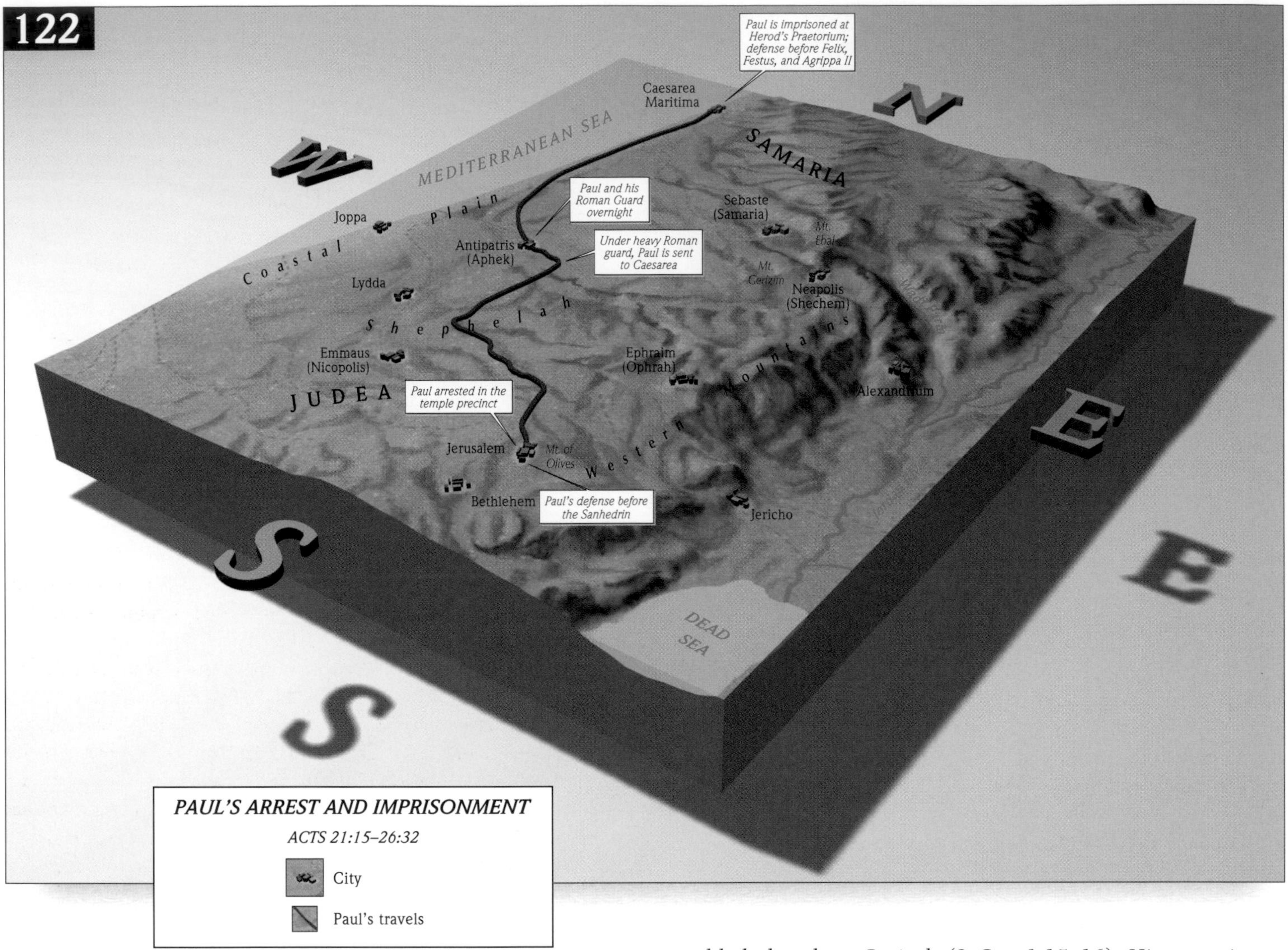

122

PAUL'S ARREST AND IMPRISONMENT

ACTS 21:15–26:32

City

Paul's travels

danger. He wrote about being "burdened immensely, beyond our strength" (2 Cor. 1:8–9), and compared his experiences in Ephesus to "fighting wild beasts" (1 Cor. 15:32). Despite the obstacles, Paul persevered, preaching first in the synagogue and then teaching daily in the lecture hall of the rhetorician Tyrannus. Paul extended his ministry through letter writing (1 and 2 Corinthians, possibly Romans) and by dispatching assistants by sea to the troubled church at Corinth (1 Cor. 4:17) and to Macedonia (Acts 19:22).

In Ephesus, Paul's labors affected local magicians, who subsequently burned their books containing magical incantations. Moreover, Paul's preaching caused a reduction in the sale of idols of Artemis to pilgrims visiting the temple of Artemis (Diana), prompting a riot led by Demetrius the silversmith. Calmer heads prevailed when the city clerk persuaded the mob that they courted Roman reprisals for such unlawful actions.

Shortly thereafter, Paul departed for Macedonia and Greece, fulfilling a previously expressed desire to revisit the troubled church at Corinth (2 Cor. 1:15–16). His route is not stated, but he probably sailed from Troas, as in his earlier visit. After exhorting believers in Macedonia, Paul went to Corinth for a three-month visit. When spring came, he determined to sail for Syria. A plot on his life forced Paul to retrace his steps back through Macedonia, where he sailed for Troas. At Troas, Paul restored life to the unfortunate Eutychus who, while slumbering during Paul's sermon, suffered a deadly fall.

Traveling on to Assos by land, Paul rejoined his ship and passed through the Samos Straits to Miletus, where he said farewell to the elders of Ephesus. From Miletus, Paul journeyed homeward to Jerusalem, going first to Patara by way of Cos and Rhodes and then to Caesarea with stops at Tyre and Ptolemais. Although repeatedly warned by friends not to go up to Jerusalem for fear of reprisals because of his work among the Gentiles, Paul nonetheless was determined to report his work to the Jerusalem church.

The warnings proved well-founded. When Paul went to the temple in the company of men (presumably Jews from Asia) to participate in purification rites, the Jews accused Paul of violating the prohibition against bringing Gentiles beyond their allotted court (Acts 21:26–36). Rescued from a mob by the Roman commander of the cohort stationed in the Antonia Fortress, Paul revealed to the officer his Roman citizenship, and was allowed to defend himself before the Sanhedrin (Acts 22:30–23:11). The next day, Paul's nephew reported a plot on the apostle's life, necessitating his speedy removal from Jerusalem under heavy guard to the safety of the Roman procurator at Caesarea, Felix (Acts 23:12–35). Traveling by way of Antipatris, Paul arrived at Caesarea probably in A.D. 58. He was kept in Herod's praetorium for two years. Felix allowed Paul some freedom and permitted visits of friends who ministered to the apostle during his enforced stay. Felix and his wife, Drusilla, listened to Paul's testimony, but were unmoved by Paul's words.

IMPORTANT CITIES IN PAUL'S MINISTRY

Paul's missionary strategy involved starting churches in the urban centers of the Roman Empire. Paul then left the new communities of faith in the hands of trusted leaders as he traveled to start new work. Still, he wrote back to many of these cities to help them as they struggled to remain loyal to Christ in a pagan environment.

ATHENS

"The glory of Athens" had faded by the time Paul briefly visited the city on his second missionary journey. Exhausted by war and overshadowed by Rome, Athens lost her political importance and most of her cultural significance. Yet the gleaming marble monuments adorning the Acropolis, built around 450 B.C. during the age of Pericles, gave mute testimony to Athens' glorious heritage.

Paul arrived in Athens by ship, debarking most likely at the Piraeus, the largest of Athens' three harbors. Clustered about the steep hill known as the Acropolis, arising out of the Attica Plain, the city of Athens had a history hearkening back to the Mycenaean era (fifteenth to thirteenth century B.C.). Mycenaean remains have been found on the Acropolis. Below the Acropolis on the north side stood the agora—the civic hub of the ancient city. The Greek agora contained the buildings that once served Athens' democracy—the *Bouleuterion* (council chamber), *Tholos*, and *Heliaia*. Several *stoas* (colonnaded halls open on one side) surrounded the Greek agora. The Middle Stoa bordered the south, a smaller Stoa of Zeus stood on the west, and the Stoa of Attalos on the east divided the Greek agora from the recently built Roman forum. Temples, altars, and numerous inscriptions recalled Athens' religious traditions. One of the best-preserved Greek temples is the Hephaestion on the west side of the agora, a temple honoring the god of craftsmen. An altar to the "Twelve Gods" and a temple to Ares added by Augustus in the center of the agora stood near a large odeum built by the emperor's son-in-law, Marcus Agrippa. The Panathenic Way, used in annual festivals honoring Athena, bisected the Greek agora on its journey up to the Acropolis.

The ancient Greek Agora of Athens as viewed from the Acropolis. The reconstructed Stoa of Attalos is visible on the right.

By Paul's time the Greek agora had become more of a museum for monuments recalling Athens' former glory. The commercial center of the city shifted to a new Roman forum east of the Stoa of Attalos. The forum was 364 feet long and 321 feet wide and had a clock tower easily visible from the market. Today known as the Tower of the Winds, it contained a sundial and a water clock. Paul probably debated with philosophers among the bustling crowds of the Roman forum.

Paul surely visited the Acropolis, where he walked among some of the most beautiful monuments of antiquity. People approached the Acropolis from the west through the Propylaea, a monumental gateway. Crowning the Acropolis was the Parthenon, the magnificent Doric temple built to honor Athens' patron goddess, Athena. A frieze running along the sides of the temple depicted scenes from the yearly Panathenaic Festival held in Athena's honor. Nearby stood a large statue of Athena that could be seen at sea for miles. An exquisite Ionic temple of Athena jutted out of the Acropolis on the south side, while the Erechtheum, with its "Porch of the Maidens," stood north of the Parthenon. A round temple to Augustus and Rome reminded citizens of Rome's political dominance. Below the Acropolis on the south side stood the Theater of Dionysius, originally built about 500 B.C., and a small temple to Asclepius, a god of healing.

The Acropolis of Athens viewed from Mars Hill (the Aeropagus). The beautiful Ionic temple of Athena Nike is visible on the right side.

Athens had been home to the chief schools of Greek philosophy since the fourth century B.C. Paul's debate with Epicurean and Stoic philosophers prompted a summons to appear before the Areopagus to have his views examined. In earlier times the Areopagus met on a rocky eminence west of the Acropolis, today called Mars Hill. In the Roman era the high court of Athens probably met in one of the buildings in the agora below. Paul's famous sermon delivered to the Areopagus failed to impress most of the skeptical Greek philosophers, but one member of the court—Dionysius—and a woman named Damaris were converted (Acts 17:22–34).

The Parthenon, the great temple of the patron goddess Athena.

CORINTH

Corinth was a commercial center famous for its bronze and pottery from before 600 B.C. The city was ideally situated on a narrow isthmus between central Greece and the Peloponnesus that controlled both the sea and land routes of the region. To the west, the port of Lechaeum on the Gulf of Corinth faced Italy and Spain, while the smaller harbor facility at Cenchreae, located on the Saronic Gulf, gave access to the rich ports of the East. After 600 B.C. the Corinthians built a paved roadway (the *diolkos*) to transfer cargo, and perhaps small vessels, from one port to the other across the three-and-one-half-mile neck of the isthmus. The cargo transfers saved a dangerous two-hundred-mile journey around the Cape of Malea. The Roman geographer Strabo described Corinth as "wealthy because of its commerce, since it is situated on the Isthmus and is master of two harbors, of which one leads straight to Asia, and the other to Italy; and it makes

The Lechaeum Road at Corinth. Lechaeum was one of two port facilities on either side of the Isthmus of Corinth that gave the city such strategic commercial importance.

easy the exchange of merchandise from both countries that are so far distant from each other" (Strabo, *Geography*, 8.6.20).

Although the Romans destroyed the city in 146 B.C., Julius Caesar rebuilt Corinth as a Roman colony in 44 B.C., and the city quickly regained its commercial importance. In 27 B.C. Augustus made Corinth the provincial capital of Achaia, adding political prominence to the city's unquestioned commercial importance. Corinth attracted pilgrims every two years to the Isthmian Games, one of the four major Panhellenic Games. The Isthmian Games honored Poseidon, god of the sea, and were held at nearby Isthmia. These pilgrims added to the rich cosmopolitan population—Romans, Greeks, and a sizeable Jewish community—of the great seaport city. Like most ports, Corinth had a well-known reputation for immorality. The colloquial expression "to Corinthianize" meant to engage in immoral behavior and loose living. Paul warned his Corinthian converts against returning to the immorality and licentiousness out of which they came (1 Cor. 6:9–11; 2 Cor. 12:21).

Corinth spread out below the 1,886-foot-high Acrocorinth that towered above the isthmus. Six miles of walls enclosed a city numbering one hundred to two hundred thousand in population. Walls connected Corinth with its western port, Cenchreae. Several structures stood on top of the rocky Acrocorinth including a small, but famous, temple to Aphrodite. Strabo's often-cited reference to one thousand prostitutes that served the goddess Aphrodite in Corinth is an exaggeration, but the city's well-deserved reputation for sexual license did have religious overtones.

Numerous temples to the older Olympian gods and newer deities dotted the city's landscape. A temple to Apollos (or Athena?), built shortly after 600 B.C., was restored after the Roman destruction. An important healing shrine sacred to Asclepius attracted pilgrims seeking a cure for various maladies. A larger temple west of the forum was used for the imperial cult. A row of smaller temples enclosing the west end of the forum have been attributed to various deities including Tyche, Venus, Apollo, and possibly Hera. The Egyptian deities Isis and Osiris also received worship at Corinth.

The Roman forum lay at the center of the city, approached from the north by the Lechaeum Road. A series of stoas on the south and northwest defined the forum; the southern section contained administrative buildings, while the northern sector housed shops and markets. A central row of shops bisected the forum east to west. In the middle of the shops was the *bema*, a tribunal where Paul probably stood before the proconsul Gallio in A.D. 51 (Acts 18:12–17).

Corinth contained the standard amenities of a great city, including a theater, odeum, basilicas, and baths. A large

The imposing rocky mass of the Acrocorinth.

meat market and numerous wine shops have been uncovered. Some of the shops used cold running spring water to keep perishables fresh. Three springs—Glauke, the Sacred Spring, and the much larger Fountain of Peirene—supplied Corinth with an abundance of water.

Paul made Corinth his home for eighteen months before traveling back to Jerusalem. He met Aquilla and Priscilla there, and together they practiced their trade of tentmaking. Paul began his mission in Corinth among the Jews in the synagogue, but after meeting opposition there, he extended his ministry to the Gentiles, preaching and teaching in the house of Titius Justus, where he met much success (Acts 18:5–11). Paul's lengthy stay in Corinth allowed the apostle time to pen letters back to the church at Thessalonica carried by his trusted fellow laborers Silas and Timothy. A similar opportunity afforded itself later in Paul's more lengthy stay at Ephesus.

The archaic temple of Apollo at Corinth.

EPHESUS

Ephesus, capital of the wealthy province of Asia, was home to Paul for more than two years. This proud city, whose heritage reached back a thousand years to the Ionian Greeks, boasted of her fame as the "Warden" of the great temple of Artemis, an ancient fertility/mother goddess worshiped by the Romans as Diana. One of the seven wonders of the ancient world, the Artemision was the largest marble temple of the Greek world (about 420 x 240 feet); it replaced an earlier structure burned in 356 B.C. The temple stood northeast of the city on a marshy plain beneath a hill. Ionic capitals crowned over a hundred columns set in double rows around the shrine. Some of the columns were sculpted with mythological scenes and overlaid with gold. A U-shaped altar stood in a forecourt. The Artemision was burned by the Goths in A.D. 263, and the emperor Justinian cannibalized the ruins shortly after A.D. 500 for building materials. Little remains of this once mighty edifice, but in Paul's day pilgrims from all over Asia Minor and beyond converged on Ephesus annually in the spring to pay homage to the mother goddess with special celebrations. Images of the goddess found in excavations show Artemis wearing an unusual corselet composed of eggs or multiple breasts.

The temple of Hadrian at Ephesus.

Ephesus' political importance increased when Domitian awarded the city a provincial imperial temple dedicated to the Flavian Dynasty. As a "temple warden" (Greek *Neokoros*) of a provincial imperial temple, Ephesus received political and commercial benefits and increased status among the cities of Asia. Prominent Ephesians served the Provincial Assembly (*Koinon*) whose mission was to cultivate and enforce emperor worship within the province. Several scholars identify this assembly with the second beast in Revelation 13 who made war on the Christians of Asia by requiring worship of the emperor (Rev. 13:11–18).

Ephesus' strategic location ensured the city was a large, important commercial center. A well–protected harbor at the mouth of the Cayster River afforded good anchorage despite the continual problem of silting. Links

The Library of Celsus at Ephesus. Though dating from a slightly later time than Paul, this beautiful building illustrates the wealth and culture of Roman Ephesus.

with the Meander and Hermus Valleys afforded access to the agricultural wealth and interior cities of western Asia Minor. Paul evangelized the interior by sending his disciples from Ephesus (for example, Epaphras, Col. 1:7), and carried on correspondence from Ephesus with churches (the Corinthian correspondence; perhaps the Prison Epistles—Colossians, Ephesians, Philippians, and Philemon—according to some scholars).

Hellenistic/Roman Ephesus occupied an area south of the Artemision between two prominences, Mounts Pion and Koressos. Lysimachus built the new city about 290 B.C., forcing the inhabitants of the earlier city to move from the earliest site. Ephesus was the third or fourth largest city of the empire when Paul visited the city, with a population estimated at 250,000. As the administrative capital of Asia, Ephesus was well endowed with monumental buildings, whose remains are impressive even today. An upper agora contained civic buildings, including an odeum used as a town council chamber, the Prytaneion used as a town hall, and an imperial temple dedicated to Augustus and Rome.

The large imperial temple built by Domitian stood nearby at the beginning of Curetes Street. Later, Hadrian and Trajan added a fountain and temple along this impressive street known for its fine monuments. Shops lurked behind colonnaded streetways, while fine houses crept up the slopes of the hill. The Library of Celsus, built shortly after 100 A.D., stood at the intersection of Curetes and Marble Streets. Close by, the 360-foot-square commercial agora with its many shops tucked behind a double-aisle *stoa* served the business needs of the city. A large theater built into Mount Pion seated about twenty-five thousand people and overlooked the harbor. From the theater, the Harbor Road stretched westward toward the busy port facilities. Later, the emperor Arcadius (A.D. 383–408) rebuilt this road into a spacious colonnaded thoroughfare with shops on either side. Several large bath complexes and gymnasia bordered the harbor area near the Harbor Road.

Ephesus' stature as a center of banking, commerce, provincial government, and religion made it one of the major centers of the Roman world. Little wonder that Paul spent more time in Ephesus than any other city on his missionary journeys. Ephesus provided a strong base of operations to evangelize the province of Asia, a province that fostered a large Christian community by A.D. 100.

The Great Theater at Ephesus as viewed from the Harbor Road.

PAUL'S VOYAGE TO ROME (ACTS 27:1–28:16)

Paul remained in Caesarea under arrest until Porcius Festus replaced Felix in A.D. 60. Festus and Agrippa II heard Paul's eloquent testimony but remained unmoved, even though they agreed Paul had done nothing to deserve imprisonment or death. Had Paul not appealed to Caesar as was his privilege as a Roman citizen, he might have been set free. However, Paul's appeal set him on a voyage to Rome (Acts 27–28).

These great ships supplied Rome with wheat; the largest freighters measured 180 feet long with a beam width of 50 feet. Paul and his party joined the 276 crew members and passengers bound for Italy. The heavy cargo and passenger load increased the risk of sailing, especially so late in the season. Making for Salmone on the eastern tip of Crete, the pilot sailed to Fair Havens, a small harbor in southern Crete. Paul considered remaining in Fair Havens for the winter, but those in charge suggested wintering at Phoenix on the Cretan coast, some forty miles to the west.

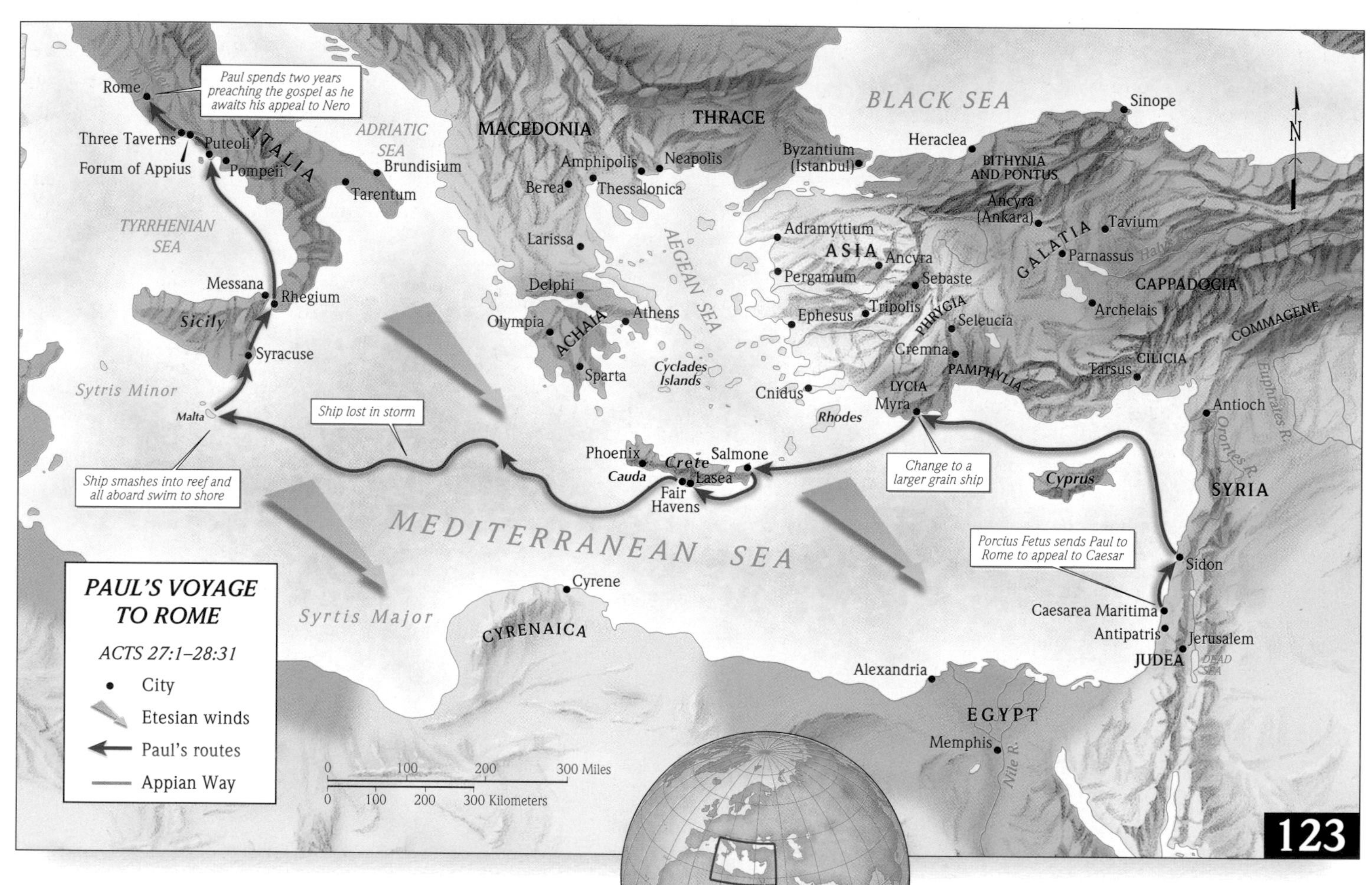

Sea journeys on the Mediterranean from east to west were difficult due to the prevailing northwesterly winds (the "Etesian Winds"). Moreover, Paul began his voyage late in the sailing season when unexpected storms threatened. Accompanied by Aristarchus from Thessalonica (Acts 19:29; 20:4), Luke, and in the custody of the centurion Julius, Paul joined other prisoners for a two-thousand-mile voyage to Rome.

Paul embarked on a small trading vessel heading to home port at Adramyttium, a city on the northeast coast of Asia Minor. The initial phase of the trip followed the coast to Sidon and then headed northwest past the lee of Cyprus "because the winds were against us" (Acts 27:4). Upon arrival at Myra in Lycia, the centurion located a much larger Alexandrian grain freighter bound for Rome.

The dash toward Phoenix following favorable light winds became a fourteen-day nightmare when gale-force winds drove the ship southwestward to the small island of Cauda. The crew fought to gain control of the vessel, using sea anchors and jettisoning cargo in a desperate bid to avoid the deadly shallows off North Africa known as Syrtis Major. Drifting helplessly for several days, the crew lost any hope of rescue.

Paul received a vision in those dark days that he and the crew would be divinely spared. On the fourteenth night, the vessel approached land, and the crew feared the ship would be smashed against the rocks. After an aborted attempt to abandon ship, the crew deployed sea anchors to slow their drift and prayed for daylight. Dawn revealed an unfamiliar land with a bay. Risking everything, the crew set a course for the beach but ran aground on a reef, the ship breaking up under the pounding waves. The centurion, ordering his soldiers not to kill the prisoners to prevent escape, gave the command to abandon ship and swim for shore. Those who could not swim clung to debris as they washed to shore.

After washing up on shore, the survivors discovered they had landed on the island of Malta. Publius, a leading citizen of the island, provided help and hospitality to Paul and his companions. The group wintered in Malta, awaiting the arrival of favorable weather conditions. This allowed Paul opportunity to exercise a healing ministry that included relief given to Publius' father. Three months later, in the custody of Julius, Paul boarded another Egyptian grain ship bound for Italy. The ship put in at Syracuse in Sicily and then sailed on to Rhegium. Catching a favorable wind, the ship sailed on to Puteoli in the Gulf of Naples.

Puteoli was a major port receiving the grain supply from Egypt vital to Rome. During the reign of Claudius, the port of Ostia increasingly supplied Rome's needs. Located at the mouth of the Tiber, Ostia had a new harbor just north of the city named Portus. Believers at Puteoli hosted Paul for a week, and then, after adequate rest, Paul's party headed north along the *Via Campana* to Capua and then by the *Via Appia* to Rome. Upon hearing of Paul's arrival in Italy, groups of Roman Christians went to greet the apostle at two way stations on the *Via Appia*—the Forum of Appius (forty-three miles from Rome) and Three Taverns (thirty-three miles from Rome). According to Acts, Paul spent two years in Rome, preaching the gospel with confidence and boldness, awaiting the adjudication of his appeal to Nero.

The Island of Malta where Paul and the crew of the wrecked Roman freighter washed ashore.

Chapter Twenty

THE FIRST JEWISH REVOLT

Introduction

After decades of Roman rule, Jewish nationalism spilled over into open rebellion against Rome in A.D. 66. This First Jewish Revolt against Rome had disastrous consequences for the Jews and Palestine; it also affected the Christian movement because of the loss of influence of the Jerusalem church. Jewish unrest was deeply rooted in the long Roman occupation of their land, but several events precipitated a crisis. When the procurator Gessius Florus confiscated seventeen talents from the Jerusalem temple treasury, the Jews violently resisted. Riots broke out between Jews and Gentiles in Caesarea Maritima over a long-simmering dispute concerning citizenship, recently decided by Nero in favor of the Gentiles. Many Jews died in Caesarea, and the riots spread to other cities where similar tensions led to bloodshed. In June A.D. 66, the daily sacrifices offered in Jerusalem on behalf of the emperor and the Roman people ceased by order of Eleazar, captain of the temple. This action signaled open rebellion against Rome.

The Opposing Armies

Recognizing the seriousness of the situation, Cestius Gallus, the Roman legate of Syria, marched south with the Twelfth Legion Fulminata ("the Thundering One") and assorted cavalry and infantry units. He took the coastal route to Caesarea then to Jerusalem via Antipatris, Lydda, and Beth-horon. Despite some initial success penetrating the city's defenses, he could not retake Jerusalem and shortly withdrew. When Roman troops suffered a serious defeat at Beth-horon at the hands of Jewish Zealots, the victory gave the Jewish insurgents confidence.

The rebels organized resistance into seven districts, each with a separate commander. The Jewish historian Flavius Josephus commanded the Jewish forces in Galilee. Many cities of mixed population refused to join the revolt; moreover, aristocratic Jews such as Agrippa II tried to prevent open rebellion, but to no avail. Factions quickly appeared in the leadership of the revolt because leaders operated with different motives and

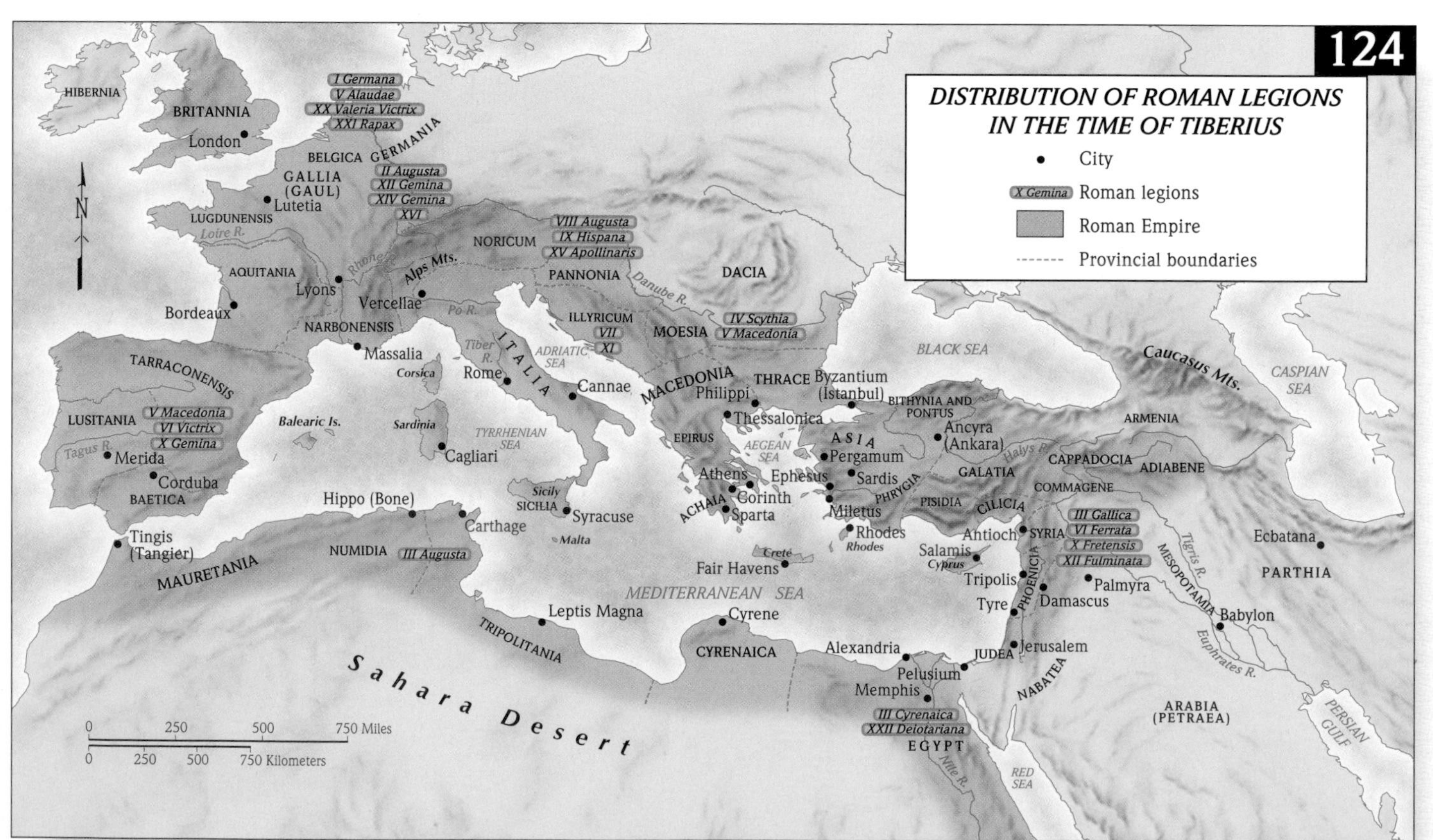

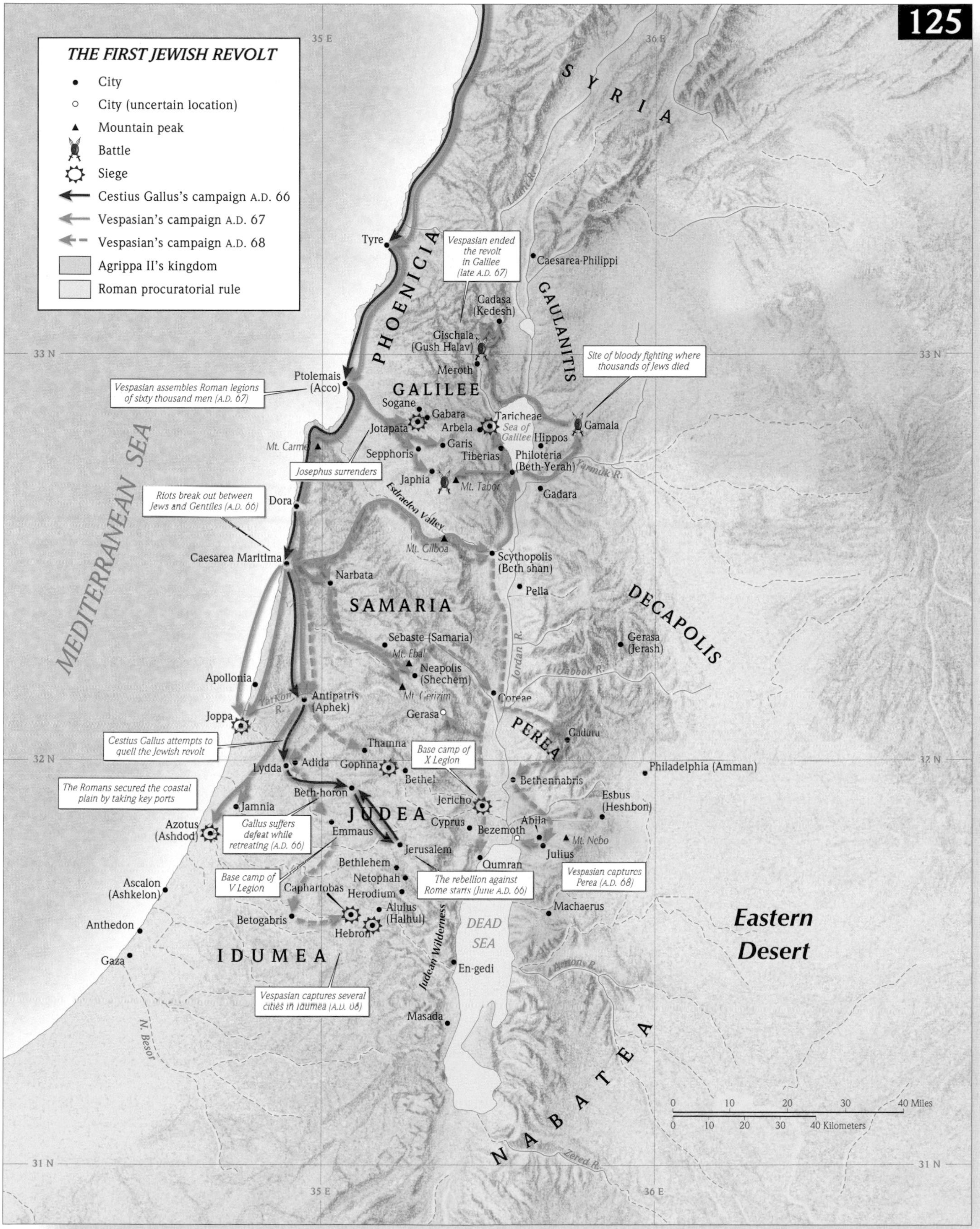

125

THE FIRST JEWISH REVOLT

- City
- City (uncertain location)
- Mountain peak
- Battle
- Siege
- Cestius Gallus's campaign A.D. 66
- Vespasian's campaign A.D. 67
- Vespasian's campaign A.D. 68
- Agrippa II's kingdom
- Roman procuratorial rule

SYRIA
PHOENICIA
GAULANITIS
GALILEE
SAMARIA
JUDEA
PEREA
DECAPOLIS
IDUMEA
NABATEA
MEDITERRANEAN SEA
DEAD SEA
Eastern Desert

Vespasian ended the revolt in Galilee (late A.D. 67)
Site of bloody fighting where thousands of Jews died
Vespasian assembles Roman legions of sixty thousand men (A.D. 67)
Josephus surrenders
Riots break out between Jews and Gentiles (A.D. 66)
Cestius Gallus attempts to quell the Jewish revolt
The Romans secured the coastal plain by taking key ports
Gallus suffers defeat while retreating (A.D. 66)
Base camp of X Legion
Base camp of V Legion
The rebellion against Rome starts (June A.D. 66)
Vespasian captures Perea (A.D. 68)
Vespasian captures several cities in Idumea (A.D. 68)

Tyre
Caesarea-Philippi
Cadasa (Kedesh)
Gischala (Gush Halav)
Meroth
Ptolemais (Acco)
Sogane
Gabara
Jotapata
Arbela
Taricheae
Sea of Galilee
Gamala
Mt. Carmel
Garis
Hippos
Sepphoris
Tiberias
Philoteria (Beth-Yerah)
Yarmuk R.
Japhia
Mt. Tabor
Gadara
Dora
Esdraelon Valley
Mt. Gilboa
Caesarea Maritima
Scythopolis (Beth shan)
Narbata
Pella
Sebaste (Samaria)
Mt. Ebal
Gerasa (Jerash)
Neapolis (Shechem)
Jabbok R.
Jordan R.
Apollonia
Mt. Gerizim
Coreae
Yarkon R.
Antipatris (Aphek)
Joppa
Gerasa
Gadora
Thamna
Lydda
Adida
Gophna
Philadelphia (Amman)
Bethel
Bethennabris
Jamnia
Beth-horon
Jericho
Esbus (Heshbon)
Azotus (Ashdod)
Emmaus
Cyprus
Abila
Bezemoth
Mt. Nebo
Jerusalem
Julius
Qumran
Bethlehem
Netophah
Ascalon (Ashkelon)
Caphartobas
Herodium
Machaerus
Alulus (Halhul)
Anthedon
Betogabris
Hebron
Judean Wilderness
Arnon R.
Gaza
En-gedi
Masada
N. Besor
Zered R.

0 10 20 30 40 Miles
0 10 20 30 40 Kilometers

35 E
36 E
33 N
32 N
31 N

goals. These factions undermined the effectiveness of resistance and led to bloody infighting among the Jews.

Nero sent the fifty-seven-year-old Vespasian to put down the insurrection (see pp. 263–65 under "The Flavian Dynasty"). A man of great military experience, Vespasian met his son Titus at Ptolemais and assembled an army of approximately sixty thousand men composed of three legions, auxiliaries, and assorted royal troops. Titus brought with him the Fifteenth Legion Apollinaris from Alexandria, while the Fifth Legion Macedonia and the Tenth Legion Fretensis arrived from Syria. Throughout the later campaigns, elements from other legions (Twenty-second Deiotariana and Third Cyrenacia) plus the Twelfth Fulminata participated in putting down the revolt. This enormous concentration of Roman forces in Palestine and Syria represented almost one quarter of the twenty-six legions available to Rome.

The Roman Forum with columns of the temple of Saturn in the foreground.

The Campaign in Galilee

Vespasian campaigned against Galilee in spring A.D. 67. Although the towns and villages of Galilee were easily defended, Vespasian made short work conquering the region. Sepphoris, along with other cities, surrendered, unwilling to oppose Rome. Other more heavily fortified fortresses required siege. The defenders of Jotapata fought to the death, although their commander, Josephus, saved his life by surrendering. Zealots at Taricheae (Magdala) resisted effectively for a time before being overwhelmed.

East of the Sea of Galilee, Gamala was the scene of bloody fighting; thousands of Jews died at Gamala, both in battle and by suicide. Mop-up actions at Mount Tabor and Gischala ended the revolt in Galilee by late A.D. 67. The Romans secured the coastal plain by taking key ports such as Joppa and Azotus. John of Gischala, the Zealot leader who bitterly opposed the tactics of Josephus, fled to Jerusalem to fight another day.

In A.D. 68 Vespasian launched a campaign to isolate Jerusalem. Moving south by way of the Wadi Farah and the Jezreel Valley, the Romans captured Perea and stationed the Tenth Legion at Jericho. The Fifth Legion moved into the Shephelah and northern Idumea, capturing several cities before encamping at Emmaus. These movements set the stage for an assault on Jerusalem that was interrupted by events in Rome.

Unrest in Rome

In June A.D. 68 Nero committed suicide after he was condemned to death by orders from the Senate. During the next twelve months a power struggle ensued in Rome for the imperial throne. Vespasian suspended plans to take Jerusalem, but Roman detachments continued to raid rebel centers from Emmaus and Jericho. Acrabeta, Gophna, Capharabis, and Hebron fell.

Three men—Galba, Otho, and Vitellius—vied for imperial power until the legions of the East proclaimed Vespasian Emperor of Rome. Vitellius retained the office of emperor until December A.D. 69 when Vespasian's supporters gained control at Rome and executed Vitellius. Vespasian's broad support ended the threat of a Roman civil war and permitted the legions to continue their work in Judea.

The Campaign of Titus against Jerusalem

Vespasian charged Titus with finishing the task of crushing the Jewish revolt. Titus assembled two legions at Caesarea and approached Jerusalem from the north, where he linked up with the Tenth Legion from Jericho and the Fifth Legion from Emmaus. Though heavily fortified, Jerusalem was completely isolated by a Roman army that may have totaled eighty thousand men.

Several Jewish factions occupied various strongholds

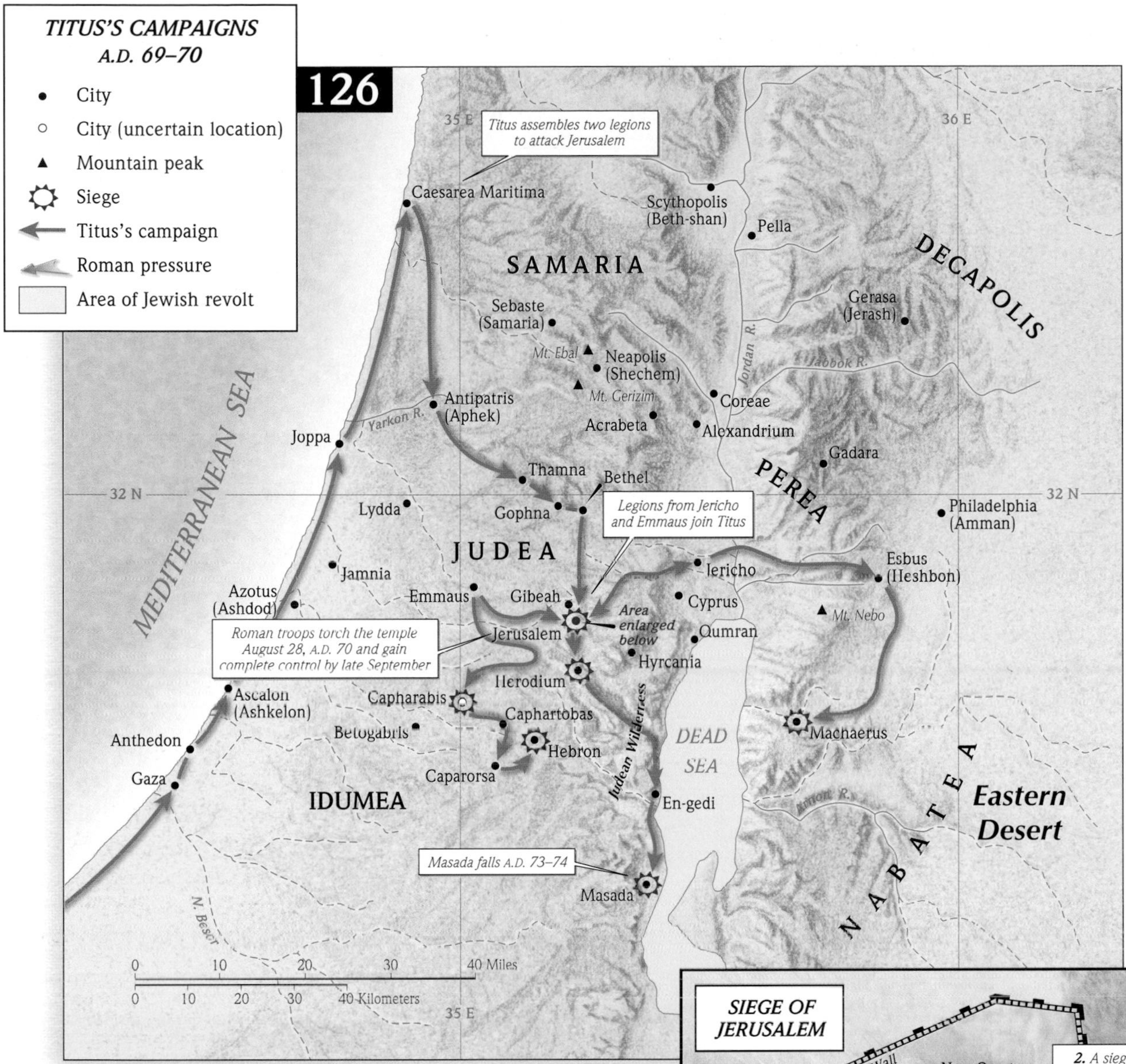

126

TITUS'S CAMPAIGNS A.D. 69–70

- City
- City (uncertain location)
- Mountain peak
- Siege
- Titus's campaign
- Roman pressure
- Area of Jewish revolt

Titus assembles two legions to attack Jerusalem

Legions from Jericho and Emmaus join Titus

Roman troops torch the temple August 28, A.D. 70 and gain complete control by late September

Masada falls A.D. 73–74

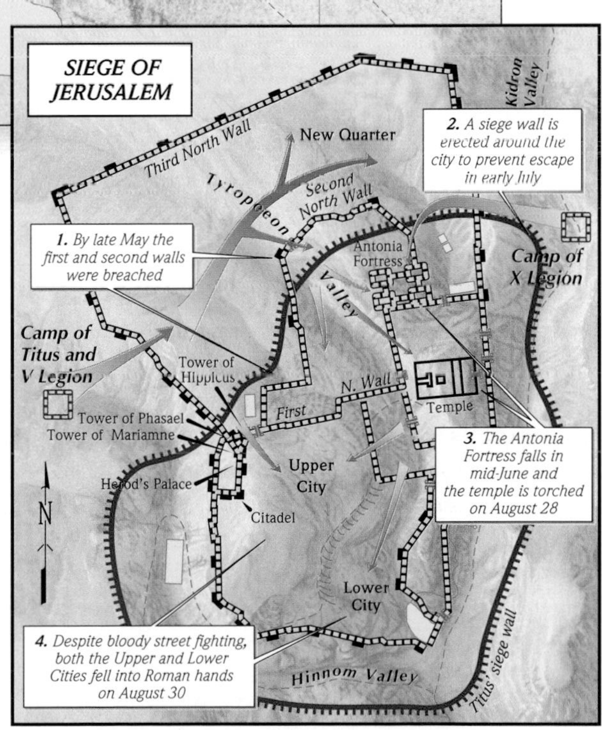

within the city. John of Gischala commanded forces holding the temple and the Antonia Fortress, while Simon ben Giora held the Upper City. Titus commanded the siege operations from his camp northwest of the city. Jerusalem's greatest vulnerability lay to the north, where Titus concentrated his efforts. By late May the first and second north walls had been breached. In July, Titus ordered a siege wall erected around the city to prevent escape. Starvation and factional infighting took a deadly toll upon the besieged Jews. The Antonia Fortress fell, and on August 6 sacrifice ceased in the temple. On the ninth of Ab (August 28, A.D. 70) Roman troops torched the temple.

During the next month both the Lower and Upper Cities fell into Roman hands despite bloody street fighting. By late September the siege of Jerusalem ended in a complete Roman victory. Titus took captive the Jewish survivors and later paraded

A closeup of the interior of the Arch of Titus in the Roman Forum showing the spoils of war taken during the First Jewish Revolt. The scene shows furnishings of the Jerusalem temple, including the seven branch candlestick (the Menorah), plundered from the temple before it was destroyed.

them along with vessels taken from the temple in an official triumph before the people of Rome. Jewish prisoners were put to death in public spectacles celebrating the Roman victory. Engraved on the Arch of Titus standing in the Roman Forum today are the spoils of war carried from Jerusalem by Roman soldiers, including the Menorah and table of Showbread looted from the temple.

Consequences of the Jewish Revolt

The First Jewish Revolt affected Jews and Christians in several ways. The province of Judea assumed a new status in Roman administration under Vespasian. Henceforth, a Roman legate commanding Roman legions governed the territory independently of Syrian administration. Roman troops settled in Palestine and built new roads that facilitated troop movement and connected legionary posts.

The Jewish population suffered greatly, both spiritually and physically. The temple and its sacrificial system were gone; Jerusalem lay in ruins and was occupied by portions of the Tenth Legion. With no temple, the influence of the high priest and the Sadducees rapidly dissolved. Only the Pharisees survived the crisis, reconstituting the Sanhedrin at Jamnia shortly before A.D. 100.

According to Eusebius, Christians fled to Pella before the destruction of Jerusalem ensued. Jerusalem, already affected by local persecutions of Christian leaders and famine, surrendered her leadership to churches in Antioch, Alexandria, and other Graeco-Roman cities that became spokes radiating the gospel into the larger Mediterranean world.

Final Jewish Resistance

Jewish Zealots held out in Judean desert fortresses despite the fall of Jerusalem. Machaerus and Herodium quickly fell to Roman forces commanded by the legate Lucillus Bassus. Zealot defenders maintained their grim hold on Masada until A.D. 73 (perhaps 74).

Flavius Silva, the Roman general, directed operations against Masada, during which a massive siege ramp built by Jewish captives gave access to the top of the fortress. As the end drew near, approximately 960 Jewish men, women, and children chose suicide rather than surrender to the Romans. Masada's fall signaled the end of Jewish armed resistance in Palestine for a time, but Zealot sympathizers in the near future again would challenge Roman authority both in Palestine and beyond (see pp. 270–73 "Life in Palestine and the Growth of the Church [A.D. 73–135]").

A view from Masada showing the main Roman camp used by the Roman General Silva during his siege of the fortress.

Chapter Twenty-One

THE CHRISTIAN CHURCH FROM A.D. 70 TO 300

The Emperors of Rome from A.D. 69 to 138

THE FLAVIAN DYNASTY

Nero's suicide in A.D. 68 ended the Julio-Claudian Dynasty that had ruled Rome since the days of Augustus. During the next year—"the year of the four emperors"—a power struggle for the imperial throne unfolded at Rome. Galba, Otho, and Vitellius claimed the title "emperor" before Vespasian finally ended the threat of civil war. Vespasian secured the throne in A.D. 69 with the support of the Roman army and quickly moved to position his two sons—Titus and Domitian—as legitimate successors. These three emperors constitute the Flavian Dynasty, a dynasty that laid the foundations for Roman power and culture that flourished between A.D. 100 and 200.

Vespasian. Vespasian rose from humble equestrian class origins to become emperor of Rome chiefly through his military accomplishments. A veteran general of the Britain campaign, Vespasian was fifty-seven years old when Nero called on him to put down the revolt in Judea. After Nero's death in June A.D. 68, Vespasian curtailed operations in Palestine until his legions acclaimed him emperor. After placing Titus in command of the Judean campaign, Vespasian eventually journeyed to Rome, where he faced serious problems.

Nero's reign had left a legacy of senatorial distrust of imperial power and a financial crisis. Moreover, the "year of the four emperors" created instability in the imperial line. Vespasian proved to be more than adequate to meet the challenge. A frugal emperor who eschewed the trappings of power and Greek culture beloved by Nero, Vespasian maximized revenues and restored the empire to solvency.

However, both Vespasian and Titus lavished funds on the rebuilding of Rome following the disastrous fire of A.D. 64. The Flavian Amphitheater—the famous Colosseum of Rome—stands as testimony to the monumental scale of Flavian patronage. Vespasian solidified the support of the army and assured the continuation of a dynasty by sharing power with his son Titus. In the provinces, the emperor's policies promoted honesty and efficiency from provincial officials. The Roman Empire had recovered strength and stability by the time Vespasian died in A.D. 79.

Titus. Titus succeeded his father in A.D. 79 but ruled only two years. The conqueror of Judea was memorialized in the Arch of Titus, commemorating a triumph granted him by Vespasian.

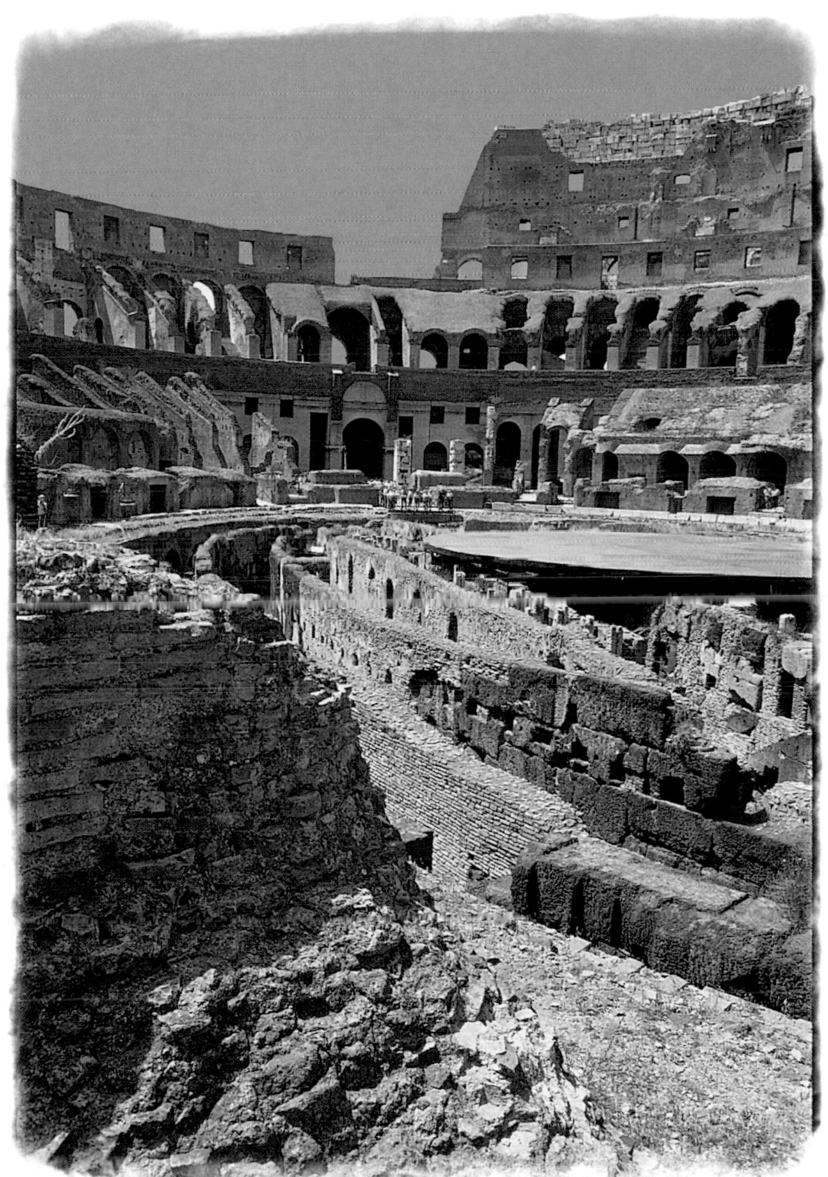

The Flavian Amphitheater in Rome, more popularly known as the Colosseum.

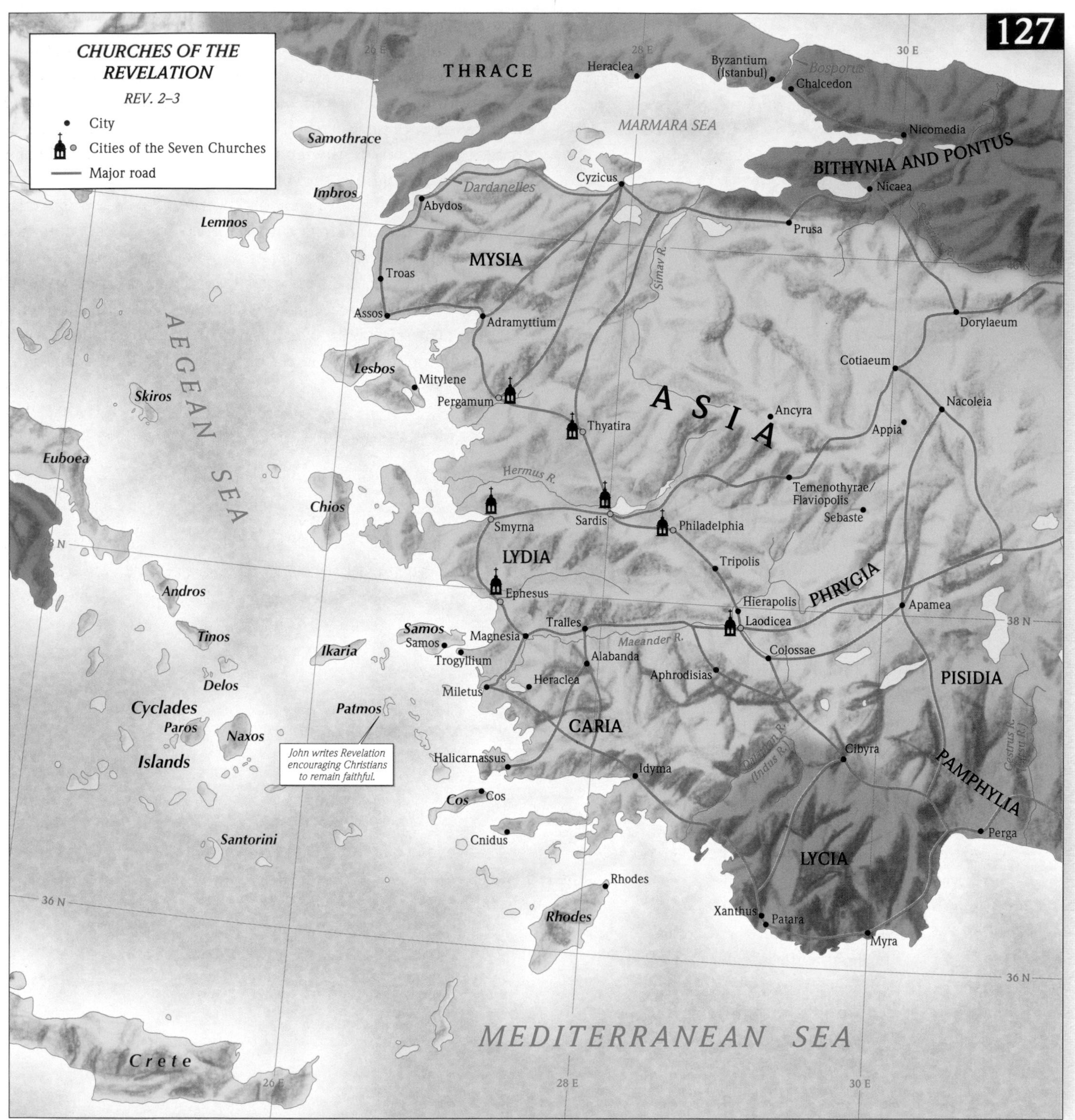

Carefully groomed by his father to be emperor, Titus served as consul seven times and commanded the Praetorian Guard, the elite force that guarded the emperor.

Although Titus initially met some resistance to his rule, he proved to be a popular emperor. His brief reign was characterized by lavish entertainments and, ironically, a concern for needy people. He provided relief for the survivors of the Mount Vesuvius eruption in A.D. 79, and continued rebuilding Rome. The Roman historian Tacitus reported that Titus had a relationship with Bernice, the sister of Agrippa II. Titus may have intended to marry her, but Rome was unwilling to accept a Jewish princess so soon after the Jewish revolt. A fever cut short the reign of Titus in A.D. 81.

Domitian. The universal verdict of ancient writers con-

demned Domitian as a cruel tyrant who abused his powerful office. Christian writers remembered him as a persecutor of the church during whose oppressive reign John wrote the Revelation. Although Domitian's reign, especially in the later years, was marked by excesses and cruelty, historians now recognize that Domitian contributed a great deal to the expansion of Roman interest.

Domitian became emperor of Rome upon the untimely death of his older brother, Titus. He had little preparation for his new responsibilities.

The Flavian emperors generally favored advancing the middle class in government service. Domitian extended that policy and, in the process, alienated powerful aristocrats and wealthy Hellenists who inevitably opposed the emperor. Yet before the situation developed into a reign of terror, Domitian accomplished much. Rome was adorned with many new public structures including the temple of Vespasian, a new forum, a new Senate building, and a large imperial palace. Domitian also secured the Roman borders along the Rhine and Danube Rivers by means of three Dacian Wars.

Cruel oppression of his powerful enemies in Rome marked the later years of Domitian's reign. Using informers to testify against his victims, Domitian executed or exiled many of his opponents. Domitian took seriously the cult of the emperor, requiring that people address him as "Lord and god." Worship of the emperor became the supreme test of loyalty to Rome. John's Revelation addressed to seven churches located in the province of Asia reflects, according to most scholars, an intense but local persecution of Christians in Asia who refused to compromise their faith by bowing to the emperor (see "Churches of the Revelation" pp. 265–67).

In Rome, Domitian attacked anyone who was suspected of divided loyalties. The persecutions had religious overtones since Domitian viewed as treason any sympathy for non-Roman religions. The proscriptions reached the highest levels, including Domitian's cousin Flavius Clemens (executed) and niece Flavia Domitilla (exiled). The classical writer Dio Cassius claims that the charge against Clemens and Domitilla was atheism—that is, they rejected the state gods. Atheism was one charge levied against Christians. It is possible, but not demonstrable, that some members of the imperial household may have been Christians.

Domitian's excesses provoked his assassination in A.D. 96. The coup was engineered from within the imperial court with the cooperation of the Praetorian Prefect. Following Domitian's death, the Senate invoked the *damnatio memoriae*, an official pronouncement that consigned the reign of Domitian to condemnation.

CHURCHES OF THE REVELATION

John addressed the Revelation to seven churches located in the province of Asia, encouraging Christians to remain faithful in the face of potent opposition and warning against any relapse into various heresies.

Domitian's persecution in A.D. 95 threatened the churches of Asia. Revelation 13 describes two fearsome beasts that waged war against the Christians in proconsular Asia: a sea beast identified with the emperor of Rome and a land beast symbolizing the provincial assembly responsible for enforcing worship of the emperor. John's vision assured believers that the ultimate victory already had been won by the sacrificial death of the Lamb of God.

Received by John on the island of Patmos, this message of hope was passed on to the churches possibly in the order they are mentioned in the Revelation: Ephesus, Smyrna, Pergamum, Thyatira, Sardis, Philadelphia, and Laodicea (for information about Ephesus, see "Important Cities in Paul's Ministry," pp. 254–55).

SMYRNA

Roman Smyrna was an impressive harbor city with vital trade connections up the Hermus Valley to Sardis. Renowned for its beauty and described by ancient writers as "the ornament of Asia," Smyrna was located thirty-five miles north of Ephesus on a prominence overlooking the Gulf of Izmir. The city was laid out along wide, beautifully paved streets and was adorned with temples, baths, gymnasia, a theater, a stadium, and a library that served the needs of the city's population, estimated at over one hundred thousand people. Tiberius granted Smyrna the honor of building an imperial temple; later Hadrian awarded Smyrna a second *neocorate* ("temple warden"—a title granted to any city awarded the right to build and maintain a temple dedicated to the provincial imperial cult). The aged bishop Polycarp, a disciple of the apostle John, suffered martyrdom in the stadium at Smyrna, a striking testimony to the tenacious faith exercised by Christians of the region.

The forum at Smyrna, modern Izmir, Turkey.

PERGAMUM

Pergamum was the capital of the Attalid Dynasty from 283 to 133 B.C., when Attalus III bequeathed his kingdom to the Romans. During the Roman era, Pergamum retained its importance. Augustus awarded the city its first of three neocorates, but Ephesus overtook its rival in 27 B.C. as the capital of Asia.

The city literally thrust forth from a series of terraces carved out of a mountain overlooking the Caicus Valley to the south. The numerous buildings still visible date primarily from the Attalid era. Eumenes II built an altar to Zeus, a massive colonnaded U-shaped altar (120 x 112 feet) built on an eighteen-foot-high platform. A 446-foot frieze around the base of the altar depicted a battle between mythological gods and giants, perhaps symbolic of an earlier Pergamene victory over invading Gauls.

The theater on the Acropolis of Pergamum.

Some scholars identify the altar of Zeus with "Satan's throne" mentioned in the Revelation (Rev. 2:13), but more likely Pergamum's close connection with the imperial cult accounts for John's use of the phrase. Pergamum's renowned library rivaled the great library at Alexandria. A major healing complex (425 x 360 feet) dedicated to the god Asclepius assured a steady stream of pilgrims to Pergamum seeking a cure for ailments. Three separate gymnasia allowed young boys and men to train body and mind. Wealthy citizens found entertainment in a theater carved out of the mountain, with a panoramic view of the surrounding region.

SARDIS

Sardis was the chief city of the Hermus Valley, the most agriculturally important of the major valleys descending westward from the Anatolian Plateau. The former capital of the Lydian Kingdom and heir to the legendary gold of King Croesus retrieved from the Pactolus River, Roman Sardis stretched out below the Acropolis perched on Mount Tmolus. Much of the city was newly constructed with generous assistance from the Emperors Tiberius and Claudius following a devastating earthquake in A.D. 17 that destroyed or seriously damaged many cities of Asia.

The Roman gymnasium complex at Sardis. In the foreground are the remains of a basilica style building eventually converted for use as a synagogue.

Sardis quickly recovered her economic status, prospering throughout the Roman era, and served as a district juridical capital *(coventus)* in the Roman administrative system. The impressive Ionic temple of Artemis, somewhat smaller than the great temple at Ephesus, amply illustrates the wealth of Sardis. During the Roman era, parts of this temple were used for the imperial cult. Sardis received the title "temple warden" *(neokoros)* three times in the second century when Asian cities competed for the honor of building provincial temples dedicated to emperor worship. Christianity took deep root in Sardis despite oppression. Bishop Mileto of Sardis was an early apologist for the Christian faith in the second century.

Roman Sardis remains largely unexcavated. Portions of an impressive thirty-five-foot-wide colonnaded street have been traced for 4,600 feet. Byzantine shops along the great thoroughfare included paint and dye shops, restaurants, and glassware shops. A massive bath/gymnasium complex, dating from A.D. 100 onward, has been reconstructed. Near the gymnasium, excavations revealed a large Jewish synagogue (60 x 20 meters) yielding numerous inscriptions, marble panels, and representations of menorahs. The structure had been converted for use as a synagogue shortly before A.D. 300 by the prominent and sizeable Jewish community in Sardis. Some commentators believe that Christian Jews in Sardis, tempted to compromise their faith, remained identified with the local synagogue because the Romans granted to the Jewish community exception to the emperor worship that was required of all other peoples.

THYATIRA, PHILADELPHIA, AND LAODICEA

Laodicea, an important banking center in the Lycus Valley.

Located thirty-five miles southeast of Pergamum, Thyatira was a minor city known principally for its textile industry. While at Philippi, Paul met Lydia, a dealer in purple fabrics, from Thyatira. Several inscriptions mention trade guilds at Thyatira (bakers, potters, tanners, and coppersmiths). The textile industry, composed of wool merchants, dyers, and linen workers, received prominent attention. Dyers used a colorfast purple dye obtained from the murex shell, much prized by the wealthy. Purple cloth exported from Thyatira boosted the economy greatly. Unfortunately, little is known of ancient Thyatira, now occupied by the modern Turkish city of Akhisar.

The ancient city of Philadelphia lies covered by the modern town of Alasehir. Neither archaeological work nor the words of classical authors provide much information about the city. Located on a tributary valley of the Hermus River southeast of Sardis, Philadelphia was near a volcanic zone susceptible to earthquakes. The city suffered severely in the A.D. 17 earthquake mentioned by Pliny, Dio Cassius, and others. Strabo described Philadelphia as "full of earthquakes, for the walls never cease being cracked" (Strabo, *Geography*, 13.4.10). Tiberius furnished funds to rebuild Philadelphia and other cities damaged by the tremor; Philadelphia added Neo-caesarea to her name in gratitude. Vineyards flourished in the volcanic soil near the city. Nothing remains of the numerous temples that once adorned the city described by pilgrims and depicted on coins.

Laodicea was one of three cities founded in the fertile Lycus Valley, an important tributary of the Meander that flowed westward to Miletus. The key city of the wealthy province of Phrygia, Laodicea lay between Colossae a few miles to the southeast and her major rival, Hierapolis, six miles to the north. John alludes to the wealth of Laodicea in the Revelation (Rev. 3:17).

In addition to being a banking center, Laodicea was known for its textile industry based on a rich black wool from sheep raised in the valley. A medical school widely known for an eye salve also brought fame and wealth to the city. The Revelation admonished believers at Laodicea to seek spiritual riches, not worldly gold, and to anoint their eyes with spiritual salve (Rev. 3:17–18).

The remains of Laodicea today, though largely unexcavated, are quite striking. Laodicea sits on top of a low, flat hill; the white cliffs of the thermal springs of Hierapolis are visible to the north, and the snowcapped peak of Mount Cadmus rises to the south. Two theaters carved into the hill and a 1,200-foot stadium are easily recognized. Some of the aqueducts that brought water to the city and a large Nymphaeum can still be seen. Inscriptions and coins mention numerous deities worshiped at Laodicea including the one honoring the city's chief deity, Zeus Laodicensis. Today nothing remains of these temples.

SUCCESSORS TO THE FLAVIAN DYNASTY

Vespasian ensured an orderly transfer of power for Rome when he positioned his sons—Titus and Domitian—to succeed him on the imperial throne. The reign of terror of Domitian's final years and his subsequent assassination called into question this manner of selecting an imperial successor. The four emperors who succeeded Nerva, Domitian's successor, came to power by a slightly different process. Each emperor "adopted" a well-qualified successor as a "son," ensuring a series of competent leaders. Under the leadership of these capable rulers—Trajan,

Hadrian, Antoninus Pius, and Marcus Aurelius—the Roman Empire reached its greatest geographical extent, and Roman culture attained its zenith.

Nerva. Upon the assassination of Domitian, the Senate turned to sixty-six-year-old Nerva, a man of good temperament, whose political cunning allowed him to escape unscathed the imperial intrigues from Nero to Domitian. Nerva also was childless, which meant he could not establish a dynasty based on inheritance.

The sixteen-month reign of Marcus Cocceius Nerva remains shrouded in mystery and intrigue. He sought to prevent financial crisis, to please the people, and to reorganize government systems. He also instituted programs designed to assist the poor with food and education. His policies toward Jews and Christians were less harsh than those under Domitian. Unfortunately, Nerva could not control the military. To counter that threat Nerva adopted Marcus Ulpius Trajan, a distinguished and admired general, granting him the title "Caesar" and the power of the imperial office. Upon Nerva's death a few months later, Trajan became Rome's emperor.

Trajan. Trajan embodied the Roman ideal of an emperor. An accomplished military leader noted for his forthrightness, hard work, and attention to administrative detail, Trajan appointed competent provincial officials and took great interest in the economic well-being of the provinces. His well-known correspondence with the governor of Bithynia—Pliny the Younger—demonstrates Trajan's direct interest in provincial affairs. Trajan advised Pliny to treat Christians in Bithynia accused of neglecting emperor worship with moderation, directing that Christians not be sought out nor condemned on the basis of unsubstantiated charges (see "Factors Enhancing the Expansion of the Church," p. 276).

Trajan sponsored a building program that upgraded harbor facilities, roads, and aqueducts. In Rome he built the largest imperial forum and adorned it with a column commemorating his military victories. He crowned the forum with a sculpture of himself.

Trajan identified closely with the Roman army, which he used to extend the empire in the east. Two Dacian Wars (A.D. 101–102 and 105–106) stabilized the Danube frontier and incorporated Dacia (roughly modern Romania) as a new Roman province. In 105/106 Trajan annexed the kingdom of Nabatea, just east of the province of Judea, and made Bostra the provincial capital garrisoned by a Roman legion. A line of Roman fortifications (the *Limes Palestina*) was extended south and east to guard the newly annexed region. Parthian pressure provoked a successful campaign in Armenia in A.D. 114, but Trajan overextended his reach in an ill-fated campaign directed against Mesopotamia in A.D. 115–117. Though Trajan's army was successful in penetrating the Tigris and Euphrates Valleys and in creating two new Roman provinces, the Parthian kingdom could not be conquered. Trajan's successor,

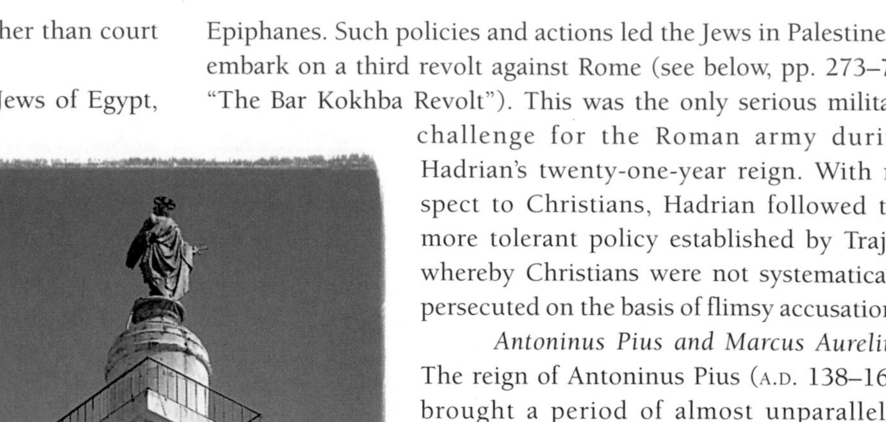

Hadrian, wisely abandoned the new provinces rather than court a disaster in the east.

During Trajan's Parthian campaign, the Jews of Egypt, Cyrenacia, Cyprus, and Mesopotamia rebelled against Rome (A.D. 115–117). During the course of the disturbances, Jewish insurgents killed many Gentiles. Rome suppressed the disorders among the Diaspora Jews, which may have impacted Palestine also, but Jewish nationalism would flare a third and final time in Hadrian's reign (see "The Bar Kokhba Revolt," pp. 274–75).

Trajan died in Cilicia in A.D. 117, apparently a victim of a weakened heart and a stroke. Late in his reign, he had adopted Hadrian as his successor.

Hadrian. Trajan adopted Hadrian, a relative and fellow Spaniard, as his successor. Unlike his predecessor, Hadrian was an intellectual whose restless mind and boundless energy drove him to travel extensively in the East. Hadrian gave up Roman claims on some peripheral territories in order to consolidate the empire's economic power. He gave up plans to hold Mesopotamia, believing that Trajan had overextended the empire. Hadrian was thus able to establish clear defensible borders for the empire. Hadrian's Wall in Britain, stretching from Tyre to Solway Firth, marked the northern limits of the empire. Like his predecessor, Hadrian strengthened the efficiency and morale of the army with his frequent visits among the soldiers.

Hadrian left his mark on Rome. He rebuilt the Pantheon and constructed the temple of Venus and Rome (the largest temple in Rome, 110 x 53 meters). Hadrian personally designed his magnificent villa at Tivoli just outside of Rome, a massive imperial estate complete with palaces, libraries, baths, and theaters.

Trajan's column in the Forum of Trajan.

Hadrian antagonized the Jews by changing the name of Jerusalem to Aelia Capitolina, by forbidding men to be circumcised, and by placing a temple dedicated to himself and to Zeus on the ruins of Herod's temple. He saw himself as another Antiochus Epiphanes. Such policies and actions led the Jews in Palestine to embark on a third revolt against Rome (see below, pp. 273–75, "The Bar Kokhba Revolt"). This was the only serious military challenge for the Roman army during Hadrian's twenty-one-year reign. With respect to Christians, Hadrian followed the more tolerant policy established by Trajan whereby Christians were not systematically persecuted on the basis of flimsy accusations.

Antoninus Pius and Marcus Aurelius. The reign of Antoninus Pius (A.D. 138–161) brought a period of almost unparalleled peace for the Roman Empire. An effective emperor who earned a reputation for honesty and piety, Antoninus dedicated his efforts to the government and his family, having never to leave Italy in a military role. His peaceful death in A.D. 161 brought his adoptive son Marcus Aurelius to the imperial throne. Known for his attachment to Stoicism, Marcus Aurelius was not so fortunate as his predecessor in matters of state. During his nineteen year reign (A.D. 161–180) Germanic tribes and Sarmatians from the Danube invaded the empire from the north—a harbinger of more serious threats to come. A plague carried by soldiers returning from yet another war in Parthia took a heavy toll on the Roman population. The death of Marcus Aurelius in A.D. 180 brought to an end decades of political stability and peace. Civil war erupted between rival exconsuls (A.D. 192–197). The third century A.D. for Rome would bring more internal instability while external threats mounted along the borders.

Life in Palestine and the Growth of the Church (A.D. 73–135)

The sixty-year period between the end of the First Jewish Revolt and the Bar Kokhba Revolt saw the transformation of Jewish political and religious life. Yet we know little about this brief but important era. Neither written sources nor archaeological data provide adequate light to write a continuous historical narrative.

The First Jewish Revolt affected Jews in several ways. The most immediate impact was political. Concerned that Judea

129

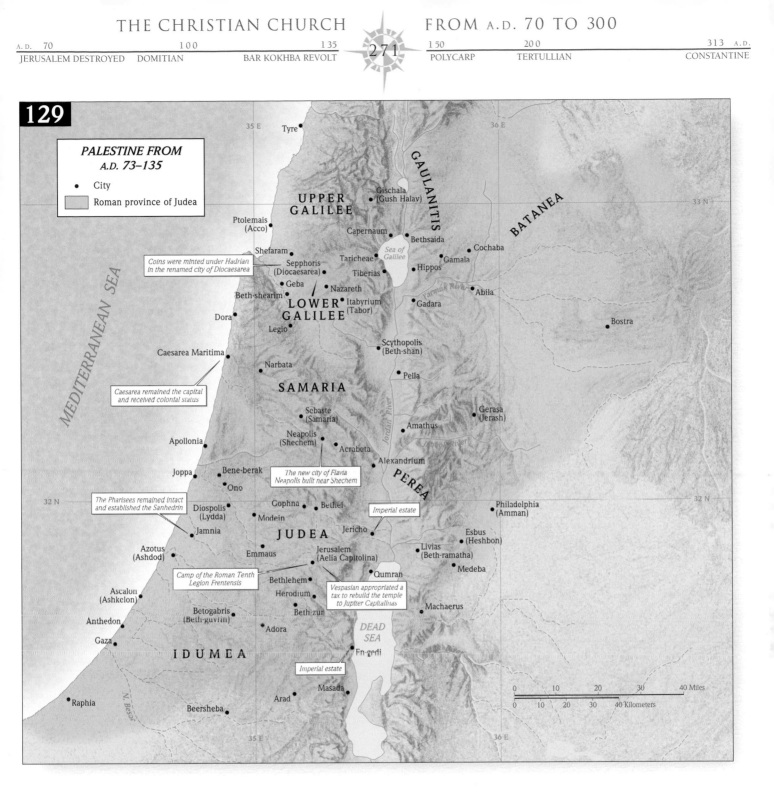

PALESTINE FROM A.D. 73–135

• City
Roman province of Judea

Coins were minted under Hadrian in the renamed city of Diocaesarea

Caesarea remained the capital and received colonial status

The new city of Flavia Neapolis built near Shechem

The Pharisees remained intact and established the Sanhedrin

Imperial estate

Camp of the Roman Tenth Legion Frentensis

Vespasian appropriated a tax to rebuild the temple to Jupiter Capitalinas

Imperial estate

was governed by magistrates of too little authority backed by too few troops, Vespasian created the new province of Judea. Henceforth, a Roman legate of Praetorian rank governed the territory independently of Syrian administration. Lucilius Bassus and Flavius Silva were the first legates of the new province, which included Idumea, Samaria, Judea, parts of Perea, and coastal cities from Raphia to Caesarea. Agrippa II governed several areas, including parts of Lebanon, territories in Galilee (Tiberias and Taricheae), and portions of Perea, until his death about A.D 92. Vespasian designated the opo balsam plantations of Jericho and En-gedi as imperial estates, funneling the taxes upon the valuable commodity into the imperial treasury.

The First Jewish Revolt also had military consequences. The Roman Tenth Legion Fretensis was garrisoned in Palestine after the war, the first Roman legionaries to be stationed in the land. Jerusalem was headquarters for the legion that established camp south of the ruins of the citadel and Herodian palace. Caesarea remained the provincial capital and under Vespasian received colonial status, a reward for loyalty to Rome that granted immunity from certain taxes. A belt of Hellenistic cities—

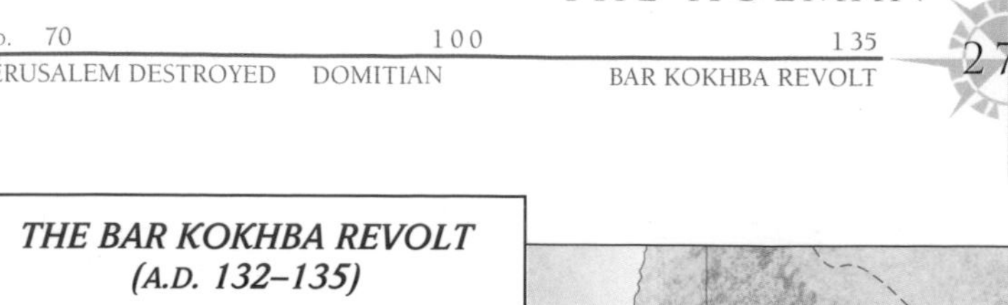

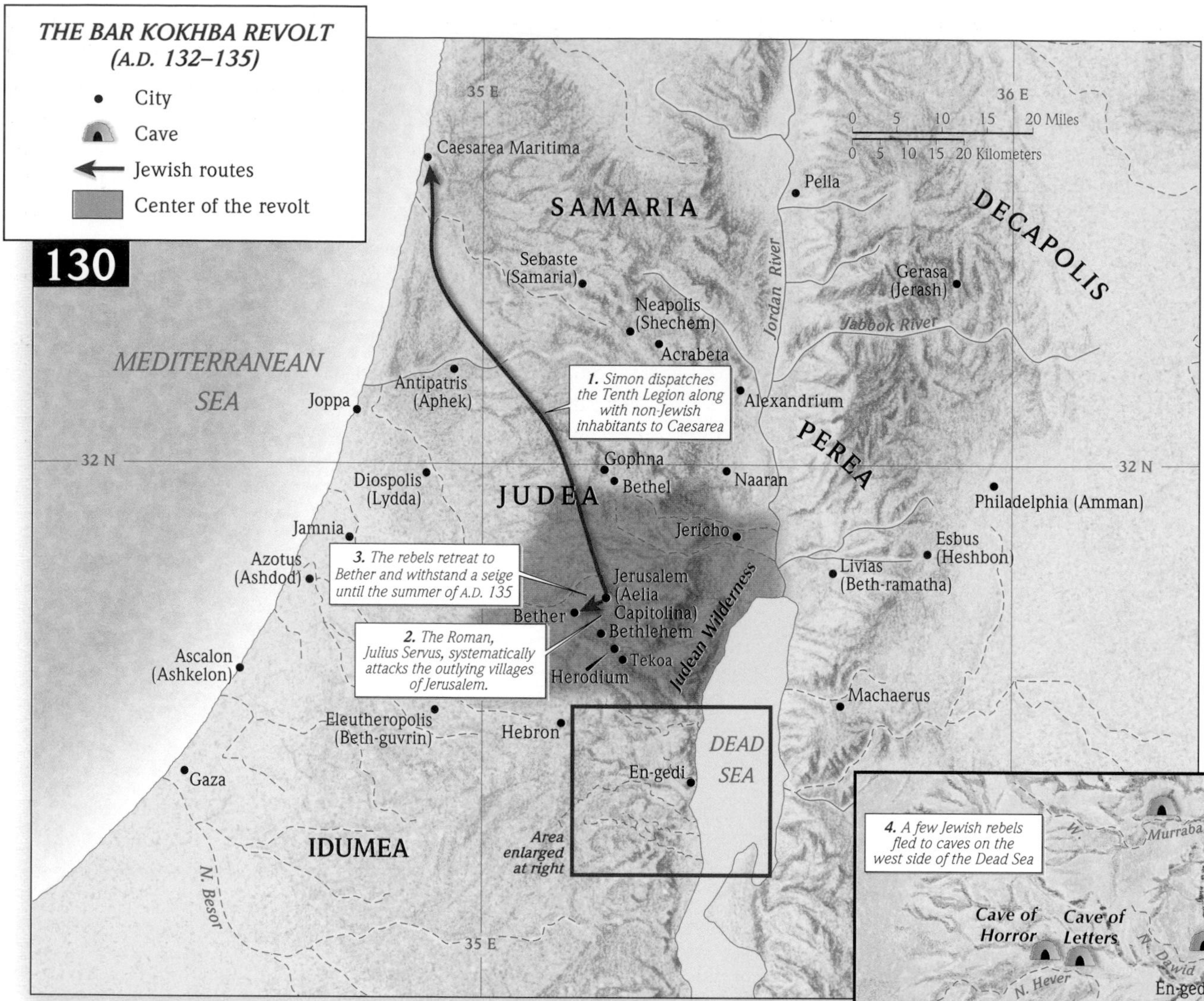

THE BAR KOKHBA REVOLT (A.D. 132–135)

• City
Cave
Jewish routes
Center of the revolt

130

1. Simon dispatches the Tenth Legion along with non-Jewish inhabitants to Caesarea

2. The Roman, Julius Servus, systematically attacks the outlying villages of Jerusalem.

3. The rebels retreat to Bether and withstand a seige until the summer of A.D. 135

4. A few Jewish rebels fled to caves on the west side of the Dead Sea

Caesarea Maritima
SAMARIA
Sebaste (Samaria)
Neapolis (Shechem)
Acrabeta
Pella
DECAPOLIS
Gerasa (Jerash)
Jabbok River
Jordan River
MEDITERRANEAN SEA
Joppa
Antipatris (Aphek)
Alexandrium
PEREA
Gophna
Bethel
Naaran
JUDEA
Diospolis (Lydda)
Jamnia
Azotus (Ashdod)
Jericho
Philadelphia (Amman)
Esbus (Heshbon)
Livias (Beth-ramatha)
Jerusalem (Aelia Capitolina)
Bether
Bethlehem
Tekoa
Herodium
Judean Wilderness
Ascalon (Ashkelon)
Eleutheropolis (Beth-guvrin)
Hebron
Machaerus
DEAD SEA
En-gedi
Gaza
IDUMEA
N. Besor
Area enlarged at right
35 E
36 E
32 N
0 5 10 15 20 Miles
0 5 10 15 20 Kilometers

Murraba'at
Cave of Horror
Cave of Letters
Cave of the Pool
N. Dawid
N. Hever
En-gedi
N. Harduf
N. Mishmar
N. Ze'elim
DEAD SEA
N

Caesarea Maritima, Sebaste, and Scythopolis—separated Judea and Galilee, the two most volatile Jewish areas. A new city, Flavia Neapolis, was built near ancient Shechem and quickly gained prominence.

The social and economic consequences of the First Jewish Revolt varied depending on geography and the degree of involvement of a city or territory in the uprising against Roman authority. Judea suffered more grievously than other regions. In addition to the destruction of Jerusalem, the region must have suffered great economic hardship. The flow of pilgrims to Judea attending the great festivals ceased, with serious economic consequence for the region. Cities loyal to Rome recovered more quickly. The Romans recognized that many cities impeded the revolutionaries and moved to reward those cities with expanded territories and privileges. In Galilee, Sepphoris minted its own coins and, under Hadrian, received the new name Diocaesarea. By the time of Hadrian, Lower Galilee was essentially dominated by two cities, Tiberias and Diocaesarea. Generally, the Roman policies strengthened the hand of the non-Jewish population in urban settings.

Josephus records Vespasian's order that Jewish lands be leased (Josephus, *JW,* VII 216–218). It seems likely that this order was directed at those Jews and lands directly involved in the revolt.

The spiritual consequences of the revolt were even greater. The temple was destroyed, along with the sacrificial system. The Sadducees and High Priestly families, both vitally connected to the temple, lost their prominence—the Sadducees disappearing as an identifiable sect. Yet Judaism retained its status as a legal religion *(religio licita)* in the Roman Empire.

Vespasian's appropriation of the half-shekel tax for use

to rebuild the temple to Jupiter Capitolinas caused great consternation for the Jews. The tax paid annually by Jewish adult males to support Herod's temple, now destroyed, henceforth went into the imperial treasury in part as a price for religious freedom. Both Jewish males and females were required to contribute annually two drachma (Josephus, *JW,* VII 216–219). Affecting both Diaspora and Palestinian Jews alike, this Jewish tax was a considerable source of revenue for the emperor and an affront to all Jews.

The spiritual crisis occasioned by the loss of the temple and sacrificial system transformed Jewish spiritual life. The Pharisees were the only religious party to survive intact. According to tradition, the Pharisee leader Rabbi Johanan ben Zakkai escaped the siege of Jerusalem in a coffin, feigning death. Roman authorities granted a request to reconstitute the Sanhedrin under Pharisee leadership at Jamnia (Jabneh). Johanan and Rabban Gamaliel II established a school of religious scholars (*Beth Din*) that provided interpretation of the Law, established the religious calendar, and generally guided Jews from both Palestine and the Diaspora in religious matters. Eventually the head of the school received the title Nasi—"Prince."

The Bar Kokhba Revolt shifted the center of Jewish spiritual life to Galilee; Shefarim, Beth-shearim, Sepphoris, and Tiberias all served as centers of rabbinic life. Eventually, the rabbis codified their interpretations and wisdom, producing the Mishnah and ultimately the Talmud, the guiding document of postbiblical Judaism.

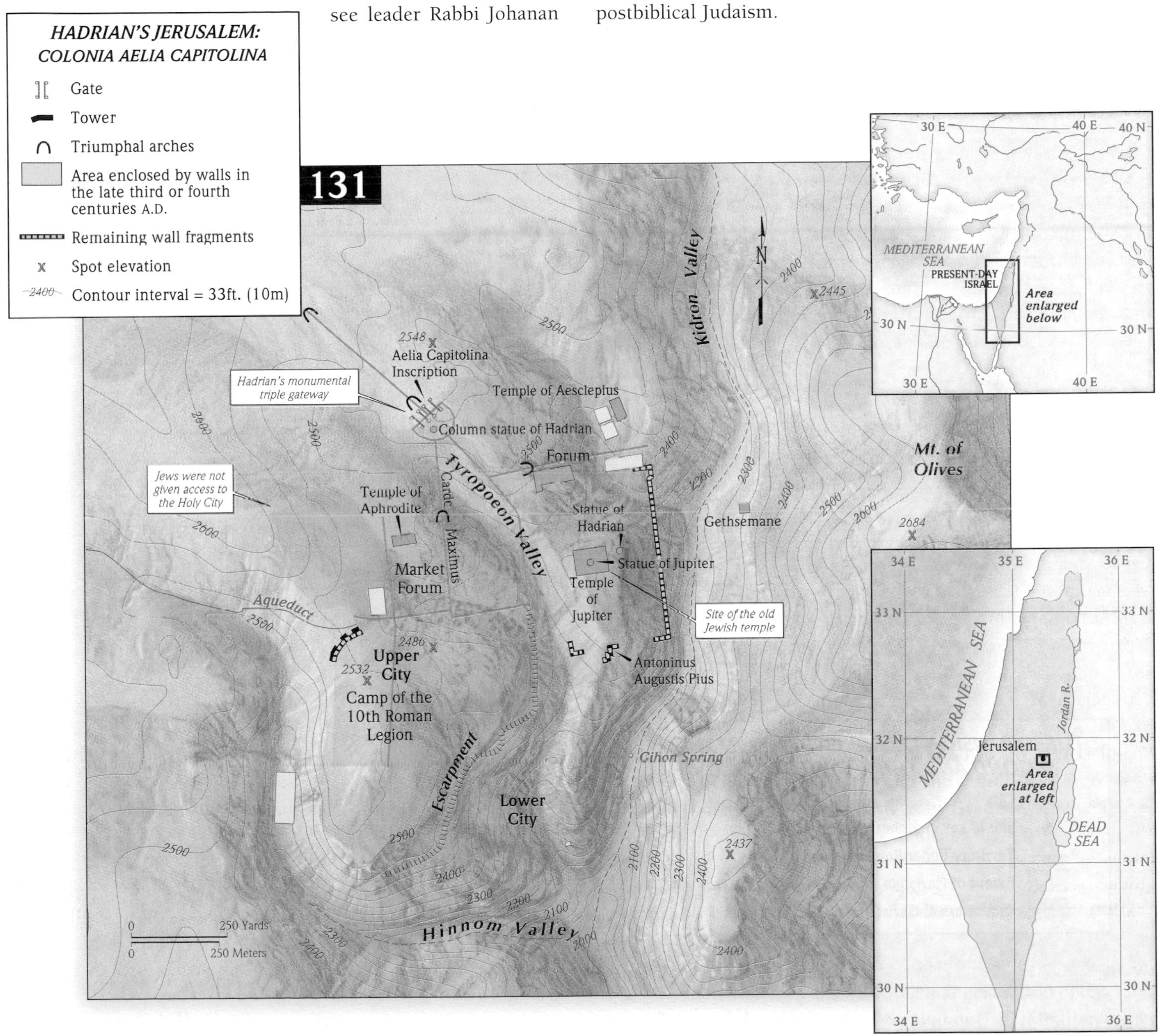

basin. The New Testament concentrates on the work of Paul and his companions, but other believers whose stories are not recounted carried with them the message of Jesus, establishing churches along the way. Although the exact circumstances surrounding their foundation eludes us, churches in Rome, Bithynia, Pontus, Cappadocia, Cyrene, and possibly Alexandria and Carthage flourished before the apostolic generation passed from the scene.

FACTORS ENHANCING THE EXPANSION OF THE CHURCH

Several factors enhanced the rapid spread of Christianity. Greek remained the common language of the empire, facilitating the preaching of the gospel. The Roman peace endured throughout the second century, allowing commerce and trade to flow freely along thousands of miles of roads and shipping lanes. Merchants, businessmen, soldiers, and others converted to the new faith spread the word of Jesus along these same conduits. The Jewish synagogues scattered throughout the Roman world provided opportunities for itinerant missionaries, although Jewish opposition to the gospel increasingly turned missionary endeavors toward Gentiles.

ASIA MINOR

Asia Minor became a stronghold of Christianity in the decades before and after A.D. 100. During the reign of Trajan (98–117), Pliny the Younger, the governor of Bithynia, complained that the "superstition" of Christianity "has spread not only in the cities, but in the villages and rural districts as well." The emperor Trajan counseled moderation in seeking out Christians for punishment, but he confirmed Pliny's policy of executing Christians who refused to recant their beliefs and worship the emperor. By the end of the first century, perhaps a quarter of an estimated 300,000 Christians in the empire lived in Asia Minor.

THE LEADING CHURCHES

By A.D. 100 several churches—Rome, Ephesus, Antioch, Alexandria, and perhaps Carthage—emerged as leaders. Clement of Rome wrote a series of letters in which he exercised pastoral concern for other churches. Bishop Ignatius of Antioch suffered martyrdom in Rome shortly after A.D. 100 during the reign of Trajan, as did Bishop Polycarp of Smyrna in A.D. 155.

Strong spokesmen appeared, including the apologists, who wrote spirited defenses of the faith in the face of Jewish and pagan attacks. Justin Martyr, a converted Samaritan philosopher, addressed his apology to the Emperor Antoninus Pius. Carthage produced the great apologist Tertullian (A.D. 160–240). The powerful voice of Irenaeus, Bishop of Lyons, who penned *Five Books against Heresies* around A.D. 200, shows the westward expansion of the church into Gaul (France).

Alexandria became a major Christian intellectual center, producing such eminent scholars as Clement of Alexandria and the greatest of the Greek theologians, Origen (A.D. 185–253). Origen's father suffered martyrdom in the Severan persecution in A.D. 202. Origen himself died of the residual effects of torture he received in the Decian persecutions (A.D. 249–51). The wide geographical distribution of writers and martyrs of the second and third centuries suggests the breadth of Christian expansion.

EXPANSION OF THE CHURCH IN THE EAST

We know much less about Christianity's expansion in the East. Under Trajan, the Roman Empire extended into Mesopotamia, but what effect this had on the spread of Christianity is unknown. Two Mesopotamian centers of Christianity, Edessa and Melitene, were established in the second century. At Dura-Europos on the Euphrates River, archaeologists have uncovered an early Christian house-church dating shortly after A.D. 200.

Despite sporadic persecutions from Roman authorities and in the face of external and internal attacks on the Christian faith, Christianity spread over the entire Mediterranean basin by A.D. 300. At the same time, Rome declined—partly the result of barbarian attacks along her borders and partly because of internal moral and political decay. Persecution of Christians became more intense under Decius (A.D. 249–51) and Diocletian (ca. A.D. 303).

The victory of Constantine over Maxentius at the Milvian Bridge in A.D. 312 paved the way for the Edict of Milan that granted toleration to Christianity. Constantine supported Christianity as a means of unifying his fragmented empire, as well as for personal reasons. He convened the first general church council at Nicaea in A.D. 325. Later, Christianity became the official religion of the Roman Empire.

However, Christianity triumphed not because of political pressure but in spite of it. Moved by the message of Christ, disciples of Jesus persevered in carrying out their Master's command. Perhaps the words of Tertullian capture the essence of the matter. In addressing the Roman provincial administrators around A.D. 197, Tertullian wrote: "The oftener we are mown down by you, the more in number we grow; the blood of Christians is seed" (Tertullian, *Apology*, 50).

GLOSSARY

acropolis: The highest elevation of a city used as a fortified citadel, often containing important public buildings such as temples and palaces.

agora: An open market or square in the heart of Greek cities where public business was conducted.

amphitheater: An oval-shaped area surrounded on all sides by seating used for gladiatorial games.

apodyterium: The dressing room of a Roman bath facility.

ashlar: Building stones cut by a stonemason to a uniform square or rectangular size and shape.

basilica: A long, rectangular building divided by a central nave and side aisles; Roman basilicas served as juridical or administrative centers; architects adapted the basilica form for churches from the fourth century A.D. onward.

baulk (balk): The unexcavated portion of a trench or a square; the vertical face of the baulk discloses to the archaeologist the layers or "strata" of an area.

boss: An untrimmed projection of a large building stone left after the edges or margins have been trimmed.

bouleuterion: In Greek cities, the building in which the city council (*boule*) met.

caldarium: The heated room of a Roman bath.

cardo maximus: The main north-south street of a city.

carytid: A support column sculpted in the form of a female.

casemate wall: A double wall composed of an outer and inner line connected by perpendicular walls forming "casemates."

cella: The central structure of the temple where the image of the god or goddess was kept.

circus (Greek: hippodrome): An elongated, narrow structure used for chariot racing.

column: A freestanding support pillar consisting of a base, shaft, and capital.

colonnade: A line of columns set at regular intervals often supporting the base of a roof.

columbarium: 1) A structure containing riches for ash urns; 2) A structure used as a pigeoncote or dovecote.

Corinthian Order: A style of Greek architecture developed in the fifth century characterized by bell-shaped capitals decorated with acanthus leaves.

decumanus: The main east-west street of a city.

Doric Order: The oldest and simplest Greek architectural order characterized by tapered, fluted columns capped by unadorned capitals.

ephebeum: Section of a Greek gymnasium complex where young men were trained in Greek culture.

fresco: Painting effected on a moist plaster surface.

forum: The Roman equivalent of the Greek agora; the most important civic building and temples as well as the markets were located in the forum.

frieze: A richly ornamented or sculpted band of reliefs; in the temples the frieze is found between the architrave and cornice (see illustration pp.__).

frigidarium: The cold room of a Roman bath.

gymnasium: A building used as a school for physical and cultural training for Greeks; the Romans often combined the gymnasium with the Roman baths.

headers and stretchers: A means of laying ashlar masonry in walls; when laid, the short ends of the headers are visible while the long sides of stretchers face outward.

hypocaust: A heating system composed of a furnace and flues to circulate heat; used in Roman baths to heat the caldarium.

in situ: A term meaning "in place." Used to describe the undisturbed position of an artifact found in excavation.

insula: Literally "island"; insula referred to lower-and middle-class apartments or tenement living quarters. The term also refers to a distinct block of houses, e.g., at Capernaum.

Ionic Order: A Greek architectural style first developed in Western Asia Minor utilizing slender columns crowned with capitals using a beautiful voluter design.

locus (loci, pl.): The smallest definable unit in archaeological excavation: each locus receives a number and all artifacts in or associated with that locus can be located three dimensionally; a locus may be a wall, a pit, a distinct layer of earth, a foundation trench, an oven, etc.

macellum: A Roman meat market.

mikveh (miqvaot, pl.): A ritual bathing installation used by Jews to maintain ritual purity. Miqvaot were found in public settings, e.g., near the southern entrance to the Jerusalem Temple, and in private houses.

mosaic: Geometric designs, pictures, or inscriptions composed by laying small cut stones of varying colors and shapes on a surface.

necropolis: A cemetery

neocorate (neocoros): "Temple-warden." A title granted to any city awarded the right to build and maintain a temple dedicated to the provincial imperial cult.

nympheum: A large public fountain.

obelisk: A monumental quarried stone, square shaped and tapered to a pyramid form at the top; often inscribed or decorated.

odeum (odeion): A small theater, often roofed, with seating in semicircular rows used for lectures and musical events.

orthostat: A large stone slab, occasionally decorated, placed within a room or entrance to form part of the lower wall.

ostracon (ostraca, pl.): A broken piece of pottery (potsherd) used as writing material; an ostracon could either be incised with a sharp tool or written on in ink. Brief letters, receipts, lists, etc. were written on ostraca.

ossuary: Stone box, often decorated, in which the bones of a deceased person were placed after the flesh had decayed.

palestra: An exercise yard found as a part of a Graeco-Roman gymnasium or bathhouse.

papyrus (papyri, pl.): Paper-like substance used for writing; made from the pith of papyrus plants that grew along the Nile River; a manuscript made of papyrus.

parchment: Treated hides of animals used for writing; vellum made of calf skin is a particularly fine parchment used for important manuscripts.

peribolos: An open area surrounded by rows of columns or walls.

piazza: An open, paved or pebbled courtyard often found inside gates in ancient cities.

pilaster: An engaged pier or beam protruding from a wall.

podium: A platform of brick or stone used to support monumental buildings or structures.

propylon: A monumental gate structure located at the entrance of a sacred enclosure or other area containing monumental buildings.

Proto-Aeolic capital: A style of decorative capitals used in the Iron Age in Palestine and elsewhere; the capitals are decorated with a stylized palmette known from Canaanite and Phoenician art.

prytaneum (prytaneion): Town hall of a Greek city.
revetment wall: A wall used to retain earth or fill.
rostra (Latin); *bema* **(Greek)**: The speakers platform located in the forum or agora.
sarcophagus: A coffin made of stone.
stele (stelae, pl.): An inscribed worked stone; steles usually were used for propaganda purposes commemorating important events (e.g., military victories) or extolling the accomplishments of kings.
stoa: A long, narrow building open to the front along a colonnade.
stratigraphy: One of the two primary principles of archaeological excavation (the other is typology). Stratigraphy is the study of the order and relative relationship among the various strata (layers) that comprise a tell. The archaeologists must distinguish the various strata in order to relate the materials found in a site to their proper period and to understand the history of the site.
stratum (strata, pl.): A self-contained layer representing a defined period in the history of a site. A stratum may evidence several phases—or stages—in the life of the stratum. Tells are composed of varying numbers of strata depending upon how long a site was inhabited.
tell (Tel): An ancient site; an artificial mound built up by and composed of successive layers (strata) of occupational debris. Tells normally have flat tops and step sides and look similar to a small mesa.
tepidarium: The warm room of a Roman bath complex.
temenos: A sacred enclosure defined by a wall containing one or more temples or high places.
tessara: Small, cube-shaped pieces of stone used to form a mosaic.
triclinium: A dining room in the Roman period, so-named for the Roman practice of placing three couches in a U-shape in the room around a table.
typology: The second major principle in archaeological excavation (see stratigraphy). Typology is the study and classification of any object or cultural features that shape important characteristics. Ceramic typology is the study of pottery vessels—their shape, composition, characteristics, and function. Because pottery was the most common artifact left by ancient people, archaeologists use pottery typology to date the level (stratum) in which the pottery was found. Certain pottery styles were characteristic of distinct periods.
volute: Spiral scroll designs used in the Ionic and Corinthian capitals.
wadi (Hebrew nahal): An Arabic term for a watercourse normally dry except for the winter rainy season. Some wadis served as roadways providing convenient access through the hills and mountains of Palestine.

BIBLIOGRAPHY

In addition to the specific listings by category below, useful information on geography, history, archaeology, and biblical sites can be located in the following dictionaries and encyclopedias under appropriate headings.

Achtemeier, Paul J., ed. *Harper's Bible Dictionary*. San Francisco: Harper and Row, 1985.

Bromiley, Geoffrey W., ed. *International Standard Bible Encyclopedia*. Rev. ed. 4 vols. Grand Rapids: Eerdmans, 1979–88.

Butler, Trent C., ed. *Holman Bible Dictionary*. Nashville: Holman, 1991.

Buttrick, George A., ed. *The Interpreter's Dictionary of the Bible* 4 vols. New York: Abingdon, 1962. See also Crim, K., ed. *Supplementary Volume*. Nashville: Abingdon, 1976.

DeVries, LaMoine F. *Cities of the Biblical World*. Peabody, MA: Hendrickson Publishers, 1997.

Douglas, J.D., ed. *The Illustrated Bible Dictionary*. 3 vols. Wheaton, IL: InterVarsity Press, 1980.

Freedman, David Noel, ed. *The Anchor Bible Dictionary*. 6 vols. Garden City, N.Y.: Doubleday, 1992.

Meyers, Eric M., ed. *The Oxford Encyclopedia of Archaeology in the Near East*. 5 vols. New York: Oxford University Press, 1997.

Roth, Cecil, et al. *Encyclopedia Judaica*. 16 vols. Jerusalem: Keter, 1972.

Sasson, Jack M., ed. *Civilizations of the Ancient Near East*. 4 vols. New York: Scribner, 1995.

Tenney, Merril C., ed. *Zondervan Pictorial Encyclopedia of the Bible*. 5 vols. Grand Rapids, Mich: Zondervan, 1975.

Part I. The Biblical Setting

A. ATLASES

Aharoni, Yohanan, Michael Avi-Yonah, Anson F. Rainey, and Ze'ev Safrai. *The Macmillan Bible Atlas*. 3d ed. New York: Macmillan, 1993.

Baines, John and Jaromir Malek. *Atlas of Ancient Egypt*. New York: Facts on File, 1980.

Baly, Denis and A.D. Tushingham. *Atlas of the Biblical World*. New York: World, 1971.

Beek, M.A. *Atlas of Mesopotamia*. Translated by D.R. Welsh. New York: Nelson, 1962.

Beitzel, Barry J. *The Moody Atlas of the Bible Lands*. Chicago: Moody Press, 1985.

Cornell, Tim and John Matthews. *Atlas of the Roman World*. New York: Facts on File, 1982.

Finley, M.I., ed. *Atlas of Classical Archaeology*. London: Chatto and Windus, 1977.

Gardner, Joseph L., ed. *Reader's Digest Atlas of the Bible*. Pleasantville, NY: Reader's Digest Association, 1981.

Grant, Michael. *Ancient History Atlas*. 4th ed. London: Weidenfeld and Nicolson, 1989.

Grollenberg, L.H. *Atlas of the Bible*. London: Thomas Nelson and Sons, 1956.

Hammond, N.G.L., ed. *Atlas of the Greek and Roman World in Antiquity*. Park Ridge, NJ: Noyes Press, 1981.

Levi, Peter. *Atlas of the Greek World*. New York: Facts on File, 1980.

May, Herbert G., ed. *Oxford Bible Atlas*. 3d ed. New York: Oxford University, 1984.

Pritchard, James B., ed. *The Harper Atlas of the Bible*. New York: Harper & Row, 1987.

Rasmussen, Carl G. *NIV Atlas of the Bible*. Grand Rapids, MI: Zondervan, 1989.

Roaf, Michael. *Cultural Atlas of Mesopotamia & the Ancient Near East*. New York: Facts on File, 1990.

Rogerson, John. *The New Atlas of the Bible*. London: McDonald & Co., 1985.

Wright, George Ernest and Floyd Vivian Filson, eds. *The Westminster Historical Atlas to the Bible*. Rev. ed. Philadelphia: Westminster, 1956.

B. GEOGRAPHIES

Abel, F.M. *Géographie de la Palestine I–II*. Paris: J. Gabalda, 1938.

Aharoni, Yohanan. *The Land of the Bible*. Translated and edited by Anson F. Rainey. Rev. ed. Philadelphia: Westminster Press, 1979. See especially Chapters I–IV.

Avi-Yonah, Michael. *The Holy Land: From the Persian to the Arab Conquest : A Historical Geography (536 B.C.–A.D. 640)*. Rev. ed. Grand Rapids: Baker, 1977.

Baly, Denis. *Basic Biblical Geography*. Philadelphia, PA.: Fortress Press, 1987

________. *The Geography of the Bible*. New rev. ed. New York: Harper & Row, 1974.

________. *Geographical Companion to the Bible*. New York: McGraw-Hill, 1963.

Borowski, Oded. *Agriculture in Iron Age Israel. The Evidence from Archaeology and the Bible*. Winona Lake, IN: Eisenbrauns, 1987.

Dorsey, Richard A. *The Roads and Highways of Ancient Israel*. Baltimore: Johns Hopkins, 1991.

Kallai, Zecharia. *Historical Geography of the Bible: The Tribal Territories of Israel*. Jerusalem: Magnes Press, 1986.

Karmon, Yehuda. *Israel: A Regional Geography*. New York: Wiley Interscience, 1971.

Orni, Ephraim and Elisha Efrat. *Geography of Israel*. 4th ed. Jerusalem: Israel University Press, 1980.

Simons, Jan J. *The Geographical and Topographical Texts of the Old Testament*. Leiden: E.J. Brill, 1959.

Smith, George Adam. *The Historical Geography of the Holy Land*. Reprint, Grand Rapids, MI: Baker, 1973.

Part II. The Old Testament Period

A. TEXTS

Beyerlin, Walter, ed. *Near Eastern Religious Texts Relating to the Old Testament*. Philadelphia: Westminster, 1978.

Breasted, James H. *Ancient Records of Egypt I–V*. Reprint, New York: Russell & Russell, 1962.

Dalley, Stephanie. *Myths from Mesopotamia: Creation, the Flood, Gilgamesh, and Others*. Oxford: Oxford University Press, 1989.

Grayson, Albert K. *Assyrian and Babylonian Chronicles*. Locust Valley, NY: J.J. Augustin, 1975.

Luckenbill, Daniel David. *Ancient Records of Assyria and Babylonia*. Chicago: University of Chicago Press, 1926–27.

Matthews, Victor H. and Don C. Benjamin. *Old Testament Parallels: Laws and Stories from the Ancient Near East*. New York: Paulist Press, 1991.

Moran, William L., ed. *The Amarna Letters*. Baltimore: Johns Hopkins, 1992

Pritchard, James B., ed. *Ancient Near Eastern Texts Relating to the Old Testament*. 3d ed. Princeton, NJ: Princeton University Press, 1969.

Smelik, Klaas. *Writings from Ancient Israel: A Handbook of Historical and Religious Documents*. Louisville, KY: Westminster/John Knox, 1991.

Walton, John H. *Ancient Israelite Literature in its Cultural Context: A Survey of Parallels Between Biblical and Ancient Near Eastern Texts*. Grand Rapids, MI: Zondervan, 1989.

Winton, Thomas D., ed. *Documents from Old Testament Times*. New York: Harper & Row, 1961.

B. GENERAL ANCIENT NEAR EASTERN SETTING

Edwards, I.E.S., C.J. Gadd, & N.G.L. Hammonds. *Cambridge Ancient History*, 3d ed. Cambridge: Cambridge University Press, 1971–1991.

Finegan, Jack. *Archaeological History of the Ancient Middle East*. Boulder, Colorado: Westview Press, 1979.

Frankfort, Henri. *The Art and Architecture of the Ancient Orient*. Supplemented by Michael Roaf and Donald Matthews. 5th ed. New Haven, Conn: Yale University Press, 1996.

Frank, Harry T. *Discovering the Biblical World*. Edited by James Strange. Rev. ed. Maplewood, N.J.: Hammond, 1988.

Hallo, William W. and W.K. Simpson. *The Ancient Near East: A History*. New York: Harcourt Brace Jovanovich, 1971.

Kitchen, Kenneth A. *Ancient Orient and Old Testament*. Downers Grove, IL: InterVaristy Press, 1966.

Knapp, A. Bernard. *The History of Culture of Ancient Western Asia and Egypt*. Chicago: Dorsey Press, 1988.

Lamberg-Karlovsky, C.C. and Jeremy A. Sabloff. *Ancient Civilizations: The Near East and Mesoamerica*. 2d ed. Prospect Heights, IL: Waveland Press, Inc., 1995.

Lloyd, Seton. *The Art of the Ancient Near East*. London: Thames and Hudson, 1961.

Rogerson, John and Philip Davies. *The Old Testament World*. Englewood Cliffs, NJ: Prentice Hall, 1989.

Saggs, H.W.F. *Civilization Before Greece and Rome*. New Haven: Yale University Press, 1989.

Schwantes, Siegfried. *A Short History of the Ancient Near East*. Grand Rapids, MI: Baker, 1965.

van der Woude, A.S., ed. *The World of the Bible*. Grand Rapids, MI: Eerdmans, 1986.

C. EGYPT AND MESOPOTAMIA

1. EGYPT

Aldred, Cyril. *The Egyptians*. Rev. ed. London: Thames and Hudson, 1984.

Gardiner, Alan. *Egypt of the Pharaohs: An Introduction*. Oxford: Oxford University Press, 1961.

Grimal, Nicolas. *A History of Ancient Egypt*. Translated by Ian Shaw. Oxford: Blackwell, 1992.

James, T.G.H. *An Introduction to Ancient Egypt*, 2d ed. London: British Museum, 1979.

________. *Pharaoh's People*. London: Pitman Press, 1984.

Kemp, Barry J. *Ancient Egypt: Anatomy of a Civilization*. London and New York: Routledge, 1989.

Kitchen, Kenneth A. *The Third Intermediate Period in Egypt*. Warminster: Aris & Phillips, 1973.

________. *Pharaoh Triumphant: The Life and Times of Ramesses II King of Egypt*. Warminster: Aris & Phillips, 1982.

Smith, W. Stevenson. *The Art and Architecture of Ancient Egypt*. The Pelican History of Art. Rev. with additions by William Kelly Simpson. England: Penguin Books, 1984.

Trigger, B.G., et al. *Ancient Egypt: A Social History*. Cambridge: Cambridge University Press, 1983.

Wilson, John. *The Culture of Ancient Egypt*. Chicago: University of Chicago Press, 1951.

2. MESOPOTAMIA

Beek, Martinus A. *Atlas of Mesopotamia*. Translated by D.R. Welsh. Edited by H.H. Rowley. New York: Nelson, 1962.

Brinkman, J.A. *A Political History of Post-Kassite Babylonia*. Rome: Pontificium Institutum Biblicum, 1968.

Kramer, Samuel Noah. *The Sumerians*. Chicago: University of Chicago Press, 1963.

Laessoe, Jorgen. *People of Ancient Assyria*. London: Routledge & Kegan Paul, 1963.

Leick, Gwendolyn. *A Dictionary of Ancient Near Eastern Architecture*. New York: Routledge: 1989.

Lloyd, Seton. *The Archaeology of Mesopotamia: From the Old Stone Age to the Persian Conquest*. Rev. ed. London: Thames and Hudson, 1984.

Moorey, P.R.S. *Ancient Mesopotamian Materials and Industries: The Archaeological Evidence*. Oxford: Clarendon Press, 1994.

Oates, Joan. *Babylon*. Rev. ed. London: Thames and Hudson, 1986.

Oppenheim, A.L. *Ancient Mesopotamia: Portrait of a Dead Civilizaiton*. Chicago: University of Chicago Press, 1964.

Postgate, John Nicolas. *The First Empires*. Oxford: Elsevier and Phaidon, 1977.

Roaf, Michael. *Cultural Atlas of Mesopotamia and the Ancient Near East*. New York: Facts on File, 1990

Roux, George. *Ancient Iraq*. 3d ed. Harmondsworth: Penguin Books, 1992.

Saggs, H.W.F. *Babylonians. Peoples of the Past*. Norman, OK: University of Oklahoma Press, 1995.

________. *The Greatness That Was Babylon: A Survey of the Ancient Civilization of the Tigris-Euphrates Valley*. 2d ed. London: Sidgwick & Jackson, 1988.

________. *The Might That Was Assyria*. London: Sidgwick & Jackson, 1984.

von Soden, Wolfram. *The Ancient Orient: An Introduction to the Study of the Ancient Near East*. Translated by Donald G. Schley. Grand Rapids, MI: Eerdmans, 1994.

Wiseman, D.J. *Nebuchadnezzar and Babylon*. Oxford: Oxford University Press, 1985.

D. HISTORIES OF ISRAEL

Ahlström, Gösta W. *The History of Ancient Palestine*. Minneapolis: Fortress, Press, 1993.

Bright, John. *A History of Israel*. 3d ed. Philadelphia: Westminster Press, 1981.
Bruce, F.F. *Israel and the Nations*. Grand Rapids, MI: Eerdmans, 1969.
Cate, Robert. *These Sought a Country*. Nashville: Broadman, 1985.
Merrill, Eugene H. *Kingdom of Priests: A History of Old Testament Israel*. Grand Rapids: Baker, 1987.
Miller, J. Maxwell and John H. Hayes. *A History of Ancient Israel and Judah*. Philadelphia: Westminster Press, 1986.
Shanks, Hershel., ed. *Ancient Israel: A Short History from Abraham to the Roman Destruction of the Temple*. Washington, D.C.: Biblical Archaeology Society, 1988.
Wood, Leon J. *A Survey of Israel's History*. Edited by D. O'Brien. Rev. ed. Grand Rapids, MI: Zondervan, 1986.

E. ISRAEL'S NEIGHBORS

1. OVERVIEWS

Finegan, Jack. *Myth & Mystery: An Introduction to the Pagan Religions of the Biblical World*. Grand Rapids, MI: Baker Book House, 1989.
Hoerth, Alfred J., Gerald L. Mattingly, and Edwin M. Yamauchi. *Peoples of the Old Testament World. With a foreword by Alan R. Millard*. Grand Rapids, MI: Baker Books, 1994.
Wiseman, D.J., ed. *Peoples of Old Testament Times*. Oxford: Clarendon Press, 1973.

2. CANAANITES

Albright, W.F. *Yahweh and the Gods of Canaan*. Garden City, N.Y.: Doubleday, 1968.
Cross, Frank M. *Canaanite Myth and Hebrew Epic*. Cambridge, Mass.: Harvard University Press, 1973.
Curtis, Adrian. *Ugarit (Ras Shamra)*. Grand Rapids, MI: Eerdmans, 1985.
Gray, John. *The Canaanites*. New York: Praeger, 1964.
Lemche, Neils Peter. *The Canaanites and their Land*. Sheffield: JSOT Press, 1991.
Ziffer, Irit. *At That Time the Canaanites Were in the Land: Daily Life in Canaan in the MB II 2000–1500*. Tel Aviv: Eretz Israel Museum, 1990.

3. PHILISTINES

Bierling, Neal. *Giving Goliath His Due: New Archaeological Light on the Philistines*. Grand Rapids, MI: Baker Book House, 1992.
Dornemann, Rudolph H. *The Archaeology of the Transjordan in the Bronze and Iron Ages*. Milwaukee, WI: Milwaukee Public Museum, 1983.
Dothan, Trude. *People of the Sea: The Search for the Philistines*. New York: Macmillan, 1992.
________. *The Philistines and their Material Culture*. New Haven: Yale University Press, 1982.

4. AMMONITES, MOABITES, AND EDOMITES

Bartlett, John R. *Edom and the Edomites*. Sheffield: JSOT Press, 1989.
Bienkowski, Piotr, ed. *Early Edom and Moab: The Beginning of the Iron Age in Southern Jordan*. Sheffield: Collis, 1992.
Dearman, J. Andrew, ed. *Studies in the Mesha Inscription and Moab*. Atlanta: Scholars Press, 1989.
Edelman, Diana Vikander, ed. *You Shall Not Abhor an Edomite for He is Your Brother*. Atlanta, GA: Scholars Press, 1995.
MacDonald, Burton. *Ammon, Moab, and Edom*. Ammon, Jordan: Al Kurba, 1994.

5. ARAMEANS

Mazar, Benjamin. "The Aramean Empire and Its Relations with Isarel." *Biblical Archaeologist* 25(1962): 98–120.
Pitard, Wayne T. *Ancient Damascus: A Historical Study of the Syrian City-State from Earliest Times until its Fall to the Assyrians in 732 B.C.* Winona Lake, IN: Eisenbrauns, 1986.
Unger, Merril F. *Israel and the Armeans of Damascus*. London: J. Clarke & Co., 1957.

6. PHOENICIANS

Katzenstein, H.J. *The History of Tyre*. Jerusalem: Schocken, 1973.
Moscati, Sabatino, ed. *The Phoenicians*. New York: Abbeville Press, 1988.
________. *The World of the Phoenicians*. Translated by Alastair Hamilton. London: Weidenfeld & Nicolson, 1968.
Muhly, J.D. "Phoenicia and the Phoenicians." in *Biblical Archaeology Today. Proceedings of the International Congress on Biblical Archaeology*, 77–91. Jerusalem: IES, 1985.

7. PERSIA

Cook, John M. *The Persian Empire*. London: Dent, 1983.
Ghirshman, Roman. *Iran: From the Earliest Time to the Islamic Conquest*. Harmondsworth: Penguin Books, 1954.
Olmstead, A.T. *History of the Persian Empire*. Chicago: University of Chicago Press, 1948.
Yamauchi, Edwin. *Persia and the Bible*. Grand Rapids, MI: Baker Book House, 1990.

F. ARCHAEOLOGY AND THE OLD TESTAMENT

1. ENCYCLOPEDIAS AND DICTIONARIES

Blaiklock, E.M. and R.K. Harrison, eds. *The New International Dictionary of Biblical Archaeology*. Grand Rapids, MI: Zondervans, 1983.
Negev, Avraham, ed. *The Archaeological Encyclopedia of the Holy Land*. Rev. ed. 4 vols. New York: Thomas Nelson, 1986.
Stern, Ephraim, Ayelet Gilboa, and Joseph Aviram, eds. *The New Encyclopedia of Archaeological Excavations in the Holy Land*. 4 vols. New York: Simon & Schuster, 1993.

2. ARCHAEOLOGY OF THE LAND OF ISRAEL

Aharoni, Yohanan. *The Archaeology of the Land of Israel*. Translated by A. Rainey. Philadelphia: Westminster Press, 1982.
Ben-Tor, Amnon, ed. *The Archaeology of Ancient Israel*. Translated by R. Greenberg. New Haven: Yale University Press, 1992.
Dever, William G. *Recent Archaeological Discoveries and Biblical Research*. Seattle: University of Washington Press, 1990.
Kempinski, Aharon and Ronny Reich, eds. *The Architecture of Ancient Israel: From the Prehistoric to the Persian Periods*. Jerusalem: Israel Exploration Society, 1992.
Kenyon, K. *The Bible and Recent Archaeology*. Revised by P.R.S. Moorey. Rev. ed. Atlanta: John Knox Press, 1987.
King, Philip J. *Amos, Hosea, Micah—An Archaeological Commentary*. Philadelphia: Westminster, 1988.
________. *Jeremiah: An Archaeological Companion*. Louisville, KY: Westminster/John Knox Press, 1993.

Lance, H. Darrell. *The Old Testament and the Archaeologist.* Philadelphia: Fortress, 1981.
Levy, Thomas E., ed. *The Archaeology of Society in the Holy Land.* New York: Facts on File, 1995.
Lewis, Jack P. *Archaeological Backgrounds to Bible People.* Grand Rapids: Baker, 1971.
Mazar, Amihai. *Archaeology of the Land of the Bible: 10,000–586 B.C.E.* New York: Doubleday, 1990.
Rast, Walter. *Through the Ages in Palestinian Archaeology.* Philadelphia: Trinity Press International, 1992.
Schoville, Keith. *Biblical Archaeology in Focus.* Grand Rapids: Baker, 1978.
Shanks, Hershel and Dan P. Cole, eds. *Archaeology and The Bible: The Best of BAR* Vol.1, *Early Israel.* Washington, D.C.: Biblical Archaeology Society, 1990.
________ and Benjamin Mazar, eds. *Recent Archaeology in the Land of Israel.* Vol.2, Washington, D.C.: Biblical Archaeology Society, 1981.
Stern, Ephraim. *Material Culture of the Land of the Bible in the Persian Period, 538–332 B.C.* Jerusalem: Israel Excavation Society, 1982.
Thompson, Henry O. *Biblical Archaeology.* New York: Paragon House, 1987.

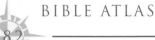

G. SELECTED ASPECTS OF ANCIENT LIFE AND CULTURE

Borowski, Oded. *Agriculture in Iron Age Israel: The Evidence from Archaeology and the Bible.* Winona Lake: Eisenbrauns, 1987.
Casson, Lionel. *Travel in the Ancient World.* London: Allen and Unwin, 1974.
Dearman, J. Andrew. *Religion & Culture in Ancient Israel.* Peabody, MA: Hendrickson, 1992.
Forbes, R.J. *Studies in Ancient Technology,* 2d ed. 9 vols. Leiden: E.J. Brill, 1964.
Matthews, Victor H. *Manners and Customs in the Bible: An Illustrated Guide to Daily Life in Bible Times.* Peabody, MA: Hendrickson, 1988.
________. and Don C. Benjamin. *Social World of Ancient Israel, 1250–587 B.C.E.* Peabody, MA: Hendrickson, 1993.
Vaux, Roland de. *Ancient Israel.* 2 vols. New York: McGraw-Hill, 1965.
Wilson, Robert R. *Genealogy and History in the Biblical World.* New Haven, Conn.: Yale University Press, 1977.
Yadin, Yigael. *The Art of Warfare in Biblical Lands in the Light of Archaeological Study.* 2 vols. Translated by M. Pearlman. New York: McGraw-Hill, 1963.

Part III. The Hellenistic Era

Avi-Yonah, Michael. *The Holy Land: From the Persian to the Arab Conquest (536 B.C.–A.D. 640): A Historical Geography.* Rev. ed. Grand Rapids, MI: Baker Book House, 1977.
Bickermann, Elias. *From Ezra to the Last of the Maccabees.* New York: Schocken Books, 1962.
Botsford, George Willis, and Charles A. Robinson. *Hellenic History.* 5th ed. Revised by Donald Kagan. New York: Macmillan, 1969.
Cary, Max. *A History of the Greek World from 323 to 146 B.C.* London: Methuen, 1951.
Cate, Robert L. *A History of the Bible Lands in the Interbiblical Period.* Nashville: Broadman, 1989.
Fraser, P.M. *Ptolemaic Alexandria.* 2 vols. Oxford: Clarendon Press, 1972.
Grant, Michael. *From Alexander to Cleopatra: The Hellenistic World.* New York: Scribner, 1982.
Green, Peter. *Alexander to Actium: The Historical Evolution of the Hellenistic Age.* Berkeley: University of California Press, 1990.
Hengel, Martin. Jews, *Greeks, and Barbarians.* Translated by John Bowden. Philadelphia: Fortress Press, 1980.
_______. *Judaism and Hellenism.* 2 vols. Philadelphia: Fortress Press, 1974.
Jagersma, Henk. *A History of Israel from Alexander the Great to Bar Kochba.* Translated by John Bowden. Philadelphia: Fortress Press, 1986.
Koester, Helmut. *Introduction to the New Testament: History, Culture, and Religion of the Hellenistic Age.* Vol.1. Philadelphia: Fortress Press, 1982.
Pearlman, Moshe. *The Maccabees.* New York: Macmillan, 1973.
Peters, Francis E. *The Harvest of Hellenism: A History of the Near East from Alexander the Great to the Triumph of Christianity.* New York: Simon and Schuster, 1970.
Pfeiffer, Charles F. *Between the Testaments.* Grand Rapids: Baker, 1959.
Reicke, Bo. *The New Testament Era: The World of the Bible from 500 B.C. to A.D. 100.* Translated by David E. Green. Philadelphia: Fortress, 1968.
Schurer, Emil. *The History of the Jewish People in the Age of Jesus Christ: 175 B.C.–A.D. 135.* 2 vols. Edited by Geza Vermes, Fergus Millar, and Matthew Black. Rev. ed. Edinburgh: T. & T. Clarke, 1973–79.
Surburg, Raymond F. *Introduction to the Intertestamental Period.* St. Louis: Concordia, 1975.
Tcherikover, Victor. *Hellenistic Civilization and the Jews.* Translated by S. Applebaum. New York: Atheneum, 1970.

Part IV. The World of Jesus and the Early Church

A. NEW TESTAMENT HISTORY

1. PALESTINE

Avi-Yonah, Michael and Baras, Zvi, eds. *The Herodian Period.* The World History of the Jewish People. New Brunswick, NJ: Rutgers University Press, 1975 .
________. *The Jews Under Roman and Byzantine Rule.* Jerusalem: Magnes Press, 1984.
Baron, Salo Wittmeyer. *A Social and Religious History of the Jews.* 2d ed., rev. and enlarged. 18 vols. New York: Columbia University, 1952–83.
Bauckham, Richard, ed. *The Book of Acts in its First Century Setting.* Vol. 4, *Palestinian Setting.* Grand Rapids, MI: Eerdmans, 1995.
Bruce, F. F. *New Testament History.* Garden City, N.Y.: Doubleday, 1972.
Farmer, William R. *Maccabees, Zealots, and Josephus: An Inquiry into Jewish Nationalism in the Greco-Roman Period.* New York: Columbia University, 1956.
Ferguson, Everett. *Backgrounds of Early Christianity.* Rev. ed. Grand Rapids, MI: Eerdmans, 1993.
Freyne, Seán. *Galilee: From Alexander the Great to Hadrian 323 B.C.E. to 135 C.E.* Notre Dame, Indiana: University of Notre Dame Press, 1980.

Hoehner, Harold W. *Herod Antipas*. Cambridge: Cambridge University, 1972.

Jagersma, Henk. *A History of Israel from Alexander the Great to Bar Kochba*. Translated by John Bowden. Philadelphia: Fortress, 1986.

Jones, A.H.M. *The Herods of Judea*. 2d ed. Oxford: Clarendon, 1967.

Koester, Helmut. *Introduction to the New Testament: History and Literature of Early Christianity* Vol. 2. Philadelphia: Fortress, 1982.

Lohse, Eduard. *The New Testament Environment*. Translated by John Steely. Nashville: Abingdon, 1976.

Nickelsburg, George W. E. *Jewish Literature Between the Bible and the Mishnah*. Philadelphia: Fortress, 1981.

Perowne, Stewart. *The Later Herods: The Political Background of the New Testament*. London: Hodder and Stoughton, 1958.

________. *The Life and Times of Herod the Great*. London: Hodder and Stoughton, 1956.

Rhoades, David M. *Israel in Revolution: 6–74 C.E.: A Political History Based on the Writings of Josephus*. Philadelphia: Fortress, 1976.

Safrai, S. and M. Stern. *The Jewish People in the First Century: Historical Geography, Political History, Social, Cultural and Religious Life and Institutions*. Compendia Rerum Iudaicarum ad Novum Testamentum. Philadelphia: Fortress Press, 1974.

Schurer, Emil. *The History of the Jewish People in the Age of Jesus Christ: 175 B.C.–A.D. 135*. 2 vols. Edited by Geza Vermes, Fergus Millar, and Matthew Black. Rev. ed. Edinburgh: T. & T. Clarke, 1973–79.

Smallwood, E. Mary. *The Jews Under Roman Rule*. Leiden: E.J. Brill, 1976.

Tcherikover, Victor. *Hellenistic Civilization and the Jews*. New York: Atheneum, 1970.

2. ROME

Boren, Henry C. Roman Society: *A Social, Economic and Cultural History.* Lexington, Mass.: D. C. Heath, 1977.

Cary, Max and Howard H. Scullard. *A History of Rome*. 3d ed. New York: St. Martin's Press, 1975.

Grant, Michael. *History of Rome*. New York: Charles Scribner's Sons, 1978.

Heichelheim, F. M. and C. A. Yeo. *History of the Roman People*. Englewood Cliffs, N.J.: Prentice-Hall, 1962.

Jones, A.H.M. *A History of Rome Through the Fifth Century.* New York: Harper & Row, 1968.

Magie, David. *Roman Rule in Asia Minor*. Princeton: Princeton University Press, 1950.

Marsh, Frank B. *A History of the Roman World from 146 B.C. to 30 B.C.* Revised by H.H. Scullard. 3d ed. London: Methuen, 1953.

McDonald, Alexander H. *Republican Rome*. New York: Praeger, 1966.

Millar, Fergus. *The Roman Near East 31 B.C.–A.D. 337*. Cambridge Mass.: Harvard University Press, 1993.

Salmon, Edward T. *A History of the Roman World from 30 B.C. to A.D. 138*. 6th ed. London: Methuen, 1968.

Scullard, Howard H. *A History of the Roman World from 753 B.C. to 146 B.C.* 3d ed. London: Methuen, 1961.

Starr, Chester G. *A History of the Ancient World*. 3d ed. New York: Oxford University Press, 1983.

________. *The Roman Empire: 27 B.C. to A.D. 476*. New York: Oxford Press, 1982.

B. ARCHAEOLOGY AND THE NEW TESTAMENT

Batey, Richard. *Jesus and the Forgotten City: New Light on Sepphoris and the Urban World of Jesus*. Grand Rapids, MI: Baker Book House, 1991.

Biers, William R. *The Archaeology of Greece: An Introduction*. Rev. ed. Ithaca, NY: Cornell University Press, 1994.

Charlesworth, James H. *Jesus within Judaism: New Light From Exciting Archaeological Discoveries*. New York: Doubleday, 1988.

Finegan, Jack. *The Archaeology of the New Testament: The Life of Jesus and the Beginnings of the Early Church*. Rev. ed. Princeton: Princeton University Press, 1992.

________. *The Archaeology of the New Testament: The Mediterranean World of the Early Christian Apostles*. Boulder, CO.: Westview Press, 1981.

Gill, David W. and Gempf Conrad, eds. *The Book of Acts in its First Century Setting*. Vol. 2, Graeco-Roman Setting. Grand Rapids, MI: Eerdmans, 1994.

Hemer, Colin J. *The Letters to the Seven Churches of Asia in Their Local Setting*. Sheffield, England: JSOT, 1986.

Horsley, Richard A. *Archaeology, History, and Society in Galilee: The Social Context of Jesus and the Rabbis*. Valley Forge, PA: Trinity Press, 1996.

McCray, John. *The Archaeology of the New Testament*. Grand Rapids, MI: Baker, 1991.

Meyers, Eric M. and James F. Strange. *Archaeology, the Rabbis, and Early Christianity.* Nashville: Abingdon, 1981.

O'Connor, Jerome Murphy. *The Holy Land: An Archaeological Guide from the Earliest Times to 1700*. 2d ed. New York: Oxford University Press, 1986.

Rousseau, John J. and Rami Arav. *Jesus and His World: An Archaeological and Cultural Dictionary*. Minneapolis: Fortress Press, 1995.

Shanks, Hershel and Dan. P. Cole, ed. *Archaeology and the Bible: The Best of BAR*. Vol 2 *Archaeology in the World of Herod, Jesus, and Paul*. Washington: Biblical Archaeology Society, 1990.

Yamauchi, Edwin. *The Archaeology of New Testament Cities in Western Asia Minor.* Grand Rapids, MI: Baker, 1980.

C. QUMRAN AND THE DEAD SEA SCROLLS

Note: The bibliography for the Dead Sea Scrolls is quite extensive. The following represents a very small selection intended to introduce the subject.

Charlesworth, James H., ed. *Jesus and the Dead Sea Scrolls: The Controversy Resolved*. New York: Doubleday, 1992.

Cook, Edward M. *Solving the Mysteries of the Dead Sea Scrolls*. Grand Rapids, MI: Zondervan, 1994.

Cross, Frank Moore. *The Ancient Library of Qumran & Modern Biblical Studies*. Rev. ed. Grand Rapids, MI: Baker Book House, 1980.

Schiffman, Lawrence H., ed. *Archaeology and History in the Dead Sea Scrolls*. Sheffield: JSOT Press, 1990.

________. *Reclaiming the Dead Sea Scrolls: The History of Judaism, the Background of Christianity, and the Lost Library of Qumran*. Philadelphia: Jewish Publication Society, 1994.

Ulrich, Eugene and James VanderKam ed. *The Community of the Renewed Covenant: The Notre Dame Symposium on the Dead Sea Scrolls*. Notre Dame, Indiana: University of Notre Dame Press, 1994.

Vermes, Geza. *The Dead Sea Scrolls: Qumran in Perspective*. 3d ed. Rev. Philadelphia: Fortress, 1981.

________. *The Dead Sea Scrolls in English*. 4th ed. Rev. and ext. New York: Penguin Books, 1995.

D. SELECTED ASPECTS OF THE WORLD OF JESUS AND THE EARLY APOSTLES

Ferguson, John. *The Religions of the Roman Empire*. Britain: Thames and Hudson, 1970.

Grant, Michael. *The World of Rome*. New York: The New American Library, 1960.

Green, Joel B., Scott McKnight, and I. Howard Marshall, eds. *Dictionary of Jesus and the Gospels*. Downers Grove, IL: InterVarsity Press, 1992.

Hawthorne, Gerald F., Ralph P. Martin, and Daniel G. Reid, eds. *Dictionary of Paul and His Letters*. Downers Grove, IL: InterVaristy Press, 1993.

Jeremias, Joachim. *Jerusalem in the Time of Jesus: An Investigation into the Economic and Social Conditions During the New Testament Period*. Philadelphia: Fortress, 1969.

Keener, Craig S. *The IVP Bible Background Commentary: New Testament*. Downers Grove, IL: InterVarsity Press, 1993.

Malherbe, A.J. *Social Aspects of Early Christianity*. Baton Rouge, LA: Louisiana State University Press, 1977.

Malina, B.J. *The New Testament World: Insights from Cultural Anthropology*. Atlanta: John Knox, 1981.

Matthews, Victor H. *Manners and Customs in the Bible: An Illustrated Guide to Daily Life in Bible Times*. Peabody, Mass: Hendrickson, 1988.

Meeks, W.A. *The First Urban Christians: The Social World of the Apostle Paul*. New Haven: Yale University Press, 1983.

Millard, Alan. *Discoveries from the Time of Jesus*. Oxford: Lion Publishing Co., 1990.

Murphy-O'Connor, Jerome. S.V. *St. Paul's Corinth: Texts and Archaeology*. Good News Studies 6. Wilmington, DE: Michael Glazier, 1983.

Sherwin-White, Adrian N. *Roman Society and Roman Law in the New Testament*. Oxford: Clarendon Press, 1963; reprint, Grand Rapids: Baker, 1992.

Stephens, William H. *The New Testament World in Pictures*. Nashville: Broadman Press, 1987.

E. JERUSALEM (OLD AND NEW TESTAMENT)

Avigad, Nahman. *Discovering Jerusalem*. Nashville: Thomas Nelson, 1983.

Bahat, Dan and Chaim T. Rubinstein. *The Illustrated Atlas of Jerusalem*. Translated by Shelomo Ketko. New York: Simon and Schuster, 1989.

Ben-Dov, Meir. *In the Shadow of the Temple: The Discovery of Ancient Jerusalem*. Translated by Ina Friedman. New York: Harper and Row, 1985.

Geva, Hillel, ed. *Ancient Jerusalem Revealed*. Jerusalem: Israel Exploration Society, 1994.

Jeremias, Joachim. *Jerusalem in the Time of Jesus*. Translated by F.H. and C.H. Cave. Philadelphia: Fortress Press, 1975.

Mare, W. Harold. *The Archaeology of the Jerusalem Area*. Grand Rapids, MI: Baker, 1987.

Ritmeyer, Kathleen and Leen Ritmeyer. "Reconstructing Herod's Temple Mount in Jerusalem." *BAR* 15 (Nov/Dec, 1989): 23–53.

Shiloh, Yigael. *Excavations at the City of David*. *Qedem* Vol. 19. Jerusalem: Hebrew University, 1984.

F. THE EARLY CHURCH

Ferguson, Everett, Michael P. McHugh, and Frederick W. Norris, eds. *The Encyclopedia of Early Christianity*. New York and London: Garland Publishing Co., 1990.

Snyder, Graydon F. *Ante Pacem: Archaeological Evidence of Church Life Before Constantine*. Macon, GA: Mercer University Press, 1985.

Tsafrir, Yoram, ed. *Ancient Churches Revealed*. Jerusalem: Israel Exploration Society, 1993.

Note on Periodicals: Periodical literature has not been included in the preceding bibliography. The array of technical and semi-technical journals containing information on the subject matter of this atlas is quite lengthy. However, a few periodicals cater to the needs of the general student of the Bible. Especially to be noted are *Biblical Archaeology Review* and *Bible Review* published by the Biblical Archaeology Society; *Biblical Archaeologists* published by the American Schools of Oriental Research; and the *Biblical Illustrator* published by Lifeway Christian Resources of the Southern Baptist Convention, Nashville, Tennessee.

INDEX OF PEOPLE AND PLACES

This index contains all geographical names (countries, regions, places, and physical features) and personal names appearing in the text. References to geographical names found in the maps of the atlas can be found in the accompanying Index of Maps.

K

L

M

N

O

P

INDEX OF MAPS

This index contains all geograpical names (countries, regions, places, and physical features) appearing in the maps. Names occurring more than fifteen times have been reduced to representative map occurrences; an asterisk after the name indicates each name so treated. Information in parentheses after the name signify an alternate spelling [e.g. Knossus (Cnossus)], another name for the same place [e.g. Acco (Ptolemais)], or a geographical annotation to distinguish sites bearing the same name [e.g. Aphek (in the Sharon)]. References to geographical names found in the text of the atlas can be found in the accompanying Index of People and Places.

291

293

T